Documents in Modern History

The origins of the First World War

Manchester University Press

DOCUMENTS IN MODERN HISTORY

Series editor:
Dr G. H. Bennett (University of Plymouth)

Series advisor:
Dr Kevin Jefferys (University of Plymouth)

The *Documents in Modern History* series offers collections of documents on the most widely debated and studied topics in modern British and international history. The volumes place fresh primary material alongside more familiar texts, and provide thought-provoking introductions to place the documents in their wider historical context.

All volumes in the series are comprehensive and broad-ranging. They provide the ideal course textbook for sixth-form students, first-year undergraduates and beyond.

Also available:

Anglo-American relations since 1939
John Baylis

Roosevelt's peacetime administrations, 1933–41: a documentary history of the New Deal years
Harry Bennett

British Communism: a documentary history
John Callaghan and Ben Harker

The Labour party: 'socialism' and society since 1951
Steven Fielding

The American Civil Rights Movement
Robert P. Green, Jr. and Harold E. Cheatham

The making of German democracy: West Germany during the Adenauer era, 1945–65
Armin Grünbacher

From Beveridge to Blair: the first fifty years of Britain's welfare state 1948–98
Margaret Jones and Rodney Lowe

Women, politics and society in Britain, c.1770–1970: a documentary history
Fiona A. Montgomery

Television and the press since 1945
Ralph Negrine

The impact of immigration in post-war Britain
Panikos Panayi

The Vietnam wars
Kevin Ruane

Britain in the Second World War: a social history
Harold L. Smith

British trade unions 1945–95
Chris Wrigley

Documents in Modern History

The origins of the First World War

Diplomatic and military documents

Edited and translated by
Annika Mombauer

Manchester University Press
Manchester and New York
distributed in the United States exclusively by Palgrave Macmillan

Published by Manchester University Press
Oxford Road, Manchester M13 9NR, UK
and Room 400, 175 Fifth Avenue, New York, NY 10010, USA
www.manchesteruniversitypress.co.uk

Distributed in the United States exclusively by
Palgrave, 175 Fifth Avenue, New York,
NY 10010, USA

Distributed in Canada exclusively by
UBC Press, University of British Columbia, 2029 West Mall,
Vancouver, BC, Canada V6T 1Z2

British Library Cataloguing-in-Publication Data
A catalogue record for this book is available from the British Library

Library of Congress Cataloging-in-Publication Data applied for

ISBN 978 0 7190 7420 2 *hardback*
ISBN 978 0 7190 7421 9 *paperback*

First published 2013

Typeset in Sabon by
Koinonia, Manchester
Printed in Great Britain by
Bell & Bain Ltd, Glasgow

For Paul

Contents

Acknowledgements

This edition has taken far longer to compile than I ever thought, and at times it has seemed like an impossible task. That I have managed to complete it at all is in no small measure due to the help I have had from friends and colleagues. In particular, I owe thanks to Paul Lawrence who has put up with more than his fair share of First World War documents and has contributed to this work in countless ways. I am also extremely grateful to John Röhl (whose unfailing enthusiasm for the project was a invaluable and much-needed boost near the end), and to Sam Williamson (who read the final manuscript with a keen eye for detail and made many valuable comments).

Others have been generous with their time, advice and expertise, or have helped by discussing aspects of the origins of the war, answering many questions, or in allowing me to cite archival sources first published in their own publications. I owe thanks to John Keiger, the late Imanuel Geiss, Bruce Menning, Joshua Sanborn, Keith Neilson, Günther Kronenbitter, Holger Afflerbach, Michael Epkenhans, Robert Foley, Matthew Seligmann, Matthew Stibbe, Stephen Schröder, Stefan Schmidt, Bernd Sösemann, Dominic Lieven, Jörg Zedler, Jackie Clarke, Mark Cornwall, Mustafa Askasal, Robert Doughty, Conan Fischer, Hartmut Pogge von Strandmann, Stefan Schmidt, Olivier Lahaie, Keith Wilson, Chris Clark, the late Fritz Fellner, Stefan Berger, Janet Clark, Chris Williams, and Silvia de Renzi. Thanks are also due to Sybille Ulinski, and to Barbara and Derek Lawrence, for helping out in many ways. Not least, The Open University has supported my work with research leave and funding, for which I am very grateful.

At Manchester University Press, Emma Brennan has waited patiently for a manuscript that was ages in the making, and has kindly agreed with me that a document collection such as this one cannot be contained within the originally agreed word-limit. George Pitcher has improved the manuscript enormously with his judicious and good-humoured copy-editing.

When I embarked upon this project, I underestimated the complexities that copyright permissions would pose. Thankfully a great number of individuals, publishers and institutions were happy to allow me to reproduce material first printed in other publications. Among them, Imanuel Geiss was particularly generous in allowing me to reproduce some of the English translations of documents published in his seminal document collection *July 1914*, and was gracious enough to encourage me to improve on those translations which both he and I found wanting.[1]

I would like to thank Her Majesty the Queen for the permission to include documents from the Royal Archives in this volume. The National Archives allowed me to cite from documents under Crown copyright in their collection, as did the Churchill Archive Centre Cambridge, the Bodleian Library Oxford, the Bayerisches Haupt-Staatsarchiv in Munich, the Bundesarchiv (Berlin and Koblenz), Bundesarchiv-Militärarchiv Freiburg, the Haus-Hof- und Staats-archiv in Vienna, Bundesarchiv Bern and the National Library of Scotland.

Thanks are also due to a number of publishers who allowed me to reprint documents which were previously published elsewhere, including Cambridge University Press, the Koehler Verlag, Chicago University Press, Stanford University Press, Edizioni scientifiche italiane, Istituto Poligrafico e Zecca dello Stato, Oldenbourg, Vandenhoeck & Ruprecht, Sutter Verlag, Peter Lang, Bedford St. Martin's and Random House. Some publishing houses and copyright holders were impossible to trace, particularly for German inter-war publications where publishers have often ceased to exist. Every effort has been made to trace the owners of the works reproduced, and if any copyright was inadvertently infringed, I will gladly endeavour to rectify this.[2]

1 See also below, 'Note on translations'.

2 Please see also below, 'A note on copyright' and the Appendix.

A note on translations and editing

If not otherwise stated, all translations from German into English are mine. Where I have used a previously published translation, I have checked every one against the original, wherever possible, and where I have amended parts of the translated text this will be indicated in the references.[1] For some Italian and French translation I was ably assisted by Anna d'Andrea and Christine Guilfoyle respectively. For the finer nuances of translations, and for identifying office-holders and matching up many names with their rightful positions I was lucky to benefit from John Röhl's patience and encyclopaedic knowledge.

While I have perhaps ironed out an archaic translation or spotted a mistake in one or other document in this way, I have tried to stay as truthful to the original text as possible. However, as everyone who translates from foreign languages knows, translation is not a science, and different styles and interpretations might lead to slightly different end results. Of course, on occasion, the nuances or words used in a document (translated or not) can be of huge importance. An example of this is the famous conversation between the British Ambassador Sir Edward Goschen and the German Chancellor Theobald von Bethmann Hollweg on 4 August 1914 in which the latter allegedly referred to the treaty guaranteeing Belgian neutrality as a mere 'scrap of paper' (**418**). Much was made of Bethmann

1 For example, many French and Italian documents are available in English translation in the English editions of the so-called coloured books and other collections. However, when checked against the original texts, these official translations turned out to be largely paraphrasing the original text (and are also, understandably, rather archaic in style), rather than rendering an exact translation. Wherever possible, I have instead provided a literal translation of these documents, based on the official document collections, rather than the coloured books. (On the somewhat dubious nature of the Coloured Books, see also below, Introduction, pp. 2ff.)

Hollweg's (and, by implication, Germany's) callousness based on this comment. And yet, we do not know for certain if the conversation was conducted in German or English and which exact phrase the Chancellor used. It is possible that the German phrase 'ein Stückchen Papier', which means literally a small piece of paper, or even more innocuously 'ein Blatt Papier', meaning simply a piece of paper, might have been wrongly, but pointedly, translated as a 'scrap of paper' by the Ambassador, with the much more derisory connotation this entails. In the ensuing international controversy which this document sparked much was made of Bethmann's dismissive summary of the Treaty that guaranteed Belgium's independence – but did he actually use those words?[2] This example highlights not only the pitfalls of translated sources, but of relying on primary source evidence in the first place, particularly when – as was so often the case – conversations were recorded that were held in different languages.[3] All the obvious disadvantages of translated texts notwithstanding, however, given that the original-language documents are often inaccessible to English-language readers, this is at least a good compromise which will allow access to documents which would otherwise be unavailable.[4]

---

2 For a detailed analysis of the evidence around the 'scrap of paper', see Thomas G. Otte, 'A "German Paperchase": the "scrap of paper" controversy and the problem of myth and memory in international history', *Diplomacy & Statecraft*, 18, 1, 2007, pp. 53–87.

3 The difficulty of using primary sources to explain the origins of the First World War is further explored in Annika Mombauer, 'The Fischer Controversy, Documents, and the "Truth" about the Origins of the First World War', *Journal of Contemporary History*, 2013, forthcoming.

4 In some cases, though, this means that documents have in fact been translated into more than one language, and while the contents of the document will still reflect the original meaning, it is probably advisable not to read too much in the nuances of the text. This is particularly the case in the Russian documents which I have translated from Otto Hoetsch's *Die Internationalen Beziehungen im Zeitalter des Imperialismus*. These documents were translated into German in the 1930s (from the original Russian or French), and I have now translated them from German into English. However, at least in this particular example we can be fairly certain that Hoetsch's rendering of the text was accurate, as he collaborated closely with the Russian editor of the documents, M.N. Pokrovsky. It had been agreed that all Soviet editing, footnotes and introductions could not be changed for the German edition, and the editions were published simultaneously in German and Russian, and even printed in Germany. For more details see Derek Spring, 'Russian Documents on the Origins of the First World War', in Keith M. Wilson (ed.), *Forging the Collective Memory. Governments and International*

This book is divided into two Parts, and consists of eleven chapters. A number of introductions locate the documents within their historical context, relate them to each other and provide the necessary background for interpreting them. The documents are arranged in chronological order, and they have been presented with all the available original information about dates, the times a telegram or despatch was sent and received (abbreviated as D. and R.), and the original telegram and despatch numbers. The documents are numbered for easier cross-referencing, and brief headings give information about the date the document was written, to whom it was sent, and by whom. Numerous cross-references have been provided throughout the volume. In addition, each document is preceded by a short summary of the most important points contained in it.

A glossary of names of the key characters precedes the documents. Details of first names, ranks and offices held, titles and so forth have only been provided in footnotes where this was strictly necessary.[5]

Spellings of names and places have been standardized: Sarajevo instead of Serajevo; Sazonov instead of Sazonoff or Sasonov; Rumania instead of Roumania; Serbia instead of Servia (and Serbian, Pan-Serbian, etc.); Isvolsky instead of Izvolsky; Pašić instead of Pasitsch or Pachitch; Bucharest instead of Bukarest, Saverne as Zabern, and so forth. Russian and Polish names can be found in a number of different transliterations in the literature, depending on when their names were recorded and by whom. Russian names have been standardized according to the Library of Congress system of transliteration. Spelling is rendered in British English, rather than American, if translations were adopted from American English. Obvious typographical errors have been corrected unless they were of significance. Omissions in the text have been indicated in square brackets, and only text which was unimportant or tangential (either because it concerned a different topic or repeated a point already made, for example) has been omitted. All salutations have been cut unless their wording might be considered significant (for example in the case of a particular familiarity of the greeting). To distinguish between different emperors, in translated text Wilhelm II is *Kaiser*

Historians through two World Wars, Berghahn, Providence, RI and Oxford, 1996, pp. 63–86, pp. 74ff.

5 For example if a person occupied a different position before and during the July Crisis.

Wilhelm, Nicholas II is *Tsar* Nicholas, and Franz Joseph is *Emperor* Franz Joseph. Where English original texts have been included the original title of Emperor for each of these monarchs has been retained. Similarly, in translations the German spelling for Wilhelm and Franz Joseph has been adopted throughout in texts, but left if their original English rendering (William and Francis Joseph) in English-language sources. Where it is difficult to translate ranks and offices held by individuals because there is no literal rendering in English, or because of different usage, the original title has been included in italics.

Abbreviations

AA	*Auswärtiges Amt* (the German Foreign Office)
AA-PA	*Auswärtiges Amt, Politisches Archiv*
AN	Archives Nationales, Paris
BA-MA	Bundesarchiv-Militärarchiv, Freiburg
Bay. HStA-KA	Bayerisches Haupt-Staatsarchiv Kriegsarchiv, Munich
BD	British Documents on the Origins of the First World War
BHST-MA	Bayerisches Haupt-Staatsarchiv-Militärarchiv
BNF	Bibliothèque Nationale de France
D.	Despatched
DD	*Die deutschen Dokumente zum Kriegsausbruch*
DDF	*Documents diplomatiques français 1871–1914*
DDI	*I documenti diplomatici italiani*
DSP	*Dokumenti o spolnoj politici Kraljevine Srbije*
FO	British Foreign Office
GP	*Die Grosse Politik*
HHStA	Haus- Hof- und Staatsarchiv, Vienna
Int. Bez.	Otto Hoetsch, *Die Internationalen Beziehungen im Zeitalter des Imperialismus*
KD	Kautsky Documents
MGM	*Militärgeschichtliche Mitteilungen*
ÖUA	*Österreich-Ungarns Aussenpolitik von der bosnischen Krise bis zum Kriegsausbruch 1914*
PA/AA	Politisches Archiv des Auswärtigen Amtes
R.	Received
RA	Reichsarchiv
RA, Kew	Royal Archives, Kew
SHAT	Service historique de l'Armée de Terre, Château de Vincennes
Tel.	Telegram
TNA	The National Archives, Kew
TNL	The National Library of Scotland
WO	War Office

Glossary of names

This list includes names of people who feature prominently in one or more of the documents. For others, please consult the index.

Aehrenthal, Alois Lexa Count von, Austro-Hungarian Foreign Minister, 1906–1912

Albert I, King of Belgium, 1909–1933

Aliotti, Carlo Count, Italian Minister in Durazzo, Albania, 1911–1922

Andrian-Werburg, Leopold Baron von, Head of Austro-Hungarian General Consulate in Warsaw, 1911–1914

Apis, see Dragutin T. Dimitrijević

Asquith, Herbert Henry, British Prime Minister, 1908–1916

Avarna di Gualtieri, Giuseppe Duca di, Italian Ambassador in Vienna, 1904–1915

Balfour, Arthur James, 1st Earl of Balfour, British Conservative politician, Prime Minister 1902 to 1905, and Leader of the Conservative Party until November 1911

Ballin, Albert, Director of Hapag shipping company

Barck, Peter L., Russian Finance Minister, 1914–1916

Barclay, Sir George, British Minister in Belgrade, 1911–1913, British Minister in Bucharest, 1913–1919

Barrère, Camille, French Ambassador in Rome 1897–1924

Below Saleske, Klaus, German Minister in Brussels

Benckendorff, Alexander Count von, Russian Ambassador in London, 1903–1916

Berchtold von und zu Ungarschitz, Leopold Count, Austro-Hungarian Ambassador in St Petersburg 1906–1911; Austro-Hungarian Foreign Minister and Chair of the Joint Ministerial Council 1912–1915

Berens, Captain, Russian naval attaché in Berlin

Beresford, Charles William de la Poer, Baron Beresford, British Admiral and MP

Bergen, Carl-Ludwig Diego von, Counsellor in the German *Auswärtiges Amt* (Balkans' desk), 1911–1919

Bergen, von, Counsellor of the Austro-Hungarian Embassy in Berlin

Berthelot, Philippe, assistant political director at the French Ministry for Foreign Affairs
Bertie, Sir Francis, British Ambassador in Paris, 1905–1918
Bertrab, von, Generalmajor, *Chef der Landesaufnahme*, in 1914 the most senior *Oberquartiermeister* in the German General Staff
Bethmann Hollweg, Dietrich von, Counsellor (*Legationsrat*) at the German Embassy in Vienna
Bethmann Hollweg, Theobald von, Imperial German Chancellor and Prussian Minister President, 1909–1917
Biedermann, Erich Freiherr von, Saxon *Legationsrat* in Berlin
Bienvenu-Martin, Jean-Baptiste, French Minister of Justice 1913–1914 and acting Premier/Foreign Minister from 15 to 29 July in 1914
Bigge, Sir Arthur (Lord Stamfordham), Private Secretary to Queen Victoria and George V
Biliński, Leon Ritter von, Austro-Hungarian Joint Minister for Finances and Administrator for Bosnia and Herzegovina, 1912–1915
Bollati, Ricardo, Italian Ambassador in Berlin 1913–1915
Bonar Law, see Law
Braham, British journalist with *The Times*
Bratiano, Joan J.C., Rumanian Minister President and Minister of War, 1914–1918
Bronevski, Arkadi Nicolajevitch, Russian Chargé d'Affaires in Berlin
Broqueville, Charles de, Belgian Prime Minister and Minister for War, 1912–1917
Buchanan, Sir George William, British Ambassador in St Petersburg, 1910–1917
Bunsen, Sir Maurice William de, British Ambassador in Vienna, 1913–1914
Burián von Rajecz, István Freiherr, Hungarian Minister in Vienna, 1913–1915
Čabrinović, Nedeljko, Serbian suspect in enquiry into assassination plot
Cambon, Jules, French Ambassador in Berlin, 1907–1914
Cambon, Paul, French Ambassador in London, 1898–1920
Capelle, Eduard von, Under- Secretary of State of the German Naval Office (*Reichsmarineamt*), 1914–1915
Carlotti di Riparbella, Marquis, Italian Ambassador in St Petersburg, 1913–1918
Carlowitz, Adolf von, Saxon Minister of War, 1914
Carol I, King of Rumania, 1881–1914
Cartwright, Fairfax, British Ambassador in Vienna, 1908–1913
Cassel, Sir Ernest, British banker
Chambrun, Charles de, First Secretary at the French Embassy in St Petersburg in 1914
Churchill, Sir Winston, British Home Secretary, 1910–1911; First Lord of the Admiralty, 1911–1915

Ciganović, Milan, Serbian government official implicated in assassination plot

Claparède, Alfred de, Swiss Minister in Berlin, 1904–1917

Class, Heinrich, President of the Pan-German League, 1908–1939

Clemenceau, Georges, French Premier and Minister of the Interior, 1906–1909

Clerk, George R., Chief Clerk of the Eastern Department of the British Foreign Office in 1914

Collon, Major, Belgian military attaché in Paris

Conrad von Hötzendorf, Franz Freiherr, Austro-Hungarian Chief of the General Staff, 1906–1911 and 1912–1917

Crackanthorpe, Dayrell Eardley Montague, British Chargé d'Affaires in Belgrade

Crowe, Sir Eyre A., Assistant Under-Secretary of State in the British Foreign Office

Czernin von und zu Chudenitz, Count Ottokar, Austro-Hungarian Ambassador in Bucharest, 1913–1916

Davignon, Julien, Belgian Foreign Minister, 1907–1916

Delcassé, Theophile, Minister of the Navy in 1912, French Ambassador in St Petersburg 1913–1914

Diamandy (Diamandi), Constantin, Rumanian Minister in St Petersburg, 1913–1914

Dimitrijević, Dragutin T. (Apis), Serbian General Staff Officer involved in the preparation of the assassination of Franz Ferdinand, founder member of the 'Black Hand'

Dobrorolski, Sergei K., Russian General, Chief of the Mobilization Section of the Russian General Staff 1914

Doumergue, Gaston, French Minister of Foreign Affairs before the July Crisis

Dumaine, Alfred, French Ambassador in Vienna, 1912–1914

Dupont, Colonel, Chief of the *Deuxième Bureau* of the French General Staff

Durnovo, Peter N., Russian Minister of the Interior 1905–1906

Eckardstein, Herrmann Freiherr von, Secretary in the German Embassy in London

Eisendecher, Karl, Prussian Minister in Karlsruhe, 1884–1914

Esher, Lord Reginald Baliol Brett, 2nd Viscount of Esher, British courtier and politician

Eulenburg, Prince Philipp, German Ambassador in Vienna, 1894–1907, and close confidant of Kaiser Wilhelm II

Falkenhayn, Erich von, Prussian Minister of War, 1913–1915; Chief of the General Staff 1914–1916

Fascotti, Carlo, Italian Minister in Bucharest

Ferry, Abel, French Under-Secretary of State for Foreign Affairs, 1913–1914

Fisher, Sir John Arbuthnot (from 1909 Lord), First Sea Lord of the British Admiralty 1904–1910 and 1914–1915
Fleuriau, A.J. de, 1st Secretary at French Embassy in London, sometimes Chargé d'Affaires in London, 1904–1921
Flotow, Ludwig Freiherr von, German Minister in Brussels, 1910–1913; German Ambassador in Rome, 1913–1915
Forgách von Ghymes and Gács, Johann Count, *Sektionschef* in the Austrian Foreign Ministry, 1913–1914
Franz Ferdinand, Archduke and heir to the Austro-Hungarian throne
Franz Joseph I, Austrian Emperor (Kaiser) and Hungarian King, 1848–1916
French, Sir John, Chief of the British General Staff, 1911–1914
Ganz, Hugo, Vienna Correspondent of the *Frankfurter Zeitung*
Gavrilović, Dragutin, Serbian military officer
Gebsattel, Ludwig von, Bavarian military attaché in Prussia
George V, British King, 1910–1936
Giesl von Gieslingen, Wladimir Baron von, Austro-Hungarian Minister in Belgrade, 1913–1914
Giolitti, Giovanni, five times Italian Prime Minister between 1892 and 1921
Goltz, Pasha Colmar Freiherr von der, Prussian General; German military instructor in Turkey, 1883–1895; vice-president of the Turkish supreme War Council, 1909–1913
Goremykin, Ivan Logginovitch, Russian Prime Minister 1906, 1914–1916
Goschen, Sir William Edward, British Ambassador in Berlin, 1908–1914
Grabez, Trifko, Bosnian Serb conspirator in the assassination of Franz Ferdinand
Granville, George Leveson-Gower, 3rd Earl Granville, British diplomat, attaché, inter alia, in Berlin in 1911, Paris in 1913
Grey, Sir Edward, British Foreign Secretary, 1905–1916
Grigorowich, Ivan K., Admiral, Russian Naval Minister, 1911–1917
Gruić, Slavko, Serbian General Secretary in the Foreign Office
Guillaume, Baron Jules, Belgian Minister in Paris 1910–1916
Haeften, Hans von, Prussian Officer in the General Staff, military writer
Haldane, Viscount (from 1911) Richard Burdon, British Minister of War, 1905–1912
Hankey, Sir Maurice, British Civil Servant, CID Secretary from 1912
Hanneken, Constantin von, German entrepreneur in China, close friend of Erich von Falkenhayn
Harcourt, Lewis V., British Minister for Colonies, 1910–1915
Hardinge, Sir Charles, permanent Under-Secretary of State in the British Foreign Office, 1906–1910
Hartwig, Nicolai, Russian Minister in Belgrade, 1909–1914
Haymerle, Franz Josef Freiherr von, *Botschaftsrat* in Austrian Embassy in Berlin
Hedeman, Jules, French journalist

Heeringen, August von, Vice Admiral, Chief of the German Admiralty Staff, 1911–1913
Heinrich (Henry), Prince of Prussia, brother of Wilhelm II
Henderson, Wilfred, British Naval Attaché in Germany
Hertling, Count Georg von, Bavarian Prime Minister, 1912–1917
Höfer von Feldsturm, Franz Ritter, General Austro-Hungarian Deputy Chief of Staff
Hopman, Albert, German Naval Officer, member of the *Reichsmarineamt* (Imperial Naval Office), 1911–1915
House, Colonel Edward, US envoy to Europe
Hoyos, Alexander (Alek) Count von, *Legationsrat* and Chief of the Cabinet in the Austro-Hungarian Foreign Ministry, 1912–1917
Huguet, Victor Jacques Marie, French Military Attaché in London, 1906–1916
Humbert, Charles, French Senator
Ianushkevitch, Nikolai N., Russian Chief of the General Staff, 1914–1915
Ignatjev, Alexei A., Russian military attaché in Paris
Imperiali di Francavilla, Marquis Guglielmo, Italian Ambassador in London, 1910–1926
Isvolsky, Alexander P., Russian Foreign Minister, 1906–1910, Russian Ambassador in Paris, 1910–1917
Jagow, Gottlieb von, German Ambassador in Rome, 1909–12; Secretary of State in the *Auswärtiges Amt*, 1913–1916
Joffre, Joseph L., Chief of the French General Staff, 1911–1914
Jovanović (Jovanovitch), Jovan M., Serbian Minister in Vienna, 1912–1914
Judet, M. Ernst, French journalist
Kageneck, Karl Count, German military attaché in Vienna 1908–1914
Kailer, Rear-Admiral von, Austro-Hungarian Deputy Chief of the Naval Staff
Kiderlen-Wächter, Alfred von, German State Secretary for Foreign Affairs, 1910–1912
Klobukowski, A.W., French Minister at Brussels, 1911–1914
Knox, A.W.F., British Military Attaché in St Petersburg, 1914
Kokovtsov, Vladimir N., Russian Minister of Finance 1904–1914; Chair of the Russian Council of Ministers and Russian Premier, 1911–1914
Kral, *Generalkonsul*, Austro-Hungarian Commissar at the international control commission for Albania, in Durrazzo
Kress von Kressenstein, Paul Otto Felix Freiherr, Bavarian Minister of War, 1912–1916
Krivoshein, Alexander Vasilievich, Russian Minister of Agriculture from 1908–1915
Krobatin, Ritter Alexander von, Austro-Hungarian Minister of War, 1912–1917
Krupenski, Anatoli N., Russian Ambassador in Rome, 1912–1915
Krupp von Bohlen und Halbach, Gustav, Chair of the Board of Krupp AG from 1909

Laguiche, General Pierre de, French military attaché in St Petersburg
Law, Andrew Bonar, British Conservative politician, opposition leader 1911–1915
Lerchenfeld-Koefering, Hugo Count von, the Bavarian Minister in Berlin 1880–1919
Leuckart von Weißdorf, Traugott Freiherr von, General of the Cavalry, Saxon Military Plenipotentiary in Berlin
Lichnowsky, Karl Max Prince von, German Ambassador in London, 1912–1914
Lichtenau, Ernst Freiherr von Salza und, Saxon Minister in Berlin from 1909
Liman von Sanders, Otto, Prussian General, Chief of German military mission in Turkey 1913–1914
Lloyd George, David, British Chancellor of the Exchequer, 1908–1915
Lodyzhenskii, I., Deputy leader of the Russian Council of Ministers
Louis, Georges, French Ambassador in St Petersburg (1909–1913)
Lucius von Stödten, Hellmuth, German Chargé d'Affaires in St Petersburg in 1911, then Consul in Durrazzo; German Minister in Stockholm 1915–1920
Ludendorff, Erich, Prussian General, Chief of Deployment Section in German General Staff, 1908–1912; 1st *Oberquartiermeister* from 1916
Ludwig III, King of Bavaria, 1913–1918
Lyncker, Moriz Freiherr von, Chief of the German Kaiser's military cabinet, 1908–1918
Macchio, Count Karl von, Under-Secretary of State for Foreign Affairs in Vienna
MacDonald, James Ramsay, British Labour politician, and Prime Minister in 1924 and 1931–1935
Maklakov, Nikolai, Russian Interior Minister, 1912–1915
Margerie, Pierre Jaquin de, Political Director in the French Foreign Ministry
Matscheko, Franz Freiherr von, *Sektionsrat* (senior section chief) and Balkan expert in Austro-Hungarian Foreign Ministry
McKenna, Reginald, First Lord of the Admiralty, 1908–1911; British Home Secretary, 1911–1915
Mérey von Kapos-Mére, Katjetan, Austro-Hungarian Ambassador in Rome, 1910–1915
Merry del Val, Rafael, Cardinal State Secretary in the Vatican
Messimy, Adolphe, French Minister of War, 1911–12; 1914
Michahelles, Gustav, German Envoy in Sofia 1913–1916
Millerand, Alexandre, French Minister of War, 1912–1913; 1914–1915
Molden, Berthold, Austro-Hungarian Consul-General in Warsaw, 1911–1914
Moltke, Helmuth von, Chief of the German General Staff, 1906–1914
Morley of Blackburn, John, Viscount, Lord President of the Council, 1910–1914 and Cabinet member

Mühlon, Wilhelm, member of the board of Krupp directors until 1914
Müller, Georg Alexander von, German Admiral, Chief of the Kaiser's Naval Cabinet, 1906–1918
Murray, Sir Archibald, British General, Commander-in-Chief of BEF in 1914
Musulin von Gomirje, Alexander Freiherr, Head of Chancellery of the Austro-Hungarian Foreign Ministry
Nicholai Nicholaevitch, Russian Grand Duke, Uncle of Tsar Nicholas II
Nicholas II, Russian Emperor, 1894–1917
Nicholson, Sir William Edward, Field-Marshall, Chief of General Staff, 1908, Chairman of the Army in India Committee, 1912
Nicolai, Walter, Prussian Officer, Head of Army's intelligence section
Nicolson, Sir Arthur, British Ambassador in St Petersburg, 1906–1910; permanent Under-Secretary of State in the Foreign Office, 1910–1916
O'Beirne, Hugh James, Counsellor of the British Embassy at St Petersburg, 1909–1914
Paĉu, Laza, Serbian Deputy Prime Minister, 1904–1905; 1906–1909; 1912–1914
Page, Walter Hines, US Ambassador in London, 1913–1918
Paléologue, George Maurice, French Ambassador in St Petersburg 1914–1917
Pallavicini, Johannes, Austro-Hungarian Ambassador in Constantinople, 1906–1918
Panouse, Colonel Louis de la, French military attaché in London
Pašić, Nikola, Serbian Prime Minister, 1904–1914
Pease, Joseph Albert, 1st Baron Gainford, British politician
Pichon, Stéphan, French Foreign Minister, 1906–1911
Pius X, Pope, 1903–1914
Plessen, Hans G.H. von, Kaiser Wilhelm's Aide-de-camp
Poincaré, Raymond, French Premier and Foreign Minister, 1912–1913; French President, 1913–1920
Pokrowsky, M.N., Russian Marxist historian, head of Central Archive and editor of *Krasnyi Arkhiv*
Pollio, Alberto, Italian Chief of the General Staff, 1908–1914
Potiorek, Oskar, Austro-Hungarian Governor of Bosnia and Herzegovina, 1911–1914
Pourtalès, Friedrich Count von, German Ambassador in St Petersburg, 1907–1914
Princip, Gavrilo, Bosnian Serb conspirator in the assassination of Franz Ferdinand
Recouly, Raymond, French journalist
Redlich, Joseph, Austrian historian
Riezler, Kurt, personal secretary to German Chancellor Bethmann Hollweg
Ritter von Grünstein, Lothar Freiherr von, Bavarian Minister in Paris

Ritter zu Grünstein (Groenesteyn), Otto Freiherr von, Bavarian Minister in the Vatican

Rodd, James Remell, 1st Baron Rennell, British Ambassador in Rome, 1909–1919

Rodzianko, Mikhail Vladimirovich, President of the Duma, 1911–1917

Rumbold, Sir Horace George Montague, British Chargé d'Affaires in Berlin 1913–1914

Rupprecht, Crown Prince of Bavaria

Sabler, W., Russian Minister in Sofia

Salandra, Antonio, Italian Premier, 1914–1920

Salza und Lichtenau, Freiherr von, Saxon military plenipotentiary in Berlin, 1904–1911; Saxon Minister in Berlin, 1911–1914

San Giuliano, Antonio Marquis di, Italian Foreign Minister, 1905–1906; 1910–1914

Sazonov, Sergei D., Russian Foreign Minister, 1910–1916

Schebeko, Nicolai N., Russian Ambassador in Vienna, 1913–1914

Schemua, Blasius, Chief of the Austro-Hungarian General Staff, 1912

Schiemann, Theodor, historian and publicist

Schilling, Count Moritz F., member of the Russian Foreign Ministry, 1911–1917

Schlieffen, Alfred von, Chief of the German General Staff, 1891–1905

Schoen, Hans von, Bavarian Chargé d'Affaires in Berlin

Sheviakov, V, Russian official in the ministry of education

Soden-Frauenhofen, Joseph Maria Graf von, Bavarian *Legationsrat* in Berlin

Squitti, Nicola, Italian Minister in Belgrade 1913–1916

Stamfordham (Sir Arthur Bigge) Private Secretary of Queen Victoria and King George V

Stevanović, Dušan, Serbian military attaché in St Petersburg, 1912, Serbian Minister of War 1914

Stolberg-Wernigerode, Wilhelm Prince zu, *Botschaftsrat* (Counsellor) in the German Embassy in Vienna

Strandtmann, Vasily N., Counsellor at the Russian Legation in Belgrade

Stumm, Wilhelm von, Director of the political department of the German *Auswärtiges Amt*, 1911–1916

Stürgkh, Count Karl von, Austrian Prime Minister, 1911–1916

Sukhomlinov, Vladimir A., Russian Minister of War, 1909–1915

Sverbejev, Sergei N., Russian Ambassador to Germany

Szápáry von Szápar, Count Friedrich, Austro-Hungarian ambassador in St Petersburg

Szécsen, Nikolaus Anton, Count von Temerin, Austro-Hungarian Ambassador in Paris, January 1911–10 August 1914.

Szögyény-Marich, Count Ladislaus, Austro-Hungarian Ambassador in Berlin, 1892–1914

Tankosić, Voija, Serbian government official implicated in assassination plot
Tatistchev, Ilja Leonidovich, Russian military plenipotentiary officer in Berlin
Timaschev, Sergei I., Russian Minister of Trade, 1906–1915
Tirpitz, Admiral von, Grand-Admiral, State Secretary of the Reich Navy Office, 1897–1916
Tisza de Boros-Jenö, Count István (Stephan), Hungarian Prime Minister, 1903–1905; 1913–1917
Trautmansdorff-Weinsberg, Karl Count, 1st Secretary (*Botschaftsrat*) at the Austro-Hungarian Embassy in London (1912–1914)
Treutler, Karl Georg von, Minister in Kaiser Wilhelm's entourage
Tschirschky und Bögendorff, Heinrich Leopold von, German Ambassador in Vienna, 1907–1916
Tyrrell, Sir William George, Private Secretary to Sir Edward Grey
Vesnić, Milonko R., Serbian Minister in Paris, 1904–1911
Victor Emanuel III, King of Italy, 1900–1946
Vitzthum von Eckstädt, Count Christoph, Saxon Minister for Foreign Affairs, 1906–1918
Viviani, René, French President of the Council and Minister of Foreign Affairs (from June 1914); French Premier 1914–1915
Wahnschaffe, Arnold von, Under-Secretary of State in the German Chancellery, 1909–1918
Waldersee, Count Georg von, *Generalquartiermeister* in the Prussian General Staff, from 1912
Waldthausen, Count Julius von, German Minister in Bucharest, 1912–1914
Warburg, Max, German banker
Wargrave, Edward Alfred Goulding, Baron Wargrave, British Conservative MP
Weizsäcker, Karl Freiherr von, Prime Minister and Foreign Minister of Württemberg, 1906–1918
Wenninger, Karl Ritter von, General, Bavarian Military Attaché in Berlin
Verëvkin, A.N., high ranking official in the Ministry of Justice
Villiers, Sir Francis Hyde, Envoy Extraordinary and Minister Plenipotentiary to Belgium, 1911–1919, Ambassador to Belgium from 1919 to 1920.
Wiesner, Friedrich von, Counsellor in the Austro-Hungarian Foreign Ministry
Wilhelm II, German Emperor (Kaiser) and Prussian King, 1888–1918
Wilson, Sir Arthur, Admiral, 1st Sea Lord, 1910–1911
Wilson, Henry Hughes, British General, Director of Military Operations, 1910–1914
Wolff, Theodor, German journalist and editor of the *Berliner Tageblatt*
Zimmermann, Arthur, Under-Secretary of State in the German *Auswärtiges Amt*, 1911–1916
Zitzewitz, Major von, German military attaché in Rome

A note on copyright

The editor has made every effort to contact copyright holders where possible wherever documents exceeded the so-called 'fair dealings' quotation limit.

Permissions to reprint documents were kindly granted by Her Majesty the Queen and the staff of the Royal Archives, The National Archives, the Churchill Archive Centre Cambridge, the Bodleian Library Oxford, the Bayerisches Haupt-Staatsarchiv, the Bundesarchiv (Berlin and Koblenz), the Bundesarchiv-Militärarchiv Freiburg, the Haus-Hof- und Staatsarchiv in Vienna, Bundesarchiv Bern, and the National Library of Scotland. Documents previously published in *Documents diplomatiques français 1871–1914* were published with permission of the Archives du ministère des Affaires étrangères et européennes where the originals can be found. Documents 12 and 17 are conserved in the Archives nationales in Paris and are reprinted here with kind permission from the archive.

Among the publishers who were kind enough to grant permission to reprint were Cambridge University Press, the Koehler Verlag, Chicago University Press, Stanford University Press, Oldenbourg, Vandenhoeck & Ruprecht, Sutter Verlag, Peter Lang and Random House. Some publishing houses were impossible to trace, particularly in the case of German inter-war publications where publishers have often ceased to exist, or have since been taken over by other publishers and their records no longer kept. In many cases, the authors were deceased and it was impossible to trace their heirs. Some potential copyright holders have not replied to enquiries. Having made these efforts to trace all copyright holders, the editor would be grateful to hear from anyone whose copyright has inadvertently been infringed.

Introduction

This book is a collection of diplomatic and military documents which illuminate the origins of the First World War. They provide an international account of the diplomatic developments of the pre-war years and the final weeks of peace, and were chosen with a focus on understanding the many remaining controversies surrounding the war's origins. Selected from a broad range of sources and countries, many of the documents are newly discovered and previously unpublished archival sources, and others have been cited in monographs but are not necessarily widely known. Some are 'standard' documents that warrant inclusion due to their significance. Others have been translated into English specifically for this volume,[1] or where translations already exist many have been updated and improved.

There was much more that could have been included if space had not been an issue. Imanuel Geiss's path-breaking document collection *Julikrise und Kriegsausbruch* exceeded a thousand pages in two volumes.[2] It only included documents that were available in the early 1960s, and it focused entirely on July 1914. Fifty years on, countless more documents have been discovered which warrant inclusion in a new document collection on the origins of the war – clearly, this volume can only contain a representative sample of documents. Taken together, they highlight the events of the years 1911–1914 in broad brushstrokes, and they illuminate in

1 Particularly if those documents, in translation, are now difficult to obtain (such as those contained in Imanuel Geiss's one-volume English document collection *July 1914. The Outbreak of the First World War: Selected Documents*, B.T. Batsford, London 1967, which is essential for any student of the subject, but now out of print).

2 Imanuel Geiss (ed.), *Julikrise und Kriegsausbruch 1914*, 2 vols, Verlag für Literatur und Zeitgeschehen, Hanover 1963/64.

more detail the diplomatic interactions of the July Crisis when the decisions which led to the outbreak of war were taken.

This introduction will outline some of the most important points of contention which are directly addressed by the documents in this volume. First, however, it is worth taking a closer look at how the documents historians have relied on in examining the origins of the war came to be public knowledge, and to position their publications against the background of the historiographical debate that started almost as soon as war began.

The 'Coloured Books'

Due to the contentious issue of war-guilt, which became divisive and passionately debated as soon as war had broken out, documents have always been crucial to the way in which governments and historians have attempted to fight their corner in the acrimonious debates on the origins of the war. In fact, documents were central to the question of the origins of the war long before historians became engaged in controversies about the war's origins. Even before the weapons of war had fallen silent, and indeed even before the World War had begun in earnest, governments published some of their secret diplomatic documents in so-called coloured books (usually named after the colour of their bindings). In this way, they tried to show they had nothing to hide, and to convince their own people, and the rest of the world, of their own innocence with regard to the war's outbreak. Germany's *White Book* was presented to the Reichstag on 4 August 1914, while Britain's first *White Paper* was presented to the House of Commons on 6 August. Additional *White Papers* were published in the following weeks and all three were combined and published as the first British *Blue Book*.[3] Russia's *Orange Book* was published on 7 August, while France waited until 1 December before publishing

3 *Great Britain and the European Crisis*, London 1914. For details about the selection process, see for example Keith Hamilton, 'Falsifying the Record: Entente Diplomacy and the Preparation of the Blue and Yellow Books on the War Crisis of 1914', *Diplomacy & Statecraft*, 18, 2007, pp. 89–108. See also Keith Hamilton, 'The Pursuit of "Enlightened Patriotism". The British Foreign Office and Historical Researchers During the Great War and its Aftermath', in Keith M. Wilson (ed.), *Forging the Collective Memory. Government and International Historians through Two World Wars*, Berghahn, Oxford 1996, pp. 192–229, p. 195.

its own documents in the French *Yellow Book*.[4] Serbia's *Blue Book* was published in November, and Austria-Hungary's *Red Book* in February 1915. Each was designed to blame the enemy for the outbreak of war by publishing carefully selected official documents.[5] In addition to offering only a highly selective number of documents, the volumes were also on occasion marred by omissions (not always marked) or additions to the text of the documents themselves, as

---

4 This delay seemed suspicious in the eyes of some critics. See for example Hermann Kantorowitz, *Gutachten zur Kriegsschuldfrage* (1927), ed. Imanuel Geiss, Frankfurt/M. 1967, p. 65. The volume did indeed include an entirely falsified document, namely the French Ambassador's telegram to Paris of 31 July, advising the French Government of Russia's mobilization which appeared in a longer form in the *Yellow Book* (**349**). Paléologue's short telegram from St Petersburg announcing Russia's mobilization was expanded to include a paragraph which justified this move with reference to alleged German and Austrian mobilization measures. (These were at that point an invention.) It is, however, possible that this document was falsified as early as 31 July, rather than just for inclusion in the *Yellow Book*. It is unclear whether the additional words were added at the Quai d'Orsay before the telegram was passed to Viviani on 31 July, as Conan Fischer argues, or whether they were added later for inclusion in the *Yellow Book*. Conan Fischer, *Europe between Democracy and Dictatorship, 1900–1945*, Wiley-Blackwell, Oxford 2011, pp. 37–38. See also Frederick Schuman, *War and Diplomacy in the French Republic*, Whittlesey House, London 1931, p. 233 who considers the earlier falsification a 'possible hypothesis'. Further, see Hamilton, 'Falsifying the Record', p. 90. The *Yellow Book* was published by the Ministère des Affaires Etrangères as: *Documents diplomatiques 1914: la Guerre européenne*, Imprimerie Nationale, Paris 1914). For a critical assessment, see Andrew Barros and Frédéric Guelton, 'Les imprévus de l'histoire instrumentalisée: le livre jaune de 1914 et les Documents Français sur les Origines de la Grande Guerre, 1914–1918', *Revue d'histoire diplomatique*, 1, 2006, pp. 3–22.

5 The publication of so-called coloured books (official document collections, usually published during or after international crises by governments intent on justifying their own positions in foreign-policy matters) was not particular to the situation in 1914, but the urgency with which all governments sought to prove their innocence in the events that led to war was unprecedented. For background about the British *Blue Books*, see e.g. H.W.V. and Temperley L.M. Penson, *A Century of Blue Books 1814–1914*, Cambridge University Press, Cambridge 1938. For details of the history of coloured books and those relating specifically to the First World War, see Sacha Zala, *Geschichte unter der Schere politischer Zensur. Amtliche Aktensammlungen im internationalen Vergleich*, Oldenbourg, Munich 2011, pp. 23–37; Mario Toscano, *The History of Treaties and International Politics: The Documentary and Memoir Sources*, Johns Hopkins Press, Baltimore 1966, pp. 88–103; John W. Langdon, *July 1914, The Long Debate 1918–1990*, Berg, New York, Oxford 1991, p. 17.

well as careful re-arranging of the chronology in which they were despatched, designed to advance a particular point of view. At times the text was rendered in paraphrase, sometimes with the intention of making it impossible for anyone to discover the codes used when the text was initially put into cypher.[6] Not surprisingly, suspicion of falsification of the coloured books was rife (and in some cases justified) during and after the war.[7]

For the purposes of historical research based on published documents it is important to realize that the coloured books were not edited by historians but by diplomats eager to advance a particular version of events. As Winfried Baumgart observes:

> A Government will only publish those documents which appear to it to be useful in rebuffing attacks. In view of a choice having been made in this way one can therefore conclude straight away that pieces that appeared unsuitable would have been deliberately excluded.[8]

In compiling their Coloured Books, the editors did not apply the criteria we would today look for in a scholarly edition of documents. Nonetheless, in the absence of other official publications, as for example in the case of Belgium, historians still rely on the Belgian *Grey Books* on the origins of the war.[9] However, official

6 Winfried Baumgart, *Quellenkunde zur deutschen Geschichte der Neuzeit von 1500 bis zur Gegenwart*, Vol. 5: Das *Zeitalter des Imperialismus und des ersten Weltkrieges (1871–1918)*, Part 1: *Akten und Urkunden*; Part 2: Persönliche Quellen, Wissenschaftliche Buchgesellschaft, Darmstadt, 1977, 2nd edn 1991, Vol. 5, Part 1, p. 69.

7 Zala, *Geschichte unter der Schere*, pp. 31–35. An example of the critique levelled at the Russian *Orange Book* is Gisbert Freiherr von Romberg (ed.), *Die Fälschungen des russischen Orangebuches*, Berlin, Leipzig 1922 (Eng. transl. *The Falsification of the Russian Orange-Book*, Allen &Unwin, London, New York 1923). A critical assessment of the French *Yellow Book* was undertaken by, among others, Bernadotte E. Schmitt, 'France and the Outbreak of the World War', in *Foreign Affairs*, 15, 1937, pp. 516–536. See also (**349**) for an example of the types of document that were falsified in the *Yellow Book*. Examples of the falsifications contained in the British *Blue Book* can be found in Kantorowitz, *Gutachten*, pp. 68–80. For a discussion of the various coloured books, see also Baumgart, *Quellenkunde*, Vol. 5, Part 1, pp. 67ff. See also below, p. 563, n. 79.

8 Ibid., p. 69.

9 Ibid. The five volumes of Belgian documents edited in Germany by Bernhard Schwertfeger are not an official Belgian document collection – rather, they were compiled in Germany with the aim of discrediting the Entente and Belgium. Schwertfeger (ed.), *Amtliche Aktenstücke zur Geschichte der Europäischen Politik 1885–1914. Die Belgischen Dokumente zur Vorgeschichte des Weltkrieges 1885–1914. Vollständige Ausgabe der vom Deutschen Auswärtigen Amt*

document collections, published after the war, are generally a more reliable source for historians, although of course here, too, caution must be exercised when using them.

Revisionists, anti-revisionists, and the world war of documents

Following Germany's defeat, the debate on the war's origins began in earnest. It is not necessary to revisit these arguments here in any detail; many publications have already summarized the long debate on the origins of the war.[10] Briefly, however, there were a number of fairly distinct phases when the outbreak of war was interpreted in different ways. During the war, each combatant power was motivated by the need to justify its own involvement in the war as essentially defensive, and maintain its innocence as regards its outbreak, in order to ensure an enthusiastic support of the war effort. As we have seen, the Coloured Books were one way in which this aim was pursued.

After the war, the efforts on Germany's side were much intensified following the Versailles Peace Settlement, which attributed sole war guilt to Germany and her Allies (Article 231). 'Revisionists' (chiefly, but not exclusively, in Germany) who objected to the war guilt allegation of the victors and wanted to revise it clashed with their opponents ('anti-revisionists') over their interpretations of the events that had led to war. Governments saw themselves involved in a 'battle by means of archive documents',[11] even, in the words of the German historian Bernhard Schwertfeger, engaged in 'a world war of documents'.[12] As a result, an enormous number of previously secret documents were made available for public scrutiny. The

herausgegebenen Diplomatischen Urkunden aus den Belgischen Staatsarchiven, 5 vols, Deutsche Verlagsgesellschaft für Politik und Geschichte, Berlin 1919.

10 Among them James Joll and Gordon Martel, *The Origins of the First World War*, Longman, London, 3rd edn, 2007; Langdon, *The Long Debate*; Annika Mombauer, *The Origins of the First World War. Controversies and Consensus*, Longman, Harlow 2002; William Mulligan, *The Origins of the First World War*, Cambridge University Press, Cambridge 2010; Dieter Hoffmann, *Der Sprung ins Dunkle. Oder wie der 1. Weltkrieg entfesselt wurde*, Militzke Verlag, Leipzig 2010.

11 Pokrovsky, cited in Derek Spring, 'Russian Documents on the Origins of the First World War', in Wilson (ed.), *Forging*, pp. 63–86, p. 71.

12 Bernhard Schwertfeger, *Der Weltkrieg der Dokumente. Zehn Jahre Kriegsschuldforschung und ihr Ergebnis*, Berlin 1929.

period following the war was characterized by an unprecedented opening of the archives, even if not all the official document editions that resulted from this can be classed as scholarly.[13]

In Russia, the new Soviet Government led the way, eager to highlight the shortcomings of the previous Tsarist regime and of imperialism in general, which it saw as the cause of the war.[14] Lenin announced two days after the beginning of the October Revolution that the new Government would immediately proceed to publish all secret treaties, and as a result the world learned for the first time, for example, about the secret London Treaty of 26 April 1915 in which the Entente Powers promised Italy territorial gains in return for her entry into the war.[15] Their motivation provides an explanation about the nature of the editions they produced in which 'objectivity' was no selection criterion. As Sacha Zala observes:

> It goes without saying that neither the desire for scholarly engagement with the past nor love for historical detail, but only immediate political interests and deficiencies of legitimization motivated the new rulers effectively to unmask the unscrupulous imperialist power policy of the preceding dynasties.[16]

The Russian historian M.N.Pokrovsky suggested as early as 1918 that Russian historical documents should be centralized in an archive, and in 1921 he was appointed head of the new central archive, and became the editor of the journal *Krasnyi Arkhiv*, a major publication whose aim it was to 'expose the secrets of imperialist policy and diplomacy'.[17] Its first volume contained a large number of previously unpublished documents, and the journal continued to publish documents, albeit in a rather ad hoc fashion. Eventually, in reaction to publications of official document collections in Germany and Britain (more on this below) a more systematic collection was deemed necessary.

The first five volumes of Russian documents, covering the first seven months of 1914 and entitled *International Relations in the Age of Imperialism. Documents from the Archives of the Tsarist and Provisional Governments*, were published between 1931 and

---

13 Zala, *Geschichte unter der Schere*, p. 50.
14 For details of the history of publication of Russian documents, see the excellent account by Spring, 'Russian Documents', pp. 63–86.
15 Zala, *Geschichte unter der Schere*, p. 48.
16 Ibid., p. 47.
17 Cited in Spring, 'Russian Documents', p. 67.

1934 by Pokrovsky, and a simultaneous German-language edition appeared in Berlin, translated by the historian Otto Hoetsch, who had collaborated with Pokrovsky.[18] The collection contained over 2,000 documents, but was regarded as disappointing by some in Germany 'because it contains [...] not one really new or weighty document which could convince our enemies and the neutrals of the error of their opinions'.[19] While disappointing for German revisionists at the time of its publication, the collection is certainly very useful for scholars today. As Derek Spring observes, the documents in this edition (and subsequent Soviet series of document collections) 'were selected and edited to such a high standard [...] that they still remain as the essential starting point for [an] examination of the Russian role in the origins of the war'.[20] A number of documents from these volumes have been included in this collection, supplemented by other sources which have subsequently been unearthed by Russian historians. They enable us to highlight and unravel the complex decision-making of military and political leaders in St Petersburg, their relationship with their French ally and the contentious decision for mobilization in 1914.

In Germany, Kurt Eisner's revolutionary government in Munich took their cue from the Soviet publication, and published the Bavarian documents about the origins of the war. This decision was also motivated by a wish to influence world opinion against the old regime by highlighting its responsibility for war, and it preceded the Treaty of Versailles.[21] 'This is the only means with which to achieve that the peace negotiations can be conducted on the spirit of mutual trust', Eisner wrote on 21 November 1918.[22]

Soon, the Socialist government in Berlin decided that in order to influence the peace negotiations at Versailles, it would be advan-

18 *Mezhdunarodnye Otnosheniya v Epokhu Imparializma. Dokumenty iz arkhivov tsarskogo i vremennogo pravitel'stv*, published also under the German title *Die Internationalen Beziehungen im Zeitalter des Imperialismus* (cited below hereafter as *Int. Bez.*) For more details on the background to this publication, see Spring, 'Russian Documents', pp. 74ff.

19 This was the complaint by the publisher. Cited in Spring, 'Russian Documents', p. 77.

20 Ibid, p. 82.

21 For details, see for example Bernhard Grau, *Kurt Eisner 1867–1919. Eine Biographie*, Beck, Munich 2001, pp. 377–391.

22 P. Dirr (ed.), *Bayerische Dokumente zum Kriegsausbruch und zum Versailler Schuldspruch*, 3rd edn, Oldenbourg, Munich, Berlin 1925, Doc. No. 22.

tageous to underline the complete rupture of the new German state with the old, and to lay bare the decisions that had led to the outbreak of war and thus perhaps bring about a more lenient peace agreement.[23] Their call for an international committee of experts to assess the origins of the war had been rejected and they decided to publish their own documents. Karl Kautsky was initially charged with this task. Despite his declared intention to approach the task in 'Rankean fashion' (i.e., striving for objectivity and attempting to portray events 'as they had really been'), he was in fact convinced of Germany's war guilt and this influenced his selection criteria.[24] His work was greeted by a heated controversy and objection from historians and politicians, and his selection was only published after two editors of more patriotic persuasion, Max Montgelas and Walter Schücking, had taken over from him. Four volumes of German Documents (*Die Deutschen Dokumente zum Kriegsausbruch*, or DD), sometimes referred to as the 'Kautsky-Documents', were published in December 1919.[25] Too late to influence the Allies' decision at Versailles as had been the original intention, it is in any case difficult to see how what was contained within them could have led to a more lenient ruling by the victorious allies in any case. The volumes are still a useful collection for historians, and a number of documents for this edition have been included in this volume. Usefully, they include the many incendiary marginal notes penned by Kaiser Wilhelm II at crucial junctures, and where those are available, they have been reproduced here.

Proving Germany's innocence had become much more pressing following the Versailles war-guilt clause which burdened a defiant Germany with sole responsibility for starting the war that most Germans felt they had not caused.[26] In the summer of 1919 the German Government decided to commission a more extensive

---

23 Zala, *Geschichte unter der Schere*, p. 50.

24 Ibid.

25 *Die deutschen Dokumente zum Kriegsausbruch. Vollständige Sammlung der von Karl Kautsky zusammengestellten amtlichen Aktenstücke mit einigen Ergänzungen*, edited by Graf Max Montgelas and Walter Schücking, 5 vols, Charlottenburg 1919 (cited hereafter as DD).

26 As Holger Herwig shows, the attempts to 'deceive Clio' with official document collections and accounts of the outbreak of war began in August 1914, when the German Government authorized publications aimed at showing that 'the ring of entente politics encircled us ever more tightly'. Holger H. Herwig, 'Clio Deceived. Patriotic Self-Censorship in Germany after the Great War', in Wilson (ed.), *Forging*, pp. 87–127.

edition of documents spanning the years 1871–1914, and the first volumes of what would eventually be a 40-volume collection were published in 1922.[27] The intention was still to prove the victors wrong regarding the origins of the war. As the German Chancellor Wilhelm Marx wrote to the British Prime Minister Ramsay McDonald in 1924, with reference to this official German document collection *Die Grosse Politik* (GP), the German Government fully intended to use the documents contained in these volumes to force the victors of 1918 to convene an international court of arbitration to re-examine the war-guilt question.[28] Germany's inter-war governments regarded the publication of these documents as an 'act of self-defence'[29] and as part of the large-scale 'innocence propaganda' which dominated publications of this period.[30] By publishing documents relating to international relations in the pre-war period, the editors sought to highlight the foreign policy pursuits of other governments in the years before the war. Their early release of official documents on such a large scale certainly ensured that almost all studies of the origins of the war had to use the voluminous German document collection as their starting points.[31]

Despite the criticism levelled at the edition for its 'legitimizing character', the selectivity employed by its editors and the confusing manner in which the documents were organized thematically rather than chronologically, historians have concluded that the edition was scholarly enough that 'the value of any single source

---

27 The last volume was published in 1927. *Die Grosse Politik der Europäischen Kabinette, 1871–1914. Sammlung der Diplomatischen Aktenstücke des Auswärtigen Amtes*, edited (on behalf of the *Auswärtiges Amt*) by Johannes Lepsius, Albrecht Mendelssohn Bartholdy and Friedrich Thimme, 40 vols, Berlin 1922–1927.

28 Wilson (ed.), *Forging*, p. 11.

29 Ibid., p. 12. For a critique of the selectivity employed by the editors see e.g. Fritz Klein, 'Über die Verfälschung der Historischen Wahrheit in der Aktenpublikation "Die Grosse Politik der Europäischen Kabinette 1871–1914"', in *Zeitschrift für Geschichtswissenschaft*, 7, 1959, pp. 318–330; and for an excellent summary of the genesis of the edition, and of the criticism levelled at it, see Zala, *Geschichte unter der Schere*, pp. 62ff.

30 As Konrad Repgen points out, Weimar historians 'did not engage in controversies with each other [...], the debates over the causes of the war of 1914 were waged as a fight, although not internally, but rather directed to the outside'. Konrad Repgen, 'Methoden – oder Richtungskämpfe in der deutschen Geschichtswissenschaft seit 1945?', *Geschichte in Wissenschaft und Unterricht*, 30, 1979, pp. 591–610, p. 600, cited in Zala, *Geschichte unter der Schere*, p. 68.

31 Herwig, 'Clio Deceived', p. 96.

remains unaffected by these criticisms',[32] and the volumes constitute 'an indispensable source for the study of late nineteenth- and early twentieth-century history.[33] For the purposes of compiling the present edition of collected documents, individual documents contained within the volumes of *Die Grosse Politik* have been included without undue concern about their authenticity.

The post-war government in the new Austrian Republic also published a three-volume edition of documents in 1919, *Die österreichisch-ungarischen Dokumente zum Kriegsausbruch*.[34] They were explicitly conceived as an addition to and extension of the Austrian *Red Book* published during the war, and it seems as if Otto Bauer, the Austrian Secretary of State for Foreign Affairs, wanted to copy attempts by Kurt Eisner in Bavaria to influence the proceedings at Saint-Germain by appearing trustworthy and to some extent remorseful (albeit by publishing documents which pointed to the guilt of governments which were no longer in existence).

In response to the official publications of both former allies and enemies, a large-scale publication of documents eventually got under way and the resulting Austro-Hungarian document collection was published by Ludwig Bittner et al. as *Österreich-Ungarns ussenpolitik von der bosnischen Krise bis zum Kriegsausbruch 1914*,[35] in nine volumes which were published simultaneously in 1930. Due to financial restrictions and time pressure, the volumes only covered the period 1908 to 1914 and focused exclusively on Austria-Hungary's Balkan policy. However, they contained 11,000 documents for this period, while Germany's GP contained 15,000 documents, covering 44 years and a much larger geographical

32 Matthias Peter and Hans-Jürgen Schröder, *Einführung in das Studium der Zeitgeschichte*, Paderborn 1994, pp. 206f., cited in Zala, *Geschichte unter der Schere*, p. 76, n. 240.

33 Hamilton, 'Falsifying the record', p. 89.

34 *Die österreichisch-ungarischen Dokumente zum Kriegsausbruch. Diplomatische Aktenstücke zur Vorgeschichte des Krieges 1914. Ergänzungen und Nachträge zum österreichisch-ungarischen Rotbuch*, ed. by Staatsamt für Äusseres, 3 vols, Vienna 1919. For details on Austria's document editions see Ulfried Burz, 'Austria and the Great War. Official Publications in the 1920s and 1930s' in Wilson (ed.), *Forging*, pp. 178–191; Rudolf Jerábek, 'Die österreichische Weltkriegsforschung' in Wolfgang Michalka (ed.), *Der Erste Weltkrieg*, Piper, Munich 1994, pp. 953–971.

35 Ludwig Bittner et al. (eds), *Österreich-Ungarns Aussenpolitik von der bosnischen Krise bis zum Kriegsausbruch 1914*, 9 vols, Österreichische Bundesanstalt für Unterricht, Wissenschaft und Kultur, Vienna and Leipzig, 1930.

range.[36] The nature of this collection is thus different from that of those published by the other Great Powers, which offered a more comprehensive account of foreign policy in a longer time-frame before the war. This makes the Austrian collection 'of a unique nature, something less than a true general collection and something more than a monographic one'.[37] The volumes contain a lot of interesting documents on the July Crisis in particular, and many of them have been included in this collection.

Other governments felt the pressure to publish their secret documents, these 'sharpest of weapons',[38] largely in response to the early document collections already published in the Soviet Union, Austria and particularly Germany whose attempt to refute the allied war-guilt ruling was showing promise in the light of published evidence which foregrounded shared responsibility rather than sole German war guilt. The publication of *Die Grosse Politik* forced Britain and France to consider adopting similar measures, as contemporaries had predicted,[39] and Britain was the first to respond with an official document publication. 'Rather late', as Max Montgelas criticized, the *British Documents on the Origins of the War* (BD) were published between 1926 and 1938.[40] The British Government's intention to publish an official document collection was announced in 1924 (when Prime Minister Ramsay McDonald decided, in G.P. Gooch's words, 'to break the seals'), although James W. Headlam-Morley had already previously been appointed to edit a collection similar to Kautsky's *Deutsche Dokumente*.[41] Now two established and well-known historians were charged with the task in an attempt to suggest 'historical accuracy & impartiality' to the outside world, an important departure from the previous attempts by govern-

36 In an early enthusiastic review, William L. Langer was impressed by the quality of the edition which he considered 'a Christmas surprise for the historian [...] which he will not soon forget'. There was 'every guarantee of its complete honesty', he concluded. Langer, review of *Österreich-Ungarns Aussenpolitik von der bosnischen Krise bis zum Kriegsausbruch 1914,* Foreign Affairs, April 1930.

37 Toscano, *Treaties*, p. 153.

38 M.N. Pokrovsky, 28 November 1927, in an article in *Pravda*, cited in Spring, 'Russian Documents', p. 72. Klaus Hildebrand also refers to 'files as weapons'. *Deutsche Außenpolitik 1871–1914*, Munich 1989, p. 52.

39 E.g. Thimme and Schwertfeger had predicted a compulsion to publish among the former enemies. Cited in Zala, *Geschichte unter der Schere*, p. 77.

40 Montgelas cited in Zala, *Geschichte unter der Schere*, p. 78.

41 Mombauer, *Controversies*, pp. 57ff.

ments to direct and influence the publication of official documents by excluding historians from this task.[42] In practice, however, the editors had to contend with historian and civil servant James Headlam-Morley whose previously compiled collection on the July Crisis became the last of the eleven-volume publication of *British Documents on the Origins of the First World War* (BD), but the first to be published.[43] His introduction, stressing the need to consider the feelings of other governments over the necessity for historical accuracy and completeness, laid the volumes open to criticism from other historians and resulted in 'serious tensions' between the editors and Headlam-Morley.[44] In subsequent forewords the editors made clear their desire for complete objectivity on their part as regards the selection process, stressing that they would have felt 'compelled to resign if any attempt were made to insist on the omission of any document which is in their view vital or essential'.[45]

Gooch's and Temperley's task was more difficult, compared with that of their German, Austrian and Russian colleagues, because in London there had been no regime change and certain continuities (of personnel or policy, for example) might have affected their editorial work. Some critics have therefore considered the *British Documents* to be even more flawed than their German equivalent.[46] However, it has also been noted that 'on more than one occasion the editors demonstrated a remarkable broadmindedness in their choices'.[47] The inclusion of the minutes added to many documents

42 Zala, *Geschichte unter der Schere*, p. 79.

43 BD, Vol. XI: *The Outbreak of the War. Foreign Office Documents* (28 June–4 August), London 1926.

44 In the words of historian Herbert Butterfield. For details see Zala, *Geschichte unter der Schere*, pp. 80f.

45 Foreword to Vol. 3, cited in ibid, p. 82.

46 Zala, *Geschichte unter der Schere*, p. 83, who cites the Soviet historian A.S. Jerussalimski as an example of this critique.

47 Toscano points out the example of Goschen's report of 6 August, which related to the infamous 'scrap of paper' conversation on 4 August in which Germany's Chancellor Bethmann Hollweg had allegedly dismissed the treaty which guaranteed Belgian neutrality as a 'scrap of paper'. By including the document it was revealed that the phrase, of which so much was made by Allied propaganda against Germany, had 'no disparaging implication whatsoever'. The very fact that this document was included 'testifies to a high degree of objectivity'. *Treaties*, p. 141. It should, however, be noted that the document had previously been published, immediately after Goschen had presented his report to Parliament, as the *Blue Book Miscellaneous No. 6*. T.G. Otte, 'A "German Paperchase": The "Scrap

by diplomats in Whitehall attests further to the collection's 'scientific value'. The minutes, written in the belief that they would not be published, allow a unique insight into the 'internal formative process of British foreign policy'.[48] The documents contained within the official British collection can be used with confidence by historians working on the topic today,[49] and a number of them, including the confidential minutes, have been selected for this collection.

In France, the 'Commission de Publication des Documents relatifs aux Origines de la Guerre de 1914–1918' was constituted in 1928 and charged with editing official government documents which would result in France's official publication *Les Documents diplomatiques français 1871–1914* (DDF).[50] The decision to publish French documents (in addition to the three volumes of *Yellow Books* published between 1918 and 1921) was announced by the Poincaré government in 1927, partly motivated by the fact that revisionist historians were basing their apologetic accounts of Germany's role in the outbreak of the war on Germany's official document collection.[51] Pierre de Margerie, who had been Political Director in the French Foreign Office in July 1914, noted in 1926: 'There can be no doubt that under the influence of the enormous quantity of documents that the *Wilhelmstrasse* has thrown on to the historical market, world opinion has begun to change to our disadvantage.'[52] The first volume was published in 1929, leading to sarcastic remarks about the delay of the French publication. Bernhard Schwertfeger considered it 'perhaps the most important success of the German document edition [GP] that France has also decided to publish [her] pre-war documents [...] France has been the last [...] to follow the German example'.[53] The last of the 42 volumes was not published until 1959, with the 3rd series, focusing on the July Crisis, having been completed in 1936.[54]

of Paper" Controversy and the Problem of Myth and Memory in International History', *Diplomacy & Statecraft*, 18, 1, 2007, pp. 53–87, pp. 57ff. See (**419**).

48 Toscano, *Treaties*, pp. 141–142.

49 Zala, *Geschichte unter der Schere*, p. 84.

50 For details see Keith Hamilton, 'The Historical Diplomacy of the Third Republic', in Wilson (ed.), *Forging*, pp. 29–62, p. 44; Mombauer, *Controversies*, pp. 65ff.

51 Zala, *Geschichte unter der Schere*, p. 85.

52 Cited in Hamilton, 'Historical Diplomacy', p. 44.

53 Cited in Zala, *Geschichte unter der Schere*, p. 84.

54 As Jean-Baptiste Duroselle points out, this was a full decade after the British documents for the same period had been published. *La Grande Guerre des Français: l'incompréhensible*, Perrin, Paris, 1994, p. 26.

The French official document collection *Documents diplomatiques français* was modelled on the German example in terms of its time-span (1870–1914) and its focus on the diplomatic causes of the war, although it adopted a chronological approach.[55]

Although the edition could be regarded as the most scholarly of the official document collections, it should not be overlooked that among the 54 members of the commission there were only 19 historians, the rest being recruited mainly among diplomats, including – controversially – some of the former ambassadors who had been in office during the July Crisis (Maurice Paléologue, Jules Cambon and Camille Barrère, for example).[56] However, the French official collection also contains many documents which were not in France's favour in the war-guilt controversy.[57] For historians working on this topic, the official French document collection is still an essential first port of call, and a number of its documents can be found in this collection.

Italy was the only one of the Great Powers not to publish any official diplomatic documents in the inter-war years.[58] There was no immediate political reason for such an edition, considering that the war-guilt question did not affect Italy which had remained neutral in 1914. Moreover, Mussolini's Government was not inclined towards a large document edition which aimed at revealing the 'historical truth'.[59] It was only after the Second World War that a commission was charged with the publication of Italian diplomatic documents. The lateness of this project meant that the time frame of the edition was extended to include the years 1861 to 1943. Five series were being worked on simultaneously and publication is still not complete. The last volumes are expected to be completed about 80–100 years after the publication of the first ones in 1954.[60] The multi-volume series *I documenti diplomatici italiani* deals with the origins of the war in Series 4 and 5.[61] Some of the documents contained therein have been translated for inclusion in this collection, particularly

55 For details see Zala, *Geschichte unter der Schere*, p. 85; Baumgart, *Quellenkunde*, p. 127; Hamilton, 'Historical Diplomacy', pp. 43ff.

56 Zala, *Geschichte unter der Schere*, p. 87.

57 Toscano, *Treaties*, p. 152.

58 Wilson (ed.), *Forging*, p. 5.

59 Baumgart, *Quellenkunde*, 5, I, p. 38.

60 Ibid., p. 39.

61 A. Torre/Ministero degli affari esteri. Commissione per la pubblicazione dei documenti diplomatici (eds), *I documenti diplomatici Italiani*, Series 1–9 (1861–1943), Rome, 1954ff.

pertaining to Italy's decision for neutrality during the July Crisis.

Clearly, the Serbian documents are of great significance, but the Yugoslav Ministry of Foreign Affairs refused to publish Serbian documents after the war. In the absence of any official government publication (to this day), historians have had to rely on a collection published by the former Serbian Minister in Berlin, Milos Boghicević, which is available in German translation.[62] This is not an official document collection, but rather the private collection of a former diplomat with a strong bias against the policies of the pre-war Serbian government.[63] Due to the collection's 'polemical character', the material might as best 'be considered adequate as an outline of the general scheme of Serbian policy, it is very nearly impossible to use in determining the roles played by individuals and in delegating responsibility'.[64] Historians working on Serbia's policy prior to 1914 can, however, benefit from a scholarly edition containing documents in Serbo-Croat, French, German and Russian. Vladimir Dedijer and Života Anić's *Dokumenti o spolnoj politici Kraljevine Srbije 1903–1914* (Documents on the Foreign Policy of the Serbian Kingdom, 1903–1914) covers the years 1903 to 1914 in seven volumes, and some of the evidence contained in its volumes has been included in this collection.[65]

The Fischer controversy and the renewed quest for archival sources

In the inter-war years, a variety of views were advocated as to why war had broken out in 1914. Most pronounced was the effort to blame the Dual Alliance Powers, and Germany in particular, as had been the case in the Treaty of Versailles. But other arguments were advanced, for example blaming primarily France and Russia (H.E. Barnes), or arguing that no single country was ultimately responsible for the escalation of the July Crisis into war (S.B. Fay).[66] By

62 Milos Boghitschewitsch (ed.), *Die auswärtige Politik Serbiens 1903–1914*, 3 vols, Brückenverlag, Berlin 1928–1931.

63 Toscano, *Treaties*, p. 156.

64 Ibid., p. 157.

65 Vladimir Dedijer and Života Anić (eds), *Dokumenti o spolnoj politici Kraljevine Srbije*, VII/2, Belgrade 1980.

66 See Holger Herwig and Richard Hamilton (eds), *The Outbreak of World War I. Causes and Responsibilities*, 5th revised edn, Lexington, MA, 1991, pp. 10–11.

the 1930s, a new war-guilt consensus had been established, and the efforts of revisionist historians, often backed up by the official document collections, were becoming the new orthodoxy. It now became widely accepted that Europe had 'slithered into war' as a result of blunders and accidents as David Lloyd George had maintained in his *War Memoirs*.[67]

After the Second World War, revisionist views continued to be widely held and the perception of European nations accidentally stumbling into war in 1914 was still predominant. Even the former enemies France and Germany were able to agree on a conciliatory interpretation which effectively negated German sole war guilt. This point of view was challenged by a number of scholars, including the Italian Luigi Albertini, but none had more impact than Fritz Fischer's interpretation of the origins of the war, advanced in the early 1960s.[68] Based on new documentary evidence (some of it contained in this collection) he and his followers exploded this comfortable orthodox view and argued that Germany had plotted with Austria-Hungary to start a war against Serbia, and that Germany's decision-makers had deliberately accepted the risk of an escalation of a localized into a European war because they had pursued aggressive foreign-policy aims.[69]

The ensuing debate divided historians into pro- and anti-Fischer camps in a controversy that was passionately fought for nearly two decades. Eventually a consensus was reached which largely

---

67 David Lloyd George, *War Memoirs*, Vol. I, Odhams Press, London, 1938. For more details on the historiographical developments in the 1930s to 1950s, see Mombauer, *Controversies*, pp. 105ff.

68 Fritz Fischer, *Griff nach der Weltmacht. Die Kriegszielpolitik des kaiserlichen Deutschlands, 1914/18*, first published 1961. Nachdruck der Sonderausgabe 1967, Düsseldorf 1984 (Eng. transl.: *Germany's Aims in the First World War*, London 1967); idem, *Krieg der Illusionen. Die deutsche Politik von 1911–1914*, paperpack reprint of 2nd edn 1970 (1st edn 1969), Droste, Düsseldorf 1987 (Eng. transl.: *War of Illusions. German Policies from 1911–1914*, Norton, London 1975); idem, *Juli 1914: Wir sind nicht hineingeschlittert. Das Staatsgeheimnis um die Riezler Tagebücher*, Rowohlt, Reinbek 1983. See also the special issue of *The Journal of Contemporary History* on the Fischer controversy, edited by Annika Mombauer, forthcoming 2013.

69 Among Fischer's followers was his assistant Imanuel Geiss, whose groundbreaking document collection *Julikrise und Kriegsausbruch* provided the documentary evidence which demonstrated design, rather than accident, in Berlin's and Vienna's decision-making. Many of the documents he published in the 1960s are now also contained in this collection.

acknowledged that Germany bore a significant amount of responsibility for the outbreak of war, that her leaders did conspire to provoke a war and that they had been willing to risk an international conflagration.[70] In recent years historians have again come to question, albeit more dispassionately than Fischer's contemporary critics, his focus on Germany, and some would consider a Fischerite interpretation to be outdated and somewhat limited, particularly in the light of international evidence which has come to light since his theses were first advanced. That is not necessarily to say that what he alleged about German intentions was not true, but rather that the intentions of the other key players also deserve our attention. As a consequence, more emphasis has been put on analysing the actions of the other great powers, and in particular on Austria-Hungary's decision-makers, whose important role in the crisis had been somewhat overshadowed during the Fischer controversy. As the documents in this volume show, it was in Vienna that the first decisions for a confrontation with Serbia were taken, and it was of course Austria-Hungary which issued the first declaration of war. Clearly, the actions of her decision-makers deserve some close scrutiny.

Historians have also increasingly focused their attention on the crises of the pre-war years which, in the Fischer interpretation, seem largely to have been the result of German posturing, and which seem – at least with hindsight – almost inevitably to have led to war. This view of an unavoidable trajectory towards a European war has recently been questioned. Instead, it has been argued that the 'concert of Europe' actually worked quite efficiently before 1914, as international crises were solved by negotiation, rather than a war involving the Great Powers. The First World War was thus preceded by a period of 'avoided wars', and the question that needs answering is why it was not avoided once more in 1914.[71]

Historians today largely argue for an internationalization in attempting to unravel the origins of the war, by acknowledging more fully the role of all the Great Powers in the pre-war years

70 In October 2011, an international symposium of historians revisited the Fischer controversy on the occasion of the 50th anniversary of the publication of *Griff nach der Weltmacht*. Some of the papers can be found in *The Journal of Contemporary History*, special issue, ed. Annika Mombauer, 2013, forthcoming.

71 See for example Holger Afflerbach and David Stevenson (eds), *An Improbable War? The Outbreak of World War I and European Political Culture before 1914*, Berghahn, New York 2007.

and months. A hundred years after the outbreak of the war, the new direction in the historiography of the war's origins appears on the face of it to hark back to some extent to the comfortable consensus of the inter-war years which emphasized shared war guilt. However, whereas in the 1930s the alliance system was blamed and the outbreak of war was considered an accident, today human agency is foregrounded – this suggests that there was no inevitability about the war's outbreak, but that it resulted from either mistakes, deliberate decisions or both. Moreover, even those who still see in Germany's actions the main cause of the war will acknowledge that she did not act in isolation, and that it was actually Austria-Hungary which took the first steps on the road to war. Others point towards Russia and France and argue that the two partners were not just victims of an Alliance plot, but that they pursued their own foreign-policy goals in and before July 1914 which ultimately did not rule out the possibility of war and that they even welcomed it when it came.[72]

Such an extensive and productive historiographical controversy which has produced countless accounts of why the First World War broke out has also resulted in an unprecedented wealth of primary evidence, as historians scoured the archives in order to arm themselves with primary sources to support their arguments. Fischer and his assistants found much of his more incendiary evidence in unpublished and previously inaccessible archival sources, many in the archives of East Germany. His publications and the ensuing controversy resulted in a quest by the so-called 'Fischer-school' and by their critics to locate further primary evidence and publish it in scholarly editions.[73] So heated was this debate, and so important

72 Sean McMeekin claims that Russia was to blame for the outbreak of the war which it unleashed because of the desire to claim the Straits for Russia. *The Russian Origins of the First World War*, Harvard University Press, Cambridge, MA 2011. The case for a reappraisal of France's role in the events leading to war is made by Stefan Schmidt, *Frankreichs Außenpolitik in der Julikrise 1914. Ein Beitrag zur Geschichte des Ausbruchs des Ersten Weltkrieges*, Oldenbourg, Munich 2007.

73 Among them (and this is no exhaustive list) are Imanuel Geiss's two-volume document collection *Julikrise und Kriegsausbruch 1914* (of which an abridged German and an English edition were published in 1965 and 1967 respectively), John Röhl's publication of memoranda by Prince Karl Max von Lichnowsky and Prince Philipp zu Eulenburg, and his 3-volume edition of the Eulenburg papers, the diaries of Kurt Riezler, edited by Karl Dietrich Erdmann, and the diaries of the journalist Theodor Wolff, edited by Bernd Sösemann, to name only a few.

were documents in proving the point for one side or the other, that arguments even ensued over the authenticity of primary sources, and the reliability of published editions of documents. In this sense, primary sources continued to be used as weapons by historians. Prominent examples include the published diaries of Alfred von Waldersee, Georg Alexander von Müller and Kurt Riezler.[74]

Indeed, it has been a characteristic of the debate that historians were unable to agree on the interpretation of certain key documents, such as Admiral von Müller's diary entry detailing the events of the so-called War Council meeting of December 1912. Did his account of the meeting suggest that something momentous had been decided (a definite decision to unleash war, postponed for exactly 18 months until July 1914), or was Müller's own conclusion that this meeting had really amounted to 'almost 0' correct, as Walter Görlitz's truncated rendering of the text had suggested?[75] Similarly, Bethmann

---

Geiss (ed.), *Julikrise und Kriegsausbruch*; Geiss (ed.), *Juli 1914* (Eng. transl. *July 1914*); Röhl (ed.), *Zwei deutsche Fürsten zur Kriegsschuldfrage*, English transl.: *1914: Delusion or Design?*; Röhl (ed.) *Philipp Eulenburgs Politische Korrespondenz*, 3 volumes, Boldt, Boppard/Rhein 1976–1983; Karl Dietrich Erdmann (ed.), *Kurt Riezler. Tagebücher, Aufsätze, Dokumente*, Vandenhoeck and Ruprecht, Göttingen 1972, republished, with an introduction by Holger Afflerbach, Vandenhoeck and Ruprecht, Göttingen 2008; Bernd Sösemann (ed.), *Theodor Wolff. Tagebücher 1914–1918*. Boppard/Rhein 1984. Other important more recent edited collection include the diaries of Albert Hopman, prominent member of the Reichsmarineamt (the German Naval Office), edited by Michael Epkenhans, *Albert Hopman. Das ereignisreiche Leben eines 'Wilhelminers'. Tagebücher, Briefe, Aufzeichnungen 1901 bis 1920*, Oldenbourg, Munich 2004. Holger Afflerbach edited letters by Generaloberst Moriz Freiherr von Lyncker, the chief of the military cabinet, and the wartime diaries of Generaloberst Hans Georg von Plessen, general adjutant and commander of the Imperial Headquarters in *Kaiser Wilhelm II als oberster Kriegsherr im Ersten Weltkrieg: Quellen aus der militärischen Umgebung des Kaisers 1914–1918*, Oldenbourg, Munich 2005.

74 For example, the debate about the so-called war council meeting of December 1912 called into question the accuracy of Walter Görlitz's edition of the Müller diaries. While some of the diary entries reflect accurately the original text, others were altered by the editor to present a more favourable version of events. Walter Görlitz (ed.), *Regierte der Kaiser? Kriegstagebücher, Aufzeichnungen und Briefe des Chefs des Marinekabinetts, Admiral Georg Alexander von Müller 1914–1918*, Musterschmidt ,Göttingen, Berlin, Frankfurt/Main 2nd edn, 1959; Walter Görlitz, *Der Kaiser ... Aufzeichnungen des Chefs des Marinekabinetts Admiral Georg Alexander von Müller über die Ära Wilhelms II.*, Musterschmidt, Göttingen 1965. For a critique of the edition see John Röhl, 'Admiral von Müller and the Approach of War, 1911–1914', *Historical Journal*, 12, 1969, pp. 651–673.

75 See for example Röhl, 'Admiral von Müller', and see docs (**44**), (**46**), (**47**).

Hollweg's attitude in the weeks before the outbreak of war, revealed in the diary of his personal assistant Kurt Riezler, could be interpreted either as evidence of the Chancellor's pessimism and fear in 1914, or of his policy of 'bluff' or calculated risk during the July Crisis.

Some documents were so contested that they were the cause of their own controversy, and the Riezler diary, published by Karl-Dietrich Erdmann, is a case in point.[76] Prior to their publication, Erdmann had claimed that the diaries – which so far only he had seen – proved Fischer wrong, particularly regarding Bethmann Hollweg's role during the July Crisis. Both sides (i.e., Fischer and his supporters on the one hand, and his critics on the other) therefore awaited the publication of the diaries with great anticipation. Riezler had been a close confidant of the Chancellor and as such in almost daily contact with him during July 1914 – his observations would surely allow us to judge Bethmann Hollweg's intentions. When the long-awaited edition appeared in 1972, doubts were soon raised about the authenticity of parts of the documents and about the fact that they did not contain the explosive evidence that one had been led to expect.[77] However, a real controversy did not begin until the early 1980s, when the principal attack against Erdmann's edition was launched by Bernd Sösemann who criticized the volume

76 The history of the publication, and of the controversy over the diaries, is detailed in Agnes Blänsdorf, 'Der Weg der Riezler-Tagebücher. Zur Kontroverse über die Echtheit der Tagebücher Kurt Riezlers', *Geschichte in Wissenschaft und Unterricht*, 35, 1984, pp. 651–684. For an account in English, see Langdon, *The Long Debate*, pp. 109ff. The diaries were published by Erdmann, *Kurt Riezler*. For a bibliography of the relevant newspaper articles and publications around the Riezler controversy, and a strong attack on Erdmann, see Bernd Felix Schulte, *Die Verfälschung der Riezler Tagebücher. Ein Beitrag zur Wissenschaftsgeschichte der 50er und 60er Jahre*, Peter Lang, Frankfurt/M., Bern and New York 1985. For the debate in the German press, see e.g. Karl-Heinz Janssen, 'August '14: Wahrheit auf Raten. Zwei Historiker streiten um Tagebücher: Wurde die deutsche Kriegsschuld am Ersten Weltkrieg im nationalen Interesse verschleiert?', *Die Zeit*, No. 24, 10 June 1983; Karl Dietrich Erdmann, 'Die Tagebücher sind echt. Streit um ein historisches Dokument, das ins Zwielicht geraten ist. Eine Antwort', *Die Zeit*, No. 28, 8 July 1983; and letters to the editor, *Die Zeit*, No. 33, 12 August 1983. The 'duel' between Erdmann and Bernd Sösemann was largely conducted in the pages of the *Historische Zeitschrift*. The extracts of the diary which are included in this collection have been checked against the original archive copy which Bernd Sösemann kindly made available to me (**135**), (**138**), (**147**), (**181**).

77 Fritz Fellner concluded: 'The Riezler diaries do not reveal anything and do not prove anything.' Review of *Kurt Riezler. Tagebücher, Aufsätze, Dokumente*', in *Mitteilungen des Österreichischen Instituts für Geschichte*, 1973, pp. 490–495.

primarily on technical grounds.[78] The suspicion was raised that some incriminating material had been removed, either by Riezler himself, or by someone else after his death. As far as critics of the edition were concerned, the reliability of the diary has to be seriously called into question.[79] The importance attached to contemporary evidence as a way of laying bare the decision-making of July 1914 added to the heated nature of the Riezler diary controversy. In the end, the diary failed to confirm the views of one or other side in the debate, while the controversy surrounding its authenticity only added to the mistrust between the different factions. Extracts from the archive copy have been included in this collection.[80] Read in conjunction with other documents, Riezler's diary illuminates Bethmann Hollweg's anxieties in 1914, and due to the importance of its author, and of the controversy it caused, it should not be missing from a document collection on the origins of the war, despite the doubts that have been raised about the edition as a whole.

At the same time as the Riezler diaries divided historians, Bernd Sösemann's own scholarly edition of the diaries of Theodor Wolff, the influential and well-connected editor of the newspaper *Berliner Tageblatt*, was published. It contains the testimony of several key witnesses who, in private conversation with Wolff, spoke of Germany's role in the events that led to war, including Bethmann Hollweg and the Foreign Secretary Gottlieb von Jagow. The evidence published by Sösemann suggested that among Germany's leading politicians and industrialists, it was believed that the Wilhelmstrasse had caused the war, albeit by miscalculation rather than design.[81]

---

78 For example, Erdmann had not mentioned that the diaries contained substantial gaps, and that some of the original material, covering the crucial years 1907–1914, was missing. He also had not alerted his readers to the fact that for the most important times, July and August 1914, the diary was not kept in its usual format in small exercise books, but on loose pages, which differed in style from the rest of the diaries, suggesting that Riezler perhaps edited crucial sections of his writings, or that they had even been tampered with at a later date, perhaps even in the light of the Fischer controversy. See Bernd-Felix Schulte, *Die Verfälschung der Riezler Tagebücher*, who suspected foul play on behalf of Fischer's critics.

79 Some have even concluded that they are 'unsuitable material for history-writing'. Lüder Meyer-Arndt, *Die Julikrise 1914. Wie Deutschland in den Ersten Weltkrieg stolperte*, Böhlau, Cologne, Weimar, Vienna 2006, pp. 3/67. This is an exaggeration, although it is true that Riezler's diary needs to be used with caution.

80 (**135**), (**138**), (**147**), (**181**).

81 Sösemann (ed.), *Theodor Wolff*, see e.g. Vol. I, No. 88, 357, 340. See also John Röhl, 'Germany', in Keith M. Wilson (ed.), *Decisions for War 1914*, UCL Press,

Recent document editions were not, of course, limited to Germany, but the nature of the Fischer controversy of the 1960s made them particularly controversial. Elsewhere, document editions have not tended to cause quite such a stir. The important diary of the Austrian journalist Josef Redlich is another key source (its publication preceded the Fischer controversy), and contains soul-searching reflections by Austrian decision-makers on their responsibility for the outbreak of war. First edited by Fritz Fellner in 1953, an expanded and updated edition was published in 2011, and several interesting excerpts which illuminate Austro-Hungarian decision-making on the eve of the war have been included in this volume.[82]

In addition to such official and scholarly collections, countless autobiographical accounts, memoirs, diaries and letters were published, most in the inter-war years, as almost all those involved in the decision-making of the pre-war years sought to commit their memories to paper. A number of extracts from such sources have been included in this collection. Naturally, these accounts have to be approached cautiously, particularly given the contentious nature of the topic. To give an obvious example: one would not want to construct an account of the origins of the First World War based solely on the (notoriously unreliable) memoirs of Kaiser Wilhelm II,[83] or even on the memoirs of other German decision-makers. Clearly, their accounts will be biased in a particular way, as will be those written by their French, Russian and British counter-parts. But bringing them all together allows us to compare in very instructive ways.

In other examples, the authenticity of memoirs is called into question by the fact that their authors were eager to clear their names of suspicion of personal wrong-doing, and to present their own (rather than just their governments') actions in a particularly

---

London 1995, pp. 27ff. Given that Wolff's diary contains records of conversations with many influential politicians in the years 1914–1919, and that the authenticity of this source is not in doubt, it is a very rewarding source for historians, and a typically revealing extract from Wolff's diary has also been included in this collection (**211**).

82 (**157**), (**205**), (**320**). Fritz Fellner and Doris A. Corradini (eds), *Schicksalsjahre Österreichs. Die Erinnerungen und Tagebücher Josef Redlichs, 1869–1936*, 3 vols, Vol. 1: *Erinnerungen und Tagebücher 1869–1914*, Böhlau, Vienna, Cologne, Weimar 2011.

83 Emperor William II, *My Memoirs, 1878–1818*, Engl. transl., Cassell, London 1922.

favourable light. Maurice Paléologue's memoirs, for example, based on his diaries written while he was France's ambassador in St Petersburg, must be read with some caution, for he was writing them with a view to combating critics who blamed his forthright support of the Russian ally for the escalation of the crisis.[84] Extracts from his memoirs have been included in this collection, not least because they add a different nuance and a personal perspective to the available diplomatic documents which highlight decision-making in St Petersburg, but the apologetic intentions behind them must not be overlooked.[85]

While Paléologue's memoirs are perhaps an extreme example, it goes without saying that all memoirs have to be approached with some caution, although this should not detract from their intrinsic value to historians. Such personal accounts offer a different perspective to that of official documents. At best, read alongside other, less biased sources, they add richness and detail to the events under scrutiny, although at worst, they are merely apologetic attempts to whitewash the actions of individuals or those of their government.[86]

84 For Paléologue during the July Crisis, see for example John Keiger, *France and the Origins of the First World War*, Macmillan, London, Basingstoke 1983, pp. 159ff. Schmidt, *Frankreichs Außenpolitik*, p. 338 provides a discussion of the various critiques of Paléologue's role during the crisis.

85 (**190**), (**300**), (**330**), (**350**), (**380**), (**395**), (**415**), (**427**). Even before it was necessary to paint his role in July 1914 in a particular light, it seems that Paléologue was prone to certain embellishments in his writing. Louis de Robien, attaché at the French Embassy in St Petersburg since early July 1914, recalled: 'Whenever he recounted an event or sought to retrace a conversation, he recreated them almost entirely in his imagination, endowing them with more vividness than truth.' Cited in Christopher Clark, *The Sleepwalkers. How Europe Went to War in 1914*, Allen Lane, London 2012, p. 435.

86 A useful summary of the most important personal accounts for the period can be found in Baumgart, *Quellenkunde*, Vol.5, Part 2. Other French memoirs included in this edition include those of Raymond Poincaré (**339**), (**344**), Joseph Joffre (**29**), (**262**), (**279**), (**303**), (**414**) and Adolphe Messimy (**263**). In this collection, excerpts were also included from the memoirs of Theobald von Bethmann Hollweg (**27**), Herrmann von Eckardstein (**93**) and Helmuth von Moltke (**363**); from Vladimir Kokovtsov (**40**), Sergei Doborolski (**280**) and Mikhail Rodzianko (**328**), from Conrad von Hötzendorf (**84**), (**105**), (**118**), (**129**), (**321**), (**325**), and from Giovanni Giolitti (**423**).

The collection's contribution to the debate on the origins of the war

The documents selected for inclusion in this collection address a number of important themes that arise in most discussions of the origins of the First World War. They are arranged chronologically. They fall into two parts, each with its own introduction which sets the documents within their historical context. The focus of Part 1 is on the pre-war crises and international tensions in the years 1911 to June 1914. An understanding of how a major conflagration was avoided before 1914, rather than how a chain of events inevitably led to war, is essential background for an analysis of the decisions made in July 1914, and the documents in this first part of the volume provide primary source evidence which help explain the tensions between the Great Powers in the pre-war years. They provide evidence on the international decision-making at critical junctures, such as the Agadir Crisis, Haldane Mission and the Balkan Wars, and provide background on international diplomacy and the arms race in the crucial pre-war years.

Part 2 contains documents which relate to the July Crisis of 1914, and here a number of threads run through the collection which reflect some of the controversial issues raised in the historiographical debates on the origins of the war. Seven in particular deserve highlighting, and can be examined in detail with the help of the documents in this volume.

1. The documents illuminate how **the decision to use the assassination of Archduke Franz Ferdinand to go to war with Serbia** was arrived at. Taken first in Vienna, this fateful resolve was enthusiastically supported in Berlin. The documents show that the assassination offered a welcome pretext to unleash a war against Serbia which had so frequently been demanded in Vienna. The concept of a 'preventive' war and of the fortuitous timing of the crisis are a recurring theme in the documents emanating from Vienna and Berlin – preventing an anticipated decline in international status (in the case of Austria-Hungary), or preventing a situation in the not-too-distant future when Russia would become too strong and too quick to deploy her troops, making a successful war against her impossible (in

the case of Germany).[87] At the same time, they highlight the attempts by the leaders of both countries to pretend to allies and to future enemies that they were not plotting to force war on Serbia and that Austria-Hungary's reaction to the assassination would not be excessive. This includes statements made by German diplomats that they had no prior knowledge of Austria-Hungary's plans to issue an ultimatum to Serbia, and efforts in Berlin and Vienna to appear outwardly calm so as not to alert the Entente Powers or Serbia to their planned diplomatic move. They also attest to the deliberate deception and secrecy which was adopted to ensure a diplomatic and military advantage for Austria-Hungary.

2. The documents provide evidence of the **reactions of the Entente powers to the assassination**, and in particular their **attempts to arrange mediation.** Once the ultimatum to Serbia had been presented, Britain's role in trying to avert the crisis particularly stands out in this regard, as the documents show, but France and Russia also appear more interested in mediation than Austria-Hungary and Germany, where lip-service was paid to Britain's mediation proposals but where a diplomatic solution to the crisis was not actually desired.

3. The documents reveal to what extent **Britain refused to declare her hand** during the crisis. Despite Sir Edward Grey's best efforts to bring about a peaceful outcome, British policy has in fact been accused of having contributed, unwittingly perhaps, to the outbreak of war. Hence the documents also highlight how Britain was, from the moment the ultimatum was delivered, caught between two impossible positions, was forced either to declare her support for France and Russia, and thus perhaps encourage them towards a tougher stance vis-à-vis Austria-Hungary and Germany, or to let the rest of Europe know that Britain would keep out of a potential war, thus encouraging Germany and Austria-Hungary towards a more belligerent attitude. The documents in this collection demonstrate the extent to which Britain was pressurized from both

87 Dieter Hoffmann has provided a list of evidence of at least 76 occasions where a preventive war was demanded in Germany in the years 1906–1914. *Der Sprung ins Dunkle*. pp. 325ff.

sides to declare her hand, and refused to do so until the very last moment. It also demonstrates that the violation of Belgium was not the main reason for the Cabinet's decision to enter the war on France's side, but that it provided a useful rallying call to win over the British public for a war on the continent.[88]

4. A further thread which emerges prominently from the available documents is **Germany's desperate hope for British neutrality**. At certain times during the crisis, there was a deeply-felt, if misguided, conviction in Berlin that British neutrality was almost assured. Documents have been included which illuminate how this misapprehension arose, and what effect it had on decisions taken in Berlin where Chancellor Theobald von Bethmann Hollweg's policy in particular rested on his hope for British neutrality.[89] The German Kaiser, too, was confident that Britain would remain neutral, and felt betrayed by his English cousin King George V when this hope turned out to have been unfounded. Due to the important role he played in the decision-making process in Berlin, this was of great significance, as a forceful cautioning word from him before Austria's declaration of war on Serbia could have influenced and perhaps still halted the unfolding crisis.

5. Primary source evidence has been included in this volume to provide an insight into **France's role in the July Crisis**. In the nearly 100 years of debate on the origins of the First World War, much effort has been put, at various times, into trying to make a case for French war guilt. France's role has been the subject of scrutiny by contemporaries and historians. Was France merely a 'minor player'[90] in the crisis, or actually a

88 During the war it continued to be seen as important to emphasize Belgium's plight. The documents do not, however, bear out Headlam-Morley's claim that the 'crucial matter is Belgium, for it cannot be too often insisted that it was the invasion of Belgium which was the definite and conclusive reason for England joining the war'. J.W. Headlam-Morley, *England, Germany and Europe*, Macmillan, London 1914, p. 12, cited in Otte, 'A "German Paperchase"', p. 61.

89 See particularly the letters by Prince Heinrich, and the telegrams by Lichnowsky: (**250**), (**281**), (**296**) (Kaiser's marginal notes), (**370**), (**371**), (**375**).

90 Eugenia Kiesling, 'France', in Holger Herwig and Richard Hamilton (eds), *The Outbreak of World War I. Causes and Responsibilities*, 5th rev. edn, Cambridge University Press, Lexington, MA and Toronto 1991, pp. 227–265, p. 227.

'forgotten belligerent'[91]? This question has recently been highlighted again as historians attempt to find new approaches to explaining why war broke out in 1914.[92] Documents have been selected with these important questions in mind, highlighting French decision-making, the role of France's military leaders, and in particular her relationship with Russia, to enable readers to address the question of whether France encouraged Russia to adopt a hostile attitude towards Austria-Hungary, and even perhaps to mobilize.

6. The following documents also provide detail concerning **the timing of Russia's mobilization**, a crucial and much-debated aspect of the events that led to war. In the long controversy on the origins of the First World War, much has been made of the timing of the Russian mobilization, in an effort to prove that Russia was responsible for the outbreak of war, owing to her early move to a partial mobilization. This was an argument that was most fervently advanced by German revisionists in the years after 1918, but it can still be encountered today.[93] The documents in this collection provide details about the chronological sequence in which mobilization orders were given to enable readers to draw their own conclusions about the importance of these orders with regard to attributing blame for the war's outbreak. While some historians still continue to argue over Russia's 'war guilt' based on her partial mobilization having been ordered on 26 July (the Army Corps of the military districts Kiev, Odessa, Kazan and Moscow were mobilized that day), it cannot be disputed that it was Austria-Hungary who was the first to *declare war* on another country, namely Serbia. *Mobilizations* did not necessarily have to lead to war, as Russia's statesmen were keen to highlight on many occasions (although this did not apply to Germany, where in fact due to the constraints of the so-called Schlieffen Plan it necessarily did), but *declarations of war* did lead to war – and

91 Langdon, *July 1914*, p. 165. Stefan Schmidt in *Frankreichs Außenpolitik*, p. 363, juxtaposes these two positions and concludes that France was 'an actor of exceptional importance' whose actions or lack of actions at various junctures shaped the international crisis of July 1914 in a way that led to the outbreak of war.

92 For example in ibid.

93 See for example McMeekin, *Russian Origins*.

while some aspects (indeed many) of the July Crisis are amatter of interpretation, the timing of the declarations of war is one of those rare 'facts' in history that cannot be disputed. What remains contentious, however, is the intention behind partial mobilizations and declarations of impending states of war, and the inevitability, or otherwise, of such measures leading to the outbreak of war.

7. And finally, perhaps the most unexpected thread emerges from the international nature of the documents in this collection. Such a focus reveals surprising similarities in Europe's capitals as regards **the conflict between military and political decision-making.** The documents included here highlight the extent to which governments were put under pressure to act decisively by their military leaders. In Germany, Austria-Hungary, Russia, France and to a lesser extent in Britain in the last weeks of July 1914, final tussles took place between the military leaders and their civilian counterparts – the desire to be ahead of the enemy in terms of military preparations motivated the military decision-makers, while the need to avoid appearing to be the aggressor, as well as obviously the desire among some civilians still to avoid the war altogether, motivated their civilian colleagues. It is striking how all the military leaders were frustrated with their civilian counterparts, how in all capitals they pushed for an earlier mobilization, or for more immediate military preparations and action, while being concerned that the enemy was gaining an advantage of time or location over them. However, in some capitals, frustrated military leaders had to accept that political arguments won the day and that their wishes were second to those of the diplomats. This was true particularly in London, but also in Paris and St Petersburg, where the Tsar controlled the military decisions and repeatedly frustrated their efforts to declare a general mobilization. However, in Berlin and Vienna, military preoccupations overruled any political decisions and relegated politics behind military concerns much sooner – a crucial difference, which influenced, for example, the way Belgium's neutrality was viewed by French and German military planners. Nonetheless, the documents show clearly that if left to their own devices, unsurprisingly, all military leaders would

> have pressed for military solutions to the July Crisis much earlier – managing and restraining these military demands until the chance of a peaceful solution had been ruled out was a common problem among Entente and Alliance powers alike.

The events to which the documents in this volume testify will be under particular scrutiny again as the hundredth anniversary of the war's outbreak brings with it renewed interest in the First World War and its causes. Undoubtedly, documents will continue to play a major role in the way historians approach the subject, and in the ongoing controversy. They have been regarded as a key to the truth about the past, a window into understanding the motivations and decision-making that led Europe into its bloody twentieth century. In the immediate aftermath of the war, governments laid them open for public scrutiny, with the implication that such willingness to reveal details of pre-1914 secret diplomacy proved that they had nothing to hide about their own role in the events. Subsequently, historians have used them as weapons in their ongoing disputes, and yet at times they have been unable even to agree on their authenticity and have differed wildly in their interpretation.

Since the Fischer controversy first raged in the 1960s, huge numbers of additional documents have been discovered, as new generations of historians scoured the archives for anything that could either prove or contradict the arguments of Fischer and his followers. Among the new pieces of evidence were letters and diaries of leading statesmen, diplomats and military leaders, as well as military documents which had not been included in the official postwar publications.[94] Since the reunification of Germany, many more such documents have come to light in the archives of East Germany, and many of them are included in this volume. Since 1991, further primary sources have emerged in the archives of the former Soviet Union, and of course for all former Great Powers,

94 In particular, the Germany military records, largely believed to have been destroyed in the Second World War, which were discovered in the former Soviet Union and can now be consulted in the Military Archive in Freiburg. Some military documents had been published, although again not by historians, but often under the auspices of the very military leaders who had been involved in planning and fighting the war. Examples of official military document collections include the German *Reichsarchiv* study *Der Weltkrieg*, which included two volumes of documents, or the French collection *Les Armées françaises dans la Grande Guerre*, edited by the Ministère de la Guerre.

increasing amounts of documents have been unearthed by historians working on this topic from different international angles.

While documents may not ultimately reveal 'the truth', they are the best chance we have of piecing together the events of July 1914 and of the preceding months.[95] This collection offers a wealth of primary sources, and its purpose is to enable its readers to draw their own conclusions, based on evidence, as to why war broke out in August 1914.

95 For a detailed discussion of this point see Annika Mombauer, 'The Fischer Controversy, Documents, and the "Truth" about the Origins of the First World War', *Journal of Contemporary History*, 2013 (forthcoming).

Part I
The period of 'avoided wars', 1911–1914

Introduction

The years immediately preceding the outbreak of war should not be regarded as inevitably leading to war in 1914. While with hindsight such an interpretation seems almost inescapable – given that the period was characterized by increasing international tension, mutual suspicion and a widespread arms race – it is worth noting that in fact these last years of peace saw a number of successful attempts by the Great Powers to avert a large-scale war. Peace conferences and mediation, not war, were the way to settle international crises, at least those involving the so-called Great Powers. While smaller states engaged in armed conflicts, the governments in London, St Petersburg, Paris, Berlin and Vienna did not, and war was avoided at several important junctures. This history of 'avoided wars'[1] is crucial background for understanding the decision-making of European statesmen and military leaders during the final crisis in July 1914 when the Great War, so frequently anticipated and so often avoided, finally broke out. Before the war, alliance systems both sustained peace and acted as deterrents, and they 'generally functioned as a restraint on war', rather than being a cause of it.[2] During the July

1 Jost Dülffer, Martin Kröger and Rolf-Harald Wippich (eds), *Vermiedene Kriege. Deeskalation und Konflikte der Großmächte zwischen Krimkrieg und Erstem Weltkrieg (1856–1914)*, Oldenbourg, Munich 1997. More recently, the thesis that war was actually improbable, rather than unavoidable, was tested by Holger Afflerbach and David Stevenson (eds), *An Improbable War?: The Outbreak of World War I and European Political Culture before 1914*, Berghahn Books, New York 2007.

2 William Mulligan, *The Origins of the First World War*, Cambridge University Press, Cambridge 2010, p. 229. Similar arguments have been made by Holger Afflerbach, *Der Dreibund. Europäische Großmacht- und Allianzpolitik vor dem Ersten Weltkrieg*, Böhlau, Munich 2003 and Friedrich Kießling, *Gegen den*

Crisis, most governments continued, at least outwardly, to try to find a diplomatic solution to the international crisis that resulted from the assassination of the Austro-Hungarian heir to the throne on 28 June 1914. In Vienna and Berlin, however, there was no desire for yet another conference or for mediation. The documents that follow go some way towards explaining why this was so. However, they also show that all governments of the Great Powers shared the fear that at some point in the near future, a major European war was inevitable. This fatalism underpinned most of the decision-making of the years 1911 to 1914.

In 1911, Europe's major powers clashed over their rival interests in North Africa.[3] When the French sent troops to Morocco in May to suppress a revolt (and thus, by implication, to extend their influence over that country), Germany considered this to be a move contrary to international agreements regulating Moroccan affairs in which the powers had guaranteed the independence of the Moroccan state, and demanded compensation (**2**). Germany tried, as before in 1905/1906, to assert her claim as a Great Power who could not simply be ignored in colonial affairs.[4] After failing to find a diplomatic solution, the German government dispatched the gunboat *Panther* which arrived at the port of Agadir on 1 July to intimidate the French. War seemed likely (**8**). However, having initially

---

'großen Krieg'? Entspannung in den internationalen Beziehungen, 1911–1914, Oldenbourg, Munich 2002.

3 For background on the Agadir Crisis, see e.g. J.-C. Allain, *Agadir 1911: Une Crise impérialiste en Europe pour la conquête de Maroc* (Paris, 1976); M.L. Dockrill, 'British Policy During the Agadir Crisis of 1911', in F.H. Hinsley (ed.), *British Foreign Policy Under Sir Edward Grey*, Cambridge University Press, Cambridge 1977, pp. 271–287; Emily Oncken, *Panthersprung nach Agadir. Die deutsche Politik während der Zweiten Marokkokrise*, Droste, Düsseldorf 1981; Geoffrey Baraclough, *From Agadir to Armageddon. Anatomy of a Crisis*, London 1982; Dülffer et al. (eds), *Vermiedene Kriege*; Ralf Forsbach, *Alfred von Kiderlen-Wächter (1852–1912). Ein Diplomatenleben im Kaiserreich*, 2 vols, Vandenhoeck & Ruprecht, Göttingen 1997; T.G. Otte, 'The Elusive Balance. British Foreign Policy and the French Entente before the First World War', in Alan Sharp and Glyn Stone (eds), *Anglo-French Relations in the Twentieth Century: Rivalry and Cooperation*, Routledge, London and New York, 2000; pp. 23–26.

4 For details of the First Moroccan Crisis, see e.g. Frederick V. Parsons, *The Origins of the Morocco Question 1880–1900*, Duckworth, London 1976; Martin Mayer, *Geheime Diplomatie und öffentliche Meinung. Die Parlamente in Frankreich, Deutschland, und Großbritannien und die erste Marokkokrise 1904–1905*, Droste, Düsseldorf 2002.

attempted to restrain France during the ensuing Agadir Crisis (**3**), Britain eventually supported France, and the Anglo-French Entente emerged further strengthened from the negotiations that followed, while Germany found herself diplomatically isolated.

Against this background, David Lloyd George's famous 'Mansion House Speech' of 21 July 1911 (**4**), rejecting 'peace at any price' and threatening to fight on France's side against Germany if the need arose, caused great indignation in Germany and set the tone for widespread and on-going anti-British sentiments (**18**). Herbert Asquith recalled after the war that the 'speech produced a *crise de nerfs* at Berlin', and that the 'situation was full of grave possibilities'.[5]

It was during this crisis, too, that the British Committee of Imperial Defence met on 23 August 1911 to discuss how to react if the situation escalated and France required military assistance (**6**).[6] Some historians have argued that this meeting marked the turning point when the British General Staff's strategy of sending the British Expeditionary Force to the Continent (the so-called Continental commitment) became accepted British military policy.[7] It has even

5 Herbert Asquith, *The Genesis of the War*, Cassell and Co., London, New York et al., 1923, pp. 93–4. He commented that 'war had been escaped over this business; no one could say, or can say now, how narrowly' (p. 95). For details of Lloyd George's speech, and his attitude towards Germany during the Crisis, see Bentley B. Gilbert, 'Pacifist to Interventionist: David Lloyd George in 1911 and 1914. Was Belgium an Issue?', *Historical Journal*, 28, 4, 1985, pp. 863–885, pp. 866ff.

6 Asquith commented that 'it seemed to me to make it opportune to institute afresh a thorough and comprehensive investigation by the Committee of Imperial Defence of the parts which our navy and army should respectively (and co-ordinately) play in the event of our being involved in a European war. Such an inquiry accordingly took place in the autumn of 1911. It furnished information, and led to the adoption of plans which, three years later, were found to be of the utmost importance and value', Asquith, *Genesis*, p. 96. For details on the workings of the CID, see John P. Mackintosh, 'The Role of the Committee of Imperial Defence before 1914', *English Historical Review*, 77, July 1962, pp. 490–503. For a detailed discussion of the genesis of this meeting see Nicholas J. d'Ombrain, 'The Imperial General Staff and the Military Policy of a "Continental Strategy" during the 1911 International Crisis', *Military Affairs*, 34, 3, October 1970, pp. 88–93.

7 See e.g. Samuel R. Williamson, *The Politics of Grand Strategy: Britain and France Prepare for War, 1904–1914*, Harvard University Press, Cambridge MA 1969, pp. 187–204; John Gooch, *The Plans of War: The General Staff and British Military Strategy, c.1900–1916*, London 1974, pp. 289–92. Less convinced about the importance of the meeting are e.g. Keith Neilson, 'Great

been argued that the meeting of 23 August 'set the course for a military confrontation between Britain and Germany', comparing it in historical importance to the German 'war council' meeting of December 1912 when war was demanded by Kaiser Wilhelm and his military advisers, decided upon and reluctantly postponed by 18 months (**44**). On balance, however, most would probably concede that the nature of the two events was very different.[8]

The Agadir Crisis was also the backdrop to the Anglo-French military and naval talks of 1911 in which the two Entente partners firmed up their commitments to each other and agreed how to proceed militarily in case of a European war (**10**), although Britain did not formally commit to supporting France in a future conflict (**14**). Such a formal commitment was, in fact, never made, which explains why Britain, in July 1914, could – in an effort to bring about a peaceful solution to the crisis – play a waiting game in which she did not commit herself either to intervene or to remain neutral in any future war.

The crisis of 1911 was resolved diplomatically following international negotiations leading to the Treaty of Fez (4 November 1911). Germany was compensated with a small part of the French Congo, but the affair amounted in fact to another diplomatic defeat for Germany (much as the First Moroccan Crisis had in 1906). As a result, Germans were becoming increasingly worried that their foreign-policy adventures were not leading to the desired breaking-up of anti-German alliances. Rightly or wrongly, they felt encircled by hostile powers. Germany had also revealed itself as an aggressive bully (as it had done previously during the First Moroccan Crisis when its aim had been to drive apart the newly-created Entente between Britain and France) and was now considered France's principal future enemy (**13**). France's relations with Britain were increasingly important, but she was also looking towards Russia,

Britain', in Richard F. Hamilton and Holger H. Herwig (eds), *War Planning 1914*, Cambridge University Press, Cambridge et al., 2010, pp. 175–197, pp. 183ff. and Hew Strachan 'The British Army, its General Staff and the Continental Commitment 1904–14', in David French and Brian Holden Reid (eds), *The British General Staff. Reform and Innovation, 1890–1939*, Frank Cass, London and Portland, OR 2002, pp. 75–94.

8 The case for the importance of the meeting is made by Niall Ferguson, *The Pity of War*, Allen Lane, London 1998, p. 65. This interpretation is not widely shared, and, according to Nielson, it is 'deeply flawed'. 'Great Britain', p. 185 n. 43.

a valuable alliance partner since their agreement of 1894. Russia also had the worrying potential to become a future enemy; Russia's military, economic and financial future seemed ominously to lead to a time when France's support might no longer be needed.

In these uncertain times, demands for a preventive war were voiced among Germany's military leaders, and calls for army increases were frequently made (**15**), (**16**). Moreover, Austria-Hungary had only provided lukewarm support for her Dual Alliance partner, leading to fears that the ally could only be counted on in a crisis pertaining to its own interests. Germany's decision-makers arrived at the realization that only a crisis in the Balkans would guarantee the all-important Austro-Hungarian support required in a future war – looking further ahead, this would be an important factor in the July Crisis following Archduke Franz Ferdinand's assassination.

In February 1912, there was a chance of an improvement of Anglo-German relations which had been tense after years of a naval arms race precipitated by Admiral von Tirpitz's naval building plan,[9] when the British Minister of War Richard Haldane travelled to Berlin to discuss the possibility of a rapprochement (**19**), (**20**), (**21**), (**22**).[10] Germany's aim was a 'definitive agreement' between the two

---

9 For details of the Tirpitz Plan, see e.g. Volker R. Berghahn, 'Zu den Zielen des deutschen Flottenbaus unter Wilhelm II.', *Historische Zeitschrift*, 210, 1970, pp. 34–100 and idem, *Der Tirpitzplan. Genesis und Verfall einer innenpolitischen Krisenstrategie unter Wilhelm II.*, Droste Verlag, Düsseldorf 1971; Rolf Hobson, *Imperialism at Sea: Naval Strategic Thought, the Ideology of Sea Power, and the Tirpitz Plan, 1875–1914*, Brill, Boston 2002. For a recent reinterpretation of British foreign policy and the naval race, see for example Dominik Geppert and Andreas Rose, 'Machtpolitik und Flottenbau vor 1914. Zur Neuinterpretation britischer Außenpolitik im Zeitalter des Hochimperialismus', *Historische Zeitschrift* 293 (2011), pp. 401–437; Andreas Rose, *Zwischen Empire und Kontinent – Zur Transformation britischer Außen- und Sicherheitspolitik im Vorfeld des Ersten Weltkrieges*, Veröffentlichungen des Deutschen Historischen Instituts London, 70, Munich 2011; Matthew Seligmann, *The Royal Navy and the German Threat, 1901-1914: Admiralty Plans to protect Britain Trade in a War against Germany,* Oxford University Press, Oxford 2012.

10 For details of the Haldane Mission, see e.g. Stephen E. Koss, *Lord Haldane. Scapegoat for Liberalism*, Columbia University Press, New York, London 1969, pp. 65ff.; R.T.B. Langhorne, 'The Naval Question in Anglo-German Relations, 1912–1914', *Historical Journal*, XIV, 2, 1970, pp. 359–370; Wolfgang J. Mommsen, *Großmachtstellung und Weltpolitik 1870–1914*, Ullstein, Frankfurt/Main, Berlin 1993, pp. 228ff.; Forsbach, *Kiderlen-Wächter*, Vol. II, pp. 579ff.

naval rivals which Britain could not undertake given her existing Entente with France and Russia, and given that Germany was in turn not willing to reduce her naval building programme (**24**), (**25**), (**26**), (**27**). The British government was divided on whether to come to an agreement with Germany (**28**), and France was assured that Britain, whatever arrangement might be made, would still support her Entente partner if she became the victim of an unprovoked attack, although this did little to assuage the French Government's fears about a possible Anglo-German rapprochement (**34**). In the words of the Russian ambassador in Paris, they displayed 'a certain nervousness'.[11] The negotiations were ultimately unsuccessful, and did not result in a formal agreement – Germany offered too little and wanted too much in return,[12] and Britain was unwilling to destabilize her existing agreements in return for such little practical gain.

In 1912, the Balkans once again demanded the attention of Europe's statesmen.[13] Bulgaria, Greece, Montenegro and Serbia formed the Balkan League, and in October 1912, the League declared war on Turkey which was defeated and driven out of most of the Balkans. 'Everyone is stunned', recorded the Russian Ambassador Benckendorff in London, commenting in particular on the new respect accorded to Bulgaria's victories. 'No one says anymore that this is a squabble among *rotten little nations*.'[14] The Great Powers were on the brink of war; would Austria-Hungary be willing to let Serbia fight a successful Balkan war and increase her power? France had assured Russia of her support if Austria-Hungary attacked Serbia, and Germany had likewise shored up her ally in case Austria-Hungary found herself embroiled in a war with

11 Friedrich Stieve, *Isvolsky and the World War. Based on the Documents recently published by the German Foreign Office*, transl. E.W. Dickes, George Allen & Unwin, London 1926, p. 77.

12 Langhorne, 'The Naval Question', p. 359, n. 5. The German government gave Haldane a copy of their forthcoming new naval law which was much more expansive than the Admiralty had expected and only worried Britain's naval leaders more.

13 For details of the Balkan Wars in the context of worsening European relations see David Stevenson, *Armaments and the Coming of War. Europe 1904–1914*, Clarendon, Oxford 1996, pp. 231ff. and Christopher Clark, *The Sleepwalkers. How Europe went to War in 1914*, Allen Lane, London 2012, p. 251.

14 Benckendorff to his wife, 27 and 26 October 1912, cited in Marina Soroka, *Britain, Russia and the Road to the First World War. The Fateful Embassy of Count Aleksandr Benckendorff (1903–1916)*, Ashgate, Farnham 2011, pp. 228–9.

Russia (**42**). In November 1912, partial mobilization measures were agreed upon in St Petersburg (**40**), and Europe faced its gravest crisis yet. In Berlin, Chief of Staff Moltke favoured 'an immediate strike' (**47**), while the French Minister of War Millerand worried about the possibility that German troops might be moved from the East to threaten France (**45**). Millerand even tried to force the Russians' hand, and it was certainly clear to the government in St Petersburg that France would play her part in a forthcoming war. However, the victors later fell out over the spoils, and ended up fighting each other in the Second Balkan War of 1913. As a result of the wars, Serbia doubled her territory, and now posed an even greater threat to Austria-Hungary, both externally, due to her size and obvious military capability, and internally by encouraging the sizeable Serbian minority within the Dual Monarchy to demand its independence. Once again, Europe was on the brink of war (**54**), (**57**). It was recognized in the Entente that Austria-Hungary could not ignore Serbia's provocations in the long term, and that the tensions between them might well lead to war in the future (**60**). What is more, Russia had kept extra troops on duty after the summer manoeuvres, an intimidating measure as far as Austria-Hungary's military leaders were concerned. They were well aware that Russian troops outnumbered Austro-Hungarian ones; in the military district of Warsaw alone, 320,000 Russian troops would be opposed by 21,000 Austrian ones, a worrying realization.[15]

In late 1912, Austria-Hungary wanted to put a stop to Serbia's expansion in the Balkans, if necessary by war (**37**), but Kaiser Wilhelm II was initially not prepared to support the ally in a war against Serbia simply 'because Austria does not want the Serbs in Albania or Durazzo' (**36**). However, Germany's military decision-makers were quick to realize that the crisis offered a welcome opportunity for war. The Kaiser, in a characteristic and dramatic change of heart, and his Chief of Staff Helmuth von Moltke eventually ended up offering their full support to the ally 'in all circumstances', in words that echoed the same assurances they would later make to their ally in early July 1914 (**39**), (**53**), (**120**), (**130**). By this point, the German Kaiser had decided that 'should Russian countermeasures or demands follow which might force Franz Joseph to declare war,

15 Günther Kronenbitter, *'Krieg im Frieden'. Die Führung der K.u.K. Armee und die Großmachtpolitik Österreich–Ungarns 1906–1914*, Oldenbourg, Munich 2003, p. 383.

then he has right on his side and I am ready [...] to accept the *casus foederis* in its fullest meaning and with all its consequences'.[16]

This is essential background for understanding Austria's reaction to the Serbian-supported assassination of the heir to the Austro-Hungarian throne on 28 June 1914 (**103**), (**106**). Given the long-standing Balkan instability, and Serbia's many provocations, this was a threat to the Empire's international reputation that Vienna's statesmen felt they could not ignore. With the moral right seemingly on their side, the assassination provided an opportunity to dispose of the Serbian threat once and for all, and this time German support in avenging an act of terrorism and regicide would be more forthcoming, and international toleration of such a move more likely.

The crisis in November 1912 brought Europe to the brink of war; with hindsight, it can be regarded as a dress-rehearsal for what was to come in the summer of 1914. While Germany assured Austria-Hungary of unlimited support, the Tsar and his Minister of War, Sukhomlinov, were at the same time discussing the possibility of partial Russian mobilization (**40**). If implemented, this decision would almost certainly have led in turn to an Austro-Hungarian general mobilization, and in the light of Germany's promise to her ally, a European war would have been difficult to avoid.[17]

During this crisis, French military experts considered the Entente's chances of victory 'with great optimism', as Poincaré told the Russian Ambassador Isvolsky on 12 September, because Austria-Hungary's forces would be tied up in the Balkans and Italy was bound to France, due to her agreement and the Italo-Turkish (or Libyan) war.[18] He based his confidence on assessments by the French General Staff who had predicted in a report of 2 September

---

16 Wilhelm II to Kiderlen-Wächter, 21 November 1912, GP, 33, No.12405.

17 This point is made, for example, by L.C.F. Turner, 'The Russian Mobilization in 1914', in Paul M. Kennedy (ed.), *The War Plans of the Great Powers, 1880–1914*, Allen & Unwin, London 1979, pp. 252–268, p. 255. See also below, Note 69, and **40** for details of the conference at Tsarskoe Selo on 23 November.

18 Luigi Albertini, *Origins of the War of 1914*, 3 vols, Eng. transl., Oxford University Press, Oxford 1952–57, Vol. 1, p. 373, who points out that after the war Poincaré kept silent about these statements to Isvolsky. In the same meeting, Poincaré assured Isvolsky that should Russia be forced to become involved in a war against Austria-Hungary, 'the French government would recognise this in advance as a *casus foederis* and would not hesitate for one moment to fulfil the obligations which it has incurred in respect of Russia.' See Clark, *Sleepwalkers*, p. 297.

1912 that the Entente would have the greater chance of victory if war were to result from an Austrian intervention in the Balkans.[19]

Germany's military leaders were not yet quite so confident of Germany's chances, leading to the infamous discussion to 'delay' the war for a while in the so-called German 'War Council' meeting of December 1912 which took place against the background of the Balkan Wars threatening to embroil the Great Powers (**44**), (**46**), (**47**). Historians have long debated the significance of this event during which Kaiser Wilhelm II and his senior military advisors reacted to news from London that Britain would support France in a future conflict by discussing unleashing a war at that moment and then deciding to postpone it, and they are divided over how to evaluate its importance. For some, the timing of the outbreak of war, exactly 18 months later as discussed in December 1912, appears too much of a coincidence (**43**), (**48**). At best, the event demonstrates the extent to which German decision-makers felt themselves to be beleaguered and convinced that war was inevitable; at worst, it has been seen as the point at which they actually decided to provoke a war in the not-too-distant future when certain conditions (such as the widening of the Kiel Canal) had been met.[20] It is undisputed, however, that Germany's military planners used the occasion of the Balkan crisis to advocate war, emphasizing their chances of winning at that moment, and at the same time using the opportunity to underline their frequent calls for army increases (**41**), (**49**).

Throughout this period, the question of Belgian neutrality was at

19 DDF, 3e série, 3, No. 359. For a discussion of the importance of this document, see Turner, 'Russian Mobilization', p. 256.

20 The most detailed discussion of the war council and the available evidence is provided by John Röhl, *The Kaiser and his Court*, Cambridge University Press, Cambridge, 1994, who also provides a detailed bibliography of the controversy around the war council (pp. 255f.). For the most recent summary of the event and its importance see John Röhl, *Wilhelm II. Der Weg in den Abgrund, 1900–1941*, Beck, Munich 2008, 2nd edn 2009, Vol. 3, pp. 963ff. (English translation forthcoming, Cambridge University Press 2013.) Historians who do not see a direct connection between the famous meeting and the outbreak of war 18 months later include W.J. Mommsen, 'Der Topos vom unvermeidlichen Krieg: Außenpolitik und öffentliche Meinung im Deutschen Reich im letzten Jahrzehnt vor 1914', in idem, *Der autoritäre Nationalstaat*, Frankfurt/Main 1990, pp. 380ff.; E. Zechlin, 'Die Adriakrise und der "Kriegsrat" vom 8. Dezember 1912', in idem *Krieg und Kriegsrisiko. Zur Deutschen Politik im Ersten Weltkrieg*. Düsseldorf 1979; L.C.F. Turner, *The Origins of the First World War*, Edward Arnold, London 1970.

the forefront of the minds of military planners in Paris and Berlin. In France, Chief of the General Staff Josef Joffre was compelled to put political above military considerations in his strategic planning. He would not be able to violate Belgian neutrality in a future war[21] (**12**), (**17**). In Germany, however, a different approach was adopted. The Chief of the General Staff Moltke made clear that political concerns were of secondary importance compared with military considerations, and that Belgium would have to be invaded when war began (**52**). In meetings with the Belgian King Albert in November 1913, Moltke and Kaiser Wilhelm II even attempted to intimidate the Belgians into allowing them to march through Belgium unopposed (**65**).[22] Moltke told King Albert unambiguously: 'It is very much in the interest of the small states to be with us, because the consequences of the war will be grave for those who go against us.'[23] The Belgians turned down this extraordinary request (which revealed not only Germany's aggressive intentions, but also details of her intended war-plan), as they would again later during the July Crisis – keen to preserve her status as an independent country, Belgium refused to allow either France or Germany access to her territory (**385**).

At the same time, Russia saw herself provoked by the close ties between Germany and Turkey (**66**). Their long-standing military association was further underlined when a German officer, Otto Liman von Sanders, was posted to a German military mission in Constantinople in late 1913, charged with reorganizing the Turkish army. Russia reacted indignantly to this apparent extension of German interest in such a strategically important part of the world, and with war once again on the cards during the crisis, the Liman von Sanders affair has subsequently been considered the 'last conflict before the catastrophe'.[24] The crisis was resolved peacefully in early 1914, but

21 For details, see e.g. Roy A. Prete, *Strategy and Command. The Anglo-French Coalition on the Western Front, 1914*, McGill-Queen's University Press, Montreal et al., 2009, pp. 21ff.

22 For details, see Jean Stengers, 'Guillaume II et le Roi Albert à Potsdam en novembre 1913', *Bulletin de la Classe des Lettres et des Sciences Morales et Politiques*, 7–12, 1993, pp. 227–253; Annika Mombauer, *Helmuth von Moltke and the Origins of the First World War*, Cambridge University Press, Cambridge 2001, pp. 153ff.

23 Cited in Jean Stengers, 'Guillaume II et le Roi Albert', pp. 227–253.

24 On the Liman von Sanders affair, see e.g. William Mulligan, 'We Can't Be More Russian Than the Russians: British Policy During the Liman Von Sanders Crisis, 1913–1914', *Diplomacy & Statecraft* 17, 2, 2006, pp. 261–282; Martin Kröger,

had further destabilized relations between the Great Powers, particularly between Russia and Germany which were characterized by mutual suspicion and hostile press campaigns (**71**), (**86**), (**97**). Russia was particularly keen to strengthen the Entente. Sazonov, encouraged by Benckendorff in London and Isvolsky in Paris, believed that Russia's Great Power status depended on support from France and Britain.[25]

That a war between the major European powers was not inevitable is underlined, to give but one prominent example, by the fact that in France, the possibility of a future rapprochement with Germany was not ruled out by leading statesmen, particularly by Joseph Caillaux, and that improved future Franco-German relations were not out of the question in 1913 (**64**).[26] In that year, Max Warburg wrote to Under-Secretary of State Wahnschaffe: 'By and large it is certainly ridiculous to speak today of the possibility of a French-English-German rapprochement, but I was told seriously in conversations that one would not be surprised if we were there in five years' time.'[27] However, in August 1913 the French and Russian General Staffs had come to an agreement about military cooperation and finally signed the Franco-Russian Military Convention on 9 September 1913.[28]

The year 1914 was dominated by speculations about Russia's

'Letzter Konflikt vor der Katastrophe: Die Liman-von-Sanders-Krise 1913/14', in Dülffer et al. (eds), *Vermiedene Kriege*, pp. 657–671; Mustafa Aksakal, *The Ottoman Road to War in 1914. The Ottoman Empire and the First World War*, Cambridge University Press, Cambridge 2008, pp. 80ff.; Hans Herzfeld, 'Die Limankrise und die Politik der Grossmächte in der Jahreswende 1913–1914', *Berliner Monatshefte*, September 1933, pp. 837–858; October 1933, pp. 973–993.

25 Soraka, *Britain, Russia and the Road to the First World War,* p. 239.

26 For details see Klaus Wilsberg, *'Terrible ami – aimable ennemi'. Kooperation und Konflikt in den deutsch-französischen Beziehungen 1911–1914*, Bouvier Verlag, Bonn 1998, pp. 99–103.

27 Warburg to Wahnschaffe, 12 April 1913, PA-AA, Frankreich 102, vol. 57, cited in Wilsberg, *'Terrible ami – aimable ennemi'*, p. 98.

28 DDF, 3e série, 3, No. 79. As Turner points out, the Franco-Russian convention highlights to what extent 'all military thinking in Europe was dominated by the implications of the Schlieffen Plan. Moreover [...] the potential application of that plan would lead automatically to intense military activity in eastern Europe. Russia would have to invade East Prussia as soon as possible to relieve pressure on France, while Austria would be compelled to attack in Russian Poland to bring relief to the German Eighth Army in East Prussia', in 'Russian Mobilization', p. 257.

current and future military strength, not just in Germany and Austria-Hungary, but also in France and Britain (**74**), (**75**). British foreign policy was determined by the fear of Russia's and Germany's future strength. With a view to protecting British interests in the Empire, Anglo-Russian naval negotiations took place in 1914[29] (**79**), (**81**), (**99**), (**100**), (**102**). On Russia's side, this was seen as a first step towards cementing a more formal defensive alliance between the three Entente partners. Sazonov was concerned about the effectiveness of the Entente, 'whose actual existence is as little proved as the existence of the Sea Serpent'.[30] The prospect of an Anglo-Russian naval convention about which Berlin learnt from a spy in the Russian Embassy in London led to further insecurity in Germany, and provided military leaders and right-wing pressure groups with ammunition for their requests to build more ships and increase armaments (**85**), (**87**), (**135**), (**143**). In the early summer of 1914, demands were made for preventive war in Germany, Austria and Italy as the outlook for the long-term future of the Triple Alliance seemed bleak (**84**), (**91**), (**92**), (**93**), (**94**). In Vienna, Chief of the General Staff Franz Conrad von Hötzendorf had demanded a war against Serbia on at least 25 occasions in 1913 alone, and his aggressive attitude towards Serbia, which extended by proxy to Russia, was well known in St Petersburg, too.[31] While frequently demanding a preventive war, German decision-makers nonetheless also continued to hope – as they would in July 1914 – that Britain might still be won over and at least remain neutral in a future war (**73**), (**76**).

While the Entente-partners France and Britain discussed whether a more formal agreement between Britain and Russia might be possible (**83**), in Russia not everyone was convinced that the future lay with the Entente. The war-party in Russia encouraged an anti-German press campaign (**97**), (**99**), while Russian conservatives advocated redirecting Russia's foreign policy towards more cordial

29 For details, see Soraka, *Britain, Russia and the Road to the First World War*, pp. 246–8; Stephen Schroeder, *Die englisch-russische Marinekonvention*, Vandenhoek & Ruprecht, Göttingen 2004.

30 Cited in I.V. Bestuzhev, 'Russian Foreign Policy, February to June 1914', *Journal of Contemporary History*, 1, 3, July 1966, pp. 93–112, p. 108.

31 Hew Strachan, *The First World War*, Vol. 1: *To Arms*, Oxford University Press, Oxford 2001, p. 69; Bruce Menning, 'Russian Military Intelligence', article MS, forthcoming.

relations with Germany (**72**). Here, too, was potential for a development which could, in time, have diffused the volatile relationship between the two Great Powers, and perhaps have prevented war. British decision-makers were certainly concerned that there was a real possibility of a Russo-German rapprochement (**81**), as indeed were the French.

While in May 1914 the US envoy Colonel Edward House recorded in dismay that the situation in Europe was 'extraordinary' and a war likely (**88**), by the early summer of 1914 the international situation was actually less tense than it had been for years, and Anglo-German relations in particular were much improved (**102**), (**112**),[32] leading Arthur Nicolson to observe: 'Since I have been at the Foreign Office, I have not seen such calm waters.'[33] He could not have known that he was observing the proverbial calm before the storm.

32 An example of this is the British naval visit to the Kiel Regatta (**86**).

33 Nicolson to Goschen, 5 May 1914, TNA, FO 800/374, cited in Zara Steiner and Keith Neilson, *Britain and the Origins of the First World War*, Palgrave Macmillan, London 2003, p. 229.

1
Documents from 1911

(1) 16 April 1911: Grey to Asquith

First Moroccan Crisis led to decision to exchange views among French and British General Staffs; Britain expects to be asked for support in case of war

---

Private

Early in 1906[1] the French said to us 'will you help us if there is a war with Germany?' We said 'we can't promise[,] our hands must be free'. The French then urged that the Mil[itar]y Authorities should be allowed to exchange views – ours to say what they could do – the French to say how they would like it done, if we did side with France – Otherwise, as the French urged, even if we decided to support France, on the outbreak of war we shouldn't be able to do it effectively. We agreed to this.[2] Up to this point. CB[3], R.B.H[aldane] and I were cognizant of what took place – the rest of the men were scattered in the Election.[4] [...]

Unless French war plans have changed, there should be no need for anything further, but it is clear we are going to be asked something.[5]

TNA, FO 800/100.

---

1 During the First Moroccan Crisis official and unofficial Anglo-French Staff talks took place between 15 December 1905 and 31 January 1906. See S.R. Williamson, Jr, *The Politics of Grand Strategy. Britain and France Prepare for War, 1904–1914*, Harvard University Press, Cambridge, MA 1969, pp. 61ff.

2 For details of Anglo-French staff talks, ibid., pp. 59ff.

3 Sir Henry Campbell-Bannermann, Liberal Prime Minister 1905–1908.

4 The General Election was held from 12 January to 8 February 1906.

5 See also (**10**).

(2) 19 April 1911: Kiderlen-Wächter in conversation with Heinrich Class

German Aims in Moroccan Crisis

It is a question whether we try for naval bases or for a colony, as you wish. The Imperial Navy Office is against naval bases, as it fears a division and weakening of the fleet. We have quite enough with Kiaochow; if only we could get rid of it with decency! Your plan is different, that of a colony which can be treated like East Africa or Cameroon and which can be left to its fate in the event of war. For the fate of colonies will be decided in Europe. It will be useful to raise demands in the press and in associations. Such a division of labour between the *Auswärtiges Amt* and national associations is desirable. I can then say, 'yes, I am ready for compromise but public opinion must be considered.' [...] We shall stand firm in Morocco though it is possibly we may seem to draw back a step. This should not disappoint you. [...] You can count on it, our Morocco policy will please you; you will be satisfied.

Heinrich Class, *Wider den Strom*, Koehler, Leipzig 1932, pp. 203–204.

(3) 20 July 1911: Crowe to Bertie

British policy during Moroccan Crisis

Private
I am, personally, sorry beyond words at the line we are taking up in this Morocco business. It seems to me our cabinet is all on the run and the strong hints we are giving to France that she must let Germany into Morocco makes me ashamed as well as angry.

TNA, FO 800/160.

(4) 21 July 1911: Lloyd George's Mansion House Speech

British Chancellor of the Exchequer warns against further German expansion; Britain will not stand aside in conflict between France and Germany

[...] I believe it is essential in the highest interests, not merely of this country, but of the world, that Britain should at all hazards maintain her place and her prestige amongst the Great Powers of the world. Her potent influence has many a time been in the past, and may yet be in the future, invaluable to the cause of human liberty. It has more than once in the past redeemed Continental nations, who are sometimes too apt to forget that service, from overwhelming disaster and even from national extinction. I would make great sacrifices to preserve peace. I conceive that nothing would justify a disturbance of international good will except questions of the greatest national moment. But if a situation were to be forced upon us in which peace could only be preserved by the surrender of the great and beneficent position Britain has won by centuries of heroism and achievement, by allowing Britain to be treated where her interests were vitally affected as if she were of no account in the Cabinet of nations, then I say emphatically that peace at that price would be a humiliation intolerable for a great country like ours to endure. National honour is no party question. The security of our great international trade is no party question; the peace of the world is much more likely to be secured if all nations realize fairly what the conditions of peace must be [...].[6]

The Times, 22 July 1911.

(5) **19 August 1911: Moltke to his wife**

Moltke bemoans the fact that war might once again be averted

The wretched Morocco-story is beginning to get on my nerves. It is certainly a sign of laudable stamina to be eternally sitting on [hot] coals, but it is not pleasant. If we once again emerge from this affair with our

6 On the Mansion House speech, see David Lloyd George, *War Memoirs*, Vol. I, Odhams Press, London, 1938, pp. 25ff. Prime Minister Asquith and Foreign Secretary Grey had previously seen and approved of the text, and Lloyd George had taken 'advantage of the opportunity to deal with the external situation'. Herbert Asquith, *The Genesis of the War*, Cassell and Co., London, New York et al., 1923. See also W.S. Churchill, *The World Crisis, 1911–1918*, 2 vols, Odhams Press, London 1938, Vol. I, pp. 46–50; Edward Grey, *Twenty-Five Years, 1892–1916*, 2 vols, Stokes, New York 1925, Vol. I, pp. 219, 222–240; Keith M. Wilson, 'The Agadir Crisis, the Mansion House speech, and the Double-Edgedness of Agreements', *Historical Journal*, XV, 3, 1972, pp. 513–532. For further references see Zara Steiner and Keith Neilson, *Britain and the Origins of the First World War*, 2nd edn, Palgrave Macmillan, London 2003, p. 316, n. 63, and this volume, p. 32, n. 3.

tail between our legs, if we cannot bring ourselves to make energetic demands which we would be ready to force through with the help of the sword, then I despair of the future of the German Reich. In that case I will leave. But before that I will make the request to get rid of the army, and to have us placed under Japan's protectorate, then we can make money without being disturbed and we can turn completely simple-minded.

Eliza von Moltke (ed.), *Helmuth von Moltke, Erinnerungen, Briefe, Dokumente 1877–1916*, Der Kommende Tag, Stuttgart 1922, p. 362.

(6) 23 August 1911: Minutes of the Committee of Imperial Defence meeting

Committee requested to consider giving support to France; discussion of how and when to despatch the British Expeditionary Force

Secret

Action to be taken in the event of intervention in a European War

The Prime Minister said he had called the Committee together as the European situation was not altogether clear, and it was possible that it might become necessary for the question of giving armed support to the French to be considered.

The Sub-Committee which examined this question in 1908 came to the following conclusions:

a) The Committee, in the first place, desire to observe that, in the event of an attack on France by Germany, the expediency of sending a military force abroad or of relying on naval means alone is a matter of policy which can only be determined when the occasion arises by the Government of the day.
b) In view, however, of the possibility of a decision by the Cabinet to use military force, the Committee have examined the plans of the General Staff, and are of opinion that, in the initial stages of a war between France and Germany, in which the Government decided to assist France, the plan to which preference is given by the General Staff is a valuable one, and the General Staff should accordingly work out all the necessary details.

The General Staff had prepared a fresh Memorandum on the subject in the light of recent developments (C.I.D. Paper 130-B), and on the second hypothesis that the United Kingdom becomes the active ally of France the important points were [...] that we should mobilise and dispatch the whole of our available regular army of six divisions and a cavalry division immediately upon the outbreak of war, mobilising upon the same day as the French and Germans. It was further suggested that additional reinforcements, consisting of two or three divisions of British and native troops might be drawn from India, and possibly the seventh division from the Mediterranean and South Africa.

Lastly, the General Staff asked from the Admiralty an assurance that the Expeditionary Force could be safely transported across the Channel and from the other directions indicated in their paper, and that the Navy will protect the United Kingdom from organised invasion from the sea. [...]

Sir Arthur Wilson said that the reply of the Admiralty to the first question was that the Navy could spare no men, no officers, and no ships to assist the Army. The whole force at the disposal of the Admiralty would be absorbed in keeping the enemy within the North Sea. Ordinarily the Navy would furnish transport officers and protecting ships. These could not be furnished in these circumstances. The Channel would, however, be covered by the main operations, and provided the French protected the transports within their own harbours, the Admiralty could give the required guarantee as to the safety of the expedition.

Sir William Nicholson said that as regards that point the General Staff asked for no more. He presumed that the General Staff could count upon the ungrudging assistance of the Transport Department of the Admiralty.

Mr McKenna said that that assistance could not be given during the first week of war. The whole efforts of the Admiralty would be absorbed in mobilising the Navy, and the Transport Department especially would be fully occupied in taking up Fleet Auxiliaries.

Sir William Nicholson said that the whole scheme had been worked out in detail. [...]

Admiral Bethell said that the demands of the Army could not be attended to if they were simultaneous with the mobilisation of the Fleet.

Mr. McKenna said that he heard of this scheme now for the first time. [...]

Sir Arthur Wilson said that the scheme had not been brought to his notice. He had understood that a scheme for dispatching the Expeditionary Force had been mooted, but that it had been abandoned.

[...]

The Prime Minister said that the plans of the General Staff as laid before the Sub-Committee of 1908 had always laid stress on the necessity for mobilisation and concentration taking place, immediately upon the outbreak of war, if military intervention was to be valuable, and he was at a loss to understand why it should be supposed that the Fleet would not be mobilising at the same time.

[...]

The Prime Minister said that it was necessary that it should be understood that the question of time was all important. The simultaneous mobilisation of our army and that of the French, and the immediate concentration of our army in the theatre of war were essential features of the scheme.

The second assurance asked for by the General Staff, that of a guarantee by the Admiralty against invasion might be postponed for the moment, and he would first ask the Committee to consider the desirability of carrying out the operations proposed by the General Staff or the alternative scheme suggested by the Admiralty on their merits.

Appreciation of the Military Situation on the Outbreak of a Franco-German War

General Wilson said that our Expeditionary Force consisted of –

1 Cavalry Division;
6 Divisions;
Army Troops;
a total of about 160,000 men.

[...] The total number of German divisions which could be considered as mobile and able to take and keep the field has been estimated at 121. [...] In the present circumstances, he thought that 84 divisions [were] the limit of a German Army invading France.

Against this force the French could put 75 divisions, less 9 required to watch against the Italian frontier, or a net total of 66 divisions. [...]

Sir Edward Grey said that he did not think that the French would have anything to fear from Italy.

General Wilson said that however that might be, there was no doubt that in the first deployment, the French would employ nine divisions to watch the Italian frontier. The French fortified lines were probably safe against any attack, and, as he had already indicated, the gap between Epinal and Toul did not form a favourable line of advance. The Germans would, of course, attack all along the line, but their main effort must be made through the 90-mile gap between Verdun and Maubeuge. Through this gap there ran only thirteen through roads. Each road could accommodate three divisions; but not more. So that the limit of numbers which the Germans could employ along this front was about 40 divisions. A similar result was arrived at upon the basis of the extent of front upon which a division could fight, namely from 2 to 2½ miles.

Against this force the French could probably place from 37 to 39 divisions. So that it was quite likely that our six divisions might prove to be the deciding factor.[7]

7 As Williamson points out, 'the military conversations [which had begun between France and England in late 1905] as such were not discussed in any detail, nor

[...]

Sir Edward Grey agreed that our military support would be of great moral value to the French.

As to the Belgians, he thought that they would avoid committing themselves as long as possible in order to try and make certain of being on the winning side.

[...]

Mr. Lloyd George asked whether the General Staff could forecast what would happen if the French were driven back from the line of the Meuse.

[...]

General Wilson said that it depended upon so many unknown factors that it was very difficult to prophesy what course the French might take, and he had no knowledge of what the views of the French General Staff on the subject were. [...]

Sir Arthur Wilson said that apart from the smallness of its numbers and other considerations, our Army would labour under disadvantages due to difference of language and training, and diversity of ammunition, arms, and equipment. It would also be handicapped by its dependence for its supplies upon French railways. In the early days of the war, when it was proposed to dispatch our forces, the French would also be mobilising, and there would be congestion on the railways.

Sir William Nicholson said that the whole question of concentration including sea and railway transport, and of supply, had been worked out, and he did not anticipate serious difficulty in these matters arising.

[...]

Sir Edward Grey [...] enquired when the first general action was calculated to take place.

General Wilson said that in all probability it would take place between the seventeenth and twentieth days after the French and German mobilisation were ordered.

Mr. McKenna said that for that action it appeared that the Germans would have a maximum of seventy divisions and the French would have sixty-six. The latter seemed to him to be ample with which to defend their frontier. Was the probable effect of our intervention with six divisions so great that without it the French would not resist German aggression, while with it they would[?]

---

did Henry Wilson reveal the existence of the signed memorandum on British help to France; on the other hand, [he] left no doubts about his intimacy with the French Staff, *Strategy*, 1969 edn, p. 191. See also John W. Coogan and Peter F. Coogan, 'The British Cabinet and Anglo-French Staff Talks, 1905–1914: Who knew what and when did he know it?' *Journal of British Studies*, 24, 1, 1985, pp. 110–131.

Sir Edward Grey said that we must postulate that the French intended to fight. The point was whether our intervention would make the difference between defeat and victory.

Mr. McKenna asked whether, if we gave the French an assurance of assistance now, it would not make the French less inclined to accept the German terms.

The Prime Minister said that the point which the Cabinet would have to decide was what we were going to do if we resolved to commit ourselves to the support [of] the French against German attack. [...]

The Committee adjourned.

On re-assembling –

[...]

Sir Edward Grey said that the problem which they had to solve was how to employ the Army so as to inflict the greatest possible amount of damage upon the Germans. So far as he could judge, the combined operations outlined were not essential to naval success, and the struggle on land would be the decisive one.

Sir Arthur Wilson said that it was a question of degree. Any direct assistance which the Army could give would be valuable. [...]

The Prime Minister asked what the naval criticism on the proposals of the General Staff was.

Sir Arthur Wilson said that the Admiralty felt confident that troops would be required to second the efforts of the Navy, and also he did not know whether the number of troops which would remain in the United Kingdom after the departure of the 6 divisions was sufficient to insure that raids would be immediately overwhelmed. [...]

Mr. McKenna said that the absence of the British Army from this country would, undoubtedly, have a great moral effect upon the English people, and there would be a great danger of interference with the freedom of action of the Fleet. There was no real danger of invasion, but many well-known officers and others had declared repeatedly throughout the country that we were not safe from invasion and there was, therefore, considerable risk of panic on the outbreak of war. That would result in great pressure being brought to bear upon the Government to tie the Fleet to the defence of our coast. The moral effect upon the English people would be so serious as to be disastrous. In addition the strain upon the Admiralty of having to provide the sea transport required by the Army immediately on the outbreak of war would, assuredly, hamper the initial operations of the Navy.

[...]

The Prime Minister said that the opinion of the Committee of 1908 was that – 'Until at least four months had elapsed after the embodiment of the Territorial Force it would seem necessary to retain two divisions of Regular Troops fully mobilized in the United Kingdom.'

Mr. Lloyd George said that he had never been convinced that the retention of the two regular divisions at home was really necessary.

[...]

Lord Haldane enquired whether, assuming that invasion was impossible, and that raids only need to be considered, it was necessary to our schemes for Home Defence – for which Sir Archibald Murray was responsible – that two regular divisions should be retained in this country.

Sir Archibald Murray said that he certainly did not consider their retention essential.

[...]

The Prime Minister said that the question which impressed him was, whether, supposing the whole of our 6 divisions had been sent abroad, we should have sufficient military force within the United Kingdom to overwhelm a serious raid. He agreed that the public would be nervous and would require to be reassured. Assuming that the Government decided to intervene on the Continent of Europe, it was obviously desirable that our intervention should be effective, but at the same time it was necessary to retain sufficient forces in this country to meet all probable contingencies. What was the least force with which we could hope to intervene on the Continent effectively[?]

General Wilson said that the view of the General Staff was that our whole available strength should be concentrated at the decisive point, and that point they believed to be on the French frontier. The moral effect of sending 5 divisions would no doubt be almost as great as the dispatch of six.

Sir William Nicholson said that from the military point of view it would be better to send 4 divisions than none.

[...]

Sir Arthur Wilson said that the Navy required at least one division to second its operations, and it was certain that many more troops would be required for our own coasts than could at present be foreseen.

Lord Haldane said that in his view, if we had nothing to fear but small raids, the risk of denuding the country of regular troops could be taken. [...]

114th meeting of the CID, TNA, Cab 2/2.[8]

---

8 Hankey would later recall that 'from that time onward there was never any doubt what would be the Grand Strategy in the event of our being drawn into a continental war in support of France. Unquestionably the Expeditionary Force, or the greater part of it, would have been sent to France as it actually was in 1914'. Cited in Williamson, *Strategy*, 1969 edn, p. 193. Immediately after the

(7) 29 August: Henry Wilson to Churchill

Considers war with Germany inevitable

[...] In my opinion a war between ourselves and Germany is as certain as anything human can be. It if does not come today it will come tomorrow or the next day, and in all probability it will come at a time which suits Germany and not us. There is only one way to victory and that is to see to it that our foreign policy and our strategy go hand in hand and that sufficient force is available to carry out the policy which has been previously determined.

TNA, Adm. 116/3474, cited in Keith M. Wilson, 'The War Office, Churchill and the Belgian Option, August to December 1911', in *Bulletin of the Institute of Historical Research*, 50, 122, 1977, pp. 218–228, p. 220.[9]

(8) 30 August 1911: Churchill to Grey

Suggests alliance with France and Russia; promise to safeguard Belgium in case of war

Perhaps the time is coming when decisive action will be necessary. Please consider the following for use if and when the Morocco negotiations fail.[10]

Propose to France and Russia a triple alliance to safeguard (*inter alia*) the independence of Belgium, Holland and Denmark.

Tell Belgium that, if her neutrality is violated, we are prepared to come to her aid and to make an alliance with France and Russia to guarantee her independence. Tell her that we will take whatever military steps will be most effective for that purpose. But the Belgian Army must

meeting, however, Hankey's assessment was that 'no decision was arrived at'. Sir Maurice Hankey to Admiral J. Fisher, 24 August 1911, as printed in Keith Wilson, 'Hankey's Appendix: Some Admiralty Manoeuvres During and After the Agadir Crisis', *War in History* 1, 1, 1994, p. 87.

9 On Henry Wilson's role in the prewar years, see Samuel R. Williamson Jr., 'General Henry Wilson, Ireland, and the Great War', in William Roger Louis (ed.), *Resurgent Adventures with Britannia. Personalities, Politics and Culture in Britain*, London, I.B. Tauris, 2011, pp. 91–105.

10 At this point war seemed an almost inevitable result of the crisis. Churchill recalled: 'I could not think of anything else but the peril of war.' *World Crisis*, I, p. 46.

take the field in concert with the British and French Armies, and Belgium must immediately garrison properly Liège and Namur. Otherwise we cannot be responsible for her fate.

Offer the same guarantee both to Holland and to Denmark contingent upon their making their utmost exertions. [...] will you kindly send this letter on to the Prime Minister.

Cited in Winston S. Churchill, *The World Crisis, 1911–1918*, 2 vols, Odhams Press, London 1938, Vol. I, p. 47.[11]

(9) 3 September 1911: Gebsattel to Kress

Preventive war favoured in Berlin

[...] in military circles, particularly here in Berlin, the mood is more war-like than a little while ago, more war-like than I myself thought a few days ago. On our side – high-ranking, too – it is emphasized that we should use the situation, which is relatively favourable for us, to strike.

Bay. HStA-KA, MKr41, Nr. 1731.

(10) 8 September 1911: Grey to Asquith

Second Moroccan Crisis; Anglo-French relations

Private
It would create consternation if we forbade our military experts to converse with the French. No doubt these conversations and our speeches have given an expectation of support. I do not see how that can be helped.[12]

The news to-day is that the Germans are proceeding leisurely with the negotiations, and are shifting the ground from Congo to economic concessions in Morocco. Cambon has just been to see me, and on the whole thinks well of the prospect.

To me it looks as if the negotiations were going to enter upon exceedingly tedious but not dangerous ground.

TNA, Grey Papers, FO 800/100.

11 For further details on Churchill's views of the Belgian question, see K.M. Wilson, 'The War Office, Churchill and the Belgian Option: August to December 1911', in *Bulletin of the Institute of Historical Research*, 50, 122, 1977, pp. 218–228.

12 See (**1**).

(11) 4 October 1911: Esher's diary

Esher talks to Asquith at Balmoral; Asquith opposed plan of landing British troops in France rather than in Belgium, but is told that French and British General Staffs have already worked out detailed plans

[...] Then we talked about the General Staff scheme of landing and [*sic*] Army in France. The P.M. is opposed to this plan. He inclines to an occupation of Belgium upon political and military grounds. He will not hear of the despatch of more than 4 Divisions. He has told Haldane so. He wants the Belgian plan worked out.

But, I reminded him that the mere fact of the W[ar] O[ffice] plan having been worked out in detail with the French G[eneral] S[taff] (which is the case) has certainly committed us to fight, whether the Cabinet likes it or not, and that the combined plan of the two General Staffs hold the field. It is certainly an extraordinary thing that our officers should have been permitted to arrange all these details [...] when the Cabinet has never been consulted.

I asked the P.M. whether he thought that it would be possible to have an English force concentrated in France within 7 days of the outbreak of war, in view of the fact that the Cabinet (the majority of them) have never heard of the plan. He thinks it impossible! How this would astound the General Staff.[13] But it confirms what I said to Huguet (the F. military attaché) nearly two years ago. The thing is unthinkable with our methods of government. The P.M. has formed a good opinion of Sir J. F[rench]. He recognises that he possesses no gifts or experience, but he is impressed by his knowledge of war and his good sense.

Altogether the P.M. showed that he had thought a good deal of these problems, but he is lazy and hesitates to act upon his vie[w]s. He despises the French Government and says that the brothers Cambon rule France in her foreign relations.

Churchill Archives Centre, Cambridge, The Papers of Viscount Esher, ESHR 2/12.[14]

13 See (**51**). Keith Neilson argues that evidence such as this shows that the importance of the CID meeting has been overstated, suggesting that the political opposition to deploying the BEF in France also needs to be taken into account: 'Great Britain', in Richard F. Hamilton and Holger H. Herwig (eds), *War Planning 1914*, Cambridge University Press, Cambridge 2010, pp. 175–197, pp. 185–186.

14 Cited in Keith Neilson, 'Great Britain', in Hamilton and Herwig (eds), *War Planning 1914*, Cambridge University Press, Cambridge 2010, pp. 175–197, p. 186. I am grateful to Keith Neilson for making this document available to me,

(12) 11 October 1911: Minutes of the French Superior Council of Defence meeting

Joffre considers political implications of potential violation of Belgian neutrality; France will wait for Germany to cross Belgian border first

[...] The Chief of the General Staff observed that concerning Belgium the question is not solely a military one, it is above all one of diplomacy. If we violate Belgian neutrality first, we will become *provocateurs*. England will not take our side; Italy will have the right to declare herself against us. We will consequently be stopped by political considerations. If only military considerations are taken into account, we would, on the contrary, have the greatest interest in taking the offensive through Belgium. [...]

The Minister of Foreign Affairs remarked that when the war had been on the point of breaking out this question had been discussed between the Chief of the General Staff and himself. He had understood that one would hold oneself ready, but that one would leave Germany to violate Belgian neutrality first, and would thus only position oneself to meet them at the Luxembourg-Belgian [border].[15]

P.V., C.S.D.N., Séance du 11 octobre 1911, Fonds Messimy, AN 509 AP/5.

(13) October 1911: French assessment of future conflict

Germany is France's main potential enemy

The General Staff of the Army considers it obvious that Germany is our principal adversary ... [O]f all the rival nations for France, Germany is the strongest, the most immediately menacing. Its allies are only satellites.

Ministère de la Guerre, État-Major de l'Armée, Note indiquant les points relatifs à la situation extérieure, Octobre 1911. SHAT 2N1, p. 2, cited in Robert Doughty, 'France', in Hamilton and Herwig (eds), *War Planning 1914*, pp. 143–174, p. 144.

---

and to the Churchill Archive Centre for allowing me to reproduce it here.

15 For context, see Robert Doughty, 'France', in Hamilton and Herwig (eds), *War Planning 1914*, p. 148, and Williamson, *Strategy*, 1969 edn, pp. 209–210.

(14) 16 November 1911: Asquith's report of Cabinet meeting for the King

Britain not formally committed to supporting France

Sir E. Grey made it clear that at no step of our intercourse with France since Jan. 1906 had we either by diplomatic or military engagements compromised our freedom of decision & action in the event of war between France & Germany.[16]

Asquith to the King, 16 November 1911, Asquith Papers I/6, Bodleian Library, Oxford, cited in Keith Neilson, 'Great Britain', in Hamilton and Herwig (eds), *War Planning 1914*, pp. 175–197, p. 187.

(15) 2 December 1911: Moltke to Bethmann Hollweg

Military justifications for army increases

The preparations for deployment and operations require long and careful work, they cannot be changed from one day to the next, and our political leadership will also have to be considerate of them. Even just the point in time when politics are to be continued by force of arms can be of decisive importance for the outcome. [...]

The equipping, perfection and strengthening of her military power in all areas makes France an ever more powerful and dangerous opponent. Everyone prepares themselves for the big war that is widely expected sooner or later. Only Germany and her ally Austria do not participate in these preparations.[17]

BA-MA, BArch RH 61/406: 'Die Militärpolitische Lage Deutschlands', pp. 57–58, pp. 14–17.

16 See (**1**) and (**10**).

17 For a discussion of Moltke's memorandum, see also David Stevenson, *Armaments and the Coming of War*, Clarendon, Oxford 1996, pp. 202–203; David Herrmann, *The Arming of Europe*, Princeton University Press, Princeton, NJ 1997, pp. 169ff.; Annika Mombauer, *Helmuth von Moltke*, Cambridge University Press, Cambridge 2001, pp. 132ff.

(16) 13 December 1911: Schlieffen to the editor of *Deutsche Revue*

Fear that Germany is not keeping up with French armaments

[...] Because 65 million Germans do not deploy more trained soldiers than 41 million French, Germany will be in a minority even vis-à-vis France alone, completely aside from the English and perhaps also Belgian troops that will come to her aid. Whether the English fleet and army as well as the French fleet have gained in spirit of enterprise for the possible war is unclear, but the self-confidence and desire for war of the French army and the whole nation has in any case increased substantially in the last summer.

PA Berlin, R 788, 13 December 1911.

2
Documents from 1912

(17) 9 January 1912: French Superior Council of National Defence meeting

---

Council refused to permit a violation of Belgian neutrality, but French forces could enter Belgium at the first news of her violation by the Germany army

---

Whereas the Swiss question is of no interest to France and Germany, the Belgian problem is totally different. Trustworthy documents suggest that Germany would not hesitate to extend her army's zone of action into Belgium.

From our point of view, it could be in our best interests, from a military perspective, to violate Belgium's neutrality in order to threaten the Rhine provinces of Prussia directly and repel the enemy masses in southern Germany by cutting them off from Berlin; but, in this case, England would refuse to lend her support, and may even declare herself against us.

The situation would be different if the Germans were the first to violate Belgian territory and it seems obvious that we would have the right to march to meet them, without taking into account Belgium's neutrality.

The question of the Grand Duchy of Luxembourg's neutrality is, from a military point of view, linked to that of Belgium; but the same does not apply from the diplomatic point of view. If we think it will help with the running of operations, we must not hesitate to cross into the territory of the Grand Duchy whose government is subservient to Germany's politics.

C.S.D.N., Séance du 9 janvier 1912, pp. 4–5, AN 509AP/5.[1]

1 See also Guy Pédroncini, 'Stratégie et relations internationales: La séance du 9 janvier 1912 au conseil supérieur de la défense nationale', *Revue d'histoire diplomatique* 91 (1977), pp. 143–158.

(18) 12 January 1912: Goschen to Nicolson

Anti-British feelings in Germany

I wish I could give a better report of Anglo-German relations, but my few England-loving German friends tell me that they have never known the feeling of irritation against England so strong and so widespread as it is at present, I am afraid that this is the case.

TNA, FO371, 1373, f.116–9.[2]

(19) 29 January 1912: Memorandum by Grey, Churchill, and Lloyd George

Memorandum intended to serve as a basis for Lord Haldane's mission

1. Fundamental. Naval superiority recognized as essential to Great Britain. Present German naval program and expenditure not to be increased, but if possible retarded and reduced.
2. England sincerely desires not to interfere with German Colonial expansion. To give effect to this she is prepared forthwith to discuss whatever the German aspirations in that direction may be. England will be glad to know that there is a field or special points where she can help Germany.
3. Proposals for reciprocal assurances debarring either power from joining in aggressive designs or combinations against the other would be welcome.

GP, 31, No. 98.

(20) 7 February 1912: Grey to Bertie

Haldane Mission

London, 7 February 1912

Last month a communication reached one of my Colleagues from the German Emperor through Ballin and Cassel. It was brought to me, and

2 Cited in Terence Cole; 'German Decision-Making on the Eve of the First World War', in John Röhl (ed.), *Der Ort Kaiser Wilhelm II. in der deutschen Geschichte*, Munich 1991, pp. 53–76, p. 57.

some further communications passed through the same channel. The Emperor expressed a strong wish that I should go to Berlin, and he sent me an invitation. I thought that this would never do; but I also thought that the communications should not go any further through unofficial channels.

It happens to be convenient for Haldane to go to Berlin about the business of a University Committee for Scientific Education, over which he presides here. He is to see Bethmann-Hollweg, and have a very frank exchange of views about naval expenditure and other things, in order to discover whether the Germans will do any thing in connection with that expenditure, and what they want in return.

I have discussed the whole ground thoroughly with him and with Goschen. The question is not very easy. The Germans are very vague about what is possible as regards naval expenditure; and, though we are quite prepared to satisfy them that we have no intention of attacking them or supporting an aggressive policy against them, we must keep our hands free to continue the relations which we already have with France.[3]

I spoke to Cambon for his information and that of Poincaré, so that it is not necessary for you to make a communication; but I think that you ought to know how things stand, in case that Poincaré should say anything to you.

BD, VI, No. 499.

(21) 8 February 1912: Haldane's diary

Haldane Mission

8 February

At the interview with the Chancellor [Bethmann Hollweg], which took place at 2 o'clock, and lasted for more than an hour and a half, [...] I told him that I felt there had been a great deal of drifting away between Germany and England, and that it was important to ask what was the cause. [...] Germany had built up, and was building up, magnificent armaments, and with the aid of the Triple Alliance she had become the centre of a tremendous group. The natural consequence was that other Powers had tended to approximate. [...] While the fact to which I had referred created a difficulty, the difficulty was not insuperable; for two

3 As Zara Steiner and Keith Neilson point out, 'this in outline remained Grey's basic position from 1912 until July 1914': *Britain and the Origins of the First World War*, Palgrave Macmillan, London 2003, p. 101.

groups of Powers might be on very friendly relations if there was only an increasing sense of mutual understanding and confidence. The present seemed to me to be a favourable moment for a new departure. The Morocco question was now out of the way, and we had no agreements with France or Russia except those that were in writing and published to the world.

The Chancellor interrupted me, and asked me whether this was really so. I replied that I could give him the assurance that it was so without reserve, and that in the situation which now existed I saw no reason why it should not be possible for us to enter into a new and cordial friendship carrying the two old ones into it perhaps to the profit of Russia and France as well as Germany herself. [...]

[Bethmann Hollweg] wished to propose a formula; the balance of power was a phrase he did not like, though he admitted that the historical considerations I had referred to made it natural that some grouping should take place, and that England should lean towards the weaker side. He had, however, proposed, in his communication to us, a formula of neutrality which might go a long way to help.

I said that I cordially agreed with the good intention of his formula, the wording of which was that neither was to enter into any combinations against the other. [...]

We then passed on to the question of the German fleet [...] What was the use of entering into a solemn agreement for concord and against attack if Germany at the same moment was going to increase her battle fleet as a precaution against us, and we had consequently to increase our battle fleet as a precaution against her? [...][4]

BD, VI, No. 506.

(22) 8 February 1912: Minute by Crowe

Opposition against Anglo-German agreement by members of the Foreign Office

It would be a political mistake of the first magnitude to allow the German government to squeeze concessions out of us and leave them quite free to pursue the policy of carefully preparing their inevitable war against us.[5]

4 Haldane's account continues below (**24**). For references on the Haldane mission, see above p. 35, n. 10.

5 This is just one of many examples which demonstrate the Foreign Office's resistance to Haldane's discussions. See Steiner and Neilson, *Britain*, p. 103 for more details.

TNA, FO 371/1572, cited in Zara Steiner and Keith Neilson, *Britain and the Origins of the First World War*, Palgrave Macmillan, London 2003, p. 103.

(23) 8 February 1912: Tirpitz to Müller

Tirpitz summarizes the political demands to be made of England

England may not participate in a war between Germany and France, no matter who the 'attacker' is. If we cannot obtain this guarantee then we will simply have to continue arming in order to be up to the Anglo-French entente which has, de facto, the character of an offensive alliance.[6]

BA-MA Freiburg, *Nachlass* Tirpitz, N 253/26a, cited in John Röhl, *Wilhelm II.*, Vol. 3, *Der Weg in den Abgrund, 1900–1941*, Beck, Munich 2008, p. 902.

(24) 9 February 1912: Haldane's diary

Haldane's meeting with Wilhelm II and Tirpitz; Tirpitz insists that naval laws cannot be altered even to accommodate an Anglo-German agreement

I lunched at 1 o'clock with the Emperor at the Schloss. [...] After luncheon the Emperor withdrew with me to his study along with Admiral von Tirpitz. [...] The Emperor tried, as I did myself, to bring his mind to the standpoint of the other country. After expressing the opinion that an agreement, if it could be come to, would improve things enormously for all of us and indeed for the whole world [...], the Emperor invited me to proceed to naval matters. [...]

Admiral von Tirpitz, and indeed the Emperor himself, said that the original programme was to have a new Fleet Law with a new ship every

6 Also printed in Alfred von Tirpitz, *Der Aufbau der deutschen Wehrmacht*, Cotta'sche Buchhandlung, Stuttgart, Berlin 1924 p. 282. See also Tirpitz to Wilhelm II., 9 October 1917, GP, 31, No. 11426, and 'Lord Haldane and Germany', *Manchester Guardian*, 1 September 1917. For a detailed discussion of Tirpitz's role in the events, and the Kaiser's views, see John Röhl, *Wilhelm II.*, Vol. 3, *Der Weg in den Abgrund, 1900–1941*, Beck, Munich 2008, pp. 889ff.

year of the six; that they had cut it down to three ships in six years beginning in 1912, and it was very difficult to get out of this. Admiral von Tirpitz said that he had to take care of the Emperor's position before the German public, and that the three new ships were, moreover, essential for the third squadron, which they desired to introduce for the purpose of having a fleet available all the year round. [...]

I insisted that fundamental modification was essential. [...] the Emperor was so disturbed at the idea that the world would not believe in the reality of the agreement unless the ship-building programme was modified that he asked me what I would suggest. I said [...] that if he could not drop the new law [...] he might as least drop out a ship. [...] After much talking we got to this, that, as I insisted that they must not inaugurate the agreement by building an additional ship, at once, they should put off building the first ship till 1913, and then should not lay down another till three years after (1916), and lay down the third till 1919. [...] The Emperor thought the agreement would affect profoundly the tendency in ship-building, and he certainly should not desire to go beyond the three ships. The fact of the agreement was the key to everything. The Chancellor, he said, would propose to me this afternoon a formula which he had drafted. I said that I would see the Chancellor and discuss any further territorial questions with him, and would then return as speedily as I could and report the good disposition which I had found to my colleagues, and leave the difficulty of not being able to stop ship-building more completely [...] to their judgment. [...]

9 February 1912 (Later)

[...] After my interview with the Emperor I dined with the Chancellor. [...] The Chancellor said that if we could not meet them in their necessity for a new Fleet Law, the idea of agreement must go to pieces ('*scheitern*') and that things would grow worse. He had done and was doing his best – what the result of failure would be was a matter of destiny ('*Schicksal*'). I observed that [...] I was as anxious for an agreement as he was, and my colleagues were anxious too. But how would our agreement look if it were followed by more ship-building? [...][7]

BD, VI, No. 506.

7 Haldane's account continues below, (**26**).

(25) 9 February 1912: Wilhelm II to Ballin

Wilhelm II's version of his conversation with Haldane

Agreement reached by me. I met [Haldane] by a long way. But this is now the end! He [Haldane] was very nice and understanding and completely understood my point of view as Supreme War Lord as well as Tirpitz on the question of the naval laws. I believe I have thus done everything in my powers!!!

Cited in John Röhl, *Wilhelm II., Der Weg in den Abgrund, 1900–1941*, Beck, Munich 2008, p. 904.

(26) 10 February 1912: Haldane's diary

Bethmann Hollweg concerned that naval building plans would jeopardize Anglo-German agreement; attempts to use Haldane to undermine Tirpitz

---

[...] On the Saturday [10th] I lunched with Baron von Stumm, of the Foreign Office [...] After luncheon he took me aside and said he had something to tell me. It was that the Chancellor was unhappy over what he had gathered from his talk with me last night was my impression that my colleagues would consider Tirpitz's concession too small to be accepted by English public opinion. The Chancellor, said Baron Stumm, was not going to let this agreement – which was the dream of his life – founder because of Tirpitz, and it would help him, Stumm thought, if I took a very strong line to the effect that there must be further naval concessions. I took the hint, and when I went [...] to [the Chancellor's] house at 5 o'clock, I began by saying that [...] English public opinion would not improbably be unmanageable and, I thought, with reason. He said he saw my point. He would do his best. But the forces he had to contend with were almost insuperable. Public opinion in Germany expected a new law and the third squadron, and he must have these. [...][8]

BD, VI, No. 506.

---

8 The next day, a despondent Bethmann Hollweg informed Admiral von Müller: 'The matter is much less favourable. Haldane had a very unfavourable impression of Tirpitz, I do not yet know what will become of this.' Müller's diary of 10 February 1912, cited in Walter Görlitz, *Der Kaiser*, Musterschmidt, Göttingen 1965, pp. 113–114.

(27) 8–10 February 1912: Bethmann Hollweg's Memoirs: the Haldane Mission

Bethmann Hollweg's retrospective account of the Haldane Mission

Lord Haldane arrived in Berlin on 8 February. Our long, confidential discussion was friendly and conducted with great openness. Haldane emphasized emphatically that the deciding personalities in England not only aimed at an improvement, but at friendly relations. The next day Haldane had a meeting with the Kaiser, with Admiral von Tirpitz in attendance.[9] The discussion seemed to be going well. We made the concession only to order the first of the three ships in our *Novelle* in 1913, the other two in 1916 and 1919, which seemed to please the Minister. In private conversation he expressed his delight at his impressions and was hopeful regarding the success of the negotiations which he considered a world-historic event.

On the German side a comprehensive draft contract was worked out, whose core was a definite agreement of neutrality between England and Germany. The formula for this was: 'Should one of the signatories be embroiled in a war with one or several powers, the other signatory will at the very least observe benevolent neutrality vis-à-vis the signatory at war and try its best to achieve a localization of the conflict.'

In turn Haldane suggested his own formula:

'Neither power will make or prepare to make any unprovoked attack upon the other or join in any combination or design against the other for purposes of aggression or become party to any plan of naval or military enterprise alone or in combination with any other power directed to such an end.'

[...] In all of this I gained the impression that Haldane was generally amenable. He attempted to combine our formulas and accepted the idea of benevolent neutrality with the proviso that it had to be wars in which the partner of the agreement could not be considered to be the aggressor. [...]

Personally I was determined to champion utmost restraint in the question of the fleet building programme, if I were able to create a political agreement as a compensating counter-weight. But this is where England failed. In long drawn-out negotiations Sir Edward Grey finally conceded the following formula:

'Because both powers share the desire to ensure peace and friendship with each other, England declares that she will not launch an unprovoked

9 See (24) and (25). For details of Haldane's visit see Röhl, *Wilhelm II.*, Vol. 3, pp. 900ff.

attack on Germany and that she will refrain from any aggressive policy against Germany. An attack is not part of any contract nor part of any combination of which England is currently a member, and England will not join any agreement that aims at such an attack.'

This formula, which only protected us from an unprovoked bellicose policy by England herself, not however from England's hostile participation in the case of a Franco-Russian attack [on Germany], could not effectively diffuse the international situation as it had developed. Therefore we suggested the addition that England would as a matter of course adopt benevolent neutrality 'if a war were forced on Germany'. But Sir Edward Grey rejected this addition categorically, as he explained to our ambassador, because of concern to be endangering the existing friendship with the other powers.

This was the decision.[10]

Theobald von Bethmann Hollweg, *Betrachtungen zum Weltkrieg*, 2 vols, Vol. 1, *Vor dem Kriege*, Hobbin, Berlin 1919, pp. 48–53, 56f.

(28) 16 February 1912: Bertie's Memorandum

Haldane Mission; British policy and suspicions of German intentions; speculations about a future war between Germany and France

---

I saw Nicolson & Grey today. The former described to me in detail and the latter in general terms the origin of and the discussion between Haldane on the one side with Bethmann-Hollweg with the Emperor and with H.M. & Admiral Tirpitz.

Instead of our having as hitherto made an Agreement to naval armaments a condition preliminary to a political conversation, Haldane left aside altogether a naval discussion, explained that we had no aggressive intentions and no surprise meditations against Germany. What were the reasons for the feeling in Germany which Bethmann Hollweg & Co. admitted – that we always stood in the way of German ambitions. What did the German Govt. want us to do?

The suggestion of Bethmann Hollweg and his spokesman, M. de Stumm, were that we should hand over to Germany Zanzibar and Pemba, renounce in favour of Germany our reversionary right under the 1898 secret agreement to the piece of territory thereby reserved to us in Portuguese Angola, undertake not to join any combination of Powers against Germany for aggression against Germany.

---

10 See also (22) and (28).

In return for these concessions by England, Germany would cede to England the German right of participation on an equality which any other Power might acquire from the Porte of a share in the Bagdad-Persian Gulf portion of the Bagdad Railway. Germany would also give to England diplomatic support in the Persian Gulf in return for a share in any railway concessions which England might obtain in Persia. Germany would also renounce her reversionary claim to the Portuguese portion of the island of Timor.

On such bases an understanding would no doubt[,] M. Bethmann Hollweg said[,] be advantageous to both parties and a formula might be signed of good intentions and of benevolent neutrality in case of an attack on Germany by France.

It would be a gratuitous sacrifice to give to Germany Zanzibar and Pemba though she has opposite on the mainland Dar es Salaam a better harbour than we have in Zanzibar and Harcourt has no objection to ceding those islands nor to the renunciation of our reversionary claim to the piece of Portuguese Angola.

I warned Grey that we had had disputes with Germany in regard to Zanzibar. She had not carried out her undertakings relative to that Sultanate. She never interpreted agreements as we did when they appeared to be injurious to her interests, and that there would be a great outcry at the renunciation of a part of Portuguese Angola, for it had been specially reserved in order to connect Rhodesia territorially with the Atlantic.

Grey was evidently disposed to make the renunciation on the plea that Germany would by the secret agreement of 1898 have Lobito Bay to which terminus the Railways would naturally be directed.

I warned Grey that the Press and public in France are very nervous and suspicious as to the result of the Haldane mission and that if we make these concessions to Germany for practically no return, it will be surmised that there must be some secret agreement to our advantage, for the diplomatic support of Germany in the Persian Gulf is not required by us and by granting her a share in Persian railway concessions we should be giving a good deal which might harm us without consideration, and that if we signed a formula binding ourselves not to join any combination to attack Germany we might tie our hands very inconveniently as regards France. He said, Do you mean that it is possible that France will attack Germany? I replied that the first attacker is not necessarily the real aggressor. The French Government are aware of recent great military preparations in Germany. What are they for? If the movements of German troops towards the French frontier and other measures indicated warlike intentions by Germany I thought that the French troops might be the first to cross the frontier, as they might thereby gain a great military advantage which with the French temperament would be of the highest importance as if a victory were gained by them it would infuse a spirit into the French troops which would count for much in a campaign. The quarrel between Germany and France might be due to the former and she would be the real aggressor though not the one to strike the first blow. In France it is feared that Germany is making preparations for an attack on France as soon as England has been hoodwinked by Germany.

The Dutch have preemptive rights by Treaty with Portugal to the Portuguese portion of the Island on Timor and the Netherlands Minister has so informed the F.O.

The Porte having acquired from Germany her interests in the Bagdad-Persian Railway at a price paid by Turkey the Porte has requested that H.M. Govt. will negotiate with Turkey and not with Germany on the subject. Germany stipulated that she should have reserved to her in case of a deal by Turkey with another Power or Powers, a share equal to that of any Foreign Power. The Porte holds that this claim cannot be transferred by Germany to another Power.

The Government are in a hesitating state. The Lord Chancellor, Harcourt and some others are for coming to arrangements with Germany. Grey is wavering. Churchill is against tying our hands. I don't know as to Lloyd George and Asquith.[11]

TNA, Bertie Papers, FO 800/188.

(29) 21 February 1912: Joffre's account of a secret meeting at the Quai d'Orsay

Military and Naval leaders provide details of their agreements with Britain; discussion of the Belgian question; military leaders outline necessity of advancing through Luxembourg and Belgium; civilians reject this for fear of losing international support

[...] The Minister of the Navy [Delcassé] explained the nature of the naval arrangements arrived at between the British Admiralty and the French Naval Staff. All operations in the North Sea, the English Channel and the Atlantic were reserved to the British Fleet, whereas the French Fleet would have charge of operations in the Mediterranean.

11 On 19 March the Germans rejected the British proposal which did not contain the promise of neutrality that Bethmann Hollweg had desired.

On my side, I informed the meeting that our conversations with the British Staff touching the land forces had taken as a basis six infantry divisions, one cavalry division and two mounted brigades, a total of one hundred and twenty-five thousand combatants. Our study had led us to agree that this army would be embarked in British and Scottish ports and would land at Boulogne, Havre and Rouen. Upon disembarking, a period of twenty-four hours in camp was provided for, after which the British units would be moved to the region of Hirson-Maubeuge. In this way our eventual allies would be prepared to start operations on the fifteenth day of mobilization.

Taking the strictly military point of view [...] I then explained to the Conference that if we could conduct our offensive across Belgium – assuming that no other consideration prevented such a course and that we could come to an understanding with the Belgian Government beforehand – the problem presented to us would be simplified and our chances of victory would be singularly increased. Asked to elaborate this idea I expressed myself as follows:

'In case of war with Germany, the plan which would be most fruitful in decisive results is taking from the very start a vigorous offensive in order to crush by a single blow the organized forces of the enemy. The existence close to the Franco-German frontier of natural obstacles and fortified barriers restricts our offensive to narrowly limited regions. [...] neither in Alsace nor in Lorraine do we find ground favourable for an offensive having in view immediate decisive results. The situation would be infinitely more advantageous if it were permissible for us to extend our left beyond our frontier into the Grand Duchy of Luxembourg. In this region we could develop all our means of action, and we would be passing far to the north of all the fortified systems constructed at a great cost by our adversaries. In case of success, our armies would throw the German masses back towards southern Germany and directly menace their principal line of retreat as well as their communications with Berlin. Moreover, a movement through Belgium would make it possible for the British Army to participate more efficaciously in our operations, and the assistance of this army would bring us a marked superiority as compared with our adversaries.'

[...] I deduced the conclusion that we had a major interest in feeling free to push our armies into Belgian territory, and do it without waiting until such time as the Germans had themselves violated Belgium, as it was probable that they would do. [...]

The Minister of War, M. Millerand, stated that he was in agreement with my conception of the results to be expected from a plan of operations having in view offensive action across Belgian territory, and M. Delcassé, Minister of the Navy, pronounced himself with equal firmness in favour of my opinion.

But the Premier, M. Poincaré, pointed out that an invasion of Belgium by France would run the risk of setting against us not only Europe but the Belgians themselves, by reason of the difficulty of coming to an understanding with them beforehand; under these conditions it seemed essential that our entrance upon Belgian territory be justified at least by a positive menace of German invasion. Indeed, it was this fear of an invasion of Belgium by the Germans which, in the first place, had led to the military agreements with Great Britain. We, therefore, had to be sure that a plan based upon a march by us through Belgium would not have for its effect the withdrawal of British support from our side. [...]

Joseph Joffre, *The Memoirs of Marshal Joffre*, 2 vols, Geoffrey Bles, London 1932, Vol. I, pp. 49–51.[12]

(30) 21 March 1912: Paul Cambon to Paléologue[13]

Likelihood of Germany advancing through Belgium in case of war; should France pre-empt such a move by violating Belgian territory?

London, 21 March 1912
Private letter
Today Sir Arthur Nicolson asked me what we think of the general situation here. I told him we were worried, and that rumours of war were spreading far and wide. I do not believe any more than he does that the German government's intentions are aggressive, but there is definitely agitation among the military, and little by little rumour is spreading that we are on the brink of war. While on this subject, I told the Permanent Secretary of State what we had been told about advice

12 (Taken from the published English translation of Joffre's memoirs, but here with minor stylistic alterations.) Present at this three-hour meeting were Prime Minister Raymond Poincaré, Minister of War Alexandre Millerand, Naval Minister Delcassé, Maurice Paléologue, Director of Political Affairs at the Foreign Office, Vice-Admiral Marie Aubert, Chief of the Naval General Staff, and Joseph Joffre, Chief of Army General Staff. See also Raymond Poincaré, *Au Service de la France: neuf années de souvenirs*, 10 vols, Librairie Plon, Paris, 1926–1933, Vol. I, pp. 224–225. For context and discussion, see S.R. Williamson Jr, *The Politics of Grand Strategy*, Harvard University Press, Cambridge, MA 1969, p. 212.

13 Paléologue was at this time Director of Foreign Affairs at the Quai d'Orsay. During the July Crisis, he was France's ambassador in St Petersburg.

given to the German banks inviting them to protect their currency and I added a piece of information that my military attaché was given just this morning by the English Chief of the General Staff about purchases of wheat by the German Government. Naturally, I came round to talking about the information our General Staff received about the plans showing the German General Staff's intention to concentrate forces on the Aix-la-Chapelle side, a concentration that could only be explained as a plan to violate Belgium's neutrality. So, I said that at some point our two Governments might ask themselves the following question: 'If it were established that an army concentrated around Aix-la-Chapelle was preparing to enter Belgium, and if we even knew this army's scouts were about to cross the border into the neutral State, should we wait for Belgium to be occupied by the German army before advancing from our side?' – 'This is very serious', said Sir Arthur. 'Yes, but it is a question that will be asked, if we are certain the German forces will march into Belgium.' I added, jokingly, that rumour of war would have to be very widespread before such questions could be asked, and while I did not give the impression that I otherwise attached any importance to going into Belgium, I was not sorry to have thrown this suggestion into the conversation. Sir A. Nicolson asked me if I knew something about the ministerial changes that are being talked about in Berlin.[14] He had heard nothing about this matter. It is likely that M. de Kiderlen will not remain in office, but it does not seem likely that M. de Bethmann Hollweg will be sacrificed.[15]

[The end of the letter is about internal affairs in England and the problem in Crete].[16]

DDF, 3e série, 2, No. 240.

14 Chancellor Bethmann Hollweg had offered his resignation on 6 March 1912, outraged by Wilhelm II's bellicose utterances and despatches following the Haldane Mission. The Kaiser did not grant his request. For details see Röhl, *Wilhelm II.*, Vol. 3, pp. 912–913.

15 Kiderlen-Wächter died suddenly on 31 December 1912. Bethmann Hollweg remained Chancellor until July 1917.

16 This text was added by the editors of DDF.

(31) 22 March 1912: Balfour to Churchill

Suspects German policy to be motivated by expansionist aims

A war entered upon for no other object than to restore the Germanic Empire of Charlemagne in a modern form, appears to me at once so wicked and so stupid as to be almost incredible. And yet it is almost impossible to make sense of modern Germany policy without crediting it with this intention.

Cited in R.T.B. Langhorne, 'The Naval Question in Anglo-German Relations, 1912–1914', *Historical Journal*, XIV, 2, 1970, pp. 359–370, p. 361.

(32) 28 March 1912: Poincaré to Paul Cambon

Relief in Paris that Britain is not signing up to an agreement with Germany concerning possible British neutrality in a future war

Despatch No. 290
Paris, 28 March 1912

As I told you in my telegram of the 23rd of this month, I was very touched by the frankness of the messages you received from the First Secretary of State for Foreign Affairs about relations between England and Germany. It was invaluable to learn that the British Government had refused to be bound by a declaration of neutrality towards the German Government, in the event that Germany should enter into conflict with a third Power.

But a meeting I had yesterday with the Ambassador [Bertie], during which he expressed himself very freely, leads me to want a little more detail about the assurances you were given.

After telling me that he wanted to talk to me 'as if he were not the Ambassador', Sir Fr. Bertie added: 'Sir Ed. Grey has just written to me that M. Cambon was very happy with his assurances concerning the declaration of neutrality Germany has asked us for. This surprises me, because the fact that any such declaration has not been agreed does not necessarily mean it has been dismissed once and for all. What Germany wanted from us was not just the promise of straightforward neutrality; she wanted that neutrality to be benevolent, which is absurd because benevolent neutrality is no longer neutrality at all. Sir Ed. Grey, to his credit, answered with a refusal: actually, he is totally surrounded at the moment by people who want to strengthen ties with Germany [...]. I do confess that I no longer understand his politics; it worries me, even. We must prevent this declaration of neutrality from being agreed, which it is in danger of being within a very short time if the German Government repeats the same demand. In truth, we are only being asked to commit to remaining neutral in the event that Germany is attacked. But, who can guarantee that France, provoked and threatened by the mobilisation of the German army will not be forced to take up the offensive? No, M. Cambon must not give the impression of being happy. If you, yourself, speak to London firmly, they will be reluctant to commit the error I am dreading.'

This advice comes from too friendly and respectful a source for me not to follow it. So I would be obliged if you would take up this matter, without delay, with the First Secretary of State for Foreign Affairs, obviously without implicating Sir Francis Bertie. It is extremely important that England should not commit to remaining neutral [in a war] between France and Germany, even in the event that the attack would seem to come from us. For example, could we legitimately be blamed for an attack, if a concentration of German forces in the region of Aix-la-Chapelle forced us to cover our northern border by crossing into Belgian territory?

On the other hand, mindful of England's loyalty and without *any written agreement having united the two Governments*, we have allowed our Staff to enter into secret talks with the English Staff and share the most important outlines of our strategic plans.[17] The British Government knows our attitude towards it has not changed. We are not asking it to limit any room for manoeuvre on our account any more today than we did before; we wholly accept it should want to retain that until the last moment. But at the very least it should not relinquish any freedom to our detriment by signing a declaration of neutrality that could only encourage Germany to renew her traditional tactics of provoking France.[18]

DDF, 3e série, 2, No. 269.[19]

---

17 For details of Anglo-French staff talks see Samuel R. Williamson Jr., *The Politics of Grand Strategy. Britain and France Prepare for War, 1904–1914*, Harvard University Press, Cambridge, Massachusetts 1969, pp.59ff.

18 See also Isvolsky's retrospective account of France's objections to the possibility of an Anglo-German rapprochement, dated 5 December 1912: 'M. Poincaré expressed himself most emphatically against such an undertaking. He pointed out to the British Government that the signature of such a treaty with Germany by Great Britain would end at a blow the existing Franco-British relations, since no written agreement of a general political character existed between France and Great Britain. This objection had its result: the London Cabinet declined Germany's proposal, to the lively dissatisfaction of Berlin.' Friedrich Stieve, *Isvolsky and the World War*, Allen & Unwin, London 1926, p. 78.

19 For context see Williamson, *Strategy*, p. 213.

(33) 9 April 1912: Grey to Bertie

British assurance that Anglo-French Entente is not compromised by Anglo-German negotiations

Telegram
Private
Foreign Office, 9 April 1912
D. 4.25 p.m.

[...] There is no new development about the formula and nothing more to be said, unless the Germans make a new suggestion. I refused to put in the word neutrality because it would give the impression that our hands were tied. If Germany attacked and forced war upon an ally or friend of ours it would be provocation to us and therefore formula as we proposed it would not tie our hands. [...]

BD, VI, No. 569.

(34) 10 April 1912: Bertie to Grey

French reservations about Anglo-German negotiations

Telegram
Private
Paris, 10 April 1912
D. 7.10 p.m.
R. 9 p.m.

I have spoken to M. Poincaré in the sense of your private telegram of yesterday.[20] He says that if a formula such as has been proposed is signed and published it will be a painful surprise to French public and will also be viewed with disappointment by some of his colleagues. The French Amb[assado]r will speak to you on the subject.

BD, VI, No. 570.

20 See (33).

(35) 15 April 1912: Nicolson to Grey

Record of Nicolson's conversation with Paul Cambon on 14 April, detailing French fears of possible Anglo-German rapprochement

[...] The French Government were convinced that an opportunity would be seized, perhaps not this year, but possibly the next year or the year after, by Germany to create some incident which would arouse public feeling on both sides of the frontier, and which would, viewing the temper in both countries, very probably lead to war. The German Emperor and the German Chancellor were, doubtless, pacifically inclined, but they were not, in reality, the influential and deciding factors. The Pan-Germans, the Navy League, and other chauvinistic elements, the military, etc., were the factors which had the greatest weight and influence. In these circumstances, M. Poincaré considered that it was necessary to take stock of the position of France, and to see on what outside assistance she could rely when the moment arrived. It was evident that the attitude of England was a very important factor, and the recent endeavours of Germany to neutralise her clearly indicated that England was regarded as the Power which held largely the balance for or against peace. Were Germany assured that England would remain neutral, her hands would be free for dealing with France. Were she in doubt, she would hesitate. But it was of great importance to France also to be assured what would be the attitude of England, and if she could count upon her. [...]

Harold Nicolson, *Sir Arthur Nicolson*, Constable, London 1930, pp. 268–269.

(36) 11 November 1912: Wilhelm II's Memorandum

Against the background of the Balkan Wars, Wilhelm II is adamant Germany should not be forced to go to war by Austria-Hungary

(Handwritten resumé of a conversation with Bethmann Hollweg and Kiderlen on 9 November)

Austria has incautiously adopted a harsh dictatorial tone vis-à-vis the Serbian demands in the press and in official decrees. This can have a provocative effect and lead to complications. Serbia demands access to the Adriatic Sea with ports, Austria refuses this wish *a limine* [*sic*].

Russia seems to want to support Serbia's aspirations and could collide with Austria about this in such a way that it could come to a conflict with weapons. Then the *casus foederis* applies for Germany because Vienna would be attacked by Petersburg – according to the [Dual Alliance] Treaty. This requires the mobilisation and a war against 2 fronts for Germany, i.e. in order to march against Moscow Paris has to be taken first.[21] Paris will undoubtedly be supported by London. Thus Germany must enter a war of survival with 3 Great Powers in which everything has to be risked and perhaps she can perish. All this happens because Austria does not want the Serbs in Albania or Durazzo. It is obvious that this goal is for Germany no rallying cry for a war of annihilation and therefore no opportunity to fire up with one word the German nation for a war fought for such reasons, and nobody can defend in front of his conscience and his responsibility before God and his people risking Germany's existence for such a reason. It would far exceed the confines of the treaty [...].

GP, 33, No. 12349.

(37) 18 November 1912: Kageneck's report from Vienna

Balkan Wars; Austrian Chief of Staff considers war between Austria and Serbia hardly avoidable

[It seemed to me] as if he [Schemua] had arrived at the opinion that one would hardly be able to avoid a call to arms. [...] Today, after a conversation with a number of General Staff officers I, too, had the impression as if the chances for war or peace stood at 50 per cent, as Poincaré remarked recently.[22]

PA Berlin, R 8627, *Militär- und Marineangelegenheiten Österreichs.*

21 This shows that the Kaiser was well aware of the implications of Germany's war planning (the so-called Schlieffen Plan). For details on this see for example Annika Mombauer, 'German War Plans', in Richard F. Hamilton and Holger H. Herwig (eds), *War Planning 1914*, Cambridge University Press, Cambridge 2010, pp. 48–78, *passim.*

22 In a memorandum of 9 November 1912 the Chief of Staff claimed that 'even in the case that we have to fight this war on our own, the chances for success are not at all unfavourable' (cited in Günther Kronenbitter, *'Krieg im Frieden'*, Oldenbourg, Munich 2003, p. 388). On 22 November, he travelled to Berlin to ascertain Germany's position if war were to break out imminently (**39**).

(38) 22 November 1912: Grey to Paul Cambon

Franco-British discussions about mutual support in case of war

Private
Foreign Office, 22 November 1912

From time to time in recent years the French and British naval and military experts have consulted together. It has always been understood that such consultation does not restrict the freedom of either Government to decide at any future time whether or not to assist the other by armed force. We have agreed that consultation between experts is not, and ought not to be regarded as an engagement that commits either Government to action in a contingency that has not arisen and may never arise. The disposition, for instance, of the French and British fleets respectively at the present moment is not based upon an engagement to co-operate in war.

You have, however, pointed out that, if either Government had grave reason to expect an unprovoked attack by a third Power, it might become essential to know whether it could in that event depend upon the armed assistance of the other.

I agree that, if either Government had grave reason to expect an unprovoked attack by a third Power, or something that threatened the general peace, it should immediately discuss with the other, whether both Governments should act together to prevent aggression and to preserve peace, and if so what measures they would be prepared to take in common. If these measures involved action, the plans of the General Staffs would at once be taken into consideration, and the Governments would then decide what effect should be given to them.[23]

BD, X, No. 416.

23 The final sentence 'if these measures involved action …' was omitted by Grey when he read this letter to the House of Commons on 3 August 1914.

(39) 22 November 1912: Schemua's report about meeting Moltke and Wilhelm II[24]

Moltke and Wilhelm II assure the Austrian Chief of Staff of Germany's support, regardless of circumstances and even if general war were to result; Germany's military strategy revealed and received with scepticism by Schemua

[...] Our discussion brought a confirmation of the agreements of March of this year,[25] and also resulted in complete agreement in the assessment of the situation as a whole.[26] Moltke showed complete understanding for the assessment of our situation vis-à-vis Russia and Serbia and also expressed that he was entertaining the thought of certain preparations on the German-Russian border, namely requesting a possible calling up of reservists. He also promised me not just passive support, but an active offensive action in parallel with ours. He emphasised repeatedly the ally's faithful attitude, that we could absolutely count on Germany's support if Russia threatened us, and that it was also for Germany of imminent interest that we were not weakened.

24 Schemua travelled in civilian clothes to Berlin for this secret meeting in which the allies wanted to discuss how to proceed in the current crisis. Archduke Franz Ferdinand also travelled to Berlin. For details see E.C. Helmreich, 'An Unpublished Report on Austro-German Military Conversations of November, 1912', *Journal of Modern History*, V, 2, June 1933, pp. 197–207, *passim*; Kronenbitter, *'Krieg im Frieden'*, pp. 396–397; Röhl, *Wilhelm II.*, Vol. 3, pp. 948ff., who shows that the editors of Germany's official document collection, *Große Politik*, deliberately downplayed the importance of this visit. The visit of Schemua and Franz Ferdinand at the height of the crisis caused concern in St Petersburg where, also on 22 November, the Tsar met with Sukhomlinov and the commanders of the military districts of Warsaw and Kiev and decided on mobilization of the Kiev district, and parts of the Warsaw district, and to prepare to mobilize the Odessa district. As Turner points out, this was the 'embryo' of the partial mobilization which was proposed in July 1914. L.C.F. Turner, 'The Russian Mobilization in 1914', in Paul M. Kennedy (ed.), *The War Plans of the Great Powers, 1880–1914*, George Allen & Unwin, London 1979, pp. 252–268, p. 254, (**201**), (**206**) and (**207**). The measure was overruled the next day. (**40**)

25 Schemua met Moltke as part of his inaugural visit to Berlin from 14–16 March. For details see Josef Mann, 'FML Blasius Schemua. Chef des Generalstabes am Vorabend des Weltkrieges 1911–1912', PhD Dissertation, University of Vienna 1978. I am grateful to Günther Kronenbitter for this reference.

26 At the same time, Archduke Franz Ferdinand was also having meetings with Kaiser Wilhelm II, and he was also assured that the monarch was willing to support Austria 'under all circumstances', even if a world war 'with the three Entente Powers' were to result. See Röhl, *Wilhelm II.*, Vol. 3, p. 951. Franz Ferdinand's account of the talks with Wilhelm II in ÖUA, IV, Nos 4571 and 4559.

He was aware of the seriousness of the situation. Germany's mobilization would automatically result in that of France, and mobilised armies side by side was an impossible situation which would necessarily result in a clash. In that case it was naturally the first intention to defeat the opponent in the West first – which he hoped for in 4–6 weeks – and then to deploy the surplus of power eastwards.

In response to my objection that this short time seemed rather questionable to me and the forces initially put aside in the East a bit small, Moltke replied he could perhaps deploy further divisions, made up of *Ersatz* troops, whose operative readiness would, however, be achieved a little later.

Further he asked me if it was planned to leave something behind against Italy, to which I replied that this was not intended, which visibly assured him.

Regarding Rumania's involvement he was also of the same opinion as me that a closer tie of Rumania's forces to our right wing would certainly be of great advantage to us.

The German Kaiser appeared. [...] He first brought some latest news [...], among others that an industrialist who had just returned from a big automobile tour through all of France had not noticed anything suspicious anywhere which pointed towards preparations for war or war-like mood; he further mentioned the contents of a letter from a high-ranking person in the Tsar's circle that they were not sufficiently prepared for a war yet; this would however be the case in 2 years – then would be the *partie remise*.

[...] In response to my remark that I could not help myself worrying about Italy's attitude H.M. told me that this was not justified [...]. The King [Victor Emanuel] was a reserved, but reliable man. During San Giuliano's last visit to Berlin the latter had expressed himself in a strictly friendly tone for the alliance, [...] and had declared himself willing to sign immediately the renewal of the alliance treaty.

H.M. expressed to Moltke that it might perhaps be advisable visibly to get together with the Italian General Chief of Staff also, in order to demonstrate publicly the military cooperation between the Triple Alliance Powers. Turning back to me H.M. emphasised emphatically that we could fully count on Germany's support in all circumstances.

[...] Moltke emphasised that he, too, was fully aware that the coming events would concern the existence of the [European] states. [...][27]

---

27 Following his meeting with Wilhelm II, Franz Ferdinand telegraphed to Vienna: 'Kaiser Wilhelm especially gracious, and declared he was willing to support us in everything. Full security in this respect. Absolutely against conference of the powers. Have clearly defined our standpoint. Kaiser Wilhelm says that as soon as our prestige demands it we should take energetic action in Serbia, and

Cited in E.C. Helmreich, 'An Unpublished Report on Austro-German Military Conversations of November, 1912', *Journal of Modern History*, V, 2, June 1933, pp. 197–207, pp. 205–207.

(40) 23 November 1912: Kokovtsov's account of a meeting between the Tsar and his military advisers

---

Meeting between Nicholas II and Sukhomlinov, Kokovtsov, Sazonov, Rukhov (Minister for Transport and Communications), Zhilinski (Chief of Staff); Tsar had agreed partial mobilization measures with Minister of War the previous day

---

In the evening of November 9 [22nd], Sukhomlinov telephoned to inform me that the Tsar wished to receive me the next morning at 10 o'clock. [...] The next morning at the station I met Sukhomlinov, Sazonov, Chief of the General Staff Zhilinski, and Minister for Transport and Communications Rukhlov. No one knew why we had been summoned. [...]

The Tsar received us in his large study. [...] Then the Tsar, opening a map on the table before him, began to explain, calmly and clearly, the ratio of Russian and Austrian military forces on our frontier, the weakness of our infantry, numbering not over 90 rifles to a company while the Austrian infantry numbered 200, the slowness of our transport, and the consequent necessity for considerably increasing the troops stationed near the frontier.

'To accomplish this purpose', said the Tsar, 'yesterday, at the conference of the commanders of the Warsaw and Kiev Military districts, it was decided to mobilize the entire Kiev district and part of the Warsaw district, and to prepare to mobilize the Odessa district.

'I wish to stress particularly the fact that this refers exclusively to our Austrian frontier and that we have no intention whatever of taking any steps against Germany. [...]'.

[...] Sukhomlinov [added] that all the telegrams pertaining to the mobilization had been already prepared and would be sent as soon as this conference had ended.

The Tsar, addressing me, added: 'The Minister of War wanted to

---

we can be certain of his support. [...] Met with great sympathy and agreement here; in respect to Russia rather an irritated attitude.' Cited in Helmreich, 'An Unpublished Report', pp. 199–200. According to Szögyény, the Kaiser had even said 'should it be a question of prestige for Austria-Hungary, he would not fear even a world war, and that he would be ready to enter into a war with all three of the Entente powers'. Ibid., p. 200. In early July 1914, similar promises would be made to Count Hoyos when he visited Berlin. See (**120**) and (**130**).

dispatch these orders yesterday,[28] but I asked him to wait another day, since I wanted to discuss the situation with those ministers who ought to be apprised of it before the final orders are given.'

We three looked at each other with the greatest amazement and only the presence of the Tsar restrained us from giving vent to the feelings which animated all of us.

I spoke first, and I had to struggle to retain my composure. I stated frankly that the Minister of War and the two commanders apparently did not perceive what danger they were preparing for Russia in planning this mobilization – a danger of war with Austria and Germany, and at a time when in consideration of our national defense every effort should be made to avert this catastrophe.[29]

The Tsar interrupted me, saying literally the following:

'I do not, just as yourself, Vladimir Nikolaevich, allow the thought of an imminent war. We are not ready for it [...]. But we have before us not the problem of war but a simple measure of precaution, consisting of augmenting the ranks of our army on the frontier and of moving up the troops now removed too far in the rear somewhat closer.'

I continued my speech, pointing out to the Tsar that no matter what we chose to call the projected measures, a mobilization remained a mobilization, to be countered by our adversaries with actual war, for which Germany was ready and only watching for a chance to begin. The Tsar again interrupted me:

'You exaggerate [...]. I have no intention of mobilizing our troops against Germany, with whom we are on the best of terms which cause us no apprehensions, but Austria is openly hostile and has taken a series of steps against us including the increased fortifications at Krakow [...].'

After this I felt compelled to point out that since Austria and Germany were bound by a treaty which amounted to a subordination of the former to the latter, these two countries could not be considered separately. Moreover, in such a mobilization we assumed a great responsibility not

---

28 See above, p. 79, n. 24.

29 For a discussion of the importance of these events in 1912 see Bruce W. Menning, 'Russian Military Intelligence, July 1914: What St Petersburg Perceived and Why It Mattered', article MS, forthcoming, and L.C.F. Turner 'The Russian Mobilization in 1914', in Paul M. Kennedy (ed.), *The War Plans of the Great Powers, 1880–1914*, George Allen & Unwin, London 1979, pp. 252–268, pp. 253ff. Turner points to the dangerous situation that would have been created by a Russian partial mobilization at this critical time: 'There seems little doubt that a Russian partial mobilisation on the scale envisaged by Sukhomlinov would infallibly have produced Austrian counter-measures on a very large scale and would probably have led to Austrian general mobilisation. The remorseless process of mobilisation and counter-mobilisation might well have followed the same fatal course as in 1914' (p. 255).

only for Russia but also for France, since under the terms of our military agreement with our ally we had no right to undertake any such measures without coming to an understanding with her. […]'

Vladimir N. Kokovtsov, *Out of My Past. The Memoirs of Count Kokovtsov*, Stanford University Press, Stanford, London, Oxford 1935, pp. 345–346.[30]

(41) 25 November 1912: Ludendorff's memorandum

Demands for further German army increases

We must adopt measures that keep the country free from attacks in breach of international law and that would make us independent from the measures adopted by our opponents. We must go further than this and give our entire army the strength that alone can guarantee ultimate success in the next war, a war that we will have to be waging with [our] allies, but on the whole with our own strength for [the aim of] Germany's greatness. We must make the decision to utilize our human resources (*Menschenbestand*). We must again become the people in arms that we were once turned into in great times by great men.

BA-MA, BArch RH 61/996: Carl Mühlmann; 'Der Feldherr Ludendorff'.

(42) 2 December 1912: Bethmann Hollweg's Reichstag speech

If Austria-Hungary finds herself threatened as a result of the Balkan Wars, Germany will support her unconditionally

[…] If [Austria-Hungary] finds herself, contrary to all expectations, attacked by a third party in trying to make her interests known, and thus [finds] her very existence threatened, then we would have to step up to her side, determined and decisive, in accordance with our alliance duty (lively applause on the Right, in the Centre and with the National Liberals).

Then we would have to fight on the side of our ally to maintain our own position in Europe, to defend the security and future of our own country (Bravo! on the right, in the Centre, and with the National Liberals).

30 Taken from the published English translation of Kokovtsov's memoirs, but here with minor stylistic alterations.

I am convinced that we will have the entire people behind us with such a policy. [...][31]

Stenographische Berichte des Reichstags, 13. Legislaturperiode, Vol. 286, 2472.

(43) 3 December 1912: Lichnowsky's report from London

News from London that Britain would become involved in a war on the side of France

London, 3 December 1912
No. 1130

Lord Haldane called on me today in order to discuss the political situation with me. During the long conversation he emphasized repeatedly the necessity to reach an agreement on the conflicts in the oriental crisis, because it could not be foreseen what results a war would have in which one or several of the Great Powers would become involved. England was completely peaceful and nobody here wanted a war, not least for economic reasons. But in the general European chaos which could result from Austria marching into Serbia if Serbia did not willingly clear the occupied Adriatic coast, it was hardly likely that Great Britain would remain a silent observer.

I replied that I did not want to pose the question if this meant as much as that England would then proceed in a hostile manner against us. He replied that this was certainly not the necessary, but the possible,[32] result of a war between the two continental groups. The roots of English politics, this is how he put it, lay in the here widespread sentiment that the balance of power of the groups should be maintained somewhat. England would therefore under no circumstances allow France to be defeated which he, as a great admirer of our army and our military institutions, foresaw with some certainty. England could not and would not want to be faced afterwards by a unified continental group led by a single power.

Should thus Germany be embroiled in the conflict by Austria, and thus end up at war with France, then currents would be created in England

31 As John Röhl points out, Moltke had insisted that the Chancellor delivered this speech. The declaration was, of course, welcomed in Vienna, but caused alarm in London, where a warning about Britain's likely role in a future war was promptly made (**43**). Röhl, *Wilhelm II.*, Vol. 3, p. 955.

32 See (**42**).

which no government could resist and whose consequences were entirely unpredictable. The theory of the balance of power of the groups was, however, for England an axiom and had also led to the closer relations with France and Russia. He could vouch for the fact that they wanted here the best relationship with Germany [...]. Also, nobody here would want to go to war with us as long as no European embroilments occurred. The results of a European war were, however, entirely unpredictable and he could then not guarantee for anything. [...][33]

GP, 39, No. 15612.

(44) 8 December 1912: Admiral von Müller's diary

The so-called 'War Council' meeting

Sunday. Ordered to see His Maj. at the Schloss at 11 a.m. with Tirpitz, Heeringen (Vice Admiral) and General von Moltke. H.M. speaks to a telegraphic report from the Ambassador in London, Prince Lichnowsky, concerning the political situation.[34] Haldane, speaking for Grey, has told Lichnowsky that England, if we attacked France, would unconditionally spring to France's aid, for England could not allow the balance of power in Europe to be disturbed. H.M. greeted this information as a desirable clarification of the situation for the benefit of those who had felt sure of England as a result of the recent friendliness of the press.

H.M. envisaged the following:

Austria must deal energetically with the foreign Slavs (the Serbs), otherwise she will lose control of the Slavs in the Austro-Hungarian monarchy.

33 Wilhelm II added several angry marginal notes, and commented at the end: 'because England is too cowardly to leave France and Russia in the lurch openly, and too envious of us and hates us, that is why the other powers are not allowed to defend their interests with the sword, because against all reassurances [...] she will proceed against us. A real nation of shop keepers! And this they call peace politics. Balance of Power! The fight to the end between Slavs and Germans finds the Anglo-Saxons on the side of the Slavs and Gauls'. Wilhelm II saw Lichnowsky's telegram on 8 December (the day of the so-called 'war council meeting) and immediately wrote to Kiderlen-Wächter that 'Haldane's conversation with Lichnowsky [...] tears apart all veils of uncertainty' about England's attitude in a future war. GP, 39, No. 15613. On 4 December, Lichnowsky reported about a conversation with Grey: 'If, however, a European war resulted from Austria advancing against Serbia, and if Russia [...] marched into Galicia, which would lead to us helping [Austria], then France's involvement would be inevitable, and the further consequences impossible to foresee.' GP, 33, No. 12481. See also (**42**).

34 See (**43**).

If Russia supports the Serbs, which she evidently does (Sazonov's declaration that Russia will immediately move into Galicia if Austria moves into Serbia) then war would be unavoidable for us too. We could hope, however, to have Bulgaria and Rumania and also Albania, and perhaps also Turkey on our side. An offer of alliance by Bulgaria has already been sent to Turkey. We have exerted great pressure on the Turks. Recently H.M. has also pressed the Crown Prince of Rumania, who was passing through on his way back from Brussels, to come to an understanding with Bulgaria. If these powers join Austria then we shall be free to fight the war with full fury against France. The fleet must naturally prepare itself for the war against England. The possibility mentioned by the Chief of the Admiralty Staff in his last audience of a war with Russia alone cannot now, after Haldane's statement, be taken into account. Therefore immediate submarine warfare against English troop transports in the Scheldt or by Dunkirk, mine warfare in the Thames. To Tirpitz: speedy build-up of U-boats, etc. Recommendation of a conference of all naval authorities concerned.

General von Moltke: 'I believe a war is unavoidable and the sooner the better. But we ought to do more through the press to prepare the popularity of a war against Russia, as suggested in the Kaiser's comments.'

H.M. supported this and told the State Secretary [Tirpitz] to use his press contacts, too, to work in this direction. T[irpitz] made the observation that the navy would prefer the postponement of the great fight for one and a half years.[35] Moltke says the navy would not be ready even then and the army would get into an increasingly unfavourable position, for the enemies were arming more strongly than we, as we were very short of money.

This was the end of the conference. The result amounted to almost 0.

The Chief of the General Staff says: War the sooner the better, but he does not draw the logical conclusion from this, which is to present

35 Wenninger recorded: 'Tirpitz demanded postponement for 1 year', and Albert Hopman heard later that Tirpitz requested 'to delay war, if possible, for 1–2 years'. John Röhl, *Kaiser, Hof und Staat*, Beck, Munich 1988 (English translation: *The Kaiser and his Court*, Cambridge University Press, Cambridge 1995), pp. 177ff. This was not the first occasion on which Tirpitz speculated on the earliest possible date at which the fleet might be ready. At a meeting with the Kaiser and Moltke in June 1909, a similar argument had already been presented. 'Admiral von Tirpitz assures that, in 5 to 6 years, when the widening of the Kaiser-Wilhelm-Canal and the position on Heligoland were completed, the danger posed by England would be removed. Already in two years' time it would be considerably less.' GP, 28, No. 10306, p. 176, 3 June 1909. In 1911, Falkenhayn also referred somewhat dismissively to the Navy being ready in 1914. See Holger Afflerbach, *Falkenhayn. Politisches Denken und Handeln im Kaiserreich*, Oldenbourg, Munich 1994, p. 79. See also (**235**).

Russia or France or both with an ultimatum which would unleash the war with right on our side.

In the afternoon I wrote to the Reich Chancellor about the influencing of the press.[36]

Cited in John Röhl, 'An der Schwelle zum Weltkrieg', *Militärgeschichtliche Mitteilungen,* 21, 1, 1977, doc. 4.

(45) 9 December 1912: Poincaré to George Louis[37]

Fears about consequences of Austro-Hungarian mobilization measures for France

Telegram No. 969
Secret. Very confidential
Paris, 9 December 1912
D 9.15 p.m.

The Minister of War [Millerand], worried about the mobilisation measures that Austria-Hungary is proceeding with, wants to know if the Russian General Staff has taken any of its own precautions. All superiority gained by Austria-Hungary in her preparations could, indeed, induce Germany to transfer to our border some of the Army Corps stationed on her eastern border.[38]

DDF, 3e série, Vol. 5, No. 22.

36 There is 'unusually abundant' documentary evidence around this secret meeting, with additional accounts being provided by the Saxon and Bavarian military plenipotentiaries and by Tirpitz's close confidant Captain Albert Hopman. For a detailed discussion of the evidence, and of the controversy around the war council, see Röhl, 'Dress Rehearsal in December: military decision-making in Germany on the eve of the First World War, in idem, *The Kaiser and his Court*, Cambridge University Press, Cambridge 1994, pp. 162ff.

37 French Ambassador in St Petersburg.

38 See also (**39**).

(46) 10 December 1912: Claparède's report about a conversation with Wilhelm II

Kaiser summarizes information received from London, and predicts that war will be likely within 1–2 years

[...] After breakfast [...] the Kaiser kept me back in the smoking room where we were alone and started talking about the political situation in a serious but also very excited tone: how quickly the matters had developed, he said, since we had seen each other in Switzerland! Who could have foreseen that the Turks would be defeated in such a way! [...]

Even worse, the Kaiser then added, is that, as I heard *just a few* days ago from my Ambassador in London, Lord Haldane, Germany's alleged friend, had explained to him that England would never allow that Germany would assume a dominant position in central Europe vis-à-vis her immediate neighbours.[39] Is this not an impertinent remark which would deserve an end to diplomatic relations with England! Is it not outrageous that England, for whose good relationship with us we have done so much, perhaps too much, that these Anglo-Saxons, related to us by shared roots, religion, [and] civilising ambitions, want to lend themselves to being a tool of the Slavs. [...]

The Kaiser [...] then said that the creation of a strong Serbian empire, aimed against Austria and Germany, must be prevented. It was the vital condition of both countries not to be encircled by a ring of Slavs. We have renewed the Triple Alliance, so they know in Petersburg how things are fixed. If this question – for us a vital question – cannot be solved by diplomacy then the weapons will decide. The solution can be postponed. The question itself will however arise again in 1 or 2 [years] and Turkey will then have to be strengthened again: that was my first policy: it will be necessary to create a state in the Balkans which does not gravitate towards Petersburg, but towards Vienna [...].

BA Bern, CH-BAR#E2300#1000/716#100*, Berlin, Politische Berichte und Briefe, Militärberichte, Band 17, 1911–1914.[40]

---

39 See (**43**).

40 Cited in Terence F. Cole, 'German Decision-Making, Records of the Swiss Embassy in Berlin', in John Röhl, *Der Ort Kaiser Wilhelm II*, Munich 1991, pp. 53–76, pp. 62–63. Cole points out that this is a draft report and that the final version is no longer contained in the files of the Swiss Government in Bern.

(47) 15 December 1912: Wenninger to Bavarian Minister of War

Berlin's decision-makers demand preventive war at 'war-council'

Moltke wanted to launch an immediate attack (*sofortiges Losschlagen*); there had not been a more favourable opportunity since the formation of the Triple Alliance. Tirpitz demanded a postponement for one year, until the Canal and the U-boat harbour on Heligoland were finished. The Kaiser agreed to a postponement only reluctantly. [...]

The Kaiser instructed the General Staff and the Admiralty Staff to work out an invasion of England in grand style.

Meanwhile his diplomats are to seek allies everywhere, Rumania (already partly secured), Bulgaria, Turkey, etc.

Your Excellency will see that the picture behind the scenes is very different from that on the official stage.

Cited in John Röhl, 'An der Schwelle zum Weltkrieg', *Militärgeschichtliche Mitteilungen*, 21, 1, 1977, doc. 22.

(48) 20 December 1912: Bethmann Hollweg to Eisendecher

Chancellor dismisses Lichnowsky's news of Britain's likely involvement on France's side in a future war

Haldane's revelation to Lichnowsky was not actually that serious.[41] It only revealed what we have known for a long time: that England still advocates the policy of balance of power and that she will therefore support France.[42]

Cited in Röhl, 'Schwelle', p. 124.

41 See (**43**).

42 In a letter to his brother Heinrich of 12 December 1912, the Kaiser outlined both the events of the war council meeting and the news from England. 'My diplomats are very concerned. But not us military [men]. We have always reckoned with the English as our likely enemies [...].' Wilhelm II to Prince Heinrich von Preussen, 12 December 1912, quoted in John Röhl, 'An der Schwelle zum Weltkrieg', *Militärgeschichtliche Mitteilungen*, 21, 1, 1977, p. 105. In fact, however, Bethmann Hollweg's rather calmer report to Eisendecher suggests the Kaiser may have got it wrong. See also Kiderlen-Wächter to Eisendecher, 19 December 1912: 'I do not attach special importance to the utterances of the minister but regard them rather as a well-intentioned attempt to warn us to be cautious.' Ibid., p. 124.

(49) 21 December 1912: Moltke to Bethmann Hollweg

Chief of Staff reassures the Chancellor that Germany is still able to win a war under current circumstances

The Triple Alliance was concluded as a *defensive* alliance. It incorporates all the weaknesses of such an alliance. If one of the allied states is being attacked, the other two must support it, that is, without being themselves attacked, enter a war for which there might not be any inclination or understanding within the nation. However, only if the entire people is permeated with the realization that a harming of the ally also endangers its own vital interests will it develop *the kind of* will to make sacrifices that every state requires in our time, [a time] that no longer wants, no longer needs cabinet wars in order to conduct an energetic war. [...]

If war occurs, there can be no doubt that the main weight of responsibility will be on Germany's shoulders which will be gripped on three sides by her opponents.

Nonetheless we will, *under the current conditions*, still face even the most difficult tasks with confidence, if we manage to formulate the *casus belli* in such a way that the nation will take up arms united and enthusiastically.[43]

Reichsarchiv, *Kriegsrüstung*, *Anlagen*, No. 54, pp. 158ff.

43 Some historians claim Ludendorff was the author of this text, e.g. Niall Ferguson, who speaks of 'Ludendorff's "great memorandum" of December 1912', 'Germany and the Origins of the First World War: New Perspectives', *Historical Journal* 35, 3, 1992, p. 744. Carl Hans Hermann also asserts Ludendorff's central position in the army increases, and credits him with authorship of the General Staff memoranda of 1911–1912. *Deutsche Militärgeschichte*, Frankfurt/Main 1966, p. 263f., and David Herrmann also considers Ludendorff was 'the driving force' behind General Staff demands: David G. Herrmann, *The Arming of Europe and the Making of the First World War*, paperback edn, Princeton University Press, Princeton, NJ 1997, p. 184. For further details and further references on the quest for German army increases in the pre-war years, see Annika Mombauer, *Helmuth von Moltke and the Origins of the First World War*, Cambridge University Press, Cambridge 2001, pp. 174ff.

(50) 31 December 1912: Henry Wilson's Diary

War seems likely in the near future

The news to-night is not good. Rumania is threatening to mobilize, and Russia is requesting Austria to demobilize or she will strengthen her Polish corps. The year opened in gloom and closes in deeper gloom. The Peace Conference of the Balkan States is sitting in St James's Palace, but it looks like breaking up, and the Great Powers are grouped in veiled hostility. It seems possible, though I think not by any means certain, that we shall have a European war this next year. And in spite of all I have written and worked during the whole year, we are *not* ready. It is disgusting and scandalous.

Cited in Charles Callwell, *Field-Marshal Sir Henry Wilson*, 2 vols, Cassell 1927, p. 121.[44]

44 For background to Wilson's demands for war, see Samuel R. Williamson, Jr., 'General Henry Wilson', in W.R. Louis (ed.), *Resurgent Adventures with Britannia*, I.B. Tauris, London 2011, *passim*.

3
Documents from 1913

(51) January 1913: Moltke's memorandum

Germany cannot afford to respect Belgian neutrality in future war; Britain will be found on the side of Germany's enemies

[...] The great difficulties which are connected with a march through Belgium must not be overlooked. It is not pleasant to begin the war with the violation of the territory of a neutral neighbouring state. However, where the existence of our state is at stake, all considerations for others must take second place. It would be very desirable if we could come to an agreement with Belgium to the extent that Belgium either joins us, in which case all desired territorial gains in the West could be assured to her, or that she at least refrains from any hostile activities against our troops. In this case Germany would guarantee the Belgian state all its full territorial integrity. We neither want to annex Belgian territory, nor to wage war against Belgium at all, we merely require the country as an area for deployment. However, right from the start I consider it to be out of the question that our diplomacy will succeed in arranging such an agreement with Belgium, rather we will have to reckon with the fact that Belgium would consider a German advance through her territory as *casus belli* and would immediately place herself on the side of our opponents.[1] [...]

But we will not just have to fight against the Belgian army. A violation of Belgian neutrality will also turn England into our opponent. It is for England a question of life and death to prevent Germany from establishing herself on the side of the Channel opposite her and thus gain the opportunity for further naval strengthening, turning her into a danger for the island Empire which would permanently tie up all of England's strength and would make her unable to maintain her world domination. [...] For Germany it would be well worth considering if it were not worth doing without the march through Belgium for the

1 See (65).

prize of English neutrality were it not for the fact that England left no doubt that she would actively participate in the war on the side of our opponents, whether we marched through Belgium or not.

I would consider it extraordinarily dangerous if, prompted by vague assurances from England, we would do without our only chance which enables us to have a quick deployment against France. We would impose on ourselves the difficulty of a frontal attack on the strong French Eastern front and would have no guarantee that England would not intervene at a given moment after all.[2] [...] Given England's political attitude, following her close connection with the Franco-Russian alliance, it cannot be expected that she will be on our side and we therefore have no certainty vis-à-vis her. Only England's active participation in the war as an ally of the Triple Alliance would give this certainty. England considers Germany to be stronger than France. She fears a defeat of the latter and German hegemony and, true to her politics which are aimed at preserving the European balance of power, she will do everything to hinder Germany's expansion of power. Therefore, we will have to count England towards the number of our opponents. [...]

In a war of the Triple Entente against the Triple Alliance not just the German, but also more or less the Austrian and Italian coasts will be blocked, and an import of victuals would be made particularly difficult for Germany. As long as Holland remains neutral an import would be possible via that country under American flag. It can hardly be assumed that England would not respect that flag. If we make Holland our enemy we block up this last windpipe through which we can breathe. I consider this to be so important that it seems better to me to accept the difficulties that result from the advancing of the German right wing, than to violate the neutrality of the Netherlands with an advance through Limburg.[3] [...]

BA-MA, BArch RH 61/406: 'Die Militärpolitische Lage Deutschlands', pp. 65–67.

2 See (**52**), (**363**) and (**367**).

3 For details of Moltke's military plans, see Annika Mombauer, 'German War Plans', in Richard F. Hamilton and Holger H. Herwig (eds), *War Planning 1914*, Cambridge University Press, Cambridge et al., 2010, pp. 48–78, *passim.*

(52) January or February 1913: Jagow in conversation with Moltke

Jagow's retrospective account of a conversation in which Moltke dismisses Britain's role in a future war

I warned Moltke seriously about the violation of Belgian neutrality which, to my mind, was bound to bring England against us into the equation. Moltke became contemplative, but then he said: Well, I think if need be we would be able to deal with those 150,000 Englishmen, too.[4]

PA Berlin, NL Gottlieb von Jagow, Vol. 8, Part I. *Politische Aufsätze.* 'Der Durchmarsch durch Belgien', pp. 48ff.

(53) 29 January 1913: Falkenhayn to Hanneken[5]

Moltke and Kiderlen-Wächter in favour of general war during Balkan crisis

If Kiderlen had stayed alive, he and Moltke would probably have pushed for the matter to have been brought to a decision now.[6] Both were of the very sensible opinion that we cannot gain anything but only lose by continuing to wait. [...] Now Moltke is on his own, a fact that gives cause for concern as regards the struggle with H[is] M[ajesty].

Cited in Holger Afflerbach, *Falkenhayn*, Oldenbourg, Munich 1994, p. 102.

4 See (**51**). For the French Chief of Staff's different take on the question of Belgium see (**12**).
5 Constantin von Hanneken, close friend of Falkenhayn's; businessman in China.
6 Foreign Secretary Kiderlen-Wächter died of a stroke on 31 December 1912. He was succeeded by Gottlieb von Jagow.

(54) 31 January 1913: Cartwright to Nicolson

Relations between Russia and Austria-Hungary declining; Austria getting exasperated with threat from Serbia

Vienna, 31 January 1913
Private

[...] It seems to me that the relations between Russia and Austria-Hungary, instead of showing any signs of improvement, are growing worse from day to day, not officially perhaps but through the steadily increasing animosity between the two nations. Serbia will some day set Europe by the ears and bring about a universal war on the Continent, and if the French press continues to encourage Serbian aspirations as it has done during the last few months, the Serbs may lose their heads and do something aggressive against the Dual Monarchy which will compel the latter to put the screw on Serbia. I cannot tell you how exasperated people are getting here at the continual worry which that little country causes Austria under encouragement from Russia. [...] It will be lucky if Europe succeeds in avoiding a war as a result of the present crisis. The next time a Serbian crisis arises, with probably the younger Emperor on the Throne here,[7] I feel certain that Austria-Hungary will refuse to admit of any Russian interference in the dispute and that she will proceed to settle the difference with her little neighbour by herself 'coûte que coûte'. [...]

BD, IX, II, No. 582.

(55) 22 February 1913: San Giuliano's speech to the Chamber of Deputies

Italy will not be a spectator but determined to play role of Great Power

[We] did not wish only to assure Italy's position in the Mediterranean through the occupation of Libya, but we wanted beyond that to show to the world and ourselves that Italy could resolve by herself and by her own efforts alone the first major problem of international relations placed before her. [...] If by the force of events, against our will and against the will of our allies and the Great Powers, there must occur, sooner or later, territorial changes in the Mediterranean, Italy cannot

7 I.e., Franz Ferdinand.

remain a passive spectator. [...][8]

In half a century of struggle to raise herself from her unhappy past condition to her present grandeur which is [only] a preparation for a still more radiant future, [Italy] has revealed herself not only with the thought and work of a few individuals which can vanish but with the virile virtù of the whole nation which [always] remains.

Cited in Richard J.B. Bosworth, *Italy, the Least of the Great Powers*, Cambridge University Press, Cambridge, New York et al. 1979, p. 359.

(56) 23 February 1913: Otto von Ritter to Hertling

Vatican in favour of Austria going to war against Pan-Slavism

---

[...] In Vatican circles I also hear more and more the point of view that Austria will only be able to rebuff the Pan-Slav attack with the use of arms, [an attack] which not only threatens her existence, but European culture per se, and that the current moment in which Russia's readiness for war still left a lot to be desired should be exploited for it.

BayHStA, MA 2567, cited in Jörg Zedler, 'Das Rittertelegramm', Munich 2010, pp. 175–202, p. 193.[9]

---

8 At this stage, the Chamber broke into shouts of 'Bravo' and 'Benissimo'. See Richard J.B. Bosworth, *Italy, the Least of the Great Powers*, Cambridge University Press, Cambridge, New York et al. 1979, p. 359.

9 See also (**195**). In January 1913, the Cardinal State Secretary in the Vatican, Merey del Val, had judged the situation in the Balkans 'very sceptically and pessimistically. [...] The political tension was increasing day by day and in the end the smallest spark could cause a general explosion.' Ritter to Hertling, 31 January 1913, cited in Jörg Zedler, 'Das Rittertelegramm', in Jörg Zedler (ed.), *Der Heilige Stuhl in den internationalen Beziehungen 1870–1939*, Herbert Utz Verlag, Munich 2010, pp. 175–202, p. 197, note 77. My thanks to John Röhl for alerting me to this publication, and to Jörg Zedler for allowing me to cite from it.

(57) 24 February 1913: Nicolson to Grey

French military consider Balkan Wars good opportunity for European war as it would ensure Russian support which would otherwise not be guaranteed

Private

Foreign Office, 24 February 1913

I met General Wilson last night, who has just come back from Switzerland and on his way through Paris saw some of the leading military men. He tells me that the soldiers are of the opinion that it would be far better for France if a conflict were not too long postponed. Their reasons are that if it would come now it would be in consequence of the Balkan difficulties, and therefore they would be able to secure the wholehearted support of Russia. Were a conflict to be postponed and eventually to arise over some difficulty between Germany and France alone, they had some doubts, treaty notwithstanding, whether Russia would go wholeheartedly on their side. They impressed upon Wilson that Russia was now exceedingly strong, both in her military organisation and also in her financial condition, and was therefore far less dependent on French support, either in a military or a financial sense. In short, that Russia was now well able to look after herself, and might be inclined to take a line of her own. (This I gather is not quite the view of the French Government, who are nervous lest they should be dragged into a war over Balkan affairs in which the French public have no great interest.) He further said that he found some doubts in the minds of the military men as to what would be our attitude – whether we should really in the case of a conflict give them any material assistance on land, and whether, indeed, such assistance would be efficient and above all timely.

General Wilson said that of course he had only seen military men and no one else, and he was repeating to me their views alone.

I also saw Braham,[10] and he told me that he had been rather disturbed by a letter which he had received from the 'Times' Correspondent in Paris. He laid great stress on the military spirit now pervading France, and which was, he thought, rather dangerous.

MINUTE

The French Gov[ernmen]t clearly do not want to be dragged into war over the Balkans and are working to prevent Russia precipitating a conflict over that. We on our side can be no party to France precipitating a conflict for the revanche. E. G[rey].

BD, IX, No. 656.

10 A journalist with *The Times*.

(58) 28 April 1913: Jagow to Tschirschky

German desire to appear provoked during the Scutari crisis to ensure British neutrality

It is very important for us to be in the role of the provoked [party], because I believe that England will then – but probably also only then – remain neutral.

PA/AA, Botschaft Wien, Vol. 6/I, cited in Stephen Schröder, *Marinekonvention*, Göttingen 2004, p. 584.

(59) 6 May 1913: Sazonov to Russian Minister in Belgrade Hartwig

Serbia will have to fight another war to secure territories which are currently part of Austria-Hungary

Serbia has passed only through the first stage of her historical career. To reach her goal she must endure another frightful struggle, in which her very existence will be staked. [...] Serbia's Promised Land lies in the territory of the present Austria-Hungary, and not in that for which she is now striving, with the Bulgarians barring the way. In these circumstances it is of vital importance to Serbia to maintain the alliance with Bulgaria, and on the other hand by patient and tenacious effort to bring herself up to the necessary standard of preparedness for the contest which is inevitably coming. Time is working for Serbia and for the destruction of her enemies, who already show plain signs of dissolution.[11]

Cited in Friedrich Stieve, *Isvolsky and the World War*, Allen & Unwin, London 1926, p. 180.

11 A week later the Serbian Ambassador in St Petersburg reported to Belgrade: 'Sazonov told me again that we must work for the future, as we shall get a great deal of territory from Austria-Hungary. I replied that we shall gladly give Monastir to the Bulgarians if we can get Bosnia and other Austrian provinces.' Cited in Friedrich Stieve, *Isvolsky and the World War*, Allen & Unwin, London 1926, p. 181.

(60) 23 May 1913: Cartwright to Nicolson

Summarizes the likely future threat posed by Serbia for Austria-Hungary

Private
Vienna, 23 May 1913

[...] The position of Serbia is a very difficult one, and one which is fraught with danger for the future tranquillity of Europe. [...] As soon as peace is restored in the Balkans, the Austrian authorities anticipate that Serbia will begin a far-reaching agitation in the Serb inhabited districts of the Dual Monarchy, and as this country cannot allow any dismemberment of her provinces without incurring the danger of the whole edifice crumbling down, we have all the elements in the near future of another violent crisis in this part of the world, which may not unlikely end in the final annexation of Serbia by the Dual Monarchy. That, however, will lead to a war with Russia, and possibly to a general conflict in Europe [...]

BD, IX, No. 994.

(61) 25 May 1913: Lord Stamfordham's[12] notes of his conversation with Wilhelm II

At talks with the Kaiser in Berlin Wilhelm II predicts future war will involve England on side of Germany's enemies; Germany will support Austria-Hungary if she is attacked by the Slavs; Britain would do better to be Germany's ally than fight her

[...] This war [in the Balkans] has upset the whole of the East and it will some day raise a question, not British, or Russian but international, for it will be racial. The Slavs have now become unrestful and will want to attack Austria. Germany is bound to stand by her ally – Russia and France will join in and then England – fighting against the Anglo-Saxons and the Culture of the world. He [Wilhelm II] cannot understand how we wish to join the Latin Races in preference to the Teutons – do you wish to fight with the Portuguese as your allies?' 'I know this, that you are engaged to help them [the French].' I said that only an unprovoked attack would involve us, and HM replied 'and will you tell me what an unprovoked attack is – Is it enough to knock your cap off or must I

12 Sir Arthur Bigge.

kick your shins. Look at that Morocco business: I know that [Sir John] French was over in France or your Staff Officers were and you promised to send 100,000 troops,[13] and *that's what made us so sore*. I am a man of peace – but now I have to arm my Country so that whoever falls on me I can crush – and crush them I will.

He had told the E[mperor] of R[ussia] that if Austria was attacked he was absolutely bound to help her: the aged Emperor [Franz Joseph], with his past defeats, sorrows etc., could *not* be left to stand alone. The R[ussian] E[mperor] quite recognized this – He was very nice to the [German] Emperor. There is no ill feeling between Russia and Germany.

You talk a deal about the balance of power and that to maintain it you joined the *Entente*: but *Germany* holds the balance of power. [...]

RA Kew, GV/M 450/18, Record of a Conversation between the German Emperor and Lord Stamfordham at Berlin, 25 May 1913.[14]

(62) 25 May 1913: Lord Stamfordham's notes of a conversation with Jagow

Summary of talks with Jagow in Berlin; Germany seeks better understanding with Britain

He [Jagow] was convinced that the one great thing to bring about was a good understanding between England & Germany: [...] but it will take time – possibly ten years or more: and he has told the Emperor so: who on the other hand 'can't wait for ten years'! He said 'Germany want nothing in Europe: she has no wish to interfere with England: but she wants elbow room and to get this she might have even to fight' – But 'we ought to work together'. By race, character, religion & culture we are similar and could command the whole world if we went together. [...].

Speaking 'not as a Minister' 'but privately to me' in the regard to the Slavs he considers war *with them* is inevitable though possibly not in the next decade. Talking of war with France he said if we defeated her 'we could take no more territory from her: we could not digest it'[.] 'We can't digest Lothringen [Lorraine] as it is'.

13 For details on the Anglo-French Staff talks, see above, p. 42, n. 29.

14 Reproduced with permission of Her Majesty Queen Elizabeth II. A slightly different version of this document is also cited in Röhl, *Wilhelm II.*, Vol. 3, pp. 990–991. Lord Stamfordham considered the conversation with Wilhelm II so significant that he made four attempts at capturing the meeting in his notes. See Röhl, *Wilhelm II.*, Vol. 3, p. 990. I am very grateful to Miss Pam Clark of the Royal Archives for her help in checking the text of (**61**) and (**62**) against the original.

RA Kew, PS/GV/M 450/18, 'Record of a Conversation between Lord Stamfordham and Herr von Jagow, Foreign Minister', 25 May 1913.[15]

(63) 12 June 1913: Guillaume to Belgian Government

The new French three-years' military service law is unsustainable unless there is a war soon

Paris, 12 June 1913

[...] Thus it is now certain that the new French legislation will contain provisions which the country is unlikely to be able to bear for long. The burdens of the new law will be so heavy for the general population, the expenditure involved will be so huge, that the country will soon protest, and France will then be faced with the alternative of either renouncing the unendurable or very shortly going to war. It will be a heavy responsibility for those who have brought the nation to this pass. They are followed in a sort of stupor, an interesting but deplorable dementia. [...]

The propaganda in favour of the law for three years' military service, aiming at producing a resurrection of chauvinism, was brilliantly prepared and carried through; it began with the demand for the election of M. Poincaré as President of the Republic; it is still going on, regardless of the risks which it is provoking; there is great uneasiness in the country.[16]

Cited in Friedrich Stieve, *Isvolsky and the World War*, Allen & Unwin, London 1926, p. 169.

(64) 15 November 1913: Schoen to Bethmann Hollweg

Signs of possible future Franco-German rapprochement

Paris, 15 November 1913
No. 384

[...] The current Government obviously wishes to maintain the improved mood between the two nations [France and Germany] and regards as the best means for this in the agreement of further formal agreements with

15 Reproduced with permission of Her Majesty Queen Elizabeth II.

16 For details of the French three years' service law see Gerd Krumeich, *Armaments and Politics in France on the Eve of the First World War*, Berg, London 1984.

us about questions which, if unresolved, would increase our opposition (*Gegensätze*) and lead to friction. [...]

[...] in any case, French current good intentions make a good impression and could, if turned into deeds, transform our relationship with our neighbour in the West to a bearable one for some time. Of course, they will neither lead to the chasm between them and us being filled in, nor to a change in the grouping of the European powers. [...]. Even if your relationship with France were to improve substantially, it will for a long time be one of thinly-applied politeness[17] which can easily become cracked and brittle. At least this development will be more desirable than the hardly bearable state in which, as the French like to say, '*on se regarde comme des chiens de fayence*' [we are silently squaring up to each other].[18]

GP, 39, No. 15657.

(65) 22 November 1913: Jules Cambon to Pichon

Wilhelm II and Chief of General Staff put pressure on Belgium to remain neutral in case of European war and allow German troops to march through Belgian territory

---

Despatch No. 698
Top secret
Berlin, 22 November 1913
Telegram No. 698
R. Dir. pol., 23 December

Baron Beyens, Minister of Belgium, has, on the 10th of this month, sent me an important message about the impressions his King has brought back from his recent trip to Germany.

In Potsdam, King Albert, the Kaiser, and the Chief of General Staff, Moltke, had a conversation that has quite struck the King.[19]

---

17 Wilhelm II's marginal note: 'correct'.

18 Wilhelm II commented at the end of the document: 'Good'.

19 This visit took place on 5–6 November. For details see Jean Stengers, 'Guillaume II et le Roi Albert', *Bulletin de la Classe des Lettres*, 7–12, 1993, pp. 227–253. See also Mombauer, *Moltke*, pp. 153ff., and Röhl, *Wilhelm II.*, Vol. 3, pp. 1040ff. In January 1904, during a visit of the Belgian King Leopold II to Berlin, similar threats were made: 'Those who are in the case of a European war not with me are against me', Wilhelm threatened the King when the latter declined to accept the prospect of 'extending his sceptre over French Flanders, Artois and

He thought until now, like everyone else, that Wilhelm II, who had used his personal influence to maintain the peace in many critical circumstances, was still of this frame of mind.[20] This time, he found him completely changed: Wilhelm II is no longer, in his eyes, a champion of the peace, opposed to the bellicose tendencies of certain German political parties. The Kaiser has thus come to believe that war with France is inevitable and this is what it will come down to, sooner or later. He thinks that French politics, far from discouraging fanaticism among her people, has, for some time, tended to make people feel suspicious all the time and to thwart Germany at every opportunity; and he is convinced that the idea of revenge never ceases to haunt the French spirit. The Kaiser, it goes without saying, believes in the overwhelming superiority of the German army and in its certain success.

General von Moltke spoke in exactly the same way as his Sovereign. He, too, declared the war necessary and inevitable but he was even more assured of success, 'because,' he said to the King, 'this time the matter must be settled; and Your Majesty cannot imagine the irresistible tide of enthusiasm which will carry the entire German people along when that day comes.'

The Belgian King protested that it was a travesty to interpret the French Government's intentions in such a way and to let oneself be misled about the sentiments of the French nation by the demonstrations of a few unscrupulous fanatics or agitators.

The Kaiser and his Chief of General Staff nevertheless persisted in their point of view.

(King Albert wishes his conversations to remain secret. The Ambassador points out that he cannot withhold a 'communication of this kind' from the knowledge of the President of the Republic and the Minister of Foreign Affairs. Baron Beyens agrees, but adds 'that he will stress that this confidence should not go any further'.) [...]

Baron Beyens tells me that apart from all this, the Kaiser seemed older, tense and irritable.

As the years weigh more heavily on Wilhelm II, family traditions, the rigorous nature of the Kaiserin, the reactionary tendencies of the court, and especially the impatience of the military, increase their influence on his state of mind. Who knows whether he feels jealous of the popularity

the Ardennes' in return for support of Germany in the coming war. See Röhl, *Wilhelm II.*, Vol. 3, pp. 348ff. He also threatened Queen Wilhelmina of the Netherlands that her country would have 24 hours to decide whether to be for or against Germany in a future European war. Ibid., p. 351.

20 See Röhl, *Wilhelm II*, Vol. 3, p. 1040, who detects 'an increased hostility' on the part of Wilhelm II vis-à-vis France from about December 1912 onwards.

gained by his son[21] who flatters the passions of the Pan-Germans and who does not regard the Empire's position in the world to be equal to its power? Also, perhaps France's answer to Germany's latest bid to establish incontestably Germanic supremacy by increasing her army is, to some extent, responsible for his bitterness, for, whatever may be said, one feels that Germany cannot do much more.

'Be that as it may,' continued the Minister of Belgium, 'the President of the Republic must be warned. The King has noted that Germany's disposition is as favourable towards England and Russia as it is unfavourable towards France.[']' So, it would seem to him that it is important that, as far as possible, we make sure that absolutely no incident occurs. [...]

The conversation ended there [...].

One may well ask oneself what lies at the heart of this conversation.

The personal loyalty of King Albert dismisses *a priori* any idea that he is becoming Germany's spokesperson. It really is the emotion he felt which Baron Beyens reported to me.

The Kaiser and especially his Chief of General Staff may have wished to impress the Belgian King and discourage him from opposing any resistance in the event of a conflict between us. Perhaps Germany would also like to make Belgium less hostile to certain ambitions that are emerging here with regard to the Belgian Congo, but this last hypothesis does not seem to me to tally with what General von Moltke said.

As for the rest, Kaiser Wilhelm is less master of his impatience than is usually supposed. More than once, I have seen him allow his real thoughts to be aired. Whatever his aim was in the conversation that was reported to me, the secret King Albert confided to me is no less serious. It tallies with the precariousness of the general situation and with the state of a certain body of public opinion in France and Germany.

If I were allowed to draw any conclusions, I would say there is no reason to be worried, but we should take account of this new fact: the Kaiser is becoming used to an order of ideas which were formerly repugnant to him, and that, to borrow a phrase from him which he likes to use, 'we must keep our powder dry'.[22]

DDF, 3e série, 8, No. 517.

21 Crown Prince Wilhelm. See (**85**).

22 The Belgian attaché Beyens summed up his impressions after the talks of November 1913: 'What we must keep in mind of Moltke's suggestions is that the military leadership considers a war against France unavoidable or rather that it desires it to be so, contrary to the allegations of the General [Moltke]. As the Kaiser is surrounded solely by generals who no doubt have received the order to speak the same language as the Chief of the General Staff, it is intended to change H.M. peace-loving attitude and to convince him of the necessity of this war.' Quoted in Fritz Fischer, *Krieg der Illusionen*, Droste, Düsseldorf 1987, p. 320.

(66) 23 November 1913: Jagow to Wilhelm II

Jagow informs the Kaiser about the latest events in the Liman von Sanders crisis

Berlin, 23 November 1913

Your Majesty's Chargé d'Affaires [Freiherr von Lucius] in St Petersburg reports: 'I have explained to M. Sazonov your position regarding the military mission. [...] The Minister hopes that we will at least comply with the Russian wishes in so far that the General at least did not reside in Constantinople. He did not doubt that England and France also considered this uncomfortable. [...] The General could just as well reside in Adrianople or Smyrna. He could find a reply to all our arguments. Reforming work was necessary everywhere. The near East was big [...].'

May I request most humbly of Your Imperial and Royal Majesty the authorization to reply to M. Sazonov along the following lines: The negotiations with Turkey had already been concluded to such an extent that a change of the conditions was currently not possible. However, the General chosen to be the Chief of the Military Mission will be authorized thoroughly to check in situ once again the question if a move of his residence to Adrianople or Smyrna would be possible. According to enquiries conducted so far, however, it seemed for technical reasons to be not conducive to undertake the reform work anywhere other than in the capital, as all military education facilities could be found here. There was no reason to see any 'acte peu amical' against Russia in our procedure, not least because your Majesty had already given notice of this intention to His Majesty Tsar Nicholas during his visit, and because the presence of an English Admiral in Constantinople had never been queried by any power.

[*Wilhelm II's marginal comments:*]

Russia fears the strengthening of Turkey by us and the increase of her military strength or rather her usability by us against her when Russia will one day attack us! She wants to keep Turkey dying and wants to keep Stambul [sic] as easy pickings! England will no doubt not want that! Russia in her greed for land pockets Manchuria, Mongolia, Northern Persia without us batting an eye-lid. But if we send officers to Turkey, then Russian 'public opinion' is excited!! If we went along with Russia's wishes, we would simply lose our prestige in the Moslem world![23]

23 According to Hans Herzfeld, this was the 'decision that destroyed all Russian hopes'. 'Die Limankrise', *Berliner Monatshefte*, September 1933, p. 847. For further details on the crisis see also B. von Siebert, *Diplomatische Aktenstücke*

GP, 38, No. 15452.

(67) 24 November 1913: Jules Cambon to Pichon

Assessment of German threat to the Belgians; views on the Zabern incident

Berlin, 24 November 1913
Private letter

I am sending you herewith two secret letters: one relating to a conversation between the Kaiser and the King of Belgium,[24] the other relating to the incident in Zabern.[25]

The first relates to the message M. Beyens sent me a fortnight ago which he made me promise to only deliver verbally to the President of the Republic and yourself. I do not think I can wait until my next trip to Paris to tell you about the King of Belgium's evaluation of the situation, his impression. So I am writing to you, but I beg that this despatch only be read by the President, yourself and Paléologue, who will put it in his safe. If this despatch were read by anybody else, who knows where it could lead?

I was not surprised by King Albert's impression. It echoes that which I myself have felt for some time. We are extremely mistrusted. Baron Beyens attributes this state of affairs, on the one hand, to the growing influence of the military elements on the Kaiser; and on the other hand, to the irritation (he can use no other word) that our nationalist newspapers cause abroad with all their boasting and teasing, obviously targeting the President of the Republic.

It is clear that in this present situation we must be very careful. I wondered, when I saw the Zabern affair come to light, if the Pan-Germans were not behind it and were trying to provoke us. In any case, this incident happened just in time to cloud the issue when the situation was easing slightly in the case of Asia Minor.

As the despatch that I am personally sending you shows, I spoke to M. Zimmermann twice about the Zabern affair. He confided his difficulties

zur Geschichte der Ententepolitik der Vorkriegsjahre, de Gruyter, Berlin/Leipzig 1921, pp. 676–708.

24 See (**65**).

25 For accounts of the Zabern Affair in English, see e.g. David Schoenbaum, *Zabern 1913. Consensus Politics in Imperial Germany*, George Allen & Unwin, London 1982; Richard W. Mackey: *The Zabern Affair, 1913–1914*, University Press of America, Lanham 1991.

to me. There is obviously discord between the civilian and the military sections of the government. We have only one way to bring agreement between them, against us, and that is for us to lose our temper. That is why it is important that we do not lose the calm that we have shown in France until now. I am convinced that Lieutenant Forstner's career is over, but in order for his punishment to be severe, it will not be immediate.[26]

Moreover, the Colonel of the Zabern[27] regiment came to Potsdam to offer the Kaiser his resignation, who refused it. Obviously, he shares some of the responsibility: perhaps, as happens in many regiments, he gave the order for talks to be held in the barrack rooms to prevent enlistments to the Legion. Also, German military authorities treat the act of repeating officers' words in quarters as treason. On this point, German public opinion agrees with the military authority's point of view – which says much about the different mentalities in France and Germany.

It is possible that the affair will reach the Reichstag. The Chancellor's situation is difficult.[28] The conservatives accuse him, notably in this Zabern affair, of having let go of the Government's reins. Others ask if there is a military government acting alongside and within a civilian government. Deep down, there is some truth in this.

The Chancellor will side with the Kaiser. Of that, there is no doubt. The last time I saw M. de Bethmann Hollweg, his language revealed pessimistic tendencies, showing that his attitude has changed and justifying the King of Belgium's secrecy.

So I think we must continue following the cautious line of conduct that we have maintained until now. [...]

DDF, 3e série, 8, No. 522.

---

26 The nineteen-year-old Second Lieutenant Günter Freiherr von Forstner caused an affront to the people of the Alsatian town of Zabern (Saverne) in October 1913. The resulting crisis led to a state of siege being declared in late November, and was even intensified in December when Forstner struck a local who had laughed at him. For both offences, the punishment was considered too lenient by the inhabitants of Alsace-Lorraine and highlighted to what extent they were at the mercy of the Germany military occupying powers. The resulting crisis even led to a vote of no confidence in the Chancellor Bethmann Hollweg, although the Kaiser refused to allow him to resign.

27 Adolf von Reuter.

28 On 4 December the Chancellor suffered a vote of no confidence, although backed by the Kaiser he refused to step down.

(68) 25 November 1913: O'Beirne to Grey

Sazonov suggests compensation for other powers over Liman von Sanders' appointment

Tel. (No. 393)
St. Petersburg, 25 November 1913
D. 7.26 p.m.
R. 10.15 p.m.

Russian Minister for Foreign Affairs to-day requested me to telegraph to you concerning engagement by Turkey of forty-two German officers with a German general in executive command of army corps at Constantinople. He is much perturbed by this arrangement, which he says greatly displeases the Emperor, and he has complained to the German Government that it was an unfriendly proceeding on their part not to mention matter to him when in Berlin.

M. Sazonov considers that foreign Ambassadors will be placed in undignified position by fact that Turkish capital will be practically in hands of a German commander. He thinks it necessary that other Powers should make some compensating demands of Turkish Government.[29]

As to forms which such demands should take, he mentioned appointments of Russian officers in Armenia and British officials in Asiatic Turkey. [...][30]

BD, X, I, No. 379.

(69) 27 December 1913: Goschen to Grey

Liman von Sanders crisis: the official German view; evidence of Sazonov's assertiveness

29 For details of the demands see Siebert, *Aktenstücke*, p. 678.

30 Sazonov decided to use the Liman appointment to 'abandon nine years of restraint in Russian foreign policy'. At a special conference on 31 December 1913, Sazonov was supported by military representatives who all agreed that war was 'fully permissible' over the affair, against the objection of Chair of the Council of Ministers, V.N. Kokovtsov, who pointed to Russia's internal weakness. It was decided that the support of the other Entente powers would be a requisite for military action. See David M. McDonald, 'The Durnovo Memorandum in Context: Official Conservatism and the Crisis of Autocracy', *Jahrbücher für die Geschichte Osteuropas*, 44, 4, 1996, pp. 481–502, pp. 494–495.

Tel. (No. 219)
Berlin, 27 December 1913
D. 8.30 p.m.
R. 11.55 p.m.

[...] The Secretary of State [Jagow] spoke to me to-day on the subject of the German Military Mission. He said that he was doing all he could to come to some amicable arrangement, but it was not easy, firstly because the Ottoman Government seemed rather inclined to make difficulties, and secondly because the Russian press and, of course, that of France were writing too much on the subject. [...]

In conversation afterwards he told me that they had been much surprised by the strong objections of Russia to the mission. The matter had been first mentioned by the Emperor to the Emperor of Russia, who had made no objections, and had in fact rather encouraged the idea. It had, unfortunately, not been mentioned to M. Sazonov when he was here; he had probably been unaware of it, and the Chancellor, thinking that the affair was all arranged, and that it was only a matter of another German officer succeeding General von der Goltz,[31] had not thought it worth while to discuss it. It was only when M. Kokovtsov came to Berlin that Russian feelings on the subject were discovered.[32]

There had been no bad faith in the matter at all, and the only reason why the Turks had insisted on General Liman being given a slightly superior position than his predecessor was that the latter had, comparatively speaking, failed owing to his not being in a position to enforce the necessary discipline. The proof that General Liman's position as commander of the 1st Army Corps was nothing very extraordinary lay in the fact that the position had previously been occupied by a Turkish colonel. He himself had been inclined to think that the position was not sufficiently important for an officer of General Liman's rank.

The reason why Constantinople had been chosen was the obvious one that all the military schools were there, and that it was absolutely necessary that the general should have them under his eye. In the meantime the German Ambassador at Constantinople [Wangenheim] was coming to Berlin in a few days, and the whole matter would be gone into thoroughly.

BD, X, I, No. 450.

---

31 After defeat in the Russo-Turkish War (1877–1878), Colmar von der Goltz (1843–1916) was sent to Turkey, at the Sultan's request, to help reorganize the Ottoman Army, and he spent 12 years in Constantinople. Under his leadership, significant improvements were made to the Turkish Army.

32 The Russian Premier Kokovtsov travelled to Berlin en route from Paris and met with Bethmann Hollweg on 17 November 1913. See GP 38, No. 15450 and 15451.

4
Documents from 1914

(70) 12 January 1914: Poincaré's conversation with the French journalist Judet

Russia is becoming increasingly powerful; war between her and Germany will come in two years' time

[...] Poincaré added: 'Russia has an immense future. Her power is in full development. She will not forget the action that Germany has just won in Constantinople.[1] In two years' time there will be war. My entire efforts are aimed at preparing ourselves for it.'

Georges Louis' diary, cited in Erwin Hölzle (ed.), *Quellen zur Entstehung des Ersten Weltkrieges. Internationale Dokumente, 1901–1914*, Wissenschaftliche Buchgesellschaft, Darmstadt 1978, p. 178.

(71) 21 January 1914: Buchanan to Nicolson

Limon von Sanders crisis nearly resolved; Russia anxious for continued good relations with Britain

Private
St Petersburg, 21 January 1914

[...] The von Sanders incident seems to be on the high road to a settlement. At the usual Diplomatic reception on New Year's Day the Emperor told the German Ambassador that he regarded the incident as 'aplani', in consequence, as Sazonov told me, of a telegram which he had received from the Emperor William. [...] Sazonov is perfectly satisfied with the arrangement under which von Sanders will become Inspector-General of the Turkish Army, while a German Officer will act as Chief of the

1 That is, during the Liman von Sanders crisis. See (66), (68) and (69).

Staff; but I rather doubt whether the Russian public will share this satisfaction. We, however, have every reason to be thankful that Sazonov is so easily satisfied, as otherwise we should have found ourselves in a very awkward position. There is still, however, one point which is not quite clear, namely whether a German General is to have command of the Scutari Division. [...]

In the few minutes conversation which I had with the Emperor I delivered the messages with which the King had charged me and told Him how anxious His Majesty was to see the relations between the two countries become more friendly every day and how much His Majesty hoped that we should always be able to overcome any little differences which might from time to time arise.[2] I added that Sir Edward had, both in his conversations with Lichnowsky and through Goschen in Berlin, done all that was possible to induce the German Government to arrange the von Sanders incident in a manner satisfactory to Russia, as he had felt that it was at Berlin and not at Constantinople that a settlement must be sought. [...]

BD, X, II, No. 469.

(72) February 1914: P.N. Durnovo, 'Memorandum to Tsar Nicholas II'

Russia should not be bound to Britain but reorient herself towards Germany; Durnovo predicts that future war will end in revolution and defeat

The central factor of the period of world history through which we are now passing is the rivalry between England and Germany. This rivalry must inevitably lead to an armed struggle between them, the issue of which will, in all probability, prove fatal to the vanquished side. The interests of these two powers are far too incompatible, and their simultaneous existence as world powers will sooner or later prove impossible. [...] Naturally, England cannot yield without a fight, and between her

2 During the crisis, the Kaiser had hoped that Anglo-Russian relations would be damaged and Anglo-German relations strengthened. In response to news in the Russian press that the Entente would remain firm and united, for example, Wilhelm II wrote one of his excited marginal notes: 'Bluff: Only you alone cannot see it! Because England plain refused, the unity stops here!' Marginal note on Pourtalès' report of 18 December 1913, BA-AA Türkei 139, Vol. 30, cited in Fritz Fischer, 'Weltpolitik, Weltmachtstreben und deutsche Kriegsziele, *Historische Zeitschrift*, 199, 2, 1964, pp. 265–346, p. 315.

and Germany a struggle for life or death is inevitable.

The armed conflict impending as a result of this rivalry cannot be confined to a duel between England and Germany alone. Their resources are far too unequal, and, at the same time, they are not sufficiently vulnerable to each other. Germany could provoke rebellion in India, in South Africa, and, especially, a dangerous rebellion in Ireland, and paralyze English sea trade by means of privateering and, perhaps, submarine warfare, thereby creating for Great Britain difficulties in her food supply; but, in spite of all the daring of the German military leaders, they would scarcely risk landing in England, unless a fortunate accident helped them to destroy or appreciably to weaken the English navy. As for England, she will find Germany absolutely invulnerable. All that she may achieve is to seize the German colonies, stop German sea trade, and, in the most favourable event, annihilate the German navy, but nothing more. This, however, would not force the enemy to sue for peace. There is no doubt, therefore, that England will attempt the means she has more than once used with success, and will risk armed action only after securing participation in the war, on her own side, of powers stronger in a strategic sense. But since Germany, for her own part, will not be found isolated, the future Anglo-German war will undoubtedly be transformed into an armed conflict between two groups of powers, one with a German, the other with an English orientation.

Until the Russo-Japanese War, Russian policy had neither orientation. From the time of the reign of Emperor Alexander III, Russia had a defensive alliance with France, so firm as to assure common action by both powers in the event of attack upon either, but, at the same time, not so close as to obligate either to support unfailingly, with armed force, all political actions and claims of the ally. At the same time, the Russian Court maintained the traditional friendly relations, based upon ties of blood, with the Court of Berlin. Owing precisely to this conjuncture, peace among the Great Powers was not disturbed in the course of a great many years, in spite of the presence of abundant combustible material in Europe. France, by her alliance with Russia, was guaranteed against attack by Germany; the latter was safe, thanks to the tried pacifism and friendship of Russia, from révanche ambitions on the part of France; and Russia was secured, thanks to Germany's need of maintaining amicable relations with her, against excessive intrigues by Austria-Hungary in the Balkan peninsula. Lastly, England, isolated and held in check by her rivalry with Russia in Persia, by her diplomats' traditional fear of our advance on India, and by strained relations with France, especially notable at the time of the well-known Fashoda[3] incident, viewed with

3 The Fashoda Crisis of 1898 was the result of territorial disputes between Britain and France in East Africa. War was narrowly averted, and the crisis resulted in a diplomatic victory for Britain.

alarm the increase of Germany's naval power, without, however, risking an active step.

The Russo-Japanese War radically changed the relations among the Great Powers and brought England out of her isolation. As we know, all through the Russo-Japanese War, England and America observed benevolent neutrality toward Japan, while we enjoyed a similar benevolent neutrality from France and Germany. Here, it would seem, should have been the inception of the most natural political combination for us. But after the war, our diplomacy faced abruptly about and definitely entered upon the road toward rapprochement with England. France was drawn into the orbit of British policy; there was formed a group of powers of the Triple Entente, with England playing the dominant part; and a clash, sooner or later, with the powers grouping themselves around Germany became inevitable.

Now, what advantages did the renunciation of our traditional policy of distrust of England and the rupture of neighbourly if not friendly, relations with Germany promise us then and at present? Considering with any degree of care the events which have taken place since the Treaty of Portsmouth,[4] we find it difficult to perceive any practical advantages gained by us in rapprochement with England. [...]

To sum up, the Anglo-Russian accord has brought us nothing of practical value up to this time, while for the future, it threatens us with an inevitable armed clash with Germany.

Under what conditions will this clash occur and what will be its probable consequences? The fundamental groupings in a future war are self-evident: Russia, France, and England, on the one side, with Germany, Austria, and Turkey, on the other. It is more than likely that other powers, too, will participate in that war, depending upon circumstances as they may exist at the war's outbreak. But, whether the immediate cause for the war is furnished by another clash of conflicting interests in the Balkans, or by a colonial incident, such as that of Algeciras,[5] the fundamental alignment will remain unchanged.

Italy, if she has any conception of her real interests, will not join the German side. For political as well as economic reasons, she undoubtedly hopes to expand her present territory. Such an expansion may be achieved only at the expense of Austria, on one hand, and Turkey, on the other. It is, therefore, natural for Italy not to join that party which would safeguard the territorial integrity of the countries at whose expense she hopes to realize her aspirations. Furthermore, it is not out of the question that Italy would join the anti-German coalition, if the scales of war should incline in its favour, in order to secure for herself the most

4 The Treaty of Portsmouth formally ended the Russo-Japanese War.

5 The Algeciras Conference was convened to end the First Moroccan Crisis.

favourable conditions in sharing the subsequent division of spoils. [...]

The main burden of the war will undoubtedly fall on us, since England is hardly capable of taking a considerable part in a continental war, while France, poor in manpower, will probably adhere to strictly defensive tactics, in view of the enormous losses by which war will be attended under present conditions of military technique. The part of a battering ram, making a breach in the very thick of the German defence, will be ours, with many factors against us to which we shall have to devote great effort and attention. [...]

Are we prepared for so stubborn a war as the future war of the European nations will undoubtedly become? This question we must answer, without evasion, in the negative. That much has been done for our defence since the Japanese war, I am the last person to deny, but even so, it is quite inadequate considering the unprecedented scale on which a future war will inevitably be fought. [...]

Another circumstance unfavourable to our defence is its far too great dependence, generally speaking, upon foreign industry, a fact which [...] will create a series of obstacles difficult to overcome. The quantity of our heavy artillery, the importance of which was demonstrated in the Japanese War, is far too inadequate, and there are few machine guns. The organization of our fortress defences has scarcely been started, and even the fortress of Reval, which is to defend the road to the capital, is not yet finished.

The network of strategic railways is inadequate. The railways possess a rolling stock sufficient, perhaps, for normal traffic, but not commensurate with the colossal demands which will be made upon them in the event of a European war. [...]

All these factors are hardly given proper thought by our diplomats, whose behaviour toward Germany is, in some respects, even aggressive, and may unduly hasten the moment of armed conflict, a moment which, of course, is really inevitable in view of our British orientation. [...]

The vital interests of Russia and Germany do not conflict. There are fundamental grounds for a peaceable existence of these two States. Germany's future lies on the sea, that is, in a realm where Russia, essentially the most continental of the Great Powers, has no interests whatever. We have no overseas colonies, and shall probably never have them, and communication between the various parts of our empire is easier overland than by water. No surplus population demanding territorial expansion is visible, but, even from the viewpoint of new conquests, what can we gain from a victory over Germany, Posen, or East Prussia? But why do we need these regions, densely populated as they are by Poles, when we find it difficult enough to manage our own Russian Poles? Why encourage centripetal tendencies, that have not ceased even to this day in the Vistula territory, by incorporating in the Russian State the restless Posnanian and East Prussian Poles, whose national demands even the German Government, which is more firm than the Russian, cannot stifle? [...]

It should not be forgotten that Russia and Germany are the representatives of the conservative principle in the civilized world, as opposed to the democratic principle, incarnated in England and, to an infinitely lesser degree, in France. Strange as it may seem, England, monarchistic and conservative to the marrow at home, has in her foreign relations always acted as the protector of the most demagogical tendencies, invariably encouraging all popular movements aiming at the weakening of the monarchical principle.

From this point of view, a struggle between Germany and Russia, regardless of its issue, is profoundly undesirable to both sides, as undoubtedly involving the weakening of the conservative principle in the world of which the above-named two Great Powers are the only reliable bulwarks. More than that, one must realize that under the exceptional conditions which exist, a general European war is mortally dangerous both for Russia and Germany, no matter who wins. It is our firm conviction, based upon a long and careful study of all contemporary subversive tendencies, that there must inevitably break out in the defeated country a social revolution which, by the very nature of things, will spread to the country of the victor. [...]

The peasant dreams of obtaining a gratuitous share of somebody else's land; the workman, of getting hold of the entire capital and profits of the manufacturer. Beyond this, they have no aspirations. If these slogans are scattered far and wide among the populace, and the Government permits agitation along these lines, Russia will be flung into anarchy, such as she suffered in the ever-memorable period of troubles in 1905–1906.[6] War with Germany would create exceptionally favourable conditions for such agitation. [...]

If the war ends in victory, the putting down of the Socialist movement will not offer any insurmountable obstacles. There will be agrarian troubles, as a result of agitation for compensating the soldiers with additional land allotments; there will be labour troubles during the transition from the probably increased wages of war time to normal schedules; and this, it is to be hoped, will be all, so long as the wave of the German social revolution has not reached us. But in the event of defeat, the possibility of which in a struggle with a foe like Germany cannot be overlooked, social revolution in its most extreme form is inevitable.

As has already been said, the trouble will start with the blaming of the Government for all disasters. In the legislative institutions a bitter

6 That is, the revolution following the disastrous Russo-Japanese War of 1904–1905.

campaign against the Government will begin, followed by revolutionary agitations throughout the country, with Socialist slogans, capable of arousing and rallying the masses, beginning with the division of the land and succeeded by a division of all valuables and property. The defeated army, having lost its most dependable men, and carried away by the tide of primitive peasant desire for land, will find itself too demoralized to serve as a bulwark of law and order. The legislative institutions and the intellectual opposition parties, lacking real authority in the eyes of the people, will be powerless to stem the popular tide, aroused by themselves, and Russia will be flung into hopeless anarchy, the issue of which cannot be foreseen.

No matter how strange it may appear at first sight, considering the extraordinary poise of the German character, Germany, likewise, is destined to suffer, in case of defeat, no lesser social upheavals. The effect of a disastrous war upon the population will be too severe not to bring to the surface destructive tendencies, now deeply hidden.

[...] Defeated, Germany will lose her world markets and maritime commerce, for the aim of the war – on the part of its real instigator, England – will be the destruction of German competition. After this has been achieved, the labouring masses, deprived not only of higher but of any and all wages, having suffered greatly during the war, and being, naturally, embittered, will offer fertile soil for anti-agrarian and later anti-social propaganda by the Socialist parties.

These parties, in turn, making use of the outraged patriotic sentiment among the people, owing to the loss of the war, their exasperation at the militarists and the feudal burgher regime that betrayed them, will abandon the road of peaceable evolution which they have thus far been following so steadily, and take a purely revolutionary path. Some part will also be played, especially in the event of agrarian troubles in neighbouring Russia, by the class of landless farmhands, which is quite numerous in Germany. Apart from this, there will be a revival of the hitherto concealed separatist tendencies in southern Germany, and the hidden antagonism of Bavaria to domination by Prussia will emerge in all its intensity. In short, a situation will be created which (in gravity) will be little better than that in Russia.

A summary of all that has been stated above must lead to the conclusion that a rapprochement with England does not promise us any benefits, and that the English orientation of our diplomacy is essentially wrong.

We do not travel the same road as England; she should be left to go her own way, and we must not quarrel on her account with Germany. The Triple Entente is an artificial combination, without a basis of real interest. It has nothing to look forward to. The future belongs to a close and incomparably more vital rapprochement of Russia, Germany,

France (reconciled with Germany), and Japan (allied to Russia by a strictly defensive union). A political combination like this, lacking all aggressiveness toward other States, would safeguard for many years the peace of the civilized nations, threatened, not by the militant intentions of Germany, as English diplomacy is trying to show, but solely by the perfectly natural striving of England to retain at all costs her vanishing domination of the seas. In this direction, and not in the fruitless search of a basis for an accord with England, which is in its very nature contrary to our national plans and aims, should all the efforts of our diplomacy be concentrated. It goes without saying that Germany, on her part, must meet our desire to restore our well-tested relations and friendly alliance with her, and to elaborate, in closest agreement with us, such terms of our neighbourly existence as to afford no basis for anti-German agitation on the part of our constitutional-liberal parties, which, by their very nature, are forced to adhere, not to a Conservative German, but to a liberal English orientation.[7]

Durnovo, 'Memorandum to Tsar Nicholas II, February 1914', in Frank Golder (ed.), *Documents of Russian History*, Century, New York and London 1927, pp. 12–19.

(73) 26 February 1914: Jagow to Lichnowsky

Jagow considers Lichnowsky's worries about British role in future war unfounded

Private Letter
Berlin, 26 February 1914
Confidential

[...] Be a little more optimistic in the assessment of our English friends. I would like to think that you sometimes see things too negatively, also when you express the view that England would *in any case* be found on the side of France against us in case of war. We did not build our fleet for nothing, and it is my conviction that when it comes to it they will consider very carefully the question in England whether it really is all that easy and devoid of danger to play France's guardian angel. [...]

GP, 37/I, No. 14697.

7 For a discussion of Durnovo's memorandum, see David M. McDonald, 'The Durnovo Memorandum in Context: Official Conservatism and the Crisis of Autocracy', *Jahrbücher für die Geschichte Osteuropas*, 44, 4, 1996, pp. 481–502.

(74) 18 March 1914: Buchanan to Grey

Russia will be militarily stronger than Germany in 3 years' time

(No. 75)
St. Petersburg
D. 18 March 1914
R. 25 March 1914

[...] The temporary advantages, which Germany has secured by her Army Bill of last year, will in a few years time be eclipsed by the counter measures which Russia has been obliged to take in self defence. By the year 1917 she will have increased by some 460,000 men the peace time strength of her army [...], while she will possess a fleet in the Baltic, which, though not very formidable in itself, will nevertheless prove a thorn in the side of Germany, should that country be at war with England. Unless therefore Germany is prepared to make still further financial sacrifices for military purposes, the days of her hegemony in Europe will be numbered; as, even without the co-operation of England, Russia and France combined will then be strong enough to confront the united forces of the Triple Alliance. There are, however, still three critical years to pass before that result is achieved. In the race for armaments Russia has more staying powers than Germany; and, as Germany is aware of that fact, there is always the danger that she may be tempted to precipitate a conflict before Russia is fully prepared to meet it. During these crucial years, therefore, Russia will stand in need of our support; and, should we fail to give it when she appeals for it, England will no longer be numbered among her friends.

BD, X, II, No. 528.

(75) 18 March 1914: Buchanan to Nicolson

Russia will win arms race with Germany; might Germany use opportunity to strike before Russia becomes invincible?

Private
St. Petersburg, 18 March 1914

[...] I have dealt fully in a despatch with the German Press campaign.[8]

8 See BD, X, II, No. 528. On that despatch, Nicolson minuted: 'My own personal opinion is that Germany will do her utmost to win over Russia – finding that threats do more harm than good – and that the new factors in Russia will not

What Germany hopes to gain by it is more than I can say, as the only result has been to make Russia more determined than before to strengthen her means of defence and to be on her guard against any possible surprises. The reason for it, however, is not so far to seek. Germany is discovering that instead of having improved her military position by the Army Bill of last year, she will in three years be much worse off than before. France has, in consequence, reverted to the three years service and Russia will, by that time, have increased her army by some 460,000 men and raised its peace effectives to the enormous figure of 1,750,000. It is not surprising, therefore, that Germany should show signs of nervous irritability. The question of absorbing interest is what will she do? Will she bring in another Army Bill? If she does, Russia will go one better; and in this race for armaments she can always outdistance Germany. Russia is conscious of her latent strength and is determined to use it. She is and will, I believe, remain thoroughly pacific, but she has had enough of the weakness and vacillation which marked her policy during last year's crisis. She is also, perhaps, aware that she cannot count on our armed support in all eventualities, and she may wish to be strong enough to act independently of us. Can Germany afford to wait till Russia becomes the dominant factor in Europe or will she strike while victory is still within her grasp? I will not attempt to answer this question but the danger and the temptation are both there. Till she has completed her armaments, Russia will have need of our support; and her eventual attitude towards us will depend on whether we stand firmly by her in any crisis which may arise during the intervening years. [...].

BD, X, II, No. 529.

(76) 23 March 1914: Carl von Weizsäcker's notes

Bethmann Hollweg speculates about likely British attitude in European war

---

23/3 Conversation with I[mperial C[hancellor] [...] In the current year probably no war. But future nonetheless very uncertain. If Austrian-

---

be indisposed to listen to overtures – especially having regard to the internal situation both here and in France.' See (**72**). The German press campaign started at the beginning of March that year with an article in the *Kölnische Zeitung* which appeared inspired by the Wilhelmstrasse and which argued that Russia was preparing for war in three to four years' time. For details see John Röhl, *Wilhelm II., Der Weg in den Abgrund, 1900–1941*, Beck, Munich 2008, 2nd edn 2009, Vol. 3, pp. 1046–1047. See also (**163**).

German-French-Russian war then England would probably initially remain neutral, [...] would intervene if France defeated.[9]

HStA Stuttgart, NL Weizsäcker, Q 1/18, Bü. 41, cited in Stephen Schröder, *Die englisch-russische Marinekonvention*, Vandenhoeck & Ruprecht, Göttingen 2004, p. 578.

(77) 24 March 1914: Colonel Knox's Memorandum for Henry Wilson

Russian military increases; favourable assessment of Russian military ability; estimation of Russia's future military strength

Attached is a most valuable and interesting despatch from Col Knox regarding the Russian army. It shows most clearly how the increases and improvements made in the Russian army since 1905 and the huge increase now being carried out will make this army the most serious factor in European policy in a few years time. One can understand better now the recent German press campaign against Russia.

The following is a summary of the most important points in this despatch:

1 – The annual contingent is to be increased next year by 111,000 men. As it is believed that the new recruiting law will give an additional 35,000 this year, the increase over former years will be 146,000 annually, giving in 3 years time an increased peace strength of nearly 450,000.

2 – This increase in the peace strength will be used partly for the creation of new units and partly to raise the peace strength of all existing units. The new units to be raised are:

2 new Army Corps, one on the Western frontier, one in Siberia.

A 4th Finland Rifle Brigade, thus bringing the XXII A[rmy] C[orps], which at present contains only 3 brigades, up to the normal strength of other AC.

A new division in the Caucasus, which presumably will be used to form, with the surplus division of the XVI AC, a IVth Caucasian AC.

The Russian army will then consist of 40 AC, 32 in Europe and the Caucasus, 8 in Asia.

26 new cavalry regiments, some of which will be used to replace the Cossack regiments in the regular cavalry divisions. There are 16

9 During the July Crisis, Bethmann Hollweg continued to believe in the possibility of British neutrality until it was too late to change Germany's policy.

regular cavalry divisions (excluding the guard) each of which contain 1 Cossack regiment. Thus there would remain 10 regiments for the formation of new units, or 2½ cavalry divisions, bringing the total in Europe to 27 or 28 cavalry divisions.

New artillery units. This includes the reorganization of the artillery in 6 gun batteries instead of 8 (giving 2 extra batteries per AC), the adding of a division of heavy artillery to each AC, and the artillery for the new formations.

We have made a rough calculation as to the number of men (peace strength) which these new formations and the increases in peace strength of existing units [...] will absorb, and estimate that after all these have been provided for, there will still remain a surplus of 100,000–150,000 men. Therefore if our calculations are approximately correct and if the Russian War Ministry are not unduly optimistic in believing that they can add 150,000 to their annual contingent without difficulty, it would seem that they could add another 3 or 4 army corps to their strength.

3 – It is interesting to note that apparently alternative proposals were laid before the Duma, i.e. to increase the term of the service in the infantry & artillery to 4 years or to increase the contingent. The effect of both proposals would be approximately the same as regards increased peace strength, but the former would mean improved training, the latter a larger number of cadres. [...]

4 – The results of the increase in the term of service (from a nominal 3, actual 2⅔, in the infantry and artillery, and a nominal 4, actual 3⅔ in the mounted & technical branches, to 3¼ and 4¼ years respectively) are most important. Formerly during the winter months the Russian army was really at only ⅔ of its nominal peace strength, for the old contingent was dismissed in November and the new one which came up at about the same time was not reckoned fit to take its place in the ranks till it had received 4 months training. Now that the two contingents overlap, this weakness is removed, and moreover by the commencement of April, when the new contingent will have received 4 months training, and before the old one is dismissed, there will be present in the ranks additional to the normal peace strength a number of trained men equal to the strength of the annual contingent. Thus, in April 1917, Russia will have under arms, if all the proposed measures are carried out, well over 2,000,000 men. The month of April will not be a propitious one in which to start a campaign against Russia.

On the other hand the dangerous moment for Russia will arise on the dismissal of the old contingent, for owing to the Russian system, whereby on mobilization men to not rejoin the units in which they served in peace, some confusion might arise. In a country like Russia there would however probably be little difficulty in retaining the men as long as there was the slightest cloud on the political horizon.

5 – Colonel Knox's estimate of the qualities of the Russian army, the virtues and defects of the leaders, subordinate officer and rank & file, agrees exactly with the opinion formed in this section from information received from other sources. The raw material is excellent, the training is good and improving very rapidly, and an immense improvement has been made in the officer, which was formerly the weakest point. The chief defects which remain are the lack of initiative inherent in the Russian character, the doubt as to whether the organization of the rear services, which is never practised in peace, can possibly be efficient in war, and the question of whether the right leader can be found for an army, which needs special handling.

6 – The development of her railway system is of course of the utmost importance to Russia but it is too early to say yet exactly what the effect of the new programme will be.

[*Note by Henry Wilson, 27.3.14*]
This is a most interesting Despatch. It is easy to understand now why Germany is anxious about the future & why she may think that it is a case of 'now or never'.

TNA, WO 105/1039.

(78) 30 March 1914: Nicolson to de Bunsen

Jagow's thoughts on the value of Austria-Hungary as an ally to Germany; Nicolson's fears that Russia might gravitate towards Germany and that the alliance system might be revised in the near future

---

[...] I have exceedingly strong doubts – whatever the Bulgarian representative at Vienna may say – that Bulgaria will for long continue to revolve in the Austrian orbit. I am quite sure that sooner or later she will feel compelled to gravitate once more to Russia, as on the broad principles of policy it is perfectly clear that it is Russia and not Austria who is destined to play, as she has hitherto in the past, a predominant part among the Slav races of the Balkan Peninsula. As regards Austria, I think the following information which I have received from Goschen may be of interest to you, but I must ask you of course to consider it as for your own information only. Jagow said to Goschen that there was one matter which caused him far more anxiety than the dissolution of the Ottoman Empire, and that was the future of the Dual Monarchy.[10] He hated to say it or to think it, but he could not unpack his mind of the fear that it was a race between the two Empires which would go to pieces first. Goschen said that he was not one of those who believed that the Dual Monarchy would necessarily break up the moment the aged Emperor passed away. Jagow replied that it was not the change of Rulers that he had so much in mind, though in a crumbling edifice like the Dual Monarchy a change from a Sovereign popular and picturesque to an unpopular one[11] was certainly a matter for some misgiving. What troubled him much more was the want of cohesion in the Monarchy which was becoming more marked every day. The people in the Monarchy who hitherto had some or at all events the most imperial feeling were the Austrian-Germans. These were also falling victims to the nationality fever and were beginning to follow the example of the other nationalities in Austria and looking entirely after their own interests and neglecting those of the Empire. This was the most disquieting symptom of all, as the Austrian-Germans had always been the best and most reliable element in the State and really the chief factor in keeping the Empire together. As to the rest Hungary was striving harder than ever to increase her independence and to magyarize her heterogeneous populations. The populations of the Serbian provinces were gravitating towards Serbia and the Hungarian-Rumanians towards Rumania; while the Slovaks and Croatians were struggling for recognition as separate nationalities. When one came to think of it, it was almost chaos, and Jagow could not help sometimes appraising the alliance value of a country in such a state. The above is the substance of what I am sure you will agree with me was an exceedingly interesting conversation between Goschen and Jagow.

My own personal idea is that this recent Press campaign against Russia was not really seriously meant on the part of Germany, and that she will do her utmost to come to terms with Russia, or in any case create more friendly and intimate relations. Of course there is no doubt that for the moment there is a very strong anti-German feeling in Russia and a determination not to accept any longer German dictation; but I have known such phases of feeling to have arisen in Russia and to have passed away without leaving much trace behind. We must always remember that there never has been any conflict between Russia and Germany and that on more than one occasion and for some lengthy periods the two countries have worked and fought together in close co-operation. We must also not forget that among many high and influential circles in Russia there is a desire to keep on the friendliest terms with Germany as representing the great bulwarks of the monarchial

10 See (**95**).

11 That is, Franz Ferdinand.

[*sic*] system.[12] I have no doubt that the people who are now coming into office in Russia are largely imbued with this feeling, which I am sorry to say has no doubt been greatly deepened and emphasized by the deplorable condition in which France and ourselves are at present placed. A country with the traditions and institutions of Russia can hardly view with much favour the events which are occurring both in France and here, and she may well consider whether it is to her interest to be linked to counties who seem to be on the high road towards revolution and ruin, and whether it would not be more to her interest to ally herself with that great central Power which in any case on the surface has the appearance of stability and where the monarchial [*sic*] system is firmly established. I do not mean that next week we shall hear that Russia has denounced her alliance with France or that she has broken off abruptly her understanding with us, but as events develop in this country and in France I do think the tendency in Russia will become more and more marked towards a friendly understanding with Berlin. One of the chief obstacles to this friendly understanding in recent times has been the strong support which Germany has always accorded to the aims and objects of Austria, but if it be true that Germany is now beginning to doubt the value of her alliance with Austria and is disposed to treat it as of little account, indeed perhaps as an encumbrance, I think it is extremely probably that before very long we shall witness fresh developments and new groupings in the European political situation. I am afraid I have treated you to rather an academical essay, but I do think we are approaching a period when we must be prepared to see a new course adopted among some of the great European Powers.

TNA, FO 800/373.

(79) 3 April 1914: Buchanan to Grey

Buchanan's audience with Nicholas II; suggestion of possible Anglo-Russian naval convention

---

No. 100
Secret
St. Petersburg
D. 3 April 1914.
R. 7 April 1914

[...] This led His Majesty to say that He would like to see a closer bond

12 See (**72**).

of union established between England and Russia, such as an alliance of a purely defensive character. On my remarking that I feared that this was impracticable at present, the Emperor said that we might at any rate conclude some arrangement similar to that which existed between His Majesty's Government and the Government of the French Republic. I replied that I was ignorant of the terms of this arrangement. His Majesty said He was also unacquainted with them but that He believed that, if we had not actually a military convention with France, we had discussed and agreed on what each country was to do in certain eventualities. On my observing that the despatch of an expeditionary corps to co-operate with the Russian army was, for material reasons, out of the question, the Emperor said that, even if it was feasible, it would serve no useful purpose, as He had men enough and to spare at home. It might, however, be advantageous to arrange beforehand for the co-operation of the British and Russian fleets. By the year 1917 He hoped to have 8 Dreadnoughts in the Baltic, and, in the event of war, the Germans would have to despatch more than the number of ships to watch them. He would never propose that a British fleet should be sent to the Baltic on account of the dangers to which it would be exposed from mines in the Belt and from attack by a superior German fleet passing through the Kiel Canal. The existence, however, of a Russian fleet in the Baltic would ease the situation for the British fleet in the North Sea. At present, His Majesty continued, our understanding was confined to Persia, and He was strongly of opinion that that understanding ought to be extended, either by some sort of arrangement such as He had suggested, or by some written formula which would record the fact of Anglo-Russian co-operation in Europe. [...]

P.S. Mr. Sazonov whom I saw this afternoon [...] said that, if an Alliance was out of the question, it must at any rate be given such a definite character that Germany would know that, were she to embark on an aggressive policy, she would in certain eventualities be confronted by the united forces of England, France and Russia. Such an understanding would, His Excellency maintained, guarantee the peace of Europe, as Germany was too much afraid of the British Fleet to risk a war in which that Fleet would be opposed to her.[13]

BD, X, II, No. 537.

13 As McDonald points out, within weeks of this meeting, Russia and Britain embarked upon talks for a naval agreement. 'The Durnovo Memorandum in Context', p. 499. For a recent study of the naval convention, see Stephen Schröder, *Die englisch-russische Marinekonvention. Das Deutsche Reich und die Flottenverhandlungen der Triple-Entente am Vorabend des Ersten Weltkriegs*, Vandenhoeck & Ruprecht, Göttingen 2004.

(80) 4 April 1914: Paléologue to Doumergue[14]

Britain seems disinterested in prospect of Anglo-Russian alliance; French Ambassador fears that rejection might lead the Russians into Germany's arms[15]

Telegram Nos 144, 145
St Petersburg 4 April 1914
D. 2.05 p.m.; 4.03 p.m.
R. 2.40 p.m.; 4.40 p.m.

Secret. Very confidential.
Yesterday, my English colleague was given a private audience with Tsar Nicholas. His Majesty has developed forceful arguments in favour of an Anglo-Russian alliance, which he shared with myself on the 17th of February.

'I only imagine this alliance as *defensive*,' said the Tsar, 'but I fervently wish it to be the best guarantee of peace.'

Sir G. Buchanan, who personally supports the idea of the alliance, did not think he would be able to hide from the Tsar the fact that his views are not shared by his Government. The Tsar was very disappointed by this response. If the British Government persists in declining the pact that is so adamantly proposed, we fear the Triple Entente will be jeopardised.

We must not forget that the idea of establishing closer links with Germany has many supporters in St Petersburg, mainly in the imperial entourage. The day the Tsar acknowledges that he cannot base any precise or lasting policies on the support of England, will he not listen to the insidious appeals that come to him from Berlin?

I add that the Tsar is following a carefully considered conviction when he asserts that the Triple Entente must be reinforced to assure the maintenance of general peace.

DDF, 3e série, 10, No. 69.

---

14 Minister of Foreign Affairs Gaston Doumergue.
15 But see also (**81**) for British fears that Russia would forge closer ties with Germany if Britain did not join her.

(81) 16 April 1914: Buchanan to Nicolson

Russia seeks defensive agreement with Britain; Britain needs to keep Russia on her side or risk losing her to Germany[16]

Private
St Petersburg 16 April 1914

[...] As regards the question of doing something to strengthen our understanding with Russia, I think that it would be better to await the result of the King's visit to Paris[17] before saying anything to the Russian Government in reply to the tentative suggestions made to me by the Emperor and Sazonov.[18] From what Paléologue tells me, I gather that the French Government are rather preoccupied with regard to the possibility of maintaining the Anglo-Russian understanding for any length of time on its present rather shaky basis and would like to see it take a more precise and definite shape. It is therefore more than probable that Poincaré will speak both to the King and to Sir Edward on the subject, though whether he is likely to put forward any concrete proposal I do not know. What the Emperor and Sazonov apparently want is a written agreement which would make it clear to the world that, in the event of Russia being involved in a defensive war, England would give her armed support. They argue that the publication of an agreement of this character would secure the peace of Europe, as the Germans would never force a war on Russia did they know that they would have to deal with the British fleet as well as with the Russian army; but as such an agreement would virtually amount to a defensive alliance I do not imagine that there is much chance of His Majesty's Government agreeing to it. The Naval agreement of which the Emperor spoke as an alternative to an alliance is perhaps more feasible, as without binding ourselves to support Russia at sea in the event of her being at war, we might enter into an interchange of views with regard to a combined naval plan of campaign, should a war break out in which both countries had become involved. The two fleets would then be in a position to co-operate effectively with one another without having to wait till the naval staffs had been able to consult together after the outbreak of hostilities.

[...] In a conversation which I had with him a few days ago, Sazonov again reverted to the subject, saying that, unless something was done, the Triple Entente would soon become a quantité négligeable. Germany,

16 But see also (**80**) for evidence of French fears that Russia might gravitate towards Germany if rejected by Britain.

17 King George V visited Paris on 21 April 1914.

18 See (**79**).

he maintained, was bent on establishing her hegemony in Turkey and she would one day push matters too far, with the result that we should all be dragged into war. We had made an alliance with Japan; but that alliance, it was true, had been directed against Russia. Why could we not then conclude an agreement with Russia that would guarantee us both against German aggression. He did not care what form that agreement took; but, if we wished to maintain peace, we must proclaim to the world the solidarity of the Triple Entente.

I fully realize all the difficulties in the way of an agreement of this nature, but I can't help feeling that we shall be running a great risk if we do nothing to consolidate our understanding. Russia is rapidly becoming so powerful that we must retain her friendship at almost any cost. If she acquires the conviction that we are unreliable and useless as a friend, she may one day strike a bargain with Germany and resume her liberty of action in Turkey and Persia. Our position would then be a very parlous one.

You will have seen from my telegram that the Russian Government want to buy the two Dreadnoughts which Armstrongs are building for the Chilean Government. Gregorovitch told me that they are required for service in the Baltic, and he expressed the hope that His Majesty's Government would do all they could to facilitate the purchase. It is quite a new departure for Russia to order battleships abroad, and the fact of her doing so now shows the serious view she takes of the international situation.

BD X, II, No. 538.

(82) 24 April: Goschen to Nicolson

Britain cannot be on friendly terms with Russia and Germany at the same time

I doubt, no I am sure, we cannot have it both ways, i.e. form a defensive alliance with Russia and at the same time be on cordial terms with Germany.

TNA, FO 800/374, cited in Zara Steiner and Keith Nielson, *Britain and the Origins of the First World War*, Palgrave Macmillan, London 2003, p. 135.

(83) 1 May 1914: Grey to Bertie

Discussions in Paris about potentially strengthening Anglo-Russian relations

No. 249
Secret
Foreign Office, 1 May 1914

On the 23rd ult[imo] I had a long conversation with [Foreign Minister] M. Doumergue at the Quai d'Orsay. Sir William Tyrrell was with me, and M. Cambon and M. Margerie were present also.

M. Doumergue spoke at length and with great emphasis on the necessity for doing something to make relations with Russia more secure. He evidently assumed that Germany would make great efforts to detach Russia from the French Alliance, and might possibly be successful. In that case, France and England would be left alone [...]. The French knew that an Alliance between Britain and Russia was out of the question, but could we not at least promise to discuss matters with Russia, if necessary?

I said that I thought it not impossible, if the French agreed, that we should communicate to the Russian Government exactly what the state of things was between France and ourselves. We might let them know of the note that I had given to M. Cambon, and of the conversations that had taken place between the Military and Naval Staffs. Russia would then be able to see exactly how things stood, and what scope they left for any conversations with her. She would understand that both the French and the British Governments were left entirely free to decide whether, in case of war, they would support one another or not. [...]

Later in the evening [...] M. Poincaré spoke to me and expressed himself satisfied with what he had heard that I had said to M. Doumergue. I pointed out [...] that it was more difficult for us in the case of Russia than in the case of France – I would not say to enter into engagements, for we had no engagements with France – but to hold out to Russia any hopes of assistance from us. Whether we engaged in a Continental war or kept aloof would depend on public opinion in Great Britain when the time came. If there were a really aggressive and menacing attack made by Germany upon France, it was possible that public feeling in Great Britain would justify the Government in helping France. But it was not likely that Germany would make an aggressive and menacing attack upon Russia; and, even if she did, people in Great Britain would be inclined to say that, though Germany might have successes at first, Russia's resources were so great that, in the long run, Germany would be exhausted without our helping Russia. Besides this, the French

Government were a free Government, while the Russian Government were not; and this affected the sympathy of public opinion in Britain.

When I made the latter remark to M. Poincaré, he said that there was the same difficulty in the French feeling for Russia.

On this I observed that I knew this to be so, but in France the utility of an Alliance with Russia was felt, while in England the matter required much more explanation.

M. Poincaré observed that it was not an Alliance that was suggested, for there could be no question of anything more between England and Russia than existed between England and France.

I found that everyone conversant with politics, both those in office and such men as MM. Clemenceau and Delcassé, were immensely impressed by the growing strength of Russia and her tremendous resources and potential power and wealth.[19]

BD, X, II, No. 541.

(84) 12 May 1914: Conrad and Moltke meet in Karlsbad

Conrad recalls the last meeting of the allied Chiefs of Staff

We initially discussed the political situation and the adherence to our previous agreements in case of a joint war. In addition to that I expressed: 'We would no longer be able to count on the Rumanians as allies, but would possibly have to consider them even as an opponent.' General von Moltke objected that Rumania would initially remain neutral and wait.

I: 'This does not alter our intention to march into Galicia with the bulk of our forces. However, I must stress all the more how desirable it would be if a bit more were done on the German side for the Russian theatre of war than is currently intended.'

M.: 'Twelve Divisions – perhaps a bit more – East of the lower Vistula.'

I: 'The Russian offensive will also be directed against the province of Prussia, and you have such few forces there.'

M.: 'There will then be even fewer Russian forces there.'

I: 'You cannot count on that. Russia will turn against us, but it is also not far from Warsaw to Berlin; I would like you to consider what could happen if *we* get in an unfavourable situation. Then the road would be clear for Russia. What will you do if you have no success

19 Grey repeated during his visit to Paris what he had already told Cambon during the First Moroccan Crisis. See Steiner and Neilson, *Britain and the Origins of the First World War*, p. 262.

in the West and the Russians attack your rear in the East in this way?'

M.: 'Yes, I will do what I can. We are not superior to the French.' [...]

We then talked about the likelihood of a war. General von Moltke felt that any delay would amount to a reduction of our chances; with Russia one could not risk being in competition about masses. He continued:

'Here they unfortunately always expect a declaration from England that she will not participate. Such a declaration will never be given by England.'

I: 'Germany's attitude in the past years has allowed the favourable opportunities to go unused. In 1908 we committed the grave error of not tackling Serbia; and again last year!'

M.: 'Why did you not strike?'

I: 'At the last moment His Majesty was against it.'

General von Moltke emphasised that he was convinced of the real loyalty of official Italian circles, especially General Pollio's.[20]

I: 'I think so, too, but even Pollio is only human, he could not be there anymore tomorrow.[21] In Italy it is public opinion which could lead to a change of heart at the last minute. We cannot count on Italy with any *certainty*.' [...]

Before I left, I asked General von Moltke again how long, in his opinion, it would take until Germany, in a joint war against Russia and France, would be able to turn to Russia with strong forces.

M.: 'We hope to be finished with France in six weeks from the beginning of operations, or at least so far that we can move the bulk of our troops against Russia.'

I: 'So for at least six weeks we have to lend our back against Russia.'

I took my leave from General von Moltke, unaware that I would shake his hand for the last time. [...]

Franz Conrad von Hötzendorf, *Aus meiner Dienstzeit, 1906–1918*, 5 vols, Rikola Verlag, Vienna, Leipzig, Munich 1922–1925, Vol. 3, pp. 669–673.

20 See (**89**), (**91**).

21 Pollio died on 28 June 1914.

(85) 18 May 1914: Waldersee's memorandum 'on Germany's military position'

Germany's enemies unlikely to want to provoke a war any time soon; Waldersee advocates army increases; fear of Russia's future strength

---

[...] For the moment we do not need to contemplate that Germany's opponents might begin a war; however, the signs are increasing that they are arming ceaselessly and are making preparations in the most manifold areas in order to attack the Triple Alliance [...] or preferably even Germany on her own when the time is right, albeit at a time a few years hence. It cannot be said that this year in particular is inviting Germany's opponents to attack the Triple Alliance. On the contrary, for the moment none of the main participants can really gain anything from bringing about the armed fight. [...]

France now has two years of young recruits who are obviously only poorly trained. They are only just starting to create useable heavy artillery for the field army. A new Chamber has been elected, but the domestic issues still have to be clarified.

Russia's large-style military organization is still in the making and requires a few years still until its greatest utility has been achieved, as well as, closely related, the large scale extension of strategic railways.

England has currently no inclination at all to be involved in military action due to the Irish question and several domestic difficulties.[...]

From this contemplation it can be deduced that Germany will not have to endure an attack in the nearest future in a normal course of events, but that, on the other hand, she not only has no reason to avoid a conflict whatever the situation, rather, that the prospects for surviving a great European war quickly and victoriously are today still very favourable for Germany and also for the Triple Alliance. Soon this will no longer be the case. [...]

It is a fact that today General Conrad in Vienna and Pollio in Rome share this point of view.[22] [...] 'Everywhere and anywhere abroad', exclaimed General Pollio recently, 'one is of the opinion that in 2 years' time France and Russia will have closed the ring around the Triple Alliance with the powers who support them.' [...]

---

22 Pollio, Conrad and Moltke had most recently met in August 1913 during the German summer manoeuvres, and in October 1913 at Salzbrunn in Silesia, in a meeting presided over by Wilhelm II. Waldersee had also met Pollio in September and December that year. See John Gooch, 'Italy', in Richard F. Hamilton and Holger H. Herwig (eds), *War Planning 1914*, Cambridge University Press, Cambridge et al. 2010, pp. 198–225, p. 220.

Even if in the language of some diplomats and in the columns of the press of the Triple Entente there is now talk of a détente of the situation, then this should not fool us as to the seriousness of the situation in which matters are worsening for Germany in a not too distant future in the most horrible way. [...]

The main burden in a future war will rest on [Germany], on her alone. Our opponents are not foolish enough not to realize that only the defeat of Germany will clear a free path for them. The geographic position is conducive to a simultaneous attack in the front and the rear. It is certain that this is planned.

We will defeat France with a quick offensive, but it will take time. As long as we can reckon with Austria's advance against Russia in certain numbers, the troops we have available in the East would suffice to keep Russia's armies away from our country until we can spare troops from the West.

But the Russian army increases with every year, it becomes more mobile. If Rumania were even to attack Austria's rear and side with her nearly 20 divisions, then Austria's help would decrease to a negligible amount.

This possibility forces us to muster all our strength to carry out the fight – which we will hardly be spared – as much as possible by ourselves. For this we require further troops for our East.

From the word go we would relinquish any chance of victory if we went on the offensive on one side [only]. If politics allows itself already to be forced onto the defensive, the Germany army may never allow it.

It will be indefensible in history if [the German army] does not attempt everything in order to prevent such a situation. We cannot therefore avoid the necessity of completely implementing general conscription. [...]

The German diplomats should realize that the successful continuation of their policy by the army is only possible if the latter is put in a position where it can defend itself to some extent against an enormous, superior power. Otherwise it would be advisable to revise the policy. What the result of that might be for the German Reich at the present moment is, however, doubtful. [...]

BA-MA, BArch RH 61/577, No 94: 'Denkschrift über Deutschlands militärische Lage, Mai 1914'.

(86) 18 May 1914: Nicolson to Goschen

Surprised at Germany's hostile stance towards Russia; concerns about Ulster question

Private
Foreign Office, 18 May 1914

[...] The account you give of the Crown Prince's conversation is certainly interesting.[23] I think he talks great nonsense when he says that an Anglo-German Alliance would keep the peace in the world. I am quite sure that if we broke away from Russia and embarked on such an engagement [with Germany] we should bitterly rue the day. Russia would be able to make herself exceedingly disagreeable to us in regions where we are unfortunately very weak and where German assistance, even if willingly offered, would be of no avail, – indeed could not be operative. The general tenor of the Crown Prince's conversation certainly makes one hope that the life of his father will be much prolonged, though I imagine that when he does come to the throne he will not be able to exert any dominating influence over German foreign policy. I was rather surprised to read Jagow's attack upon the attitude and tone of the Russian press. I thought that the press polemic had been buried for ever, and I do not quite understand why Jagow should go out of his way to revive it. I should have thought that Germany would now do her utmost to get on the friendliest footing with Russia, but it does not look from Jagow's speech as if for the moment she was particularly anxious to do so. Buchanan's French colleague [Paléologue] is starting a hare that Russia is becoming a little uneasy as to Germany's attitude, and even goes so far as to say that the Russian Minister of War

23 See BD, X, II, No. 508, Goschen to Nicolson, 15 May 1914: 'The Crown Prince, as everybody knows who is at all intimately acquainted with him, requires holding back and not urging on. He has many charming and lovable qualities, but discretion is not one of them [...] only recently in conversation with a young member of my staff [...] he gave his opinion on various subjects with extraordinary freedom. He said among other things that unless Russia changed the present order of her going, Germany would one of these days read her a bitter lesson which she would not easily forget [...]. For France he expressed the greatest contempt, and he maintained that the day of the Latin races was past. [...] The future was to the Anglo-German race, and if England and Germany were wise they would join together in a regular Alliance and keep the other nations to order. I confess that I have heard at all events some of these opinions expressed in still higher quarters but I expect that there would be ructions if it was ever known that the Heir Apparent poured them into the ears of his young friends in the intervals of a game of Lawn Tennis.'

considers that war is almost inevitable within the next year. I do not myself believe that there is anything at all in this. There is no question at present existing which would necessarily lead to any strained relations between Russia and Germany, and I am quite sure that neither Sovereign has the slightest intention or desire to break the peace. The French Ambassador at Petersburg is well known as an alarmist and disseminates some exaggerated reports. [...]

I expect that the Germans will make great capital out of our squadron's visit to Kiel, and I do consider it rather unfortunate that the visit should fall within the Kiel week.[24] However, we are sending a squadron to visit three Russian ports, so I hope that no jealousy will be created in Russia. [...]

I am afraid that the health of the Austrian Emperor [Franz Joseph] is causing a good deal of uneasiness in his immediate entourage. It is naturally not very satisfactory that a man of his age should have been an invalid during six or seven weeks without any marked improvement. I do not myself think that there will immediately be a great change on the accession of his successor, although there is no doubt that the advent of Franz Ferdinand will cause a good deal of disquietude. [...]

We are entering into a phase of great anxiety and crisis in this country. Though I do not intend to bother you with my views on the question I must say that I do not see much hope for a peaceful solution, though everybody is crying out that it is absolutely necessary that one should be found. Next week will be an important one. I do not know for how long it will be possible for Ulster to passively maintain the severe strain which has been put upon her.[25] [...]

BD, X, II, No. 510.

24 See (**116**).

25 As D.C. Watts points out, British public opinion was almost entire preoccupied with the Irish question before and during the July Crisis and he speculates that 'had the war in Europe not intervened Ireland might well have been the scene of civil war by September, 1914, which could hardly have avoided spreading to England'. 'The British Reactions to the Assassination at Sarajevo', *European Studies Review*, 1, 3, 1971, pp. 233–247, p. 233.

(87) 28 May 1914: Sazonov to Benckendorff

Anglo-Russian naval convention seen as important step towards creating Franco-Russian-British alliance

We are exceedingly gratified at the readiness of the British Government to begin without delay the negotiations for the conclusion of an agreement between Russia and Great Britain concerning the joint operations of our naval forces in the event of joint military action. Apart from the desirability of such an agreement from a specially military point of view, we attach great importance to it from general political considerations. We see in the conclusion of such an agreement an important step towards associating Great Britain more closely with the Franco-Russian alliance, and an effective means of strengthening the recognition of the common interests of Great Britain and Russia, which, we are convinced, will be of great advantage in all questions affecting British and Russian interests. [...]

Cited in Friedrich Stieve, *Isvolsky and the World War*, Allen & Unwin, London 1926, p. 201.

(88) 29 May 1914: Edward House reports from Berlin

Colonel Edward House, the American president's special envoy to London, reports on the European situation in May 1914

The situation is extraordinary. It is militarism run stark mad. Unless someone acting for you can bring about a different understanding, there is some day to be an awful cataclysm. No one in Europe can do it. There is too much hatred, too many jealousies. Whenever England consents, France and Russia will close in on Germany and Austria. England does not want Germany wholly crushed, for she would then have to reckon alone with her ancient enemy, Russia; but if Germany insists upon an ever increasing navy, then England will have no choice. The best chance for peace is an understanding between England and Germany in regard to naval armaments and yet there is some disadvantage to us by these two getting too close.

Edward House, *Intimate Papers*, 2 vols, Houghton Mifflin, London 1926, Vol. I, *Behind the Political Curtain, 1912–1915*, pp. 254ff.

(89) 31 May 1914: Waldersee to Kageneck

Moltke and Conrad ready to start war if good opportunity arises; Pollio encourages and supports this view

Baden Baden, 31 May 1914.
Very confidential

[...] The talks in Karlsbad proceeded to the satisfaction of the participants on this side. They[26] were both agreed on the fact that at the moment things were still favourable for us, that one should therefore not hesitate on a suitable occasion to proceed with vigour and, if necessary, to begin the war. With every passing year the chances were diminishing. It is interesting [...] that P[ollio] in Rome communicated to me this point of view as his own, too; he compared the current situation of the Triple Alliance with that of our great King in 1756 and advised to proceed according to his recipe! However, in Karlsbad they were of the opinion that the statesmen could not be won over for any energetic measures. C[onrad] has promised for now to stick with the offensive in Galicia with the previously agreed strengths. However, we have our doubts if he will have the opportunity to carry out his intention. Matters in Rumania continue to be bad. [...]

This situation has led us to consider seriously deploying Italian troops in the Eastern theatre of war. To my great satisfaction P[ollio] has in principle agreed to this idea and C[onrad] has welcomed it warmly when talking to M[oltke]. It has not yet been decided to what extent and in which circumstances the matter is to be instigated, but negotiations have begun and it is possible that I will personally shortly be having oral discussions about this. [...].

Cited in Günther Kronenbitter, 'Die Macht der Illusionen', *Militärgeschichtliche Mitteilungen*, 57, 1998, pp. 525–526.

26 Moltke and Conrad had met in Karlsbad on 12 May. See (**84**).

(90) May 1914: Moltke to Bethmann Hollweg[27]

Moltke demands army increases following 3–year service law in France

[…] In my memorandum of 21 December 12[28] I outlined for Your Excellency the military and political situation as it presented itself at the end of 1912 and I explained the demands for the continuing expansion of the German army which resulted from it. These demands were only partially met with the army increases of 1913.[29] In the main, the provision of three new army corps which I considered necessary was not carried out, also the troops at the border and those destined for special orders have not had their peace budget increased to the level which they require for their tasks.

Apart from this failure to carry out an important part of the measures which I already considered important at the end of 1912, since then the situation among our potential opponents has shifted in a very significant way to our disadvantage.

France has introduced the three-year term of service and raised a new army corps;

Russia [has introduced] the 3½- and 4½-years service under provision of 4–5 new army corps. At the same time Russia is in the process of improving her entire army from the bottom up in an unimagined manner within a few years.[30]

In addition, the situation in the Balkans has in recent times become a completely different one: we can no longer count on Rumania on our side, but rather she will probably be found on the side of our opponents. Thus Austria will be tied up on the Balkans in such a way that we can no longer seriously count on an Austrian offensive into Russia.[31]

Thus we must realise that the offensive of almost the entire Russian army will be directed against our remaining forces in the East, and that is to say of a Russian army which will, already from about the year

27 This memorandum was not sent to the Chancellor, but rather served as notes for a meeting with the Kaiser in May 1914 in which Moltke attempted to convince the monarch of the need to implement actual universal conscription.

28 See (**49**).

29 The army increases of 1913 were the largest since the founding of the Empire in 1871. Following Russia's decision to modernize and increase her army substantially, the *Heeresvorlage* planned for an additional 135,000 men which would, by 1915, equate to a total peace-time strength of 800,000.

30 See also (77) for a similar British assessment of Russia's increasing strength.

31 Germany's deployment plan (the so-called Schlieffen Plan) relied on Austria's support in the East while German troops defeated France in the first few weeks of the war.

1917 onwards, most likely be fitted out and equipped in everything in the modern way, and which, thanks to its 3½- and 4½-year service and its budgets for war strength, will already be prepared in peace-time to cross the border in the shortest space of time, possibly even without prior declaration of war.

We must not close our eyes to these facts which are so unfavourable for us!

According to my dutiful opinion it is high time that we train every capable German man for military service if we do not want one day to be accused of not having done everything to protect the German Empire and the German race. For there cannot be any more serious doubt about the fact that a future war will be about the existence [*Sein oder Nichtsein*] of the German people.[32]

[...] I consider this measure, the implementation of general conscription, far more practical than the introduction of a 2½- or 3-year service in our army. [...]

BA-MA, BArch RH 61/577, No. 95, 'Entwurf eines Schreibens des Chefs des Generalstabs an den Reichskanzler'.[33]

(91) May 1914: Pollio in conversation with Zitzewitz

Pollio advocates preventive war while the Triple Alliance is still strong

The ring which is forming around the Triple Alliance is getting stronger every year and we are calmly looking on! I honestly believe that the years 1917 or 1918 which are generally (*partout, mais partout*) named by the opponents of the Triple Alliance as the date for a military strike [*Losschlagen*] are not just a product of fantasy. They could very well have a real basis. Do we now really wait until the opponents are prepared and ready? Is it not more logical for the Triple Alliance to abandon all pretence of civility and to start a war ourselves which will one day be forced upon us, while there is time? And this is why I ask, completely in the spirit of your great King Friedrich, I believe, when he broke through the iron ring of his opponents in 1756: Why do we not begin the unavoidable war now?[34]

32 For Moltke's demands for preventive war, see also (**92**).

33 Also printed in *Kriegsrüstung und Kriegswirtschaft, Anlagenband*, Document No.65.

34 Waldersee reported on 2 May to Kageneck that Pollio 'regards the situation of

Cited in Wolfgang Foerster, 'Der deutsche und der italienische Generalstab vor dem Weltkriege', *Deutscher Offizier-Bund*, No. 20, 1926, pp. 874–878, pp. 877–878.

(92) May or June 1914: Jagow recalls conversation with Moltke

Moltke demands preventive war

The military superiority of our enemies would [in the next two to three years] be so great that he [Moltke] did not know how we could overcome them. Today we would still be a match for them. In his opinion there was no alternative to making preventive war in order to defeat the enemy while we still stand a chance of victory. The Chief of the General Staff therefore proposed that I should conduct a policy with the aim of provoking a war in the near future.[35]

Cited in John Röhl (ed.), *From Bismarck to Hitler*, Barnes & Noble, London 1970, p. 70.

the Triple Alliance as so serious that he advises one should take an energetic step until in two years time at the latest the ring of opponents is entirely closed'. Cited in Günther Kronenbitter, '*Krieg im Frieden*', Oldenbourg, Munich 2003, p. 443. See also (**89**). Pollio died on 28 June 1914. He was replaced by General Cadorna on 27 July, an 'unknown quantity' (Foerster) for the German and Austrian allies. Although the German military attaché in Rome, Major von Zitzewitz, reported on that day that 'General Cadorna takes on all obligations that Pollio committed to' (and Cadorna wrote to Moltke on 27 July accepting the agreements made by his predecessor), Italy's government did not accept that the *casus foederis* arose from Austria's quarrel with Serbia. As late as 2 August, Moltke stated: 'It is not important if Italy supports us actively with strong forces, but rather, that the Triple Alliance as such appears united in the war. This [goal] is reached with the smallest dispatch of troops imaginable.' Cited in Wolfgang Foerster, 'Der deutsche und der italienische Generalstab vor dem Weltkriege', *Deutscher Offizier-Bund*, No. 20, 1926, pp. 874–878, p. 878. See also Gooch, 'Italy', p. 224.

35 See also Fritz Fischer, *Krieg der Illusionen*, Droste, Düsseldorf 1987, pp. 583–585, and (**90**).

(93) 1 June 1914: Eckardstein's Memoirs

Eckardstein records a conversation with Moltke; German military consider Britain's military strength to be negligible

The General [von Moltke] to whom I relayed my observations which I made during my recent stay in Paris, in particular the highly pressured war-like machinations of the Russian Ambassador Isvolsky, listened to my report with great attention. After I had finished my report, he said literally the following: 'What you have told me is of great interest to me. If only it would finally boil over – we are ready and the sooner the better for us.' I replied to the General that I could not at all imagine that we could at the present moment engage in a war at all, as we and Austria stood politically completely isolated and would in case of war have the entire world against us. [...] When I maintained that England, in case that we forced a march through Belgium by breaking their neutrality, would declare war immediately and would support France not just on the sea, but also on land, he initially shrouded himself in deep silence, but then soon made the following short remark. 'You are also mistaken regarding England; in any case, what she will do in the event of war we can await calmly'.[36]

Hermann von Eckardstein, *Lebenserinnerungen*, 3 vols, Paul List, Leipzig 1921, Vol. III, p. 186.

36 The underestimation of Britain continued right into the war. On 30 August, for example, the Bavarian Crown Prince Rupprecht noted in his diary: '[Falkenhayn] said that 5000 English [troops] had landed in our rear at Oostend. That is fine by us. We'll get them!' Kronprinz Rupprecht von Bayern, *In Treue fest. Mein Kriegstagebuch*, ed. Eugen von Frauenholz, 3 vols, Deutscher Nationalverlag, Munich 1929, Vol. I, p. 72. The French opponent was similarly underestimated. See for example Wenninger's diary entry of 31 July, when rumours of an ultimatum to France led to speculation in the Ministry of War whether this was necessary as France seemed to be shying away from an armed conflict. Wenninger recorded: 'General von Wild says: "Well, we would like to have the brothers take part, too."' Bernd-Felix Schulte, 'Neue Dokumente zum Kriegsausbruch und Kriegsverlauf 1914', *Militärgeschichtliche Mitteilungen*, 25, 1, 1979, p. 140.

(94) 4 June 1914: Lerchenfeld to Hertling

Discussion with Chancellor about missed opportunity for preventive war in 1905

[...] The discussion then moved onto [the topic of] the preventive war that many military men were demanding.[37] I expressed the point of view that the right moment for it had already been missed. The Chancellor confirmed this by identifying the military situation in the year 1905 as the one that would have offered us the greatest chances.[38] But the Kaiser had not waged a preventive war [then] and will not wage one [now].

Ernst Deuerlein (ed.), *Briefwechsel*, 2 vols, Harald Boldt, Boppard am Rhein 1973, No. 97.

(95) 11 June 1914: Nicolson to Hardinge

Germany fears Austrian decline and Russia's growth

[...] Germany is becoming anxious as to the future, as she knows very well that Austria may not exist for any appreciable length of time as a coherent country, and that before long the disintegrating forces in the Dual Monarchy may become seriously operative. She therefore does not look upon Austria as a very strong ally; while, on the other hand, the growth of Russia in all directions is inspiring her with some apprehension. [...][39]

TNA, Nicolson papers, FO 800/374.[40]

37 See for example (**85**), (**90**) and (**91**).

38 It was felt that during and after the Russo-Japanese war Germany would have had a chance to fight successfully against France as Russia was neutralized by her defeat. As a result the Chief of Staff Alfred von Schlieffen demanded preventive war in 1905. See Annika Mombauer, *Helmuth von Moltke*, Cambridge University Press, Cambridge 2001, pp. 44–45.

39 See for example (**78**] and (**85**).

40 Cited in Stephen Schröder, *Die englisch-russische Marinekonvention*, Vandenhoeck & Ruprecht, Göttingen 2004, p. 143.

(96) 16 June 1914: Wenninger to Kress

Ministries of War of Bavaria, Saxony and Württemberg are no longer to receive written reports, but await information by special emissaries

Berlin, 16 June 1914
Confidential

In today's meeting *Generalquartiermeister* Count Waldersee requested that we should refrain from written reports to the Ministries of War. The Ministers of War of the Federal States will be informed orally by special emissaries of the General Staff. In Munich, Colonel Krause will present himself on the 25th of the month.[41]

Bay. HStA Munich, Abt. IV, Mkr. 41.[42]

(97) 16 June 1914: Bethmann Hollweg to Lichnowsky

Russian anti-German press campaign might lead to further calls for arms increases in Germany; Russia well-prepared for war but probably does not want it; guarantee for future peace in Anglo-German cooperation

Very confidential!
Written by own hand!
Berlin, 16 June 1914
D. p.m.

It will not have escaped Your Excellency's notice that the article in *Birchewija Wjedomosti*, which we know to have stemmed from the [Russian] Minister of War, General Suchomlinov, caused a considerable stir in Germany. As a matter of fact, no officially inspired article has probably ever revealed the warlike tendencies of the Russian military faction as recklessly as this press statement does. It is probably written too clumsily to strengthen French chauvinism permanently. However, the repercussions for German public opinion are inescapable and worrying.

41 Quite what the Bavarian Ministry of War was to be informed about is not clear. John Röhl points out that on the same day that this directive was issued, the Kaiser talked to Bethmann Hollweg about preventive war (**97**). He raises the question of whether Waldersee had prior knowledge of the assassination plot, but with no further evidence available this is merely a matter for speculation. See Röhl, *Wilhelm II.*, Vol. 3, p. 1074.

42 I am grateful to John Röhl for making a copy of this document available to me.

If hitherto only the most extreme Pan-Germans and militarists insisted that Russia was deliberately scheming a war of aggression against us, then now calmer politicians are also beginning to incline to that view. The next result will be a demand for renewed, immediate, extensive strengthening of the Army. This will, given how things are with us, produce competition with the navy, which refuses to be short-changed when anything is done for the army. Since, as I mention *very confidentially*, His Majesty the Kaiser is already quite set in these views, I fear that the summer and autumn will see a fresh outburst of armaments fever.[43]

Even though the uncertainty of conditions in Russia makes it difficult to discover the real aims of Russian policy with any certainty, and although, disposed as we are politically, we must consider that Russia, more than all the Great European Powers, is most prepared to run the risk of a great warlike adventure, nevertheless I still do not think that Russia is planning a war against us soon. She wishes rather – and we cannot reproach her for it – in case of a renewed eruption of the Balkan crisis, secured by more extensive military armaments to be able to act more forcefully than during the last troubles in the Balkans. Whether there is then a European conflagration will depend entirely on the attitudes of Germany and England. If we act together as joint guarantors of peace in Europe, and in doing so are neither hampered by the engagements of the Triple Alliance nor of the Triple Entente, *so far as we pursue that aim from the start according to a jointly conceived plan*, it will be possible to avert the war. Otherwise a minor conflict of interests between Russia and Austria-Hungary may light the war-torch. [...]

It is obvious that more violent agitation by German chauvinists and armament fanatics will hamper such Anglo-German cooperation just as much as an attitude by the British Cabinet which secretly supports French and Russian chauvinism. Germany will never be able to give up on a corresponding growth of her army in relation to the growth of her population. [...]

It is certainly gratifying that Sir Edward Grey firmly denied in the House of Commons those rumours of an English-Russian naval agreement and that his denial was emphasized in the *Westminster Gazette*.[44] If these rumours had turned out to be true, even if only to the extent

43 For an assessment of Wilhelm II's warlike mood in June 1914, see Röhl, *Wilhelm II.*, Vol. 3, p. 1074. On 20 June, Wilhelm II suggested a preventive war, as he and his military advisers had done previously. The banker Max Warburg recorded his conversation with him: 'Russia's armaments [and] the extensive Russian railway building were in his opinion preparations for a war which will break out in 1916. [...] Besieged by his worries the Kaiser even speculated if it were not better to strike, rather than to wait.' Warburg's advice was to wait as Germany was only increasing in strength each year. Ibid, p. 1074.

44 See also (87) and (99).

that the English and Russian navies planned cooperation in a future war against Germany – similar to the agreements which England made with France at the time of the Morocco crisis – it would not only have highly agitated Russian and French chauvinism, but public opinion here would also have reacted in justified alarm that would have stimulated a navy scare and a renewed poisoning of relations with England which have slowly been improving. In the midst of the nervous tense state in which Europe has been for the last few years, the further consequences would have been unforeseeable. In any case, the idea of a common English-German effort to guarantee peace would have been fatefully endangered from the very beginning by emerging complications. [...]

DD, No. 3.

(98) 24 June 1914: Pollio to Italian Ministry of War

Chief of Staff warns that Austria has nearly as many troops on Italy's border as on Russia's and that Italy needs to increase her military capacity to be able to meet Austria's potential threat

Under the current political and military circumstances, it is a duty to explain to this Ministry the considerations which emerge both from the Austro-Hungarian military preparation and consolidation, which are monitored closely by these headquarters, and also from the tendencies of the neighbouring Monarchy which manifest themselves through several symptoms about which one can have no doubts. For years Austria has methodically and restlessly been developing a wide programme of military measures at different levels on our borders: the political relations between Italy and the Monarchy, so much improved in these last few years, have done nothing to diminish this impressive activity. [...]

As can be seen from irrefutable documents, Austria, by doing so, aims at securing her position as far as we are concerned, in order to have, if necessary, freedom of movement in the event of new developments in the Balkans. [...]

At present Austria, having seen her plans to expand in the Balkans frustrated by events, aims, however, to assert her supremacy over Albania. This supremacy has been desired and prearranged, at least for the time being, mostly in the event of a military intervention in that region and is aimed, more than at conquering new land, at consolidating Austrian prestige and political influence over the new State.[45] [...]

45 In December 1913, the new Albanian state had been formed, following the Second Balkan War.

It seems that so much violence stems from the opinion that this is the best way to discourage and scare us to the point of letting the events in Albania happen under the exclusive aegis of Vienna. Unfortunately, Italy is the only nation that Austria feels can be treated this way. This mirrors exactly the Austrian mentality, which is narrow-minded and lacking in feelings, modelled on the idea of bullying those who are weak or those *who pretend to be so*. And this simplistic and brutal course of action, especially in a country such as Austria where only the irresponsible factors prevail, are fed and supported by an ancient legacy of resentment towards us, in the way the Slavs, the aristocracy and the clergy feel and, most of all, in the way the military authorities feel. Despite a significant change in the way the military elements think, it cannot be denied that, especially among those who are subordinate to the Hereditary Archduke [Franz Ferdinand] whose malevolent intentions towards Italy were never hidden,[46] there still persists a barely repressed feeling of hostility which, should something happen, could reveal itself in a tangible way. And I am firmly of the opinion, comforted by my knowledge of the neighbouring Monarchy, that it is not by acquiescing that we will obtain the approval and respect of Austria, but by showing that we are strong and that entering agreements with us is necessary, more than ever, for the future of the Dual Monarchy. [...]

Under such circumstances, in regard to the consequences of the military preparations, I think that it is my duty to show to Your Eminence the advantage I would have from knowing what our Government thinks of the various intentions towards us of the Austro-Hungarian Government and in which way this Government plans to act in case the divergence of interests on the part of both States would definitely become apparent.

And this is not so much a worry for the present, because, after all, the old Emperor has fairly positive feelings towards Italy and has shown himself to be, even in recent times, averse to war. [...]

Certainly I am not inclined to believe that, in spite of the seriousness of the local situation in Albania and the excesses of the language of the Austrian press, there could be immediate and dangerous repercussions to the overall relationship between Italy and Austria.

However, keeping in mind the Austrian mentality which, not letting itself be influenced by the political fluctuations, drives that Government to continuously devolve large amounts of money to the ongoing plans against us, and keeping in mind also the impulsivity of our people as regards Austria, I have tried, up until now, to do my best to reach, as far as that is concerned, the required degree of preparation. However, the means placed at our disposal by the Army are now so scarce that they are not enough to reach a minimum preparation even close to what Austria has achieved on our borders. And I have no doubt that only when we

46 See (**104**).

reach the above minimum degree of preparation will our policy have the necessary strength to support effectively our rights vis-à-vis Austria. And I believe that only then would peace be guaranteed in that area, because Austria, due to her national character, would show herself in every way more respectful of our dignity as a great nation than she has been recently.[47]

Cited in Massimo Mazzetti, *L'esercito italiano nella triplice alleanza*, Naples 1974, pp. 409–412.

(99) 24 June 1914: Grey to Goschen

Anglo-Russian Naval Agreement 1914

No. 197
Foreign Office, June 24, 1914

I saw the German Ambassador [Lichnowsky] to-day, before he went for ten days or so to Germany.

He spoke at some length about my reply in the House of Commons the other day, referring evidently to the reply I had given to a question about an alleged new naval agreement with Russia, though the Ambassador did not mention such an agreement by name. He said that the statement that I had made had given great satisfaction in Berlin, and had had a reassuring effect.[48] There was anxiety in Germany about the warlike intentions of Russia. The Ambassador himself did not share this anxiety, as he did not believe in the hostile intentions of Russia. But there had been an article in the *Novoe Vremya* lately very hostile in tone to Germany. The Pan-Germanic element was really apprehensive, and, though Herr von Bethmann Hollweg did not share these views any more than Prince Lichnowsky himself, he did feel that there was danger of a new armaments scare growing up in Germany. Herr von Bethmann Hollweg had instructed Prince Lichnowsky to tell me that he hoped, if new developments or emergencies arose in the Balkans, that they would be discussed as frankly between Germany and ourselves as the difficulties that arose during the last Balkan crisis, and that we should be able to keep in as close touch.

I said to Prince Lichnowsky that I felt some difficulty in talking to him about our relations with France and Russia. It was quite easy for me to

47 This was Pollio's last word on the subject of the Triple Alliance, as he died on 28 June 1914 of a heart attack. See Massimo Mazzetti, *L'esercito italiano nella triplice alleanza*, Edizioni Scientifiche Italiane, Naples 1974, p. 413.

48 See (97).

say, and quite true, that there was no alliance; no agreement committing us to action; and that all the agreements of that character that we had with France and Russia had been published. On the other hand, I did not wish to mislead the Ambassador by making him think that the relations that we had with France and Russia were less cordial and intimate than they really were. Though we were not bound by engagement as allies, we did from time to time talk as intimately as allies. But this intimacy was not used for aggression against Germany. France, as he knew, was now most peacefully disposed.

The Ambassador cordially endorsed this.

Russia, as he himself had said, was not pursuing an aggressive anti-German policy, or thinking of making war on Germany. It was quite true that Russia was much interested, and often anxious, concerning developments in the Balkan peninsula; but anti-German feeling was not the motive of this anxiety. For instance, when the Emperor of Russia had visited Rumania the other day, the Russian Government had not talked to us about the visit as a matter of policy, or tried in any way to bring us into it as a matter of policy. I most cordially reciprocated what Herr von Bethmann Hollweg had said, that as new developments arose we should talk as frankly as before, and discuss them in the same spirit as we had discussed things during the Balkan crisis. Let us go on as we had left off when that crisis was over. I was most anxious not to lose any of the ground that had been gained then for good relations between us.

The British Government belonged to one group of Powers, but did not do so in order to make difficulties greater between the two European groups; on the contrary, we wished to prevent any questions that arose from throwing the groups, as such, into opposition. In the case, for instance, of the German military command in Constantinople,[49] which had caused us some anxiety early this year, we had done all we could to ensure its being discussed between Germany and Russia direct and not made the subject of formal representations in Constantinople by one group, and thereby an occasion for throwing the two groups, as such, into opposition, and making them draw apart.

Prince Lichnowsky cordially agreed. He said that our being in the group we were was a good thing, and he regarded our intimacy with France and Russia without any misgiving, because he was sure that it was used for peace.

I said that he was quite justified in this view. We should never pursue an aggressive policy, and if ever there was a European war, and we took part in it, it could not be on the aggressive side, for public opinion was against that.

Prince Lichnowsky expressed, without qualification, that the view he

49 See (**66**), (**68**) and (**69**).

held of our intentions was the same as the one that I had just explained to him.

In conclusion, he spoke again of the apprehension of his Government lest a new armaments scare should grow up in Germany.[50] He added that he had frankly told Herr von Bethmann Hollweg that there were certain things that would make friendly relations with us impossible.

I presume that he meant by this an addition to the German Naval Law, but I did not press him on the point.

I said that I realised that our being in one group, and on intimate terms with France and Russia, had been used in past years in Germany to work up feeling for expenditure on armaments, and there was always the risk that that might be done again. I sincerely hoped, however, that too much importance need not be attached to articles in the *Novoe Vremya*, for, just as he had had to read an article of which I had not heard before, an article hostile to Germany, so, as recently as last night, I had had to read an article from the *Novoe Vremya* containing a violent attack on us in connection with the Anglo-Persian oil concession.

In the course of conversation I also said, in order to emphasise the point that Russia did not pursue a really anti-German policy, that there were three persons through whom we learnt the disposition of the Russian Government: one was Count Benckendorff, who, I was sure, Prince Lichnowsky would recognise was not anti-German; another was M. Sazonov, who was sometimes anxious, owing to attacks made on him in the Russian press, as to whether the Triple Entente was not contrasting unfavourably with the Triple Alliance, and proving to be a less solid force in diplomacy, but who never showed any indication of desiring to use the Triple Entente for aggressive policy against Germany, and who used it solely as an equipoise; the third person was the Emperor of Russia, and, as I was sure Prince Lichnowsky would know, he did not favour an aggressive policy against Germany, or, indeed, against anyone.[51]

BD, XI, No. 4.

50 See (**97**).

51 For Prince Lichnowsky's account of this conversation see DD, No. 5.

(100) 25 June 1914: Grey to Buchanan

Rumours of Anglo-Russian Naval Agreement

No. 243.
Foreign Office, June 25, 1914.

I observed to Count Benckendorff to-day that immense harm was being done by the persistent reports about a naval agreement between Russia and England. I heard that Germans like Professor [Theodor] Schiemann were receiving information from friends in Paris and St. Petersburg that, in spite of all I had said in the House of Commons, there was a naval agreement, and it was even assumed that it included a bargain about the opening of the Straits. No doubt the information came from unofficial people, who did not know the facts, and assumed them to be other than they were. A question was to be addressed to me in the House of Commons on the subject of the opening of the Straits to ships of war, and I intended to reply that this had not been discussed for the last five years, and that the treaties remained in force, but that from time to time, though not within the last five years, the question of the conditions on which the Straits might be opened to warships had been discussed with us. As Count Benckendorff would remember, we did go into this question with M. Isvolsky when he was in London in 1908. We had not discussed it since then. The persistent reports would do great harm in Germany. They might lead to a new 'Novelle' in connection with the German fleet, and they might impair our good relations with Germany, which had improved very much during the last Balkan crisis, and which I wished to maintain. I told Count Benckendorff the gist of my conversation yesterday with Prince Lichnowsky as to our relations with France and Germany.[52] I knew that Prince Lichnowsky held the same view as I did about these relations.

Count Benckendorff entirely endorsed what I had told him that I had said to Prince Lichnowsky, and said that he was very glad that I had said it, as Prince Lichnowsky would make excellent use of it.[53]

BD, XI, No. 5.

52 See (**99**). See also (**128**), note 49.

53 Count Benckendorff's account of this conversation has been published in Benno von Siebert, *Diplomatische Aktenstücke*, De Gruyte, Berlin and Leipzig 1921, p. 824.

(101) 26 June 1914: Hoyos to Pallavicini

Discussions about alliance with Rumania

I have the honour of sending you on behalf of the Minister [Berchtold] as an enclosure a copy of a private letter by Czernin.[54] The Minister replied to him that we share his views about the Rumanian danger, but that we could not believe in his cure-for-all[55] about which you know. In the meantime a long memorandum for Berlin is being drafted which is to be sent soon,[56] and the Minister is doing his utmost to open Tschirschky's eyes. Hopefully we will decide upon a different political orientation when this final attempt to maintain relations with Rumania has failed. [...]

ÖUA, VIII, No. 9926.[57]

(102) 27 June 1914: Bertie Memorandum

Rumours of Anglo-Russian Naval Talks; Anglo-German détente; Russia's military preparedness; Home Rule Question

Written at Paris 27/6 from notes made on journey from London to Paris June 25th.

I had an interview with Grey this afternoon at the House of Commons in his private room.

He is much exercised at a leakage which has occurred somewhere in regard to what has been represented to the German Government to be a Naval Convention or alliance between England and Russia.[58]

The German Ambassador has spoken to Grey on the subject of the

54 Copy of the letter, dated 22 June 1914, in ÖUA, VIII, No. 9902.

55 H. Bertil A. Petersson speculates that this was most likely trying to add Rumania and Serbia to the Triple Alliance. H. Bertil A. Petersson, 'Das österreichisch-ungarische Memorandum an Deutschland vom 5. Juli 1914', *Scandia*, 29, 1963, pp. 138–190, p. 184, note 56.

56 See (**117**).

57 For more details see Petersson, 'Das österreichisch-ungarische Memorandum', p. 184.

58 The secret information was leaked by a German spy in the Russian embassy in London. For details about the Anglo-Russian naval talks see Steiner and Neilson, *Britain*, pp. 129ff.; Stephen Schröder, *Die englisch-russische Marinekonvention*. See also (**87**) and (**99**).

reported agreement under instructions from the German Government.[59] Bethmann-Hollweg credits Grey's denial in the House of Commons of the existence of any Alliance or Convention and so does the German Emperor, but information of its reality has reached the German Government from a Russian Grand Duke at St. Petersburg and from Paris.

Grey is inclined to suspect Isvolsky or even Poincaré who is very indiscreet to newspaper people.

Bethmann Hollweg says that the Pan-Germanists will make use of the reports of such an Agreement to agitate for additions to the German Fleet which is most regrettable just as the relations between Germany and England have so much improved. Grey wishes me to inquire of Isvolsky whether he has mentioned the subject to any outsider.

I said that Isvolsky is such a liar that he would deny anything that it might suit him to repudiate. I might pump Viviani but the Quai d'Orsay might be the divulging culprit. As however the naval conversations with Russia are not to be of any binding character and the arrangements under them would only come into force in the contingency of the British and Russian Governments agreeing to put them into force in certain circumstances not defined it might be an advantage that while England's position would be one of freedom from actual engagement, the impression should exist in Germany that in the event of a conflict between Germany and Russia and France acting in alliance a British Fleet would give active aid to Russia. It was fear of British naval intervention that prevented Germany from going to war with France about Morocco. Yes, said Grey, but we are on good terms with Germany now and we desire to avoid a revival of friction with her, and we wish to discourage the French from provoking Germany.

I reminded Grey that the German Government in order to obtain money from the Reichstag for an increase in the German Fleet had invented an encircling policy on the part of England. If they desired to continue the naval competition with us they would find some pretext such as an alleged Anglo-Russian agreement. The truth is that whereas formerly the German Government had aggressive intentions under the impression that Russia was not prepared and was not willing to come to the aid of France unconditionally, that France was in a weak condition and that England would stand aloof, they are now genuinely alarmed at the military preparations in Russia, the prospective increase in her military forces and particularly at the intended construction at the instance of the French Government and with French money of strategic railways to converge on the German frontier. They will enable the Russian Government to place an enormous military force on that frontier. Whether the Russian Government will be able to provide all the

59 See (**97**).

requirements for the troops and continue the supplies and find competent Generals is a debatable question.

The French people do not desire war. They are afraid of the calamities which would result even from a successful war. What might bring about a conflict would be a further increase in the military strength of Germany with which France having a much smaller population could not compete in the long run. This might make the French desperate and an incident might bring about a conflict.

Grey thinks that the German Government are in a peaceful mood and they are very anxious to be on good terms with England, a mood which he wishes to encourage.

The German Ambassador asked whether H.M. Government would if a fresh crisis arose in the Balkans be willing to continue the consultations with the German Government which had lately so much contributed to the avoidance of conflict between the Great Powers. Grey said certainly so far as it might be possible without a separation from the present relations between England, France and Russia.

I supposed[,] and Grey said correctly, that he would continue the intimate conversations and consultations with France and to a lesser degree with Russia and consult with Germany so far as it might be expedient so as to be a connecting link between Germany and the Triple Entente and a restraint on the hastiness of Austria and Italy.

Grey is angry with the French Government on the subject of the French arms traffic through Jibuti to Abyssinia and to the Somali Mahdi.

He is very anxious about the state of affairs in Persia and the intemperate conduct of the Russian Officials and officers in that country, the northern portion of which they treat as though it was Russian territory. Sazonow has no grasp of subjects or authority over Russian officials in Persia and is often obstinate and tiresome and raises unnecessary questions in Balkan affairs.

I told Grey that the French are perturbed at the internal state of England resulting from the Home Rule Controversy[60] and that the Viviani ministry would very likely fall in the Autumn through a combination of the Unified Socialists who are hostile to the three years' military service law[61] and the Centre & Right who are in favour of it. [...]

---

60 In 1914 the controversy over granting Irish 'home rule' led to bitter debates in Parliament and fears of civil war in Ireland.

61 In order to meet the challenge posed by Germany's larger population and their army increases of 1912, the three-year service law was agreed by the Chamber in the middle of 1913, extending military service by one year. The Socialist victory in the elections in April to May 1914 threatened the Three Year Law, and even Joffre's position, who would have been replaced by General Maurice Sarrail in the autumn, had it not been for the outbreak of war. Roy A. Prete, *Strategy and Command. The Anglo-French Coalition on the Western Front,*

Grey is, he says, much more anxious about the prospective Railway Strike in England than concerning the home rule question.[62] [...]

TNA, FO 800/171.

1914, McGill-Queen's University Press, Montreal et al., 2009. p. 31. For details on the Three Year Law, see Gerd Krumeich, *Armaments and Politics in France on the Eve of the First World War*, Leamington Spa 1984.

62 Since 1904 Grey had been a director of the North-Eastern Railway Company.

Part II
The July Crisis

Introduction

In view of the tensions of the years before July 1914, it is perhaps not surprising that war would eventually result from such international rivalries, although as we have seen, such a development was arguably far from inevitable. Moreover, a general war would need a trigger, and would depend on a certain amount of desire for war in favour of diplomacy which had so far ensured that a great war had been avoided. The trigger for such a conflict was provided by the murder of the Austrian heir to the throne, Archduke Franz Ferdinand and his wife in Sarajevo on 28 June 1914 (**106**). The assassination has often been described as the spark that would set light to a continent that was riddled with international tensions. However, even in July 1914 a European war was not inevitable, as the following documents show. Right until the last moment, some European statesmen were desperately trying to avoid an escalation of the crisis by advocating mediation, while others did everything in their power to make ensure that a war would break out.

Samuel R. Williamson and Russel Van Wyk have convincingly pointed to the role of contingency and the importance of the decisions taken by individuals during July 1914 to show that a different outcome to the crisis is easily imaginable:

> The events of July 1914 provide the historian with ample examples of the role of contingency in human affairs. If Princip had missed the archduke or had killed only his wife; if Pašić had jettisoned Apis; if Wilhelm II had already departed on his North Sea cruise before Hoyos arrived; if Tisza had continued to resist Berchtold; if the Italian indiscretions about Habsburg action had become public;[1] if Poincaré had been more

1 The German ambassador in Rome had hinted in conversation with San Giuliano that Austria-Hungary was intending to make far-reaching demands of Serbia,

restrained in his enthusiasm for Russia; if the Russians had worried less about Pan-Slavism and more about the future of the Romanovs; or if actual civil war had broken out in Dublin – any one of these possibilities could have changed the situation dramatically.

> Furthermore, it is important to note the significance of personalities as contingent factors. If any one of these leaders had acted differently (save Cadorna), he might well have interrupted the slide to war: if, for example, Pašić had exposed Apis and accepted a Habsburg investigation into the assassination; or if Bethmann had reversed course when the Habsburgs delayed so long in their move against Belgrade and warned Vienna to rethink its policies.[2]

The documents which follow provide evidence that it would indeed have been possible for some of these contingent factors to have played out differently, and while it is futile to speculate 'what if', it is at least important to realize that war was not the only possible outcome in July 1914.

It is of course important to consider the background of the assassination, and the trail leads to Serbia, to Apis and Pašić – the former, a high-ranking officer in the Serbian military, a secret conspirator who helped organise the assassins, the latter aware of the plan, however vaguely, but too worried about Apis' influence in Serbia to raise the alarm.[3] However, in order to understand why the crisis escalated into full-scale war, we must look at Vienna and Berlin in the first instance, for it was here that war (that is to say a war between Austria-Hungary and Serbia) was consciously risked and planned. As Leopold Baron von Andrian-Werburg recalled after the war had ended: '*We* started the war, not the Germans and even less the Entente – that I know.' He continued:

> I have the distinct impression that the war was decided on by that circle of younger talented diplomats who formed Berchtold's political council, who influenced him strongly and who, if they were – as they were in this case – in agreement, decided things. Musulin, the impetuous chatterbox, who, when the prospects were good in the war, used to call himself 'the man who caused the war', Alek Hoyos, Fritz Szápary [...] they made the

---

while Austria-Hungary had hoped to present Italy, like all the other great powers, with a *fait accompli*. (**164**)

2 Samuel R. Williamson Jr and Russel van Wyk (eds), *July 1914. Soldiers, Statesmen, and the Coming of the Great War*, Bedford St Martin's, Boston, New York, 2003, p. 259.

3 For a detailed study of the background of the assassination, see Christopher Clark, *The Sleepwalkers. How Europe Went to War in 1914*, Allen Lane, London 2012.

war. I myself was in lively agreement with the basic idea that only a war could save Austria. As the world situation was then, I am also quite sure that, two or three years later, war for Austria's existence would have been forced on us by Serbia, Rumania and Russia, and under conditions which would make a successful defence far more difficult than at that time.[4]

France, Russia, Britain and Italy entered the stage much later in July 1914, when most decisions had already been taken, and consequently the documents that follow reflect the comparative silence from Paris, St Petersburg and London until the Austro-Hungarian ultimatum was delivered on 23 June (**180**), (**191**).[5] Until this point, most European statesmen had been deliberately kept in the dark about the nature of their plan by the decision-makers in Vienna and Berlin, although the ultimatum was not a complete surprise to them when it was finally delivered.[6]

When the war was barely a month old, the former British Ambassador to Vienna, Sir Maurice de Bunsen, explained the extent of the secrecy exercised vis-à-vis the foreign representatives at Vienna:

The delivery at Belgrade on the 23rd July of the Austrian note to Serbia was preceded by a period of absolute silence at the Ball[haus]platz. Except Herr von Tschirschky who must have been aware of the tenour [*sic*], if not of the actual words of the note, none of my colleagues were

4 Cited in Fritz Fellner, 'Austria-Hungary', in Keith M. Wilson (ed.), *Decisions for War, 1914*, UCL Press, London 1995, pp. 9–25, p. 14.

5 For further information on the diplomatic events of the July Crisis see, *inter alia*, Imanuel Geiss (ed.), *July 1914. The Outbreak of the First World War. Selected Documents*, Scribner, London 1967; Luigi Albertini, *The Origins of the War of 1914*, 3 vols, Eng. transl., Oxford University Press, Oxford 1952–1957; Fritz Fischer, *War of Illusions. German Policies from 1911–1914*, Norton, London 1975; James Joll and Gordon Martel, *The Origins of the First World War*, Longman, 3rd edn, London 2007; Keith M. Wilson (ed.), *Decisions for War, 1914*, London 1995; David Stevenson, *Armaments and the Coming of War*, Clarendon, Oxford 1996; John W. Langdon, *July 1914. The Long Debate 1918–1990*, Berg, New York, Oxford 1991; David Stevenson, *The Outbreak of the First World War*, Macmillan, London 1997. Further references can be found in Annika Mombauer, *Helmuth von Moltke*, Cambridge University Press, Cambridge, 2001, Chapter 4. The most recent and comprehensive account is Christopher Clark's *The Sleepwalkers. How Europe went to War in 1914*, Allen Lane, London 2012.

6 Flotow's indiscretion in conversations with San Giuliano between 14 and 16 July had given some of the game away, and the French military secret service were also aware of the Austro-Hungarian intention to issue an unacceptable ultimatum. See Stefan Schmidt, *Frankreichs Außenpolitik in der Julikrise 1914*, Oldenbourg, Munich 2007, p. 68 and (**169**), (**179**). Bunsen was able to report on 16 July that Vienna was planning a move against Serbia (**161**).

allowed to see through the veil. On the 22nd and 23rd July M. Dumaine, French Ambassador, had long interviews with Baron Macchio, one of the Under-Secretaries of State for Foreign Affairs, by whom he was left under the impression that the words of warning he had been instructed to speak to the Austro-Hungarian Government had not been unavailing, and that the note which was being drawn up would be found to contain nothing with which a self-respecting State need hesitate to comply. At the second of these interviews he was not even informed that the note was at that very moment being presented at Belgrade, or that it would be published in Vienna on the following morning.

Count Forgach, the other Under-Secretary of State, had indeed been good enough to confide to me on the same day the true character of the note, and the fact of its presentation about the time we were speaking.

So little had the Russian Ambassador [Schebeko] been made aware of what was preparing that he actually left Vienna on a fortnight's leave of absence about the 20th July. He had only been absent a few days when events compelled him to return. It might have been supposed that Duc Avarna, Ambassador of the Allied Italian Kingdom, which was bound to be so closely affected by fresh complications in the Balkans, would have been taken fully into the confidence of Count Berchtold during this critical time. In point of fact his Excellency was left completely in the dark, no doubt for the good reason that Italy would certainly have rejected the policy embodied in the note of July 23rd if she had been invited to endorse it. As for myself, no indication was given me by Count Berchtold of the impending storm, and it was from a private source that I received on the 15th July the forecast of what was about to happen which I embodied in my telegram No. 85[7] of the following day.[8]

In Vienna, the official reaction to the assassination was indignant outrage, but this outward appearance was in stark contrast to the privately held thoughts of some important decision-makers. Franz Ferdinand had not been universally popular, on account of his spiky character and his political views. The Germans within the Dual Monarchy had considered him to be too Slavophile, the Slavs too German, and the Hungarians too Austrian.[9] Moreover, some of the decision-makers in Vienna had been keen for a 'reckoning' with Serbia for some time, a move that had always been opposed by the Archduke, and considered this a golden opportunity. It is a tragic irony that Franz Ferdinand, whose assassination would

7 See (**161**).

8 BD, XI, No. 676, de Bunsen to Sir Edward Grey, letter of 1 September 1914.

9 Jürgen Angelow, *Der Weg in die Urkastrophe. Der Zerfall des alten Europa 1900–1914*, Be.bra Verlag, Berlin 2010, p. 118. See (**109**).

provide the pretext for war, had in his lifetime opposed war. He had even attempted to limit the influence of the General Staff (**205**).[10] For its Chief, Franz Conrad von Hötzendorf, the Archduke's demise offered a welcome excuse for a war against Serbia. He still regretted what he (as well as his German counterpart Helmuth von Moltke) had considered the 'missed opportunity' for a 'reckoning with Serbia' in 1909.[11] Other so-called 'hawks' in Vienna were also keen to seize the opportunity of waging a war against Serbia whose pan-Slav agitation threatened to undermine the cohesion of the Austro-Hungarian empire (**117**), (**126**).[12]

In Berlin, the possibility of a Balkan crisis was greeted favourably by military and political decision-makers, for it was felt that such a crisis would ensure that Austria would definitely become involved in a resulting conflict (unlike during the earlier Moroccan crises, for example). When the Austrian envoy Count Alexander (Alek) Hoyos arrived in Berlin to ascertain the powerful ally's position in case Austria made demands of Serbia, he was assured that Germany would support Austria unconditionally, even if she chose to go to war over the assassination, and even if such a war were to turn into a European war. This was Germany's so-called 'blank cheque' to Vienna (**119**), (**120**), (**130**).

While most decision-makers in Vienna and Berlin did not actually want a *European* war, the available evidence shows that they were certainly willing to risk it. In Vienna, they were motivated by a growing awareness of Austria-Hungary's increasing loss of prestige and by a fatalism of what the future would hold which meant they preferred an 'end with terror to a terror that never ends'. In Berlin, the political decision-makers had been encouraged to accept the risk of a European war by Germany's leading military advisers who had advocated war 'the sooner the better' on many occasions and who had assured the politicians that Germany stood a good chance of defeating her enemies. Germany's military leaders had been conjuring up the image of a Russia that could still be defeated

austro-hungarian war hunger

10 Ibid., p. 118.

11 Franz Conrad von Hötzendorf, *Aus meiner Dienstzeit 1906–1918,* 5 vols, Rikola, Vienna, Leipzig, Munich 1921–1925, Vol. I, p. 165.

12 On the decision for war in Vienna, see for example Günther Kronenbitter, *'Krieg im Frieden'*, Oldenbourg, Munich 2003, *passim* and Samuel Williamson Jr, *Austria-Hungary and the Origins of the First World War*, Macmillan, London 1991, *passim.*

by Germany at this time, but that in future would be too strong to be taken on successfully (**181**).[13] Their fatalistic views were shared by their military colleagues in Rome and Vienna, and in London and Paris, too, there was growing concern of Russia's predicted future strength (**163**), (**174**). Neither France nor Britain felt they could abandon Russia for fear of what would happen if she emerged victorious from a future war.

On the road to war which followed the assassination, the Hoyos Mission was a crucial juncture at which the 'basic idea that only a war could bring Austria's salvation' became accepted in Vienna.[14] Armed with such reassurances from Germany, the Austro-Hungarian Joint Ministerial Council decided on 7 July to issue an ultimatum to Serbia, after the Austrian Premier István Tisza objected to a more immediate strike. This intervention influenced the subsequent timetable significantly. The ultimatum was designed to be deliberately unacceptable, and its wording would not be revealed to anyone but the German ally until the day it was presented in Belgrade. (**134**). The time limit for Serbia's answer was deliberately kept short to avoid the possibility of negotiations (**144**), (**146**). However, much time would pass before the ultimatum was finally delivered to Belgrade: first the harvest had to be completed, for which most soldiers of the Dual Monarchy were on harvest leave. Moreover, it was decided to wait until the state visit of Raymond Poincaré, the French president, to Russia was over, so that the two allies would not have a chance to coordinate their response to Austria's ultimatum (**146**), (**154**).[15] Throughout these early days of the crisis, Vienna kept Berlin informed of their

13 See Mombauer, *Moltke*, pp. 121ff.

14 The words of Leopold von Andrian-Werburg, cited in John Leslie, 'Österreich-Ungarn vor dem Kriegsausbruch', in Ralph Melville et al. (eds), *Deutschland und Europa in der Neuzeit*. Halbband, Stuttgart 1988, pp. 661–684, p. 668. For details of the Hoyos Mission see Chapter 6, pp. 183ff.

15 The state visit had been planned since the spring of 1914. On 16 July, President Poincaré, Premier Viviani and the political director of the Quai d'Orsay Pierre de Margerie departed from Dunkirk, and would only return to French soil on 29 July, leaving the running of foreign affairs in the hands of the inexperienced Minister of Justice Jean-Baptiste Bienvenu-Martin (**233**). French and Russian political leaders had conducted a number of visits in the preceding years: in 1912, Poincaré visited Russia to discuss matters relating to Italy, Grand Duke Nikolaevitch attended French military manoeuvres in the same year, and Joffre made a similar visit to Russia in 1913. Roy A. Prete, *Strategy and Command. The Anglo-French Coalition on the Western Front, 1914*, McGill-Queen's University Press, Montreal et al., 2009, p. 6.

plans, while to the outside world, they both gave the impression of calm, even sending their main decision-makers on holiday to keep up this illusion – Wilhelm II considered this to be 'childish', but it was arguably much more devious than that.[16] It certainly put the other powers off the scent. As Jean Jacques Becker has put it, 'it is hard to imagine the leaders of the country indulging in the joys of tourism [...] having plotted the outbreak of a European war', and yet, this was the case for Austria-Hungary and Germany, where under the pretence of holidaying a war was plotted behind the scenes.[17]

The Italian alliance partner was also deliberately kept in the dark, save for Flotow's indiscretions (**140**), (**197**), (**210**), (**225**). It is due to this deception that the other major powers did not play a role in the July Crisis until 23 July, when the ultimatum was finally presented in Belgrade (**180**), (**191**). While increasingly suspicious of her intentions and aware that some kind of action was being planned, the governments of the other European powers expected that Austria-Hungary would seek redress, but they were largely unaware of the secret plotting in Vienna and Berlin. In the capitals of the other Great Powers, Vienna's outrage at this act of terrorism was certainly shared, and it was expected that she would demand redress of some kind. Both Russia and France, however, denied that Serbia was in any way linked to the assassination. Sazonov stated confidently that 'no proof that the Serbian government had tolerated such machinations would ever be produced', and Poincaré similarly denied that Belgrade had been involved in the plot.[18] They were taken by surprise by the severity of the demands made of Serbia and suspected immediately that Vienna's decision-makers were determined to provoke a war.

The Serbian response to the 'unacceptable' ultimatum astonished everyone (**227**). The Belgrade Government agreed to all but one of the demands, making Austria's predetermined decision to turn down Serbia's response look suspicious in the eyes of those European powers who wanted to try to preserve the peace. Even Kaiser Wilhelm II now thought that every reason to go to war had gone (**276**). Britain suggested (repeatedly) that the issue could be resolved at the conference table, but her mediation proposals were only given

16 (**144**). See also (**142**), (**171**).

17 Becker cited in John Keiger, *Raymond Poincaré*, Cambridge University Press, Cambridge 1997, p. 165.

18 Clark, *The Sleepwalkers*, p. 409.

half-hearted support by Berlin and not taken up by Vienna (**204**), (**225**), (**260**).

Instead, from 23 July the crisis was dominated by attempts by France and Russia as well as the Alliance to get British Foreign Secretary Sir Edward Grey to declare Britain's hand. Britain, at this point still preoccupied with events in Ireland, refused until the very end of July to commit to her allies, in an effort to try to prevent an escalation of the crisis. It has been argued that Britain could have played a more decisive role by declaring her intentions to support France earlier, and that the outcome of the crisis might have been different as a result. According to this point of view, if Germany's decision-makers had known earlier and with certainty that Britain would be involved in a war on the side of the Entente, they would have accepted mediation proposals and would have counselled peace in Vienna. Certainly Berlin worked on the (misconceived) assumption that British neutrality was possible, and even likely (**148**). However, the British cabinet was divided over a British involvement in a European war, and no definite decision to support France was possible until Germany's violation of neutral Belgium provided Grey with a much-needed reason for joining the war. By then, he was so convinced that Britain needed to declare her support for France and Russia that he threatened to resign over the issue (**388**).

In the crucial last days of July, Britain's decision-makers were divided on how to deal with the threat of war on the continent and torn between their fear of a victorious Germany and a victorious Russia, if the latter managed to win the war without British support. We can of course only speculate if an earlier declaration of British involvement would have changed the minds of decision-makers in Vienna or Berlin and made them more inclined to accept mediation instead of war. Nonetheless, the ambivalence of Sir Edward Grey's policy should not really be seen as a cause of the war, not least because his hesitant attitude was motivated by the desire to *avoid* an escalation of the crisis. Moreover, British public opinion, the press (with the exception of *The Times*), and the majority of the Cabinet were not ready for Britain to go to war over Serbia until Belgium's demise finally provided a reason to become involved in continental affairs. Until that point Grey had feared that a definite promise of support might have led France or Russia to accept the risk of war more willingly, and had consistently refused to declare Britain's hand one way or the other.

In France, decision-making was hampered by the fact that the senior statesmen were abroad for many of the crucial days of the crisis. (This was, as we have seen, the result of a deliberate decision to present the ultimatum at the least opportune moment for French decision-makers.) France's attitude vis-à-vis her Russian ally has been much scrutinized by historians in order to ascertain if undue pressure, or at least too much support, too readily offered, influenced decisions in St Petersburg and if war-guilt can thus be attributed to France (an argument first advanced by revisionists in the inter-war years).[19] France was caught uncomfortably between two stools, and her desire to ensure British support even affected her military plans. Nothing should suggest to the Entente partner that France might be responsible for the onset of hostilities, and mobilization measures had to be postponed until reliable news had been received of German moves, while French troops were deliberately withdrawn ten kilometres behind the border to ensure that hostile acts would not even result accidentally (**303**), (**332**), (**337**).

In the weeks following the assassination, Russia's decision-makers reacted with alarm to the rumours that Austria might be planning to act harshly against Serbia. Having initially been reassured by Vienna's denials, the surprise at the ultimatum was all the greater, and the text of the ultimatum suggested to Sazonov immediately that war would be 'unavoidable'.[20] In a meeting of the Council of Ministers on 24 July, the Ministers discussed the fact that demands had been made of Serbia which were 'wholly unacceptable to the Kingdom of Serbia as a sovereign state'. Nonetheless, the decision was made to advise Serbia not to offer any resistance to any armed invasion, while Vienna was to be asked to extend the time limit, and permission for mobilization was to be sought to cover all eventualities (**206**).[21] On 25 July measures were decided on for a partial mobilization which began on 26 July. However, crucially this mobilization did not make war unavoidable, as Russia's decision-makers were at pains to stress. At the same time, the Russian Government was keen to support Britain's mediation proposals.

19 For details of the historiographical debate on the origins of the First World War see for example Annika Mombauer, *The Origins of the First World War. Controversies and Consensus*, Longman, Harlow 2002.

20 See Dominic Lieven, *Russia and the Origins of the First World War*, St. Martin's Press, New York 1983, p. 140.

21 Ibid., p. 144.

The prospect of Russia's support was a great relief to Prime Minister Nikola Pašić in Belgrade, and it has been argued that Serbia's rejection of one of the points of the ultimatum may have been made on the basis of this support (**227**).[22] However, it would arguably have been impossible for Pašić to accept all of Austria-Hungary's conditions, not least because of Serbia's recent military successes. Public opinion would hardly have condoned such an outwardly visible expression of weakness, even if the Prime Minister had been inclined towards acceptance. Moreover, an investigation of the background of the assassination would have led the Austrians to Dragutin Dimitrijević, head of the Serbian Military Intelligence, who was also known as Apis, the leader of the 'Black Hand' organization which had been behind the assassination. The demand of an Austrian-led enquiry was unacceptable because it would have revealed that the Serbian Government, while not the instigators of the plot, had nonetheless had prior knowledge of it, and had failed to prevent the murder from taking place.

Only at the very last minute, when it was clear that Britain, too, would become involved if war broke out, did the German Chancellor try to restrain the Austrians, but his mediation proposals arrived far too late and were in any case not forceful enough. They also did not have the backing of Germany's military leaders (**317**). Austria declared war on Serbia on 28 July, and thus set in motion a domino-effect of mobilization orders and declarations of war by Europe's major powers, and her decision-makers were unwilling to stop their war against Serbia in order to make negotiations possible. By the time Britain had declared war on Germany on 4 August, following Germany's invasion of neutral Luxembourg on 2 August and Belgium on 4 August (necessitated by Germany's deployment plan, the so-called Schlieffen Plan[23]), the Alliance powers (without Italy, which had decided to stay neutral) faced the Entente powers in the 'great fight' that had so long been anticipated.

---

22 Albertini, *Origins*, Vol. 2, pp. 352–362.

23 For details on the debate on the nature of the Schlieffen Plan, see for example Annika Mombauer, 'Of War Plans and War Guilt: the Debate Surrounding the Schlieffen Plan, *Journal of Strategic Studies*, 28, 5, October 2005, pp. 857–885; Hans Ehlert, Michael Epkenhans and Gerhard P. Groß (eds), *Der Schlieffenplan. Analyse und Dokumente*, Schöningh, Paderborn 2006. For details of Germany's war plans, see Annika Mombauer, 'German War Plans', in R. Hamilton and H. Herwig (eds), *War Planning 1914*, Cambridge University Press, Cambridge 2010, pp. 48–79.

5

Immediate reactions to the assassination

28 June–3 July: Documents (103)–(116)

In all European governments, the immediate reaction to the news of the assassination was one of horror and outrage. This act of terrorism – a regicide – was immediately regarded by many as a possible cause for war (**103**). It is tragic, with hindsight, that this was also a time that had seen some improvements in the relations between Britain and Germany (and much was made, therefore, of the naval visit to Kiel in early July), but it was too little too late (**116**). Without willingness in all the European capitals to settle once more for a diplomatic solution to an international crisis, the assassination provided the trigger to an international crisis that could not be contained.

(103) 28 June: Nicolai's Diary

News of assassination received; fear that this will mean war

Motorboat trip to view the Kiel Canal.[1] Upon my return, in the afternoon, I receive the news of the assassination of the Austrian heir to the throne and his wife.[2] The Kaiser receives the news from the Chief of the Naval Cabinet [Georg Alexander von Müller] while participating at the race on board the Meteor, the flags are on half-mast, all festivities have been cancelled. In the evening I eat in the Krupp-house. Very serious mood. Often I hear the view that the event means war.

Sonderarchiv Moscow, NL Nicolai, Fond 1414: 1–10.[3]

1 See (**47**), (**235**), (**335**).

2 See (**106**) for details of the assassination.

3 The entry in the transcript is wrongly dated 24.6.1914. My thanks to Michael

(104) 28 June: Salandra's conversation with San Giuliano

News of assassination causes some relief in Italy

[...] Suddenly my work was interrupted by the telephone, a special line connecting the Prime Minister's apartment with the other Ministries. It was the Marquis di San Giuliano [...]: 'Are you there, Salandra? – Have you heard? We are rid of that tedious affair of the Villa D'Este!'

'Is it possible?'

'The Archduke Franz Ferdinand was assassinated at Sarajevo this morning.'[4]

Antonio Salandra, *Italy and the Great War*, Edward Arnold, London 1932, p. 18.

(105) 29 June 1914: Conrad's conversation with Berchtold

Conrad advocates mobilization against Serbia; Berchtold counsels diplomatic resolution of crisis and awaiting the outcome of the investigation into the assassination

On 29 June in the evening, before a Ministerial Council scheduled for 8 o'clock, I saw Berchtold. I had greeted him with the words: 'We meet again under circumstances which are quite different from when we parted.'

Count Berchtold remarked that Kaiser Wilhelm would come to the funeral, which would offer an opportunity to discuss the situation. I replied that this was certainly desirable, but that this had been an attack against the Monarchy, which ought to be followed by an immediate step. In my opinion it would consist of mobilization against Serbia. This seemed to me to be unavoidable, however little it suited the Monarchy

Epkenhans who has kindly made this document available to me, prior to its forthcoming publication in an edition of the Nicolai diaries.

4 In March 1914 the Italian Parliament had agreed to purchase the villa from Franz Ferdinand, but negotiations had become protracted because the price was too high, and because of anti-Austrian feelings (and antipathy towards Franz Ferdinand) in the Italian Chamber. Antonio Salandra, *Italy and the Great War*, Edward Arnold, London 1932, pp. 18–19. Salandra sums up the Archduke's qualities, but particularly his perceived failings, not least the fact that he was 'rightly supposed to be no friend to Italy. Notoriously disliked as he was by his relatives in Vienna and even by his august uncle [...] Franz Ferdinand, in spite of his tragic end, was little regretted'. Ibid., pp. 20–21.

at present. The Minister replied that the outward occasion was lacking and that public opinion must also first be prepared.

Count Berchtold: 'Do you not think that a revolution might break out?'

I: 'But where?'

Count B.: 'In Bohemia.'

I: 'Do not let anyone persuade you of such a thing.'

Count B.: 'I thought of a different procedure. We make the demand of Serbia to dissolve certain societies, dismiss the Minister of Police, etc.'[5]

I: 'The Serbs will quietly dismiss the Minister of Police; it will have no effect whatsoever; only the use of force will have an effect. The Moslems and the Croats are against the Serbs. Vis-à-vis Russia one ought to stress the anti-monarchic element of the murder, and King Carol could hardly be actively hostile considering this circumstance.'

Even Count Berchtold agreed that the moment had indeed come to solve the Serbian question and that he would discuss the matter with His Majesty. Above all, however, one would have to wait for the outcome of the investigation.

Franz Conrad von Hötzendorf, *Aus meiner Dienstzeit, 1906–1918*, 5 vols, Rikola Verlag, Vienna, Leipzig, Munich 1922–1925, Vol. IV, pp. 33–34.

(106) 29 June: Bunsen to Grey

British Ambassador reports on assassination of Franz Ferdinand

No. 129
Vienna, June 29, 1914
(Received July 2)

The Archduke Franz Ferdinand and the Duchess of Hohenberg were both murdered yesterday morning by a Slav nationalist or anarchist at Sarajevo.

His Imperial Highness had left Vienna on Tuesday evening, 23rd June, on his journey to Bosnia. He embarked on Wednesday morning at Trieste onboard the battleship 'Viribus Unitis', proceeded on Thursday morning onboard a smaller vessel up the river Narenta to Metkovitch in Dalmatia, whence he took the train for Mostar, the Herzegovinian capital, and after a drive round the town continued his journey to Ilidze,

5 Note how the beginnings of the subsequent ultimatum demands can be found in this early conversation.

a small Bosnian watering place near Sarajevo, where the Duchess of Hohenberg was awaiting him. On Friday and Saturday, 26th and 27th June, the Archduke was present at the mountain exercises of portions of the 15th and 16th Army Corps, which took place immediately to the south of Sarajevo. Yesterday, Sunday, 28th June, His Imperial Highness, after attending Mass at Ilidze, proceeded by train, with the Duchess, to Sarajevo, as arranged, for the purpose of making a progress through the town and receiving loyal addresses. On their way from the station to the Town Hall the official account states that a bomb was thrown at them but was warded off by the Archduke, exploding behind the Imperial motor car and wounding slightly the two officers who occupied the next car, and more or less seriously some 20 persons in the crowd of onlookers. At the Town Hall speeches were exchanged between the *Burgermeister* and the Archduke, the latter expressing his satisfaction at the cordiality of his reception and alluding to the failure of the dastardly attempt on his life. Undeterred, it is said, by suggestions that it would be wiser to abandon the remainder of the programme, His Imperial Highness and the Duchess proceeded in the direction of the Town Museum, or as some accounts have it of the hospital to which the wounded had been carried after the bomb outrage. A man ran in from the crowd and fired rapidly several shots from a Browning pistol into the car. The Archduke's jugular vein was severed and he must have died almost instantaneously. The Duchess of Hohenberg was struck in the side and expired immediately after reaching the Konak to which both were carried. The Governor, General Potiorek, who had also conducted the manoeuvres and was with them in the car, was unhurt. A few steps from the scene of the murders an unexploded bomb was found. It is presumed that it was thrown away by a third conspirator, on perceiving that the second assault had been successful.

From what has hitherto come to light regarding this atrocious crime it is conjectured that the murdered pair were probably the victims of a carefully prepared plot. The Archduke, it is true, is known to have been a sympathiser with the aspirations of the subject nationalities of the Emperor, in so far as these can be regarded as reasonable and capable of realisation without peril to the unity of the Dual Monarchy. He had been given therefore, according to all accounts, an enthusiastic reception at every stage of his journey through Dalmatia, Herzegovina and Bosnia. Even the opposition Press had accorded him a welcome, with the exception of the 'Narod', a Serbian irredentist organ, which made no allusion to the Archduke's visit, but published instead, on a sheet bearing the Serbian colours, a glowing article in commemoration of the battle of Kossovo, which marked the downfall of the Serbian Empire before the Turkish onslaught in the [fourteenth] century. A telegram from Agram[6] appears this morning in the official 'Fremdenblatt', to the effect that since the intention of the Heir Apparent to attend the Bosnian manoeuvres became known a violent Pan-Serbian agitation has been raging in the Serbo-Croatian capital. The Archduke is said to have been warned in vain against undertaking his projected journey, and to have himself endeavoured to dissuade the Duchess from meeting him in Bosnia. Her Highness was however determined to share the danger with her husband. The Agram telegram proceeds to state that since 1908 (the year of the [Bosnian] annexation) the revolutionary Serbian organisation has displayed an ever increasing activity; that Gabrilović and Prinzip, the first of whom threw the bomb and the second fired the pistol, are said to be members of the terrorist Great Serbian organisation; and that in Agram no one doubts that a carefully prepared plot had been set on foot against the Archduke.

Those who remember the circumstances of the notorious Agram and Dr. Friedjung trials in 1908 and 1909,[7] when the efforts of the Austro-Hungarian Government to justify the expected war with Serbia by publishing proofs of a widespread irredentist Serbian plot so woefully broke down, will hesitate to accept without adequate proof wholesale denunciations of the Serbian patriotic societies which may now be expected to be made.[8]

Though Vienna is outwardly very calm, all public performances have been stopped, and at Brunn, the capital of Moravia, where a great 'Sokol' or Slav nationalist gathering of gymnasts was being held, and some fears prevailed of a conflict with simultaneous German demonstrations, both sides seem to have agreed to stay further proceedings in sign of mourning.

The news of the murders was broken about midday yesterday to the Emperor at Ischl, where His Majesty had arrived only the day before. His Majesty has thus lived to see his nephew and heir added to the list of his nearest relations who have died violent deaths.[9] His Majesty returned to Vienna to-day. He has made a most happy recovery from his recent severe illness.

BD, XI, No. 21.

6 Zagreb.

7 During the infamous trial in 1909 of the Austrian historian Heinrich Friedjung it was proved that his claim that three prominent members of the Croato-Serbian Coalition were agents of 'Greater Serbia' was based on forged evidence.

8 See for example (**108**), (**111**).

9 His daughter Sophie died in 1857, his son Rudolf committed suicide in 1889, and his wife Empress Elizabeth was assassinated in 1898.

(107) 30 June 1914: Jovanović to Pašić

Serbia is blamed for assassination of Franz Ferdinand

Telegram
Vienna, 17/30 June 1914

The tendency at Vienna to represent in the eyes of Europe the outrage committed upon the Austro-Hungarian Crown Prince as the act of a conspiracy engineered in Serbia is becoming more and more apparent. The idea is to use this as a political weapon against us. The greatest attention ought, therefore, to be paid to the tone adopted by our press in its articles on the Sarajevo outrage.

Serbian *Blue Book*, No. 2.[10]

(108) 30 June: Tschirschky to Bethmann Hollweg

Tschirschky urges caution in Vienna; Wilhelm II disagrees and urges for action against Serbia 'now or never'

Vienna, 30 June 1914
Received 2 July, afternoon

Report 212

[*Wilhelm II's emphases and marginal notes of 3 July*[11]]

Count Berchtold told me today that everything pointed to the fact

10 Engl. transl. from *Collected Diplomatic Documents relating to the Outbreak of the European War*, HMSO, London 1915, pp. 370.

11 The Kaiser's friend Philipp Eulenburg commented after the war on Wilhelm II's infamous marginal notes: 'Psychologically, however, the markedly belligerent, aggressive character of the Kaiser's *marginalia*, the reflection of which appears in the Vienna Cabinet meeting of 7 July (**134**), does not mean that he necessarily had belligerent *intentions*. One needs to know Kaiser Wilhelm as well as I do to be able to explain this contradiction. The explanation is that the Kaiser's super-vivacious nature in fact knows *only the superlative*. To him something is either: magnificent, splendid, incomparable – or: atrocious, infamous, intolerable. The intermediate notes desert him entirely [...] whenever he chooses his words. That is why his speeches always impressed *strongly* – and offended strongly. That is why, too, his marginalia are so dangerous, for they all, without exception, have the character of exclamation marks. Eulenburg to Kurt Breysig, 22 September 1919, cited in John Röhl, *1914: Delusion or Design?*, Elek, London 1973, pp. 131.

that the threads of the conspiracy to which the Archduke fell victim ran together at Belgrade. The affair was apparently so well thought out that very young men were intentionally selected for the perpetration of the crime, against whom only a mild punishment could be decreed. The Minister spoke very bitterly about the Serbian plots.	*hopefully not.*
I frequently hear expressed here, even among serious people, the wish that at last a final and fundamental reckoning should be had with the Serbs. The Serbs should first be presented with a number of demands, and in case they should not accept these, energetic measures should be taken.[12]	*Now or never.*
I take opportunity of every such occasion to advise quietly but very impressively and seriously against too hasty steps. First of all, they must be certain of what they want, for so far I have heard only very imprecise expressions of opinion. Then the chances of any action should be carefully weighed up,	*who authorized him to act that way? that is very stupid. none of his business, as it is solely Austria's matter what she plans to do in this case. Later, if it goes wrong, it will be said that Germany did not want it! Let Tschirschky be good enough to drop this nonsense! The Serbs must sorted, and that right soon!*[13]

12 See (**105**).

13 We do not know how Tschirschky was informed of the Kaiser's view. However, there is plenty of evidence to show that his initially cautious attitude changed after 3 July and that he started to put extensive pressure on Viennese decision-makers. For a detailed discussion of all the relevant evidence, see Luigi Albertini, *The Origins of the War of 1914*, 3 vols, Eng. transl., Oxford University Press, Oxford 1952–1957, Vol. II, pp. 150ff. See also Imanuel Geiss, *July 1914*, Scribner, London 1967, p. 63 who points out that Wilhelm II's marginal note and Tschirschky's change of heart pre-dated the so-called 'blank cheque' (**120**), (**130**) and that the Kaiser 'had decided on war against Serbia even before he knew whether that was what the Austrians really desired'. See also John Röhl, *Wilhelm II.*, Vol. III: *Der Weg in den Abgrund, 1900–1941*, Beck, Munich 2008, pp. 1075ff. for a discussion of the background to Wilhelm II's infamous marginal note '*jetzt oder nie*' (now or never). Eugen Fischer, Secretary to the

and it should be kept in mind that Austria-Hungary does not stand alone in the world, that it is her duty to think not only of her allies, but to take into consideration the entire European situation, and especially the attitude of Italy and Rumania on all questions that concern Serbia.	*Goes without saying; nothing but truisms.*

DD, No.7.[14]

(109) 30 June: Bollati to San Giuliano

Zimmermann reveals that Archduke had not been held in high regard in leading German diplomatic circles; fears that unreasonable Austrian demands of Serbia might lead to conflict and that Germany will have to restrain Austria-Hungary

Reichstag Commission of Inquiry into the War Guilt Question, commented after the war: 'Kaiser Wilhelm II wrote many a marginal note which he himself did not take seriously, many to which no attention was paid at the Foreign Ministry. But the one of 3 July 1914, to the report of the Ambassador to Vienna of 30 June, at once became a *mot d'ordre*. In Herr von Tschirschky at Vienna a transformation took place. On 30 June he had confidently reported home his serious attitude of warning. On 2 July he still manifested to Emperor Francis Joseph and on the 3rd to Berchtold his aversion for a violently emotional policy in the Serbian question. On that same 3rd the Kaiser wrote his marginal note and on the 4th the daily report of the Viennese Foreign Ministry records that Tschirschky had said [...] with the obvious intention that it should be passed on: "Germany would support the Monarchy through thick and thin, no matter what it should decide to do against Serbia; the sooner Austria-Hungary started off the better" etc. [...] The transformation took place soon after the Kaiser had intimated his opinion. One must assume that the Kaiser's standpoint was at once telegraphed or telephoned on to Tschirschky. Any such telegram sent neither by nor on the instruction of the Chancellor or the Secretary of State need not have been preserved in such a way as to be available to us today.' Eugen Fischer, *Die kritischen 39 Tage von Sarajevo bis zum Weltbrand*, Berlin 1928, pp. 63–64 (cited in Albertini, II, pp. 151–152, note 3). See also Albertini, II, p. 150, on the conversation between Tschirschky and Ganz, the Vienna correspondent of the *Frankfurter Zeitung*, which underlines this change of position.

14 Engl. translation based on Geiss, *July 1914*, No. 2, here with minor amendments.

Berlin, 30 June 1914
D. 9.15 p.m.
R. 1 July, 1.15 a.m.
Telegram No. 4828/490

In the conversation I had this morning with Zimmermann we talked, of course, first of all about the horrible misdeed of Sarajevo and of the political consequences that can derive from it. While paying the rightful homage to the unhappy victims, he told me in all confidentiality that the personality of the heir to the Austrian throne was not, after all, such that could have fully inspired confidence here. He certainly was keen on the Triple Alliance, called himself a friend of Germany and, in the last few years, had formed a cordial relationship with Kaiser Wilhelm, but at home he sided preferably with the Slavs and dreamed of that project of Trialism which, in many people's opinion here, would have put an end to the German superiority in the monarchy. He also had too many dislikes and prejudices: against the Hungarians, against the Italians, against everything liberal; he was moody, violent, subject to backward and exclusivist influences. Without wanting to deny his qualities and merits, especially regarding the army, one can assume that his disappearance could simplify rather than complicate the situation of the Monarchy, at home and abroad. That is, if there were men capable of imprinting on its politics a wise and energetic course, now that the will of the old Emperor,[15] so easy to dominate these days, would no longer encounter that resistance and adverse tide which, in recent years, had so often paralysed the actions of the rulers of Vienna. But one must doubt that such men really exist.

For the time being Zimmermann detects as the principal danger that the legitimate indignation breaking out in Austria-Hungary against Serbia could lead to measures too severe and provocative for the neighbouring Kingdom. And he foresees for the German Government a continuous and laborious task of restraining the Cabinet in Vienna from compromising decisions.

The German press in general does not express such judgements, which Zimmermann naturally told me strictly in confidence. Here all the newspapers greatly praise the character of the late Archduke and consider his death an insurmountable loss for the Monarchy to which he, with his willpower and keen awareness of his rights and duties, would have known how to give new life and to raise it to a greater power.

DDI, 4th series, XII, No. 25.

15 Franz Joseph, Emperor of Austria and King of Hungary.

(110) 1 July: Ferry's note about conversation with Serbian Ambassador Vesnić

Serbia had warned Austria of planned plot against the Archduke

I received a visit from M. Vesnić, the Serbian Minister, with whom I have a long-standing relationship and who told me 'as a friend':

1 That he considered the assassination of the Archduke to be a response to the annexation of Bosnia. The Prince, moreover, was renowned as a 'man of authority'. The Serbian government had even informed the Austrian Government that they had got wind of the plot.[16]
2 Having contemplated the demise of the old Emperor, he told me the transfer of power would be straightforward: the Yugoslav problem is developing slowly and will only reach a conclusion in about thirty years, so long as no persecution and politics *à la Metternich* hasten the course of this evolution.
3 Concerning the Greco-Turkish conflict, he appeared sceptical to me. 'These are the waves after the storm.' [...]

DDF, 3e série, 10, No. 466.

(111) 1 July: Tisza to Franz Joseph

Tisza counsels against war at the present time

[...] First of all we have so far no sufficient grounds for holding Serbia responsible and for provoking a war with her in spite of possible satisfactory explanations from the Serbian Government. We should find ourselves in the weakest position imaginable, appearing before the whole world as the disturber of peace and kindling a great war in the most unfavourable conditions.

Secondly I regard the present moment generally as highly unfavourable, when we have practically lost Romania without gaining any compensation for it, while Bulgaria, the only state on which we can count, is exhausted.

16 There is further mention of this warning in the report by M. d'Apchier de Maugin, DDF, 3e série, 10, No. 463. For details of Jovanović's warning to Austria see Mark Cornwall, 'Serbia', in Keith M. Wilson (ed.), *Decisions for War, 1914*, UCL Press, London 1995, pp. 55–96, p. 66, and Christopher Clark, *The Sleepwalkers. How Europe went to War in 1914*, Allen Lane, London, 2012.

In the present Balkan situation my least concern would be finding a suitable *casus belli*. When the moment to strike presents itself, a reason for war can always result from the various questions. But first a diplomatic constellation must be created which creates less unfavourable power relations for us.

The definitive inclusion of Bulgaria in such a way which does not offend Rumania and which leaves open the door for an understanding with her as well as with Greece becomes more urgent by the day, therefore, a last approach much be made to Germany to bring about the open accession of Rumania to the Triple Alliance.[17] If Germany cannot or will not carry out this mission, she must put up with our securing at least Bulgaria for the Triple Alliance.[18] [...]

ÖUA, VIII, No. 9978.

(112) 2 July: Lichtenau to Vitzthum

Auswärtiges Amt in Berlin think war between Austria-Hungary and Serbia will be avoided and that neither Russia, France nor Britain desire a war at the present time; early evidence of Berchtold's resolve

---

Berlin, 2 July 1914 (despatched 2 July 1914)
No. 1045
Confidential

[...] Austria-Hungary is now planning to take vigorous action against Serbia on account of the murder. The German Government has advised the Serbian Government to afford the maximum cooperation in this matter in which it finds all Europe against Serbia, and the Russian Ambassador to Berlin has also been approached to influence Serbia accordingly, which has also been promised. In the *Auswärtiges Amt* they believe that a war between Austria-Hungary and Serbia will therefore be avoided. Should it break out nonetheless, Bulgaria would immediately declare war on Greece – the dispute between Greece and Turkey

17 See also H. Bertil A. Petersson who points out that the memorandum that Count Hoyos presented in Berlin on 5 July made precisely this request: 'Das österreichisch-ungarische Memorandum an Deutschland', *Scandia*, 29, 1963, pp. 138–190, p. 185. See (**115**).

18 For details on the relationship with Rumania see for example Paul Schroeder, 'Romania and the Great Powers before 1914', *Revue Roumaine d'Histoire*, XIV, 1, 1975, pp. 39–53.

fortunately having been settled – Russia would mobilise and world war could no longer be prevented. There is a renewed pressure from the military side for allowing things to drift towards war while Russia is still not yet ready, but I do not think that his Majesty the Kaiser will allow himself to be induced to this.

The *Auswärtiges Amt* believes, as before mentioned, that it will not come to a war between Austria and Serbia. As far as our relations with our neighbours are concerned, neither Russia nor France has any desire to start a war. France is too preoccupied with her internal affairs and her financial troubles. Russia, it is true, has been rattling the sabre, but the reason for this is apparently only to ensure that she receives the 500 million promised by France for next year, as she, too, is suffering from a lack of money. Our relations with England have improved, even though we should not succumb to the illusion that we are popular on the other side of the Channel. But England also does not desire a war, as the times are past when she could leave the peoples on the continent to slaughter each other; she would herself be drawn in and her trade would be destroyed as well; in addition our Fleet was still a factor with which England would now have to reckon. Her colonies were also giving her much to worry about. Therefore if it does not come to a war between Serbia and Austria, then my informant believes that peace will be preserved. [...]

The death of the Italian Chief of the General Staff Pollio was referred to as a great loss for the Triple Alliance.[19] [...]

August Bach (ed.), *Deutsche Gesandtschaftsberichte zum Kriegsausbruch*, Quaderverlag, Berlin 1937, No. 2.[20]

19 See, however, (98) which demonstrates Pollio's strong anti-Austrian feelings. General Alberto Pollio was Italian Chief of Staff from 1908 until his death on 28 July 1914. See also DD, No. 11, Tschirschky to Bethmann Hollweg, 2 July: 'The Kaiser [Franz Joseph] also mentioned that General Pollio's sudden death was a serious loss for Italy and also for us. "Everyone is dying around me", said H.M., "it is too sad."'

20 Engl. transl. based on Geiss, *July 1914*, No. 4, but here with amendments.

(113) 2 July: Dumaine to Viviani

Bitter reaction in Austria to the assassination; rumours that it won't come to more than posturing on Austria's part; Austrian authorities in Bosnia failed to curb nationalist agitation over last few months

Telegram No. 91
Vienna, 2 July 1914
D. 1.40 p.m.
R. 4.50 p.m.

Within Austrian military circles and for all those who are not resigned to letting Serbia retain the position she has won in the Balkans, the crime of Sarajevo incites the most hateful bitterness.

The enquiry into the cause of the assassination, which is being insisted upon under intolerable conditions for the dignity of Belgrade's Government, would, if refused, give rise to grievances that would allow for a military intervention. But it is said that the Austrian Emperor disagrees with this kind of provocation because of his old age and the ever-mounting problems in Albania; once again they will probably have to make do with mere threats.

Our press, especially the *Temps*, is being attacked by the least justified of recriminations. My Russian colleague is very offended by the insinuations made about his country which the English *Standard* has also repeated.

General Potiorik, the commander in Bosnia, has established that, in the past months, none of the rigorous measures he has been calling for to curb Pan-Serbian party propaganda have been approved in Vienna. Responsibility for this falls to M. de Bilinski, Governor of the annexed provinces, who was experimenting with conciliation and appeasement methods. Given the stark facts putting him at fault, it seems certain he will be replaced.[21]

DDF, 3e série, 10, No. 470.

21 He was, in fact, not replaced.

(114) 3 July: Leuckart to Carlowitz

German General Staff considers German involvement in war likely and favours it at the present time.

No. 73/3472
Berlin, 3 July 1914
[Handwritten letter]

I have to report to your Excellency that in responsible circles here the political situation is regarded as very serious – also for us. At the memorial service[22] for His Imperial Highness Archduke Franz Ferdinand I had the opportunity to talk things over with *Generalmajor* Count Waldersee, *Generalquartiermeister* in the Great General Staff. What he said seemed to be the opinion of the Chief of the General Staff of the Army. He opined that we might become involved in a war from one day to the next. Everything depended on what attitude Russia took in the Austro-Serbian business. In any case the course of events was also being closely watched by the Great General Staff. I gained the impression that they would regard it with favour if war were to come about now. Conditions and prospects would never become better for us.[23]

However H.M. the Kaiser is said to have pronounced in favour of maintaining peace.

The Royal Minister [Lichtenau] has learned the same – as far as I know from the *Auswärtiges Amt*.[24]

One very much doubts here that the reason for the cancellation of H.M. the Kaiser's trip to Vienna is an indisposition. There is also disbelief that the trip has not occurred due to the state of health of H.M. the Emperor of Austria; rather often the opinion is expressed that political considerations were decisive.[25] One wanted to avoid that the situation was aggravated, e.g in case of a demonstration or similar by Serbian elements during the [Kaiser's] presence in Vienna.

August Bach (ed.), *Deutsche Gesandtschaftsberichte zum Kriegsausbruch*, Quaderverlag, Berlin 1937, No. 3.[26]

---

22 At St Hedwig's Church in Berlin, on 3 July.

23 See for example (**89**).

24 See (**112**). But cf. (**108**) for Kaiser's bellicose attitude.

25 It was in fact due to concerns about possible terrorist attacks on the Kaiser. See DD, No. 6b, Bethmann Hollweg to Tschirschky, 2 July 1914. See also Röhl, *Wilhelm II.*, Vol. 3, p. 1076. According to Nicolai, the Kaiser's planned trip to Vienna was cancelled 'due to the wishes of the Austro-Hungarian Government which felt that it could not guarantee sufficient personal security of the Kaiser'. Nicolai Papers, Moscow, 29 June (wrongly dated as 25 June in the transcript).

26 Engl. transl. based on Geiss, *July 1914*, No. 5, but here with amendments and

(115) 3 July: Rumbold to Grey

Austrian and German reactions to the assassination

No. 269
Berlin, July 3, 1914
Received July 6th

As far as can be judged, the assassination of the Archduke Francis Ferdinand and of his Consort at Sarajevo produced an impression almost amounting to consternation in Germany. The Emperor had only quite recently returned from Konopischt[27] and the intimacy existing between His Majesty and the Austro-Hungarian Heir Apparent was a matter of common knowledge as well as of great satisfaction to Germans. The measure of the association of the German people with all that concerns their Emperor enables the observer to gauge the horror with which the news was received of the crime which deprived His Majesty of his intimate friend. Added to this was great and universal sympathy for the aged Emperor Francis Joseph, who has lost the support of a Prince to whom he had entrusted the general supervision of the army and whose object it was to create a strong fleet. The foregoing were the considerations which suggested themselves to the German press on first hearing the news, and the possible political results of the crime to Germany's future relations with her ally have been little touched upon.

It may, perhaps, be observed generally that the relations between the Austro-Hungarian and German Empires fall into two parts, viz., the relations of the two Empires and of their Rulers *inter se* and the extent of the military and naval assistance they can give one another in the event of a war. The two questions are, of course, closely connected. In regard to the first point, the intimacy existing between the Emperor [Wilhelm] and the late Archduke seemed to constitute one certain factor in the future relations between the two Empires. This factor has now disappeared. It is now a matter of academical speculation whether, had the Archduke lived, there would have been found room in the Triple Alliance for two such masterful personalities as the Emperor and the late Austro-Hungarian Heir Apparent, in other words, whether the intimacy between them would have lasted. Complications might have arisen had any attempt been made to alter the line of succession in Austria-Hungary and these complications would not have left this country indifferent. But as regards this part of the question, such opinion as has found expression

additions.

27 Franz Ferdinand had met the German Kaiser in Konopischt, 50 kilometres south-east of Prague, on 12–13 June 1914.

in the press is to the effect that nothing will be changed in the relations between the two allies. It is devoutly hoped here that the Austrian Emperor may yet live for several years to come and be able to train up the new Heir Apparent.[28]

You are aware that, since the Balkan wars, doubts have sprung up in Germany as to the extent to which she can reckon on military assistance from her neighbour in the event of a general war.[29] The idea is that Austria-Hungary would be hampered by having to prepare for eventualities on the Serbian frontier. This idea has been strengthened by the recent crime at Sarajevo. One or two organs of the press at once pointed out that the aspirations of those working for a greater Serbia constitute a danger to the peace of Europe. One paper says that the question of the Southern Slavs is the one which will determine the destiny of Austria. The attitude of the Austro-Hungarian Government at this juncture is therefore being watched with anxious interest, as people here have had little doubt from the first that the plot which led to the death of the Archduke was hatched in Serbia.

On learning the news of the assassination of the Austro-Hungarian Heir Apparent the Emperor [Wilhelm] at once altered his plans and returned to Potsdam on the 29th ultimo. His Majesty expressed his intention of personally attending the funeral of the Archduke, and it was given out that he would be accompanied by Prince Henry.[30] It was announced in the course of yesterday, however, that owing to a sudden indisposition (attributed to lumbago), His Majesty had been obliged to abandon his intention of being present at the funeral.[31] I have learnt privately that the abandonment of His Majesty's journey to Vienna was due to a letter from the Emperor of Austria. It is announced this morning that Prince Henry has likewise given up his intention of attending the funeral.

A memorial service for the Archduke Francis Ferdinand and his Consort took place to-day at St. Hedwig's Church in Berlin. The Emperor was represented by Prince Eitel Friedrich and the service was attended by

28 Franz Joseph's great-nephew Karl.

29 See (**78**).

30 Prince Heinrich of Prussia, the brother of the German Kaiser.

31 BD, XI, No. 24, Rumbold to Grey, Berlin, 2 July 1914: 'It is officially announced that the Emperor has, owing to a slight indisposition, given up the intention of going to Vienna to attend the funeral of the Archduke Franz Ferdinand. Great stress is laid in the press announcements on the fact that this decision has in no way been influenced by political considerations or by fear for the safety of the Emperor.' But see (**114**), note 25. Kaiser Franz Joseph regretted not being able to discuss 'the political situation with you' and instead sent a hand-written letter outlining the details of the threat Serbia posed to Austria-Hungary. See ÖUA, VIII, No. 9984.

the principal Government officials at present in Berlin as well as by the entire diplomatic corps.[32]

BD, XI, No. 26.

(116) 3 July 1914: Henderson to Rumbold[33]

Visit of British Squadron to Kiel; anti-British feelings among conservative Germans

I have the honour to submit the following report on the visit of our Second Battle Squadron and three light cruisers to Kiel during Kiel Regatta Week:–

From the moment it was known at the Reichs-Marine-Amt that a visit was in contemplation, I was approached by many German naval officers in Berlin, who gave honest expression to the satisfaction with which they looked forward to the occurrence.

His Majesty the German Emperor spoke to me with evident pleasure about it, and I do not doubt that the lavish hospitality which was subsequently shown to our squadron was due largely to His Majesty's desire that we should be well entertained [...]. The German press was at first reticent about the approaching visit, and very little was said about it beyond the bare publication of the fact that it was going to take place. Later on, however, some of the leading Conservative organs let themselves go. [...]

The *Dresdner Nachrichten* (Conservative) published an unfriendly article, headed 'No Illusions', in which it stated that the obvious intention of the simultaneous visit of another of our squadrons to Cronstadt was to take the shine out of the visit to Kiel.[34]

It is said that in spite of Sir Edward Grey's denial of any formal understanding with Russia, his *démenti* was not as exact as it might have been and that in Germany it was still accepted as a fact that a verbal understanding has been arrived at as to co-operation of the British and Russian fleets against Germany, Russia to contain part of the German fleet in the Baltic while England annihilated the remainder in the North Sea. It warned its readers not to lose their heads over the prospective

32 See also (**114**).

33 Wilfred Henderson, British Naval Attaché; Sir Horace Rumbold, British Chargé d'Affaires in Berlin.

34 This was indeed the case. See (**86**). See also (**79**), (**81**), (**87**), (**97**), (**99**), (**100**), (**102**).

festivities at Kiel, and ended up by saying that on the German side the motto should be 'Watchfulness and holding-back'. [...]

It must be remembered when reading the above that I have brought into prominence the views of those who distrust us, that is to say, the Conservative view, but it would be wrong to take these articles to which I have given prominence as exemplifying the views of the majority of Germans. They are distinctly the views of the minority, although of an influential minority. [...]

The people whom we met (chiefly naval people) were honestly glad to see us. The attitude towards us of the German naval officers was the very opposite of that insincere toadyism and sickly sentimentality which we are not infrequently treated to elsewhere. [...]

In fine, it may be said that the Kiel visit was a great success, all the more because of its non-political character. It has achieved more in its non-political garb than it could have in any other disguise, and each individual German naval officer is anxiously looking forward to the return visit in the hope that he may take part in it. [...]

Matthew Seligmann (ed.), *Naval Intelligence from Germany*, Ashgate, Naval Records Society, Aldershot 2007, doc. 219.

6

The Hoyos Mission

4 July–12 July: Documents (117)–(148)

The documents in the following section demonstrate clearly that many of Vienna's decision-makers were eager to grasp the opportunity of a 'reckoning' with Serbia which presented itself in the aftermath of the assassination. Particularly a younger generation of diplomats who had participated in Alois von Aehrenthal's expansionist foreign policy in the early years of the century were of the opinion that an active foreign policy was the only way out of the internal stagnation they all felt Austria-Hungary was experiencing.[1]

In this, they were vigorously supported, even encouraged, by their alliance partner in Berlin. Some evidence for Austria-Hungary's acute desire to break out of a perceived 'encirclement' and to arrest their alleged decline can be found in the Matscheko memorandum (**117**), composed before the assassination of Franz Ferdinand and then adapted to the new circumstances and presented to the German Kaiser on 5 July.[2] Berthold Molden's memorandum

---

1 See Fritz Fellner, 'Austria-Hungary', in Keith M. Wilson (ed.), *Decisions for War, 1914*, UCL Press, London 1995, pp. 9–25, p. 11, and John D. Leslie, 'The Antecedents of Austria-Hungary's War Aims. Policies and Policy-Making in Vienna and Budapest before and during 1914', *Wiener Beiträge zur Geschichte der Neuzeit*, 20, 1993, pp. 307–394. Fellner identifies the three most decisive of these diplomats: 'Forgách was the planner and theorist of the anti-Serbian policy; Hoyos the instrument for securing the endorsement of the anti-Serbian policy by the German Empire; and Musulin the draftsman who drew up the decisive documents that put the plan and the political conviction into action, namely the ultimatum and the declaration of war.' Fellner, 'Austria-Hungary', p. 12.

2 The differences between the two versions (that drafted by Matscheko on 24 June, and the one handed to the German ally together with Franz Joseph's hand-written letter) are analysed in detail in H. Bertil A. Petersson, 'Das österreichisch-ungarische Memorandum an Deutschland vom 5. Juli 1914', *Scandia*, 29, 1963, pp. 138–190, *passim*.

(**126**) also demonstrates clearly the extent of Austria-Hungary's foreign-policy aims even before Count Hoyos had received the infamous blank cheque during his visit to Berlin (**120**), (**130**). Germany's pledge of support delivered during the Hoyos Mission was necessary for Austria-Hungary's resolve and played a part in their decision to issue an ultimatum to Serbia during their Ministerial Council meeting on 7 July (**134**), but their determination to act decisively predated the visit (**112**).[3] Of course we cannot know with any certainty what Vienna's decision-makers would have decided if their alliance partner Germany had not offered unconditional support at this early stage, although it is certain that the 'hawks' in Vienna did not need any encouragement and that the cautious Tisza was unable to halt them for long: their minds were made up that the time had come for dealing energetically with the troublesome Serbs (**105**).[4] However, they did receive encouragement from Berlin, where the decision-makers declared 'emphatically' that an action of the Monarchy against Serbia was 'expected' (**139**). On 7 July, the decision to issue an unacceptable ultimatum was taken, leading to the order being given to Wladimir Baron von Giesl, the Austro-Hungarian Minister in Belgrade: 'However the Serbs react to the ultimatum, you must break off relations and it must come to war.'[5] As we will see, Serbia's surprisingly compliant reply ensured that this predetermined attitude would cause suspicion in the eyes of the other Great Powers.

Among the Entente powers, but also in Rome, there was suspicion that Germany was disingenuous in her vigorous denials to have had any prior knowledge of Vienna's intentions. The available evidence shows without doubt that German decision-makers knew about the plan, hatched in Vienna, to despatch a deliberately unacceptable ultimatum to Belgrade and that they were well aware of the reasons for its delay. This intention was known to the German ally almost

---

3 For details of the Hoyos Mission, see for example Fritz Fellner, 'Die "Mission Hoyos"', in Wilhelm Alff (ed.), *Deutschlands Sonderung von Europa 1862–1945*, Peter Lang, Frankfurt, Bern, New York 1984, pp. 283–316.

4 Hoyos was one of the 'hawks': Diary of Joseph Redlich, 3 November 1916: 'Yesterday evening alone at Alek Hoyos'. We talked very confidentially and companionably. He does not regard peace as near! I was very touched when he told me openly that he has for a long time been depressed by the feeling really to have been the actual cause of the war because he had held and used decisive influence over Berchtold [...].' Cited in Fellner, 'Die "Mission Hoyos"', p. 290.

5 Cited in Fellner, 'Austria-Hungary', p. 15.

as soon as the decision was taken, and Berlin's decision-makers were also aware of its likely contents before anyone else in the crisis, despite their protests to the contrary, although they did not know the exact terms of the ultimatum until 22 July (**132**), (**224**), (**245**).

(117) 5 July: Matscheko-Memorandum[6]

Summary of Austro-Hungarian foreign-policy concerns; fear of Russia; evidence for Austria-Hungary's desire to break out of her perceived 'encirclement'

Following the great upheavals of the last two years relations on the Balkans have been clarified to an extent that it is now possible to oversee the results of the crisis somewhat and to determine to what extent the interests of the Triple Alliance, in particular those of the two central Imperial powers, have been affected by the events and which conclusions result from this for the European and Balkan policies of these powers.

6 This is the date when the memorandum was handed to Kaiser Wilhelm in Berlin, not the date when it was drafted. As well as Kaiser Franz Joseph's letter, Hoyos also delivered this memorandum, first drafted by Franz von Matscheko on 24 June 1914 (ÖUA, VIII, No. 9918), finalized on 28 June and subsequently modified to reflect the new situation following the assassination at Sarajevo (the updated version is dated 1 July but delivered to Kaiser Wilhelm II on 5 July). Some historians have credited Tisza with the authorship (for example Fay, Albertini, Fischer), but Petersson ('Das österreichisch-ungarische Memorandum', p. 142) argues that the memorandum was based on previous drafts by Tisza, but written under the auspices of Berchtold. The memorandum advocated a more assertive foreign policy which would require the support of the Hungarian Prime Minister Istvan Tisza and of the German ally. It demanded 'energetic' steps to break Russia's encirclement and saw Bulgaria as a potential ally and Rumania as a potential enemy. After 28 June the memorandum was amended and asked for a more aggressive military policy. It has been argued that there is a notable difference between the two versions of the memorandum. The earlier one advocated a diplomatic-political campaign against Rumania without the use of force, designed to improve Austria-Hungary's position in the Balkans, the latter called for an immediate war against Serbia. However, Paul Schroeder notes the 'essential continuity and logical connection between these two phases of the planned Austro-German offensive'. Schroeder, 'Romania and the Great Powers before 1914', *Revue Roumaine d'Histoire*, XIV, 1, 1975, p. 45. For details on the memorandum, see also G. Kronenbitter, *'Krieg im Frieden'*, Oldenbourg, Munich 2003, p. 467; S. Williamson, *Austria-Hungary and the Origins of the First World War*, Macmillan, London 1991, p. 165; Petersson, 'Das österreichisch-ungarische Memorandum', pp. 138–190.

If one compares without prejudice today's situation with that before the great crisis [i.e. the Balkan Wars] one has to conclude that the result, if seen from the point of view of Austria-Hungary as well as the Triple Alliance, can hardly be regarded as favourable. However, the balance shows a few plusses. It has been possible to create an independent Albanian state as a counter-weight against Serbia's advance [...]. The relations of the Triple Alliance with the strengthened and enlarged Greek kingdom have eventually been created in such a way that Greece, despite her alliance with Serbia, need not necessarily be regarded as an opponent.

In the main, however, due to the development which led to the Second Balkan War, Bulgaria has awoken from Russia's spell and can today no longer be regarded as an exponent of Russian policy. On the contrary, the Bulgarian government strives to adopt a closer relationship with the Triple Alliance.

These favourable developments are, however, faced by some unfavourable ones which weigh more heavily. Turkey, whose unity of interests with the Triple Alliance was a given and which posed a strong counterweight against Russia and the Balkan states has been almost entirely pushed out of Europe and has suffered a substantial loss of her great power status.

Serbia, whose policy has for years been led by hostile tendencies against Austria-Hungary and who is entirely under Russia's influence, has achieved an increase in territory and population which has far exceeded her own expectations; through the territorial neighbourhood with Montenegro and the general strengthening of the pan-Serbian idea the possibility of a further increase of Serbia by way of a union with Montenegro has come closer. Finally, during the course of the crisis the relationship between Rumania and the Triple Alliance has substantially altered.

While the Balkan crisis has thus led to results which are in themselves already not favourable for the Triple Alliance and which carry in them the germ of further development which is particularly undesirable for Austria-Hungary, we see on the other hand that Russian and French diplomacy has initiated a unified and orchestrated action aimed at further expanding these advantages and to modify those developments which are disadvantageous from their point of view. [...]

While the policy of the two Imperial powers and, to some extent, also that of Italy is conservative and the Triple Alliance has solely a defensive character, the policy of Russia and France pursues certain tendencies which are aimed against the status quo and the Russo-French alliance is [...] ultimately of an offensive nature. That the policy of the Triple Alliance could so far prevail and that the peace of Europe has been protected from disturbances by Russia and France was due to the military superiority which the armies of the Triple Alliance, in particular

Austria-Hungary's and Germany's, undoubtedly possessed in comparison with those of Russia and France, while Rumania's alliance with the Imperial powers was a factor of high esteem. [...]

Until now, Austria-Hungary's military plans in case of a conflict with Russia were based on the condition of Rumania's cooperation. If this condition falls away, if there is not even absolute certainty of new Rumanian aggression, then the Monarchy must make other arrangements for the case of war and must even consider the building of fortifications against Rumania.

Politically this is about proving to Rumania through deeds that we are in the position to create a different basis for Austria-Hungary's Balkan policy. [...] In the current Balkan situation this [...] can only be achieved if the Monarchy agrees to Bulgaria's request, already suggested a year ago and since then repeated several times, and enters into an agreement with her. Concurrently, the Monarchy's policy should seek to arrange an alliance between Bulgaria and Turkey [...]. Rumania's attitude almost pushes the Monarchy by necessity to grant Bulgaria any rapprochement that she has been seeking for so long, in order to scupper the otherwise hardly stoppable success of Russia's encircling policy. [...]

However, before Austria-Hungary attempts the action in question [arriving at an agreement with Bulgaria], she attaches the highest value to arriving at a complete agreement with the German Empire, and not just due to concerns which result from the tradition and the close alliance but particularly because important interests of Germany and of the Triple Alliance are at stake [...].

For, if Russia, supported by France, seeks to unite the Balkan states against Austria-Hungary, if she attempts to increase the deterioration of the relationship with Rumania, then this enmity is not solely aimed at the Monarchy but also against the ally of the German Empire, against the part of the central-European block which, due to its geographic position and internal structure is the most exposed and most vulnerable to attacks and which blocks Russia's path to the realisation of her global plans.

However, to break the military superiority of the two Imperial powers with the help of troops from the Balkans is the aim of the Dual Entente, but not Russia's final aim. While France is aiming for a weakening of the Monarchy because she expects from this the support of her *revanche* plans, the intentions of the Tsar's Empire are much more expansive still.

If one surveys Russia's development during the last two centuries, the continual increase of her territory, the enormous increase of her population, far in excess of that of all other European great powers, and the immense advance of her economic resources and military strength and considers that this large Empire is still, due to its position and agreements as good as cut off from the sea, then one understands the necessity of the traditionally innate aggressive character of Russian policy.

Sensibly one cannot accuse Russia of having territorial ambitions against the German Empire; nonetheless the extraordinary armaments and military preparations, the expansion of strategic railways against the West and so on in Russia are certainly directly even more against Germany than against Austria-Hungary.

For Russia has recognized that the realization of her [...] plans in Europe and Asia primarily injure important interests of Germany and would therefore meet with inescapable resistance. [...]

Russia's manifest encirclement tendencies against the Monarchy, who does not pursue *Weltpolitik*, have the final aim of making it impossible for the German Empire to mount any resistance against those final Russian aims and against her political and economic supremacy.

For these reasons the leadership of Austria-Hungary's foreign policy is also convinced that it is in the joint interests of the Monarchy as much as Germany's in the current state of the Balkan crisis to oppose promptly and energetically a development, aspired to by Russia and supported by her, which it will later perhaps no longer be possible to revert.

This memorandum had just been completed when the terrible events of Sarajevo occurred.

The whole consequences of this heinous murder cannot yet be fathomed today. At least, however, it has delivered the indubitable evidence, if such was still required, for the unbridgeable difference between the Monarchy and Serbia as well as for the danger and intensity of the pan-Serbian movement which will stop at nothing.

Austria-Hungary has not been lacking in good will and accommodation in order to achieve a bearable relationship with Serbia. But it has recently been shown that these attempts have been entirely in vain and that the Monarchy will also in future have to reckon with Serbia's stubborn, irreconcilable and aggressive enmity.

All the more important is for the Monarchy the necessity to tear apart with a determined hand the threads which her opponents want to weave into a net above her head.

ÖUA, VIII, No. 9984.

(118) 5 July: Conrad's audience with Emperor Franz Joseph in Schönbrunn

Germany's support essential for Austria-Hungary's decision for a war against Serbia

The conversation immediately turned to the political situation.

His Majesty had a complete grasp of it and was fully aware of its seriousness. I expressed my view of the unavoidability of a war against Serbia.

H.M.: 'Yes, this is quite right, but how do you want to wage war if then everyone will attack us, particularly Russia?'

I: 'But Germany will cover our rear?'

His Majesty looked at me doubtfully and said: 'Are you certain of Germany?' He had charged the heir to the throne Archduke Franz Ferdinand to demand of the German Kaiser in Konopischt a declaration whether we could also in future count unconditionally on Germany.[7] The German Kaiser had avoided the question and not given an answer.

I: 'Your Majesty, but we must know how we are placed.'

H.M.: Yesterday evening a note has been despatched to Germany in which we demand a clear answer.'[8]

I: 'If the answer is that Germany is on our side, will we then wage the war against Serbia?'

H.M.: 'In that case, yes (after a brief pause contemplating this question His Majesty continued:) but if Germany does not give us that answer, what then?'

I: 'Then we are indeed on our own. We would need the answer soon, as the big decision depends on it.'

H.M.: 'The German Kaiser is on his North Sea Cruise.[9] In any case we will have to await the answer.'

I was under the impression that His Majesty was not certain of Germany and therefore hesitated in his decision. [...]

At the end of the audience His Majesty was friendly as always and remarked: 'On Tuesday I will be going to Ischl.'

I requested of His Majesty, if the crisis were to dissipate and the situation would allow for it, to be allowed to go to the Tyrol for a few days, which His Majesty granted with the words: 'Of course, you too need a holiday.'

7 Franz Ferdinand had met the German Kaiser in Konopischt, 50 kilometres south-east of Prague, on 12–13 June 1914.

8 This refers to the letter and memorandum taken by Hoyos to be presented to Wilhelm II by the Austrian Ambassador Szögyény (**120**), (**130**).

9 In fact, Wilhelm II was still in Berlin and would only depart on 7 July.

I mention these details here because they prove that a decision for a war against Serbia had then by no means been taken. [...]

Franz Conrad von Hötzendorf, *Aus meiner Dienstzeit*, 5 vols, Rikola Verlag, Vienna, Leipzig, Munich 1922–1925, Vol. IV, pp. 36–38.

(119) 5 July: Hoyos' personal account of his 'mission' to London

Germany aware of likely risk of European war, but nonetheless encourages Austria-Hungary to proceed with action against Serbia; Hoyos informs ally that Italy is to be kept in the dark; outlines territorial annexation plans which were not condoned widely in Vienna

[...] I arrived on Sunday morning in Berlin. Szögyény advised me to go to Understate Secretary Zimmermann in Jagow's absence,[10] who would arrive that same evening, and to give him copies of the documents while he drove to Potsdam to Kaiser Wilhelm where he was invited for lunch. The Kaiser was prepared for Kaiser Franz Joseph's hand-written letter and also that Szögyény had to bring him important news.

[...] Zimmermann [...] read the two documents and his first observation [...] was 'yes, 90% likelihood of a European war if you do something against Serbia'. The conversation which then developed and which lasted over an hour could only be interpreted by me that in Berlin they expected an energetic strike by us against Serbia and that they were determined to grant us the necessary support. Zimmermann said much about the readiness for battle [*Schlagfertigkeit*] of the German army, its strength since the acceptance of the last army bill. Among other things he remarked that we would probably be sufficiently occupied in the Balkans and hardly be able to muster significant numbers of troops against Russia. But this did not matter, for Germany was strong enough to wage the war on both fronts alone. ([...] When I returned to Vienna I told General Conrad what Zimmermann had said to me and our Chief of Staff, who knew the exact arrangements, laughed at me and thought that Zimmermann did not know what he was saying.)

On parting I said to Zimmermann: 'You could not really have thought that Austria-Hungary would quietly accept the murder of the heir to the throne at Sarajevo and not react to it.' He replied: 'No, but we did fear it a little bit.'

The meeting with the Reich-Chancellor, Jagow[11] and Zimmermann

10 Jagow was on his honeymoon in Switzerland.

11 Jagow returned from his honeymoon on 6 July.

which took place the next day was of course of more formal character. But even here there was no sense of the German gentlemen wanting to restrain us or to limit the action to the realm of diplomacy. [...] In reply to the question what we intended to do with Serbia when we had carried out the action I took the liberty, much resented by Tisza, to declare that Serbia would have to be divided between us, Bulgaria and Rumania.[12] I did this because I knew that the Germans would waver in the support of our plans if, as had been the case in the Balkan War and in the following years, we could not formulate out plans precisely and had uncertain aims. [...]

My conversation with the three German statesmen ended with me repeating to the Chancellor that we considered a war with Serbia unavoidable, sooner or later, but that we were willing for now to make do with closer ties with Bulgaria if Germany felt that a [different] moment would be more advantageous from a European point of view. In reply Bethmann Hollweg told me that it was not for Germany to give us advice regarding our policy vis-à-vis Serbia, that she would cover our back and fulfil her alliance obligations in every way if we considered it necessary to proceed against Serbia. If I wanted to know his personal view about the opportunity afforded by the present moment, then he could tell me that war was unavoidable and the current point in time was more advantageous than a later one.

I had one more task to fulfil in Berlin, and that was to convince the German statesmen that it would not be possible for us to inform Italy in advance of our intentions vis-à-vis Serbia, on the one hand because we would have to worry about indiscretions, and on the other because we knew exactly that Italy, based on Article VII of the Triple Alliance Treaty, would approach us with the demand of the cessation of the South Tyrol and in case of our refusal would immediately adopt a hostile attitude against us.[13] I succeeded in convincing the German gentlemen of the accuracy of this argument. [...][14]

Alexander Hoyos, ‘My Mission to Berlin’, cited in Fritz Fellner, ‘Die “Mission Hoyos”’, Peter Lang, Frankfurt am Main, et al. 1984, pp. 311–313.

12 In the Ministerial Council meeting of 7 July, it was Tisza who objected strongly to any territorial gains made by Austria-Hungary as a result of action against Serbia (**134**). See also (**167**).

13 Article VII of the Triple Alliance Treaty specified Italy’s right to compensation if Austria-Hungary acquired Balkan territory. For the text see Holger Afflerbach, *Der Dreibund*, Böhlau, Munich 2003, Appendix C, p. 886.

14 Hoyos wrote this account after the war had ended.

(120) 5 July: Szögýeny to Berchtold

Hoyos Mission; account of Szögýeny's meeting with Wilhelm II; Kaiser Wilhelm promises support; Germany's so-called 'blank cheque' to Austria-Hungary[15]

Berlin 5 July 1914
D. 7.35 p.m.
R. 10.00 p.m.
Telegram 237
Strictly Confidential

After I had informed Kaiser Wilhelm that I had a hand-written letter from His Imp[erial] and Roy[al] Apostolic Majesty, which Count Hoyos had brought me today and which I was to give to him, I received an invitation to lunch with Their Majesties at noon in the *Neues Palais*. I gave His Majesty the hand-written letter and the enclosed memorandum.[16] In my presence the Kaiser read both with the greatest attention. The first thing he assured me was that he had expected some serious step on our part towards Serbia, but that at the same time he must confess that the detailed statement of His Majesty made him regard a serious European complication possible and that he could give no definite answer before having taken council with the Imperial Chancellor.

After lunch, when I again called attention to the seriousness of the situation, the Kaiser authorised me to inform our Gracious Majesty that we might in this case, as in all others, rely upon Germany's full support. He must, as he said before, first hear what the Imperial Chancellor had to say, but he did not doubt in the least that Herr von Bethmann Hollweg would entirely agree with him. This was especially so regarding an action on our part against Serbia. But it was his (Kaiser Wilhelm's) opinion that this action must not be delayed. Russia's attitude would in any case be hostile, but for this he had been prepared for years, and even if a war between Austria-Hungary and Russia were to result, we could be convinced that Germany would stand by our side with the usual

15 See (**171**), in which the Bavarian Chargé d'Affaires in Berlin, Hans von Schoen, refers to the agreement given to the Austrians as a 'blank cheque'.

16 (**117**). The letter and the memorandum can be found in ÖUA, VIII, No. 9984 (also in DD No. 13 and 14). In addition to the two documents, Hoyos also delivered some verbal instructions for the Ambassador, as Berchtold confirmed in his memoirs: 'When he took over the two documents intended for Berlin Hoyos received verbally from me the order to inform Count Szögyény that we considered the moment to have arrived perhaps to have a reckoning with Serbia.' Cited in Fellner, 'Die "Mission Hoyos"', p. 295.

faithfulness of an ally.[17] Russia was, by the way, at the present time not prepared for war, and would certainly think very hard before appealing to arms. But it would agitate against us among the Triple Entente and add fuel to the fire in the Balkans.

He understood perfectly well that His Apostolic Majesty, given his well-known love of peace, would find it difficult to march into Serbia; but if we had really recognised the necessity of warlike action against Serbia, then he (Kaiser Wilhelm) would regret if we did not make use of the present moment, which was so favourable for us.

As regards Rumania he would ensure that King Carol and his advisors would act correctly.

Concluding an alliance with Bulgaria 'was hardly favoured by him', now as ever he did not have any trust in King Ferdinand, nor his former or present advisers. Still he would make not the slightest objection to a treaty between the Monarchy and Bulgaria, though this treaty must contain nothing to offend Rumania and it must – as the memorandum also proposes – be communicated to Rumania.[18]

Kaiser Wilhelm intends leaving tomorrow morning for Kiel, and from there to go on his North Sea tour; but before leaving, His Majesty will discuss the subject in question with the Imperial Chancellor. For this purpose he has called him from Hohenfinow[19] to the *Neues Palais* for this evening.

I shall certainly have an opportunity of talking to the Imperial Chancellor during the course of tomorrow.[20]

ÖUA, VIII, No. 10058.[21]

---

17 Konrad Jarausch has termed this 'one of the most momentous assurances of European history'. 'The Illusion of Limited War: Bethmann Hollweg's calculated risk, July 1914', *Central European History*, 2, 1, 1969, pp. 48–76, p. 56.

18 On Rumania's position in 1914 see Schroeder, 'Romania and the Great Powers before 1914', *passim*.

19 The Chancellor's country estate about 70 kilometres north-east of Berlin.

20 For Bethmann Hollweg's account of these events, see Theobald von Bethmann Hollweg, *Betrachtungen zum Weltkrieg*, 2 vols, Vol. 1, *For dem Kriege*, Hobbin, Berlin 1919, pp. 134ff.

21 English translation based on Imanuel Geiss, *July 1914*, Scribner, London 1967, No. 6, but here with minor differences.

(121) 5 July: Bollati to San Giuliano

Zimmermann promises that Germany would urge restraint on Austria but that Serbia would do well to exercise the same

Berlin, 5 July 1914.
D. 1.15 a.m.
R.2.50 p.m.
Telegram 5967/501

[...] I have already informed Your Excellency of the intensely hostile language towards Serbia, all over the German press, [...] and, on the other hand, of the reassurance given to me by Zimmermann that he would try to influence the Vienna Cabinet towards moderation. He told me yesterday that he had started working on this and that he would not fail to continue. He added, however, that it would have been better if Belgrade also realized the requirements of the situation, since the evidence of the Serbian origin of the Sarajevo plot is indisputable and the language used by the Serbian press, even the unofficial one, is singular to say the least.[22]

DDI, 4th series, XII, No. 78.

(122) 5 July: Plessen Diary

Hoyos Mission: Wilhelm II discusses Austrian request for support with his advisers; German approval of Austrian policy and encouragement to use opportunity for war against Serbia

H.M. has ordered me to the *Neues Palais* at 5 pm. There I find the Chief of the Military Cabinet Lyncker and Minister of War Falkenhayn.[23] H.M. reads to us a letter of the Austrian Emperor and a memorandum of the Austrian Foreign Minister, Count Berchtold, according to which the Austrians are preparing themselves for war against Serbia and want first to assure themselves of Germany.[24] The Chancellor and Secretary of State [Jagow] were also present. Our opinion is that the Austrians should

22 The next day, San Giuliano urged Serbia to exercise restraint, and – via Berlin – tried to do the same in Vienna. DDI, 4, XII, Nos 89 and 90. See Richard J.B. Bosworth, *Italy, the Least of the Great Powers*, Cambridge University Press, Cambridge, New York et al. 1979, pp. 380–381.

23 See (**123**).

24 (**117**).

act against Serbia the sooner the better and that the Russians – though friends of Serbia – nonetheless will not participate. There is the threat of Rumania abandoning the Triple Alliance,[25] and an alliance between Turkey and Bulgaria is on the horizon. – H.M.'s departure for his North Sea cruise is to proceed undisturbed.[26]

August Bach (ed.), *Deutsche Gesandtschaftsberichte zum Kriegsausbruch*, Quaderverlag, Berlin 1937, p. 14.

(123) 5 July: Falkenhayn to Moltke[27]

Hoyos Mission: Minister of War Falkenhayn and Chancellor Bethmann Hollweg did not gain impression that war would break out

Berlin, 5 July 1914

To be delivered by hand.
Strictly confidential

This afternoon H.M. the Kaiser and King sent for me at the *Neues Palais* to inform me that Austria-Hungary seemed resolved no longer to tolerate the hatching of intrigues against Austria on the Balkan Peninsula and therefore, if necessary, to march into Serbia as a beginning; if the Russians refused to tolerate this, Austria would not be disposed to give way.

H.M. felt justified in drawing this inference from the words of the Austrian Ambassador, when the latter this afternoon delivered a memorandum from the Government in Vienna and a hand-written communication from Emperor Franz Joseph.[28]

I was not present during this conversation, so am unable to permit myself to form any opinion in this matter. On the other hand, H.M. read aloud both the hand-written letter and the memorandum. Insofar as the hurriedness of the proceedings gave one a chance to arrive at any opinion, these documents did not succeed in convincing me that the

25 For details see Schroeder, 'Romania and the Great Powers before 1914', *passim*.

26 Wilhelm II departed on his annual North Sea Cruise on 7 July. (**123**), (**125**).

27 Helmuth von Moltke was in Karlsbad (today Karlovy Vary in the Czech Republic, 350 kilometres south of Berlin) for his annual cure. He returned to Berlin on 25 July. During his absence he was kept informed about events by a number of colleagues. See Annika Mombauer, *Helmuth von Moltke*, Cambridge University Press, Cambridge 2001, pp. 193–197.

28 (**117**), (**120**), (**130**).

Vienna Government had taken any firm resolution. Both paint a very gloomy picture of the general situation of the Dual Monarchy as a result of Pan-Slav agitations. Both consider it necessary that something should be done about this with the greatest urgency. But neither speaks of the need for war, rather both expound 'energetic' political action such as the conclusion of a treaty with Bulgaria, for which they would like to be certain of the support of the German Reich.

This support should be granted with some indication that it would, in the first place, be a matter for Austria-Hungary to take the requisite steps which are in her own interest.

The Chancellor, who was also in Potsdam, appears to have as little faith as I do that the Austrian Government is really in earnest, even though its language is undeniably more resolute that in the past. At any rate, not only has he raised no objections about the Scandinavian journey taking place, but he has even recommended it. Certainly under no circumstances will the coming weeks bring any decisions. It will be a long time before the treaty with Bulgaria is concluded. Your Excellency's stay at the Spa will therefore scarcely need to be curtailed. Nonetheless, although I have not been authorized to do so, I considered it advisable to inform you of the gravity of the situation so that anything untoward which could, after all, occur at any time, should not find you wholly unprepared.[29]

DD, 2nd edn, 1927, p. XII.[30]

(124) 5 July: Haldane to Grey

German ambassador concerned that Austria will take drastic action against Serbia and drag Germany into a conflict; Austria determined to humiliate Serbia

Lichnowsky who has just come back from Berlin came to see me yesterday. He appears to be very worried about the state of opinion in Germany. Austria he says is in a white heat of indignation over the murder of the Archduke and is contemplating drastic action. I asked him if he meant by this war, and he replied that that would depend on Serbia, but that Austria felt strongly that Serbia must be publicly humiliated. The general feeling in Berlin was, he said, that Serbia could not be allowed to

29 Wilhelm II instructed Generalmajor von Bertrab to inform Moltke. See August Bach (ed.), *Deutsche Gesandtschaftsberichte zum Kriegsausbruch*, Quaderverlag, Berlin 1937, p. 14.

30 Engl. transl. based on Geiss, *July 1914*, No. 7, with minor amendments.

go on intriguing and agitating against Austria and that Germany must support Austria in any action she proposed to take. There was naturally apprehension in Germany that Russia would support Serbia and that led him on to say that he had heard the opinion expressed in authoritative quarters that we had entered into a naval treaty with Russia. I told him that that was nonsense and advised him to see you at once and tell you what he had told me. He brought me a letter from Ballin, which was the reason of his visit and Ballin too takes a pessimistic view and evidently thinks that Austria may drag Germany into trouble.[31]

Cited in Frederick Maurice, *Haldane 1856–1915. The Life of Viscount Haldane of Cloan*, Faber & Faber, London 1937, p. 348.

(125) 6 July: Hopman to Tirpitz

Despite German support for Austria-Hungary there is general expectation that the crisis would blow over

[...] Yesterday Kaiser Franz Joseph had a memorandum handed to H.M. by the Austrian Ambassador, in which it is argued that the investigation about the assassination in Sarajevo had shown without doubt that high-ranking Serbian officials, active officers, even perhaps members of the royal family had known about the murderous plan before it had been executed.[32] The Austrian government would approach Serbia with demands for the most extensive satisfaction and, as soon as this had not been fulfilled, to have her troops march into Serbia.[33] H.M. does not consider it likely that Russia would intervene because the Tsar would not support regicides and because Russia was currently not entirely ready for war militarily and financially. The same was true, particularly in

31 The timing of the meeting Haldane had with Lichnowsky is significant, for it points to determination in Vienna, and knowledge of such determination in Berlin, before Hoyos had officially informed the ally of Austria's intention to explore all options. For details on the naval treaty see **(79)**, **(81)**, **(87)**, **(97)**, **(99)**, **(100)**, **(102)**.

32 This had not, in fact, been established.

33 It would only transpire later in the crisis that in fact Austro-Hungarian troops would not be able to mobilize for more than two weeks after mobilization was declared. The Saxon Military Plenipotentiary Leuckart reported to the Saxon Minister of War on 29 July: 'In the Great General Staff one is of the opinion that the Austrian army will not be operational before 12 August. Rumour has it that the Austrian mobilization has been hindered by difficulties and that we might therefore also have to postpone our mobilization – if mobilization becomes necessary – if possible.' BA-MA, W-10/50890.

financial regards, in France. H.M. did not speak about England. He let it be known to Kaiser Franz Joseph that he could rely on him. H.M. believes that the situation will be clarified in 8 days' time with Serbia giving in, but nonetheless considers it necessary also to be prepared for a different outcome. He had therefore already spoken yesterday with the Imperial Chancellor, the Chief of the General Staff, the Minister of War and the deputy Chief of the Admiralty Staff. Measures which might lead to creating political alarm or which cause particular costs are to be avoided for now. [...]

H.M., who according to His Excellency v. Capelle, makes a calm and determined impression, has departed for Kiel this morning to board ship to leave for the North Sea Cruise.[34]

Volker R. Berghahn and Wilhelm Deist, 'Kaiserliche Marine und Kriegsausbruch 1914', *Militärgeschichtliche Mitteilungen*, 4, 1970, pp. 37–58, No. 1.

(126) 6 July: Berthold Molden's memorandum[35]

Doubts about the future of the monarchy; impressions of Austria-Hungary's decline must be countered with decisive action against Serbia; fears of an encirclement of the Empire by hostile powers and of Germany abandoning her weakened ally; Serbia should be given a short time to comply with Austrian demands or face military action; German support has been assured and she must relieve Austrian troops in the North

34 Wilhelm II boarded the royal yacht *Hohenzollern* on 6 July and set sail for his annual Scandinavian cruise on the 7th. Hopman also left a record of his conversation with Capelle in his diary. See Michael Epkenhans (ed.), *Albert Hopman. Das ereignisreiche Leben eines 'Wilhelminers'*, Oldenbourg, Munich 2004, pp. 382ff.

35 Molden was Austro-Hungarian Consul-General in Warsaw from 1911–1914, as well as a journalist and editor. He was one of a small circle of diplomats in the *Ballhausplatz* in July 1914. Though not directly involved in actual decision-making he was in close contact with members of the so-called Belvedere Circle around Archduke Franz Ferdinand. His memorandum of 6 July was intended for internal use (one copy went to Forgách, section chief in the Foreign Ministry and close adviser to Berchtold). Solomon Wank points to the similarities between some of Molden's arguments and those made by Berchtold on 7 July in the Ministerial Council meeting, although there is no evidence that proves that he read the memorandum prior to the meeting. Solomon Wank, 'Desperate Council in Vienna in July 1914', Berthold Molden's unpublished memorandum', *Central European History*, 26, 3, 1993, pp. 281–310.

against Russia; danger that a war with Serbia would lead to a war with Russia; the present time is right for political and military action against Serbia and might not be again in future

---

The monarchy is now living through one of those moments that will be decisive for a long time. The history of the next years, probably of the next decades, will bear the imprint of the decisions that are being made in these days. [...]

[...] public opinion of educated people, at least those who do not subscribe to pacifism, would approve of strong and decisive action. Everywhere among the educated classes one finds almost heavy despondency regarding what appears to them as giving in or weakness; everywhere one finds the view that by continuing such a policy the empire is heading towards collapse, after the decline has already allegedly begun; everywhere one finds doubts about the future of the monarchy, which is torn by conflicts internally and which is no longer respected by even her smallest neighbours. [...] it has long been the opinion that, in order to erase the impression of decline and disintegration, a striking deed, a punch of the fist would be necessary. This was the mood during and after the Balkan War and also during the last Albanian crisis. [...] It is undeniable that the moral effect of an action would be extremely favourable. Austria-Hungary would again believe in herself. I have the will, therefore I am, is what would be said.

The general international situation as it has developed over the years increasingly pushes the Monarchy into the most exposed position. It cannot be too much longer before it will be so surrounded that its enemies will feel themselves downright challenged to attack it, and who knows if it then will still make the impression on the German ally of being worth a life-and-death struggle. [...]

For the moment, the Serbian government is still deeply dismayed over the murderous act in Sarajevo; in the absence of the consequences that it fears it will begin to pocket the gains that the event can have for it. To this terrible turn of events for us, quite apart from the profound loss of the Heir to the throne, as an extraordinary personality, a new one will have been added. Everywhere one will say that Austria-Hungary has indeed hurled insults at Serbia and persecuted the defenceless Serbs in Bosnia, but that she lacks the courage to take action against Serbia herself. Not only Serbia will profit from that, but everyone who wants to advance at our expense – Rumania, Russia, Italy. All diplomatic negotiations which we will have to have will be made more difficult, one will close in on us ever more tightly, [and] step on our feet more and more. [...]

If we crush Serbia, Serbian imperialism within and beyond our borders will also be crushed for a long time to come. Obviously we do not first have to prove that we are stronger than Serbia; however, by an action, we will have offered proof that we are not afraid of Serbia's backer, of Russia, while, on the other hand, if Russia does not intervene she will prove that she is afraid of us and the German Empire and that the role of protector which, as Sazonov's last speech shows, she has assumed even in regard to the Orthodox church in Galicia and Hungary, is useless lies. [...]

The suppression of Serbian megalomania would exert a most favourable influence on the Croatians and the Mohammedans of Bosnia and Herzegovina and the Croats of Austria and Hungary. This is all the more important because the South Slav provinces in particular must in a certain sense first be won over to our side or be won back over particularly because they constitute our access to the sea. To lose them would mean drying up, approaching certain downfall; therefore all the peoples of the Monarchy have an interest in the preservation of these territories, and one cannot put the fight for them on the same level with the fight for Lombardy and Venetia. [...] The extraordinary importance of our relations with Serbia derives from the very fact that, because of the support provided to Serbia by Russia, she incessantly lays mines in those territories and in addition now wants to force us through criminal acts to leave her those territories. Certainly, it is not the government which inspires such plots, but they lead in the same direction as that pursued by the government. The aim is our coastland, the lungs with which we breathe. There is no peace between us and Serbian imperialism; we can live in peace with Serbia, but not with her imperialist policy. This conviction has become so firm among all people who think for and with Austria-Hungary that one could hear often enough in the last years that the next Serbian challenge, the next Serbian proof of flagrant hostility must be used to present the bill. Conciliation as long as possible, but, at the next blow, strike back. This next blow has now been struck – the whole world can see which convictions have come to the fore in Serbia. It is not a matter of revenge, but of security for the future. Revenge might be the most understandable motive for the feeling of the simplest people in our population. For many others it will mean that Serbia has now revealed her evil intentions – politics however has to demand either guarantees or subjugation.

Several paths can be chosen in order to push Serbia to the wall. If Serbia, after a specified, very short period of time, does not yield, then certainly war,[36] for this we must be determined from the outset. Of course a quick success in such a war is urgently necessary; misfortune would be fatal, slow development worrying. We must march only if we

36 In the event, Serbia would only be given 48 hours to reply to the ultimatum (**180**), (**191**).

are certain of decisive victory; for this reason alone it is important that Germany relieve us as much as possible in the north, thereby allowing us to act vigorously in the south. Very important, therefore, is that article of the alliance treaty [of 1879] that calls for a war against Russia also in the case when, while the ally is engaged in a war with a third power, Russia threatens it by a concentration of troops.[37] [...]

The danger that a war with Serbia could lead to a war with Russia is, as stated, not completely to be disregarded, despite the indignation over the assassination which may initially have prevailed at the Petersburg imperial court. However, precisely because it cannot be ruled out, the effect of our forceful action will be all the stronger; in Serbia, Rumania, Bulgaria one will see that we do not shrink from that possibility. Of course it is better if the chance of war with Russia is reduced; it will be reduced, apart from Germany's adherence to alliance,[38] probably also by England's attitude. It cannot be assumed that England would consider a war involving the entire European continent as lying in her interest, quite apart from economic considerations which must confront her. For England, a German victory would be unwelcome, a victory of Russia would also be extremely uncomfortable; she will therefore strive, as much as it lies in her power, to work for localization of an Austro-Hungarian war.[39] Sensibly England would welcome a defeat of Serbia and the accompanying moral defeat of Russia, for English politicians would have to be blind not to see that Russia is at the centre of a conspiracy directed against the integrity and autonomy of Austria-Hungary, a conspiracy which, in the final analysis, is as threatening to England's existence, because this conspiracy will be ever more violently pursued the longer and the more undisturbed one allows it to grow. Its success would mean the predominance of the Tsarist Empire in the entire region between the borders of Germany and India. [...]

A political and, if it must be, military demonstration of force against Serbia would have an effect everywhere. It would perhaps also bear positive fruits, although for the immediate future it would be only a defensive measure in the political strategy – albeit a tactically offensive one. It would make an impression on Russia, which for some time now has again become intoxicated with visions of her own greatness and knows how to get others to share this image of herself. It would have an

37 Molden was clearly unaware that while he was hoping for Germany to bail out Austria-Hungary, Germany was relying on Austro-Hungarian troops to be deployed against Russia first in order to implement her deployment plan against France. This would become obvious at the end of the crisis. See (**353**).

38 Following the Hoyos Mission to Berlin, Vienna's decision-makers knew that they could count on the German ally whatever action they chose to take (**120**), (**130**).

39 This was a very astute observation and summed up Britain's foreign policy endeavours for much of the July Crisis.

effect on Austria-Hungary and would restrain the destructive tendencies which stem from the belief in the weakness and the hopeless future of the state, and this effect would be at least as valuable as that made on the outside world. [...]

Politically and probably militarily, an action at the present moment would be much less precarious than at any future one – psychologically it would be far more favourable now. Today we still have our fate in our hands; tomorrow, perhaps we will not.

Cited in Solomon Wank, 'Desperate Council in Vienna in July 1914', *Central European History*, 26, 3, 1993, pp. 281–310.[40]

(127) 6 July: Wilhelm II in conversation with Krupp von Bohlen und Halbach

Kaiser determined to show resolve during the crisis

[Notes written by Dr Mühlon, member of the board of Krupp directors]

[Wilhelm II announced] he would immediately declare war if Russia mobilized. This time all would see that he would not back down [*umfalle*]. The Kaiser's repeated emphasis that in this case nobody would again be able to accuse him of indecision had even appeared almost comical.[41]

Cited in Fritz Fischer, *Griff nach der Weltmacht*, first published 1961. Nachdruck der Sonderausgabe 1967, Droste, Düsseldorf 1984, p. 51.

(128) 6 July: Grey to Rumbold

Conversation with Lichnowsky about Germany's response to assassination; German concerns about increase in Russian military strength and rumours of Anglo-Russian naval convention

(No. 214.) Secret.
Foreign Office, July 6, 1914.

The German Ambassador spoke very warmly to-day of the satisfaction and pleasure which had been given to the Emperor, and generally, by the

40 Translation here by Annika Mombauer.

41 This conversation took place in Kiel the evening of 6 July, before the Kaiser embarked on his North Sea cruise. He would later change his mind. See (**277**), (**374**).

visit of the British Admiral to Kiel.[42]

I said that I knew that it had given great satisfaction and pleasure on our side.

The Ambassador then went on to speak to me privately, he said, but very seriously, as to the anxiety and pessimism that he had found in Berlin. He explained that the murder of the Archduke Franz Ferdinand had excited very strong anti-Serbian feeling in Austria; and he knew for a fact, though he did not know details, that the Austrians intended to do something and it was not impossible that they would take military action against Serbia.

I said that surely they did not think of taking any territory?

The Ambassador replied that they did not wish to take territory,[43] because they would not know what to do with it. He thought their idea was that they must have some compensation in the sense of some humiliation for Serbia. The situation was exceedingly difficult for Germany; if she told the Austrians that nothing must be done, she would be accused of always holding them back and not supporting them; on the other hand if she let events take their course there was the possibility of very serious trouble. The Ambassador earnestly hoped that, if trouble came, we would use our influence to mitigate feeling in St. Petersburg.

A second thing which caused anxiety and pessimism in Berlin was the apprehension in Germany about the attitude of Russia, especially in connection with the recent increase of Russian military strength. He was told that Russia now had a peace footing of one million men and the impression in Germany was that Russian feeling towards Germany was very unfavourable.

A third thing was the idea that there was some Naval Convention between Russia and England.[44] He had reported to his Government all that I had said to him recently,[45] just before he went to Germany on holiday, about our relations with Russia and France, and he had assured his Government that they could trust every word, and that there was no secret agreement on our part. They accepted the statement that there was nothing between the British and Russian Governments, but they felt that, nevertheless, there might be some understanding between the British and Russian Naval authorities. If there was such an understanding for co-operation directed against Germany, it would strengthen chauvinistic

42 Vice-Admiral Sir George John Scott Warrender of Lochend (1860–1917) was in command of HMS *George V* and a squadron of British ships which attended the Kiel Regatta in June 1914. See (**86**) and (**116**).

43 In fact, Hoyos favoured this early in the crisis and it was largely due to Tisza's objections that territorial gains were not part of Vienna's demands. See (**119**) and (**134**).

44 See (**79**), (**85**), (**87**), (**97**), (**99**), (**100**), (**102**), (**135**), (**143**).

45 See (**99**).

feeling in Russia, it would make pan-German feeling quite irresistible, and lead to an increase of the German Naval law, which otherwise was not intended, and it would also impair good feeling between England and Germany generally. This was what had been impressed upon him very strongly in Berlin.

The Ambassador went so far as to say that there was some feeling in Germany, based more especially upon the second and third things that he had mentioned to me this afternoon, that trouble was bound to come and therefore it would be better not to restrain Austria and let the trouble come now, rather than later. He impressed upon me more than once that he was speaking quite privately and on very delicate matters, but he was anxious to keep in touch with me. Though he did not share the belief of some people in Berlin that Russia was ill-disposed towards Germany, he was so anxious that he felt he must speak to me immediately on his return from Germany. He quoted Herr von Bethmann Hollweg as being pessimistic.[46]

The Ambassador said that he had asserted at Berlin that though England would remain firmly in the group of the triple entente, for she must preserve the balance of power and could not see France annihilated, yet we did not wish to see the groups of Powers draw apart. I cordially confirmed this.

I said that I would look up the record of what I said to him recently before he went to Berlin about our relations with France and Russia and I would show it to him.[47] We had had no indication from St. Petersburg, ever since the question of the German command in Constantinople was settled,[48] that the Russians had any feeling of anxiety or irritation or ill-will as regards Germany. I recalled what I had said to him at the time of the German command at Constantinople as to how strongly Russia felt on that point, but since it had been settled I had heard nothing unfavourable from St. Petersburg as regards Germany. I was disturbed by what the Ambassador had told me about the form that anti-Serbian feeling might take in Austria. If trouble did come, I would use all the influence I could to mitigate difficulties and smooth them away, and if the clouds arose to prevent the storm from breaking. I was glad that he had spoken to me, and I should like to talk the whole matter of his conversation over with him later on, when I had had time to consider it.[49]

46 See (**135**).

47 See (**99**). See also (**143**).

48 On the Liman von Sanders crisis see (**66**), (**68**), (**69**).

49 Prince Lichnowsky's account concurs with Grey's. The Ambassador reported to the German Chancellor that he discussed 'the entire European situation confidentially' with Grey. He pointed out that one 'could not blame the Austro-Hungarian Government if it were not to leave unpunished this new provocation,

BD, XI, No. 32.

(129) 6 July: Conrad's conversation with Berchtold and Forgách

Conrad stresses need for war to solve the situation; importance of Germany's support discussed; answer expected imminently

Count B[erchtold] said to me: 'Yesterday you were with His Majesty. The Emperor told me that you regard the situation very calmly.'

I: 'Yes – but I have also said to His Majesty that a thorough solution can only be expected from a war.'

I then told Count Berchtold about the course of the audience of the previous day and repeated my view that the assassination was not just directed against one person, but against the Monarchy, and that it had emanated from Serbia. Returning to the possibility of a war against Serbia I emphasized that we would above all need to know with certainty whether Germany would be on our side.

Count B.: 'We will have an answer tomorrow. The German Kaiser

---

given the support which the plotters had evidently received from Belgrade, and if it demanded satisfaction from the Serbian government'. He also discussed that there were concerns in Berlin over 'Russia's massive armaments and certain other signs, such as the building of strategic railways'. 'Russia's mood towards us and Austria-Hungary was without a doubt not friendly. This fact, coupled with the Bosnian outrage, had led to a somewhat pessimistic assessment of the external situation with us.' Finally Lichnowsky touched on 'a somewhat delicate topic'; 'We knew from his assurances that there were no secret agreements of a political nature between England and Russia. Naturally we did not have the slightest reason to doubt the sincerity of his words, but we regretted all the more the fact that rumours repeatedly arose which reported on a naval agreement which aimed at cooperation of both sides against us in case of war. I was not in a position to check the accuracy of such rumours but could well imagine that any discussions of the two sides' naval authorities did not fall in the realm of political agreements and binding treaties, and that they would therefore be in accordance with his explanations. In this case however I believed I needed to alert him to the fact that such agreements would necessarily lead to a strengthening of the nationalist tendencies in Russia which doubtless exist already and on the other hand lead to a desire of armaments increases with us and would make it harder for the Government to oppose such demands which exceed the level of legally stipulated increases known to him. Sir Edward replied [...] that he had already told me recently that no new or secret agreement existed, however that the relations with the Entente partners nonetheless were of a very intimate character. [...] In any case he did not directly deny discussions [*Fühlungnahme*] of the two navies for the case of a joint war. [...] 6 July 1914, Lichnowsky to Bethmann Hollweg (received in Berlin 9 July), DD No. 20, pp. 40–42. See (**99**).

said 'yes', but he would still have to speak with Bethmann Hollweg. How will His Majesty react to this?'

I: 'If Germany agrees His Majesty will be in favour of the war against Serbia.' [...]

Count B. asked my views on which point in time to choose for the war. He pointed out that it was currently harvest time and that the Monarchy would have to exist for a whole year on the harvest. Count Berchtold suggested initially to order a trial mobilization.

I was decidedly against this and remarked that if we mobilize at all, then it could only be a full mobilization (Plan B[alkans]).

Count Berchtold continued: 'Tisza is against the war, he is afraid of a Rumanian advance into Transylvania. What will happen with Galicia if we mobilize against Serbia?'

I: 'There would be no mobilization in Galicia for now. However, if the Russians threaten [us], then the three corps in Galicia must mobilize.'

Count Forgách: 'I have no doubts that Germany has to be with us, first because of her alliance obligation, and secondly because Germany's own existence is threatened.'

I: 'When can I expect the answer from Germany?'

Count B.: 'Tomorrow. But the Germans will ask us what will happen after the war.'

I: 'Then you will say that we do not know that ourselves.'

Finally Count Berchtold told me that a Ministerial Council meeting would take place on 7 July.[50]

Franz Conrad von Hötzendorf, *Aus meiner Dienstzeit*, 5 vols, Rikola Verlag, Vienna, Leipzig, Munich 1922–1925, Vol. IV, pp. 39–40.

(130) 6 July: Szögyény to Berchtold[51]

Germany pledges full support to Austria-Hungary; German pressure to use the present opportunity

Berlin 6 July 1914
D. 5.10 p.m.
R. 8.00 p.m.
Telegram 239
Chiffre – Strictly Confidential

50 (**134**).

51 In 1933 Hoyos maintained in conversation with the historian Luigi Albertini that he, not Szögyény, had written this report. See Fellner, 'Die Mission Hoyos', p. 295.

In addition to my telegram 237 of yesterday.[52]

Have just had a long discussion with the Imperial Chancellor and the Under-Secretary of State [Zimmermann], together with Count Hoyos. Herr von Bethmann Hollweg began by saying that Kaiser Wilhelm had instructed him to express orally his thanks for the hand-written letter which he would answer personally in a few days.

He (the Imperial Chancellor) was also authorized by his Imperial Master to give a precise account of the position of the German Government towards the imperial letter and memorandum, which he did as follows:

The German Government perceives all the dangers arising for Austria-Hungary and thus also for the Triple Alliance from Russia's plan of a Balkan league; it perceives also that in this situation we should be desirous to induce Bulgaria to join the Triple Alliance formally, but it must insist that this should be done in a way – as indeed is intended – not to affect our obligations towards Rumania. The German Envoy in Sofia [Michahelles] was therefore authorized immediately to negotiate in this sense with the Bulgarian government if his Austro-Hungarian colleague asks him to. At the same time he (the Imperial Chancellor) intends instructing the German Envoy in Bucharest [von Waldthausen] to speak openly with the King of Rumania, to inform him of the negotiations in Sofia and to call his attention to the fact that he ought to suppress the Rumanian agitation against us. Herr von Bethmann Hollweg will also ask for the King to be told that he (Chancellor) had in the past always advised us to make up with Serbia, but that after the late events he realizes that this is as good as impossible; Rumania should also take this into account.

As regards our relations with Serbia the German Government is of the opinion that we must judge what is to be done to clarify the relationship; in this we could – whatever form our decision might take – certainly count on Germany, as ally and friend of the Monarchy, to be right behind her.

During the further course of conversation I ascertained that the Imperial Chancellor like his Imperial Master considers immediate intervention on our part as the most radical and best solution for our difficulties on the Balkans. From an international point of view he considers the present moment as more favourable than a later one; he is happy for us not to inform either Italy or Rumania beforehand of an intended action against Serbia. However, Italy should now already be informed of the intention to allow Bulgaria to join the Triple Alliance.[53]

Both the Imperial Chancellor and the Under-Secretary of State were of the opinion that it would be best at present to negotiate a treaty

52 (**120**).
53 (**120**).

with Bulgaria only, and to leave it to the future whether Turkey and eventually Greece would bind themselves to Bulgaria. The Chancellor remarked that in view of the great interests which Germany has in Turkey, this country's accession would be most desirable.

With regard to the step to be undertaken in Bucharest by the representative of Germany, Herr von Bethmann Hollweg thinks it might be useful if, once King Carol's answer has reached Berlin, Count Czernin would a few days later speak with the King in a similar way.

At the conclusion of our discussion, the Chancellor asked about the current state of play in Albania and warned earnestly against any plans which might endanger our relations towards Italy or the duration of the Triple Alliance.

Herr von Tschirschky will be informed of our discussion in strict secrecy.

ÖUA, VIII, No. 10076.[54]

(131) 6 July: Forgách to Tisza

Germany urges Austria-Hungary to use present opportunity for a strike against Serbia

Telegram
D. 1.30 p.m.

Top secret.

Kaiser Wilhelm had it reported to His Majesty that we could rely on the full support of Germany in a potential action. According to Kaiser Wilhelm's opinion we should now not wait any longer with an action against Serbia. We should not let this present favourable moment remain unused. Russia was today not ready for war and Germany stood on our side as a faithful ally.

ÖUA, VIII, No. 10091.

54 Engl. transl. based on Geiss, *July 1914*, No. 8, here with some amendments.

(132) 7 July: Kageneck to Moltke

Austro-Hungarian demands will be unacceptable to Serbia; Russia likely to support Serbia in case of war; Austrian military certain that war will come

This morning a Joint Council of Ministers[55] will take place in Vienna.[56] It has to concern itself with the most important question which steps [...] will have to be taken against the Serbian Government.

This time they seem to have grasped the seriousness of the situation in the Foreign Ministry and to understand that now or never again the moment has come in which to solve the Serbian question.[57]

As I have been told by someone in the know, the Austro-Hungarian demands for Serbia are to be so strong that avoidance or giving in are out of the question. Thus the war against Serbia would be a given. The question is now what Russia will say, for Serbia will naturally first go there for advice. If however the demand is so damaging to Serbia's national feeling, which seems to be the case, then in my opinion Russia cannot allow that the Slavic sentiment on the Balkans would suffer such a loss of prestige. Thus Russia would also be actively involved.

Were it not for the embarrassing uncertainty regarding Rumania's attitude one could look towards the future with less concern.

The above-mentioned person in the know (a General Staff officer) just told me with a triumphant smile: 'This time the war is certain.' [...]

Cited in Günther Kronenbitter, 'Die Macht der Illusionen', *Militärgeschichtliche Mitteilungen*, 57, 1998, pp. 530–531.[58]

---

55 Hungary and Austria maintained separate parliaments, each with its own prime minister. The two were linked by a common government responsible to the Emperor. The common government had responsibility for the army, the navy, for foreign policy and for the customs union. A Common Ministerial Council (sometimes called Joint Council of Ministers or Joint Ministerial Council in English) ruled the common government: it comprised the three ministers for the joint responsibilities (finance, military, and foreign policy), the two prime ministers, some Archdukes and the monarch.

56 See (**134**).

57 N.B. this is being discussed even before the Ministerial Council meeting has taken place.

58 This document, cited from archive files, is not completely identical to the version published in Bach, *Gesandtschaftsberichte*, p. 15.

(133) 7 July: Vesnić to Pašić

Austro-Hungarian government still undecided how to react; ambassador suspects that decision will only be made following investigation into the crime

Paris, 21 June/7 July 1914

I had a long conversation on Wednesday last on the subject of the Sarajevo outrage with M. Viviani, the new Minister for Foreign Affairs,[59] who was somewhat concerned at what had occurred. I made use of this opportunity to describe to him briefly the causes which had led to the outrage, and which were to be found, in the first place, in the irksome system of Government in force in the annexed provinces, and especially in the attitude of the officials, as well as in the whole policy of the Monarchy towards anything orthodox. He understood the situation, but at the same time expressed the hope that we would preserve an attitude of calm and dignity in order to avoid giving cause for fresh accusations in Vienna.

After the first moment of excitement public opinion here has quieted down to such an extent that the Minister-President himself considered it advisable in the Palais de Bourbon to soften the expressions used in the statement which he had made earlier on the subject in the Senate.

Serbian *Blue Book*, No. 13.[60]

[134] 7 July: Minutes of the Joint Council of Ministers for Common Affairs

Decision to provoke a war by presenting deliberately unacceptable demands to Belgrade; Tisza insists on diplomatic move before military intervention; possibility of localizing the conflict discussed but it seems likely that Russia will become involved eventually; Germany's support considered essential and on this occasion willingly given; occasion favourable but in the long run likely to deteriorate

Minutes of the Joint Council of Ministers held on 7 July 1914 chaired by the Minister of the Imperial and Royal House and Minister for Foreign

59 He had become President of the Council and Minister for Foreign Affairs on 13 June and was Premier from 13 July.

60 Engl. transl. in *Collected Diplomatic Documents relating to the Outbreak of the European War*, HMSO, London 1915, pp. 375–376.

Affairs Count Berchtold.

Present: The Imperial and Royal President of the Council of Ministers Count Stürgkh, the Roy. Hungarian Premier Count Tisza, the Imp. and Roy. Joint Minister of Finances Ritter von Biliński, the Imp. and Roy. Minister of War *Feldzeugmeister* Ritter von Krobatin, the Imp. and Roy. Chief of the General Staff G. d. I. Baron von Conrad, the Deputy Chief of the Naval Staff, Rear-Admiral von Kailer

Minutes taken by: Secretary of Legation Count Hoyos

Subject of Council: Bosnian Concerns. The diplomatic action against Serbia.

The Chair [Berchtold] opens the meeting remarking that the Council of Ministers had been called together to advise on the measures to be taken for addressing the evils which in Bosnia and Herzegovina have resulted from the catastrophe of Sarajevo. According to his view there would be a number of internal measures which the crisis in the state of Bosnia has made desirable; but first there should be clarity whether the moment had not come when a show of force would deal with Serbia once and for all. A decisive stroke of this kind could not be dealt without previous diplomatic preparation,[61] and for this reason he had contacted the German Government. The discussions in Berlin had brought about a very satisfactory result, as both Kaiser Wilhelm as well as Herr von Bethmann Hollweg had emphatically promised us the absolute support and aid of Germany in the eventuality of a warlike complication with Serbia.[62] Now we must still take into account Italy and Rumania, and in this he agreed with the Berlin Cabinet that it would be better to act and await eventual claims to compensation.

He realized that a war with Serbia could lead to a war with Russia. However, Russia's present policy was in the long run aimed at a league of the Balkan states including Rumania, which it could at a suitable moment play out against the Monarchy. It was his belief that we must take into account that in the face of such policy our situation must deteriorate as time goes on, all the more because our own South Slavs and Rumanians would interpret any inaction as weakness, and it would give credence to the persuasions of the two neighbours bordering our frontier.

The logical result of what has been said would be to get in advance of our foes and by a timely reckoning with Serbia, to stop the development of the process at present going on, which we would not be able to do later.

61 In the Engl. transl. in Geiss, *July 1914*, No. 9, this was erroneously printed as: 'A decisive stroke of this kind could be dealt without previous diplomatic preparation'.

62 (**120**), (**130**).

The Royal Hungarian Premier [Tisza] agrees that during the last days the situation had changed on account of the facts which the judicial examination has brought forth and due to the attitude of the Serbian press, and emphasizes that the possibility of a warlike action against Serbia seems nearer than he believed immediately after the crime of Sarajevo. However, he would never consent to a surprise attack upon Serbia without a previous diplomatic action, such as seemed to be intended and had unfortunately also been discussed by Count Hoyos in Berlin, because in this case, in his opinion, we would have a sorry standing in the eyes of all Europe, and would very likely have to reckon with the enmity of all the Balkan states – except Bulgaria – which is too weak just now to be of any effective help.

It was absolutely necessary that we formulated demands for Serbia and only issued an ultimatum if Serbia did not meet them.[63] These demands should be hard, but not impossible to meet. If Serbia accepted them, we should have a splendid diplomatic success and our prestige in the Balkans would increase immensely. If our demands were not met, he would also be in favour of warlike action, but even now he had to stress that by means of a war we could aim to reduce the size of Serbia, but we could not completely annihilate it, because on the one hand Russia would fight to the death before allowing this, and also because he, as Hungarian Premier, could never consent to the Monarchy's annexing any part of Serbia.

It was not for Germany to decide whether we ought to strike against Serbia now or not. Personally he held the view that it was not absolutely necessary to wage a war at the present moment. Presently we must remember that agitation against us in Rumania is exceedingly strong just now and that in view of the excited feelings of the population we would have to reckon with a Rumanian attack, and we should doubtless have to keep substantial powers in Transylvania to intimidate the Rumanians. Now that Germany has happily opened the way to Bulgaria's joining the Triple Alliance, a promising perspective for successful diplomatic action in the Balkans had opened up, in that by the accession of Bulgaria and Turkey to the Triple Alliance we may create a counterbalance to Rumania and Serbia and thus force Rumania to return to the Triple Alliance. With regard to Europe it must also be considered that

63 In October 1913, Austria-Hungary had successfully prevented Serbia from re-occupying territory that had been given to Albania at the London Conference of 30 May. Like in July 1914, an ultimatum had been presented, Germany's support had been secured, but the ultimatum had forced Serbia to back down, due not least to lack of support from Russia. See Richard C. Hall, 'Serbia', in Richard F. Hamilton and Holger H. Herwig (eds), *The Origins of World War I*, Cambridge University Press, Cambridge 2003, pp. 92–111, p. 104.

the balance of power between France and Germany was deterioriating on account of the lower [French] birth-rate, and that thus Germany will in future have increasingly more troops at her disposal against Russia.

All these were circumstances which had to be considered when arriving at a resolution involving such exceedingly heavy responsibility as was being taken today, and he must again declare that despite the crisis in Bosnia, where in any case a great deal might be done by a reform of the administration, he could not make up his mind in favour of war, but still thought that a marked diplomatic success – which would cause a deep humiliation of Serbia, would be suitable decidedly to improve our situation and allow an advantageous policy in the Balkans.

The Chair responds that the history of the last years had shown that diplomatic successes against Serbia had increased the Monarchy's prestige for the time being, but had in the end also increased the tension in our relations with Serbia. Neither our success in the annexation crisis, nor that of creating the Albanian state, nor subsequently Serbia having had to give way after our ultimatum of the autumn of last year[64] changed the actual circumstances. A radical solution of the question raised by the propaganda for a Greater Serbia, which is systematically undertaken in Belgrade, and whose corrupting effects we feel from Agram to Zara,[65] was only possible by energetic intervention.

With regard to the danger of a hostile attitude in Rumania, mentioned by the Hungarian Premier, the Presiding Minister is of the opinion that it was less to be feared at the present time than in the future, when the partnership of interests between Rumania and Serbia would crystalize more and more. King Carol had indeed occasionally expressed doubts whether under present circumstances he would be able to do his duty as an ally vis-à-vis the Monarchy by giving active help. But we could hardly assume that he would consent to a warlike operation against the Monarchy, or that he would be unable to oppose public feeling in such an eventuality. Besides it must be remembered that Rumania stands in fear of Bulgaria which would impede her ability to act freely, even under present circumstances.

As to the Hungarian Premier's remark with regard to the proportion of forces between France and Germany, he thought it right to call attention to the fact that the reduction of the growth of the population in France was more than balanced by the increasing population of Russia, so that the assertion that Germany would in time have more troops at her disposition against France[66] cannot be taken into account.

64 The ultimatum of 18 October 1913 following Serbia's attempt to reclaim some Albanian territory.

65 Today known as Zagreb and Zadar.

66 This is a mistake in the minutes and should have read 'Russia'.

The Imp. and Roy. Premier [Stürgkh] points out that the present Council of Ministers had been called for the purpose of discussing the measures to be taken in Bosnia and Herzegovina, to ensure the success of the judicial examinations on the assassination and to counteract the Pan-Serbian movement that is taking place in Bosnia. These questions must recede if the main question arises, whether we might not solve the Bosnian difficulty by exercising force against Serbia.

Two reasons had made this main question very pressing just now; in the first place the Governor in Bosnia and Herzegovina [General Potiorek], based on his own perceptions and on his thorough knowledge of the country, declares that it is his belief that no successful measures could be applied in the interior of these provinces unless we deal Serbia a forcible stroke first. These perceptions on General Potiorek's part make it imperative to ask whether we are at all able to stop the subversive activity which originates in Serbia, and whether we are able to keep the two provinces in question if we do not promptly deal a blow to Serbia.

During the last few days the whole situation had changed, and a psychological situation had been created which in his opinion was decidedly pointing to a war with Serbia. He agreed with the Hungarian Premier that it is for us and not for the German Government to decide whether a war is necessary or not; still he must say that our decision should be influenced strongly by the fact that when we looked for the most faithful support of our policy in the Triple Alliance, we were promised unreserved loyalty and advised to act without delay. Count Tisza should consider this circumstance and remember that by a weak and hesitating policy we might risk not being so certain of German support at some future time. This was the second consideration, next to the interest we have in restoring order in Bosnia, which should be considered.

It was a question of detail how the conflict should begin and if the Hungarian Government thinks that a surprise attack, 'sans crier gare', as Count Tisza expressed it, was not feasible, then some other way would have to be found; but he urgently wished that whatever happened, we acted without delay and spared our national economy a protracted period of suspense. But all this was mere detail next to the question of principle, whether it was absolutely necessary to have a war or not, and here the prestige and the existence of the Monarchy were decisive, whose south Slav provinces he considered lost if nothing happened.

We should therefore decide in principle today that action must and shall follow. He also shared the presiding Minister's belief that a mere diplomatic success would not at all improve the situation.[67] If a foregoing diplomatic action is therefore resorted to for international

67 This attitude did not change in Vienna throughout the Crisis. See for example (333).

reasons, it should be taken with the firm resolve that this action can only end in war.

The Imp. and Roy. Minister of Finance [Biliński] remarks that Count Stürgkh had referred to the fact that the Governor [of Bosnia and Herzegovina, Potiorek] wanted war. For two years General Potiorek had been of the opinion that we had to survive a test of strength with Serbia in order to keep Bosnia and Herzegovina. We should not forget that the Governor was *in situ* and able to judge these matters better. Herr von Bilinski, too, is convinced that the decisive fight was unavoidable sooner or later. He had never doubted that Germany would be on our side in the event of war and had already received the most definite assurances in this regard from Herr von Tschirschky in November 1912.[68] The recent events in Bosnia had led to a very dangerous mood among the Serbian population, particularly the pogrom against the Serbs in Sarajevo had led to all Serbs feeling very agitated and bitter, so that one could no longer decide who among the Serbs was still loyal and who was a Pan-Serb. In the country itself it would no longer be possible to amend this situation; the only means would be a definite decision whether a Pan-Serb idea could have a future or not.

Even if the Royal Hungarian Premier were happy with a diplomatic success at the moment, he could not be so from the point of view of Bosnian interests. The ultimatum which we presented to Serbia last autumn had made the mood in Bosnia worse and had increased the hatred against us. There was general talk among the people that King Peter would come and free the country. Serbs only respond to violence, a diplomatic success would make no impression in Bosnia whatsoever and would rather be damaging than anything else.

The Roy. Hungarian Premier [Tisza] remarks that he has the highest opinion of the current Governor as a military man, but as regards the civilian administration it could not be denied that it had failed utterly and that a reform was urgently needed. [...] He did not see why the affairs in Bosnia could not be substantially improved by a thorough reform of the administration.

The Imp. and Roy. War Minister [Krobatin] is of the opinion that a diplomatic success would be of no value at all. A success of this kind would be interpreted as weakness. From a military point of view he must stress that it would be better to go to war immediately, rather than at

68 Kiderlen-Wächter had instructed Tschirschky on 19 November 1912 to advise the ally that Germany 'would in case of further occurrences [...] not shrink for a moment from fulfilling our alliance duties.' GP, 33, No. 12397. See also (**39**). For details of the assurances made to Austria-Hungary in November 1912 ('you can count on us') see John Röhl, *Wilhelm II.*, Vol. III: *Der Weg in den Abgrund, 1900–1941*, Beck, Munich 2008, 2009, pp. 943ff.

some later point, because the balance of power would in future change to our disadvantage. As to the manner of the beginning of war, he must highlight the fact that the two big wars of recent years, the war between Russia and Japan as well as the Balkan war, began without a prior declaration of war. It was his belief that we should at first only carry through the mobilization intended against Serbia, and wait with the general mobilization until it could be seen if Russia was stirring or not.

We had already lost two opportunities for solving the Serbian question and had postponed the decision each time. If we did this again and did not react to this new provocation, then this would be taken as evidence of weakness in all south Slav provinces and we would cause a strengthening of the agitation against us.

From a military point of view it was desirable that the mobilization should be carried out immediately and as secretly as possible, and that an ultimatum should be addressed to Serbia only when the mobilization was complete. This would also be advantageous with regard to the Russian forces, as just now the Russian border corps are incomplete due to the harvest leave.

After this a discussion begins on the aims of a war against Serbia, during which the Royal Hungarian Premier's view that Serbia might be reduced as to size but not annihilated out of consideration for Russia, was adopted. The Imp. and Roy. Premier [Stürgkh] stresses that it would also be advisable that the Karageorgevich dynasty be removed, and the crown be given to a European prince, as well as placing the reduced kingdom in a certain position of military dependency vis-à-vis the Monarchy.

The Royal Hungarian Premier [Tisza] still holds the belief that a successful Balkan policy could be created by the addition of Bulgaria to the Triple Alliance, and calls attention to the terrible calamity of a European war under present circumstances. It should not be overlooked that all kinds of eventualities are possible in the near future – Russia might be absorbed by Asian complications, a recovered Bulgaria might want to wage a war of revenge against Serbia, etc. which would all improve our position vis-à-vis the problem of Greater Serbia, compared to today's.

The Chair replies that certainly one might imagine many possibilities in the future which would place us in a favourable situation. But he feared that there was no time for such developments. The fact must be considered that our enemies were preparing for a decisive conflict with the Monarchy and that Rumania was lending a helping hand to the diplomacy of Russia and France. We must not assume that our policy with Bulgaria would be a full equivalent for the loss of Rumania. It is his belief that Rumania cannot be won back as long as Serbian agitation continues, because agitation for Greater Rumania follows the Serbian and will not meet with opposition until Rumania feels isolated by the annihilation of Serbia and sees that her only chance of being supported is to join the Triple Alliance. We must moreover not forget the fact that with regard to Bulgaria's accession to the Triple Alliance the very first step has not yet been made. All we know is that the present Bulgarian government a few months ago expressed this wish and was then about to conclude an alliance with Turkey. This has not been accomplished; on the contrary, Turkey has since come under Russian and French influence. The attitude of the Radoslawoff Ministry, however, gave no reason to doubt that Bulgaria is still disposed to lending a willing ear to any positive propositions we might make in the sense referred to. Still we cannot make these assumptions a safe cornerstone of our Balkan policy because the present Bulgarian government has no sound basis; public opinion to joining the Triple Alliance and Radoslawoff's Ministry might be turned out. We must also remember that Germany accepted the accession of Bulgaria to the Triple Alliance on the condition only that the agreement should not be directed against Rumania.[69] This condition is rather difficult to comply with and might at some future time cause uncertainties.

A lengthy and detailed debate on the question of war follows. The result of the discussion may be summarized as follows:

1 That all present wish for a speedy decision of the controversy with Serbia, whether it be decided in a warlike or a peaceful manner;
2 that the Council of Ministers is prepared to adopt the view of the Royal Hungarian Premier according to which the mobilization is not to take place until after concrete demands have been addressed to Serbia and after being refused, an ultimatum has been sent.

All present except the Royal Hungarian Premier hold the belief that a purely diplomatic success, even it if ended with a glaring humiliation of Serbia, would be worthless, and that therefore such far-reaching demands must be addressed to Serbia which will make a refusal almost certain, so that the road to a radical solution by means of a military action should be opened.

Count Tisza remarks that he was anxious to meet the others halfway and was prepared to concede that the demands addressed to Serbia should be hard indeed, but not such as to make our intention of raising unacceptable terms clear to everybody. Otherwise we should have an impossible legal basis for a declaration of war. The text of the note must be studied very carefully and he should value being allowed to see it before it is sent. He must also clearly state that if his point of view was disregarded he would draw the consequences.

69 See (**120**).

After this the sitting is suspended to be reopened in the afternoon. When the Council of Ministers meets again, the Chief of the General Staff [Conrad] and the Deputy Chief of the Naval Staff [Kailer] are also present.

The War Minister [Krobatin] at the request of the presiding Minister spoke first to ask the Chief of the General Staff three questions as follows:

1. Whether it is possible to mobilize against Serbia only at first and against Russia only when the necessity arises.
2. Whether it is possible to retain a large numbers of troops in Transylvania to intimidate Rumania.
3. Where the fight with Russia would be taken up.

The Chief of the General Staff gives secret answers to these questions and asks that they should not appear in the minutes.

A lengthy debate followed these explanations, about the proportion of forces and the probable course of a European war, which being of a secret nature are not suitable to be included in the minutes.

At the end of the debate the Hungarian Premier [Tisza] again explains his point of view regarding the question of the war and appeals again to all present to consider their decision carefully.

The points which are to be contained in the note to Serbia are then discussed. No definite decision was made regarding these points; they were only formulated so as to give a clear idea of what might be asked of Serbia.

At this point the Chief of the General Staff and the Deputy Chief of the Naval Staff leave the Council, which discusses the internal situation of Bosnia and the necessary measures to be taken. [...]

The Chair concludes that though there remained differences of opinion between all the members of the Council and Count Tisza, still an agreement had been arrived at, since even the proposition of the Hungarian Premier would in all probability lead to a war with Serbia, the necessity of which he and all the other members of the Council had understood and admitted.

Count Berchtold then told the Council that he intended going to Ischl on the 8th of the month to report to His Imp. and Roy. Apostolic Majesty.[70] The Royal Hungarian Premier asks the Minister also to present to His Majesty a memorandum in which he [Tisza] would record his views of the situation.[71]

After a communication to the press had been composed the Chair closes the meeting.[72]

---

70 Kaiser Franz Joseph was on vacation in Bad Ischl.

71 See ÖUA, VIII, No. 10146.

72 In the afternoon, the meeting reconvened and discussed the military balance of power, the probable course of a European war and details of mobilization.

I have acknowledged the contents of these minutes.
Vienna, 16 August 1914
[signed]Franz Joseph

ÖUA, VIII, No. 10118.[73]

(135) 7 July: Riezler's Diary[74]

Bethmann Hollweg pessimistic about the future; outlines his fears about Russia's future strength

Hohenfinow, 7 July 1914

Drove out here[75] yesterday with the Imperial Chancellor. The old castle, the wonderful immense lime trees, the avenue like an old gothic vault. Everywhere still weighed down by the death of the wife.[76] Melancholy and composure in countryside and people.

In the evening on the veranda under the night sky long conversation about the situation. The secret news which he tells me gives a devastating impression. He considers the Anglo-Russian negotiations about a naval convention, the landing in Pomerania, as very serious, the last piece in the chain.[77] Lichnowsky much too blue-eyed [*vertrauensseelig*]. Was being duped by the English. Russia's military power increasing fast; if strategic expansion of Poland, the situation can be held in check [*hinhaltbar*].[78] Austria increasingly weaker and immobile; the burrowing from the North and South-East very much advanced. In any case unable to go to war as our ally for a German cause. The Entente knows that we

---

These discussions were not recorded in the minutes. Conrad pressed for an 'early initiation of the action'. See Jürgen Angelow, *Der Weg in die Urkastrophe. Der Zerfall des alten Europa 1900–1914*, Be.bra Verlag, Berlin 2010, p. 134.

73 English translation based on Geiss, *July 1914*, No. 9, but here with a number of amendments.

74 The authenticity of Riezler's diary entries for the July Crisis have been the subject of an acrimonious debate. For details, see p. 20, n. 76.

75 To Hohenfinow, the Chancellor's summer residence, about 60 kilometres north-east of Berlin.

76 Bethmann Hollweg's wife Martha died on 11 May 1914.

77 For details see (**79**), (**85**), (**87**), (**135**), (**143**).

78 In the published version of Riezler's diary, the editor misread the German '*hinhaltbar*' (kept in check, to be delayed) for '*unhaltbar*' (untenable). I am grateful to Bernd Sösemann for pointing out this mistake. The original Riezler diary can be consulted in the Bundesarchiv Koblenz, N 1584 (Nachlass Kurt Riezler).

are entirely paralysed as a result.

I am very startled, I had not considered [the situation] as gravely. One does not hear the secret news if one does not belong properly to the initiated ones [*zur Zunft*] – and everything that is high-politics and moreover military is 'top secret'.

The Chancellor speaks of difficult decisions. Murder of Franz Ferdinand. Official Serbia involved. Austria wants to pull herself together, message from Franz Joseph to the Kaiser with a query regarding the *casus foederis*.[79]

Our old dilemma with every Austrian Balkan action. If we encourage them, they will say we have pushed them into it; if we advise against it, it will be said that we have left them in the lurch, and we will lose the last middling ally. This time it is worse than in 1912;[80] as this time Austria is on the defence against Serbian-Russian machinations. An action against Serbia can lead to world war. The Chancellor expects from a war, however it ends, a revolution of everything that exists. [...] The future belongs to Russia which grows and grows and lies on us like an ever-heavier nightmare.

Karl Dietrich Erdmann (ed.), *Kurt Riezler, Tagebücher, Aufsätze, Dokumente*, Göttingen 1972, pp. 181–183.[81]

(136) 7 July: Nicolson to Grey

Germany is requesting that Britain will not enter naval talks with Russia

I hope that you will allow me to make an observation to you in regard to that portion of the conversation which Prince Lichnowsky had with you yesterday relating to a naval understanding with Russia. He practically warned us that if we were to enter into any kind of naval arrangement with Russia certain unpleasant consequences would ensue and we may, therefore, infer that if we wish to avoid consequences we must abandon any naval conversations with Russia. In short we are to abstain from taking the most elementary precautions and from discussing any arrangements which might be necessary to our defence in certain contingencies. This request or suggestion is a pretty strong one for one Power to make

79 (**119**), (**120**).

80 This refers to the Balkan War, when Austria-Hungary wanted to intervene to avoid Serbia's annexing of additional territory.

81 For references about the controversy on the authenticity of Riezler's diaries see p. 20, n. 76.

to another and it comes oddly from a Power who quite rightly makes secret arrangements with her allies – arrangements which for aught we know may comprise certain measures against us in possible eventualities. We must not forget that only a year or two ago Germany pressed Russia to engage to remain neutral in the event of hostilities between Germany and England – and she also strove to secure our neutrality in case of a Franco-German conflict. She, therefore, very rightly looks ahead, and seeks to avert any possible danger or combination against herself, whether near or remote. This liberty apparently she wishes to deny us. I sincerely trust we shall not walk into this trap but keep our hands perfectly free and our friendships unimpaired.

Minute by Grey:

Certainly what Lichnowsky has said is not going to alter our conversations with Russia or France or our relations to them. The difficult question is whether I should say nothing to Lichnowsky or whether I should admit that we have had and may continue to have such conversations both with France and Russia. [...].

Harold Nicolson, *Sir Arthur Nicolson*, Constable, London 1930, pp. 407–408.

(137) 7 **July: Jovanović to Pašić**

Serbian Ambassador uncertain about what attitude Austria-Hungary will adopt

---

Vienna, 24 June/7 July 1914

In influential circles the excitement continues undiminished. Though the Emperor had addressed a letter to the Prime Ministers of Austria and Hungary respectively, and to the Minister of Finance, Herr Bilinski, in which an appeal is made for calmness, it is impossible to determine what attitude the Government will adopt towards us. For them one thing is obvious; whether it is proved or not that the outrage has been inspired and prepared at Belgrade, they must sooner or later solve the question of the so-called Greater Serbian agitation within the Habsburg Monarchy. In what manner they will do this and what means they will employ to that end has not as yet been decided; this is being discussed especially in high Catholic and military circles. The ultimate decision will be taken only after it has been definitely ascertained what the enquiry at Sarajevo has brought to light. The decision will be in accordance with the findings of the enquiry.

In this respect, Austria-Hungary has to choose on the following courses: either to regard the Sarajevo outrage as a national misfortune and a crime which ought to be dealt with in accordance with the evidence obtained, in which case Serbia's co-operation in the work will be requested in order to prevent the perpetrators escaping the extreme penalty; or, to treat the Sarajevo outrage as a Pan-Serbian, South-Slav and Pan-Slav conspiracy with every manifestation of the hatred, hitherto repressed, against Slavdom. There are many indications that influential circles are being urged to adopt the latter course: it is therefore advisable to be ready for defence. Should the former and wiser course be adopted, we should do all we can to meet Austrian wishes in this respect.

Serbian Blue Book, No. 17.[82]

(138) 8 July: Riezler's Diary

Likely outcomes of the crisis: a war from the East with a good chance of winning it, or breaking up the Entente

---

Hohenfinow, 8 July 1914

Message from Kaiser Franz Joseph delivered by Hoyos.[83] Hoyos with Zimmermann. The Chancellor[84] thinks that perhaps the old Kaiser will not decide. If war comes from the East, so that we have to go to war for Austria-Hungary and not Austria-Hungary for us, then we have a chance of winning it. If war does not come, if the Tsar does not want it or concerned France counsels peace then we still have the chance to break the Entente apart over this.

Karl Dietrich Erdmann (ed.), *Kurt Riezler, Tagebücher, Aufsätze, Dokumente*, Göttingen 1972, p. 184.[85]

---

82 Engl. transl. in *Collected Diplomatic Documents relating to the Outbreak of the European War*, No. 13, pp. 377–378.

83 (**119**), (**120**), (**130**).

84 In the loose draft pages Riezler originally wrote 'Zim' [Zimmermann], but then crossed this out. My thanks to Bernd Sösemann for pointing out this omission in the published diary. The original can be found in BA Koblenz, N 1584 (Nachlass Kurt Riezler).

85 For a discussion of the controversy on the authenticity of Riezler's diaries see p. 20, n. 76.

(139) 8 July: Berchtold to Tisza

Germany pressing Austria-Hungary not to miss the opportunity to deal with Serbia

Private Letter
Vienna 8 July 1914

Tschirschky has just left me, who told me that he had received a telegram[86] from Berlin by which his Imperial Master instructs him to declare emphatically that in Berlin an action of the Monarchy against Serbia is expected and that in Germany it would not be understood if we were to neglect this opportunity without dealing a blow.

My remark that in taking a decisive resolution it would of course be of the greatest importance to know how far we could rely upon Germany's influence being used in Bucharest, and what result we might hope for, was answered by the Ambassador to the effect that Berlin thinks it is altogether out of question that Rumania would in this case be against the Monarchy. Incidentally, Kaiser Wilhelm has already addressed a letter on the subject to King Carol and we might be very sure that it left nothing to be desired in plainness of speech!

The Ambassador's further remarks showed me that Germany would consider further negotiating with Serbia a confession of weakness on our part, and that this would not be without repercussions for our position in the Triple Alliance and Germany's future policy.

Tschirschky's remarks seem to me of such significance that I thought they might in some degree influence your ultimate decisions, and for this reason I am informing you without delay and begging you, if you are of the same mind, to send a telegram (in cipher) to Bad Ischl, where I shall be all of tomorrow and shall be glad to be your interpreter with His Majesty.

ÖUA, VIII, No. 10145.[87]

86 This telegram has never been traced. See also Geiss, *July 1914*, p. 102, note 1.

87 English translation based on Geiss, *July 1914*, No. 11, here with minor amendments.

(140) 8 July: Forgách to Mérey

Austrian determination to have a war against Serbia; support from Berlin, even at the risk of a world war

[Private letter]

The Minister [Berchtold] is determined – if this word can be applied to him – to use the horrible deed of Sarajevo for a military clearing-up of our impossible relationship with Serbia. The Austrian government, as well as of course the military and Biliński [...] are in favour. Tisza is rather opposed, wants to make only such demands of Serbia which will humiliate her but whose acceptance is not totally impossible, perhaps pose an ultimatum and only mobilize afterwards. With Berlin we are in complete agreement. Kaiser & Reich-Chancellor etc. as decided as never before; they take on board complete cover against Russia,[88] even at the risk of a world war which is not at all ruled out, they consider the moment as favourable & advise to strike as soon [as possible] without asking or consulting the 2 other allies Italy and the more than dubious Rumania in any way.

HHStA, NL Mérey, K. 10, cited in Günther Kronenbitter, *'Krieg im Frieden'*, Oldenbourg, Munich 2003, p. 472.

(141) 9 July: Hopman to Tirpitz

Hopman doubts if Austria will have the necessary resolve to fight Serbia

My general impression is that the *Auswärtiges Amt* does not consider the situation to be very threatening. Personally I am convinced that the Austrians were never quite as fired up as H.M. has portrayed it and that they have already lost steam and are still losing it. I would also consider it not very advantageous if we were to associate come what may with their business which is more or less leaning towards bankruptcy. England will have the last laugh.[89]

Volker R. Berghahn and Wilhelm Deist, 'Kaiserliche Marine und Kriegsausbruch 1914', *Militärgeschichtliche Mitteilungen*, 4, 1970, pp. 37–58, No. 4.

88 Clearly a mistake, as the German military plan actually intended that Austria would cover Russia while Germany initially concentrated her efforts in the West.

89 See also Hopman's diary entry, in Epkenhans (ed.), *Albert Hopman*, pp. 386–387.

(142) 9 July: Soden to Hertling

Members of the *Auswärtiges Amt* doubt Austro-Hungarian resolve

Berlin, 9 July 1914

Under-Secretary of State Zimmermann would consider the current point in time for Austria as very favourable for, as he put it, launching a 'war of revenge' (*Rachezug*) against the southern neighbour and he believes firmly that it would be possible to localize the war. But he doubts that one would decide on this in Vienna.

From Berlin's side one would not dissuade the Viennese Government from proceeding with all means against Serbia, rather to let her know that Austria, come what may, will see the ally by her side. Vis-à-vis the representatives of the other powers the *Auswärtiges Amt* emphasised that it regards the situation without any nervousness, and as evidence has pointed to the fact that otherwise H.M. the Kaiser would have refrained from starting on his North Sea cruise, that the Chancellor would not have gone to Hohenfinow, the Chief of Staff not gone on holiday.

Ernst Deuerlein (ed.), *Briefwechsel Hertling-Lerchenfeld*, Boppard am Rhein 1973, No. 103.

(143) 9 July: Lichnowsky to Bethmann Hollweg

Grey denies existence of any secret agreements between Britain, France and Russia; ready to exert mediating influence on Russia if Austria decides to adopt stern attitude towards Serbia

Confidential!
London, 9 July 1914
R. 11 July, morning

Sir E. Grey asked me to call on him today and first of all communicated to me the notes which he made concerning our discussion which took place shortly before my visit to Berlin and Kiel.[90] He said that he could add nothing today to the words he had uttered at that time, and could only repeat to me that secret agreements between Great Britain on the one hand and France and Russia on the other, which would entail obligations on Great Britain in case of a European war, did not exist. England

90 He refers to his meeting of 24 June. See BD, XI, No. 4, Sir Edward Grey to Sir E. Goschen, 24 June 1914, and DD, No. 5, Lichnowsky to Bethmann Hollweg.

wished to preserve an absolutely free hand, in order to be able to act according to her own judgement in the event of continental complications. The Government had to an extent obligated itself to Parliament not to commit itself to any secret liabilities. In no case would the British Government be found on the side of the aggressors in the event of continental complications.

But as he did not wish to put me on the wrong track – 'as I did not want to mislead you' – he at once added that his relations to the said Powers had none the less lost nothing of their earlier intimacy. Thus, even if there exist no agreements which imposed any obligations, he did not wish to deny that from time to time 'conversations' had taken place between the naval or the military authorities on both sides, the first of them as early as the year 1906, then again during the Morocco crisis, when they had believed here, he added, laughing, that we had intended to attack the French. But even these conversations, about which he mostly knew nothing more definite, had absolutely no aggressive edge, as English policy, now as before, was aimed towards the maintenance of peace, and would find itself in a very embarrassing situation if a European war were to break out.

I repeated to the Minister about the same as I had already told him recently,[91] and gave him to understand that it would be desirable if such military conversations could be reduced to a minimum, as otherwise they might easily lead to unintended consequences.

Since our last conversation, added Sir Edward, he had informed himself thoroughly about the mood in Russia towards us, and had found no reason for a concerned view; he also seemed quite ready, if we should so desire, to use his influence in some way on the attitude of Russia. He had also already been endeavouring, in case the Vienna Cabinet should find itself compelled as a result of the murder at Sarajevo to adopt a sterner attitude towards Serbia, to persuade the Russian Government to adopt a more peaceful view and to assume a more conciliatory attitude towards Austria. Very much would of course depend, Sir Edward thought, on the kind of measures that were under consideration, and on whether they might not arouse Slavic sentiment in such a fashion as to make it impossible for Mr Sazonov to remain passive.

In general, the Minister was certainly in a confident mood, and declared in cheerful tones that he saw no reason for taking a pessimistic view of the situation.

DD, No. 30.[92]

---

91 See (**128**), and Lichnowsky to Bethmann Hollweg, DD, No. 20.

92 Engl. transl. based on Geiss, *July 1914*, No. 14, here with minor amendments.

(144) 10 July: Tschirschky to *Auswärtiges Amt*

Franz Joseph agrees with his Government's decision that demands need to be made of Serbia; formulation of demands being discussed in Vienna; Germany informed of Austrian deliberations; attempts to feign calm by sending military leaders on holiday

Telegram 85
Vienna, 10 July 1914
Absolutely confidential
D. 8.30 p.m.
R. 10.32 p.m

[*Wilhelm II's marginal comments and emphases in the text, dated 12 July*]

Count Berchtold advises me as follows regarding his audience yesterday with H. M. the Kaiser Franz Joseph at Ischl:
H. M. the Kaiser discussed the state of affairs with great calmness.
He first expressed his warm gratitude for the attitude of our Most Gracious Master and of the Imperial Government, and stated that he was quite of our opinion that it was necessary now to come to some decision, in order to put an end to the intolerable conditions in connection with Serbia. Count Berchtold added that His Majesty was quite clear as to the gravity of such a decision.

as H.M.'s memorandum is about 14 days old, this is taking a long time!
This was actually drafted as the reason for the decision itself!

The Minister then informed the Kaiser of the two options under discussion[93] here as to the approaching action against Serbia. H. M. seemed to think that the difference between them might perhaps be bridged.

93 He referred here to Tisza's position on the one hand, and that of his colleagues on the other.

	On the whole, however, H.M. tended towards the view that concrete
very much so! *and unambiguous ones!*	demands should be made of Serbia. He, the Minister, did not want to deny the advantages of such an approach. The odium of an unexpected attack on Serbia, which would otherwise fall upon the Monarchy, would thus be avoided and Serbia would be put in the wrong. Also this procedure would make it much easier for Rumania and England to adopt a neutral
they have had enough time for that	stance at least. At present the formulation of appropriate demands on Serbia constituted the main worry here, and Count Berchtold stated that he would be glad to know what was thought about it in Berlin. He thought that among other things, one could demand that an agency of the Austro-Hungarian Government be established at Belgrade in order to keep an eye from there on the Greater Serbia machinations, perhaps, also, to insist upon the dissolution of the associations and the dismissal of some compromised
all!	officers.
	The time-limit for the reply must be short, probably 48 hours.[94] Naturally even this short time frame
Hartwig is dead![95]	would suffice to enable Belgrade to

94 This is the first reference to the short time limit which Vienna decided upon. At least from this date onwards this intention was a known fact in Berlin.

95 The Russian Minister to Serbia, Hartwig, had been particularly close to Prime Minister Pašić and the two had met almost daily ('your beard is consulting with our beard', junior diplomats in the Russian mission would comment. Clark, *Sleepwalkers*, p. 91). Hartwig died of a heart failure on 10 July. See also Crackanthorpe to Grey, 11 July, BD, XI, No. 48. 'M. de Hartwig, Russian Minister here, died suddenly last night of heart failure.' *MINUTES. 'In the political and diplomatic world, M. de Hartwig's death will not cause much grief.'* E. A. C[rowe]. July 11. '*He was a faithful and active supporter of Russian policy, although his methods were peculiar. His Serbian policy was, so far as Russian interests were concerned, distinctly a success.'*

get advice from St Petersburg. Should the Serbs accept all the demands made of them then this would be a solution which was 'very disagreeable' to him, and he was still pondering which demands one could make which would make it absolutely impossible for Serbia to accept.

evacuate the Sanjac! Then the row would be on at once! Austria must absolutely get that back at once, in order to prevent the union of Serbia and Montenegro and the gaining of the sea by the Serbs.

Finally the Minister again complained about Count Tisza's attitude, which made an energetic procedure against Serbia difficult for him. Count Tisza maintained one had to proceed 'like gentlemen', however this was hardly appropriate where such important interests of the state were concerned and particularly against such an opponent as Serbia.

When faced with murderers after all that has happened! Nonsense!

The Minister would be glad to follow the suggestion of the Imperial Government – about which Count Szögyény had already telegraphed – already now to influence public opinion in England against Serbia via the press. Only in his opinion this must be done cautiously in order not to alarm Serbia prematurely.

The Minister of War will go on holiday tomorrow, also Baron

childish![96]

A. N[icolson]. 'I can only say "de mortuis nil."' *E. G[rey]*. For more details of the suspicious circumstances surrounding his death see (**152**).

96 Wilhelm II was unaware that his own government was attempting a similar cover-up, a fact that was no secret among officials in Berlin. On 18 July, for example, Chargé d'Affaires Hans von Schoen reported from Berlin to the Bavarian Prime Minister Count Georg Hertling in Munich: '[...] In the interest of localizing the war the German Government will initiate diplomatic action with the Great Powers immediately following the presentation of the Austrian note. It will claim to have been surprised by Austria's actions just like the other powers, pointing out that the Kaiser is on his North Sea cruise and the Chief of the Great General Staff as well as the Prussian Minister of War are on holiday. [...]'. DD, Appendix IV, No.2. See also Röhl, *Wilhelm II.*, vol.3, p.1088, who points out that Bethmann's additional motive for sending the Kaiser away was to remove him from the decision-making process in Berlin.

Conrad von Hötzendorf will leave Vienna temporarily. This is happening, as Count Berchtold tells me, on purpose, so as to prevent any disquiet.

about as it was at the time of the Silesian war! 'I am against all councils of war and conferences, since the more timid party always has the upper hand.' Frederick the Great

DD, No. 29.[97]

(145) 10 July: Dumaine to Viviani

Summary of Austrian press reports on Serbia; speculation that Austria will shy away from harsh demands on Serbia, particularly as enquiry into assassination did not so far reveal evidence of Serbian complicity

Telegram no. 177
Vienna, 10 July 1914
R. Cabinet, 15 July; Dir. Pol., 17 July.

If violence can now be contained and measures to control it eased, and if the danger for Serbia of an urgent ultimatum is finally dismissed, it is thanks to the great wisdom and foresight of Emperor Franz Joseph. As he said in his deeply moving letter to his Ministers,[98] the ordeal that has just been inflicted upon him 'affirmed his resolve to stay on the best course for the good of his people'; he asks only for their affection to repay him for his paternal solicitude. As for the appalling crime of Sarajevo, he wants it to be attributed 'only to the fever of a small number of misguided men'. Which is the same as declaring he condemns excessive severity and refuses to punish a whole race for the crime of a few. [...]

According to the *Reichspost*, for example, which is usually in favour of the strong-arm tactics of Baron Burian and M. de Biliński's long-running overly lenient administration, the civil authorities' passiveness helped to ruin order and discipline in schools; and by tolerating quasi-anarchic agitation, they allowed the corruption of minds. When the regicide Čabrinović [99] was expelled from Sarajevo, was not the request

97 Engl. transl. based on Geiss, *July 1914*, No. 16, here with minor amendments.
98 The monarch sent a letter to Biliński, Stürgkh and Tisza.
99 Nedeljko Čabrinović had thrown the bomb which narrowly missed the car

of a social-democrat deputy enough to make sure that he was brought back straight away? And since the crime: the papers relating to these efforts – have they not been searched for without any trace of them being found either in Bosnia or Vienna? 'This is how the government goes about its business', the newspaper concludes.

According to my colleague, M. Jovanovitch, M. de Biliński thought he could suppress nationalist ambitions in Bosnia by using the same corrupt methods as were used in Galicia. Thus, by offering them every opportunity to enrich themselves, he has done everything possible to reunite the Catholics and the Muslims with the Monarchy. But the popular and orthodox sector, around 44 per cent of the population, which is kept in an inferior position, excluded from all jobs and reduced to misery, has become even more fierce in its demands, even though the Minister in charge thought he was sufficiently looking after this sector by only moderately suppressing it. M. de Biliński is today up against both the complaints of nearly one half of his staff and of criticism from the military elements for whom the severe methods are the sole reason for dissatisfaction.

Nevertheless, even though he is directly responsible, he does not seem to have lost the trust of his old Monarch, since he is, along with the Counts Stürgkh and Tisza, one of the three people to whom the imperial letter is addressed. And it is with his agreement that the Council is considering the rigorous inspection which Bosnia's domestic administration should now undergo. One can thus allow oneself to suppose that at the end of the day this great effort will only result in quite mediocre modifications.

It is, moreover, of more general interest to observe what influence the crime of Sarajevo could have on the Monarchy's foreign policy. [...]

The notion of fairness and common sense which have been invoked in France in order to apportion responsibility for the assassination of Archduke Franz Ferdinand have undoubtedly rekindled mistrust and antipathy towards us. I have often felt that it is enough to take a neutral stand towards Serbia in order immediately to be seen as Austrophobic. This prejudice is so stubborn that the President of the Chamber of Deputies, Dr Sylvester, without any regard for the importance that his position [...] adds to his words, proclaimed in Salzburg during a meeting that the French, by applauding Serbian fanaticism, distanced themselves from civilization and soon it would be advisable to suppress the study of their language, very wrongly considered to be of universal use; he recommended that it be replaced by English, which is much more generally

carrying Franz Ferdinand, and was convicted as one of the conspirators responsible for the assassination. For details about all the conspirators see Clark, *Sleepwalkers*, pp. 47–64 and David James, *One Morning in Sarajevo*, Phoenix, London 2009, *passim.*

widespread, or Italian – each of these being infinitely more practical and more in keeping with Austria's real interests. 'The French will have only themselves to blame if they find themselves thus demoted.'

If we are banished from all nations because we quite rightly observed that before incriminating the Serbs the Austrians perhaps could have worried about their own functionaries' negligence, then what about the Russians? [...]

For [...] others – and it is the *Neue Freie Presse* that proposes this theory – the danger to Europe's peace which the spread of Pan-Serbianism is causing will inevitably have a direct impact on all the great Powers who will therefore want to join with Austria-Hungary to help suppress these revolutionaries' attacks.

The scale of the problem will thus increase, which will allow the Habsburg Monarchy to conceal the most excessive and carelessly hasty of its accusations against Serbia. It is no longer just a case of a few conspirators being involved, even though their nationality and backgrounds have not been ascertained: Pan-Serbianism is an immense and formidable conspiracy that is 'equally dreadful for all Governments and the murderous assassinations are finally waking up and raising Europe's conscience to that fact.'

And the writer obligingly lists the members on whom we can totally safely rely: first Germany, who, in fact, is more agitated about the Serbians than the Austro-Hungarians are. 'In Berlin we have seen from the very first that the bullet that severed the Archduke's carotid artery hit the Monarchy and that Pan-Serbianism triggered the bloody work of dismembering our old Empire.' We also remember the Chancellor's promise that Germany would draw her sword and take up the battle if any of her allies' interests were threatened.

German feelings will, no doubt, be shared by Italy, where they have suffered too much from regicidal attacks not to be horrified by the assassinations in Sarajevo. 'Rome is fully aware that peace in Europe is threatened by Pan-Serbian activities, behind which lie the threat of war; this begins with bombs and ends with cannon fire ... In these circumstances, Italy will remain loyal to her allies, whatever they expect will follow.'

'Will England not use her powerful influence to make Serbia listen to reason? For a matter of this importance, minor political affiliations must disappear. The assassinations of Monarchs are as deplorable to the Triple-Entente as they are to the Triple Alliance. Also, neither France nor Russia will separate herself from England. Why does the French nation treat the Austro-Hungarian Monarchy with hostility, when it has so abundantly proven its most friendly disposition and only asks for what it is due: peaceful borders and the assurance that criminal plots are not being hatched among its neighbours? Finally, Russia too has gone through the trials of assassinations of her Monarchs and is conscious that after the results obtained at Sarajevo, other maniacs can be tempted to resort to bombs' ... 'So because Europe does not want Pan-Serbianism, the approach that the Monarchy will undertake in Belgrade is not only in its own interests or in the interest of peace, it will most of all be in the name of civilization and humanity.'

Such is the theme on which the grandiloquence of Viennese publicists dwells at the present time. They implicate all Governments in the business and claim that their cause becomes that of all the Powers together.

To recap, behind these exaggerations and superfluities is probably hidden the desire not to continue in the direction to which they were committed. The Emperor, it is claimed, has shown himself to be opposed to it. Furthermore, I recall that the enquiry did not provide the accurate results that were expected[100] and which would have allowed Serbia to be clearly accused of abominable complicity. It will, as ever, make a great deal of noise to no effect, which will satisfy Austria's vanity with the thought that the Serbians will have been very alarmed by it.[101] [...]

DDF, 3e série, 10, No. 493.

(146) 11 July: Tschirschky to *Auswärtiges Amt*

Berchtold reveals details about the ultimatum's contents and its timing to the German ally; absolute secrecy essential

Private letter
Absolutely confidential
Vienna, 11 July 1914
R. 12 July

I took the opportunity again today to discuss the proceedings against Serbia with Count Berchtold, principally to impress upon the Minister once more, emphatically, that quick action was called for.

The Minister expressed himself upon the matter as follows:

In order finally to obtain exact information as to what the investigation at Sarajevo had so far brought to light, a confidential agent[102] had been sent from here to Sarajevo, whom he expected back Tuesday or Wednesday. A closer agreement had been arrived at since yesterday with the president of the Hungarian Council concerning the note to be

100 (**149**).

101 As Stefan Schmidt points out, Dumaine did not revise his assessment over the next few days, either: Schmidt, *Frankreichs Außenpolitik*, Oldenbourg, Munich 2007, p. 67.

102 Sectional Adviser Friedrich von Wiesner. See (**149**).

directed to Serbia, and he hoped by Tuesday to be able to determine the final version of this document. So far as he could say, the principal demands on Serbia would consist of the requirement that the King should officially and publicly proclaim, in a formal declaration and through an order to the army, that Serbia discarded her Greater Serbian policy; secondly, the institution of an agency of the Austro-Hungarian Government to see to the strict keeping of this promise would be required. The term granted for the answering of the note would be made as short as possible, say, perhaps, forty-eight hours. If the reply is not regarded here as satisfactory, mobilization will take place at once.

The question was now, at what time would it be best to deliver the note. He believed that it would not be advisable to deliver the note at the time when Mr Poincaré was in St Petersburg,[103] and thus give the French and the Russians the opportunity of discussing their attitude together in St Petersburg. The note should be delivered at Belgrade, if possible, before the departure of Mr Poincaré from Paris or after his departure from St Petersburg. Sometime, therefore, about 18 July, or on 24 July. The latter date might perhaps be preferable on account of the fact that at that time the harvest work in the Monarchy would be finished, lightening the difficulties of mobilization and preventing great losses from an economic point of view. [...]

May I conclude by saying that the Minister and Count Forgách, who was present at this conference, begged me *not* to telegraph in regard to the preceding and very confidential information, but to mention it only in private letters, in order that absolute secrecy may be assured. I got the impression that the gentlemen feared a leak *here in Austria* if I should telegraph in cipher.

DD, 2nd edn, No. 34a.[104]

(147) 11 July: Riezler's Diary

Riezler knows about Austrian plans for ultimatum; does not approve of long delay before mobilization can begin

---

Hohenfinow, 11 July 1914.

Two days in Berlin. With a number of tasks. In Austria there seem to

103 Poincaré, Viviani and de Margerie left France on the 15th and arrived in St Petersburg on the 20th of July for an official state visit. They were due to depart from there on the 23rd.

104 Engl. transl. from Geiss, *July 1914*, No. 17.

be differences as to the method between Berchtold and Tisza.[105] Hardly possible to guide their hand from Berlin. They seem to want a short ultimatum and, if Serbia declines, to march [*einrücken*]. Apparently they need awfully long to mobilize. 16 days says [Conrad von] Hoetzendorf.[106] That is very dangerous. A quick *fait accompli*, and then friendly towards the Entente, then the shock can be endured. And hand over good and overwhelming material against the Serbian machinations which does not allow any objections.

Karl Dietrich Erdmann (ed.), *Kurt Riezler. Tagebücher, Aufsätze, Dokumente*, Göttingen 1972, pp. 184–185.[107]

(148) 12 July: Szögyény to Berchtold

Summary of Germany's reasons for unconditional support for Austria; Russia is preparing for a future war but is currently not ready; relations with Britain are improved and Germany thinks she won't be involved in a war over Serbia

---

Concerns Germany's position in the current Serbian crisis

Report 60
Berlin, 12 July 1914
R. 13 July

As Your Excellency will have gathered from my telegraphic reports during the last days and from Count Hoyos' personal impressions, His Majesty Kaiser Wilhelm as well as all the other persons in authority are not only standing firmly and faithfully behind the Monarchy, but are encouraging us most emphatically not to neglect the present moment, but to treat Serbia most energetically, so as to clear out the revolutionary conspirators' nest once and for all, and are leaving it entirely up to us which means we consider appropriate to choose.[108]

I never for a moment doubted that Kaiser Wilhelm and all the German Empire would loyally fulfil the duties of an ally in any case, and I have

---

105 (**134**).

106 See Tschirschky to Jagow, 8 July 1914, in Imanuel Geiss, *Julikrise und Kriegsausbruch*, 2 vols, Hannover 1963/64, Vol. 1, No. 52.

107 See p. 20, n. 76 on the controversy over the authenticity of Riezler's diary.

108 On 14 July Tschirschky reported to Bethmann Hollweg that Tisza had explained to him that 'Germany's unconditional assumption of a stand by the side of the Monarchy had a great influence on the firm attitude of the Emperor'. Geiss, *July 1914*, No. 21.

been faithful to this conviction during the whole period of my ambassadorship in Berlin. I was not in the least surprised when in the present moment Germany assured us of her perfect loyalty and assistance.

However I think the fact that leading German circles and not least His Majesty Kaiser Wilhelm himself urge us, one could say, to undertake an action against Serbia which may even end in war needs some explanation. It is clear that after the recent events which cannot be deplored enough the monarchy must deal most energetically with Serbia, however, the fact that the German Government considers the present moment politically opportune also from its own point of view requires further illumination.

According to the German way of thinking, entirely shared by myself, general political considerations, and specific ones inspired by the murder of Sarajevo, form the conclusive argument for choosing the current moment in time.

Germany has recently found her conviction confirmed that Russia is preparing for a war with her western neighbours, and that she no longer regards that war as a future possibility, but positively includes it in the political calculations of the future. But only her future calculation, that is to say that she [Russia] intends waging war and that she is preparing for it with all her might, but that she does not propose it for now, or we should rather say, is not adequately prepared for it at the present time.

It is therefore anything but certain that if Serbia were engaged in a war with us, Russia would assist her with an armed hand; and should the Tsar's empire decide on war it would not be ready from a military point of view, and not by any means as strong as it will be in a few years' time.[109]

In addition, the German Government believes that it has certain signs that England would not take part in a war caused because of a Balkan country, not even if it were to lead to a war with Russia, perhaps also France.[110] Not only have the relations between England and Germany improved so far that Germany believes she no longer needs to fear direct hostilities on England's part, but England just now desires anything rather than a war and is not at all willing to bail out Serbia or, in the last instance, Russia. When all is said it must be admitted that the political constellation is at present as favourable as it possibly can be.

Add to this the specific political moment that has been caused by the assassination itself. Whereas until now a large part of our population refused to believe in the anti-monarchic separatist tendencies of a part of our Serbs, and expressed doubts that Serbia's intrigues reached across the frontier to us; all are now convinced and there is a general outcry for

109 For an assessment of Russia's potential future strength see for example (77).

110 This hope underpinned Bethmann Hollweg's policy throughout the crisis, but was completely unfounded.

an energetic treatment of Serbia which will finally suppress all agitation for a Greater Serbia.

In a similar manner the eyes of the whole civilized world have been opened and every nation condemns the bloody deed of Sarajevo and all understand that we must make Serbia responsible for it. And if Serbia's foreign friends will not adopt a stance against the Kingdom for political reasons, they will most likely not stand up in favour of her (at least not with force of arms) in the current moment.

These I believe to be the political reasons why the German Empire, with a clear perception of the opportunity offered, unreservedly encourages us to clarify our relationship with Serbia, which she also considers to be untenable, in such a manner as to stop Pan-Slav agitation for all time. [...]

ÖUA, VIII, No. 10215.[111]

111 Engl. transl. based on Geiss, *Juli 1914*, No. 18, here with some amendments.

7
Planning the Ultimatum

13 July–22 July: Documents (149)–(189)

While the Austrian ultimatum to Serbia (deliberately unacceptable and with a short time limit) was secretly being prepared, despite the fact that there was no conclusive evidence of the Serbian government's complicity in the assassination (**145**), (**149**), most of Europe was in the dark about the conspiratorial dealings in Vienna. The German ally was, however, informed of these events and being kept abreast of developments. Contrary to what they would later maintain (**209**), (**216**) Berlin's statesmen were well aware of Austria's plans – the unacceptable nature and the contents of the ultimatum were known in Berlin well before it was handed over on 23 July (**146**), (**147**), (**154**). The delivery of the ultimatum was deliberately delayed due to the French state visit to Russia (**153**). Vienna's statesmen were eager to explain to their German ally that the hold-up was not through a change of heart or lack of nerve (**156**); however, they were forced to admit that any military action resulting from Serbia's anticipated rejection of the demands would also entail considerable delay (**177**), (**225**).

The first three weeks of July were a period of outward calm while behind the scenes it was a time of secret planning and plotting. It was not a foregone conclusion in Vienna and Berlin that war would result from the assassination. Meanwhile, in London, Paris and St Petersburg, there was much uncertainty and guesswork on the part of the Great Powers' governments and their Ambassadors in Vienna and Berlin who picked up on rumours but were unable to provide definite information about Austria-Hungary's intentions (**151**), (**161**), (**168**), (**188**), (**187**). By 17 July French intelligence was aware of the plan to present Serbia with an ultimatum, but this information did not reach the French Foreign Ministry until 24 July (**169**).

Not just the Entente powers were reduced to guesswork. Throughout this period Italy was being deliberately kept in the dark by her allies while Austria-Hungary wanted to place her before a *fait accompli* (**166**), (**173**). However, Italy became aware of Austria's plans, due to the indiscretions of the German ambassador in Rome (**164**). The German ally was keen to entice Italy to stay with the Alliance by offering compensation, but Austria-Hungary – not surprisingly, as such recompense would be made from her territory – was less willing (**171**), (**173**).

Serbia's government reacted with concern to the developing crisis. It had suspected since Tisza's speech of 15 July that Austria-Hungary would seek some kind of redress.[1] Prime Minister Pašić wrote to all Serbian missions abroad (**176**) and explained that he hoped that the Great Powers might diffuse the crisis. In the weeks following the assassination, the Serbian Government made it known that it was willing to comply with any requests that were compatible with the country's independence (**165**), and to do anything 'reasonable' to help address the crime (**168**).

The hopes that an amicable solution might be found were dashed at 6:00 p.m. on 23 July, when the Austrian Minister in Belgrade, Wladimir Giesl, delivered a 48–hour ultimatum to the Serbian Foreign Ministry (which he had received three days earlier and held back under instruction, until the French President and his colleagues had embarked on their ship for their two-day voyage home) (**180**), (**191**).

Presenting Serbia and the world with a fait accompli had not quite worked, as details of the planned diplomatic move had leaked in various places, but the secrecy and deliberate deception nonetheless ensured that most Europeans were taken by surprise, and that many decision-makers were caught off-guard, or were even away from their posts for some of the crucial 48 hours which followed. In Paris, foreign policy was in the hands of the Minister of Justice Bienvenu-Martin, inexperienced in foreign affairs, while Viviani and Poincaré were embarked on their long journey home, and the shortness of time afforded to Serbia also ensured that the Great Powers could not intervene and suggest mediation, just as Austria-Hungary's and Germany's decision-makers had intended.

1 See Chapter 7, p. 244, n. 12.

(149) 13 July: Wiesner[2] to Berchtold

Investigation into the assassination so far reveals no evidence that Serbian Government was involved in the crime; crime plotted and prepared in Belgrade; Serbian frontier-guards helped smuggle the assassins and their weapons into Bosnia

Telegram without number
Sarajevo, 13 July 1914
D. 1.10 p.m.; 2.00 p.m.
R. 5.00 p.m.; 5.40 p.m.

It is the firm belief of all persons in authority here that Serbia is busily spreading propaganda for a Greater Serbia – apart from the press – also through societies and other organisations, and that everything is done with the knowledge and approval of the Serbian Government.

The material presented to me by civil and military authorities which forms the basis of this belief may be classified as follows: The material of the time before the assassination contains no proof that the Serbian Government promoted propaganda. There is little, but sufficient, material to prove that the movement originates in Serbia and is supported by societies, and is tolerated by the Serbian Government.

Judicial inquiry on assassination

There is nothing to prove or even to suspect that the Serbian Government is party to the inducement of the crime, or its preparation or the furnishing of weapons.[3] On the contrary, there are reasons to believe that this is altogether out of the question.

Evidence provided by the accused shows almost without doubt that

2 Sectional Adviser in the Austro-Hungarian Foreign Ministry, charged with obtaining information about the investigation into the background to the assassination in Sarajevo.

3 On the lack of evidence of any involvement of the Serbian Government in the planning or execution of the attack, see for example Richard C. Hall, 'Serbia', in R. Hamilton and H. Herwig (eds), *The Origins of World War I*, Cambridge University Press, Cambridge 2003, p. 106. The fact that the Government was aware of arms smuggling across the border before the assassination was proved by Vladimir Dedijer in the expanded Serbo-Croat edition of his book on Sarajevo. See Mark Cornwall, 'Serbia', in Keith Wilson (ed.), *Decisions for War, 1914*, UCL Press, London 1995, pp. 56–57. However, the Serbian Government did have warning of the planned assassination attempt, and failed to prevent the would-be assassins from travelling to Bosnia. For more details see Christopher Clark, *The Sleepwalkers. How Europe went to War in 1914*, Allen Lane, London 2012, pp. 56–64.

the crime was resolved upon in Belgrade and that preparations were made with the cooperation of Serbian state-officials Ciganović and Major Tankosić, who jointly provided bombs, Brownings, ammunition and prussic acid. Guilt of Pribićević not ascertained and the first reports about him [were] based on regrettable misunderstandings on the part of examining police organs.

It has been objectively and completely proven that bombs came from Serbian army stores in Kragujevać, but there is no evidence that they were obtained just now ad hoc, as they might stem from the supplies of the Komitadschis from the war.

Evidence of accused leaves scarcely any doubt that Princip, Čabrinović, Grabez, with bombs and weapons upon them, were secretly smuggled across the frontier to Bosnia by Serbian organs, under the direction of Ciganović. These organised transports were directed by the frontier-captains at Schabatz and Loznica and were contrived by frontier guards. Though it is not ascertained that they knew the purpose of the journey, still they must have realised the secrecy of their mission.

Other investigations following the assassination give insight into the organisation of propaganda carried out by '*Narodna odbrana*'. They contain valuable useable material, but [it] has not yet been checked; will be delivered without loss of time.

If the intentions of the time I left are still valid, the demands [of Serbia] could be extended:

A) Suppression of Government organs' cooperation in smuggling of persons and goods across frontier.

B) Dismissal of Serbian frontier-captains at Schabatz and Loznica and the implicated frontier-guards.

Prosecution of Ciganović and Tankosić.

I leave for Vienna this evening, arrive on Tuesday evening and will go directly to the Foreign Ministry.

Verbal explanation of report necessary.

ÖUA, VIII, No. 10252/53.[4]

(150) 13 July: Hopman to Tirpitz

Germany's attitude to encourage Austria and pretend to the rest of Europe that situation is harmless

Our position is still under no circumstances to discourage the Austrians and we are letting them know that we will tolerate and support their

4 English translation based on Geiss, *July 1914*, No. 19, here with amendments.

steps vis-à-vis Serbia. On the other hand we are attempting to portray the situation from a general European point of view as harmless.

Volker R. Berghahn and Wilhelm Deist, 'Kaiserliche Marine', *Militärgeschichtliche Mitteilungen*, 4, 1970, pp. 37–58, p. 50.

(151) 13 July: Bunsen to Grey

Fear of loss of prestige in Vienna; press demands strong steps against Serbia

Vienna, 13 July 1914 (Received 18 July)
From an Austrian gentleman in touch with the Ball[haus]platz I hear that, while Count Berchtold is himself peacefully inclined, a feeling that strong steps should be taken against Serbia exists in the minds of several members of the Austro-Hungarian Foreign Office whose opinions carry weight.[5] These gentlemen argue that the Dual Monarchy will lose its position as a Great Power if it does not once for all make it clear at Belgrade that Serbian provocation will no longer be tolerated on this side of the frontier, and they press for military measures to compel acceptance by Serbia of what they hold to be a necessary demand for the participation of Austrian agents in the work of discovering and bringing to condign punishment the instigators and accomplices of the plot against the heir to the Austrian Throne. The *Reichspost* and other more or less independent organs of the Vienna press are conducting a vigorous campaign on these lines. The '*Neue Freie Presse*' has distinguished itself in clamouring for vengeance against Serbia. On many sides regret is expressed that this country did not go to war with Serbia in 1908, when Bosnia and Herzegovina were annexed, so that a blow might have been struck at the neighbouring monarchy which would have reduced it to impotence for a generation.[6] Russia, it is alleged, was then not in a position after her war with Japan to render effective aid to Serbia.[7] That opportunity having been lost, as well as that offered by the recent Balkan wars, Austria-Hungary cannot afford once more to leave unpunished the insolence and audacity of the Serbian nationalists.

5 (**126**).

6 This was certainly the case among German and Austro-Hungarian military leaders, such as Moltke, Conrad and Colmar von der Goltz, as well as Wilhelm II. For evidence see Annika Mombauer, *Helmuth von Moltke*, Cambridge University Press, Cambridge 2001, pp. 112–115.

7 After the Russo-Japanese war of 1905–1906, Russia was widely regarded as weakened.

The *'Neue Freie Presse'* claims that this time the Dual Monarchy would have the sympathies of the whole of Europe with her if she took severe measures against Serbia. Even Russia would approve a campaign undertaken against a nation tainted with the crime of regicide at home, and ostentatiously condoning the Sarajevo assassination, and the rest of Europe would certainly stand by Austria in a war of righteous self-defence against murder and outrage.

Against language such as this I have already reported in my despatch No. 140 of the 11th July[8] that a note of warning has been published in the form of an official communiqué describing as entirely unfounded all the firebrand accounts which the press had been allowed to publish of the results of the recent council of the Common Ministers[9] and of the consultation held at Ischl[10] between the Emperor and Count Berchtold on the 9th July. It is indeed generally assumed that the Emperor himself would be with difficulty moved to sanction an aggressive course of action leading almost certainly to international complications of the gravest kind. That more moderate counsels are more likely to prevail is also rendered probable by the studied caution of the language held by the Hungarian Premier in his replies to interpellations in the Chamber at Budapest on the 8th July.[11] While admitting that the Archduke had fallen a victim to a deliberate plot and that six or eight bombs at least were ready to be hurled at his carriage on the fatal day, Count Tisza denied that the population of Bosnia as a whole was disloyal to the connection with the Dual Monarchy, or that any far-reaching conspiracy against Hapsburg rule existed among its people. The Government, therefore, would take no precipitate action. It would 'do its duty in every direction'. What would be done in the area of foreign affairs, he was not competent to say. He condemned the wholesale assaults on Serb property which had unhappily taken place in Bosnia, and he expressed the hope that the modus vivendi now existing between the rival sections of the Slavonic race in Croatia would be maintained in future.

The declarations of Count Tisza have had the more effect in calming the public mind in view of the fact that the Austrian Reichsrat has been suspended since March last owing to Czech obstruction, and that the

8 See BD, XI, No. 46, Bunsen to Grey, 11 July 1914.

9 (**134**).

10 The Emperor was at Bad Ischl, 270 kilometres west of Vienna.

11 See (**162**) for Bunsen's account: 'Count Tisza's first statement was made on July 8th when he declared in effect that, though he was then only in a position to give a very general reply, he might state that the investigation of the Sarajevo crime was being pursued in every direction, and it was the duty of all concerned to have regard certainly to the importance of the interests involved in the maintenance of peace, but to give due weight also to those great interests which are bound up with the existence and prestige of the Monarchy.'

Hungarian Chamber offers, therefore, at the present time, the only means of enlightening the representatives of the people regarding the intentions of the Government. Count Tisza had attended the deliberations of the Common Ministers of Foreign Affairs, War and Finance, on the day preceding his statement, and he expressed no doubt in his speech the sentiments that prevailed in that important council.[12]

But though some restraint has thus been placed on the cry for vengeance against Serbia, this country is still in a very angry mood, and the extracts daily published in Vienna from a portion of the Belgrade press serve to inflame still further the public mind. The Serbian Minister, M. Jovanovitć, condemns these utterances, but points out that they are partly accounted for, though certainly not justified, by the memory of innumerable attacks, couched in the most insulting language, which the Vienna press has been in the habit of making on the Serbian people. He also points to the language recently held by the Serbian Prime Minister as expressing the true sentiments of the nation. M. Pašić is reported to have said that the Serbian Government are willing to assist in any manner required by the obligations of a civilised State in investigating the ramifications of the crime of the 28th June on Serbian territory.

BD, XI, No. 55.

(152) 13 July: Crackanthorpe to Grey

Rumours of suspicious circumstances surrounding the death of Hartwig

(No. 129.) Very Confidential.

Belgrade, 13 July 1914 (Received 20 July)

[...] I have the honour to report that by a strange fatality M. de Hartwig, the Russian Minister to Serbia, succumbed to heart failure within the precincts of the Austrian Legation on the evening of the 10th instant.[13]

It appears that M. de Hartwig was desirous of offering to the Austrian Minister [Baron Giesl], who had returned to Belgrade the same day, a personal explanation in regard to certain rumours which had become public concerning his behaviour and attitude subsequently to the

12 On 15 July Tisza again answered questions in the Hungarian chamber. For Bunsen's account see (**162**). For Tisza's speech see *Int. Bez.*, Vol. IV, No. 249. For the reaction in the Austrian Press see (**159**).

13 BD, XI, No. 48 (see also (**144**), n. 94).

assassination of the Archduke Francis Ferdinand. I have no first-hand knowledge of what transpired at the interview and will therefore merely mention some of the reports which had been circulated, and which may have been discussed in the course of conversation.

(1.) The *Reichspost* of Vienna had recently published an article attacking the Russian Minister for holding a bridge party on the evening of the Archduke's murder. It is true that M. de Hartwig was having a quiet game of bridge that evening with the Roumanian and Greek Ministers and the Italian Chargé d'Affaires, but, under the circumstances, the article in the '*Reichspost*' seems to have contained some very unnecessary animadversions.

(2.) The Russian Minister had been accused of not hoisting the Russian flag at half-mast on the day of the funeral service for the Archduke. Though M. de Hartwig himself affirmed the flag was flying, several of my colleagues state that this was not the case. The Austrian Legation took a strong view of the matter and doubtless the Russian Minister was anxious to smooth matters over.

(3.) I regret to state that M. de Hartwig had recently been using very inappropriate and ill-advised language in regard to the private life and character of the present heir to the Austro-Hungarian throne,[14] in the presence, among others, of my Italian colleague. I do not know whether his remarks were repeated at the Austrian Legation, but if this was so, it is probable that the interview must have been, on M. de Hartwig's side, somewhat emotional, sufficiently so to hasten an end which, according to doctors' evidence, could in any case have been only deferred a few days. I am however assured that the conversation between the two Ministers was quite friendly, and from what I have seen of Baron Giesl, I should judge that he would most certainly have met M. de Hartwig's explanations in a conciliatory spirit.

On news being received in Belgrade of the strange circumstances attending the Russian Minister's death, sinister reports were at once circulated to the effect that M. de Hartwig had taken a 'cup of tea' at the Austrian Legation. I merely mention this as affording an indication of the somewhat mediaeval morals prevailing in this city.[15]

BD, XI, No. 62.

14 Franz Joseph's great-nephew, later Kaiser Karl I.

15 (**144**).

(153) 14 July: Berchtold to Franz Joseph

Berchtold informs Kaiser Franz Joseph about intended timing of delivery of ultimatum in an *Immediatsvortrag*

Vienna, 14 July 1914

In today's conference,[16] in which both Premiers and the Hungarian Minister at the court of Vienna took part, a perfect agreement was established with regard to the demands to be addressed to Serbia. The text of the note is at present being settled and will be submitted for approval in a conference of the Governments on Sunday, 19 inst.[17] When the text of the note has been agreed upon, it will be presented in Belgrade on Saturday, 25 inst.,[18] and the Serbian Government will at the same time be informed that the term for the answer to the note has been fixed at forty-eight hours, within which space of time our demands must be accepted.

The date was selected out of consideration for the visit of the President of the French Republic to the Tsar, which is to last from 20 to 25 July.[19] All those present shared my opinion that if we sent the ultimatum during the meeting in St Petersburg, this might be regarded as an affront, and that a personal discussion between the ambitious President of the Republic and the Tsar about the new situation created by the despatch of the ultimatum would increase the probability that France and Russia may join in a war.

Count Tisza has given up his objections to an ultimatum with a short term, because I alerted him to the military difficulties which would arise from delayed action.[20] I also argued that even after the mobilisation a peaceful arrangement might be possible if Serbia were to give way in good time.

In this case we would, however, have to make Serbia pay the cost of the mobilisation, and until payment was made we should have to ask for a pledge in Serbia.

Count Tisza also decidedly declared that he could only give his consent to the intended action on the condition that, even before the ultimatum was sent, a Council of the Ministers of Austria and Hungary agreed that the Monarchy was not aiming to acquire territory by the war

16 The Ministerial Council meeting of 14 July.

17 See below, Minutes of the Council of Ministers' meeting of 19 July.

18 On 17 July it was decided to bring that date forward to 23 July. See Stolberg (Counsellor at the German Embassy in Vienna) to Bethmann Hollweg, 17 July, in Geiss, *July 1914*, No. 27.

19 The state visit actually ended on 23 July.

20 See (**134**) for Tisza's objections.

against Serbia, apart from small regulations of the frontier lines.

The text of the note to be sent to Belgrade, as it was settled today, is such that we must reckon with the probability of war. Should Serbia nonetheless decide to give in and to concede to demands, then such action would signify not only a downright humiliation for the Kingdom, but *pari passu* a blow to Russian prestige in the Balkans, but it would also no doubt procure for us certain guarantees that Serbian underground work on our territory would be restrained.

ÖUA, VIII, No. 10272.[21]

(154) 14 July: Tschirschky to Bethmann Hollweg

Decision in Vienna to delay delivery of ultimatum until after Poincaré's visit to St Petersburg; promise to reveal the contents of the note to Berlin before delivering it to Belgrade

Absolutely confidential
Vienna, 14 July 1914
(Received 15 July p.m.)

[*Wilhelm II's emphases in the text and marginal notes*]

After Count Tisza left me,[22] Count Berchtold requested me to come and see him, so that he might inform me for his part of the results of today's discussion. To his

21 Engl. transl. based on Geiss, *July 1914*, No. 20, here with minor amendments.

22 See Tschirschky to Bethmann Hollweg, 14 July, in Geiss, *July 1914*, No. 21: '[...] The Count said that he had always been the one who had advised caution, but that every day had strengthened him in the conviction more and more that the Monarchy would have to come to an energetic decision in order to prove its vitality and to put an end to the intolerable conditions in the south-east. [...] Fortunately full agreement and determination prevail among the authorities here. H. M. Franz Joseph judges very calmly of the situation [...] and will certainly hold out to the bitter end. Count Tisza added that Germany's unconditional assumption of a stand by the side of the Monarchy had a great influence on the firm attitude of the Emperor. [...] The note is being composed so that the possibility of its acceptance is practically excluded. It was considered particularly important that it should demand not only assurances and promises, but deeds. In the composition of the note it was necessary, according to his view, to take care that it should be intelligible to the great general public – particularly in England – and that it should put Serbia plainly and clearly in the wrong. [...]' (DD, No. 49).

great pleasure, a general agreement on the tenor of the note to be transmitted to Serbia had been arrived at. Count Tisza had agreed to his, the Minister's, views in a very pleasing way, and had even introduced a sharper tone at various points. However, the impossibility of delivering the note at Belgrade by the sixteenth or eighteenth had been demonstrated on technical grounds. The French text was to be gone over once again definitively at a ministerial meeting next Sunday morning at nine o'clock. He would then probably submit the note to the Emperor at Ischl on Tuesday. He would guarantee that H. M. would give his approval to it.

At today's conference[23] it was unanimously agreed that it would be advisable in any case to await the *pity!* departure of Mr Poincaré from St Petersburg before taking the step at Belgrade. For it was best to avoid if possible the celebration of a fraternization at St Petersburg, influenced by champagne and by Messrs Poincaré, Isvolsky and the Grand Dukes, which might influence the attitude and possibly fix it on the part of both empires [*sic*]. It would also be much better to have the toasts delivered before the note is handed over. *!* Thus the delivery could follow on 25 July.

Count Berchtold begged me, as Count Tisza had also done, expressly and repeatedly, not to leave my Government in any doubt that merely the presence of Poincaré at St Petersburg was the reason for the delay of the delivery of the note at Belgrade, and that one could feel absolutely certain in Berlin that there could be no talk of hesitation or uncertainty here.[24]

The Minister finally told me that after the final rendering of the text on Sunday, he would immediately forward the note to the Imperial Government for its absolutely confidential information, even before submitting it to his own Emperor.[25]

DD, No. 50.[26]

---

23 The Austro-Hungarian Ministerial Council meeting of 14 July. See also (**153**).

24 See also (**156**).

25 But note how Germany would later deny having had any prior knowledge of the ultimatum. See for example (**182**).

26 Engl. transl. based on Geiss, *July 1914*, No. 22, here with minor amendments.

(155) 14 July: Letter by Pourtalès

Rumours of friction between Russia and Britain

St Petersburg, 14 July 1914
[draft letter, no addressee]

Things currently not going particularly well between Russia and England, but it is of course difficult to find out anything positive about the existing frictions which Sasonov and Buchanan do not admit to vis-à-vis the representatives of the Triple Alliance.

PA/AA, R 2062, cited in Stephen Schröder, *Die englisch-russische Marinekonvention*, Vandenhoeck & Ruprecht, Göttingen 2004, p. 641, note 60.

(156) 15 July: Berchtold to Szögyény

Berchtold reassures Germans that tactical reasons are behind the delay in delivering the ultimatum to Serbia

Telegram 234
Vienna, 15 July 1914
Strictly confidential
D. 10.30 p.m.

I have already explained to Herr von Tschirschky the reasons of the delay in our forthcoming explication with Serbia,[27] but I am anxious that your Excellency should inform strictly in private the Imperial Chancellor and the Secretary of State of the following.

Although the judicial enquiry in Sarajevo has furnished us with sufficient material,[28] still we believe that we should delay the exceedingly energetic démarche in Belgrade until the President of the French Republic, currently on the way to St Petersburg, shall have left Russian territory. To begin the action we are proposing at the very moment when the President is being celebrated as the guest of the Tsar might naturally be regarded as a political affront, which we should like to avoid. On the other hand, we should consider it unwise to undertake the threatening step in Belgrade at the very time when the peace-loving, reserved Tsar

27 See (**154**).
28 There was actually little concrete evidence to suggest that the Serbian Government had been behind the assassination. See (**149**).

Nicholas and undeniably cautious Herr Sazonov are under the influence of the two war mongers [*Hetzer*] Isvolsky and Poincaré.

Under these circumstances we do not think that we ought to realise the plans we have already discussed with Herr von Tschirschky before the end of next week.[29]

This delay, which is in itself unwelcome, will explain the attitude of our official press.

We are obliged to prevent public opinion in the Monarchy, which favours our policy, from cooling, and yet we cannot allow the press to get up too much steam so that other powers might think of mediation.[30]

ÖUA, VIII, No. 10276.[31]

(157) 15 July: Redlich's Diary

Austrian decision-makers favour war

Today half an hour with Alek Hoyos: he told me highly confidentially that the war was as good as decided on. But patience was needed, there were important reasons for a delay. In 14 days time he would tell me the secret and most interesting story of the last two weeks. Berchtold is of the same opinion as Tisza, Stürgkh, Burián. Biliński pretends the same! The Kaiser [Franz Joseph] himself is entirely ready for war. Hoyos thinks: 'If this leads to the world war, it does not matter to us.' He reads to me a very beautiful and comprehensive letter which he has just finished and which is to be handed to the English Lord Chancellor Haldane on the day of the declaration of war. He is actually a close friend of Haldane's. Germany is completely in agreement with us. Hoyos says: 'If our army

29 Among members of the German navy, it was wrongly believed that the delay had been due to Bulgaria's request. See Hopman to Tirpitz, 17 July: 'The Austrian ultimatum has been delayed by 10 days due to Bulgaria's wish, so that Bulgarian readiness for war can be completed. Bulgaria is to benefit to a large extent from the results of the action.' Volker Berghahn and Wilhelm Deist, 'Kaiserliche Marine', 1970, p. 52. See also *Reichsmarineamt*, RM3/10398, for an almost identical report by Walter Nicolai, the chief of the Intelligence Bureau, dated 17 July 1914. It is not clear where this information came from.

30 Szögyény's reply in Geiss, *July 1914*, No. 24: 'State Secretary understands perfectly that the intended energetic step in Belgrade cannot be undertaken before the President of the French Republic has left St Petersburg, but regrets this delay extremely.'

31 English translation based on Geiss, *July 1914*, No. 23, here with minor amendments.

is no good, then the Monarchy cannot survive anyway for it is today the only cohesion of the Empire.' [...] The news that Conrad and Krobatin are going on holiday is intended to obscure our intentions. [...] Mérey in Rome is the pinnacle of the war-mongers: I suspect that he has already created the accord between Italy and us. Valona will only be achievable for Italy if we carry out territorial changes on the Balkans. I tell Hoyos that I did not wish for Serbia's independence to be removed by us. Her reduction and the lessening of her independence would suffice. Whether we offer anything to Rumania is doubtful: I think it will not happen. Here in Vienna nobody believes in the possibility of war: very noticeable are the three bad days on the stock exchange last week and this week. [...]

Fritz Fellner and Doris Corradini (eds), *Schicksalsjahre Österreichs*, 3 vols, Böhlau, Vienna, Cologne, Weimar 2011, Vol. 1, pp. 613–614.

(158) 15 July: Kageneck to Waldersee

Update on intended Austrian military measures; Austrian fear that engagement with Serbs might be delayed; assurance that fight against Serbia would be abandoned if Russia intervenes; unacceptability of note to Belgrade and proposed date of its delivery

Vienna, 15 July 1914
(received 17 July)

Unfortunately General v. Conrad is currently away and has been on holiday for two days in Innichen in the Tyrol, but he should return here by the middle of next week. The Minister of War also leaves Vienna today for the same reason of 'apparent calm' ['*anscheinenden sauren Gurkenzeit*'].[32] However I was able to speak with his [Conrad's] deputy, General v. Höfer, whom I asked with reference to the specific questions[33] of Your Highness to inform me as far as he could. It is intended to

32 This was an unfortunate result of the plan to demonstrate outward calm by sending key men on holiday. Key decision-makers, such as Conrad and Moltke, could not coordinate or confirm their strategies, and military discussions had to be conducted by less senior figures. See also (**171**).

33 On 11 July Waldersee had sent specific questions to Kageneck, requesting information about Conrad's strategic intentions: 'Is the entire army to be mobilized? Is it planned to March into Galicia at the same time? Or are only a few corps, partially strengthened, to march into Serbia? Or is nothing decided yet?' (Waldersee to Kageneck, in Günther Kronenbitter, 'Die Macht der Illusionen', *Militärgeschichtliche Mitteilungen*, 57, 1998, p. 533).

declare 'Mobilization Balkans' alone. This meant until now the Corps IV, VII, XIII and XII, finally the two Bosnian-Herzegovinian XV and XVI. From a remark made by Höfer I concluded that they will initially not remove Corps XII from Transylvania because of Rumania's uncertain attitude. This should transpire (says Höfer) relatively quickly after the mobilisation order. In Galicia they intend initially to do nothing, not least so as not to give Russia reasons for counter-measures. Very sensible procedure. The company establishments of 120 men and squadrons of 150 mounted men [which have] finally been achieved there will guarantee initial security.

Höfer did express a concern (known to me already from the last trip to Scutari). Apart from the long duration of the mobilization, which gives the other powers time for possible intervention, there is the possibility that the Serbian forces, two-thirds of which are currently distributed in the new southern areas, would approach very slowly, or rather, which would be the worst scenario, would in any case only present themselves for battle in the southernmost old-Serbia in the area around Niš. It could then take perhaps three weeks after the declaration of mobilization for decisive battles to occur. The financial aspect is also important in this. Should the Serbs present themselves for battle at the lower Morava, then the General Staff here confidently expects that there will be an uprising in all of Macedonia and that the new areas will want to free themselves of the hated Serbian yoke. The question is then if Greece and also Bulgaria will want to profit from this. Then Rumania would likely turn against Bulgaria. According to the newest revelations from Senator Humbert, which are very timely for us, about the not so good state of French armaments chances are increasing that Russia will not intervene.[34] Poincaré will most likely not have too rosy a reception in Neva. I seek in vain for reasons why just at this moment this really rather dirty French linen is being washed in public. Perhaps a deliberate peaceful hint for the Russian address, if it is not a domestic lever for higher military credits.

---

34 On 13 July 1914, the French Senator Charles Humbert had publicly revealed serious shortcomings within the French army during a speech to the Senate, for example that French field artillery was inferior to Germany's, that there was a lack of officers, that fortification-artillery was out of date, that France did not have the necessary means to cross the Moselle or Rhine, and that the fortifications between Toul and Verdun had not been improved since 1875. This was welcome news in Germany and Austria-Hungary, but caused concern in Britain. See for example (**160**). On Humbert's revelations, see Gerd Krumeich, *Armaments and Politics in France on the Eve of the First World War. The Introduction of the Three-Year Conscription 1913–1914*, Berg, London 1984, p. 214; John Keiger, *France and the Origins of the First World War*, Macmillan, London 1983, p. 149. See also (**159**).

I can today report this much about the diplomatic preparations of the démarche: of late Count Tisza himself is convinced (according to his own admission vis-à-vis our Ambassador) of the necessity of energetic action of A.H. against Serbia. 'It cannot go on like this'. The old Emperor, says Berchtold, will see things through to the end. The note to be delivered to Serbia will be finished next Sunday,[35] then Berchtold will drive to Ischl for an audience. On 25 July the note is to be delivered in Belgrade and the other powers will be notified (after it has previously gone only to Berlin for confidential information).[36] As I have heard today, the note is going to be designed in such a way that an acceptance is entirely out of the question. But what if the second case scenario occurred, that following initial refusal of the note and 'Mobilization" immediately afterwards the Serbian Government succumbs to the pressure, what then? Should this great run-up again come to nothing? Berchtold fears such a turn of events. In my opinion the military leaders will then have to ensure that there can be no turning back. Getting paid for the costs of the mobilization and the turning back would hardly amount to getting half the job done. From a hint I conclude that Belgrade will be bombed with heavy artillery. Very worrying is the weak attitude of the Viennese stock exchange which has already lost more than 488 million in values. This has to open eyes abroad that something is being planned. It will not be possible to keep it a secret for long.

As regards the military measures one has to assume that they will work out, something which in this country usually cannot be taken as given. In the last 5 years people have had nothing else to do but to busy themselves with 'Mobilization Balkans and Russia', in practice and in all war games. Only it will all come off slowly, with the here usual lethargy [*Schlendrian*] about which one could fill volumes in every-day life. Perhaps there will also be uprisings with advancing south-Slav reservists which will hopefully be nipped in the bud. I have often described the still-not-resolved question of light howitzers as the pinnacle of that lethargy. I have heard today from Höfer's mouth that, if Russia intervenes, the operations against Serbia will not be continued, but all corps will be deployed against the main enemy.[37] The General Staff seem much

35 19 July.

36 Moltke commented in the margin of Kageneck's report: 'If the démarche is only presented on 25 July a lot of water will flow down the Danube before it may come to anything further.' Quoted in Theobald von Schäfer, 'Generaloberst von Moltke in den Tagen vor der Mobilmachung und seine Einwirkung auf Österreich-Ungarn', *Die Kriegsschuldfrage. Berliner Monatshefte für Internationale Aufklärung*, August 1926, p. 515. The date was later changed to 23 July.

37 This would have been welcome news in the General Staff in Berlin as Germany's military plans relied on this shift towards what they regarded as the main enemy, Russia. This was not, however, what actually occurred once war had broken out.

occupied with this dynamic and as a result fear that the Serbs might at first present themselves only far in the South.

Under these circumstances I will of course remain at my post in Vienna. As soon as the *k.u.k.* Chief of the General Staff is back in Vienna I will consult him regarding the military details.[38]

BA-MA W-10/50891.[39]

(159) 15 July: Dumaine to Viviani

Reports in the Viennese Press call for war against Serbia

Despatch No. 184
Vienna, 15 July 1914
R: Cabinet, 18 July; Dir. pol., 20 July

It was inevitable that the annoying debate responsible for revealing to the French Senate the gaps and errors in our military organization should be put to profitable use, either directly against us, or against the causes that we support.[40] This theme which lends itself so well to facile exaggerations: 'anarchy in the national defence of France,' has become a warning to Russia on how little confidence they can have in their friendship with the French Republic 'which no longer counts as a military factor in international politics'.

'It will therefore be necessary to correct very little the plans that the Tsar devised, with the help of French regiments', declares the *Neues Wiener Journal*. Better informed, the *Neue Freie Presse* is looking to use these sensational revelations to their advantage against Serbia. 'It is not by chance that just the day before a meeting between President Poincaré and Tsar Nicholas and conversations of such high importance for the

38 Waldersee received Kageneck's reply on 17 July and immediately summarized the information about the likely Austrian military measures in a letter to Jagow, warning him that 'we would do well not to reckon with a very speedy result to the Austrian military measures'. However, he assured Jagow that there was no need for action from Germany's military authorities, adding: 'General Moltke plans to return to Berlin on the 25th of this month. I remain here [in Ivenack] ready to pounce; we in the General Staff are ready, in the meantime there is nothing for us to arrange.' Waldersee to Jagow, private letter, DD, No. 74. See also Waldersee to Kageneck, 17 July 1914, cited in Kronenbitter, 'Macht der Illusionen', pp. 533f.)

39 Also in AA-PA Berlin, R8627, and in Geiss, *Julikrise*, I, No. 102, with minor differences to archive copy.

40 See (**158**), and p. 252, n. 34.

management of the vast Empire, the reporter of the military budget has divulged the state of the army and quite bluntly told the country of the reality of the situation ... Why let Europe know, at such a time, that the French army, whose strength is certainly not questionable, would still need several years in order to be completely ready? Because the French Senate, before the visit to St Petersburg, wanted clearly to affirm that it is resolved to keep the peace ... Such declarations, which it would have been easy to delay until the autumn, constitute the most energetic and spontaneous manifestation in favour of a peaceful politics. It is reasonable to suspect, moreover, that the Russian armaments, paid for from French coffers, are equally quite far from being finished. The forces of the debtor are hardly better prepared than the creditors', which does not prevent the French and Russian troops from being able to go to war any minute. But both deputies and senators reject the idea of spilling blood on behalf of Pan-Serbianism with as much horror as if were a question of a crime being committed against their own nation. Referring to Parliament discussions, the President of the Republic will have to declare to Petersburg that the country he represents will never go to war to allow the freedom of assassins and facilitate the growth of Serbia ...'. After that, it is up to Serbia to work out what help she can depend on.

With their capacity for harbouring comforting illusions, the Austrians thus already do not consider Russia and France to be in a position to have their say in European affairs, which would assure the Dual Monarchy, supported by Germany, many opportunities to subject Serbia to whatever régime she wants to impose upon her. The *Militärische Rundschau* acknowledges in plain language. 'Time is still on our side. If we do not decide to go to war, the war that will take place in two or three years at the very latest will happen in far less favourable circumstances. Right now, the initiative is ours: Russia is not ready, and both moral and legal factors are on our side, as is strength. Since one day we must accept the struggle, let us provoke it straight away ... Our prestige, our position as a great Power, and our honour are at stake. Even more than this, for it is probably a question of our very existence: to be or not to be, that really is the big question today.'

And, adding to what it has already said, today's *Neue Freie Presse* takes Count Tisza to task for the restraint of his second speech in which he said: 'our relationship with Serbia would, however, need to be clarified!'[41] These words provoke its indignation. For *Neue Freie Presse*, appeasement and security can only come from a war ('*une guerre à couteau*') against Pan-Serbianism, and it is in the name of humanity that it demands the extermination of the accursed Serbian race.

41 For details of Tisza's two speeches (8 and 15 July) see (**151**) and (**162**). See also Chapter 7, pp. 243–244, nn. 11 and 12.

All in all, there is perceptiveness in this crazy reasoning. The Habsburg Monarchy is undermined by its Slavic section; it is the Serbo-Croats who will create the catastrophe.

Staying in the present, I have consulted M. Jovanović about a possibility that seems more dangerous for his country than the more or less threatening démarche concerning the judicial enquiry. It is possible that Austria, after having put together a legal case of the kind she is very good at preparing, intends to obtain guarantees from the Belgrade Cabinet against the subversive activities of Pan-Serbianism, not only through harsh policing at the borders, but also by the dissolution of various nationalist groups and war veterans' associations which, as she will point out, are suspected of stirring up the Yugoslavian element.

'In that case,' my colleague immediately replied, 'it is the whole of Serbia that should be dissolved. There is not one among us who fosters hope of a union of all Serbs. It has come to the point that it did formerly when, in order to obtain union, M. Milovanović resigned himself to the idea of creating it, even under the Habsburg sceptre. He would have gone so far as to sacrifice the independence of our little kingdom. Austria-Hungary has not understood this; she has committed one mistake after another. The damage is now irreparable. Nevertheless, if she asks us politely, by treating us with the consideration that is customary between independent States, to help with her enquiries, to support her protection measures, we will not refuse. But if she compromises our national dignity then she will find us ready to stand up to her.'

He added, moreover, that he does not think that the Austro-Hungarian Government is taking the risk of speaking too loudly. The level of agitation is at a peak for the Bosnians, the Croats, and the Dalmatians, who are exasperated by the crushing regime that the old Monarchy upholds against the awakening of nationalities. On the other hand, he says he is assured of the unity between all the southern Slavs, irrespective of their denomination, by the obvious evidence gathered every day by the Austro-Hungarian Government. Faced with the imminent danger of disintegration, it seems one must content oneself here with a vague satisfaction of amour-propre, that Serbia will no doubt grant, certain of the compensations that the future holds for her.

DDF, 3e série, 10, No. 516.

(160) 16 July: Memorandum by F. Bertie

Conversation between Grey and Lichnowsky reveals German fears of Anglo-Russian Naval Convention; Germany afraid of Russia's military increases; might decide to fight Russia before she becomes too strong

London, 16 July 1914

I saw Grey by appointment this afternoon. [...] The German Ambassador has again interrogated Grey on the subject of the alleged Anglo-Russian Naval Convention.[42] Grey thinks that the leakage of information concerning the Anglo-Russian conversations has been due to boastings by Iswolsky.

Grey has not denied to Prince Lichnowsky that there have been military and naval conversations with France during the past 8 years, and that recently there have been conversations with Russia; but these conversations have not impaired England's liberty of action. She is quite free from any binding engagements.

Grey says that whereas hitherto Germany has feigned alarm at the encircling policy against Germany falsely attributed to H.M. Government under the inspiration of King Edward, and has made it the excuse for largely increasing her Navy, she is now really frightened at the growing strength of the Russian Army, and she may make another military effort additional to the recent large expenditure to meet which the special capital tax was instituted, or bring on a conflict with Russia at an early date before the increases in the Russian Army have their full effect and before the completion of the Russian strategic railways to be constructed with French money.

I told Grey that if Germany make a further military effort of any importance France will be bound to do something to counteract it and a very dangerous situation will be created.

Grey referred to the disclosures in the French Senate respecting the deficiencies in war material and artillery.[43] Our officers reported that the French Artillery is the best in the world. He hopes that the accusations against the French War Office will prove to be exaggerated. [...]

TNA, FO 800, 161.

42 (**79**), (**87**), (**102**). For details see Stephen Schröder, *Die englisch-russische Marinekonvention*, Vandenhoeck & Ruprecht, Göttingen 2004.

43 On French Senator Humbert's revelations see (**158**).

(161) 16 July: Bunsen to Grey (1)

Information about likely Austrian demands of Serbia; Germany appears to be backing her; likelihood of Russian intervention not seen as an obstacle in Vienna

Tel. (No. 85.) Confidential.
Vienna, 16 July 1914
D. 1.50 p.m.
R. 3.15 p.m.

From language held by Minister for Foreign Affairs [Berchtold] to a friend of mine,[44] who has repeated it to me, I gather that situation is regarded at the Ministry for Foreign Affairs in a serious light and that a kind of indictment is being prepared against the Serbian Government for alleged complicity in the conspiracy which led to assassination of the Archduke. Accusation will be founded on the proceedings in the Sarajevo Court. My informant states that the Serbian Government will be required to adopt certain definite measures in restraint of nationalist and anarchist propaganda, and that Austro-Hungarian Government are in no mood to parley with Serbia, but will insist on immediate unconditional compliance, failing which force will be used.

Germany is said to be in complete agreement with this procedure, and it is thought that the rest of Europe will sympathise with Austria-Hungary in demanding that Serbia shall adopt in future more submissive attitude. My informant states that Count Forgách entirely shares these views with his chief and that they are very generally held by all classes in this country. I asked if Russia would be expected to stand by quietly in the event of force being used against Serbia. My informant said that he presumed that Russia would not wish to protect racial assassins, but in any case Austria-Hungary would go ahead regardless of results. She would lose her position as a Great Power if she stood any further nonsense from Serbia. This language is also held by a portion of the press, including the 'Neue Freie Presse', which is now in touch with the Ministry of Foreign Affairs. The official 'Fremdenblatt' is more moderate.

I hope to see Minister for Foreign Affairs Friday.

(Repeated to Belgrade.)

44 In a later communication, he identified his informant as Count Lützow, ex-Ambassador at Rome (**168**).

MINUTE

Count Trauttmansdorff spoke to me (quite informally) at great length to-day, giving expression to very much the same views.–E. A. C[rowe]. July 16.

BD, XI, No. 50.[45]

[162] 16 July: Bunsen to Grey (2)

Bunsen reports on Tisza's position; speculation about likely Austro-Hungarian action against Serbia; public and foreign observers largely in the dark about Vienna's intentions

No. 148
Vienna, 16 July 1914
(Received 20 July)

The Vienna Press being almost exclusively taken up with speculation as to whether and when and how the expected diplomatic protest at Belgrade will be put in by the Austro-Hungarian Government, much interest attaches to the only authentic declarations which have yet been made concerning the intentions of the Common Government, namely to the replies given to his interpellators in the Hungarian Chamber by Count Stephan Tisza, Hungarian Minister President.

Count Tisza's first statement was made on July 8th[46] when he declared in effect that, though he was then only in a position to give a very general reply, he might state that the investigation of the Sarajevo crime was being pursued in every direction, and it was the duty of all concerned to have regard certainly to the importance of the interests involved in the maintenance of peace, but to give due weight also to those great interests which are bound up with the existence and prestige of the Monarchy.

Yesterday he again replied to several interpellations, and though his words were characterised by the same caution as before they attained greater precision on one or two points. He said that a clear understanding must be reached with Serbia. How this would have to be done, in what direction and by the use of what form of words, he was not yet in a position to state. He repeated that the Government was fully conscious of the great importance attaching to the preservation of peace. They did not believe that the settling of accounts with Serbia would necessarily lead to war. He would not prophecy, but would merely say that war

45 See also (**168**).
46 (**151**).

was the ultima ratio, to be resorted to only when a friendly solution proved absolutely impossible. But every nation should be in a position to make war as a last resource. Exaggerated language had been used about Bosnia. There was no danger of revolution there, and the forces maintained in Bosnia were sufficient to keep the peace. But the revolutionary societies and the schools were the field of a dangerous agitation, which must be resolutely put down.[47]

Count Tisza's speech is generally interpreted as confirming the expectation that a diplomatic protest will be addressed to Serbia, founded on the results of the investigation which is still proceeding at Sarajevo. It is also held to foreshadow a period of great tension leading possibly even to war, if the desired object proves unattainable by other means.

The proceedings in the Hungarian Chamber disclosed no difference of opinion between the Government and the Opposition as regards the necessity of calling Serbia severely to account. [...]

BD, XI, No. 65.

(163) 16 July: Granville to Grey

French newspaper reports on Russian plans to increase the annual contingent of recruits and prolong the period of service

No. 347.
Paris, 16 July 1914
(Received 17 July)

The *Temps* in its issue of to-day's date publishes a leading article on the increase, present and prospective, of the Russian Army which is worthy of note, not only on account of the information which it contains of the details of the Russian military forces, but also because of the effect which it is likely to have on French public opinion which forms its judgement on the military situation of foreign nations largely on information supplied to it by newspapers of the standing of the *Temps*. The following is the gist of the *Temps* article:

> Although the Douma [*sic*] and the Council of the Empire have taken the military vote in secret session and the Russian press has been absolutely silent about the matter, it is none the less possible to discern the chief lines of the new military plan conceived by the Russian General staff. The fundamental idea is the systematic and

47 See BD, XI, No. 82, Max Müller to Grey, Budapest, 17 July, for details on Pan-Serbian agitation.

> general numerical increase of the peace strength of the Army. Russia, which has a population of one hundred and eighty millions, is able to proceed to this measure with the greatest ease. She has only to take one soldier out of every hundred of her subjects to form an active army of one million eight hundred thousand men. She has adopted this formula and in future her army will correspond with the progress of her birthrate. The Russian Military authorities, however, are not only going to increase the annual contingent of recruits, they are also prolonging the period of service with the colours. The Ukase of the 20th March, 1906, modifying the military law of 1874 had lowered the duration of service for the infantry and mounted artillery to three years and for the other branches to four years. An alteration in this system has now been adopted; the men who in the ordinary course of events would have finished their period of service in October will be kept with the colours until the following April. As regards the increase in the annual contingents of recruits, it is to be observed that from 1908 to 1913, the figures were practically the same each year, that is to say about 450,000 men were annually incorporated. This resulted in an Army on a peace footing of 1,300,000 men. The next contingent will, however, number 580,000 men, viz., an increase of 130,000 men compared with the 1908–13 period, but this number will progressively increase. By 1918 the Russian Army on a peace footing will reach a total of 1,700,000 men; and, if the calculation be made for the first months of 1919 before the contingent which will have already done three years' service is liberated, the total of the Russian Army on a peace footing must be estimated at 2,300,000 men.

The *Temps* concludes this review of the Russian military strength by observing that the dead-weight of these new masses of soldiers is bound to have its effect on the balance of power. France is more interested than any other nation in the new state of affairs in the Russian Army, and the French contribution towards the common military effort involves the integral maintenance of the three-years' Service Law in France.

BD, XI, No. 52.

(164) 16 July: San Giuliano to Avarna, Bollati, Carlotti and Squitti

German Ambassador reveals that Austria-Hungary plans to make severe demands of Serbia[48]

Rome, 16 July 1914
D. 3.15 a.m.
Telegram 4121

These last few days I have had several talks with the German Ambassador [Flotow] on the likely conflict between Austria and Serbia. He thinks that Austria will ask Serbia to take serious measures against Pan-Serbian propaganda and that, if Serbia resists, Austria will use force. He does not think that the aim of Austria is territorial expansion and he has asked me to wield some influence on our press so that it champions the localization of the eventual conflict.

I answered that I shall continue to wield influence on the press to encourage the most friendly approach towards Austria, but I shall have no chance of succeeding if Austria's demands are not just and do not conform to the liberal principles of our public law. I repeated that we consider that a territorial expansion of Austria is against our interests and that we shall do whatever possible to prevent it. I added that, if Austria's requests are excessive and reactionary, our press and our public opinion will be unanimous against Austria and if the press lets itself be induced into supporting the localization of the conflict, this certainly shall not persuade Russia to let Serbia be crushed. I communicate the above to Your Excellency (for Vienna and Berlin) for whatever use you might consider appropriate.

DDI, 4th series, XII, No. 272.

(165) 17 July: Crackanthorpe to Grey

Attitude in Belgrade conciliatory but determined to resist foreign intervention in domestic affairs

Belgrade, 17 July 1914
D. 12 30 p.m.
R. 4.25 p.m.
Tel. (No. 44.)

48 France did not benefit from this German indiscretion until 21 July, because the French Ambassador Camille Barrère was absent from Rome at that time.

Vienna telegram No. 5 of 16th July.[49]

Present attitude of Serbian Government is prudent and conciliatory. Serbian Prime Minister has declared to Austrian Minister in unofficial conversation that Serbian Government are prepared to comply at once with any request for police investigation and to take any other measures compatible with dignity and independence of State.

But general feeling is that a demand on the part of Austro-Hungarian Government for appointment of a mixed commission of enquiry, for suppression of nationalist societies or for censorship of press, could not be acceded to, since it would imply foreign intervention in domestic affairs and legislation.

(Repeated to Vienna.)

BD, XI, No. 53.

(166) 17 July: Biedermann to Vitzthum

Auswärtiges Amt supportive of Austria-Hungary and optimistic that conflict can be localized

Berlin, 17 July 1914
Report 1076
Confidential

I have the honour most respectfully to report the following from a discussion which the Under-Secretary of State for the *Auswärtiges Amt* [Zimmermann] accorded me today:

The development of the international political situation depends entirely upon the way in which the relations between Austria-Hungary and Serbia take shape, in other words upon the demands posed by the Danube Monarchy in her long-awaited note and the reply which it will receive from Belgrade. The Government in Vienna seems only with some difficulty to be summoning up the requisite energy for a démarche and has now definitely postponed until 25 July the delivery of the Note, originally planned for 15 July.[50] It remains to be seen what form the demands will take, but it cannot be discounted that for Serbia they will be 'difficult to swallow'.

Although no attempt is being made to 'incite' our ally from this end, there is an equal determination to avoid in any way 'discouraging'

49 See (**161**).

50 Berlin did not learn until 18 July that the final date for the delivery of the Note was to be 23 July.

it; rather, energetic measures would be welcomed since it is held that this would enhance the prestige of Austria-Hungary abroad, especially with the Balkan States, and resolute action would be a suitable means of retarding, for some time at least, the inner decomposition of the Monarchy.[51] Germany can only expect support from a strong, internally united ally. As the well-known pro-Slav sympathies of the murdered Archduke continue for the present to exercise a beneficially unifying after-effect, Austria can now well afford to show a firmer hand. Efforts are therefore being made over here to ensure that the press, too, presents the idea of an Austrian intervention as a kind of mandate from Europe to perform the praiseworthy task of clearing up the nest of anarchists in Belgrade.

Italy's co-operation in those unsettled questions is not taken for granted here, so that negotiations are being conducted in strict secrecy between Berlin and Vienna alone. On the whole I have the impression that Italy is not regarded here as an especially reliable partner. The latter has, by the way, officially informed the Imperial Government that the calling up of reservists born in 1891 was to be attributed solely to domestic reasons.

If, contrary to expectations, Austria-Hungary should be compelled to take measures against Serbia, officials here count upon a localization of the conflict, as England is altogether peacefully disposed, and France and Russia seem to be equally free from any belligerent inclinations. Senator Humbert's disclosures on the state of the French army are seen as having come at a most opportune moment for the interests of world peace.[52] To sum up, there is no pessimistic view here of the situation and it has therefore also been decided not to disturb the holiday and travelling arrangements of the decisive people; after all one is prepared for eventualities. [...]

August Bach (ed.), *Deutsche Gesandtschaftsberichte zum Kriegsausbruch*, Quaderverlag, Berlin 1937, No. 4.[53]

51 (**120**), (**130**), (**139**), (**146**), (**148**).

52 On Humbert's revelations see (**158**).

53 Engl. transl. based on Geiss, *July 1914*, No. 28, here with minor amendments.

(167) 17 July: Jagow to Tschirschky

Berlin requests information about Austria-Hungary's likely aims in a war with Serbia

Decree 917
Berlin, 17 July 1914
Confidential

As Your Excellency knows from having read Count Hoyos's notes on his conference with the Under-Secretary of State, Count Hoyos stated here that Austria would have to partition Serbia completely.[54]

Count Berchtold and Count Tisza remarked on this that this declaration represented only the personal view of Count Hoyos,[55] and have therefore expressly *not* identified themselves with it; but they have not apparently expanded any further on their own territorial plans.

For the benefit of the diplomatic handling of the conflict with Serbia it would not be unimportant to know from the beginning what the ideas of the Austro-Hungarian statesmen concerning the future shape of Serbia really are, as this question will have a substantial influence on the attitude of Italy and on the public opinion and attitude of England.

That the plans of the statesmen of the Danube Monarchy may be influenced and modified by the course of events is, of course, to be regarded as self-evident; at the very least we must assume that the Vienna Cabinet has in mind some sort of a picture of the aims to be sought, even in the matter of territory. Your Excellency are to endeavour to get some clarification on this question in your talks with Count Berchtold, however, while avoiding giving any impression that we are attempting to put any obstacles in the path of Austrian activities or that we are trying to prescribe certain limits or aims. It would merely be useful for us to be informed to a certain extent about where the road is likely to lead.

DD, No. 61.[56]

54 (**119**) and (**134**). In the original concept Jagow wrote 'smash up', then changed it to 'partition'.

55 This was stressed in a meeting between Berchtold, Stürgkh, Tisza, Hoyos and Tschirschky which preceded the Ministerial Council meeting of 7 July and in which Hoyos gave a verbal report of his mission to Berlin. See DD, No. 18, Tschirschky to Jagow, 7 July. Fritz Fellner points out how unusual it was to invite the German Ambassador to such an internal discussion. Fellner, 'Die "Mission Hoyos"', in Wilhelm Alff (ed.), *Deutschlands Sonderung von Europa, 1862–1945*, Peter Lang, Frankfurt am Main 1984, pp. 283–316, p. 295.

56 Engl. transl. based on Geiss, *July 1914*, No. 26, here with minor amendments.

(168) 17 July: Bunsen to Nicolson

Speculation in Vienna about likely action against Serbia

Private
Vienna, 17 July 1914

There is only one topic in the Vienna press, even Albania in its throes being almost crowded out namely, when will the protest against Serbia be put in, and what will it contain? That there will be a protest nobody doubts, and it will probably be coupled with demands intended to humiliate Serbia. From all I hear the Ball[haus]platz is in an uncompromising mood, but very likely Count Berchtold, whom I am to see this afternoon, will be Sphynxlike as ever. The authority for the telegram I sent yesterday[57] was Count Lützow, ex-Ambassador at Rome. He has a place near us in the country and we motored over to luncheon. He had seen both Berchtold and Forgách at the Ball[haus]platz the day before, and had long conversations. He put on a serious face and said he wondered if I realised how grave the situation was. This Government was not going to stand Serbian insolence any longer. No great Power could submit to such audacity as Serbia had displayed, and keep her position in the world. A note was being drawn up and would be completed when the Sarajevo enquiry was finished, demanding categorically that Serbia should take effective measures to prevent the manufacture and export of bombs, and to put down the insidious and murderous propaganda against the Dual Monarchy. No futile discussion would be tolerated. If Serbia did not at once cave in, force would be used to compel her. Count Lützow added that Count Berchtold was sure of German support and did not believe any country could hesitate to approve not even Russia.

All this of course is only repetition of what Count Lützow understood Count Berchtold to say, and he may have made the most of it but it all agrees strangely with the language of most of the Press, and almost all the people one meets. I expressed my doubts whether, if it really came to fighting, which I could not believe, Russia would allow Austria and Serbia to have it out in a cockpit. Count Lützow said Austria was determined to have her way this time and would refuse to be headed off by anybody. Count Tisza's speech does not seem to me to read very reassuringly. He said: 'We must have a settlement (*Klärung*) with Serbia, and we may possibly achieve it without war.'[58]

I cannot yet believe Austria will resort to extreme measures, but I think we have an anxious time before us. Tschirschky I feel sure is doing

57 See (**161**).
58 See (**162**) for Bunsen's report of 16 July.

nothing to restrain this country.[59] He confessed to me lately that he did not believe in the possibility of improved relations between Austria and Serbia, and the German Military Attaché [Kageneck][60] does not conceal his belief that the hour of condign punishment for Serbia is approaching. Schebeko told me this. Schebeko says Russia would inevitably be drawn in, if this happened. I hope the private information you kindly give me in confidence in the postscript dated the 7th July to your letter of the 6th is correct and that Berlin would be against strong measures against Serbia being taken from Vienna.[61]

Jovanović came to see me again this morning. He can get nothing out of the Ball[haus]platz and rather dreads the end of the ominous silence which now prevails there. He says Serbia will do anything that can be reasonably asked to put down crime, but that it is useless to ask for the suppression of sentiments felt by every Serbian.[62] It would be just as reasonable, he says, to ask the Poles, Ruthenes, Rumanians and Italians within the Dual Monarchy to surrender the dream of eventual coalition with the main stock of their respective races beyond the border. Holding these sentiments does not necessarily make the different nationalities bad subjects. They will all keep quiet as long as they are well treated, but they keep in the back of their heads the idea that, if some day the Empire went to pieces, they would join hands with their kith and kin.

BD, XI, No. 56.

(169) 17 July: French military intelligence report

French intelligence aware of Austria's intention to present unacceptable ultimatum

Communiqué from the General Staff of Army
Paris, 22 July 1914[63]
R. Dir. pol., 24 July

59 Tschirschky did, in fact, initially try to restrain the Austrians, but was then instructed not to do so. See (**108**).

60 See (**158**).

61 BD, XI, No. 33.

62 See (**176**).

63 Despite the early date of the intelligence report, the French Government did not benefit from this information until much later in the crisis, as the General Staff only passed the report to the Foreign Office on 22 July who only received it on the 24th. See Stefan Schmidt, *Frankreichs Außenpolitik in der Julikrise*, Oldenbourg, Munich 2007, p. 69.

Note about Austro-Serbian relations[64]

Vienna, 17 July 1914

Confidential

The situation to which today's notes and those that will follow relate contains too many uncertainties for us to suggest that it is positively threatening, but we believe it to be no less worthy of attention than the situation of 1908–1909 and that of 1912–1913. We will begin by establishing where things started.

The Austro-Hungarian Government has let it be known that the assassination in Sarajevo will lead to diplomatic action, in other words, a 'démarche' to Belgrade, by means of a 'delivery of a note'. Yet, this approach can have, must have, and will have, in fact, a dual purpose:

First: It will focus on the origins of the assassination and will deal with the direct or indirect cooperation the perpetrators might have found in Belgrade or Serbia. It [the note] will list Austro-Hungary's wishes, if not demands, in the form of a notice or summons addressed to the Serbian Government, asking it or ordering it to search for and arrest the accomplices, to punish them, and perhaps to hand them over for trial in Austria-Hungary.

Secondly: Extending its concerns beyond the crime itself as well as beyond its direct upholders and supporters, it will consider the action of Serbian internal propaganda or Pan-Serbian nationalism, in other words not only that of the protest movement of Bosnia-Herzegovina, but also of the irredentism which dreams of a Serbia where all Serbs belonging to the Austro-Hungarian political community are reunited. Just like the first part of the note relating to the assassination, this second part will draw up a list of Austro-Hungary's wishes, her possible demands and will perhaps summon Serbia to repress irredentist propaganda and to make it known, clearly and solemnly, that she condemns all targeting of Austro-Hungarian territories.

Such is the scope of the note. What we mean is that such are the possibilities we must take into account as far as its content and importance are concerned: in other words, it can be anodyne, banal, purely nominal, but it can also be an ultimatum. Here lies one part of the uncertainty we have mentioned; the second part relates to the manner in which Serbia would receive a threatening note, and this question merges with the problem of knowing what Russia will advise Serbia, because Russia will certainly be behind them in this ordeal as they were during the two crises of these last years. Thus, even while the Cabinet in Vienna would have firmly fixed intentions which we would know about, we would still have to resolve

64 The editors of DDF added the following explanation: 'A document sent by the Intelligence service to the Minister of Foreign Affairs. This document evidently came from an agent.'

the other half of the problem, and supposing that we come to understand these two points, who can guarantee that the problem will not arise in a new and sudden way tomorrow, today, perhaps in two hours?

Certainly, Austria has entered the Serbo-Slavic hornets' nest, exactly as she entered the Italian hornets' nest towards the middle of the nineteenth century. There we are: we must walk, and we will walk; the Archduke's murder is an episode, nothing more. They have, it seems, shot three Serbs in Bosnia, carrying out martial law, and this fact, which we judge to be of great importance, has been confirmed to us this very night. Another episode: the Serbs, such as we know them, are not people to leave executions for long without reprisals: more episodes, more assassinations, and what of it? So, we think about the problem as if it were entirely related to the question of the 'démarche', carried out in such and such a manner, received in such and such a way: but it is not. And if there is a happy solution on this side, then danger will reappear on another and we will not have long to wait because, we repeat: the Serbo-Slav question has now taken the place of the Italian question of old, and we must remember that. Let us now leave this framework open for the facts to come and arrange themselves in their own good time while we come back to the concrete question of the present moment: *la démarche*, the note.

We hear it said: 'Nothing will be done; there will be no démarche; passions will calm down: after which a general communiqué will announce that the observations presented by the Cabinet of Vienna have been received with courteous goodwill and that their response provides the required guarantees.' This is only conceivable if Austria-Hungary gives way and accepts the decline of her prestige, or if she has been warned by her allies that she will not be supported in any way. We do not believe her to have fallen to that level; as for the attitude of her allies, at least of Germany, it is quite the opposite. We have it on good authority, and we have been told three separate times over the course of several days, that Germany guaranteed her full support, whatever happens. This attitude is new, for in 1912 and 1913, Germany not only restrained Austria but thwarted her. According to our informant, it is likely that the Jews had knowledge of the secret, for the collapse of the stock exchange, during the period from 11 to 14 [July], is absolutely inexplicable. There are several financiers to whom people in high places tell everything. [...]

It is this panic at the stock exchange that has made the three [*sic*] Ministers of War and the Chief of Staff decide to go on holiday and to send out very reassuring official notices, letting it be understood that nothing would be done that might result in bellicose complications. These notices, just like those in the newspapers, claim that Austro-Hungary's démarche is being held back pending the results of the judicial investigation in Sarajevo. Yet, we have had a long conversation with a very highly placed functionary, who has unwittingly admitted to us that the results of the investigation regarding any direct complicity or instigation by Belgrade are worthless. Consequently, we will be forced to go back to the second group of recriminations: the intellectual and moral genesis of the crime; the influence of Serbian irredentism on Austro-Hungarian territory; the sending of emissaries; the stimulation of national fanaticism leading to assassinations, etc. It is obvious that this terrain is more dangerous than the other. If they were to succeed in proving to Serbia that she was responsible for arming assassins, she would have to humble herself before Austria and the whole of Europe: if they order her to gag Serbian nationalism, they strongly provoke the patriotic fervour that has been consolidated by the victories in the two [Balkan] wars and is running very high at the moment. Instead of a criminal convicted of murder, we have before us a State whose dignity and sovereignty has been threatened. It is difficult for her to comply, and yet this is what the Cabinet in Vienna expects: it has no illusions about Serbian nationalist tendencies; it knows that this is the 'Italian question' all over again; it wants to take a firm stand. At least, it wants to try. In this respect, we have clear statements from excellent Austrian sources. As well as this, we have been informed of an urgent task that the Ministry has delivered to the foreign press. The *Daily Telegraph*'s correspondent has been asked to publish a long article given to him by the Ministry: that article has already appeared. The Ministry summoned the correspondent from the *Daily Chronicle* and has given him another one for the same purpose. We have seen this article: the correspondent has only sent a short extract to London. The same approach was made to the *Matin*'s correspondent who, having received verbal and written instructions from his newspaper ordering him to maintain close ties with the Ministry, was given a very long memorandum of which he must at least publish an extract. All these articles are indictments of Serbia with undisguised threats levelled at her if she does not guarantee to modify her policies. It seems that the Cabinet in Vienna wants to influence public opinion in France and England so that these two countries take action against Russia because, although it is in Russia's power to hold back the Serbs and to induce them to give in to Vienna's injunctions, we do not know if she would not prefer to encourage them either to engage Austria in a war complicated by the uprising of these Serbs and Romanians, or to throw her into a new mobilisation which would swallow up 200 million which she does not have.

Right now, they are playing for time. They have calmed the stock exchange first of all. Then, they want to avoid disrupting the tourist season that brings millions to the spas in Bohemia, the Tyrol and to other Alpine regions. Then they have to complete the harvest and, while waiting, they are endeavouring to create favourable international public opinion. This intermediary period could last four months under the pretext of waiting for the end of the investigation.

Until now, there have been no military measures. But the General Staff has received notice that the Serbs are taking some.[65]

DDF 3e série, X, No. 558.[66]

(170) 18 July: Buchanan to Grey

Sazonov worried about Austria's attitude towards Serbia; stresses Russia's peaceful intentions, but warns that ultimatum might lead to precautionary military measures in Russia

St. Petersburg, 18 July 1914
D. 8:50 p.m.
R. 10:30 p.m.
Tel. (No. 161.)

In the course of conversation to-day Minister for Foreign Affairs expressed the great uneasiness which Austria's attitude towards Serbia was causing him. He had received disquieting telegrams from the Russian Ambassadors at London, Berlin, and Rome, and proposed to ask the French Government to give a word of warning at Vienna. He had just seen the German Ambassador and had impressed on him that Russia's sole desire was to be left in peace. She cherished no aggressive designs against anyone, and wished to devote all her efforts to the development of her internal resources, and to the construction of the railways of which she stood in such need. The period of expansion through which she had passed was now over. The increase in her armaments was not directed against any other Power, but was necessary for the peaceful development of her vast Empire. Germany was, relatively speaking, in a far stronger position than Russia, as she had not the same length of frontiers to defend or such an extent of territory.

The Pan-Serb agitation in Austria was an internal growth, and blame could not be thrown on Serbia any more than Germany could be held responsible for the Pan-German or Italy for the Italian propaganda that was carried on within the Austrian Empire.

In reply to a question of mine, his Excellency said that anything in the shape of an Austrian ultimatum at Belgrade could not leave Russia

65 This does not seem to have been correct. The Serbian Minister of War Stefanović ordered some military preparations only after learning about the ultimatum, and Regent Alexander signed the order for general mobilization in the evening of 25 July. I am grateful to Mark Cornwall for this information.

66 (**179**).

indifferent, and she might be forced to take some precautionary military measures.[67]

BD, XI, No. 60.

(171) 18 July: Schoen to Hertling

Date for handing over the note in Belgrade; reason for the delay; nature of demands and short period for reply

Report 386
Berlin, 18 July 1914

I have the honour most respectfully to report as follows to Your Excellency concerning the prospective settlement between the Austro-Hungarian Government and Serbia, on the basis of conversations I have had with Under-Secretary of State Zimmermann, and further with the man charged with special responsibility for the Balkans and Triple Alliance,[68] and with the *Botschaftsrat* of the Austro-Hungarian Embassy.[69]

The step which the Vienna Cabinet has decided to undertake at Belgrade, and which will consist in the presentation of a note, will take place on 25 inst.[70] The reason for the postponement of the action to that date is that they wish to await the departure of Messrs Poincaré and Viviani from St Petersburg, in order not to facilitate an agreement between the Dual Alliance Powers on any possible counter-action.[71]

67 Such measures were decided upon at the meeting of the Council of Ministers on 24 July, and implemented on 26 July (**206**), (**215**). However, as Turner points out, it is significant that partial mobilization was contemplated by Sazonov before the ultimatum had been delivered: L.C.F. Turner, 'The Russian Mobilization in 1914', in Paul M. Kennedy (ed.), *The War Plans of the Great Powers, 1880–1914*, George Allen & Unwin, London 1979, pp. 252–268, p. 260.

68 Dr Carl Ludwig Diego von Bergen, *Vortragender Rat* (Counsellor) and *Dirigent der politischen Abteilung* (Director of the political department) in the *Auswärtiges Amt*.

69 Dr Franz Josef Freiherr von Haymerle.

70 Berlin became aware of the changing of the date to the 23rd only after this report was despatched. This document was one of the pieces of evidence used by the Allied Commission at Versailles to determine Germany's war guilt. For details see for example Jörg Zedler, 'Das Rittertelegramm. Bayern und der Heilige Stuhl in der Julikrise 1914', in Jörg Zedler (ed.), *Der Heilige Stuhl in den internationalen Beziehungen 1870–1939*, Herbert Utz Verlag, Munich 2010, pp. 175–202, p. 177.

71 See for example (**146**).

Until then, by the granting of leave of absence simultaneously to the Minister of War and the Chief of the General Staff, the Vienna authorities will have the appearance of being peacefully inclined; and they have not been without success in influencing the press and the stock exchange. It is recognized here that the Vienna Cabinet has been proceeding quite cleverly in this matter, and it is only regretted that Count Tisza, who at first is said to have been against any severe action, has somewhat raised the veil of secrecy by his statement in the Hungarian House of Deputies.[72]

As Mr Zimmermann told me, the note, so far as has yet been determined, will contain the following demands:

1 The issuing of a proclamation by the King of Serbia which shall state that the Serbian Government has nothing to do with the Greater-Serbia movement, and fully disapproves of it.
2 The initiation of an enquiry to discover those implicated in the murder of Sarajevo, and the participation of Austrian officials in this enquiry.
3 Proceedings against all who have participated in the Greater-Serbia movement.

A respite of 48 hours is to be granted for the acceptance of these demands.

It is perfectly plain that Serbia cannot accept any such demands which are incompatible with her dignity as a sovereign state.[73] Thus the result would be war.

Here they are absolutely willing that Austria should take advantage of this favourable hour, even at the risk of further complications. But whether they will actually rise to the occasion in Vienna still seems doubtful to Herr von Jagow and to Herr Zimmermann. The Under-Secretary of State made the statement that Austria-Hungary, thanks to her indecision and her desultoriness, had really become the Sick Man of Europe as Turkey had once been, upon the partition of which the Russians, Italians, Romanians, Serbians and Montenegrins were now waiting. A powerful and successful move against Serbia would make it possible for the Austrians and Hungarians to feel themselves once more to be a national power, would again revive the country's collapsed economic life, and would suppress foreign aspirations for years. Given the indignation in the entire Monarchy at the bloody deed, it looked as if they could even be sure of the Slav troops. In a few years, with the continuance of the operation of the Slavic propaganda, this would no longer be the case, as even General Conrad von Hötzendorf himself had admitted.

So they are of the opinion here that this is a fateful hour for Austria, and for this reason they declared here without hesitation, in reply to an

72 (**151**), (**161**).
73 But see (**227**) below for Serbia's reply in which almost all conditions are met.

enquiry from Vienna, that we would agree to any method of procedure which they might determine on there, even at the risk of a war with Russia. The blank cheque that was given to Count Berchtold's Chief of the Cabinet, Count Hoyos, who came here to deliver an All-Highest hand-written letter together with a detailed memorandum, went so far that the Austro-Hungarian Government was empowered to negotiate with Bulgaria concerning her entrance into the Triple Alliance.[74]

In Vienna they do not seem to have expected such unconditional support of the Danube Monarchy by Germany, and Mr Zimmermann has the impression that it is almost embarrassing to the always timid and undecided authorities at Vienna not to be admonished by Germany to caution and self-restraint. To what extent they waver in their decisions at Vienna is shown by the circumstance that Count Berchtold, three days after he had enquiries made here concerning the alliance with Bulgaria, telegraphed that he still had concerns about closing with Bulgaria.[75]

Therefore it would have been preferred here if they had not waited so long with their action against Serbia, and the Serbian Government had not been given time to make an offer of satisfaction on its own account, perhaps acting under Russo-French pressure.

What attitude the other Powers will take towards an armed conflict between Austria and Serbia will chiefly depend, according to the opinion here, on whether Austria will content herself with a chastisement of Serbia, or will demand territorial compensation for herself. In the first case, it should be possible to localize the war; in the other case, however, more serious complications would probably be inevitable.

The German Government will, immediately upon the presentation of the Austrian note at Belgrade, initiate diplomatic action with the Powers in the interest of the localization of the war.[76] It will claim that the Austrian action has been just as much of a surprise to it as to the other Powers, pointing out the fact that the Kaiser is on his North Sea Cruise and that the Prussian Minister of War, as well as the Chief of the General Staff are away on leave of absence. (As I take the liberty to insert here, not even the Italian Government has been taken into confidence.[77]) It will point out the fact that it is in the shared interest for all the monarchical states that 'the Belgrade nest of anarchists' be destroyed once and for all; and it will make work towards getting all the Powers to take the view that the conflict between Austria and Serbia is a matter concerning those two nations alone. The mobilization of the German

74 (**120**).

75 See ÖUA, VIII, No. 10126.

76 See Geiss, *July 1914*, No. 39: Bethmann Hollweg to the Ambassadors at St Petersburg, Paris and London, 21 July 1914.

77 See also (**172**) on the concerns of the Italian Government which suspected that Austria-Hungary might proceed against Serbia.

Army is to be refrained from, and they are also going to use the military authorities to prevent Austria from mobilizing her entire Army, and especially not those troops stationed in Galicia, so as not to bring about an automatic counter-mobilization on the part of Russia which would then force ourselves, and then France, to take the same measures and thereby conjure up the European war.

The attitude of *Russia* will, above all else, determine the question whether the attempt to localize the war will succeed.

If Russia does not want war against Austria and Germany in any case, she can, in that event – and that is the most favourable factor in the present situation – very well remain inactive, and justify herself toward the Serbs by announcing that she approves of the kind of fighting that involves the throwing of bombs and revolver shots just as little as any of the other civilized nations; this, especially, so long as Austria does not question Serbia's national independence. Mr Zimmermann assumes that both England and France, neither of whom desire a war at the present moment, will try to exert a pacifying influence on Russia; in addition, he is counting on the fact that 'bluffing' constitutes one of the most favoured requisites of Russian policy, and that while the Russian likes to threaten with the sword, he does not like very much to draw it on behalf of others at the critical moment.

England will not prevent Austria from calling Serbia to account; it is only the destruction of the nation that she would scarcely permit, being far more likely – true to her traditions – presumably to take a stand, even in this case, for the principles of nationality. A war between the Dual Alliance and the Triple Entente would be unwelcome to England at the present time, if only in consideration of the situation in Ireland. Should it, however, come to that, then according to all opinion here we should find our English cousins on the side of our opponents, because England fears that France, in the event of a new defeat, would sink to the level of a second-class Power, and that the 'balance of power', the maintenance of which England considers to be necessary for her own interests, would be upset thereby.

Italy would have very little delight in a chastisement of Serbia by Austria as she would not approve of her strengthening of her influence in the Balkans. As the envoy van Bergen, who is in charge of matters of the Triple Alliance in the *Auswärtiges Amt*, told me, the relationship between Vienna and Rome is once again less than friendly. [...]

As I have heard in the utmost secrecy that Counsellor (in the German Embassy) in Vienna, Prince Stolberg, who was here a few days ago, has been charged with discussing the question of compensation for Italy with Count Berchtold and to add unofficially that one might win over Italy permanently if Austria, in case of larger territorial acquisitions, could agree to handing over the southern Trentino to Italy [...]. However, it is hardly expected that the Cabinet in Vienna will accept this thought, and they have deliberately charged the Counsellor, and not the Ambassador who is also currently in Vienna, with raising the topic of the Trentino, so as not to cause offence with such an official suggestion. [...][78]

DD, 2nd edn, App. IV, No. 2.[79]

(172) 18 July: Memorandum of the Russian Ministry for Foreign Affairs

St Petersburg receives warning from Italy regarding Austrian intentions vis-à-vis Serbia; Russia assures Austria-Hungary that she would not allow action which would affect Serbia's independence; Austro-Hungarian Ambassador assures Sazonov of Vienna's benign intentions

St Petersburg, 18 July 1914

S. D. Sazonov returned from a short country sojourn. Wishing to inform himself as to the state of affairs prior to his meeting with the Austrian Ambassador [Szápáry], Baron Schilling went to meet him at the station, and on the way from thence to the Ministry acquainted him with the contents of a telegram[80] received from N. N. Schebeko the preceding evening from Vienna, and also with his conversation with the Italian Ambassador [Carlotti] on July 16.[81] The Minister was troubled by this information and concurred with the views of Baron Schilling that it was necessary to inform Austria in advance of Russia's determination on no account to permit any blow to Serbia's independence. The Minister was determined to express himself in the most decided manner to the Austro-Hungarian Ambassador regarding this matter.

78 On the question of compensation for Italy, see also (**173**) and (**318**).

79 Engl. transl. based on Geiss, *July 1914*, No. 33, here with minor amendments and additions.

80 On 16 July Schebeko reported that the Viennese Government intended 'to make certain demands' (*Int. Bez.*, I, 4, 247).

81 The Italian Government, despite not having been informed by Austria of her intentions vis-à-vis Serbia, had some idea and had sent a warning to the Russian Foreign Minister through its Ambassador at St Petersburg, Carlotti, asking how Russia would react if Austria decided to proceed against Serbia. As a result, Sazonov advised Szápáry that Russia would 'in no circumstances ... agree to any blow to Serbia's independence.' Szápáry reassured Sazonov sufficiently for him to be described to have been 'gentle as a lamb' by the end of the conversation (**172**). See Geiss, *July 1914*, p. 101.

Soon after reaching the Ministry, S. D. Sazonov received Count Szápáry, who spoke in the most peaceable manner of an entire absence in Austria of any intention of rendering relations with Serbia more acute. His assurances were so positive that they completely quieted the Minister's apprehensions, who after this interview said to Baron Schilling that he had had no need to resort to threats, as the Austro-Hungarian Ambassador had sufficiently emphatically assured him of the love of peace of his Government. 'Il a été doux comme un agneau.' ('He was as gentle as a lamb')

Int. Bez., I, 4, 272.[82]

(173) 18 July: Stolberg to Jagow

Berchtold against enticing Italy with compensation though this is favoured by Germany

Private letter
Vienna, 18 July 1914
R. 20 July

Yesterday I saw Berchtold, who told me that the note in question is to be handed over at Belgrade on the 23rd. As I reported yesterday,[83] Berchtold hopes that the Austrian demands, about which he did not go into particulars, will not be accepted by Serbia. He is not, however, quite sure, and I gathered the impression from his statements as well as from those of Hoyos that Serbia *can* accept the demands. To my question what would happen then, should the matter come to nothing in this fashion, Berchtold said that then they could exercise considerable latitude in the practical execution of the various demands. If they really want a final settlement of the relations with Serbia here, as Count Tisza claimed in a recent speech to be a peremptory necessity, it is certainly incomprehensible why they should not have preferred such demands as would make a breach unavoidable. If this action again ends up like a storm in a tea-cup [*das Hornberger Schiessen*] and remains nothing but a so-called diplomatic victory, then the view already taken here that the Monarchy is no longer capable of any expression of vigour will be confirmed. The results that this would have, both at home and abroad, are obvious.

I also asked Berchtold whether he intended to get in touch with Italy before finally acting against Serbia, to which he replied that so far he

82 Engl. transl. based on Geiss, *July 1914*, No. 34, here with minor amendments.
83 Geiss, *July 1914*, No. 27.

had not uttered a single word, and that his intention was to place the Italian Government before a *fait accompli*, as it appeared to him not very reliable with regard to secrecy, and as it might easily, in view of its Serbophile attitude, let something drop at Belgrade.[84] Even at Berlin they had agreed that Hoyos, with whom the matter was discussed, was right on this point. This was also confirmed to me by Hoyos himself. At that, I explained at length to the Minister, according to the tenor of the secret despatch of 15 inst. (No. 911[85]), of what tremendous importance it appeared to us they should here come to an understanding with Rome regarding the aims to be sought in case of war, and attempt to keep Italy on their side. Berchtold showed great optimism and thought that Italy could not possibly be so despicable an ally as to turn against the Monarchy. I said in reply that in case of a prospective conflict with Serbia only the alliance would not come into call and that Italy could very easily take a stand on Serbia's side, if only morally; but that this might be fateful for the stability of the Triple Alliance, and that it would unquestionably inflame Russia's lust for war. This struck the Minister as very evident, yet he would not of his own accord mention the question of compensation;[86] even when Hoyos, who had been drawn into the conference, expressed the conviction that the Italians would have to be given something, he did not take up the point. As the Ambassador [Tschirschky] is to return early tomorrow morning, I thought it better for me [not] to go any more deeply into the details of this question, which will in any case necessitate a series of lengthy discussions.

On the other hand, I had a long conversation with Hoyos immediately afterwards, during which he mentioned the subject of the Trentino of his own accord, and asked me whether this was the compensation that we had in mind, which I affirmed. He did not by any means reject this, nor did he show himself in any way deaf to the argument that in this manner irredentism could be done away with. I told him also that, if the occasion arose, it would be a question only of the comparatively small territory of the diocese of Trent. He listened to everything in a very friendly fashion, and then mentioned as a possible compensation for Italy the ceding of the Dodecanese to her. He furthermore, however, advanced the point of view that, as a matter of fact, Italy had no right to claim compensation on the strength of the agreement, as it referred only to Turkey. But I argued in reply that in this case the question could only be a political and not an equitable one, and that Austria would have to do everything possible, in consideration of the alliance, to keep Italy on board. Finally, I advised him, in the event of the outbreak of

84 See (**166**).
85 See DD, No. 46.
86 See (**171**).

any conflict with Serbia, to give Rome the assurance that they had no intention of making any territorial acquisitions but that, in case events should necessitate any such, they would compensate Italy in the most thorough manner.

I have just seen Berchtold again. He told me that tomorrow the note is finally to be put into shape with the aid of Tisza, and that it still might be modified according to the events of the day (interview with Pašić, article in the *Samouprawa*, etc.). Hoyos has just told me that the demands were really of such a nature that no nation that still possessed self-respect and dignity could possibly accept them. […]

DD, No. 87.[87]

(174) 18 July: Granville to Grey

French views of Russia; French newspapers predict huge Russian military strength by 1916; Germany afraid of Russia

(No. 354.)
Paris, 18 July 1914
(Received 20 July)

I had the honour, when communicating to you in my despatch No. 347 of the 16th instant[88] the substance of a leading article in the *Temps* on the increase of Russian military strength, to state that that article appeared to me of interest, not only on account of the information therein given, but also because of the effect which information on such a subject and from such a source was likely to have on French public opinion.

The same observation applies to an article to which the *Matin* of to-day's date gives prominence and which has been written for that newspaper by M. Jules Hedeman, who is now in St. Petersburg, for the visit of the French President. M. Hedeman is perhaps the best known special correspondent in France and his articles always attract much attention here. The following is the gist of the article published by the *Matin*:

The visit of M. Poincaré to Russia is taking place at a moment when the extraordinary awakening of Russia is manifesting itself in the most signal manner. The development of Russia to-day, in all fields of human activity, is only comparable to that of the United States of America some thirty years ago. Russian public opinion, realising the formidable power

87 Engl. transl. based on Geiss, *July 1914*, No. 31, here with minor amendments.
88 See (**163**).

of the nation, has desired to make it visible to the foreigner ... to Russia's adversaries. Measures have accordingly been taken (M. Hedeman gives the figures) for bringing about a huge increase in Russian military power. By the winter of 1916 the Russian army, on a peace-footing, will have been almost doubled, that is to say, its total will have progressed from 1,200,000 to the colossal figure of 2,215,000 men. Russia will then possess an active army greater in numbers than the joint forces of the Triple Alliance Powers. She will, moreover, thanks to new strategical railways, be able to mobilise as quickly as the other military Powers. The same effort is to be seen in naval matters, and the Russian navy estimates now exceed the British ones. Russia, who was 'militarily discredited' after the Manchurian war, is now well on the way to becoming the greatest military Power which the world has ever seen. She is animated, like France, with pacific intentions, and the Emperor Nicholas said a short time ago to a French diplomatist: 'Nous voulons être assez forts pour imposer la paix.' But Russia will no longer put up with certain proceedings on the part of Germany, such as the despatch of the Liman von Sanders mission to Constantinople[89] and the assumption by its chief of the command of the Constantinople army corps; or the arrest of honourable Russian subjects on a charge of spying; or the violence of language on the part of the Berlin press. Russian diplomacy is already adopting a new tone when it speaks to German diplomacy, and to-day Germany fears her eastern neighbour.[90] Besides the eternal animosity between Slavs and Germans a severe economic struggle between the two countries is beginning which more than ever makes an improvement of Russo-German relations impossible.

The *Temps* published yesterday a further leading article on the additions to the Russian army which have already taken place or are shortly to be carried out. It mentioned, in particular, three new Russian army corps which are to be stationed in Western Russia. The Austrian

89 For details see (**71**), (**86**), (**97**).

90 See for example (**181**). For other examples see Mombauer, *Moltke*, p. 179 and (**90**). Faced with Moltke's fear of Russia's future strength, Minister of War Falkenhayn thought that the answer did not lie in army increases, but rather in preventive war: 'Such a small increase (of our peace-time strength by 30–40,000 men) will not deter our opponents from striking in the spring of 1916 if, as Your Excellency's hints suggests, they are determined to do so, and would on the other hand only give us a small advantage in case of war compared to the disadvantages [...]. It is not my job to express, without being requested to do so, my opinion on the question whether in such a case an immediate action from our side would not be preferable to awaiting the threatening attack.' Falkenhayn to Bethmann Hollweg, July 1914 (no exact date, but written in response to Moltke's letter of 18 July) quoted in BA-MA, W-10/50276: 'Die Militärpolitische Lage Deutschlands', pp. 54/56.

newspapers, so the *Temps* article observed, anticipate that these new army corps will be quartered round Kiev and Odessa, while the German press, probably better informed, expects to see them stationed near Warsaw and Vilna.

MINUTE

Russia is a formidable Power and will become increasingly strong. Let us hope our relations with her will continue to be friendly. A. N[icolson].

BD, XI, No. 66.

(175) 18 July: Rumbold to Grey

Negotiations between Germany and Austria have been kept secret and German public is in the dark; German press impatient with lack of action on the part of Austria; relations between France and Germany unfriendly; German fear of Russia's military strength

No. 295.
Berlin, 18 July 1914.
(Received 20 July)

I have the honour to report that I had some conversation with M. [Jules] Cambon [the French Ambassador] yesterday about the general political situation. His Excellency has just returned from leave of absence. He said that he had seen the Austro-Hungarian Ambassador, and for the first time since he had known him, had found Count Szögyény pessimistic as to the outlook. This pessimism may, perhaps, be partly due to the regret and depression felt by Count Szögyény at having in a few weeks to leave a post which he has held for over twenty years. M. Cambon wondered what was the role of the German Government in the matter of any démarche contemplated at Belgrade by their ally. The Italian Ambassador is equally curious on this point. If there has been an exchange of views between Berlin and Vienna about the nature of the steps to be taken at Belgrade, the result has been kept absolutely secret. The public are in the dark, with the result that a feeling of irritation has revealed itself in some quarters which was expressed a few days ago by the 'Kreuz-Zeitung' in the following terms:-

'We notice the same hesitation and indecision as regards the contemplated démarche at Belgrade as were shown by the Austro-Hungarian Government during the crisis in the Balkans.

The Austrian Government are either in possession of sufficient evidence to be able to make representations at Belgrade, in which case they should act quickly and vigorously; or they have not got adequate proof, in which event they should not irritate Serbia by foreshadowing diplomatic action which cannot take place for want of sufficient grounds.

We are prepared in Germany to give the Austrian Government the widest support in this question, but we have a right to expect that the Austrians should make up their mind what they are going to do.'

I then asked the French Ambassador whether he did not consider that Russia and her supposed plans occupied public opinion in Germany to the same extent as England had done until lately – that in fact we had made way for Russia in this respect. M. Cambon quite agreed, and added that matters as between France and Germany were by no means what they should be. The Germans were not behaving in a friendly way towards his country. The air would have to be cleared some time or other. His Excellency alluded to the extreme sensitiveness in Germany at the present time on the question of espionage. The same point has struck me. The development of aircraft has, of course, been largely responsible for this result. It frequently occurs that aeroplanes, &c, cross the eastern or western frontiers of Germany. It was reported yesterday, for instance, that the airship 'Z 4', in a flight along the Russian frontier had crossed on to Russian territory and been fired at by the Russian frontier guards. [...]

As regards the general question of the relations between Germany and her eastern neighbour, I venture to think that the supposed hostile intentions of Russia have been largely conjured up by the German press itself. That press has no doubt given expression to the feeling of irritation and anxiety caused by the determined efforts of France and Russia to develop their armaments to the utmost possible extent. Whatever confidence the Germans may have in the efficiency and quality of their army, the enormous masses of men at the command of Russia are a constant source of preoccupation to them. Speculation as to the events which might set those masses in motion against Germany seems to follow almost as a matter of course.

BD, XI, No. 63.

(176) 18 July: Pašić to Serbian Ministers

Pašić hopes the Great Powers might help prevent the crisis turning to war

Telegram to all Serbian Missions Abroad (except Vienna)
July 18–19, 1914 [despatched at midnight]

Immediately after the Sarajevo assassination the Austro-Hungarian press began to attack Serbia and views of Serbian nationalism which are supported by different groups and associations such as the Narodna Odbrana and Others. The press accused the Serbian government of tolerating these activities. The Serbian Government regrets the events in Sarajevo. It has asked for the punishment of the assassins. It also cancelled all celebrations on the day of the deaths. But the Austro-Hungarian press has continued to charge Serbia with guilt and to give false reports which have prompted the Belgrade press to respond and defend Serbia.

The Serbian Government has asked the Belgrade press to remain calm, but daily news reports from Austria-Hungary revealed that the assassination would be used against Serbia, as well as against Serbians in the Austro-Hungarian monarchy.

The polemic between Austria-Hungary and the free Belgrade press has been aggravated by certain stories from the papers. They have spread the reports with only one goal – to make Serbia appear in European eyes as an unstable and arrogant country. Everyone who has followed this polemic knows that the Belgrade papers were simply defending against these attacks and lies. But foreign governments have not had time to note the tendency of the Austro-Hungarian press to spread alarms, not only in that country, but outside of it as well.

The Serbian government has been ready to turn over to the courts anyone connected with Sarajevo if there was evidence. The Serbian Government has also been willing to change its law about explosives and has given this project to the Privy Council. The project has not been completed because the Parliament is dissolved. Serbia has shown that she is ready – like all European countries – to perform her neighbourly duties [...].

But Austria-Hungary constantly continues the press campaign against Serbia. The Austro-Hungarian Government as well as the rest of Europe has become irritated with Serbia – an irritation seen by the actions of the political leaders who respond to questions in the Hungarian Parliament. This has prompted different discussions and demands for some answers from the Prime Minister [István Tisza].[91]

91 See Chapter 7, p. 244, n. 12 for details of Tisza's speech on 15 July.

From all of these discussions we can see that the Habsburg Government will act against Serbia; it is not possible to see in which direction.[92] All measures, especially military ones, will depend upon the answers and cooperation of the Serbian Government. There has indeed been muted talk of armed conflict if the Serbian government does not give satisfactory answers.

The sudden death of [Russian Minister] Hartwig prompted another journalistic quarrel [...].[93]

Everything that has happened has been used against Serbia. In the Hungarian Parliament it has been asserted that conflict could have very bad consequences. Nor do they limit the attacks to the investigation of the assassins, but also Serbia and greater Serbian ideals.

The Serbian Government has worked to keep peace and good relations with all of its neighbours. It has worked especially to improve relations with Austria-Hungary, which were not really good during the (Balkan) war. We have sought to settle all of the railroad issues, including security for the transportation of Austro-Hungarian products to Constantinople, Sofia, Salonika, and Athens.

The Serbian Government asserts that peace and calmness are vital interests. But Serbia is afraid that the angry people in the Austro-Hungarian Government will take a step that could humiliate Serbia and that Serbia will not accept.

Serbia wants friendly governments to know that Serbia desires 'friendly' relations with Austria-Hungary and has prevented attempts from our territory that would disturb the peace and security of the neighbouring empire. The Serbian Government would also accept any Austro-Hungarian request that demanded that the participants of the crime, if they could be found, be brought before an 'independent court'.

But Serbia cannot accept demands which would not be acceptable to any government that presumes its own independence and dignity.

---

92 As Mark Cornwall explains, Serbia suspected since Tisza's speech of 15 July that Austria-Hungary would demand satisfaction and would not shy away from armed conflict: 'Serbia', p. 69. He points out that in addition to Tisza's speech, Pašić also had the evidence of Austrian troop movements on the border. See Strandtmann to Sazonov, 19 July 1914, *Int. Bez.*, Vol. IV, No. 286 and (**162**). St Petersburg and Belgrade were also aware of Vienna's secret plans from news received from San Giuliano about his conversations with Flotow. On 16 July the Italian Minister of Foreign Affairs reported that Flotow 'believes that Austria will ask Serbia for serious measures against Pan-Serbian propaganda, and if Serbia resists, [Austria] will use force.' Cited in Samuel R. Williamson and Russel van Wyk (eds), *July 1914, Soldiers, Statesmen, and the Coming of the Great War: A Brief Documentary History*, Bedford/St Martin Press 2003, p. 161.

93 Hartwig died on 10 July. See (**152**).

We hope that the present situation will calm down. I ask that friendly governments take these reports seriously and help and work if there is need for it.

V. Dedijer and Ž. Anić (eds), *Dokumenti o spolnoj politici Kraljevine Srbije*, Belgrade 1980, No. 462.[94]

(177) 19 July: Minutes of the Austro-Hungarian Joint Council of Ministers meeting

Final text of ultimatum agreed; question of future territorial changes debated; Tisza still threatens to withdraw his support unless territorial changes are ruled out; unanimous agreement that minor border changes might be necessary for strategic reasons.

Minutes of the meeting of the Austro-Hungarian Joint Council of Ministers on 19 July 1914, chaired by the Ministers of the Imperial and Royal House and Minister for Foreign Affairs Count Berchtold

Present: The Imperial and Royal President of the Council of Ministers Count Stürgkh, the Royal Hungarian Premier Count Tisza, the Imp. and Royal Common Minister of Finances Ritter von Biliński, the Imp. and Royal Minister of War F.Z.M. Ritter von Krobatin, the Imp. and Roy. Chief of the General Staff G. d. I. Baron von Conrad, the Deputy Chief of the Naval Staff, Rear-Admiral von Kailer. Secretary of Legation Count Hoyos (minutes)

Subject under discussion: the forthcoming diplomatic action against Serbia.

Before the Joint Council of Ministers is constituted and the sitting is opened by the Minister in the chair, an informal discussion on the text of the note to be presented to the Serbian government takes place and the text is definitely agreed.

The Chair [Berchtold] then opens the Council of Ministers and proposes that the note should be presented to the Royal Serbian Government on 23 July at five in the afternoon, so that the term of 48 hours would expire on Saturday, 25 inst. at five in the afternoon and the order for mobilization could be published in the night from Saturday to Sunday. It is Count Berchtold's belief that it is improbable that the news of our step would be publicly known before the President of the

94 Engl. transl. from Williamson and Wyk, *July 1914*. Used with permission of the publisher.

French Republic had left St Petersburg; but even if this were the case, he does not think that it would do any harm, since we had fully considered the duties of etiquette and had waited until the visit was over. To a prolongation of the delay he must object on diplomatic grounds. Berlin was beginning to get nervous and news of our intentions had already transpired in Rome, so that untoward incidents could not be guarded against, if action were again postponed. Based on this explanation by the Presiding Minister, the Council votes unanimously that the note is to be presented on the 23 inst. at five in the afternoon.[95]

The *Royal Hungarian Premier* [Tisza] reserves the right to make a declaration on the subject in the Hungarian House of Deputies if the news of the presenting of the ultimatum should already reach Budapest from Belgrade on Thursday evening. This was acknowledged.

The *Chief of the General Staff* [Conrad] emphasizes that for military reasons he too is in favour of a speedy initiation of the action. The news he had lately received from Serbia showed that three situations had been created consecutively.

Initially large numbers of troops had been gathered along the Bulgarian and Albanian frontiers; next there were reports of great numbers of soldiers having been transported to Old Serbia. Those had turned out to be benign, because it was shown that this had only been an exchange of reserves, but for the last three days, he had received more serious news. First he was informed that two regiments, the 6th and the 17th, had been transferred from New Serbia to Old Serbia, and yesterday he heard from a very trustworthy confidential source in Bulgaria that three divisions had been directed north. He would yet have to get these reports verified. If they proved true, he would have to advocate speedy counter-measures.

Next the question of proclaiming the state of siege in all the territory of the monarchy inhabited by South Slavs is discussed and after a long debate it is unanimously agreed that the state of siege would not be proclaimed before the mobilization was published, not only to avoid a bad impression in foreign countries, but also among our own population. The same applies to Bosnia and Herzegovina, where the state of siege would also be put in force only at the beginning of the mobilization.

The *Imp. and Royal War Minister* [Krobatin] then explains the various measures for mobilization which he had prepared. His explanations show that everything necessary could be completed for the Imperial sanction on Wednesday, 22 inst. and that agreement with both Governments with regard to the measures to be taken by the administrative authorities in both countries had already been achieved.

The Council of Ministers then resolves to send a private letter to the Chief Commander of Bosnia and Herzegovina through the Common

95 This was later changed to 6 o'clock.

Finance Minister, informing him of the intentions of the Imp. and Royal Government with regard to Serbia.

At the request of the Royal Hungarian Premier the *Chief of the General Staff* gives confidential information on the mobilization, and answers in the affirmative Count Tisza's question whether, in the case of a general mobilization, the garrisons remaining in Transylvania for its safety were sufficiently strong to ensure order in case of internal disturbances. The garrisons were *Landsturm*-formations, commanded by officers. An experienced general would take the command. However, these troops would not be sufficiently strong to resist an attack on the part of the Rumanian army, but they could delay the advance of the Rumanian army. These troops were recruited in such a manner that only a small percentage of Hungarian Rumanians were among them. [...]

The *Royal Hungarian Premier* then requests the Council to vote on the resolution, of which he had spoken at their last meeting, and on which the Royal Hungarian Government made its consent to the whole action depend. The Council of Ministers must declare unanimously that the action against Serbia was not in any way connected with plans of aggrandisement on the part of the Monarchy, and that no part of Serbia should be annexed by us, except slight frontier corrections, necessitated by military considerations. He had to insist absolutely that such a unanimous decision be reached.[96]

The *Chair* declares that he can only accept the Royal Hungarian Premier's point of view with certain reservations. In the present political situation he was also of the opinion that, should it come to war with Serbia and we were the victors, we should annex no part of this country, but by making her surrender large portions of her territory to Bulgaria, Greece and Albania, eventually to Rumania, reduce her size so much that she would cease to be dangerous. The situation in the Balkans might change; it was not impossible that Russia should succeed in overthrowing the present Cabinet in Sofia and appointing a government hostile towards us; Albania was no reliable factor as yet; and he must, as leader of foreign affairs, reckon with the possibility that after the war there might be circumstances which would make it impossible for us to renounce all annexation, if we are to improve our frontiers.

The *Royal Hungarian Premier* declares that he cannot accept Count Berchtold's reservations and must, in consideration of his responsibility as Hungarian Premier, ask the conference to agree to his point of view unanimously. He asks this not only for reasons of domestic politics, but particularly because he is firmly convinced that Russia would resist *à outrance* if we were to insist upon the complete annihilation of Serbia, and because he believes that the best card we hold for improving our

96 See (**119**) and (**135**).

international situation is to declare to the Powers as early as possible that we have no intention of annexing any territory whatever.

The *Chair* declares that in any case he had the intention of declaring as much in Rome.

The *Imp. and Royal Premier* [Stürgkh] declares that even if the annexation of Serbian territory by the Monarchy remained out of the question, Serbia might be made dependent upon the Monarchy by the deposition of the dynasty, by a military convention, and by other corresponding measures. Moreover, the resolution of the Council of Ministers must not render impossible corrections of the borders, which might become necessary from a strategic point of view.

After the *Imp. and Royal War Minister* declares that he would vote for the resolution on the condition that besides corrections of the borders the occupation of a bridgehead on the other side of the River Save, for instance in the Schabatz district, would not be excluded, the following resolution was unanimously agreed:

The Joint Council of Ministers at the proposition of the Royal Hungarian Premier resolves that as soon as the war begins a declaration is made to the foreign Powers that no war for conquest is intended by the Monarchy, nor is the annexation of the Kingdom contemplated. Of course, strategically necessary corrections of the frontier, or the reduction of Serbia's territory to the advantages of other states or the unavoidable temporary occupation of Serbian territory are not precluded by this resolution.

The *Chair* concludes that gratifyingly on all points the Council is perfectly agreed and closes the conference.[97]

I have noted the contents of these minutes. Vienna, 5 August 1914.

(signed) Franz Joseph

ÖUA, VIII, No. 10393.[98]

97 Following the meeting, Conrad told Krobatin: 'We will see; before the Balkan Wars, the powers also talked of the status quo – after the war nobody was bothered about it.' Franz Conrad von Hötzendorf, *Aus meiner Dienstzeit, 1906–1918*, 5 vols, Rikola Verlag, Vienna, Leipzig, Munich 1922–1925, Vol. IV, p. 92.

98 Engl. transl. based on Geiss, *July 1914*, No. 35, but here with substantial amendments.

(178) 19 July: Crackanthorpe to Grey

Serbia prepared to comply with requests for investigation but confident of Russian support in case of war

Belgrade, 19 July 1914
D. 11:30 a.m.
R. 3:30 p.m.
Tel (No. 46.)

In the course of private conversation with the Under-Secretary of State for Foreign Affairs yesterday I alluded to the *Times* article of the 16th instant, suggesting that the Serbian Government should of their own motion undertake to enquire into alleged South Slav conspiracy on Serbian soil. Under-Secretary of State pointed out that, until result of proceedings at Sarajevo was made public, the Serbian Government had no material on which such an enquiry could be based. He assured me that on the publication of the findings of the Court the Serbian Government would be fully prepared to comply with whatever request for further investigation the circumstances might call for and which would be in accordance with international usage.

He said he was aware that there was an influential party in Austria who wished to take advantage of the present situation to press Serbia to extremes; but the Serbian Government had certain knowledge that restraint would be exercised on Austria from Berlin. Should, however, Austria force on a war, Serbia would not stand alone. Russia would not stand by and see Serbia wantonly attacked, and Bulgaria would be immobilised by Rumania.

(Sent to Vienna.)

BD, XI, No. 61.

(179) 19 July: French military intelligence report

Confirmation that Germany will support Austria-Hungary

No. 1717 Confidential
Vienna, 19 July 1914
[R. 24 July 1914]

Austro-Serbian relations

We have been told today, one more time, that the German Government has formally let it be known here that it will support Austria-Hungary, even in the event of complications. On this subject, our informant told us that, even if we do not believe that complications might result, the situation has to be described as uncertain because serious consequences are likely:

Germany's promises may increase Austria-Hungary's demands on Serbia and influence the manner in which those demands are made. In other words, Germany's promises may make Austria-Hungary's attitude such that, in content as in form, Serbia would be bound to receive it badly. It is clear that in this case the situation would, in fact, be serious.

We do not understand Germany's attitude which, during the 1912 and 1913 crisis [*sic*], acted as a calming influence on Austria, when not openly standing in the way of her plans. It is possible that the Cabinet in Berlin has received assurance from St Petersburg that things will not go far under any circumstances and that Berlin is seizing this opportunity to prove, at very small cost, its allegiance to its Austro-Hungarian ally. It is also possible there are other reasons for this assurance of a peaceful solution apart from St Petersburg's opinion. Such as, for example, precise knowledge of the ulterior motives of the Cabinet in Vienna which is perhaps only posturing – a hypothesis that brings us back to the preceding one. Kaiser Wilhelm has been put in an awkward position by the death of Archduke Franz Ferdinand. He had become too involved with him; he antagonized both the old Emperor and the young nephew by too obviously showing that he regarded one as already non-existent and the other as very distant and problematic. One can see that he is in a hurry to remove unpleasant impressions, and that is why we see him also trying to have the new heir present at the big [army] manoeuvres to which he had already invited the old one. According to these suppositions, Germany's attitude could all the more lead to new disappointment for Austria, who might change her tune depending on the promises received and would find herself abandoned as soon as the conversation with Belgrade took a worrying turn.

But it is not unreasonable to suppose that Berlin is alarmed at the Franco-Russian alliance's apparent display of practical efficiency. With danger appearing to increase in such a short time, Kaiser Wilhelm may consider it necessary to act first, seizing an opportunity that obliges Austria-Hungary to make the first move.

We have been assured that the Austro-Hungarian intervention will take place at the beginning of August. If we are really looking for complications, tension will appear in one month or thereabouts. Here, nothing is being done at the moment. We are told the call up for reservists in Germany is planned for September. We are alerting all people in a position to provide us with information to find out what they can about these matters.

DDF, 3e série, 11, No. 32.

(180) 20 July: Berchtold to Giesl

The Austro-Hungarian ultimatum to Serbia, sent to Giesl with a request to present it to the Serbian Government on 23 July

Vienna, July 20, 1914[99]

Your Excellency will present the following note to the Royal Government on the afternoon of Thursday, July 23, no later than between 4 and 5 pm:

[French Original] On 31 March 1909, the Royal Serbian Minister at the Court of Vienna made, in the name of his Government, the following declaration to the Imperial and Royal Government:

Serbia recognizes that her rights were not affected by the state of affairs created in Bosnia, and states that she will accordingly accommodate herself to the decisions to be reached by the Powers in connection with Article 25 of the Treaty of Berlin. Serbia, in accepting the advice of the Great Powers, binds herself to desist from the attitude of protest and opposition which she has assumed with regard to the annexation since October last, and she furthermore binds herself to alter the tendency of her present policy toward Austria-Hungary, and to live on friendly and neighbourly terms with the latter in the future.

Now the history of the past few years, and particularly the painful events of 28 June, have proved the existence of a subversive movement in Serbia, whose object it is to separate certain portions of territory from the Austro-Hungarian Monarchy. This movement, which came into being under the very eyes of the Serbian Government, subsequently found expression outside of the territory of the Kingdom in acts of terrorism, in a number of assassination attempts, and in murders.

Far from fulfilling the formal obligations contained in its declaration of 31 March 1909, the Royal Serbian Government has done nothing to suppress this movement. It has tolerated the criminal activities of the various unions and associations directed against the Monarchy, the outrageous language of the press, the glorification of the instigators of the assassinations, the participation of officers and officials in subversive intrigues; it has tolerated an unhealthy propaganda in its public instruction; and it has tolerated, finally, every manifestation which could betray the people of Serbia into hatred of the Monarchy and contempt for its institutions.

This toleration, of which the Royal Serbian Government was guilty, was still in evidence at that moment when the events of 28 June exhibited

99 See also the version in the Austro-Hungarian *Red Book*, No. 7, dated 22 July 1914.

to the whole world the dreadful consequences of such tolerance.

It is clear from the statements and confessions of the criminal perpetrators of the assassination of 28 June that the murder at Sarajevo was conceived at Belgrade, that the murderers received the weapons and the bombs with which they were equipped from Serbian officers and officials who belonged to the Narodna Odbrana, and, finally, that the dispatch of the criminals and of their weapons to Bosnia was arranged and carried out by Serbian frontier authorities.[100]

The results brought out by the inquiry no longer permit the Imperial and Royal Government to maintain the attitude of patient tolerance which it has observed for years towards those agitations which center at Belgrade and are spread thence into the territories of the Monarchy. Instead, these results impose upon the Imperial and Royal Government the obligation to put an end to those intrigues, which constitute a standing menace to the peace of the Monarchy.

In order to attain this end, the Imperial and Royal Government finds itself compelled to demand that the Serbian Government give official assurance that it will condemn the propaganda directed against Austria-Hungary, that is to say, the whole body of the efforts whose ultimate object it is to separate from the Monarchy territories that belong to it; and that it will obligate itself to suppress with all the means at its command this criminal and terrorist propaganda. In order to give these assurances a character of solemnity, the Royal Serbian Government will publish on the first page of its official press organ of 26/13 July the following declaration:

'The Royal Serbian Government condemns the propaganda directed against Austria-Hungary, that is to say, the whole body of the efforts whose ultimate object it is to separate from the Austro-Hungarian Monarchy territories that belong to it, and it most sincerely regrets the dreadful consequences of these criminal actions.

The Royal Serbian Government regrets that Serbian officers and officials should have taken part in the above-mentioned propaganda and thus have endangered the friendly and neighbourly relations which the Royal Government had most solemnly pledged to cultivate by its declarations of 31 March 1909.

The Royal Government, which condemns and rejects every thought and every attempt to interfere in the destinies of the population of any part of Austria-Hungary regards it as its duty to warn the officers, officials, and the whole population of the Kingdom that in future it will proceed with the utmost rigor against any persons who shall become guilty of any such activities, which the Government will make every effort to suppress.'

---

100 See (**149**).

This declaration shall be brought to the attention of the Royal army simultaneously by an order of the day from His Majesty the King, and by publication in the official organ of the army.

The Royal Serbian Government will furthermore pledge:

1. To suppress every publication which might incite to hatred and contempt of the Monarchy, or whose general tendency is directed against the territorial integrity of the latter;
2. To proceed at once to the dissolution of the Narodna Odbrana; to confiscate all of its means of propaganda, and in the same manner to proceed against the other unions and associations in Serbia which occupy themselves with propaganda against Austria-Hungary; the Royal Government will take such measures as are necessary to make sure that the dissolved associations may not continue their activities under other names or in other forms;
3. To eliminate without delay from public instruction everything, whether connected with teachers or with the methods of teaching, that serves or may serve to nourish the propaganda against Austria-Hungary;
4. To remove from military service and from the administration in general all officers and officials who have been guilty of carrying on the propaganda against Austria-Hungary, whose names the Imperial and Royal Government reserves the right to make known to the Royal Government when communicating the material evidence now in its possession;
5. To agree that organs of the Imperial and Royal Government assist in Serbia in the suppression of the subversive movement directed against the integrity of the Monarchy;
6. To institute a judicial inquiry against every participant in the conspiracy of 28 June who may be found in Serbian territory; the Imperial and Royal Government will delegate organs for this purpose who will take part in the proceedings held for this purpose;
7. To undertake with all haste the arrest of Major Voija Tankosić and of one Milan Ciganović, a Serbian Government official, who have both been compromised by the results of the enquiry;
8. To take efficient measures to prevent the participation of Serbian authorities in the smuggling of weapons and explosives across the frontier; to dismiss from service and to punish severely those members of the frontier service at Schabatz and Loznica who assisted the perpetrators of the crime of Sarajevo to cross the frontier;
9. To give explanations to the Imperial and Royal Government concerning the unjustifiable utterances of high Serbian functionaries in Serbia and abroad, who, without regard for their official position, have not hesitated to express themselves in a manner hostile toward

Austria-Hungary since the assassination of 28 June;[101]

10. To inform the Imperial and Royal Government without delay of the execution of the measures summed up in the above points.

The Imperial and Royal Government awaits the reply of the Royal Government by Saturday, 25 inst., at 6 p.m., at the latest.

A memorandum of the results of the investigation of Sarajevo, to the extent they relate to the functionaries named in points 7 and 8, is enclosed.

Appendix:

The investigation undertaken at the tribunal at Sarajevo against Gavrilo Princip and his comrades, guilty of and accessory to the assassination committed on 28 June this year, has up until now led to the following conclusions:

1. The plan of murdering Archduke Franz Ferdinand during his stay in Sarajevo was devised in Belgrade by Gavrilo Princip, Nedeljko Čabrinović, a certain Milan Ciganović, and Trifko Grabez with the assistance of Major Voija Takosić.
2. The six bombs and four Browning pistols along with ammunition – used as tools by the criminals – were procured and given to Princip, Čabrinović and Grabez in Belgrade by a certain Milan Ciganović and Major Voija Takosić.
3. The bombs are hand grenades originating from the weapons depot of the Serbian army in Kragujevac.
4. To guarantee the success of the assassination, Ciganović instructed Princip, Čabrinović and Grabez in the use of the grenades and gave lessons on shooting Browning pistols to Princip and Grabez in a forest next to the shooting range at Topschider.
5. To make it possible for Princip, Čabrinović and Grabez to cross the Bosnia-Herzegovina border and to smuggle their weapons, a secret transportation system was organized by Ciganović. The entry of the criminals and their weapons into Bosnia and Herzegovina was carried out by the main border officials of Schabatz (Rade Popović) and

101 This refers, inter alia, to some of the public statements made by the volatile Miroslav Spalajković who in the early days after the assassination justified Bosnian agitation against Vienna in the Russian press and who claimed that Jovan Jovanović had warned Vienna about potential dangers for Franz Ferdinand's visit. As Mark Cornwall points out, 'Spalajković's tactless language embroiled "official Serbia" deeper in the Sarajvo plot and its consequences, at a time when Pašić was trying to be conciliatory but reserved' ('Serbia', p. 66). The Serbian envoy in Constantinople, Milan Djordjević, also made provocative statements which were reported in the Italian press, and was reproached for this by Pašić (Ibid.).

Loznica as well as by the customs agent Radivoj Grbić of Loznica, with the complicity of several others.

At the same time as delivering this note, would Your Excellency please also add orally that – in the event that no unconditionally positive answer of the Royal Government might be received in the meantime – after the course of the 48–hour time limit referred to in this note, as measured from the day and hour of your announcing it, you are commissioned to leave the Imp. and Royal Embassy of Belgrade together with your personnel.

ÖUA, VIII, No. 10395.[102]

(181) 20 July: Riezler Diary

Chancellor's fear of Russia's future strength

Hohenfinow, 20 July [1914]

[...] Again [conversation] about the entire situation. Russia's increasing demands and incredible explosive power. In a few years no longer possible to fend off, particularly if the current European constellation remains. If it is possible to change or loosen it then it has to be considered whether and how the entire current alliance system can be dislodged and changed. But whether that is possible? Only if Russia, not supported to the last in the Serbian matter by the Western powers, understands that she needs to communicate with us. But even then Russia will be very expensive. She has become too powerful and needs to be engaged in Pan-Slavism even just for domestic policy reasons and as a counterweight to the revolutionary mood. [...]

Karl Dietrich Erdmann (ed.), *Kurt Riezler, Tagebücher, Aufsätze, Dokumente*, Vandenhoeck & Ruprecht, Göttingen 1972, p. 187.[103]

102 Engl. transl. based on Geiss, *July 1914*, No. 37, with minor amendments.

103 The edited published text of the diary corresponds to the unpublished original. I am grateful to Bernd Sösemann for providing me with this information. For references about the controversy on the authenticity of Riezler's diaries see above p. 20.

(182) 21 July: Jules Cambon to Bienvenu-Martin (1)

Germany feigns ignorance of contents of Austro-Hungarian ultimatum; German troops put on military alert

Despatch No. 424
Berlin, 21 July 1914
R: Cabinet, 24 July; Dir. pol., 28 July

The *Leipziger Neueste Nachrichten* of the 17th of this month have published some statements that M. Pašić made on the 12th July to their correspondent in Belgrade. I am sending the text to the Department, enclosed herewith, with a brief analysis, because a lot of newspapers have referred to it and attributed importance to it without, however, printing the content. It is quite forceful and shows the Prime Minister's resolve not to allow Austria to intimidate him, as well as his strong confidence that he will not be alone in resisting if the peace were disturbed.

The authenticity of the interview in question has been challenged, notably in an article by the *Kreuz-Zeitung*'s correspondent in Vienna, enclosed herewith.[104] It is possibly not entirely accurate in form. The Minister of Greece, for example, considers it very unlikely that M. Pašić would have talked about Greece in the relatively unenthusiastic terms that have been attributed to him, relations between the two countries being very close. But its content certainly, as we understand it, matches Serbia's state of mind.

Word has reached me, moreover, that yesterday the representative of this Power [Serbia] in Berlin went to the Wilhelmstrasse to say that his Government was ready to consider Austria's request, motivated by the assassination at Sarajevo, provided that she asked only for judicial cooperation in the punishment and prevention of political crimes: however, he was told to warn the German Government that it would be dangerous to try to use this investigation to undermine Serbia's prestige.

In confidence, I may also tell Your Excellency that the Russian Chargé d'Affaires at today's audience spoke to Herr von Jagow about this problem. Taking passages from the note in the *Norddeutsche Allgemeine Zeitung* of 19th July (see my despatch 419 of the 20th [105]), he said that he supposed that the German Government now had full knowledge of the note prepared by Austria, and was therefore willing to offer assurance that the Austro-Serbian difficulties would be localized. The Secretary of State protested that he was in complete ignorance of the contents

104 The article of 20 July was entitled 'Pašić's threats'.
105 DDF, 3e série, 10, No. 538.

of this note,[106] and said as much to me, as I pointed out in my telegram 178.[107] I could not help but be surprised by a statement that conforms so little with what the circumstances lead one to think.

Like Count Szögyény, whose impressions I have told you about, and like myself, M. Bronevski is struck by the more or less vague precautions taken by the Triple Alliance. It is forecast that it will have at its disposal, without any mobilization and simply by calling up reservists, around 650 000 more soldiers than in peacetime at the beginning of autumn (480 for Germany, 100 for Austria and 50 for Italy).

Furthermore, I have been assured that, from today, the preliminary notices for mobilization, that put Germany in a kind of 'stand to attention' alert in times of tension, have been sent to those ranks which receive them in such circumstances. This is a measure to which the Germans, given their usual procedures, can resort without exposing themselves to indiscretion and without worrying the population. It is not a sensational measure, and is not necessarily followed by full mobilization, as we have already seen, but it is no less significant for all that.

P.S. – 22 July
The Stock Exchange was better today. I get the impression from certain signs that, even while preparing to lean on Austria, the Berlin Cabinet would want to calm her.

APPENDIX

Résumé of the declarations attributed to M. Pašić

1. Relating to the help that it is said Serbia gave to the Albanian rebels.

The Minister replies that Serbia herself needs her guns, cannons, ammunition, officers and soldiers. 'Who knows if we will not soon need them? We will not start an argument with anyone, but at the end of the day [*à la fin*], the insults against us must stop and we must be left in peace. In any case, we will not be alone if any Great Power comes down on us. There are several small ones who will settle their scores with that great one. As far as Albania is concerned, we have already predicted in London what would happen if it were given a Christian Prince ... If some Turks cross our territory, we cannot stop them. Neither can we prevent the rebels from doing their shopping in our markets...'.

'The re-establishment of peace is only possible if we share the country, little matter between which Powers. We would have liked to have a narrow band of Albanian coast, with a port; this was refused; now, Antivari is at our disposal.'

2. Question about the possibility of a reunion between Serbia and Montenegro.

106 But cf. for example (**171**).
107 (**182**).

This will not take place as long as the present two aged Sovereigns are there. Most of the big Powers are in favour of it. Italy is pushing for it. Both States already have the same foreign policy.

3. Question about relations with Turkey.
   These are improving greatly.
4. Question about relations with Bulgaria.
   M. Pašić thinks these are improving, even though King Ferdinand is still hoping for the creation of a 'great Bulgaria' thanks to the support of Austria.

DDF, 3e série, 10, No. 548.

(183) 21 July: Lyncker to his wife

Waiting for news aboard the royal yacht *Hohenzollern* in Balholm, Norway

[...] Since yesterday things have been looking a bit war-like again; namely because a worsening of the situation is expected on the 25th of this month.[108] We are ready to return at any moment. However, this will probably not be necessary. [...]
[2nd letter of the day]
[...] The political situation is doubtless worsening and I wish that we were in Germany. If need be we can reach Cuxhaven in 22 hours; this is still a consolation. We have no more news, by the way, and something decisive is only expected for 25/7. [...]
[Continuation of the letter on 22 July:]
[...] I have nothing new to report; we – that is a small circle of those in the know – are really in a position of some tension regarding how matters will develop. How will Russia act if it comes – as is very likely – to a war between Austria and Serbia? Our own role is prescribed. [...]

Cited in Holger Afflerbach, *Kaiser Wilhelm II.*, Oldenbourg, Munich 2005, pp. 125/127.

108 The date when the ultimatum's 48-hour time limit would elapse. The fact that Lyncker anticipated complications on 25 July is further evidence that Germany's decision-makers were well aware of Austria's plans regarding the ultimatum, contrary to Jagow's statement to Cambon in (186)–(188).

(184) 21 July: Jules Cambon to Bienvenu-Martin (2)

Rumours that Germany will support Austria-Hungary when she makes a move against Serbia

Telegram No. 178
Berlin, 21 July 1914
D. 0.55 a.m.
R. 3.40 a.m.

The Stock Exchange in Berlin was very weak today. This fall is attributed to several factors: more stable prices; the worries that are beginning to arise on the subject of Serbia. This evening's *Lokal Anzeiger* has published a note, the purpose of which is to present the opinion that there is no reason for concern.

Confidential. I am, however, authorized to believe, according to intelligence that comes to me from trustworthy sources, that when Austria makes whatever approach to Belgrade is necessary following the assassination at Sarajevo, Germany will back her up with her authority and has no intention of playing the role of mediator.

DDF, 3e série, 10, No. 539.

(185) 21 July: Poincaré's Diary

Summary of his talks with Tsar Nicholas II

[...] But his most urgent preoccupation concerns Austria. He wonders what she is planning to do following the assassination in Sarajevo. He tells me that, in the present circumstances, he thinks it more than ever necessary for our two governments to be in complete agreement.[109]

109 As Schmidt points out, Paléologue's later assertion that Nicholas II and Poincaré had discussed a conference of the great powers to resolve the issue is a fabrication and was a later addition to his diary. *Frankreichs Außenpolitik*, p. 71, n. 77. In his memoirs, Paléologue writes: 'They concluded their review with the problem of the Austro-Serbian dispute, a problem which becomes more worrying every day owing to the arrogant and mysterious attitude of Austria. Poincaré has insisted with great force that the only way of saving the peace of the world is an open discussion between all the Great Powers, taking care that one group is not opposed to another. 'It's the method that served us so well in 1913,' he said. 'Let's try it again ...!' Nicholas II entirely agreed. Paléologue, *Memoirs*, pp. 15–16.

Notes journalières, Poincaré papers, BNF, Nafr. 106026, f. 104, cited in Stefan Schmidt, *Frankreichs Außenpolitik in der Julikrise 1914*, Oldenbourg, Munich 2007, p. 71.

(186) 22 July: Jules Cambon to Bienvenu-Martin

Germany denies knowledge of ultimatum

Telegram No. 181 Confidential
Berlin, 22 July 1914
D. 0.10 a.m.
R. 2.10 a.m.

I questioned Herr von Jagow as to the contents of the Austrian Note. He assured me that he knew nothing about it. I was astonished at this, all the more because Germany purports to stand by Austria with particular vigour.

DDF, 3e série, X, No. 551.

(187) 22 July: Dumaine to Bienvenu-Martin

Uncertainty about Vienna's intentions and date of intended démarche; speculation about nature of demands of Serbia

Telegram No. 102.
Vienna, 22 July 1914
D 4.30 p.m. (R. 8 p.m.)

Response to Telegram No. 233

There is still complete uncertainty as to the decisions which Count Berchtold, who is prolonging his stay at Ischl, is trying to obtain from the Emperor. It was believed the Government intended, while forestalling conflict between the two countries, to act with great vigour against Serbia, to dispose of her once and for all, 'to treat her like another Poland'.

Eight army corps are said to be ready to begin the campaign. But M. Tisza, who is very worried about the agitation in Croatia, is said to have actively intervened in order to restrain the warlike tension.

In any case, it is believed that Belgrade will be approached this week. The Austro-Hungarian Government's requests relating to the repression of the assassination, and to certain surveillance and policing guarantees are acceptable to Serbia's dignity; M. Jovanović believes they will be welcomed. M. Paŝić wishes for a peaceful solution, but declares he is ready for all resistance.[110]

He has confidence in the strength of the Serbian army; he counts, furthermore, on the union of all the Slavs of the Monarchy to paralyse the effort directed against his country.

Unless one is absolutely blind it should be recognized here that offensive action has the greatest chances of being disastrous as much for the Austro-Hungarian army as for the cohesion of the nationalities governed by the Emperor, which is already so compromised.

Herr von Tschirschky, the German Ambassador, is proving to be in favour of violent measures, although he acknowledges that the Imperial Chancellery does not entirely agree with him on this point.[111] The Russian Ambassador [Isvolsky], who left yesterday for Russia, confided to me that his Government will not object to steps aimed at the punishment of the guilty parties and the dissolution of notoriously revolutionary societies, but would not allow demands humiliating to Serbian national sentiment.[112]

DDF, 3e série, X, No. 554.

(188) 22 July: Bienvenu-Martin to the French Ambassadors at London, St Petersburg, Vienna, Rome

French decision-makers still in the dark; Germany still insists not to know about content of Austrian note to Serbia

Telegram Nos 307, 377, 238.
Paris, 22 July 1914
D. 9.10 p.m.

M. Jules Cambon asked M. de Jagow what the Austrian note in Belgrade contained and the Chancellor [*sic*] replied that he had no idea.[113] Our Ambassador expressed his surprise at this. He commented that the fall of the stock market in Berlin continues and that pessimistic news is circulating.

M. Barrère discussed the Austro-Serbian tensions with the Marquis di San Giuliano, who is worried about it.[114] He confirms that he is bringing

110 (**173**).

111 Note the curious reversal of his stance from earlier in the crisis when he had counselled caution and had been reprimanded for this by the Kaiser. See (**108**).

112 Telegrams No. 102 and 103, merged into one, were sent on 23 July at 10.30 a.m. to London No. 309, Berlin No. 307, Petersburg No. 370, Rome No. 288.

113 See DDF, 3e série, 10, No. 551.

114 See DDF, 3e série, 10, No. 546.

pressure to bear on Austria so that Serbia is only asked to undertake realistic measures, for example, the dissolution of the Bosnian Club and not an enquiry into the causes of the assassination in Sarajevo.

In a general way, it seems that the Austrian Government, feeling outflanked by its press and by the military party, is looking to obtain the maximum from Serbia, initially with intimidation, directly and indirectly, and is relying on Germany for this purpose.[115]

DDF, 3e série, 10, No. 555.

(189) 22 July: Lyncker to his wife

Lyncker does not believe a world war will result from the crisis

[Balholm, Norway, aboard the *Hohenzollern*]

[…] The thunderclouds on the political horizon are getting ever darker. [...] Impossible to say how it will pan out. Do not worry yourself prematurely, however; such crises have often passed and one can hardly imagine that a big world war might be unleashed because of this gang of murderers in Serbia. […]

Cited in Holger Afflerbach, *Kaiser Wilhelm II.*, Oldenbourg, Munich 2005, p. 127.

115 In the French *Yellow Book* an additional paragraph was included which is not contained in the version printed in the DDF: 'I have asked the French Ambassador at Vienna to use all his influence with Count Berchtold and to represent to him, in a friendly conversation, how much Europe would appreciate moderation on the part of the Austrian Government, and what consequences would likely be entailed by violent pressure on Serbia. French *Yellow Book*, No. 17, Engl. transl. in *Collected Diplomatic Documents on the Outbreak of the European War*.

8

Reactions to the Ultimatum

23 July–27 July: Documents (190)–(268)

'On 23 July at 6 o'clock', Wladimir von Giesl later recalled, 'I had given the ultimatum to the [Serbian] Deputy Prime Minister Paču. [...] The next day, the swarm of bees was fully active.'[1] (**191**) Paču was startled to receive what was clearly a significant document, and assembled the ministers who were present in Belgrade. (191) Crucially, Prime Minister Pašić was absent, spending the day campaigning in Niš for the forthcoming elections. Having read the document, the first person to speak was Ljuba Jovanović, the Minister of Education, who proclaimed: 'We have no other choice but to fight it out.'[2]

The delivery of Austria-Hungary's ultimatum spelt the end of a period of uncertainty during which Europe's Great Powers had been playing a guessing game about Austria-Hungary's likely move against Serbia. In Europe's capitals, the reaction was largely one of surprise at the severity of the demands (**232**), followed by immediate attempts to find a way of defusing the crisis and arranging mediation. While Vienna's (and Berlin's) decision-makers expected Serbia to refuse to accept the demands made of her and use this non-compliance as pretext for a war, in the other capitals of Europe, the quest for mediation (at best) and a localization of the conflict (at worst) began in earnest.

France, Russia and Britain now started to play major roles in the crisis of which they had so far been largely unaware. In that, they were

1 Wladimir von Giesl, 'Konnte die Annahme der serbischen Antwortnote den Ausbruch des Weltkrieges verhindern?' *Berliner Monatshefte*, May 1933, pp. 454–469, p. 464.

2 Cited in Christopher Clark, *The Sleepwalkers. How Europe Went to War in 1914*, Allen Lane, London 2012, p.459.

motivated by more than just a desire to preserve peace in Europe – alliance consideration and the desire to maintain great-power status were influencing their decisions and were to affect the outcome of the crisis. Thus, for example, France did not play an entirely negligible role in escalating the crisis because she accepted the risk of a war by pursuing her goal of maintaining France's position as a great power. Even when the Russian Foreign Minister Sazonov was still cautious, Poincaré and Paléologue were encouraging a tough stance vis-à-vis Austria-Hungary (**190**), (**202**), (**203**).[3] Following their departure from St Petersburg, the French Ambassador Paléologue repeatedly assured the Russians of unlimited French support (seemingly speaking on behalf of the French Government, but actually exceeding his authority), but the ground had already been prepared by Poincaré's demands for firmness during his state visit (**190**), (**272**). However, this did not mean that the French were forging ahead with their military preparations. The French Minister of War, Messimy, decided in consultation with Chief of Staff Joffre that the French army should wait for Germany to commit the first acts of hostility along their shared border, a stance that would characterize French policy for the rest of the crisis, although increasingly the Chief of Staff began to worry about the effects this would have on France's ability to wage a successful war against Germany (**244**), (**279**), (**303**), (**338**), (**379**). Joffre was, however, confident in the ability of the French Army, telling Messimy in response to the news

3 Stefan Schmidt argues for a revision of the traditional view (largely based on Renouvin's post-war publications) that France attempted to find a diplomatic solution to the crisis. His evidence suggests a much more calculating element to French policy in July 1914. With the aim of preventing German hegemony in Europe, Schmidt claims, Poincaré advocated a 'firm' policy vis-à-vis Austria-Hungary's demands in his talks with the Russian ally during his state visit to St Petersburg. In Schmidt's interpretation, such a demand carried the implicit assurance of military support if the crisis led to war. Schmidt, *Frankreichs Außenpolitik in der Julikrise 1914*, Oldenbourg, Munich 2007, p. 355. In 1931, Frederick L. Schuman argued that the French President's visit to Russia had had a significant effect in that it 'impress[ed] Nicholas and Sazonov with French willingness to follow them in any course they might choose and to strengthen their determination to resist the Austrian demands on Serbia. This was not an incitement to war, nor even, in so many words, a "blank check" to St Petersburg. [...] But it was the inevitable result of Poincaré's insistence on Entente solidarity, which he regarded as essential to French security'. Schuman, *War and Diplomacy in the French Republic*, Whittlesey House, London 1931, p. 215. See also (272).

on 24 July that France might go to war: 'Very well, sir, we will do it if it is necessary.' Messimy's enthusiastic 'Bravo!' and Joffre's confidence were a long way removed from Joffre's pessimism in 1911, when he had told the Premier Joseph Caillaux that France's chance for victory was not even 70 per cent.[4]

Russia, too, now reacted to the crisis which had so far been only of Austria-Hungary's and Germany's making. Her decision-makers took their first steps on the road to mobilization in a 'crucial meeting' of the Council of Ministers in the afternoon of 24 July in which the Foreign Minister told his colleagues that he was convinced that 'Austria-Hungary and Germany were resolved to deal a decisive blow at Russian authority in the Balkans by annihilating Serbia'[5] (**206**). Once the Tsar had approved his Ministers' decision, war had become 'more probable', given Austria-Hungary's determination to go to war with Serbia, and Germany's decision to support her ally, come what may.[6] The meeting on 24 July is also important because, in the absence of any written evidence as to the conversations between the Russian and French allies during the French state visit to St Petersburg, it has been argued that the record of that first meeting following the news of the ultimatum might reflect a plan that the allies had previously agreed upon, 'if any plan was concerted with France before the departure of the French Mission'.[7] Russia's decision-makers felt compelled to support Serbia

---

4 Robert A. Doughty, 'France', in Richard Hamilton and Holger Herwig (eds), *War Planning 1914*, Cambridge University Press, Cambridge 2010, pp. 143–174, p. 167.

5 Dominic Lieven, *Nicholas II. Twilight of the Empire*, St Martins Griffin, New York 1993, p. 201. As Schuman points out, these decisions were made 'before the expiration of the forty-eight hour time limit of the Austrian note to Serbia and before any rupture of diplomatic relations between Vienna and Belgrade, and they reflect Sazonov's determination to resort to war in the event of an Austrian attack on Serbia.' *War and Diplomacy*, p. 219.

6 Dominic Lieven, *Russia and the Origins of the First World War*, St Martin's Press, New York 1983, pp. 146–147.

7 Robert C. Blinkley makes this speculative point, and also argues that the document 'strongly testifies that the original intent of the Russian Government (perhaps, by implication, of the French Government also) was honorable and pacific'. 'New Light on Russia's War Guilt', *Current History*, 23, 4, January 1926, pp. 531–533, p. 533. A counter-argument for such interpretations of Russia's role has recently been advanced by Sean McMeekin, who claims that Russian ambitions to capture the Straits motivated her actions in July 1914. *The Russian Origins of the First World War*, Belknap Press, Cambridge MA, London 2011.

and to stand up to this provocation from Vienna in the same way as Austria-Hungary's decision-makers felt compelled to put their foot down in the light of the perceived Serbian provocation: not to react would mean suffering a decline of their national honour and prestige. If Russia allowed herself to be pushed out of the Balkans, Finance Minster Bark recorded, 'she would be considered a decadent state and would henceforth have to take second place among the Powers'.[8] Much the same worries motivated Vienna's decision-makers,[9] and indeed all the Great Powers worried about a potential loss of prestige and of 'Great Power status'.

In the evening of 25 July the Council of Ministers decided on a 'period preparatory to war' (the equivalent of Germany's '*Zustand drohender Kriegsgefahr*') to come into effect the next day. On 26 July the partial mobilization of four military districts was confirmed[10] (**229**), (**246**). The Chief of the Mobilization Section of the Russian General Staff would later remember: 'The war was already a settled matter, and the whole flood of telegrams between the governments of Russia and Germany [which followed] represented merely the stage setting of a historical drama.'[11]

France learnt of Russia's decision for preparations for war and a partial mobilization of four districts the day it was decided, on 26 July (**246**), but did not choose to restrain her ally. She also did not try to intervene on 29 July when the news was received that Russia

8 Bark's notes of the meeting of 24 July cited in Lieven, *Nicholas II*, p. 201.

9 See for example (**117**), (**126**), (**134**).

10 See for example Alfred von Wegerer, 'Russian Mobilization of 1914', *Political Science Quarterly*, 43, 1928, pp. 201–228. Wegerer's revisionist account argues that Russia would have had no need to declare her partial mobilization in response to Austria's declaration of war on Serbia on the 28th, and he accuses Russia of implementing '*de facto* a secret introduction to mobilization, a masked pre-mobilization' on 26 July (p. 202). Ulrich Trumpener has shown the extent to which German intelligence services went to try to get news of Russia's moves during those crucial days of July: 'War premeditated? German Intelligence operations in July 1914', *Central European History*, 9, 1, 1976, pp. 58–85, pp. 65f. For a detailed discussion of the measures implemented, see L.C.F. Turner, 'The Russian Mobilization in 1914', in P. Kennedy (ed.), *War Plans of the Great Powers*, Allen & Unwin, London 1979, pp. 261ff. and most recently, Bruce W. Menning, 'Russian Military Intelligence, July 1914: What St. Petersburg Perceived and Why It Mattered', article MS, forthcoming. For a recent interpretation which emphasizes the importance of Russia's mobilization see McMeekin, *The Russian Origins*, *passim*.

11 Sergei K. Dobrorolski, *Die Mobilmachung der russischen Armee, 1914*, Berlin 1922, pp. 21–22.

would initiate a partial mobilization against Austria-Hungary in response to that country's declaration of war on Serbia[12] (**299**). At a meeting of the Ministerial Council in Paris that day, the Ministers approved of the Russian decision.[13]

In Britain, the government had been preoccupied with events in Ireland, and news of the ultimatum came as a surprise to the Cabinet (**198**), (**221**). The Industrialist Albert Ballin reported from London: 'The Austrian note to Serbia is considered very calmly here. This is probably partly due to the current situation, for the Ulster question dominates the hour. The Gentlemen [Grey and Haldane] were yesterday evening extremely pessimistic.'[14] In fact, though, Sir Edward Grey considered the document 'extraordinary', and it caused widespread consternation in Britain and instantly overshadowed the worries about Ireland.[15] Grey's efforts to arrange a solution by mediation began immediately.

The British Government was intent on arranging mediation to solve the crisis peacefully and asked for Germany's help in trying to convince the Austrians to accept this (**204**). However, Germany's statesmen merely passed on the suggestion to Vienna to save face, advising their ally in no uncertain terms that they did not expect them to accept the British proposal, thus continuing the underhand game they had already played throughout July. Rather than counselling restraint, Vienna was urged to follow up her diplomatic move with immediate military measures, 'to place the world before a *fait accompli*' (**225**), (**260**). Still in defiant mood, and thus encouraged by Germany, Austria-Hungary did not take the other great powers up on their suggestion to extend the deadline for Serbia's answer (**209**), (**212**), (**214**), (**223**).

Following Prime Minister Pašić's return to Belgrade, the defiant mood of 23 July (when Paču had informed the Serbian missions

12 Schmidt, *Frankreichs Außenpolitik*, p. 318.

13 Ibid. Schmidt points out that Poincaré destroyed the relevant notes in his diary, and it is not possible to reconstruct what was discussed in this meeting based on contemporary evidence. However, based on the report by Minister of the Interior Maly to Caillaux, the French Ministerial Council expressly approved of the Russian move.

14 Ballin to Jagow, 24 July 1914, GP, 39, No. 15889.

15 Ballin was right about the preoccupation with Irish matters which threatened, in July, to lead to a 'head-on clash between the Liberals and Conservatives'. D.C. Watts, 'The British Reactions to the Assassination at Sarajevo', *European Studies Review*, 1, 3, 1971, pp. 233–247, p. 234.

abroad that 'no Serbian Government could accept [the Austrian demands] in their entirely') had turned into one of resignation. Now Pašić informed Serbia's missions on 25 July that Vienna would be offered 'full satisfaction'. However, news from the Serbian Minister in St Petersburg, Spalajković, that acceptance of the Austrian demands would amount to 'committing suicide' and assurances that Serbia could 'count unofficially on Russian support' led to a hardening of the Serbian attitude. In the evening of 25 July, Spalajković reported: 'In all circles without exception, the greatest resolve and jubilation reigns on account of the stance adopted by the tsar and his government.'[16] The Serbian Government crafted a reply which 'create[d] the appearance of offering the maximum possible compliance without compromising Serbian sovereignty'.[17]

The Serbian response to the 'unacceptable' ultimatum astonished everyone (**227**), (**242**), (**264**). In large parts the Government agreed to accept it (they would not allow Austro-Hungarian officials to conduct the Serbian enquiry into the assassination), making Giesl's hasty departure (he had been instructed to leave no matter what Serbia's reply) and Austria's predetermined decision to turn down Belgrade's response look suspicious in the eyes of the other European powers who wanted to try to preserve the peace (**242**), (**251**), (**257**), (**275**), (**278**). Even the Kaiser now decided that there was no longer any reason to go to war, much to the dismay of his military advisers (**276**). However, Chancellor Bethmann Hollweg chose not to alert the ally in Vienna to the Kaiser's suggestion of stopping the Austro-Hungarian advance outside of Belgrade (the 'Halt in Belgrade') in time[18] (**277**).

For Sir Edward Grey, this was a particularly difficult time. The days following the ultimatum were characterized by Germany's hope for British neutrality, by France's and Russia's demands for Britain's involvement in any potential conflict on their side (**202**), (**218**), (**234**), and by the British Cabinet's refusal to commit the country one way or another. Grey was trying to convince a reluctant Cabinet that the time had come to make a decision as war seemed

16 Cited in Clark, *Sleepwalkers*, pp. 460–463. Clark concludes that '[i]t was reassurance from the Russians that stiffened the backs of the Serbs.' (p. 462) However, cf. (**201**): in a conversation following the Council of Ministers meeting on 24 July, Sasonov advised Spalajković that Serbia should exercise 'extreme caution'.

17 Ibid, p. 463.

18 See Imanuel Geiss (ed.), *July 1914*, Scribner, London 1967, No. 115.

unavoidable, and as Britain would be dragged inevitably into it, regardless of her decision (**259**).

If war could not be avoided, at least an attempt could be made to localize it (**231**). Britain invited all the Great Powers to join in a mediation effort (**209**), (**220**), and Russia encouraged Serbia to support British proposals 'energetically' (**218**). Following the Serbian reply Britain put pressure on Germany to urge Vienna towards 'some moderation' (**257**), while Russia had even suggested to Serbia that she allow Austrian troops to occupy her territory and then appeal to the Powers for help, rather than mobilizing and fighting (**200**), (**206**). Sazonov also urged 'extreme moderation' to the Serbian Minister in St Petersburg (**201**).

For Vienna's decision-makers, these were very unwelcome developments. On 27 July, Berchtold asked for the Emperor's signature on the draft declaration of war for Serbia, arguing that he 'did not interpret it impossible that the Triple Entente Powers could make still another attempt to achieve a peaceful solution of the conflict unless a clear situation is created by a declaration of war.'[19] Austro-Hungarian policy was still, as it had been at the beginning of July, based on the premise that a diplomatic success would be undesirable and tantamount to failure, and that a war against Serbia was the only worthwhile outcome of the crisis.

Italy, not having been consulted by Austria-Hungary, did not consider it her duty to support her alliance partner in what she interpreted to be an aggressive move in which the *casus foederis* did not apply (**197**). Compensation might still have been a way of swaying the Triple Alliance partner and was favoured by Germany, though unsurprisingly not by Austria-Hungary. It was of course easier for Germany to advocate compensation, as it was Austro-Hungarian territory that would have to be offered to compensate and entice

19 ÖUA, VIII, No. 10855. As Fritz Fellner points out, 'This justification, with which Berchtold presented the declaration of war for signature, should have been sufficient to silence from the start all historical and, indeed, all political, debate about the question of responsibility for the unleashing of the war. However dangerous subversive activity in the South Slav provinces of the Habsburg Monarchy might have been, however hostile Russian politicians might have been towards Austria-Hungary, until July 1914 the will to make war was present only in Austro-Hungarian government circles. [...] The will to this third Balkan War dominated the thoughts and actions of Austrian politicians and military men.' Fellner, 'Austria-Hungary', in K. M. Wilson (ed.), *Decisions for War, 1914*, UCL Press, London 1995, pp. 9–25, pp. 16–17.

Italy (**318**), (**326**). At this point in the crisis, it seemed too high a price to pay.

In Germany it was still hoped that Britain would remain neutral (**235**), (**237**), but this was a policy largely based on misunderstandings and wishful thinking (**266**), (**267**), (**281**). It was a misapprehension with serious consequences, and once Berlin's decision-makers realized that they could not, in fact, count on Britain, it was too late to restrain their ally (**317**), (**321**). Underlying the German decision-makers' reasoning was the fear of what the future would bring, in particular given Russia's predicted military strength in a few years' time (**181**), (**211**). This prediction of Russia's future invincibility was shared in Vienna, London and even in Paris, though crucially not in St Petersburg: 'in marked contrast to the decision-makers in the German Empire, in Great Britain or even in France, who had formed an almost sinister judgement of the strength of Russia's power, the [Russian] Foreign Minister considered the military possibilities of his country to have been modest'.[20] For those in charge in Vienna and Berlin, waiting for Russia to become invincible was not an option in 1914, a time when they were still quietly confident of being able to wage a war successfully.

(190) 23 July: Paléologue's Memoirs

Tsar and Poincaré still in the dark about Austria's intentions vis-à-vis Serbia

The Tsar made me sit behind him in the stern of the yacht [*Alexandria*] and told me of the conversation he had just had with Poincaré:

'I'm delighted with my talk with the President. We see absolutely eye to eye. I am not less peace-loving than he, and he is not less determined than I to do everything necessary to prevent the cause of peace being compromised. He fears some Austro-German manoeuvre against Serbia and thinks we should reply with the united front of a common diplomatic policy. I think the same. We must show ourselves firm and united in our efforts to find possible solutions and the necessary adjustments. The more difficult the situation becomes the more important will unity and firmness become.'

20 Schmidt, *Frankreichs Aussenpolitik*, p. 357.

[Paléologue] 'That policy seems to me the essence of wisdom; I'm afraid we shall have to resort to it before long.' [...]

[Tsar] 'Have you any fresh reason for your apprehension?'

[Paléologue] 'I have at least one – the unexpected return of my colleague Szapary,[21] and the air of cold and hostile reserve he adopted towards the President of the Republic the day before yesterday. Germany and Austria are preparing a shock for us.'

[Tsar] 'What can they want? A diplomatic success at the expense of Serbia? To score a point off the Triple Entente? ... No, no; notwithstanding appearances the Emperor William is too cautious to launch his country on some wild adventure, and the Emperor Francis Joseph's only wish is to die in peace.' [...]

Maurice Paléologue, *An Ambassador's Memoirs*, George H. Doran, New York 1925, pp. 27–28.

(191) 23 July: Giesl to Berchtold

Describes delivery of ultimatum and problems caused by short time in which to draft reply

Telegram 175
Belgrade, 23 July 1914
D. 8.00 p.m.
R. 24 July, 2.15 a.m.

Ultimatum.[22]

Premier *ad interim* Paču after some hesitation conceded a conversation for six o'clock, and received me at the striking of the clock with Secretary-General Gruić present (because Paču does not know French). I gave him the note and added that the term for the answer had been fixed for Saturday at 6 p.m. and that if by that time I had received no answer or an unsatisfactory one, I should leave Belgrade with the entire legation [...].

21 The Austro-Hungarian Ambassador had been absent from St Petersburg for two months to attend to his ill wife and son and had returned unexpectedly on 20 July, leading Paléologue to suspect 'that the Austro-Serbian difference is getting more acute'; 'there is going to be a rupture and the ambassador must be at his post to play his part in the dispute and take his share of responsibility.' Diary entry 21 July 1914, *An Ambassador's Memoirs*, Doran, New York 1925, p. 18.

22 Text of the ultimatum (**180**).

Paču, without reading the note, answered that the elections were being carried out and some of the Ministers were absent from Belgrade.[23] He feared it would be physically impossible to assemble a complete Council of Ministers in time for taking what he must believe to be an important decision. The Council of Ministers had been assembled since five o'clock.

I answered that in our age of railways, telegraphs and telephones and given the size of the country, it could only be a question of a few hours to assemble the Ministers, and that in the forenoon I had advised to inform Herr Pašić. But this was an internal Serbian concern, that I had no right to judge. Nothing more was discussed.

ÖUA, VIII, No. 10526.[24]

(192) 23 July: Lyncker to his wife

Tense mood among the Kaiser's party aboard the *Hohenzollern*

[Balholm, Norway, aboard the *Hohenzollern*]

[...] All of us here, that is to say those in the know, are somewhat tense; the Austrian note has been handed over today in Belgrade; it is supposed to be very harsh. What will the Serbs do? Undoubtedly this will depend on whether they have Russia behind them or not. Austria has probably only granted them 48 hours, so that we will perhaps see more clearly in 2 to 3 days. [...]

Cited in Holger Afflerbach, *Kaiser Wilhelm II.*, Oldenbourg, Munich 2005, p. 128.

23 Elections were to be held on 14 August. Pašić was away in the provinces when the ultimatum was delivered, and reluctantly returned early the next morning (Richard Hall, 'Serbia', in Hamilton and Herwig (eds), *Origins of World War I*, Cambridge 2003, p. 109). As a result of the election campaign, as Mark Cornwall points out, Pašić had 'to play the nationalist card' during the crisis. Cornwall, 'Serbia', in Keith M. Wilson (ed.), *Decisions for War, 1914*, UCL Press, London 1995, pp. 55–96, p. 58.

24 Engl. transl. based on Geiss, *July 1914*, No. 45, here with minor amendments.

(193) 23 July: Hoyos to Haldane[25]

Hoyos attempts to convince Haldane that Serbia was behind the plot against Franz Ferdinand and that Austria-Hungary needs to proceed against her; Russia backs Serbia for her own aims; alerts Haldane to the danger that Russia might pose for India in the future if her ambitions in the Balkans and Constantinople are not resisted

I venture to write to you with Count Berchtold's knowledge in the serious crisis which my country is passing through because I learned to value your sense of justice during my stay in England and feel sure that you will judge the difficulties which have driven Count Berchtold to the step he has taken with impartiality and be able to realise, apart from European politics and the present groupment of powers, in an unbiased manner, that no other way was open to us but to try to force Serbia to renounce her ambitions and to suppress the agitation against us in her country. [...]

The assassins all came from or had been in Belgrade, three of them have confessed, independently from the other, that they received bombs and revolvers from a Serbian officer belonging to the Panserb secret society, Narodna Odbrana, and that Serbian frontier guards and customs officials helped them to smuggle the bombs while crossing the border and to get to Sarajevo safely. About 70 people were in the plot and our poor Archduke had six more bomb throwers and assassins waiting for him in case he escaped the first two.[26]

And behind all these deadly intrigues looms Russia as the protector of the Southern Slavs, as the missionary of militant orthodoxy in Galicia and Hungary, as the aggressive force, whose political aims and ambitions coincide with those of Serbia and also with those lately to be traced in Rumania. All to destroy Austria-Hungary to bar any interference in the future, when Russia decides to go to Constantinople and further. That is how matters really stand and that is why we can hesitate no longer but must try to break through the chain of iron that is being forged to bind and destroy us. [...]

All these symptoms have been watched here carefully for some time, the murder of the Archduke brought a slow and steady development

25 No precise date is given. The letter arrived 'simultaneously with the arrival of the news of the Austrian ultimatum'. Hoyos had known Haldane personally from his time at the Austro-Hungarian Embassy in London in 1911. See Frederick Maurice, *Haldane 1856–1915*, Faber & Faber, London 1937, p. 349.

26 For details of the conspiracy, see Clark, *Sleepwalkers*, pp. 47–64, 367–403 and David James Smith, *One Morning in Sarajevo*, Phoenix, London 2009, *passim*.

to a hasty climax and if we are now taking matters in hand seriously, even at the risk of a general European war breaking out, we do so fully conscious that our country's existence is in danger and that Austria would be signing her own death warrant, if she continued passively enduring while her enemies are scheming to break her up as old iron.

I trust and hope that this will be realised in England. Many I know who have suffered from the uncertainty of the political situation of the last 2 years will blame us for disturbing the peace of Europe, but they should consider that this uncertainty cannot cease as long as Russia and her friends in the Balkans remain convinced that we are going to pieces and that they will get a large share when this happens. It is this false impression which creates the unstable atmosphere from which we have all suffered in the last years.

And lastly Englishmen should realise what the whole world would look like if the Russian daydreams came true, if Russia held the Balkans and Constantinople in undisputed sway and need fear no one in her back and flanks, when once she followed the example of Alexander the Great and turned her eyes towards India. [...]

Haldane's comment: 'This is very serious. Berchtold is apparently ready to plunge Europe into war to settle the Serbian question. He would not take this attitude unless he was assured of German support. Hoyos' letter is clearly intended to prepare us for the ultimatum and is an attempt to scare us into neutrality with the Russian bogey. The one hope is that Bethmann Hollweg's influence in Berlin will prevail.'

Frederick Maurice, *Haldane 1856–1915*, Faber & Faber, London 1937, pp. 349–352.

(194) 23 July: Fascotti to San Giuliano

Rumanian King raises doubts whether *casus foederis* would apply to Rumania and Italy in case of a war resulting from Austria's ultimatum to Serbia

---

Telegram No. 776
Sinaia, 23 July 1914
D. 7.30 p.m.
R. 24 July, 12.50 a.m.

[...] King Carol then spoke of the consequences of an eventual Austrian-Serbian-Russian conflict from which, on the basis of the alliance, Germany, Italy and Rumania would not be able to abstain. His Majesty said that the *casus foederis* would be controversial and that we would in any case not be involved in a war without having been informed and consulted with reasonable warning; on this point His Majesty insisted very much [...].[27]

DDI, 4th series, XII, No. 443.

(195) 24 July: Otto von Ritter to Hertling

Pope Pius X approves of Austria-Hungary going to war with Serbia over the assassination

Vatican, 24 July 1914

Chiffre[28]

Pope approves of strong measures by Austria against Serbia and in case of war with Russia does not regard Russian and French army highly. Cardinal State Secretary [Merry del Val] also hopes that Austria will this time persevere and did not know when else she would want to conduct a war if she were not determined to reject a foreign agitation which had led to the assassination of the heir to the throne and furthermore in the current constellation threatens Austria's existence.[29] This also testifies to the Curia's great fear of Pan-Slavism.

BayHStA, GPS 918 and MA2568, cited in Jörg Zedler, 'Das Rittertelegramm', in idem (ed.), *Der Heilige Stuhl*, Munich 2010, pp. 175–202.[30]

27 For details see Glenn E. Torrey, 'The Rumanian-Italian Agreement of 23 September 1914', *Slavonic and East European Review*, 44, 103, 1966, pp. 403–420, p. 406, where he points out that Rumania was the first to raise doubts about the *casus foederis* and thus influenced Italy to adopt the same stance, rather than the other way round as is usually maintained. See (**196**), (**197**), (**230**), (**326**), (**336**).

28 Ten year later Ritter admitted that he considered the contents of this telegram to be so sensational that he personally put it in cipher, rather than, as was usual, giving it to a secretary to do. Jörg Zedler, 'Das Rittertelegramm', in Zedler (ed.), *Der heilige Stuhl*, Herbert Utz Verlag, Munich 2010, pp. 175–202, p. 179.

29 In 1912 the Pope had already remarked that 'Austria-Hungary was threatened in her existence by the Slavic strangle-hold'. Ritter's report of 29 December 1912, cited in Zedler, p. 193. See also (**56**).

30 Zedler points out that this revealing telegram was not passed from Munich to Berlin and that Ritter did not mention it to his Prussian colleague in the Vatican. It is likely that its contents were news to the Government in Berlin when it was first published in 1919. Likewise there is no evidence to suggest that its contents were made known to Vienna. Zedler, 'Das Rittertelegramm', pp. 188–190. (I am grateful to John Röhl for alerting me to this document.)

(196) 24 July: San Giuliano to Bollati and Varna

Italy does not accept *casus foederis*; intervention on side of Allies only possible if Italy receives compensation

Rome, 24 July 1914
D. 10.40 p.m.
Telegram 759

Today the Prime Minister [Salandra], Flotow and myself had a long conversation.[31] For your personal information and by way of guidance as to what to say, we give you a résumé. Salandra and I at once called the attention of the Ambassador to the fact that Austria had no right to take such a step as she has taken at Belgrade without previously coming to an agreement with her Allies.

In fact, the wording of the Note and the nature of its demands show clearly that Austria wishes to provoke a war. We have therefore pointed out to Flotow that, because of Austria's manner of proceeding and because of the defensive and conservative nature of the Treaty of the Triple Alliance, Italy is under no obligation to come to Austria's assistance if through her action she finds herself involved in war with Russia; for this would be due to her own provocation and aggression.

The fact, however, that there is no obligation does not preclude the possibility that it might be convenient for us to take part in an eventual war, should that correspond to our vital interests.

But, given the political regime of our country, it would be quite impossible for us to participate unless the Government were able to furnish the assurance that an advantage corresponding to our risks would be secured – an advantage, that is, sufficient to overcome the resistance of public opinion to a war fought in the interests of Austria, who has recently made many mistakes that have hindered the work of progressive reconciliation which was being effected – thanks to Your Excellency's wise co-operation.

We have also drawn Flotow's attention to the fact that it would not be possible for His Majesty's Government to decide on the lines of its policy in the present instance without first consulting our Allies and ascertaining whether they agree with our interpretation of Article VII.[32] [...]

Flotow mentioned several times, in the course of the conversation, the need for territorial compensation for us in case of a territorial expansion of Austria.

31 For Flotow's account see (**197**).

32 Italy insisted that under the terms of Article VII of the Alliance Treaty she would be compensated with territory in return for agreeing to Austria-Hungary making any territorial acquisitions on the Balkans.

Salandra and I have also drawn to Flotow's attention, and he agreed, that the communication from Austria at present does not require any response and, consequently, at the moment we do not have any reason to speak. I shall add, for the information of Your Excellency only, that Flotow did not have a good impression of the note from Austria, because it looked to him randomly compiled and aimed at causing conflict.

DDI, 4th series, XII, No. 488.

(197) 24 July: Flotow to Jagow

Italian Prime Minister and Foreign Minister offended at not having been consulted; doubtful why Italy should support Austria-Hungary

Telegram 20
Fiuggi, 24 July 1914[33]

In a rather heated meeting with Prime Minister Salandra and Marquis di San Giuliano which lasted several hours the latter was of the opinion that the spirit of the Triple Alliance agreement had demanded of such a serious and aggressive move by Austria that she consulted with the ally beforehand. As this had not occurred with regard to Italy she could consider herself not involved in any further consequences of this step.

In addition Article 7 of the Triple Alliance Agreement (which I do not have here) demanded that with any changes on the Balkans the partners communicated beforehand and that, if one of the two partners effected any territorial changes, the other would be compensated.[34]

In response to my remark that, as far as I knew, Austria had declared not to want any territorial acquisitions, the Minister said that such a declaration had only been made very conditionally. Rather, Austria had declared not to intend to make any territorial acquisitions *now*, conditional on potential later decisions which might become necessary. The Minister opined that one could not hold it against him if he was taking precautionary measures in time.

The text of the Austrian note was so aggressive and composed so clumsily that public opinion in Europe and also in Italy would be against Austria; no Italian government could fight against that.[35]

33 San Giuliano was in the resort of Fiuggi Fonte, 50 miles south-east of Rome.

34 For the text of the Article, see Holger Afflerbach, *Der Dreibund*, Böhlau, Munich 2003, Appendix C, p. 886. See also (**196**).

35 The Italian Government was not told until 22 July of Austria-Hungary's

Following Marquis di San Giuliano's energetic explanation, based on the Triple Alliance agreement, that the treaty carried the obligation of a defensive war, but that Austria was proceeding aggressively, and that therefore Italy would not be further engaged in case of a Russian intervention I disputed this point of view energetically and, following prolonged discussion, achieved the declaration that this, as Marquis di San Giuliano's other declarations above, was merely an observation of his position in principle which did not exclude different decisions by the Italian Government. I explained that at this stage it was not important what might have to happen later, but rather that at the current moment the world needed to be shown the closeness and unity of the Triple Alliance and to avoid everything which could lead Russia and France to suspect an internal disagreement among the Allies. Therefore I had to request urgently also to influence the press in this way. [...]

My impression is that the only way to keep Italy on side is to promise her compensations at the right moment, when Austria is carrying out the acquisition or occupation of the Lowtschen.[36]

I found Salandra to be reasonably understanding. He comprehended that vital interests of Austria were affected. My task is made much more difficult by the fact that the Austrian Ambassador [Mérey] is ill in bed. Counsellor[37] incapable. [...][38]

[*Wilhelm II's marginal comment*] '*This is a lot of nonsense and will sort itself out in the course of events.*'

DD, Nos 156 and 168.

intention to make demands of Belgrade, and the content of the ultimatum had only become known in Rome on 24 July. On 20 July Tschirschky had expressed the German Government's worry that Italy would 'not only not find sympathy in Italy but perhaps direct resistance', to which Berchtold replied 'that it was very regrettable that Italy has seemingly caught wind of our intended move against Serbia', and he blamed Flotow for indiscretion in Rome and considered it 'highly worrying' that Italy had found out about the planned move. 'We intended to inform the Cabinet in Rome one day before delivering the note to Serbia, which seemed to me as an act of courtesy entirely sufficient with an unreliable ally.' He also affirmed that as Austria-Hungary had vowed to refrain from annexing Serbian territory, Italy's attempt to invoke Article VII was not justified. ÖUA, VIII, No. 10398.

36 A mountain top in Montenegro.

37 The two Counsellors (*Botschaftsräte*) were Ludwig Graf Ambrózy von Séden and Freiherr de Baux.

38 For a discussion of this meeting, see William A. Renzi, 'Italy and the Great War', *American Historical Review*, 73, 5, June 1968, pp. 1414–1432, pp. 1421–1422.

(198) 24 July: Churchill remembers the arrival of the ultimatum

British Cabinet meeting; Ministers preoccupied with Ireland until the delivery of the ultimatum; Churchill's reaction to the ultimatum

The Cabinet on Friday afternoon sat long revolving the Irish problem. [...] The discussion had reached its inconclusive end, and the Cabinet were about to separate, when the quiet grave tones of Sir Edward Grey's voice were heard reading a document which had just been brought to him from the Foreign Office. It was the Austrian note to Serbia.[39] He had been reading or speaking for several minutes before I could disengage my mind from the tedious and bewildering debate which had just closed. We were all very tired, but gradually as the phrases and sentences followed one another, impressions of a wholly different character began to form in my mind. This note was clearly an ultimatum; but it was an ultimatum such as had never been penned in modern times. As the reading proceeded it seemed absolutely impossible that any state in the world could accept it, or that its acceptance, however abject, would satisfy the aggressor. The parishes of Fermanagh and Tyrone faded back into the mists and squalls of Ireland, and a strange light began immediately, but by perceptible graduations, to fall and grow upon the map of Europe. [...]

Winston S. Churchill, *The World Crisis*, 2 vols, Odhams Press, London 1938, Vol. I, pp. 154–155.

(199) 24 July: Viviani to Bienvenu-Martin

French and Russian Governments keen to counsel moderation in Vienna; hope that Britain will support this approach

Telegram (unnumbered)
St Petersburg, 24 July 1914
D. 2.05 a.m.
R. 5.30 a.m.

I should be obliged if you would urgently send the following telegram to our Ambassador in Vienna:

For your confidential information. In the course of my conversations with M. Sazonov we were brought round to considering the dangers

39 See (**180**) and (**191**).

which might result from any step taken by Austria-Hungary towards Serbia in relation to the assassination of the Archduke heir. We agreed it was advisable that everything possible must be done to prevent a request for explanations, or some formal demand which would amount to an intervention in Serbia's home affairs which could justifiably be considered an attack on her sovereignty and independence.

Consequently, we thought there was good cause to have a friendly conversation with Count Berchtold to give him some cautious advice so that he understands how ill-advised it would be to make any approach in Belgrade which could be seen as a threat by Austria-Hungary.

The British Ambassador [Buchanan], brought up-to-date by M. Sazonov, expressed the idea that his Government would no doubt contribute to efforts aimed at removing any danger which might threaten general peace, and he has telegraphed his Government in this respect.[40]

M. Sazonov has sent instructions to that effect to M. Schebeko.[41] Without there being any question here of collective or concerted action by representatives of the Triple Entente in Vienna, I would request you to discuss the matter with your two colleagues and to agree between you the best way for each of you urgently to make Count Berchtold understand that the present situation requires restraint.

Please pass on this telegram to our representatives abroad.[42]

DDF, 3e série, 11, No. 1.

---

40 See (**202**).

41 *Int. Bez.*, I, 4, No. 322. The editors of DDF added the following footnote: 'The telegram M. Sazonov sent to Vienna on 22 July [...] indeed contains the instructions M. Viviani talks about and this telegram refers to very similar instructions given to the French Ambassador in Vienna. So there is an interval of over twenty-four hours between the sending of the Russian and the French instructions.' If this date if 22 July is correct, it suggests that the Franco-Russian allies knew even more about what Vienna was planning than has previously been suspected.

42 The document contains an annotation by M. Berthelot: 'Sent by telegram, 24 July, 9.30 a.m., to London, Berlin, Rome, indicating that the de facto situation created by the sending of the Austrian Note yesterday evening no longer corresponds with that envisaged at the time of the instructions and new ones are required from the three Governments of the Triple Entente. Petersburg, London, asked by telegram for the plans and intentions of the Russian and British Governments. Telegraphed via the Eiffel Tower in France, 24 July, 10.00 a.m.'

(200) 24 July: Sazonov to Strandtmann

Serbia should try to appeal to the Powers rather than offering resistance

Telegram 1487
Urgent

St Petersburg, 24 July 1914

Personal. Please decipher yourself.

If Serbia is really in such a helpless condition as to leave no doubt regarding the result of an armed struggle with Austria, it would perhaps be better that in the event of an invasion by Austria the Serbs should not even try to offer resistance, but should retreat and allow the enemy to occupy their territory without fighting, and make a solemn appeal to the Powers. In this appeal the Serbs, by pointing out the difficulty of their position after the recent war during which their moderation gained them the recognition of Europe, might refer to the impossibility of their surviving an unequal struggle, and ask for the protection of the Powers based upon a sense of justice.

Int. Bez., I, 5, 22.[43]

(201) 24 July: Memorandum of the day of the Russian Ministry for Foreign Affairs

Reaction in Russia to the news of the ultimatum in Belgrade; Serbian Minister advised to exercise caution in formulating a reply

St Petersburg 24/11 July

Early this morning a telegram was received at the Foreign Ministry from Belgrade confirming the information given yesterday by the Counsellor of the Italian Embassy. Baron Schilling immediately warned the Ambassadors Isvolsky and Schebeko by telephone of the necessity of their returning immediately to their posts.

Around 10 o'clock in the morning S.D. Sazonov arrived from Tzarskoe Selo; Baron Schilling immediately communicated the above-mentioned information to him. This news made a very strong impression on the Minister who exclaimed spontaneously: 'C'est la guerre européenne.' The

43 Engl. transl. based on Geiss, *July 1914*, No. 60, here with minor amendments.

Austro-Hungarian Ambassador was immediately called to the Ministry by telephone; while waiting for the Ambassador S.D. Sazonov personally reported to the Tsar, also by phone from Baron Schilling's office, regarding the ultimatum presented to Serbia by Austria.[44] His Majesty exclaimed: 'This is outrageous!' and ordered to be kept informed. [...]

The French Ambassador invited S.D. Sazonov, the English Ambassador [Goschen] and the Rumanian Envoy [Diamandy] for breakfast for an exchange of opinions.[45] On this occasion the Minister asked these representatives urgently to communicate his request to their respective governments that they would immediately design a plan of action with us. This request was naturally also directed at the Rumanian Minister, which resulted in Rumania also being drawn into this joint matter. For us it was advantageous to involve Rumania on our side in this matter, on the other hand it was obviously flattering for Rumania to participate equally in the diplomatic steps to be taken by the Great Powers.

At three o'clock a Council of Ministers took place [...].[46]

After the meeting of the Council of Ministers there was a meeting between S.D. Sazonov and the Serbian Minister during which the [Foreign] Minister advised extreme moderation in respect of the reply of the Serbian Government to the Austrian note.

At 7 o'clock the German Ambassador [Pourtalès] came to the Foreign Minister. He attempted to justify Austria's action on the grounds that the investigation of the murder of Sarajevo had produced evidence which proved the guilt of the Serbian Government.[47] In addition he endeavoured to prove the correctness of Austria's procedure by pointing to the necessity to defend the 'monarchic principle'. S. D. Sazonov addressed Count Pourtalès in a very firm tone and condemned strongly the method of the Viennese Cabinet, while insisting on the unacceptable nature of the note handed to Serbia, and that furthermore a lack of courtesy existed vis-à-vis the Great Powers in that Austria, in turning to them while at the same time according to Serbia so short a period for meeting the demands that the Powers were not afforded the possibility to consider the matter and to express their views in time.

Those who saw Count Pourtalès when he left the Minister testify that he was very agitated and that he did not conceal the fact that S. D. Sazonov's words and particularly his firm determination to resist the Austrian demands had made a strong impression on the Ambassador.[48]

44 This was the first time that Sazonov had ever made a report to the Tsar on the telephone. Lieven, *Nicholas II*, p. 199.

45 For Buchanan's account see (**202**).

46 For details of the discussion and conclusions see (**206**).

47 But see (**149**) on lack of evidence of Serbia's complicity.

48 Count Pourtalès' account in Geiss, *July 1914*, No. 58.

While the German Ambassador was with the Minister, the French Ambassador [Paléologue] arrived at the Ministry and, not wishing to meet his German colleague, went to Baron Schilling and waited there in his office [...]. The French Ambassador expressed the opinion that despite the events which had occurred he considered that the President of the French Republic ought not to change any aspect of the programme for his journey to the Scandinavian capitals, but should return quietly to France, as previously proposed, with stops in Stockholm and Copenhagen. Otherwise, in the opinion of the Ambassador, a general panic might arise because there would be an impression that the head of the French Republic regarded the political situation as threatening. Meanwhile the Ambassador considered the situation as by no means hopeless. He founded his optimism on the assumption that Germany would hardly decide to support Austria since she knew to what serious consequences this would inevitably lead at the present moment. [...]

Int. Bez., I, 5, 25.[49]

(202) 24 July: Buchanan to Grey

Sazonov hopes that England will proclaim her solidarity with France and Russia; result of French state visit was agreement that France was willing to fulfil her alliance obligation vis-à-vis Russia; firm and united attitude was only chance of averting war

---

St Petersburg, 24 July 1914
Urgent
D. 5:40 p.m.
Tel. (No. 166.) Urgent.
R. 8 p.m.
[...] Minister for Foreign Affairs [Sazonov] telephoned to me this morning saying that he had just received text of ultimatum presented by Austria at Belgrade yesterday that demands a reply in forty-eight hours. Step thus taken by Austria meant war, and he begged me to meet him at the French Embassy.

Minister for Foreign Affairs and French Ambassador [Paléologue]

49 Engl. transl. based on Geiss, *July 1914*, No. 61, here with minor amendments. A different English translation can be found in M. F. Schilling, *How the War Began in 1914, Being the Diary of the Russian Foreign Office from the 3rd to the 20th (Old Style) of July, 1914*, Allen & Unwin, London 1925, pp. 28–32.

told me confidentially that result of the visit of the President of the French Republic had been to establish the following points:

1 Perfect community of views on the various problems with which the Powers are confronted as regards the maintenance of general peace and balance of power in Europe, more especially in the East.

2 Decision to take action at Vienna with a view to the prevention of a demand for explanation or any summons equivalent to an intervention in the internal affairs of Serbia which the latter would be justified in regarding as an attack on her sovereignty and independence.

3 Solemn affirmation of obligations imposed by the alliance of the two countries.[50]

Minister for Foreign Affairs expressed the hope that His Majesty's Government would proclaim their solidarity with France and Russia. He characterised Austria's conduct as immoral and provocative. Some of the demands which she had presented were absolutely inacceptable [*sic*], and she would never have acted as she had done without having first consulted Germany. The French Ambassador gave me to understand that France would not only give Russia strong diplomatic support, but would, if necessary, fulfil all the obligations imposed on her by the alliance.

I said that I could not speak in the name of His Majesty's Government, but that I would telegraph all that they had said. I could personally hold out no hope that His Majesty's Government would make any declaration of solidarity that would entail engagement to support France and Russia by force of arms. We had no direct interests in Serbia, and public opinion in England would never sanction a war on her behalf. Minister for Foreign Affairs replied that the Serbian question was but part of general European question and that we could not efface ourselves.[51]

---

50 Stieve points to the fact that this document was omitted from the British Blue Book and alleges that these agreements were made before the ultimatum to Serbia had been handed over, but he does not cite the entire document which clearly refers to the ultimatum having been handed to Serbia the previous day. It is, however, unclear from the document whether the conversation with Paléologue did predate the ultimatum, and whether the agreements between Poincaré and Sazonov did so, also. Stieve asserts that this amounted to a blank cheque for Russia. Friedrich Stieve, *Isvolsky and the World War*, Allen & Unwin, London 1926, pp. 214–215.

51 Paléologue recorded in his *Memoirs*: 'Buchanan assumed that his government would desire to remain neutral and was therefore apprehensive that France and Russia would be crushed by the Triple Alliance. Sazonov protested: "At the present juncture England's neutrality would be tantamount to her suicide!" "I'm certain of that", Sir George replied sadly. "But I'm afraid public opinion with us is still far from realizing what our national interests so imperiously require." I emphasized the decisive part England could play in quenching Germany's

I said that I gathered that His Excellency wished us to join in telling Austria that we could not tolerate her active intervention in Serbian internal affairs. If she paid no attention to our representations and took military action against Serbia, did Russia propose to declare war upon her? Minister for Foreign Affairs said that the whole question would be considered by a Council of Ministers to be held this afternoon,[52] but that no decision would be taken till a further Council of Ministers had been held under the presidency of the Emperor, probably tomorrow.[53] He personally thought that Russia would at any rate have to mobilise.

I suggested that the first thing to be done was to try to gain time by bringing our influence to bear to induce Austria to extend term of delay accorded to Serbia. The French Ambassador replied that time did not permit of this; either Austria was bluffing or had made up her mind to act at once. In either case a firm and united attitude was our only chance of averting war. I then asked whether it would not be advisable to urge Serbian Government to state precisely how far they were prepared to go to meet Austria's wishes. Minister for Foreign Affairs said that some of the demands contained in [the] ultimatum might no doubt be accepted, but that he must first consult his colleagues.

As they both continued to press me to declare our complete solidarity with them, I said that I thought you might be prepared to represent strongly at Vienna and Berlin danger to European peace of an Austrian attack on Serbia. You might perhaps point out that it would in all probability force Russia to intervene, that this would bring Germany and [?France] into the field, and that if war became general, it would be difficult for England to remain neutral. Minister for Foreign Affairs said that he hoped that we would in any case express strong reprobation of Austria's action. If war did break out, we would sooner or later be dragged into it, but if we did not make common cause with France and Russia from the outset we should have rendered war more likely, and should not have played a 'beau rôle.'

From French Ambassador's language it almost looked as if France and Russia were determined to make a strong stand even if we declined to join them. Language of Minister for Foreign Affairs, however, was not so [?decided] on this subject.

---

warlike ardour; I cited the view the Tsar Nicholas expressed to me four days ago – "Unless Germany has lost her reason altogether, she will never dare to attack Russia, France and England combined." [See (**208**)]. Thus it was urgently necessary for the British Government to announce its adhesion to our cause, which was the cause of peace. Sazonov warmly advocated the same course. Buchanan promised to make strong representations to Sir Edward Grey in favour of the policy of resistance to Germanic arrogance.' Paléologue, *Memoirs*, pp. 31–43.

52 See (**206**).

53 See (**215**).

Austrian Government seemed purposely to have presented their ultimatum at moment when President of the French Republic and President of the Council were leaving Russia on their return to France, where they cannot arrive for four or five days.[54]

Towards the close of our interview we were joined by Rumanian Minister [Diamandy], with whom Minister for Foreign Affairs had a private conversation in which His Excellency invited also Rumanian Government to make representations at Vienna.

(Repeated to Paris, 1:20 p.m., No. 217.)

MINUTES [by Crowe, Nicolson and Grey]

The moment has passed when it might have been possible to enlist French support in an effort to hold back Russia.

It is clear that France and Russia are decided to accept the challenge thrown out to them. Whatever we may think of the merits of the Austrian charges against Serbia, France and Russia consider that these are the pretexts, and that the bigger cause of Triple Alliance versus Triple Entente is definitely engaged.

I think it would be impolitic, not to say dangerous, for England to attempt to controvert this opinion, or to endeavour to obscure the plain issue, by any representation at St. Petersburg and Paris.

The point that matters is whether Germany is or is not absolutely determined to have this war now.

There is still the chance that she can be made to hesitate, if she can be induced to apprehend that the war will find England by the side of France and Russia.

I can suggest only one effective way of bringing this home to the German Government without absolutely committing us definitely at this stage. If, the moment either Austria or Russia begin to mobilise, His Majesty's Government give orders to put our whole fleet on an immediate war footing, this may conceivably make Germany realise the seriousness of the danger to which she would be exposed if England took part in the war.

It would be right, supposing this decision could be taken now, to inform the French and Russian Governments of it, and this again would be the best thing we could do to prevent a very grave situation arising as between England and Russia.

It is difficult not to agree with Sazonov that sooner or later England will be dragged into the war if it does come. We shall gain nothing by not making up our minds what we can do in circumstances that may arise to-morrow.

---

54 This suspicion was correct. See (**171**). For other documents that prove this point, see for example Geiss, *July 1914*, Nos 17, 20–24, 27, 33, 35.

Should the war come, and England stand aside, one of two things must happen:

(a.) Either Germany and Austria win, crush France, and humiliate Russia. With the French fleet gone, Germany in occupation of the Channel, with the willing or unwilling cooperation of Holland and Belgium, what will be the position of a friendless England?

(b.) Or France and Russia win. What would then be their attitude towards England? What about India and the Mediterranean?

Our interests are tied up with those of France and Russia in this struggle, which is not for the possession of Serbia, but one between Germany aiming at a political dictatorship in Europe and the Powers who desire to retain individual freedom. If we can help to avoid the conflict by showing our naval strength, ready to be instantly used, it would be wrong not to make the effort.

Whatever therefore our ultimate decision, I consider we should decide now to mobilise the fleet as soon as any other Great Power mobilises, and that we should announce this decision without delay to the French and Russian Governments. – E. A. C[rowe] July 25.

The points raised by Sir Eyre Crowe merit serious consideration, and doubtless the Cabinet will review the situation. Our attitude during the crisis will be regarded by Russia as a test and we must be most careful not to alienate her. – A. N[icolson]

Mr. Churchill told me to-day that the fleet can be mobilised in twenty-four hours, but I think it is premature to make any statement to France and Russia yet. – E. G[rey]

BD, XI, No. 101.

(203) 24 July: Paléologue to Bienvenu-Martin

Immediate reaction to ultimatum in Russia

Telegram No. 282
St. Petersburg, 24 July 1914
D. 9.12 p.m.
R.11.10 p.m.

As the President of the Republic and the President of the Council have been able to confirm for themselves, the attitude of the Russian Emperor and his Ministers is of the most peaceful kind. But the ultimatum which the Austro-Hungarian Government has just delivered to the Cabinet of Belgrade introduces a new and worrying element to the situation. Public opinion in Russia would not tolerate Austria attacking Serbia.

The shortness of the time limit set by the ultimatum makes it even more difficult for the Triple Entente Powers to exercise any moderating influence they may have in Vienna. On the other hand, M. Sazonov suspects that Germany will want to support her ally and I fear this impression may be correct. The solidarity of the Triple Entente's Powers must therefore remain firm. Any weakness would encourage the Germanic Powers to intensify their provocative attitude and would speed up events. Talking to me some months ago about the aggressive ulterior motives of Germany, the Russian Emperor said, 'If France and Russia really want peace, they must put themselves in a position to maintain it, if necessary, by force.' (See my despatch no. 23 of 17 February[55]). The Triple Entente does in fact have sufficient force at its disposal to safeguard peace, and it must not hesitate to demonstrate this force.

Sent by radiogram to the President of the Council [aboard the *France*]

DDF, 3e série, 11, No. 21.

(204) 24 July: Paul Cambon to Bienvenu-Martin

Mediation proposal from London supported by Cambon and Benckendorff; suspicion that Germany had encouraged Austria

---

Telegram Nos 134, 135
London, 24 July 1914
D. 5.53 p.m.
R. 6.06 p.m.

Further to my telegrams 132 and 133.

This morning, the Austrian Ambassador [Mensdorff] gave Sir Edward Grey a copy of a telegram from Count Berchtold containing the text of the ultimatum sent to the Serbian Government yesterday.[56]

After having read it, the Secretary of State for Foreign Affairs remarked that never had such a fearsome declaration been addressed by one Government to another and that serious complications could arise from it. He drew Count Mensdorff's attention to the responsibilities his Government assumed under these circumstances. This afternoon, Sir Edward Grey, anticipating the possibility of conflict between Austria and Russia with all its consequences for peace, told me that he had written to my German colleague [Lichnowsky] and that he offered to

55 See DDF, 3e série, 9, No. 322.
56 See (**180**) and (**191**).

ask the Cabinet in Berlin to support the idea of mediation by the four Powers not directly involved in the Serbian affair: England, France, Italy and Germany. This mediation would take place in both Vienna and Petersburg.

I pointed out to Sir Edward Grey that we did not yet know Petersburg's intentions and that an attempt at mediation from this side would not be justified and could be badly received; that Russia's intentions would only become clear after the opening of hostilities between Austria and Serbia; and that roused Russian opinion would, no doubt, force the Russian Government to send an ultimatum to Vienna and it would be too late to suggest any compromises. I added that it would be preferable to ask the German Government to take the initiative of approaching Vienna to offer mediation between Austria and Serbia by the four uninvolved Powers. If Germany agrees, we will, most importantly, gain time. Sir Edward Grey has abandoned his idea of mediation between Russia and Austria and he seemed prepared to meet with Prince Lichnowsky in keeping with my suggestion. I have informed Sir A. Nicolson and my colleague from Russia [Benckendorff] of this. Both of them dread a surprise from Germany and assume that Austria would not have sent her ultimatum without prior agreement with Berlin. When I observed that it was not in Germany's interest to stir up a general war,[57] Count Benckendorff said that Prince Lichnowsky, returning from leave about a month ago, had shared his pessimistic views about relations between Petersburg and Berlin. He had noticed the worry caused in Berlin by the rumours of a naval entente between Russia and England,[58] by the Tsar's visit to Bucharest,[59] and by the reinforcement of the Russian army. Count Benckendorff had concluded from this that an encounter with Russia would be readily accepted in Germany.

The Under-Secretary of State [Nicolson] has been struck, as have we all, by how worried Prince Lichnowsky has seemed since his return from Berlin, and he thinks that if Germany had wanted to, she could have prevented the delivery of the ultimatum. The situation, therefore, is as serious as it can be, and we see no way of halting the course of events. However, Count Benckendorff believes it right to try the approach I have suggested to Sir Edward Grey.

DDF, 3e série, 11, No. 23.

---

57 In the version published in the French *Yellow Book*, the sentence 'l'Allemagne n'avait pas intérêt à soulever une guerre générale' had been omitted. Sacha Zala, *Geschichte unter der Schere*, Oldenbourg, Munich 2001, p. 35.

58 See (**79**), (**85**), (**87**), (**135**), (**143**).

59 The Tsar visited Bucharest in mid-June, leading to fears that Rumania, secretly allied to Germany, Italy and Austria-Hungary, might defect.

(205) 23–24 July: Joseph Redlich's diary

Conversation with Hoyos; better for Austria-Hungary to perish than be the sick man of Europe

1 o'clock a.m.

[…] The note[60] was mainly written by him [Hoyos] and Forgách and does not really allow for acceptance by Serbia at all: it is a 48-hour ultimatum and then war begins. That Russia will go with Serbia can be assumed to be certain, not least because the revolutionary strike movements will make an external diversion advisable. If Russia abandoned Serbia to her fate without action, the nationalists would depose the Tsar. Germany, however, is ready and willing herself to opt for war. Alek was in Berlin 14 days ago[61] and spoke there first with the Under-Secretary of State Zimmermann, then with Bethmann Hollweg, who completely agreed: even if he displayed some diplomatic clumsiness, nonetheless he was completely on board right from the beginning. […] We do not want to obliterate Serbia, but to reduce her size, and take Northern Albania. […] Our note is very forceful and will, as I put it with Alek's agreement, conjure up a terrible storm in Europe. We are thus still able to want! We do not want to and cannot be a sick man, says Alek, better to perish quickly! In England the mood is against us! I predicted this. […]

Thus today a big day dawns: Hopefully it will lead to a healthier Austria! […]

We both speak about the Archduke-legend: the world does not know that the Archduke was always opposed to war. Thus through his death he has helped us to gain the energy that he never wanted to rally as long as the Kaiser lived!

Fritz Fellner and Doris Corradini (eds), *Schicksalsjahre Österreichs*, 3 vols, Böhlau, Vienna et al. 2011, Vol. 1, pp. 615–616.

60 That is, the ultimatum to Serbia. See (**180**), (**191**).
61 See (**119**).

(206) 24 July: Russian Council of Ministers meeting

Russia's response to the Austro-Hungarian ultimatum; agreed to try to gain time for Serbia to reply; to advise Serbia not to fight but entrust her fate to the support of the Great Powers; to request consent for mobilization of four military districts if the need arose; to stockpile war materials; to reduce money deposited in Germany and Austria

Special Journal of the Russian Council of Ministers[62]
St Petersburg, 24/11 July 1914

Concerning the communication of the Foreign Minister about the latest measures of the Austro-Hungarian Government in relation to Serbia

The Foreign Minister told the Council of Ministers that, according to information he had received and the note delivered by the Austro-Hungarian Ambassador at the Imperial Court, the Austro-Hungarian Government had issued demands to the Serbian Government which were in essence wholly unacceptable to the Kingdom of Serbia as a sovereign state, and were expressed in the form of an ultimatum imposing a deadline of 6.00 tomorrow evening, 25 July, for the reply. As it was likely that Serbia would seek our advice and perhaps also request our assistance the need arose immediately to prepare an answer which we could give Serbia.

After discussing the statement submitted by Sazonov, the Council of Ministers passed the following resolutions, in conjunction with the commentaries of the present political and military situation made before the Council by the War Minister, Naval Minister and Finance Minister:

I. To endorse the proposal of the Foreign Minister that he should make contact with the Cabinets of the Great Powers in an effort to persuade the Austro-Hungarian Government to grant Serbia a certain postponement of her reply to the ultimatum demands set by the Austro-Hungarian Government in order to give the Governments of the Great Powers the opportunity to inspect and study the documents on the crime committed in Sarajevo that the Austro-Hungarian Government has at its disposal and which, as the Austro-Hungarian Ambassador confirms, it is willing to communicate to the Russian Government.

62 For a discussion of the Council of Ministers' meeting and for Russia's reaction to the ultimatum, see D.C.B. Lieven, *Russia and the Origins of the First World War*, New York, St Martin's Press, 1983, pp. 140ff, and Lieven, *Nicholas II*, p. 201. See also (**207**), (**215**).

II. To endorse the proposal of the Foreign Minister that the Serbian Government should be advised, in the event of Serbia's position being such that she is not strong enough to defend herself unaided against a possible Austrian attack, not to offer any resistance to armed invasion of Serbian territory, if an attack of this kind were to take place, but rather to declare that Serbia would yield to superior force and entrust her fate to the judgement of the Great Powers.

III. To charge the War and Naval Ministers, as may be most appropriate, with the task of entreating the most gracious assent of Your Imperial Majesty to a proclamation of mobilization of the four military districts of Kiev, Odessa, Moscow and Kazan, and of the Baltic[63] and Black Sea Fleets, depending on the subsequent course of events.

IV. To charge the War Minister without delay to speed up the stock-piling of war materials for the army.

V. To charge the Finance Minister to take measures for the immediate reduction of sums belonging to the Finance Department at present deposited in Germany and Austria-Hungary.

The Council of Ministers considers it to be its most humble and obedient duty to bring its resolutions to the most exalted attention of Your Imperial Majesty.

I. Goremykin, V. Sabler, V. Sukhomlinov, I. Grigorovich, P. Kharitonov, A. Krivoshein, S. Sazonov, P. Bark, A Verëvkin, V. Sheviakov, I. Lodyzhenskii

Agreed.[64] [*Nicholas II*]
Krasnoje Selo, 25/12 July.

Int. Bez., I, 5, No.19.[65]

63 The word Baltic was added by Nicholas II who approved the decision on 25 July.

64 As Dominic Lieven explains, once the Tsar approved this decision to support Serbia against Austria-Hungary, Russia's stand 'made a European conflict probable', given Austria-Hungary's decision to go to war with Serbia and Germany's support of that policy. And yet, as Lieven concludes, 'it is not easy to see how Russia could have acted differently'. *Russia*, pp. 146–147.

65 Engl. transl. based on Geiss, *July 1914*, No. 59, here with minor amendments. A slightly different English translation can be found in Blinkley, 'New Light on Russia's War Guilt', p. 533, in which the minutes of the Council of Ministers meeting of 24 July were published for the first time from the files of the Hoover War Library.

(207) 24 July: A.V. Krivoshein's[66] summary of Russian Council of Ministers meeting of 24 July 1914

Agriculture Minister summarizes discussions of the Russian Council of Ministers; favours a firm stance vis-à-vis Austria-Hungary and Germany

[Krivoshein's views expressed during the meeting, as recorded by Finance Minister Peter Bark]:
However, our rearmament programme had not been completed and it seemed doubtful whether our Army and our Fleet would ever be able to compete with those of Germany or Austro-Hungary [*sic*] as regards modern technical efficiency [...]. On the other hand, general conditions had improved a great deal in Russia in the past few years and public and parliamentary opinion would fail to understand why, at the critical moment involving Russia's vital interests, the Imperial Government was reluctant to act boldly [...]. Our exaggeratedly prudent attitudes had unfortunately not succeeded in placating the Central European Powers [...]. No one in Russia desired war. The disastrous consequences of the Russo-Japanese War had shown the grave danger which Russia would run in case of hostilities.[67] Consequently, our policy should aim at reducing the possibility of a European war [but] if we remained passive we would not attain our objective. War could break out in spite of our efforts at conciliation [...]. In his view stronger language than that we had used hitherto was desirable. All factors tended to prove that the most judicious policy Russia could follow in present circumstances was a return to a firmer and more energetic attitude towards the unreasonable claims of the Central-European powers.

[After the meeting, Bark had a private conversation with Krivoshein:]

He thought that the only hope of influencing Germany was to show them, by making a firm stand, that we had come to the end of the concessions we were prepared to make. In any case, we should take all the steps which would enable us to face an attack.[68]

66 The Germanophobic Minister of Agriculture was a powerful member of the Russian government and enjoyed Nicholas II's full confidence.

67 During the Russo-Japanese war of 1904–1905, Russia had been defeated by the Japanese and also suffered serious domestic consequences as a result, leading to the 1905 Revolution. On the war and its impact see for example John Steinberg et al. (eds), *The Russo-Japanese War in Global Perspective. World War Zero*, Brill, Leiden and Boston 2005.

68 For more details on the meeting see Lieven, *Russia*, pp. 142–143.

Memoirs of Peter A. Bark, Columbia University, Bakhmetev Archive, New York, MS. Bark, 7, pp. 1–17, cited in Dominic Lieven, *Russia and the Origins of the First World War*, St Martin's Press, New York 1983, pp. 142–143.

(208) 24 July: Peter Bark's account of his meeting with Tsar Nicholas II

Tsar Nicholas II does not believe that war will break out as the Powers would come to an agreement, as they had done so often in the past

---

[...] the Emperor [...] remained quite calm and told me that he thought Sazonov was exaggerating the gravity of the situation and had lost his nerve. In latter years conflicts had frequently arisen in the Balkans, but the powers had always come to an agreement. None of them would wish to let a war loose in Europe to protect the interests of a Balkan state. War would be disastrous for the world and once it had broken out it would be difficult to stop. The Emperor did not think it likely that the Note had been sent after consultation with Berlin. The German Emperor had frequently assured him of his sincere desire to safeguard the peace of Europe and it had always been possible to come to an agreement with him, even in serious cases. His Majesty spoke of the German Emperor's loyal attitude during the Russo-Japanese War and during the internal troubles that Russia had experienced afterwards. It would have been easy for Germany to level a decisive blow at Russia in these circumstances – they were particularly favourable for such an attempt – since our attention was engaged in the Far East and we were left with insufficient protection against an attack from the West.

Memoirs of Peter A. Bark, cited in Dominic Lieven, *Nicholas II*, St Martin's Griffin, New York 1993, pp. 199–200.

(209) 25 July: Jules Cambon to Bienvenu-Martin

Jagow maintains not to have known about the ultimatum beforehand; expresses desire for localized conflict

Telegram No. 185
Berlin, 25 July 1914
D. 1.15 a.m.
R. 2.50 a.m.
Confidential. Top secret.

During the interview I had today with the Secretary of State [Jagow], I asked him if it was correct, as announced in the newspapers, that Austria had presented a note to the Powers on her dispute with Serbia. I asked if he had received it, and what view he took of it. Herr von Jagow answered in the affirmative, adding that the note was forcible and he approved of it, the Serbian Government having for a long time exhausted Austria's patience, who had [already] put up with so much. Moreover, this problem is, in his eyes, a domestic one for Austria, and he hopes that it will be localized. I went on to say to him that, having received no instruction at all, I only wanted to exchange very personal views with him. So I asked him if the Berlin Cabinet had really been entirely ignorant of Austria's requirements before they were communicated to Belgrade, and as he confirmed this was so,[69] I expressed my surprise at seeing him thus undertake to support claims, the scope and limits of which he was ignorant. Herr von Jagow interrupted me, and said, 'It is only because we are talking between ourselves personally that I allow you to say that to me.' 'Certainly', I said, 'but if Peter I humiliates himself, domestic trouble will probably break out in Serbia: that will open the door to fresh possibilities, and do you know where you will be led by Vienna?' I added that the language of the German newspapers was not the language of people indifferent to, and unacquainted with the affair; rather, it announced active support. Finally, I pointed out that the shortness of the deadline given to Serbia to submit would make a bad impression in Europe.

Herr von Jagow replied that he quite expected a little excitement (*un peu d'émotion*), but that he hoped that Serbia's friends would give her good advice. 'I have no doubt', I said to him, 'that Russia will endeavour to persuade the Cabinet in Belgrade to make acceptable concessions;[70] but why not ask from one what is being asked of the other, and if one allows that advice will be given at Belgrade, is it not legitimate to allow, on the other hand, that advice will also be given in Vienna?'

69 But cf. for example (**171**).
70 See (**200**) and (**206**).

M. de Jagow went on to say that that depended on circumstances, but immediately checking himself, he repeated that the problem ought to be localized. He asked me if I really thought the situation serious. 'Certainly', I answered, 'because if what is happening is the result of due reflection, I do not understand why all the bridges have been burnt.'

We parted company, once again assuring each other that this conversation was of a completely personal nature.[71]

DDF, 3e série, 11, No. 33.

(210) 25 July: Jules Cambon to Bienvenu-Martin

Belgian Minister in Berlin fears that Russia, France and Britain might not become involved in a war provoked by Germany

Telegram No.191
Berlin, 25 July 1914
D. 11.48 p.m.
R. 26 July, 1.10 a.m.

Top secret

The Belgian Minister [Beyens] appears very anxious about the course of events. He is of opinion that Austria and Germany have desired to take advantage of the fact that, owing to a combination of circumstances at the present moment, Russia and England appear to them to be threatened by domestic troubles, while in France our military system appears shaken.[72] Moreover, he does not believe in the feigned ignorance of the Government of Berlin on the subject of Austria's *démarche*. He thinks that if the form of it has not been submitted to the cabinet at Berlin, the

71 In the French *Yellow Book*, an additional paragraph was included which is not printed in the DDF: 'An article which appeared in the *Lokal Anzeiger* this evening shows also that at the German Chancery there exists a state of mind to which we in Paris are naturally not inclined to pay sufficient attention, I mean the feeling that Monarchies must show solidarity. I am convinced that great weight must be attached to this point of view in order to appreciate the attitude of Kaiser Wilhelm, whose impressionable nature must have been affected by the assassination of a Prince whose guest he had been a few days previously. It is not less striking to notice the pains with which Herr von Jagow, and all the officials placed under his orders, pretend to every one that they were ignorant of the scope of the note sent by Austria to Serbia'. French *Yellow Book*, No. 30, in *Collected Diplomatic Documents*, HMSO, London 1915.

72 This refers to Senator Humbert's damaging revelations about the state of the French army. See Chapter 7, p. 252, n. 34.

moment of its despatch has been cleverly chosen in consultation with that Cabinet in order to surprise the Triple Entente at a moment of disorganization.[73] [...]

He has seen the Italian Ambassador, who has just interrupted his holiday in order to return. It looks as if Italy would be surprised, to put it no higher, at having been kept out of the whole affair by her two allies.[74]

Baron Beyens thinks that one should not be astonished if Belgium takes certain precautionary military measures. As for me, I naturally assured the Belgian Minister as to our situation and of the cohesion of the Triple Entente.

DDF, 3e série, 11, No. 60.

(211) 25 July: Theodor Wolff's Diary

Editor of *Berliner Tageblatt* meets officials in the *Auswärtiges Amt*; Jagow does not believe war will result from the crisis, but is confident of Germany's abilities if it does; war unavoidable in the long run, but now circumstances still good

In the morning to the *Auswärtiges Amt*, where St[umm] immediately tells me that Jagow wants to talk to me. [...] I have not seen him for a long time, because we had stopped our relationship – which had also only been superficial – since the Tripoli affair.[75] He appears to me very changed, I particularly notice his shuffling gait and his bent posture, also his smile. He thanks me first of all for the 'big' service which I had given to the German Government in another matter and made compliments about the attitude of the *Berliner Tageblatt* so far in the Serbian question although naturally otherwise – he means concerning domestic policy – he does not share our views. We should continue to be firm. I tell him that I rather support the attitude of my editorial team, but that there seemed to me a lack of caution so that one could retreat later. I considered the Austrian note not very clever. – He, very animated and smiling: He thought so too, it was a hotchpotch of assembled demands, two or three big points would have been better. But more than anything one had to remain firm now. I said that it was not my intention to change the attitude of the *B[erliner] T[ageblatt]*, except perhaps in nuances. But could we not be embroiled in a world war? If Russia now did not retreat...? Jagow:

73 This was a correct assumption. See for example (**171**).

74 See for example (**166**), (**173**), (**196**), (**197**), (**225**).

75 In September 1911, Italy began a war against Turkey over possession of Tripoli.

He did not believe that; the diplomatic situation was very favourable. Neither Russia, nor France, nor England wanted the war. *And if it had to be (smiling) – war would come at one point anyway, if we let things go, and in two years Russia would be stronger than now.[76] During [our] good-bye: 'I do not consider the situation to be critical.'*[77]

I return to Stumm who explains to me the advantages of the current diplomatic situation. As always, if one shows firmness all sorts of friendships pipe up on which one had no longer counted. I say: 'If only we don't get stuck!' He indicates that one would then find a way back. Like Jagow he says that the war would be unavoidable in two years' time if we did not free ourselves from this situation. It was about trying to ascertain if Austria was still worth anything to us as an ally. She must not back away. The Russians would shout about loudly and it could lead to hot days. Perhaps Russia would mobilise and then it would of course be necessary to restrain our military. But Russia would think twice before she struck. In a war with Russia we would see all sorts: revolution in Finland and in Poland – and we would see that everything has been stolen, even the locks on the guns, and that no ammunition was left. As regards France – the revelations of Senator Humbert about the state of the army were worth their weight in gold.[78] France could not want a war. Such a good situation will not come again. Just keep it up and firmness.

Bernd Sösemann (ed.), *Theodor Wolff*, 2 vols, H. Boldt, Boppard/Rhein 1984, No. 3.

(212) 25 July: Bienvenu-Martin to Dumaine

Russian and French attempts to extend the deadline to Serbia

Telegram No. 252
Paris, July 25, 1914
D. 11 a.m.
Very urgent

The Russian Government has instructed its representative in Vienna to ask the Austrian Government for an extension of the time limit set for Serbia so as to enable the Powers to formulate an opinion on the note which Austria has offered to communicate to them, and with a view to avoiding incalculable and undesirable consequences for everyone.

76 See (**135**), (**174**), (**181**).
77 The text between the asterisks was crossed out in the diary in pencil.
78 For detail's on Senator Humbert's statements see Chapter 7, p. 252, n. 34.

A refusal of this demand by Austria-Hungary would remove all meaning from the approach she made to the Powers by passing them her Note, and would put her in conflict with international morality.

The Russian Government has asked that you urgently make a similar approach to Count Berchtold; I beg you to support your colleague's request. The Russian Government has sent the same request to London, Rome, Berlin and Bucharest.

DDF, 3e série, 11, No. 36.

(213) 25 July: Jules Cambon to Bienvenu-Martin

Germany offers little support for British mediation proposal

Telegram No. 187
Berlin, July 25, 1914
D. 4.35 p.m.
R. 6 p.m.
Very confidential

This morning the British Chargé d'Affaires, acting under instructions from his Government,[79] asked Herr von Jagow if Germany were willing to join with Great Britain, France and Italy to intervene in Vienna and St. Petersburg in order to prevent a conflict and, in the first instance, to ask Vienna to grant an extension of the time limit imposed on Serbia by the ultimatum.

Herr von Jagow replied that he had already, this very morning, immediately on receipt of Prince Lichnowsky's despatch informing him of Sir Edward Grey's intentions, telegraphed his Ambassador in Vienna to tell him to ask Count Berchtold for this extension. Unfortunately Count Berchtold is at Ischl. Moreover, the Secretary of State does not think this request would be well received.

The British Chargé d'Affaires asked Herr von Jagow, as I did yesterday, if Germany had had no knowledge of the Austrian note before it was despatched, and the Secretary of State confirmed this in such a manner that the Chargé d'Affaires sincerely believes him; but he could not refrain from expressing his surprise at the blank cheque Germany had given to Austria.[80] Herr von Jagow having replied that this was a domestic matter for Austria, the British Chargé d'Affaires remarked that it had become exceedingly international.

DDF, 3e série, 11, No. 45.

79 See BD, XI, No. 122.
80 See (**120**), (**209**).

(214) 25 July: de Fleuriau to Bienvenu-Martin

News of British mediation attempts in Vienna

Telegram No. 136
London, 25 July 1914
D. 3.26 p.m.
R. 6.40 p.m.

Sir Edward Grey has been informed this morning of the instructions given to the Russian Ambassador in Vienna asking him to request an extension of the time limit given to Serbia referred to in Austria's note of the day before yesterday.[81] M. Sazonov asked that the Russian initiative be supported by the British Embassy.

Sir Edward Grey, who does not completely approve of the last paragraph of the Russian note, telegraphed to Sir M. de Bunsen to convey the same view as his Russian colleague, and to quote the Austrian note, under whose terms Serbia's failure to comply with the conditions of the ultimatum would, as from today, lead only to diplomatic rupture and not to immediate military operations.

Sir Edward Grey concluded from this that there would be time for the Powers to intervene.

DDF, 3e série, 11, No. 46.

(215) 25 July: Special Journal of the Russian Council of Ministers

The Council of Ministers decides to request the Tsar's permission to order period preparatory to war

St Petersburg, 25/12 July 1914

Concerning the extension of the order for the period preparatory to war[82] graciously approved on 2 March/17 February 1913.

81 See BD, XI, No. 118, (**212**).

82 Bruce Menning points out the differences between the 'period preparatory to war' and actual mobilization. 'The intent behind the period preparatory to war was to initiate military readiness measures short of actual mobilization and war declaration. These measures included the imposition of military censorship, the recall of furloughed officers to their units, the verification of unit military records and the stocks required for possible mobilization, the retention on active duty of reservists scheduled for rotation to inactive status, the recall of troops training in the field to their quarters, and elevating troop readiness levels under the guise of

On 25/12 July of this year Your Imperial Majesty graciously agreed to approve the Special Journal of the Council of Ministers of 24/11 July 1914 concerning the statement of the Foreign Minister about the latest moves of the Austro-Hungarian Government in relation to Serbia.[83] Through this Journal, among other things, the War and Navy Ministers have been entrusted in their respective capacities with requesting the gracious consent of Your Imperial Majesty to the mobilization, as events require, of the four Military Districts of Kiev, Odessa, Moscow and Kazan, and of the Baltic and Black Sea Fleets, in addition to the speeding up of the completion of supplies of army equipment.

In response to the present turn of the diplomatic negotiations and in order that all departments may take the necessary measures for the preparation and smooth extension of the mobilization of the Army, the Navy and the Fortresses, as well as the deployment of the Army on the frontiers opposite the threatened opponents, the Council of Ministers now considers it advisable from 26/13 July of this year to enforce throughout the entire Empire the order for the period preparatory to war laid down in both schedules, while at the same time it empowers the War Minister to solicit the gracious consent of our Imperial Majesty to the implementation in the military department of other measures not provided for in the aforementioned schedules such as he may consider necessary in the circumstances and on the condition that he subsequently informs the Council of Ministers of the measures taken. In accordance with Article 2 of the above-mentioned order the beginning of the period preparatory to war is to be determined by ordinances of the Council of Ministers after they have been graciously approved by Your Majesty.

In the light of this the Council of Ministers resolves to put into operation the decree for the period preparatory to war in accordance with both schedules and in conformity with the particulars set out in this Journal.

The Council of Ministers regards it as its most humble and obedient duty to submit this decision for the gracious approval of Your Imperial Majesty.[84]

---

maneuvers and exercises among forward-deployed reconnaissance and covering forces.' As Menning points out, these measures 'could easily be misunderstood by contemporary observers and historians as actions synonymous with troop mobilization'. Menning, 'Russian Military Intelligence', unpublished MS, forthcoming. (I am grateful to Bruce Menning for making an advance copy of this article available to me.)

83 See (**206**), (**207**).

84 As Schmidt points out, the head of a mobilization department of the General Staff had alerted the Chief of Staff on 24 July that Russia did not, in fact, possess a plan for partial mobilization against Austria-Hungary, and that such improvised measures would put the actual mobilization plan in jeopardy, but this did not

I. Goremykin, V. Sabler, V. Sukhomlinov, I. Grigorovich, P. Kharitonov, A. Krivoshein, S. Sazonov, N. Maklakov, S. Timashev, P. Bark, A Verëvkin, P. Dumitrashko, V. Sheviakov, the deputy leader of the Council of Ministers I. Lodyzhenskii

Agreed. [*Nicholas II*]
Krasnoye Selo, 25/12 July 1914

Int. Bez., I, 5, No. 42.[85]

(216) 25 July: Pourtalès to Sazonov

Germany officially denies prior knowledge of contents of the ultimatum; localization of war desired outcome

---

Written communication, handed to the Russian Foreign Minister Sazonov by the German Ambassador in St Petersburg

(French original)

25/12 July 1914

We have heard from a reliable source that the news, spread by some newspapers, that the démarche of the Austro-Hungarian Government to Belgrade had been delivered at Germany's bidding was absolutely false. The German Government had no knowledge of the wording of the note of the Austrian Government before it had been delivered,[86] and it had no influence over its contents. Hence Germany is wrongly accused of a threatening demeanour.

As Austria's ally Germany naturally supports the demands of the Cabinet in Vienna vis-à-vis Belgrade which she considers justified. Above all she wishes – as she has already declared at the beginning of the Austro-Serbian argument – that the conflict will remain localized.[87]

Int. Bez., I, 5, No. 46.

---

stop the decision on 25 July to initiate a partial mobilization. Only on 28 July did the Chief of Staff concede that a partial mobilization was not really possible, and Sazonov was asked to explain to the Tsar the dangers associated with a partial mobilization order. Schmidt, *Frankreichs Außenpolitik*, pp. 327–328. On Russia's '*Kriegsvorbereitungsperiode*', see Gunther Frantz, *Rußlands Eintritt in den Weltkrieg. Der Ausbau der russischen Wehrmacht und ihr Einsatz bei Kriegsausbruch*, Berlin 1924 and Gunther Frantz, 'Wie Rußland mobil machte', *Berliner Monatshefte*, 14, 1, April 1936, pp. 277–319, here pp. 289ff.

85 Engl. transl. based on Geiss, *July 1914*, No. 76, here with minor amendments.

86 But see for example (**146**), (**154**), (**171**).

87 The communication was based on a telegram that Zimmermann had sent to Pourtalès, Schoen and Lichnowsky. See DD, No. 153.

(217) 25 July: Draft report of the Russian Foreign Minister for Nicholas II

Sazonov's analysis of current political questions to inform the Tsar's reply to the King of England; Persian matters of no concern in the current crisis; European balance of power is threatened

[...] The Persian matters do not cause any concern, because Russia and England, given their shared desire to reach an understanding, will not have any problems in agreeing on this terrain. The Russian Government is willing to meet the main wishes of the English Government in the conviction that the latter will itself respect the vital interest of Russia. Because Russia attaches great importance to the agreement reached in 1907 and knows to value the beneficial consequences which the agreement has already produced, she desires honestly also to maintain in future the orderly and friendly relations and the agreement with England in this, as in other areas.

At the present moment everything which concerns Persia recedes into the background on account of the complications arising out of the exacerbation of Austro-Serbian relations.

The demands made by Austria in Belgrade bear no relation either in form or in content to those omissions for which a measure of blame might possibly be imputed to the Serbian government. Though it was admissible to request the latter for an enquiry to be instituted in Serbia on the basis of the facts brought to light in Austria-Hungary by the enquiry into the murder in Sarajevo, there can nevertheless be no justification for the posing of political demands which would be unacceptable to any state.

The clear aim of this procedure – which is apparently supported by Germany – is the total annihilation of Serbia and disturbance of the political equilibrium in the Balkans.

There can be no doubt that deceitful and provocative actions of this kind will meet with no sympathy in England from either the Government or public opinion.

If Austria persists any longer with this line of policy, Russia will not be able to remain indifferent and the possibility of grave international complications will have to be taken into account. It is to be hoped that in this event Russia and England will both find themselves on the side of right and justice and that the disinterested policies of Russia, whose sole aim it is to prevent the establishment of Austrian hegemony in the Balkans will find active support on the part of England.

It is absolutely essential to see beyond the limits of the present complications and to face the fact that it is now a question of the maintenance of the balance of power in Europe which is seriously threatened. It is to be hoped that England, whose policies for centuries have been directed at the maintenance of this balance, will likewise now remain faithful to the legacy of the past.

Int. Bez., No. 47.[88]

(218) 25 July: Sazonov to Benckendorff

Britain could still exert mediating influence and condemn Austria's action and war could still be avoided

St Petersburg, 25/12 July 1914

Given the turn which events have now taken, the attitude which England will adopt is of utmost significance. There is still the possibility that a European war will be avoided. It is easier for England than for the other powers to exert a mediating influence on Austria, as she is considered in Vienna to be the most impartial and therefore they are more minded to listen to her voice. Unfortunately, according to information available to us, Austria felt entitled to hope before her steps in Belgrade that her demands would not be met by objections from England's side, and her decision was based to an extent on this speculation. Therefore it would be very desirable that England should declare clearly and firmly that she condemns Austria's action which is not justified by circumstances and exceedingly dangerous for European peace, particularly as she could easily achieve by peaceful means those of her demands which are grounded in law and compatible with Serbia's honour.

In case of further worsening of the situation which might possibly lead to corresponding steps of the Great Powers, we anticipate that England will not hesitate to place herself definitely on the side of Russia and France in order to maintain the balance of power in Europe for which she has also always stood up in the past and which, should Austria be triumphant, would doubtless be disturbed.[89]

Int. Bez., I, 5, No. 48.

88 English translation based on Geiss, *July 1914*, No. 77, here with amendments.
89 See (**220**) for Grey's clarification of Britain's position.

(219) 25 July: Sazonov to Strandtmann and Benckendorff

Still possible to avoid war if Serbia accepts British mediation

25/12 July
Urgent

Due to England's special position, whose impartiality in the matter in question is without doubt, the war between Austria and Serbia could perhaps still be avoided if the Serbian Government were to turn to the English Government with a request for mediation and if the latter were to accept this role. Could you consult in this matter with Pašić and suggest this thought to him.

[Additional text] to the Ambassador in London:

If the Serbs undertake such a step in London, will you please support it energetically. Sazonov.

Int. Bez., I, 5, No. 49.

(220) 25 July: Grey to Buchanan

Russian Ambassador urges Grey to declare support for France and Russia

(No. 295.)
Confidential.
Foreign Office, July 25, 1914

I told Count Benckendorff to-day of what I had said to the German Ambassador this morning as to the possibility of Germany, Italy, France and ourselves working together in Vienna and St. Petersburg to secure peace after Austria and Russia had mobilised.[90]

Count Benckendorff was very apprehensive that what I said would give Germany the impression that France and England were detached from Russia.

I said that France and ourselves, according to my suggestion, would be no more detached from Russia than Germany would be detached from her ally Austria. I had emphasised to Prince Lichnowsky that the participation of Germany in any such diplomatic mediation was an essential condition, and surely the situation was not made unsatisfac-

90 See **(218)**, **(221)**, **(222)**, **(224)**.

tory for Russia if France and England held their hands, provided that Germany also held hers.

Count Benckendorff urged that I should give some indication to Germany to make her think that we would not stand aside if there was a war.

I said that I had given no indication that we would stand aside; on the contrary, I had said to the German Ambassador that, as long as there was only a dispute between Austria and Serbia alone, I did not feel entitled to intervene; but that, directly it was a matter between Austria and Russia, it became a question of the peace of Europe, which concerned us all. I had furthermore spoken on the assumption that Russia would mobilise, whereas the assumption of the German Government had hitherto been, officially, that Serbia would receive no support; and what I had said must influence the German Government to take the matter seriously. In effect, I was asking that, if Russia mobilised against Austria, the German Government, who had been supporting the Austrian demand on Serbia, should ask Austria to consider some modification of her demands, under the threat of Russian mobilisation. This was not an easy thing for Germany to do, even though we would join at the same time in asking Russia to suspend action. I was afraid, too, that Germany would reply that mobilisation with her was a question of hours, whereas with Russia it was a question of days; and that, as a matter of fact, I had asked that if Russia mobilised against Austria, Germany, instead of mobilising against Russia, should suspend mobilisation and join with us in intervention with Austria, thereby throwing away the advantage of time, for, if the diplomatic intervention failed, Russia would meanwhile have gained time for her mobilisation. It was true that I had not said anything directly as to whether we would take any part or not if there was a European conflict, and I could not say so; but there was absolutely nothing for Russia to complain of in the suggestion that I had made to the German Government, and I was only afraid that there might be difficulty in its acceptance by the German Government. I had made it on my own responsibility, and I had no doubt it was the best proposal to make in the interests of peace.

BD, XI, No. 132.

(221) 25 July: Benckendorff to Sazonov (1)

Britain unwilling to declare her hand but convinced that mediation has to be conducted via Berlin

London, 25/12 July 1914
(French original[91])

I am not entirely clear on what basis, the radical press aside, Austria was able to reckon with the sympathy of the English Government. In the most recent conversation with the German Ambassador and the Austrian Ambassador Grey has emphasized the difference between questions of a police nature, as far as justified by enquiries, and the general question of a political nature, that is to say interference in Serbia. He conceded to the first and excluded the second. But it is true that Grey continues to be of the opinion that Berlin, more so than Vienna, is the centre of action, to such an extent that mediating action can only have a serious outcome via Berlin. As regards an articulated position which might resemble an alliance, my talks with Grey today have once more convinced me that England will not declare herself before a general war has been declared and thus the European balance of power is being questioned.[92] Until [then] it will maintain the position which in its mind conforms with the role of keeper of the peace. In any case Grey did not hide from the German or the Austrian Ambassador the impression that the Austrian note had made on him. [...]

Int. Bez., I, 5, No. 55.

(222) 25 July: Benckendorff to Sazonov (2)

British reactions to the ultimatum; speculation that Britain may not remain neutral

25/12
Letter
(French Original[93])

91 N.B. This document was translated into German by the editors of *International Beziehungen*, and has now been translated into English by the editor of this volume.

92 See (**220**).

93 N.B. This document was translated into German by the editors of *International Beziehungen*, and has now been translated into English by the editor of this volume.

[…] The text of the Austrian Note has exploded like a bomb in London, so much that despite the very acute crisis in the Ulster-Question England has this time woken up and understood the threatening danger.[94] […]

Sir Edward Grey's excitement when reading the note which Count Mensdorff delivered was extraordinary. He told him it was the most astonishing document that had ever been produced by diplomacy, he could however not add anything further as the situation was serious in the extreme.[95]

It is without doubt for Grey as for everyone else that Austria proceeded with full agreement with Germany, at least I think so.

When Mensdorff appeared this morning to declare that military measures would not follow immediately after the expiration of the ultimatum he was able to instil in Grey the idea that the attitude of Austria and Germany perhaps contained a certain amount of bluff. Then arrived your suggestion to increase the [period] of truce[96] which he [Grey] immediately supported in Vienna.

Thus in his [Grey's] mind the suggestion could emerge to stop the other mobilizations – apart from the Russian and Austrian – which could, in his mind, be a means to feel Germany's pulse and perhaps, if the will for war was not so completely real in Berlin as certain symptoms seem to suggest, a peaceful solution without a humiliation for Serbia might be found.

I think that he reckons little as to the effectiveness of the solution he has thought up. He doubts – and this he has confessed to me in confidence – that Germany would give up on the advantage of the speed of her mobilization. But he maintains that if it were possible at least momentarily for Germany to loosen her ties with Austria a chance for peace would develop again, and he feels obliged to continue on this path. […]

While I cannot give you any formal assurance of English military cooperation I have not observed a single symptom – not with Grey, nor with the King, or anyone of importance – that England seriously intends to remain neutral. My observations lead me strongly to the opposite impression. […]

Int. Bez., I, 5, No. 56.

94 See (**198**).

95 See also DD, I, No. 157, Lichnowsky to Jagow: 'the note, which in his opinion exceeded everything which he had ever seen of this kind'.

96 See Geiss, *July 1914*, No. 61, and (**202**), (**223**).

(223) 25 July: Bronevski to Sazonov

Last minute attempts by Britain and Russia to achieve an extension of the time limit for Belgrade

Telegram 124
Berlin, 25/12 July 1914

Request urgent instructions. No. 1488[97] received.

I have expressed my opinion to Jagow in the manner indicated.[98] He told me that the English Government had likewise requested him to recommend an extension of the time limit to the Vienna Government; he had telegraphed Vienna about this, and would also telegraph on the subject of our move but feared that his telegrams would be of no avail, on account of Berchtold's departure for Ischl and since insufficient time remained; besides, he is in doubt whether it would suit Austria to give way at the last moment and whether it might not increase Serbia's self-confidence.[99]

I replied that a Great Power such as Austria could give way without damage to her prestige and cited all the relevant arguments in support of this but could obtain no more definite promises. The Foreign Minister stated, *inter alia*, that we must be satisfied with the assurance given to Kudachev yesterday[100] that Austria was not seeking any territorial acquisitions; perhaps Giesl's forthcoming departure after the expiry of the time limit indicated that the encounter would not follow immediately. Austria had, however, requested the German Government to assume responsibility for the protection of the interests of Austrian subjects in Serbia in the event of a diplomatic rupture, and this it had consented to do. In reply to vague hints that pressure would have to be exerted on Vienna for the avoidance of possible threatening consequences, the Foreign Minister each time answered evasively that he did not even want to think about such matters.

Int. Bez. I, 5, No. 63.[101]

97 See Geiss, *July 1914*, No. 61.

98 That is, requesting an extension of the time limit so that the other powers could study the results of the Austrian enquiry. See Geiss, *July 1914*, No. 61, and (202), (223).

99 See DD, No. 171, Jagow to Tschirschky, 25 July 1914.

100 ÖUA, VIII, No. 10615, Daily Report about a visit of the Russian Chargé d'Affaires, 24 July 1914.

101 Engl. transl. from Geiss, *July 1914*, No. 78.

(224) 25 July: Grey to Rumbold

Britain suggests mediation if conflict extends to Russia and Austria-Hungary; surprise at Berlin's assurance to have had no prior knowledge of the ultimatum

Foreign Office, July 25, 1914.
Tel. No. 197
D. 3 p.m.

I have told German Ambassador that Austrian Ambassador has been authorised to inform me that rupture of diplomatic relations and military preparations but not operations on part of Austria would be the method of procedure on expiry of time limit. I said this interposed a stage of mobilisation before actual crossing of frontier, which I had urged yesterday should be delayed.

We should now apparently be soon confronted by a moment at which both Austria and Russia would have mobilised. The only chance of peace would be for the four Powers, Germany, Russia [*sic*],[102] France and ourselves, to keep together if Russia and Austria did both mobilise, and to join in asking Austria and Russia not to cross frontier till there had been time for us to endeavour to arrange matters between them.

German Ambassador read me a telegram from German Foreign Office saying that Germany had not known beforehand and had had no more than other Powers to do with the stiff terms of Austrian note to Serbia, but that having launched the note Austria could not draw back.[103] The Ambassador said, however, that what I contemplated was mediation between Russia and Austria; this was a different question, and he thought Austria might with dignity accept it, and he expressed himself personally favourable to what I had suggested.

I endorsed his observation, saying that between Serbia and Austria I felt no title to intervene, but as soon as the question became one between Austria and Russia it was a question of the peace of Europe, in which we must all take a hand.

I impressed upon him that if Austria and Russia mobilised the participation of Germany would be essential to any diplomatic action for peace. We could do nothing alone. I had had no time to consult the French Government, who were travelling at the moment,[104] and I could not be sure of their views; but if German Government were prepared to agree with my suggestion I was prepared to say to the French Govern-

102 This should have said 'Italy'.
103 See DD, No. 153.
104 Poincaré, Viviani and de Margerie left St Petersburg on 25 July.

ment that I thought it the right thing to do.[105]

(Repeated to Paris No. 221/2; Rome No. 192/3; Vienna No. 355/6; and St. Petersburg No. 154/5: 'For your own information only.')

BD, XI, No. 116.

(225) 25 July: Szögyény to Berchtold

Berlin urges immediate military operations against Serbia and a *fait accompli*

Telegram 285
Confidential
Berlin, 25 July 1914
D. 2.15 a.m.
R. 8.00 p.m.

With regard to the concluding words in Your Excellency's telegram 258 of yesterday (Count Mensdorff's answer to Sir Edward Grey[106]) I should like to remark that here [in Berlin] it is generally regarded as certain that an unsatisfactory answer by Serbia will immediately be followed by our declaration of war *coupled* with military operations.

Here every delay in the beginning of military operations is seen as signifying danger that other powers might interfere. We are urgently advised to proceed without delay and to place the world before a *fait accompli*.

I entirely share the views of the *Auswärtiges Amt*.

ÖUA, VIII, No. 10656.[107]

105 For Prince Lichnowky's account of this conversation see DD, Nos 179 and 180.
106 ÖUA, VIII, No. 10580 (Berchtold had added the sentence: 'The state of war will only arise after a declaration of war.')
107 Engl. transl. based on Geiss, *July 1914*, No. 71, here with minor amendments.

(226) 25 July: Tisza's report to Kaiser Franz Joseph

Tisza advocates immediate mobilization if Serbian reply unsatisfactory

Budapest, 25 July 1914

The responsibility which is resting on all advisers of the Crown in these decisive days makes it my duty to turn with the sincere request to Your Majesty to order mobilization immediately in case of an insufficient answer from Serbia.[108] Given the contents of our note it seems to me there is no other possible way. The slightest hesitation or wavering would severely impair the impression of the Monarchy's energy and her ability to act, would influence the attitude of our friends and our opponents as well as those undecided elements, and would result in potentially fateful consequences.

ÖUA, VIII, No. 10708.

(227) 25 July: Serbian Government to Giesl

Serbia's reply to the Austro-Hungarian ultimatum

Belgrade, no date

The Royal Serbian Government have received the communication of the Imperial and Royal Government of the 10th [23rd] of this month, and are convinced that their reply will remove any misunderstanding which may threaten to impair the good neighbourly relations between the Austro-Hungarian Monarchy and the Kingdom of Serbia.

Conscious of the fact that the protests which were made both from the tribune of the national Skupština and in the declarations and actions of the responsible representatives of the State – protests which were cut short by the declarations made by the Serbian Government on 18 [31] March 1909 – have not been renewed on any occasion as regards the great neighbouring Monarchy, and that no attempt has been made since that time either by the successive Royal Governments or by their organs to change the political and legal state of affairs created in Bosnia and Herzegovina, the Royal Government draw attention to the fact that in this connection the Imperial and Royal Government have made no representation except one concerning a school book, and that on that occasion the Imperial and

108 See also (**225**) for Germany's views on this.

Royal Government received an entirely satisfactory explanation. Serbia has several times given proofs of her pacific and moderate policy during the Balkan crisis, and it is thanks to Serbia and to the sacrifice that she has made in the exclusive interest of European peace that that peace has been preserved. The Royal Government cannot be held responsible for manifestations of a private character, such as articles in the press and the peaceable work of societies – manifestations which take place in nearly all countries in the ordinary course of events, and which, as a general rule, escape official control. The Royal Government are all the less responsible, in view of the fact that at the time of the solution of a series of questions which arose between Serbia and Austria-Hungary they gave proof of a great readiness to oblige, and thus succeeded in settling the majority of these questions to the advantage of the two neighbouring countries.

For these reasons the Royal Government have been pained and surprised at the statements, according to which members of the Kingdom of Serbia are supposed to have participated in the preparations for the crime committed at Sarajevo; the Royal Government expected to be invited to collaborate in an investigation of all that concerns this crime, and they were ready, in order to prove the entire correctness of their attitude, to take measures against any persons concerning whom representations were made to them. Falling in, therefore, with the desire of the Imperial and Royal Government, they are prepared to hand over for trial any Serbian subject, without regard to his situation or rank, of whose complicity in the crime of Sarajevo proofs are forthcoming, and more specially they undertake to cause to be published on the first page of the *Journal officiel*, on the date of 13/26 July, the following declaration:

'The Royal Government of Serbia condemn all propaganda which may be directed against Austria-Hungary, that is to say, all such tendencies as aim at ultimately detaching from the Austro-Hungarian Monarchy territories which form part thereof, and they sincerely deplore the baneful consequences of these criminal movements. The Royal Government regret that, according to the communication from the Imperial and Royal Government, certain Serbian officers and officials should have taken part in the above-mentioned propaganda, and thus compromised the good neighbourly relations to which the Royal Serbian Government was solemnly engaged by the declaration of 31 March 1909, which declaration disapproves and repudiates all idea or attempt at interference with the destiny of the inhabitants of any part whatsoever of Austria-Hungary, and they consider it their duty formally to warn the officers, officials and entire population of the kingdom that henceforth they will take the most rigorous steps against all such persons as are guilty of such acts, to prevent and to repress which they will use their utmost endeavour.'

This declaration will be brought to the knowledge of the Royal Army in an order of the day, in the name of His Majesty the King, by his Royal Highness the Crown Prince Alexander, and will be published in the next official army bulletin.

The Royal Government further undertake:

1 To introduce at the first regular convocation of the Skupština, a provision into the press law providing for the most severe punishment of incitement to hatred or contempt of the Austro-Hungarian Monarchy, and for taking action against any publication the general tendency of which is directed against the territorial integrity of Austria-Hungary. The Government engage at the approaching revision of the Constitution to cause an amendment to be introduced into article XXII of the Constitution of such a nature that such publication may be confiscated, a proceeding at present impossible under the categorical terms of article XXII of the Constitution.

2 The Government possess no proof, nor does the note of the Imperial and Royal Government furnish them with any, that the *Narodna Odbrana* and other similar societies have committed up to the present any criminal act of this nature through the proceedings of any of their members. Nevertheless, the Royal Government will accept the demand of the Imperial and Royal Government and will dissolve the *Narodna Odbrana* Society and every other society which may be directing its efforts against Austria-Hungary.

3 The Royal Serbian Government undertake to remove without delay from their public educational establishments in Serbia all that serves or could serve to foment propaganda against Austria-Hungary, whenever the Imperial and Royal Government furnish them with facts and proofs of this propaganda.

4 The Royal Government also agree to remove from military service all such persons as the judicial enquiry may have proved to be guilty of acts directed against the integrity of the territory of the Austro-Hungarian Monarchy, and they expect the Imperial and Royal Government to communicate to them at a later date the names and the acts of these officers and officials for the purposes of the proceedings which are to be taken against them.

5 The Royal Government must confess that they do not clearly grasp the meaning or the scope of the demand made by the Imperial and Royal Government that Serbia shall undertake to accept the collaboration of the organs of the Imperial and Royal Government upon their territory, but they declare that they will admit such collaboration as agrees with the principle of international law, with criminal procedure, and with good neighbourly relations.

6 It goes without saying that the Royal Government consider it their duty to open an enquiry against all such persons as are, or eventually may be implicated in the plot of 28 June, and who happen to be within the territory of the Kingdom. As regards the participation in this enquiry of Austro-Hungarian agents or authorities appointed for this purpose by the Imperial and Royal Government, the Royal Government cannot accept such an arrangement, as it would be a violation of the Constitution and of the law of criminal procedure; nevertheless, in concrete cases communications as to the results of the investigation in question might be given to the Austro-Hungarian agents.

7 The Royal Government proceeded, on the very evening of the delivery of the Note, to arrest Commandant Voija Tankosić. As regards Milan Ciganović, who is a subject of the Austro-Hungarian Monarchy and who up to 28 June was employed (on probation) by the directorate of railways, it has not yet been possible to arrest him.

The Austro-Hungarian Government are requested to be so good as to supply as soon as possible, in the customary form, the presumptive evidence of guilt, as well as the eventual proofs of guilt which have been collected up to the present, at the enquiry at Sarajevo for the purposes of the later enquiry.

8 The Serbian Government will reinforce and extend the measures which have been taken for preventing the illicit traffic of arms and explosives across the frontier. It goes without saying that they will immediately order an enquiry and will severely punish the frontier officials on the Schabatz-Loznica line who have failed in their duty and allowed the authors of the crime of Sarajevo to pass.

9 The Royal Government will gladly give explanations of the remarks made by their officials whether in Serbia or abroad, in interviews after the crime which according to the statement of the Imperial and Royal Government were hostile towards the Monarchy, as soon as the Imperial and Royal Government have communicated to them the passages in question in these remarks, and as soon as they have shown that the remarks were actually made by the said officials, although the Royal Government will itself take steps to collect evidence and proofs.

10 The Royal Government will inform the Imperial and Royal Government of the execution of the measures comprised under the above heads, in so far as this has not already been done by the present note, as soon as each measure has been ordered and carried out.

If the Imperial and Royal Government are not satisfied with this reply, the Serbian Government, considering that it is not to the common interest to precipitate the solution of this question, are ready, as always, to accept a pacific understanding, either by referring this question to the decision of the International Tribunal of The Hague, or to the Great

Powers which took part in the drawing up of the declaration made by the Serbian Government on 31 March 1909.[109]

ÖUA, VIII, No. 10648.[110]

(228) 25 July: Czernin to Berchtold

Suggestions from Russia for Rumania to intervene; Rumanian Prime Minister Bratiano suggests negotiations even once Austro-Hungarian troops have entered Serbia

Telegram
Bucharest, 25 July 1914
D. 9 p.m.
R. 26 July 9 a.m.

Secret. Herr Bratiano receives telegram from Petersburg asking if Rumania could not intervene, so that ultimatum would be extended and possibility of accepting the demands would be made easier for Serbia. As the ultimatum was already expired, the Prime Minister added if it might not be possible, following a likely deployment of our troops [into Serbia], to stop and to resume the negotiations while continuing with a provisional occupation, following the assurance that we do not intend to make any lasting annexation.

ÖUA, VIII, No. 10662.

(229) 25 July: Journal of the Russian General Staff Committee

Pre-mobilization period to be declared on 26 July for four military districts

25/12 July 1914

The Chief of the General Staff informed the members of the General Staff Committee that his Majesty the Emperor deigned to declare that it was necessary to support Serbia, even if that required declaring mobilization

109 As Mark Cornwall explains, Pašić and his colleagues agreed that Serbia needed a period of consolidation following the Balkan Wars. The Minister of War, Dušan Stevanović, wanted a 10-year programme to rebuild the army which was in a poor state. Therefore, Pašić was 'bound to act cautiously towards Austria-Hungary' following the ultimatum. In the weeks after the assassination Serbia hoped that with 'a conciliatory yet not wholly submissive stance they could ward off an Austro-Serbian confrontation'. Cornwall, 'Serbia', 58–60.

110 French original. English translation from Geiss, *July 1914*, No. 72.

and starting acts of war, however not before Austrian troops had crossed the Serbian border.

According to news received some preparatory actions for mobilization were already being conducted in Austria-Hungary and Italy. Thus His Majesty the Emperor deigned to confirm the decree of the Council of Ministers that the period prior to mobilization will commence in the night from 25/12 to 26/13 July.

Should it prove necessary to declare mobilization, it is ordered by the highest authority, due to the fact that one had to restrict oneself to actions against Austria alone, to mobilize the military districts of Kiev, Odessa, Kasan and Moscow. The other military districts will only mobilize in case of Germany joining Austria, no sooner, so that greater diplomatic entanglements can be avoided. [...]

Int. Bez. I, 5, No. 79.

(230) 25 July: Szögyény to Berchtold (2)

Italy expresses astonishment at not having been informed as an ally

---

Telegram No. 283
Berlin, 25 July 1914
D 8.45 p.m.
R 26 July 12.30 p.m.

Very confidential

Secretary of State [Jagow] told me today that [Bollati] the Italian Ambassador here had expressed his astonishment that Your Excellency had not told his Government, as an allied Power, sooner about our step in Belgrade. Herr von Jagow replied that Germany had also not been informed by us any earlier[111] which he, Jagow, considered to be the right procedure as the current conflict was to be regarded as a matter between Austria-Hungary and Serbia.

The above will be telegraphed to the German Ambassador in Rome to inform his talks with the addition to add vis-à-vis Marquis [di] San Giuliano if necessary that in the past Italy also had not informed her allies of her 24-hour ultimatum to Turkey.[112]

ÖUA, VIII, No. 10655.

111 This was not true. See for example (**171**).

112 On 28 September 1911 Italy issued an ultimatum to Turkey to agree to Italy's military occupation of Tripolitania and Cyrenaica (today's Libya). Even before the ultimatum expired the next day, Italy began hostilities leading to a war that lasted until October 1912.

(231) 25 July: Lyncker to his wife

Wilhelm II's decision to return home following news that Serbian Government has not accepted all Austro-Hungarian demands

[Balholm, Norway, aboard the *Hohenzollern*]

[…] Today's news sounds serious enough. As was to be expected, Russia has placed herself on Serbia's side, and the Austrian envoy in Belgrade [Giesl] will depart this evening, if the ultimatum has not been answered satisfactorily.[113] This will almost certainly mean war. We are all ready to go home, and we actually should do it straight away. I do not understand why this is not happening. Instead he [Wilhelm II] is torturing himself here.[114] Our fleet, too, is still dispersed up here, however I assume that it will sail home soon and that we will follow speedily. […]

5 o'clock pm [...] On the basis of a telegram from Belgrade the Kaiser has just decided to depart for Cuxhaven in one hour (has since been changed to Kiel). The Serbian Government has seemingly refused to meet the demands made by Austria and intends to move its seat to Niš. That looks worrying enough and we are all glad that we are homeward bound. Perhaps this journey home is for us also the first step towards war. Well, we will survive it honourably. The army is good, at least that is what we think, and will do its duty. Of course, though, it will be a difficult fight with 2 fronts, such as we have not ever had to such an extent.

[Continued on Sunday, 26 July:]

[…] The news received is that yesterday afternoon the entire Serbian army was mobilized[115] and that the Austrian envoy Baron Giesl left Belgrade together with his staff. Thus war seems unavoidable there. On the other hand the Reich-Chancellor reports to the Kaiser that he was busy with England trying to localize the war, that is to limit it to the two powers or, in other words, to keep Russia out. For us everything will depend on whether this will succeed. Judging by the views of the Russian press, it is doubtful.

---

113 See (**191**) and (**227**).

114 The Chancellor had tried to dissuade the Kaiser, bent on cutting short his trip, from returning too early. See DD, No. 193, Bethmann Hollweg to Wilhelm II, 25 July and DD, No. 221, Bethmann Hollweg to Wilhelm II, 26 July. See also John Röhl, *Wilhelm II.*, Vol. III: *Der Weg in den Abgrund, 1900–1941*, Beck, Munich 2008, 2009, pp. 1100ff.

115 Giesl had erroneously informed Vienna that Serbia had mobilized at 3 p.m. Although Belgrade had been on war footing all day and conscripts had been called up, King Alexander did not sign the mobilization order until the evening of 25 July and the official announcement of general mobilization was not made until later that night. See Cornwall, 'Serbia', p. 82.

Cited in Holger Afflerbach, *Kaiser Wilhelm II.*, Oldenbourg, Munich 2005, pp. 128–129.

(232) 26 July: Lothar Freiherr von Ritter to Hertling[116]

Austro-Hungarian ultimatum to Serbia comes as a complete surprise to Paris

Report 318
Paris, 26 July 1914
(arrived 28 July 1914)

The French Government, the French press, and French public opinion have been unimaginably surprised by the handing-over of the Austrian note to the Serb Government.

Following the heated debates on income tax, deputies and senators have turned their backs on the capital and since then Paris has been almost dead.

All the ambassadors, except Freiherr von Schoen, are absent from Paris. The Italian Ambassador, M. Tittoni, is in Iceland.

The ambassadors of the Triple Entente were not in Belgrade and the calming explanations of Count Berchtold for the Russian Ambassador Schebeko in Vienna before the start of his holiday did not lead anyone here to believe in an impending conflict.

The running of the Ministry for Foreign Affairs has been passed to the Minister of Justice, Bienvenu-Martin, who has little experience in foreign policy.

Together with the President of the Council [Poincaré] and the Minister for Foreign Affairs, M. Viviani, the Chief of the Cabinet de Margerie is also taking part in the official trip of the President to Russia and the Scandinavian countries.

M. Cambon in Berlin was about to go on his big summer holiday and on Thursday the press in Paris announced the impending departure of the German Ambassador to Germany.

All this shows how utterly unprepared political circles here were when met with the suddenly arising danger of war. [...]

On the stock exchange the note has created a real panic. [...]

Pius Dirr (ed.), *Bayerische Dokumente zum Kriegsausbruch*, Oldenbourg, Munich and Berlin 1925, No. 31.

116 Report for the attention of King Ludwig III of Bavaria (*Immediatbericht*).

(233) 26 July: Otto Freiherr von Ritter to Hertling[117]

Pope in favour of Austria taking on Serbia and fighting Pan-Slavism

It is the general opinion of the Curia that Austria must now finally be serious with the Serbs so as not to lose the prestige of a Great Power and perhaps also to achieve again a little more respect for the Catholic element in the big looming battle with Slavdom. I am therefore very surprised that in the press here, albeit in the press that is hostile to the Vatican, there was talk of the Pope's mediation attempts in the Austro-Serbian conflict. According to the enquiries I have made these rumours are entirely invented. [...] The Curia is in this case, I would almost say, inclined towards war [*kriegerisch gesinnt*] and if we lived in the times of Julius II it might even be capable of drawing the sword against Slavdom, so great does it consider the danger which threatens the Catholic Church from that quarter.

BayHStA, MA 2568, cited in Jörg Zedler, 'Das Rittertelegramm', in idem (ed.), *Der Heilige Stuhl*, Herbert Utz, Munich 2010, pp. 175–202, p. 194.

(234) 26 July: Benckendorff to Sazonov

Britain still not willing to offer support to Russia and France in case of war; British politics and public opinion absorbed by Ulster question; Grey still hopes for possibility of negotiations

Letter
London, 26/13 July 1914

[...] Grey, who had been absent during the day [...] returns this evening. God willing that your clear and appropriate language will make an impression upon him. He told me further that his language in Berlin would not allow them in any way to reckon on English neutrality in case of war.[118] Lichnowsky was indeed very despondent, but because he bemoans the war. I am not entirely certain that he understood Grey's words as Grey wanted them to be understood. This I now repeat to Grey every day and in all registers. He barricades himself behind hopes

117 Report for the attention of King Ludwig III of Bavaria (*Immediatbericht*).

118 Nonetheless, Germany's decision-makers continued to hope for British neutrality for several more days.

of negotiations. I do not succeed in pushing him further. Unfortunately Cambon is away and will only return on Tuesday morning.[119] I have asked for him to speed up his return. I believe that the decisive factor is that Grey is not certain of public opinion and is worried that he would not find any support if he engaged himself too far. [...]

England, entirely absorbed, completely absorbed by Ulster, is only just waking up.[120] She has known since yesterday that a war is on the cards, she has worried about it since yesterday. But that England could be drawn into it is not understood in England's slow realization process.

This is deplorable, but it is as it is.

It is clear that the eyes are opening more quickly in the Foreign Office, elsewhere not. I do not give up hope to achieve that I can get Grey to lift the mask in these days. I cannot promise you.

I congratulate you wholeheartedly to your attitude, which is heartfelt by me, also your measured language and the caution which you observe with the disposition of our future actions. Very necessary, absolutely necessary to ensure English cooperation for us. Even if it came too late it would be immeasurably valuable. But I repeat that England has not yet woken up sufficiently. It might be possible that Grey suffers under this as we do, which by the way would not benefit matters at all.

If it is true that Austria, as is being said, is not planning on starting the war immediately then there is still a spark of hope. But I am more pessimistic than you regarding Germany's role. And that is what I emphasize here. England is less frightened about Austrian hegemony in the Balkans than by German hegemony in the world. [...].

Int. Bez., I, 5, No. 91.

119 As John Keiger shows, Cambon was unhappy in London and away in Paris as often as possible, including in July 1914. See Keiger, *France and the Origins*, p. 105. He was still in London on 24th, and expected back on Tuesday 28th, which suggests that he spent the weekend in Paris, as was often his habit. (My thanks to John Keiger for helping me to piece together Cambon's movements at that time).

120 See (**198**).

(235) 26 July: Captain Berens to Chief of Russian General Staff Rusin[121]

Assessment of situation from Russian navy's perspective; mood in Berlin anticipates war; Kiel canal widened and allowing quick transfer of ships from Baltic to North Sea; public opinion in Berlin in favour of war

Report

Berlin, 26/13 July 1914
[D. 28 July]

[...] However, due to the fact that I have spent three and a half years here and have during that time experienced several serious political crises I consider it my duty to inform Your Excellency that according to all external signs one has to regard the mood here as very worrying: the press is without difference of party colouring very determinedly in favour of supporting Austria. On the main streets there are continuous demonstrations for Austria and occasionally also demonstrations against us which has never before happened during my stay here.[122] However one has to take into consideration that in the main the youth and often very young people participate in this. The newspapers publish many extra editions which are immediately sold out.

It can be expected that all these worrying signs will increase following tomorrow's return of the Kaiser, who is hurriedly returning from Norway, five days before the originally set date.[123]

The French here, and in particular their naval attaché, are very concerned and regard the situation as extraordinarily serious; today he came to find out if we have any news about the return of the fleet from Norway and asked that we would tell him immediately if we found out anything. Regarding this news our naval agents have already taken measures for our timely update about the main movements of the fleet. At the moment there is no news of the return, a newspaper report just mentioned that yesterday the Dreadnought *Kaiserin* had sailed from the Elbe through the [Kiel] Canal for the first time.[124]

121 Admiral A.I. Rusin, Chief of the Russian Naval General Staff in 1914; became Chief of the Naval Field Staff in 1916.

122 See also (**239**).

123 He arrived back in Potsdam on 27 July. See (**231**), (**266**).

124 The Kiel Canal (or Kaiser Wilhelm Canal) was opened in 1895 and connected the Baltic and the North Seas. In order to accommodate dreadnoughts and allow the German navy to move ships quickly from one potential theatre of war to another, it was necessary to widen the Canal. Its completion, predicted

[…] The local press notes with particular satisfaction England's more than reserved attitude towards the conflict[125] which naturally exceptionally eases Germany's situation.

For now until tomorrow's return of the Kaiser hardly any military measures are to be expected. Nothing has occurred in this regard until now. However one has to bear in mind that their mobilization times are very short and that they need not hurry with their mobilization. As soon as the fleet has returned from Norway some news will probably be available as to their dislocation, although one has to consider that the Canal is now open for all ships and that their movement from one sea to another requires no more than ten to eleven hours. There cannot be any difficulties with the mobilization of the fleet because they have well-trained personnel and the German distances allow for it to be conducted in a short space of time.

[…] I believe that one would be very content to withdraw if a way out of the current situation could be found, but that it is feared here that one had gone too far, and they now pay attention only to what Russia will do and whether one will have to proceed. The huge noise which is being made by demonstrators in the streets […] has of course to be considered, however, I believe that the responsible circles would want to resolve the matter peacefully, of course not without embarrassing Austria much.

[…] The entire press screams that the decision over war and peace is in Russia's hand and that Germany has to fulfil her obligations against Austria.

Persons who have lived here for more than thirty years do not recall such a mood in the streets as it is currently manifesting itself.

Int. Bez., I, 5, No. 99.

---

for the summer of 1914, had been alluded to during the so-called war-council meeting of December 1912 (see (**44**) and (**47**)), and this issue had played a central role in discussion in Berlin since the Agadir Crisis of 1911. On 3 July 1914 the Chief of the Admiralty Staff, Hugo von Pohl, had enquired urgently of the Imperial Naval Office 'whether the state of works at the Kaiser Wilhelm Canal now allows the passage of dreadnoughts and when the planned attempt to pass it will go ahead' (cited in Röhl, *Wilhelm II.*, Vol. 3, p. 1080). Early on 25 July the dreadnought *Kaiserin* successfully undertook the trial passage.

125 See for example (**234**).

(236) 26 July: Grey to Missions in Paris, Vienna, St Petersburg, Niš, Berlin and Rome

British mediation proposal

Telegrams No. 232, 159, 365, 18, 204, 198
London, 26 July 1914
D. 3 p.m.

Ask Minister of Foreign Affairs if he would be disposed to instruct Ambassador here to join with representatives of Italy, Germany, France and myself in a conference to be held here at once in order to endeavour to find an issue to prevent complications. With this view representatives at Vienna, St Petersburg and Belgrade should be authorised in informing Governments to which they are accredited of above suggestion to request that pending results of conference all military operations should be suspended.[126]

BD, XI, No. 140.

(237) 26 July: Nicolson to Grey

British statesmen aware that Germany did not support mediation proposal; Germany convinced that Britain would stand aside

No. 144.
58, Cadogan Gardens, S.W. [London]
26 July 1914

I telegraphed to you[127] an idea which occurred to me after reading Buchanan's telegram No.169.[128] It seems to me the only chance of avoiding a conflict[,] it is I admit a very poor chance[,] but in any case we shall have done our utmost. Berlin is playing with us. Jagow did not really adopt your proposal to intervene at Vienna, and to be backed up by us and France, but simply 'passed on' your suggestion and told his ambassador to speak about it.[129] This is not what was intended or desired. Mensdorff asked to see me this afternoon. It was only to announce officially that

126 For Goschen's reply from Berlin see (**254**). The other replies can be found in BD, XI, Nos 175, 183, 185, 189, 198, 202.

127 See BD, XI, No. 139.

128 See BD, XI, No. 125.

129 This was indeed the case. See DD, I, No. 171.

relations had been broken off with Serbia, and that Serbia was mobilising. He asked me what news we had from St. Petersburg. I told him that the situation was most gravely viewed there, as was natural, but I gave him no details. I saw Benckendorff to whom I read Buchanan's 169. He had no news, but impressed on me that Lichnowsky was convinced we could stand aside and remain neutral[;] an unfortunate conviction as were they to understand that our neutrality was by no means to be counted upon and that we could not be expected to remain indifferent when all Europe was in flames, a restraining influence would be exercised on Berlin.

I have just heard you have approved my proposal[.] I am glad, though I am not hopeful. Still no chance should be neglected.

I lunched with Stamfordham. He told me Prince Henry came over yesterday and breakfasted with the King this morning.[130] Prince Henry said if Russia moved there would be an internal revolution and the dynasty be upset. This is nonsense but it shows how anxious they are to make out to us that Russia will remain quiet and to spread about that we will be equally quiescent[,] a foolish procedure (Prince Henry has gone back to Germany).

BD, XI, No. 144.

(238) 26 July: Henry Wilson's Diary

Serbia has agreed to terms of ultimatum; decision for war depends on Germany

Went to see Sir A. Nicolson and found a lot more dispatches, all warlike. Austria, Russia, and Serbia seem to be going to mobilize, but, so far, no news of Germany moving. Until she moves there is no certainty of war. The Serbians have agreed to almost all the Austrian terms, making it difficult [for] Austria and Germany to have a European war. My own opinion is that if Germany does not mobilize to-day there will be no war.

Cited in Charles E. Callwell, *Field-Marshal Sir Henry Wilson*, 2 vols, Cassell, London 1927, Vol. 1, pp. 151–152.

130 At this meeting Prince Heinrich gained the impression that Britain would remain neutral (**281**). See also DD, No. 207, German naval attaché to Imperial Navy Office: 'King of Britain expressed to Prince Heinrich of Prussia that England would remain neutral if war were to break out among the continental powers'. King George's account does not bear this out (**250**).

(239) 26 July: Bronevski to Sazonov

Anti-Russian demonstrations in Berlin

Telegram
Berlin, 26/13 July 1914

Last night, after the news of Serbia's non-acceptance of the Austrian demands and the mobilization of Serbian troops had been received in Berlin, a large crowd which, according to newspaper reports consisted partly of Austrians, conducted a number of noisy demonstrations of sympathy for Austria. Late in the evening the demonstrators repeatedly got together in front of the building of the Imperial Embassy and exclaimed calls against Russia, while the police was hardly to be seen and, because they were obviously unprepared, also did not adopt any measures. I therefore wrote today to the State-Secretary for Foreign Affairs, alerted [him] to the occurrences [...], and asked him to let me know which measures the police would adopt in future fully to protect the embassy against similar occurrences. Just now the director of the political department of the Foreign Office visited me, gave an official apology for the events on behalf of the German Government and assured me that all measures had been taken so that such cases would not be repeated.

Int. Bez., I, 5, No. 96.

(240) 26 July: San Giuliano to Salandra

Possibility of territorial compensation if Italy plays her cards right

Fiuggi, 26 July 1914
D. 8 p.m.

[...] Immediate decisions are not at all necessary, rather they would be extremely dangerous; for the moment, everybody, at home and abroad, should be left in uncertainty about our attitudes and our decisions in order to try to get some positive advantage. For the first time since the Kingdom of Italy has existed, a German Minister of Foreign Affairs says that it is the right moment to have the Trentino. The only thing I deplore, to achieve success, is the impossibility to get farther than Fiuggi or Vallombrosa! As for demonstrations against the war in association with Austria it seems to me that they can be of more use than harm to our negotiations, but we cannot reassure public opinion and say that we shall not make war at any cost, because in that case we shall not get anything anywhere. Therefore, in my opinion, we must work in silence, speak little, not be too hasty, and stay away from Rome as much as possible.

I am confident that everything will be fine and today's news is also good and I am using it to work for peace. [...]

DDI, 4th series, XII, No. 560.

(241) 26 July: Berchtold to Kral

Berchtold requests spreading of false rumours in Albania

Telegram No. 192
Vienna, 26 July, 3 p.m.
Secret

Declaration of war against Serbia not yet made, but is imminent. I ask your Highness (while avoiding any compromise of your person) to have spread the rumour among Albanian insurgents that the state of war has already occurred, that Belgrade has been deserted by the court and the Government, that Kossovo is entirely devoid of troops and that Austro-Hungarian troops have already crossed the Serbian border.

ÖUA, VIII, No. 10728.

(242) 26 July: Szécsen to Berchtold

French Foreign Office astonished that conciliatory Serbian reply considered inadequate by Vienna

Tel. No. 125
Paris, 26 July 1914
D. 4.20 p.m.
R. 27 July, 11 a.m.

Serbia. In the Ministry of Foreign Affairs I was granted confidential access to a telegram of the French Ambassador in Belgrade which summarized content of Serbian answer which had been shown to him before it was handed over. According to this account Serbia accepts all our wishes without condition, concedes to modifying her press law and merely requests further details regarding the participation of our organs in the investigation in Serbia, which she also accepts in principle. M. Berthelot expressed his astonishment that this answer, which amounts to a total capitulation, was not accepted. I replied that I did not know the text of the Serbian note, but that I suspected that it contained nuances which modified the seemingly accommodating character and which made the answer seem unacceptable. Should Serbia indeed have accepted our wishes without reserve then our intransigent attitude would, I fear, create a very unfavourable impression here. Otherwise M. Berthelot's language was very conciliatory; he expressed the hope that in any case Serbia's very substantial agreement would offer a basis for further negotiations. [...]

ÖUA, VIII, No. 10740.

(243) 26 July: Szápáry to Berchtold

Sazonov considers all but three points of Austrian ultimatum acceptable; suggests alternatives and mediation by Italy or Britain, but Austrian Ambassador advises that it is probably too late

Tel. No. 165
Secret
St Petersburg, 26 July 1914[131]
D. 2.15 p.m.
R. 4.30 p.m.

[...] Our goal, as I had described it to him [Sazonov], was an entirely legitimate one, but he thought that the path which we were following in order to attain it was not the most secure. The Note[132] which we had presented was unfortunate in the state that it was. He had since studied it and if I had time he wanted to go through it once more with me. I remarked that I was at his disposal but that I was neither authorized to discuss the text of the note with him nor to interpret it. His remarks were, however, of interest to me. The Minister then went through all points of the note and considered today 7 of the 10 points to be acceptable

131 According to the official Austrian document edition, this document was dated 27 July. However, as Geiss points out, the conversation between Szápáry and Sazonov took place on 26 July. It is possible, however, that the document was not despatched until the 27th. See Imanuel Geiss, *Julikrise und Kriegsausbruch*, 2 vols, Hanover 1963/64, Vol. 2, p. 19, note 1.

132 The Austro-Hungarian ultimatum (**180**).

without great difficulties, only the 2 points regarding the involvement of *k.u.k.* functionaries in Serbia [points 5 and 6] and the point regarding the dismissal of officers and officials named *ad libitum* by us [point 4] he considered unacceptable in their current state.[133]

As regards point 5 I was able to provide an authentic interpretation along the lines of Your Excellency's telegram No. 172 of 25 July,[134] regarding the other two I expressed that I did not know their interpretation by my Government, but that these two were however necessary demands.

Mr Sazonov suggested that one could, for example, consider an intervention by consuls in the examinations, and regarding the dismissals that evidence would have to be presented against the culprits. Otherwise King Peter would immediately risk being assassinated. I replied that this assessment by the Minister amounted to the best reasons for our Serbian action.

Mr Sazonov said that we must be aware that the Kargeorgević dynasty was likely the last Serbian dynasty and that we did not want to create an anarchic witches' cauldron on our border? – I replied that we were certainly interested in preserving the monarchic state but that this remark by the Minister also proved how necessary it was that we acted accordingly against Serbia.

In summary the Minister declared that he thought that the matter of the note was really just about words and that perhaps a way forward could be found that was agreeable to us as to how to overcome these difficulties. Would we accept the mediation of our ally the King of Italy, or that of the King of England? – I replied that I was not in a position to utter an opinion in this regard, as the disposition of my Government was unknown to me, that matters were in place [*dass die Dinge im Rollen seien*] and that certain things could not be undone. Moreover the Serbs had already mobilized yesterday[135] and what had happened since was not known to me. [...]

ÖUA, VIII, No. 10835.

133 Serbia accepted all points except for No. 5 (**227**).

134 See Berchtold to Szápáry, ÖUA, VIII, No. 10682, 25 July 1914: 'As the involvement of *k.u.k.* functionaries in the suppression of the subversive movement in Serbia (Point 5 of our demands) raised Sazonov's particular objection, will Your Excellency please declare on this point in strict confidence that this interjection merely stemmed from practical considerations and not at all from the intention to affect Serbia's sovereignty. With regard to Point 5 "collaboration" we are thinking of the setting up of a secret "bureau de sûreté" in Belgrade which would function in the manner of similar Russian institutions in Paris and Berlin and co-operate with the Serbian police and administrative body.'

135 For details on Serbia's mobilization see above, p. 358, n. 115.

(244) 26 July: Messimy's Diary

Military plans for mobilization ready; Messimy and Joffre agree to wait for Germany to take first steps

Sunday 26 July – Baron Schoen's third and fourth visits

News has reached us from Vienna and Berlin that the announcement of Austria-Hungary's breaking of ties with Serbia has been greeted in both capitals by delirious demonstrations of enthusiasm for war.

At 9 o'clock this morning, Joffre was in my office, accompanied by Ebener, second-in-command to the Chief of Staff. Ebener brought the *Memento*, updated in April 1914, which details the series of multiple measures to be taken when the political tension intensifies. These are many and diverse and not only deal with the military domain but also civil administration (internal affairs, general security, railways, telecommunication, police headquarters, etc. ...). It will be up to me to take these measures or to ensure they are taken if the situation worsens.

The *Memento* classes them in order of urgency:

Precautionary measures
Surveillance measures
Protective measures
Preliminary organizational measures
Measures for the preparation of operations.

A similar list had already been given to me in 1911, at the onset of political tension after the Agadir Crisis. But, straight away, looking at it on the 26th of July, I notice the list has since been completed, clarified and prepared in the minutest detail. Right now, I fully grasp the remarkable results achieved by the preparation work for mobilization, under General Joffre's methodical input. I wholly congratulate him.

I am in a hurry to recall all soldiers on leave (officers and troops) right away.

[*dialogue follows*]

– 'Are you sure, Sir, that all soldiers on leave have been called back to Germany?'

– 'I have every reason to believe that the information I have gathered on this point is accurate; but I cannot officially confirm it yet. In any case, what does it matter? You are perfectly free to recall soldiers from leave!'

– 'Of course, from both a national and an international point of view, I am totally free to do that. But the game that seems to me to be in play is too serious for us not to be explicitly in agreement. What I mean is that I will not take any measures that might stir up opinion without

first consulting the Cabinet. There, I will back the propositions that you and I will have finalized together – you can count on this – but with one particular condition which is this: I will not decide on any measure that prepares for mobilization if I am not certain beforehand that a similar step has already been taken in Germany.
– I would entirely agree with you if we were not, in this regard, very obviously in a state of legal inferiority compared to the Germans. I need no other proof than the Ludendorff document.'
– 'I know absolutely nothing about this.'
[*dialogue ends*]

Ebener, present during this conversation, then gives me a copy of the document [*factum*] known by this name.[136] It constitutes a general list of measures to be taken in Germany to allow the secret mobilization of the whole nation: by disguising the call up of reservists as routine drafts; by hiding the measures being taken to concentrate forces strategically; and by attacking suddenly, by surprise and forcefully, at one or several unanticipated locations.[137]

I do not hide from Joffre my own surprise at finding myself presented with this document – in truth, such an important one – just when it becomes necessary to draw serious conclusions from it that could have dramatic consequences: either that we are being too hasty and thus overtaking our adversaries who will try to make us look like the aggressors; or that we are losing time and letting Germany take a perilous lead over us.

Joffre and I agree that we will not be the first to take any initiative whatsoever but that we will carry out, without the slightest delay, all precautionary measures corresponding to those being taken by our enemies. I must admit that while, on Belgium's side, our intelligence service has been non-existent and appalling, the Intelligence Office in Nancy and even more so that of Belfort, have admirably carried out their task.

During the daytime of the 26th July, I gave the order for officers to be recalled from leave and for all regiments on manoeuvres who can return to their garrisons by road to do so – in other words, without any use of rail transport which would inevitably be seen as preparation for mobilization.

---

136 This was apparently, according to the editors of DDF, a secret German report from 1913, by Erich Ludendorff, written in order to obtain agreement for further army increases from the Reichstag. It is, however, more likely that this was a document drafted by Ludendorff and Moltke in December 1912 when they were trying to convince the Chancellor of the need for more army increases. For this purpose, they revealed for the first time their strategic intentions for a future war. See Annika Mombauer, *Helmuth von Moltke*, Cambridge University Press, Cambridge 2001, p. 158, and (**49**).

137 Comment from the editors of DDF: 'This is exactly, to the letter, the plan for the surprise attack of Liège.'

But contrary to General Joffre's opinion, the Cabinet agrees with me that we must delay recalling soldiers on leave, of whom there are very many during this period of the farming year – 6000 in the 2nd Army Corps, 8 500 in the 6th Army Corps, 6 600 in the 20th Army Corps, etc. ... almost 100,000 throughout the whole country.

This very Sunday Baron Schoen made two consecutive visits to the Quai d'Orsay. At 5 p.m. he saw the Minister, then, coming back at 7 p.m., he went to see Philippe Berthelot who was acting as chef de cabinet.[138] In short, he is asking France to hold back Russia, but he refuses to understand that we are asking Germany for the same thing with regard to its ally in Vienna.

The memory of this splendid Sunday remains vivid in my memory. Late in the evening, I walked home along the river; groups of happy people were coming out of the Orsay railway station with their arms full of flowers and plants.

I feel awfully anxious when I think that the Kaiser's insane pride will perhaps unleash a bloody and horrifying cataclysm on this world that as yet suspects nothing. [...]

Adolphe Messimy, *Mes Souvenirs*, Librairie Plon, Paris 1937, pp. 131–135.

(245) 26 July: Berthelot's note for Bienvenu-Martin

French incredulity about Germany's alleged ignorance of ultimatum; German Ambassador reaffirms Germany has not been consulted by Vienna and confirms Germany's peaceful intentions

Paris, Sunday evening, 26 July 1914.

After his visit to the Minister at 5.00 p.m., Baron Schoen went at 7.00 p.m. this evening to the Political Director's office in order to ask whether a short communiqué on the interview of the German Ambassador and the Minister of Foreign Affairs could be given to the press in order to avoid tendentious commentaries in newspapers, such as that of the *Echo de Paris* from the day before, and so as to properly outline the meaning of the German Government's actions.

M. de Schoen suggested, to clarify his thinking, the following terms which the Political Director noted as it was being dictated: 'The Ambassador of Germany and the Minister of Foreign Affairs have had a new meeting this afternoon in the course of which they examined, in the most

138 This was not correct. Berthelot was actually assistant political director at the French Ministry for Foreign Affairs, standing in for Margerie while he was abroad. I am grateful to John Keiger for this information.

friendly spirit and in an ambiance of peaceful solidarity, the means that could be employed for the maintenance of general peace.'

The Acting Political Director replied immediately: 'So you offer assurance that Austria will accept the Serbian note or will participate in conversations with the Powers in this respect?' The Ambassador having appeared surprised and having denied this, it was put to him that if Germany's negative attitude had not changed, the terms of the suggested note to the press were excessive and of a kind to give false security to French public opinion by creating illusions about the actual situation, the dangers of which were only too obvious.

The German Ambassador gave lavish assurances of the optimistic impression he had formed, to which the Acting Political Director replied by asking if he might speak to him in a very personal and private capacity, man to man, quite freely and without regard to their respective duties. Baron von Schoen urged him to do so.

The Director then said that, to any simple mind, Germany's attitude could only be explained if it was set on going to war: a purely objective analysis of the facts and the psychology of Austro-German relations logically led to this conclusion. In view of the repeated statement that Germany was ignorant of the Austrian note's contents, it was no longer permissible to raise any doubts on that point, but was it likely that Germany would, with her eyes closed, have fallen in with Austria on such a venture? Did the insight gained from all Vienna and Berlin's past relations allow it to be supposed that Austria had taken up a position without any possible retreat, before having weighed up with her ally all the consequences of her uncompromising attitude? Germany's refusal to advise Vienna to take a moderate line seemed very surprising, now that she knew the extraordinary contents of the Austrian note! What responsibility would the German Government take, and what suspicions would weigh on them if they persisted in intervening between Austria and the Powers, after what could be called the absolute submission of Serbia, when the slightest advice given by them to Vienna would put an end to the nightmare that was weighing on Europe! The breaking off of diplomatic relations by Austria, her threats of war and the mobilization she is undertaking make Germany's peacekeeping work particularly urgent, because on the day that Austrian troops cross the Serbian frontier, we will be faced with a fact that would no doubt oblige the Cabinet in St Petersburg to intervene, and would risk unleashing a war that Germany says she wants to avoid.

Herr von Schoen, who listened smiling, once more affirmed that Germany had been ignorant of the text of the Austrian note, and had approved it after its delivery because Serbia needed to be taught a lesson she would not forget, and Austria owed it to herself to put an end to a situation which was intolerable for a Great Power. He declared, moreover, that he had no knowledge of the content of Serbia's reply to the note, and he was personally surprised that it had not satisfied Austria, if, that is, the newspapers, so often badly informed, had accurately represented it. He insisted again on Germany's peaceful intentions and on the effect that good advice might have if given in a friendly way to Vienna, for example, by England. According to him Austria was not uncompromising; what she rejects is the idea of formal mediation, the spectre of a conference. A peaceful word from St Petersburg, or sensible words said in a conciliatory tone by the Powers of the Triple Entente, would stand a good chance of being well received. He added, finally, that he was not saying Germany would not give some advice in Vienna.

Under these conditions, the Political Director said he would ask the Minister to allow him to send a short, moderate note to the press.[139]

DDF, 3e série, 11, No. 109.

(246) 26 July: Paléologue to Bienvenu-Martin

Russian mobilization of the Army Corps of the military districts Kiev, Odessa, Kazan and Moscow; intention to leave to Germany the initiative of an attack on Russia

Telegram No. 288
St Petersburg, 26 July 1914
D. 1.55 p.m.
R. 4.00 p.m.

To the Minister of War, on behalf of General Laguiche:

Yesterday at Krasnoe Sélo, the Minister of War confirmed the mobilization of the army corps from Kiev, Odessa, Kazan and Moscow. One is anxious to avoid any measures that could be interpreted as directed against Germany, however, the military districts of Varsovie, Vilna and Petersburg are taking secret precautionary measures.

The cities and governments of Petersburg and Moscow are declared to be under martial law. Following the decree is a list of subjects newspapers must not mention which, in fact, only targets reports which deal with military issues.

The commissioning of young officers which normally takes place on

139 For Schoen's accounts of this meeting, see DD, Nos 240 and 241. During his conversation with Berthelot, Schoen gained the impression that Viviani would be willing to attempt to exert a calming influence on Russia if Germany were willing to advise Vienna to restrain herself. DD, No. 241.

the 10th August, was carried out as a matter of urgency yesterday evening at 6pm at the same time as the order was given to break camp at Krasnoe. At this very moment all troops are heading back to their winter garrisons. The Minister of War has reiterated that he intends to leave it up to Germany to carry out any initial attack on Russia. The information coming from Berlin is that they would be willing to take this initiative.[140]

Yesterday evening, at the theatre in Krasnoe Sélo, rumours of mobilization having filtered through the military milieu, the Emperor was given an enthusiastic welcome.

DDF, 3e série, 11, No. 89.

(247) 26 July: Carlotti to San Giuliano

Paléologue convinced of unavoidability of war; France would fulfil her alliance duty

St Petersburg, 26 July 1914
D. 12.40 a.m.
R. 1.30 p.m.
Telegram 824/11

The French Ambassador [Paléologue] reassured me that this morning's Council of Ministers, under Sukomlikov's proposal, has specified all the directives and arrangements for war, now considered imminent, against Austria and Germany. He added that France is ready to do her full duty as an ally. When I asked him whether he considered the situation as irreparable, he answered that, in his opinion, the question does not present itself anymore as exclusively Austro-Serbian, but as German-Russian and that the attitude of the Cabinet of Berlin, inaccessible to any idea of reconciliation, shows its firm intention to provoke war [...].[141]

140 In reply, Messimy wrote on 27 July to Laguiche: 'I urge you with all my might that, in spite of the slowness of the Russian mobilization, the Tsar's armies should as soon as possible take the offensive in East Prussia.' Cited in Turner, 'Russian Mobilization', p. 263. This urgency arose from the military convention between France and Russia, and from the fact that it was well known that Germany's strategic plan would require her to fight with most of her troops in the West first. Turner concludes that the pressure France put on Russia on 27 and 28 July drove the Russian General Staff to demand general mobilization. Paléologue added his own pressure, despite the fact that he had been instructed by Viviani, now on board the *France*, to make every effort to secure a peaceful outcome. Turner, p. 264.

141 Missing group in the telegram.

He answered that the facts will prove his assertion, but that, nevertheless, the Triple Entente, while certain of the futility of its efforts, will do all in its power to avert a European catastrophe or at least, to make it clear on whom the terrible responsibility rests. Paléologue concluded by noting that the only gleam of hope comes again from London or Rome where they are perhaps thinking to take advantage of their great influence over Berlin to attempt to bring some peace.

DDI, 4th series, XII, No. 537.

(248) 26 July: Bunsen to Grey (1)

Tschirschky believes that Russians will not become involved in war between Austria-Hungary and Serbia; claims that Serbia ordered mobilization before sending reply to Vienna

Tel. (No. 106.)
Vienna, 26 July 1914.
D. 7 p.m.
R. 10 p.m.

Confidential.

German Ambassador [Tschirschky] has expressed to me his confidential belief that Russia, having received assurance that Austria-Hungary will annex no Serbian territory, will keep quiet during chastisement which Austria-Hungary is determined to inflict on Serbia.[142] I asked if he did not think public opinion might compel Russian Government to intervene on behalf of kindred nationality. He said that days of Pan-Slav agitation in Russia were over. Moscow was perfectly quiet, and everything depended on personality of Russian Minister for Foreign Affairs, who could easily resist, if he chose, pressure of a few newspapers. His Excellency did not think Russian Minister for Foreign Affairs would be so imprudent as to take step which would probably bring into melting-pot many frontier questions in which Russia was interested, such as Swedish, Polish, Ruthene, Rumanian, and Persian questions. Nor was France at all in a condition to face war.[143]

I said that I thought that the Austro-Hungarian Government had made matters a little difficult for other Powers by the tone of ultimatum to Serbia, with many requirements of which one naturally sympathised if only they had been expressed in a more temperate manner. German

142 (**268**).

143 For Senator Humbert's revelations, see Chapter 7, p. 252, n. 34.

Ambassador said that it was impossible to speak to Serbia effectively in any other way. Germany knew very well what she was about in backing up Austria-Hungary in this matter. Serbia required lesson and was about to receive one, but there ought to be no extension of the quarrel to other countries; Russia had no right to assume protectorate over Serbia, and he doubted her acting as if she made any such claim.

Italian Ambassador says that the German Ambassador has held exactly the same language to him, and that it is founded on similar opinions of both German and Austrian Ambassadors at St. Petersburg. Italian Ambassador fears that it is oversanguine as to Russian inaction.

German Ambassador asked me if I had heard that Serbian Government had made a pretence of giving way at the last moment. His Excellency had heard of a letter which you had addressed to the German Ambassador [in London] yesterday hoping that the Serbian concessions would be regarded as satisfactory.[144] I said that I had heard that Serbia had been willing to give in practically on every point. He said that it was all a sham, for Serbia had ordered mobilisation and retirement of Government from Belgrade before making her offer,[145] thus proving that she well knew it to be insufficient to satisfy legitimate demands of Austria-Hungary.[146]

MINUTES

This is only Herr v. Tschirschky. E. A. C[rowe]. July 27.
That is all and he is spreading the belief that Russia will keep quiet if no annexations occur! How little can he grasp the real situation. A. N[icolson].

BD, XI, No. 150.

144 BD, XI, No. 115: Grey wrote to Lichnowsky: 'I enclose a forecast that I have just received of the Serbian reply. It seems to me that it ought to produce a favourable impression at Vienna, but it is difficult for anybody but an ally to suggest to the Austrian Government what view they should take of it. I hope that if the Serbian reply when received in Vienna corresponds to this forecast, the German Government may feel able to influence the Austrian Government to take a favourable view of it.'

145 Serbia had ordered full mobilization on 25 July, and the Government relocated to Niš. See above, p. 358, n. 115.

146 This point is also made by Clark, *Sleepwalkers*, who considers the Serbian reply 'a highly perfumed rejection on most points', rather than largely an acceptance of the Austrian demands, as is usually maintained (pp. 465–466). For Serbia's answer to Austria-Hungary see (**227**).

(249) 26 July: Bunsen to Grey (2)

News about Austro-Hungarian mobilization measures

Tel. No. 108
Vienna, 26 July 1914
D. July 26, 12 midnight.
R. July 27, 9:30 a.m.

Military attaché's information is that mobilisation will be completed 31st July, and concentration near the Serbian frontier about 5th August. Russian Ambassador, just returned from leave, does not propose to press for more time in sense of last paragraph of your telegram No. 153 of 25th July.[147] He thinks that the Austro-Hungarian Government are determined on war, and that Russia cannot possibly remain indifferent. French and Russian Ambassadors were with me when repetition of your telegram No. 232 of 26th July to Paris arrived.[148] I informed them of its content, with which they both expressed their great satisfaction, though doubting if either Austro-Hungarian Government or German Government would accept the principle that Russia is an interested party entitled to have a say in the settlement of a purely Austro-Serbian dispute.

Italian Ambassador was also instructed to support Russian request for postponement of time limit, but too late to take any useful action. Italian Ambassador expressed to me in confidence his strong disapprobation of terms of ultimatum, and generally of Austro-Hungarian policy regarding Serbia.

(Repeated to Embassies.)

BD, XI, No. 166.

(250) 26 July: King George's record of his conversation with Prince Henry

George V's last meeting with Prince Henry; King hopes Britain can stay neutral but does not promise neutrality

Prince Henry of Prussia came to see me on Sunday July 26 at 9.30 a.m. and asked me if there was any news.[149] I said the news was very bad &

147 BD, XI, No. 118: Grey's suggestion that the Russian Ambassador at Vienna should ask for an extension of the time limit given to Serbia.

148 See (**236**).

149 Prince Heinrich [Henry, Kaiser Wilhelm's brother] visited England from 25–27 July. He gives a different account of the meeting in (**281**).

it looked like a European war & that he better go back to Germany at once. He said he would go down to Eastbourne to see his sister (Queen of Greece) & he would return to Germany that evening. He then asked what England would do if there was a European war. I said 'I don't know what we shall do, we have no quarrel with anyone & I hope we shall remain neutral. But if Germany declared war on Russia, & France joins Russia, then I am afraid we shall be dragged into it. But you can be sure that I and my Government will do all we can to prevent a European war!' He then said – 'Well, if our two countries shall be fighting on opposite sides, I trust that it will not affect our personal friendship'. He then shook hands & left the room, having been with me for about eight minutes.[150]

Cited in Harold Nicolson, *King George V*, 2nd edn, Constable, London 1967, p. 327.

(251) 27 July: Lichnowsky to Jagow

Serbia has agreed to almost all Austrian demands; Grey irritated with Germany and expects her to intervene

Telegram 164
London, 27 July 1914
D. 1.31 p.m.
R. 4.37 p.m.

Sir E. Grey had me call on him just now and requested me to inform Your Excellency as follows:

The Serbian Chargé d'Affaires had just transmitted to him the text of the Serbian reply to the Austrian note. It appeared from the reply that Serbia had agreed to the Austrian demands to an extent such as he would never have believed possible; except in one point, the participation of

150 The King's diary for that day only recorded 'Henry of Prussia came to see me early: he returns at once to Germany' (Harold Nicolson, *King George V*, Constable, London 1967 [1952], p. 327), and it is likely that the King's record of his conversation, written on a loose piece of paper, was written later when the importance of what had been said became clear. Nicolson notes that Lichnowsky's official report of the conversation merely stated that the King expressed the hope that the crisis would be resolved peacefully. The German Naval Attaché Captain Erich von Müller had, however, spread the rumour that the British King had assured Prince Heinrich of Britain's neutrality. See Nicolson, *King George V*, p. 328. For a detailed discussion, see also Röhl, *Wilhelm II.*, Vol. 3, pp. 1122ff.

Austrian officials in the judicial investigation, Serbia had actually agreed to everything that had been demanded of her.[151] It was plain that this compliance of Serbia's *was to be attributed solely to the pressure exerted from St Petersburg.*[152]

Should Austria fail to be satisfied with this reply, or rather should this reply not be accepted by Vienna as a foundation for peaceful negotiations, or should Austria even proceed to the occupation of Belgrade, which lay quite defenceless before her, it would then be absolutely evident that Austria was only seeking an excuse for crushing Serbia. And thus that Russia and Russian influences in the Balkans were to be struck at through Serbia. It was plain that Russia could not regard such action with equanimity, and would have to perceive it as a direct challenge. The result would be the most frightful war that Europe had ever seen, and no one could tell where such a war might lead.

We had repeatedly, even yesterday, turned to him with the request to *make a plea for moderation at St Petersburg,* stated the Minister. *He had always gladly complied with this request* and during the last crisis had subjected himself to reproaches from Russia to the effect that he was placing himself too much on our side and too little on theirs. Now he was turning to us with the request that we should make use of our influence at Vienna either to get them to accept the reply from Belgrade as satisfactory or as the basis for negotiations. He was convinced that it lay in our hands to bring the matter to a settlement by means of the relevant representations, and he would regard it as a good augury for the future *if the two of us should once again succeed in assuring the peace of Europe by means of our mutual influence on our allies.*[153]

I found the Minister irritated for the first time. He spoke with great seriousness and seemed absolutely to expect that we should successfully make use of our influence to settle the matter. He is also going to make a statement in the House of Commons today[154] in which he is to express his point of view. In any event, I am convinced that in case it should come to war after all, we should no longer be able to count on

151 See (**227**) and (**242**).

152 '?' added in the margin of the Kaiser's copy. See (**200**). Mark Cornwall argues that 'there is no evidence that Russian advice substantially altered the terms of Serbia's reply'. 'Serbia', p. 77. He also shows that Albertini wrongly claimed that Serbia was prepared to accept all conditions until encouraged to offer resistance by Russia. See also Luigi Albertini, *Origins of the War of 1914*, 3 vols, Oxford University Press, Oxford 1952–1957, Vol. II, p. 352.

153 See also DD, I, No. 179, Lichnowsky to Jagow, 25 July: 'I would like to draw attention again to the importance of Grey's suggestion of mediation of the four [of us] with Austria and Russia. In my opinion this is the only possibility of avoiding a world war in which we risk everything and will gain nothing.'

154 See (**257**).

British sympathy or British support, one would perceive every evidence of ill-will in Austria's procedure. Also, everybody here is convinced, and I hear it also from the mouths of all my colleagues, that the key to the situation is to be found in Berlin, and that, if peace is seriously desired there, Austria can be restrained from prosecuting, as Sir E. Grey expresses it, a foolhardy policy.[155]

DD, No. 258.[156]

(252) 27 July: Pourtalès to Jagow

Relaying information gleaned by German military attaché Eggeling in a conversation with Sukhomlinov on 26 July; Germans assured that no military measures decided against them; Russians still hopeful for mediation

St Petersburg, 27 July
D. 1 a.m.
R. 2.35 a.m.

The military attaché reports on a conversation with the Minister of War: Sazonov had asked him [Sukhomlinov] to inform me about the military situation. The Minister of War gave me his word of honour that no mobilization order had yet been issued. At the moment only preparatory measures had been ordered, not a horse was being requisitioned, not a reservist called up. If Austria crosses the Serbian border the military districts directed against Austria, those of Kiev, Odessa, Moscow, [and] Kasan, will be mobilized. Under no circumstances on the German front, Warsaw, Vilna, Petersburg. They wished urgently for peace with Germany.

In answer to my question as to the object of the mobilization against Austria, he shrugged his shoulders and indicated the diplomats. I told the Minister that we appreciated the friendly intentions but that even a mobilization against Austria alone would be regarded as very threatening. Minister reiterated expressly and repeatedly urgent desire and wish for peace.

Had impression of great nervousness and concern. Consider the wish for peace genuine, military information in so far correct that complete

155 For Germany's responses see Bethmann Hollweg's reply in Geiss, *July 1914*, No. 101, and (**254**). For a later summary of this conversation, see Karl Max Prince Lichnowsky, *My Mission to London, 1912–14*, Cassell, London 1918, pp. 34–35.

156 Engl. transl. based on Geiss, *July 1914*, No. 97, here with minor amendments.

mobilization has probably not been ordered but preparatory measures are very far reaching. They are evidently striving to gain time for new negotiations and for continuing of armaments. Also the internal situation is unmistakably causing serious anxiety. Underlying mood, hope for Germany and for H.M's mediation.

DD, No. 242.

(253) 27 July: Bertie to Grey

French Government accepts British mediation proposal

Tel. No. 88
Paris, 27 1914
D. 2:45 p.m.
R. 4:45 p.m.

Your telegrams Nos. 232 and 234 of yesterday: Austria and Serbia.

French Government accept your proposal and have sent instructions accordingly to French Ambassador in London, who returns there this evening. French Ambassador in Berlin instructed to concert with British Ambassador as to advisability of joining him in speaking to the German Government. French representatives at Vienna, St. Petersburg and Belgrade have also received necessary instructions, but Ministry for Foreign Affairs thinks that it would be dangerous for Entente Ambassadors to speak at Vienna until it is known that Germans have done so with some success.

Ministry for Foreign Affairs gathers from German Ambassador that Austrians are particularly suspicious of words 'intervention', 'mediation' and 'conference' and suggests therefore that care should be taken to speak of conversations, moderating advice, &c.

(Repeated to Embassies and Niš.)

BD, XI, No. 183.

(254) 27 July: Goschen to Grey

Germany rejects British mediation proposal

Telegram No. 96
Berlin, 27 July 1914
D. 6.17 p.m.

R. 9 p.m.

Your telegram 232 of 26 July to Paris.[157]

Secretary of State for Foreign Affairs [Jagow] says that conference you suggest[158] would practically amount to a court of arbitration and could not, in his opinion, be called together except at the request of Austria and Russia. He could not therefore, desirous though he was to co-operate for the maintenance of peace, fall in with your suggestion. I said I was sure that your idea had nothing to do with arbitration, but meant that representatives of the four nations not directly interested should discuss and suggest means for avoiding a dangerous situation. He maintained, however, that such a conference as you proposed was not practicable. He added that news he had just received from St. Petersburg showed that there was an intention on the part of M. Sazonov to exchange views with Count Berchtold. He thought that this method of procedure might lead to a satisfactory result, and that it would be best, before doing anything else, to await outcome of the exchange of views between the Austrian and Russian Governments.

In the course of a short conversation Secretary of State for Foreign Affairs said that as yet Austria was only partially mobilising, but that if Russia mobilised against Germany [the] latter would have to follow suit. I asked him what he meant by "mobilising against Germany". He said that if Russia only mobilised in south[,] Germany would not mobilise, but if she mobilised in north Germany would have to do so too, and Russian system of mobilisation was so complicated that it might be difficult exactly to locate her mobilisation. Germany would therefore have to be very careful not to be taken by surprise.

Finally, Secretary of State said that news from St. Petersburg had caused him to take more hopeful view of the general situation.

(Repeated to Embassies and Niš.)

MINUTE

So far as we know, the German Government has up to now said not a single word at Vienna in the direction of restraint or moderation. If a word had been said, we may be certain that the German Government would claim credit for having spoken at all. The inference is not reassuring as to Germany's goodwill.

At the same time the rapid succession of fresh proposals and suggestions coming from St. Petersburg made it easier for Germany to find fresh excuses for her inactivity. E. A. C[rowe]. July 28.

BD, XI, No. 185.

157 See (**236**).
158 See (**251**).

(255) 27 July: Rodd to Grey

Italy supports British conference proposal

Tel. No. 125
Rome, 27 July 1914
D. July 27, 9:15 p.m.
R. July 28, noon.

My telegram No. 123 of 26th July: Austria and Serbia.[159]

I have just seen Minister for Foreign Affairs, who has returned to Rome. He greatly doubts whether Germany will be willing to invite Austria to suspend military action pending conference, but had hope that military action may be practically deferred by fact of conference meeting at once. He does not, as at present informed, see any possibility of Austria receding from any point laid down in note to Serbia, but believes that if Serbia will even now accept it Austria will be satisfied, and if she had reason to think such will be advice of Powers, Austria may defer action. Serbia may be induced to accept note in its integrity on advice of four Powers invited to conference. This would save her face in allowing her to think she had yielded to Europe and not to Austria alone.

This is also view of Serbian agent here, provided some explanation could be given as to how points 5 and 6 of conditions would be applied.

Minister for Foreign Affairs assured me both before and after communication of note and again to-day he has assurances from Austria that she demands no territorial sacrifices from Serbia. [...][160]

(Repeated to Embassies and Niš)

BD, XI, No. 202.

159 See BD, XI, No. 148.

160 See also Arthur Nicolson's note of a conversation with the Italian Ambassador in London that day: 'The Italian Ambassador informs me that the Italian M[inistry of] F[oreign] A[ffairs] entirely agrees with you as to a Conference à quatre here. As to question of asking Russia, Austria and Serbia to suspend military operations pending results of the Conference he would recommend it warmly to Berlin and he will enquire of the Cabinet of Berlin as to the procedure to be followed at Vienna.' BD, XI, No. 189.

(256) 27 July: Bunsen to Grey

Austrian Government not willing to accept British conference proposal and determined to have a war with Serbia

Tel. No. 109
Vienna, 27 July 1914
D. 1 p.m.
R. 2:45 p.m.

After conversations with all my colleagues of the Great Powers, I believe that Austria- Hungary is fully determined on war with Serbia, that she believes her position as a Great Power is at stake, that her note was drawn up so as to make war inevitable, and that she is unlikely to listen to proposals for mediation until punishment has been inflicted on Serbia. If Russian Ambassador is rightly informed, effort of Germany to isolate conflict must fail, as he believes that Russia will be compelled to act. Postponement or prevention of war with Serbia would undoubtedly be a great disappointment in this country, which has gone wild with joy at prospect of war. Italian Ambassador is greatly concerned, and is casting about for a means of circumscribing conflict which he regards as inevitable. He asked me this morning if I thought following might be usefully proposed:

Austria to repeat to Powers in form of positive engagement promise already made to Russia to the effect that she desires neither to annex any territory nor to crush Serbia, nor to deprive her of her independence, but merely to obtain guarantees for future.[161]

His Excellency thought that possibly Russia might consent to keep quiet. He would think it over and perhaps communicate with Italian Minister for Foreign Affairs as to terms of possible formula. He begged that his name might not be mentioned as having thrown out this suggestion, which was still in a very crude form.

I informed his Excellency of proposal you are making for a conference of less interested Powers in London. He spoke gratefully of your efforts for peace, which had been so useful before, but feared that proposed inclusion of Russia among the directly interested Powers would be obstacle to acceptance.

Minister for Foreign Affairs cannot receive me till 11 a.m. tomorrow. Unless you have any special directions to send me, I propose to express hope of His Majesty's Government that war may yet be avoided, and to ask whether his Excellency cannot suggest even now way out.

161 See also (**268**).

(Repeated to Paris No. 245; Berlin No. 209; Rome No. 204; St. Petersburg No. 378; Belgrade (Niš) No. 22.)

BD, XI, No. 175

(257) 27 July: Grey to Goschen

Grey warns of consequences if conflict escalates into European war; Serbia's reply more accommodating than expected; moderation now required in Vienna

Foreign Office, 27 July 1914.
Tel. (No. 208.)
D. 3 P.M.

German Ambassador has informed me that German Government accept in principle mediation between Austria and Russia by the four Powers, reserving, of course, their right as an ally to help Austria if attacked.[162] He has also been instructed to request me to use influence in St. Petersburg to localise the war and to keep up the peace of Europe.

I have replied that the Serbian reply went further than could have been expected to meet the Austrian demands. German Minister for Foreign Affairs has himself said that there were some things in the Austrian note that Serbia could hardly be expected to accept. I assumed that Serbian reply could not have gone as far as it did unless Russia had exercised conciliatory influence at Belgrade,[163] and it was really at Vienna that moderating influence was now required. If Austria put the Serbian reply aside as being worth nothing and marched into Serbia, it meant that she was determined to crush Serbia at all costs, being reckless of the consequences that might be involved. Serbian reply should at least be treated as a basis for discussion and pause. I said German Government should urge this at Vienna.

I recalled what German Government had said as to the gravity of the situation if the war could not be localised, and observed that if Germany assisted Austria against Russia it would be because, without any reference to the merits of the dispute, Germany could not afford to see Austria crushed. Just so other issues might be raised that would supersede the dispute between Austria and Serbia, and would bring other Powers in, and the war would be the biggest ever known; but as long as Germany would work to keep the peace I would keep closely in touch. I repeated

162 For a different account see (**254**).
163 See p. 377, n. 146, on how this was not the case.

that after the Serbian reply it was at Vienna that some moderation must be urged.

(Repeated to Paris No. 241/2; Vienna No. 165/6; Rome No. 202/3; and St. Petersburg No. 375/6: 'You should inform M[inister] F[oreign] A[ffairs].'[164]

BD, XI, No. 176.

(258) 27 July: Grey addresses the House of Commons

Grey informs the House of proposed conference in London to solve the crisis; consequences of an extension of the dispute beyond Austria and Serbia would be catastrophic

Mr. Bonar Law: I rise to ask the Foreign Secretary a question of which I have given him notice: whether he would communicate any information to the House as to the situation which exits between Austria and Serbia?

The Secretary of State for Foreign Affairs (Sir E. Grey): The House will, of course, be aware, through the public Press of what the nature of the situation in Europe is at this moment. I think that it is due to the House that I should give in short narrative form the position which His Majesty's Government have so far taken up.

Last Friday morning I received from the Austro-Hungarian Ambassador the text of the communication made by the Austro-Hungarian Government to the Powers, which has appeared in the Press, and which included textually the demand made by the Austro-Hungarian Government upon Serbia.[165]

In the afternoon I saw other Ambassadors, and expressed the view that, as long as the dispute was one between Austria-Hungary and Serbia alone, I felt that we had no title to interfere, but that, if the relations between Austria-Hungary and Russia became threatening, the question would then be one of the peace of Europe: a matter that concerned us all.[166]

I did not then know what view the Russian Government had taken of the situation, and without knowing how things were likely to develop I could not make any immediate proposition, but I said that, if relations between Austria-Hungary and Russia did become threatening, the only

164 For Prince Lichnowsky's account of this conversation see DD No. 258. See also the British aide-mémoire to Sasonov of 28 July in *Int. Bez.*, No. 161.
165 See (**180**).
166 See (**220**), (**221**), (**222**), (**224**).

chance of peace appeared to me to be that the four Powers Germany, France, Italy, and Great Britain, who were not directly interested in the Serbian question should work together both in St. Petersburg and Vienna simultaneously to get both Austria-Hungary and Russia to suspend military operations while the four Powers endeavoured to arrange settlement.

After I had heard that Austria-Hungary had broken off diplomatic relation with Serbia, I made by telegraph yesterday afternoon the following proposal, as a practical method of applying the views that I had already expressed:[167]

I instructed His Majesty's Ambassadors in Paris, Berlin and Rome to ask the Governments to which they were accredited whether they would be willing to arrange that the French, German and Italian Ambassadors in London should meet me in a Conference to be held in London immediately to endeavour to find a means of arranging the present difficulties. At the same time, I instructed His Majesty's Ambassadors to ask those Governments to authorise their representatives in Vienna, St. Petersburg and Belgrade to inform the Governments there of the proposed Conference and to ask them to suspend all active military operations pending the result of the Conference.

To that I have not yet received complete replies, and it is, of course, a proposal in which the co-operation of all four Powers is essential. In a crisis so grave as this, the efforts of one Power alone to preserve the peace must be quite ineffective.

The time allowed in this matter has been so short that I have had to take the risk of making a proposal without the usual preliminary steps of trying to ascertain whether it would be well received. But, where matters are so grave and the time so short, the risk of proposing something that is unwelcome or ineffective cannot be avoided. I cannot but feel, however, assuming that the text of the Serbian reply as published this morning in the Press is accurate,[168] as I believe it to be, that it should at least provide a basis on which a friendly and impartial group of Powers, including Powers who are equally in the confidence of Austria-Hungary and of Russia, should be able to arrange a settlement that would be generally acceptable.

It must be obvious to any person who reflects upon the situation that the moment the dispute ceases to be one between Austria-Hungary and Serbia and becomes one in which another Great Power is involved, it can but end in the greatest catastrophe that has ever befallen the Continent of Europe at one blow: no one can say what would be the limit of the issues that might be raised by such a conflict, the consequences of it,

167 See (**236**).
168 See (**227**).

direct and indirect would be incalculable.

Mr. Harry Lawson: May I ask the right hon. Gentleman whether it is true that this morning the German Emperor accepted the principle of mediation which he has proposed?[169]

Sir E. Grey: I understand that the German Government are favourable to the idea of mediation in principle as between Austria-Hungary and Russia, but that as to the particular proposal of applying that principle by means of a Conference which I have described to the House, the reply of the German Government has not yet been received.[170]

BD, XI, No. 190.

(259) 27 July: British Cabinet Meeting, Viscount Morley's account

Grey informs the Cabinet that the time had come to decide between intervention and neutrality and threatens to resign in case of neutrality

On or about July 24–27[171] Grey took a very important line in the Cabinet. He informed us of the contents of Buchanan's telegram of July 24 from Petersburg:[172] describing Sazonov's hopes that England would not fail to proclaim her solidarity with France and Russia; his warnings to us that the general European question was involved and England could not afford to efface herself from the problems now at issue; that she would sooner or later be dragged into war if it did break out; and, as Buchanan thought, even if England declined to join, France and Russia were determined to make a strong stand, *i.e.* in plain language, to fight Austria and Germany.

Then Grey in his own quiet way, which is none the less impressive for being so simple, and so free from the *cassant* and over-emphatic tone

169 For Germany's reply, rejecting British mediation, see (**254**).

170 The emergency Cabinet meeting on 27 July showed that the majority of the Cabinet were not prepared to go to war to defend France from a German attack. Asquith thought Britain 'should be no more than spectators' in a European war resulting from the Austro-Serbian crisis. Grey, who did favour intervention (and had made it known that he would resign as Foreign Secretary if Britain did not support France) changed the emphasis of the debate away from support for France to support for Belgium. Frank McDonough, *The Conservative Party and Anglo-German Relations, 1905–1914*, Macmillan, New York 2007, pp. 128–129.

171 In the manuscript 26 was crossed out and replaced with 24–27.

172 See (**202**).

that is Asquith's vice on such occasions, made a memorable pronouncement. The time had come, he said, when the Cabinet was bound to make up its mind plainly whether we were to take an active part with the two other Powers of the Entente, or to stand aside in the general European question, and preserve an absolute neutrality.

We could no longer defer decision. Things were moving very rapidly. We could no longer wait on accident, and postpone. If the Cabinet was for Neutrality, he did not think that he was the man to carry out such a policy. Here he ended in accents of unaffected calm and candour. The Cabinet seemed to heave a sort of sigh, and a moment or two of breathless silence fell upon us. I followed him, expressing my intense satisfaction that he had brought the inexorable position, to which circumstances had now brought us, plainly and definitely before us. It was fairer to France and everybody else, ourselves included. Though he had at least once, talking to an ambassador, drawn a distinction between diplomatic and military intervention, it was henceforth assumed that intervention meant active resort to arms. We rambled, as even the best Cabinets are apt to do, from the cogent riddle that the European Sphinx or Sphinxes had posed, into incidental points and secondary aspects. I could not, on the instant, gather with any certainty in which direction opinion was inclining. No wonder. Everybody had suddenly awakened to the startling fact that nothing less than the continued existence of the Ministry was this time the first time in sharp peril from differences within, and not from the House of Commons.

Later, we were pressed by the Prime Minister and Grey to examine the neutrality of Belgium and our obligations under the Treaty of 1839.[173] But it was thrown back day after day as less urgent than France. I took down to the Cabinet the words of Lord Derby about the Luxemburg guarantee of 1867; mentioning the opposition to his language from the Duke of Argyll and others. But, perhaps quite as much my fault as that of anybody else, the discussion was thin and perfunctory. Simon contributed scarcely anything and the Lord Chancellor even less. A Cabinet usually thinks of one thing at once, and the question of Belgium was up to this date, and in truth up to the morning of August 3rd, when Grey had to set out his whole case in the House of Commons, secondary to the pre-eminent controversy of the Anglo-French Entente. One of these days Grey rather suddenly let fall his view, in the pregnant words that German policy was that of a great 'European aggressor, as bad as Napoleon'.

'I have no German partialities', I observed, 'but you do not give us evidence'. Perhaps he might have cited the series of Naval Laws. [...]

173 At the Treaty of London in 1839, all Great Powers had agreed to protect Belgium's neutrality.

Then they were rather surprised at the stress I laid upon the Russian side of things. 'Have you ever thought', I put to them, 'what will happen if Russia wins? If Germany is beaten and Austria is beaten, it is not England and France who will emerge pre-eminent in Europe. It will be Russia. Will that be good for Western civilisation? I at least don't think so.' [...][174]

John Morley, *Memorandum on Resignation, August 1914*, Macmillan, London 1928, pp. 1–4; 6.

(260) 27 July: Szögyény to Berchtold

Germany does not want Austria-Hungary to accept Britain's mediation proposal; Berlin merely passed it on to save face

Telegram 307
Berlin, 27 July 1914
D. 9.15 p.m.
R. 28 July, 9 a.m.

Strictly confidential

Secretary of State informed me strictly confidentially that shortly possible English proposition of mediation would be communicated to Your Excellency by the German Government. The German Government assures in the most decisive way that it does not in any way identify with these propositions, that it was even decidedly against their consideration and that it passed them on only to comply with the English request. In this it was working from the point of view that it was of the utmost importance that England should not at the present moment side with Russia and France. Therefore everything would have to be avoided which would interrupt the so far well-functioning wire between Germany and England. If Germany were candidly to declare to Sir E. Grey that she would not pass on to Austria-Hungary his wishes, which England believes would be more likely to find consideration here if Germany mediated them, then the above mentioned eventuality, which should be avoided at all costs, would occur. The German Government would, by the way, in any case where England expressed such desire declare in Vienna that it did not in any way support such demands for intervention

174 For background and additional discussion see Zara Steiner and Keith Neilson, *Britain and the Origins of the First World War*, Palgrave Macmillan, London 2003, p. 238; G.P. Gooch, *Recent Revelations of European Diplomacy*, Longman, London 1940, p. 376; McDonough, *The Conservative Party*, pp. 128–129.

and would only pass them on to comply with England's wishes. Thus already yesterday the English Government had approached him [Jagow] via the German Ambassador in London and directly via their Ambassador [Goschen] here in order to effect that he would support England's wishes with regard to our modifying the note to Serbia.[175] Jagow had answered that he would fulfil Sir E. Grey's wish to pass on England's request to Your Excellency, but that he could not support it because the Serbian conflict was a question of prestige for the Austro-Hungarian monarchy in which Germany also participated. He, Secretary of State, had therefore passed on Sir E. Grey's note to Herr von Tschirschky, but without instructing him to present it to Your Excellency; afterwards he had then been able to report to the English Cabinet that he had not directly rejected the English request but that he had even passed it on to Vienna. At the end of our conversation the State Secretary repeated his view and requested, in order to avoid any misunderstanding, to assure your Excellency that although he had acted as mediator in this case he was absolutely not in favour of a consideration of the English proposal.

ÖUA, VIII, No. 10793.

(261) 27 July: Viviani to Bienvenu-Martin

French state visit cut short due to severity of the international situation

Telegram No. 12
On board *France*, 27 July 1914
D. 7 a.m.
R. 2.20 p.m.

I have come to the decision, as has the President of the Republic, to return immediately to France without our stopping at Copenhagen or Christiania. It is not possible to take a quicker route than by sea [...]. We will arrive in Dunkerque on Wednesday morning and will return to Paris where we will arrive in the afternoon.

DDF, 3e série, 11, No. 127.[176]

175 See DD, No. 186; BD, XI, No. 149.

176 Viviani then instructed the French Ministers in Copenhagen and Christiania to that effect, citing the German Kaiser's return to Kiel as a reason for the French decision to return ahead of schedule. See DDF, 3e série, 11, No. 126, (**263**).

(262) 27 July: Joffre's Memoirs

Negotiations with Russia to ensure she would immediately take offensive in East Prussia in case of war

Among the measures to be put into effect there was one especially which demanded the decision of the Government. The question was, whether all the troops of eastern and western Morocco should remain at the disposal of the Resident General, or whether those near the border of Algeria would be assigned to the XIX Army Corps with a view to their transfer to the Continent. M. Messimy submitted this question to the Cabinet, which decided that the largest possible number of combatant units compatible with the security of our North-African possessions should be withdrawn from Morocco and Algeria.[177]

The direction which events were taking left me with no illusion – we were headed straight for war and Russia was going to find herself drawn in at the same time as ourselves. My first thought, therefore, was to strengthen the liaison between us and our Allies and I asked the Minister [Messimy] to endeavour through all possible means to make sure that, if hostilities broke out, the Government of St. Petersburg, would immediately take the offensive in East Prussia, as had been agreed upon in our conventions.[178]

It will be recalled how important I considered this immediate offensive to be; we had requested our Allies to promise to undertake it, and they had agreed to do so. Our Military Attaché and, as I have been given to understand, our Ambassador were asked to inquire of the Russian General Staff whether we could count upon them in this matter, while at the same time indicating the great importance we attached to their offensive taking place in conjunction with ours. This question was answered by the announcement made the moment war was declared, that the Russian attack would open at once.

Joseph J.C. Joffre, *The Memoirs of Marshal Joffre*, 2 vols, Geoffrey Bles, London 1932, Vol. I, pp. 117–118.

177 On July 27 Joffre asked General Hubert Lyautey to begin preparations for abandoning most of Morocco and Algeria and sending the bulk of his troops – except for those guarding the cities – to France. Guerre à commissaire résident général Rabat, 27 juillet 1914, AN 509AP/5. My thanks to Robert Doughty for supplying this reference.

178 For details of French war planning, see for example Robert Doughty, 'France', in Hamilton and Herwig (eds), *War Planning*, 143–174.

(263) 27 July: Messimy's Diary

News of sudden return of Wilhelm II leads to nervousness outside of Germany; troops are readying themselves in Alsace-Lorraine; Austria-Hungary mobilizes eight army corps

Monday 27 July–Sudden return of Wilhelm II to Berlin

News has come to us in the night of the 26th to the 27th that the Kaiser has suddenly cut short his cruise in Norwegian waters.[179] Whilst Viviani and Poincaré, in accordance with the planned itinerary, are paying an official visit to Stockholm, Wilhelm II, without consulting the Chancellor,[180] is coming back to Berlin. This sudden return, decided upon on his own initiative, increases the nervousness and anxiety of all those who see the catastrophe approaching, but it fills the military and Pan-German elements with joy.

News arriving from Nancy and Belfort becomes more detailed and worsens.

At Metz, not only are troops confined to barracks, but the military garrisons have been positioned in the forts. Batteries are being built all round these. – The troops in Alsace-Lorraine have donned *feldgrau* combat dress. The youngest reserve recruits have been alerted and advised to be ready to rejoin as soon as they receive the alert. – The recall of all soldiers on leave (officers and troops) is confirmed by multiple cross-checks. – Finally, our military attaché in Vienna announces the mobilization of at least eight Austro-Hungarian army corps.

Adolphe Messimy, *Mes Souvenirs*, Librairie Plon, Paris 1937, pp. 131–135, p. 135.

179 See (**231**).

180 This impression was shared by the British Chargé d'Affaires in Berlin, Sir Horace Rumbold, who wrote to Grey on 26 July 1914: 'Emperor returns suddenly to-night, and Under-Secretary of State for Foreign Affairs says that Foreign Office regret this step, which was taken on His Majesty's own initiative. They fear that His Majesty's sudden return may cause speculation and excitement.' BD, XI, No. 147. In fact, Wilhelm had wanted to return even earlier, but had been prevented by Bethmann Hollweg who feared that this would alert the other Powers, and Britain in particular, to the potential danger. See for example Röhl, *Wilhelm II.*, Vol. 3, pp. 1103ff.

(264) 27 July: Sazonov to Russian Embassies

Highlights conciliatory nature of Serbia's reply to Austria

Isvolsky (Paris), Benckendorff (London), Schebeko (Vienna), Krupenski (Rome), Giers (Constantinople), Bronevski (Berlin)

Telegram, 27/14 July 1914

We have just received the answer which Pašić has handed to Count Giesl.[181] The answer exceeds all our expectations by its restraint and the willingness to give Austria fullest satisfaction. We cannot comprehend wherein Austria's demands can still lie, unless she is looking for a pretext for an expedition against Serbia.

Int. Bez., I, 5, No. 119.

(265) 27 July: Pašić's Minute

Serbia defiant after making concessions

27 July, 6.50 p.m.

We have made our last concession – further we will not go, nor will we seek mediation, for that would suggest that we are ready to yield even more. Russia is resolute. Italy neutral.

DSP, No. 588, cited in Mark Cornwall, 'Serbia', in Keith M. Wilson (ed.), *Decisions for War, 1914*, UCL Press, London 1995, pp. 55–96, p. 83.

181 See (**227**).

(266) 27 July: Plessen's Diary

Wilhelm II's arrival in Potsdam; discussions with Chancellor and military leaders; no operations possible until early August; Austrians hope to localize the conflict; Britain declares intention to stay neutral

At 10 past 3 arrival of H[is] M[ajesty] at Wildpark.[182] All the *Generaladjutanten* and *Flügeladjutanten*, the *Oberst-Kämmerer* and the Chancellor were present. H[er] M[ajesty] had also come from Wilhelmshöhe[183] to welcome the Kaiser. Everyone was under the impression of the looming war. H.M. took the Chancellor, Chief of the General Staff of the Army, Chief of the Military Cabinet and myself immediately to the *Neues Palais*.[184] First long discussion of H.M. with the Chancellor alone, then with us soldiers. The Austrians won't be ready for a long time! It will take until the beginning of August before operations can begin. They hope to be able to localize the war! England declares to want to stay neutral.[185] I have the impression that nothing at all will come of this matter.

August Bach (ed.), *Deutsche Gesandtschaftsberichte zum Kriegsausbruch*, Quaderverlag, Berlin 1937, p. 22.

182 The railway station in Potsdam. Count von Dohna was also present when the Kaiser returned from his cruise, and recorded after the war: 'At Wildpark station there were H.M. the Kaiserin, Bethmann and many other important people. It was a moment during which peace seemed once again in the offing; the war-party seemed disappointed.' Alfred Graf von Dohna, 'Der Feldzug in Ostpreußen 1914', 24 April 1920, in BA-MA, W-10/51032, pp. 136f.

183 The Kaiser's summer castle near Kassel.

184 The Kaiser's castle in Potsdam.

185 There was clearly no intention to declare neutrality, hence discussion in Potsdam must have laboured under a misconception. Crowe commented on a report of 27 July that staying out of the war would have detrimental consequences for Britain: 'It is difficult not to remember the position of Prussia in 1805, when she insisted on keeping out of the war which she could not prevent from breaking out between the other Powers over questions not, on their face, of direct interest to Prussia. The war was waged without Prussia in 1805. But in 1806 she fell a victim to the Power that had won in 1805, and no one was ready either to help her or to prevent her political ruin and partition.' E. A. C[rowe] July 27. Minute on telegram by Buchanan to Grey, 27 July 1914, BD, XI, 170. However, in Germany the belief in British neutrality was based on seemingly authentic news. See for example (**281**) which would only have confirmed the (wrong) impression of Britain's intentions. See also (**250**).

(267) 27 July: Admiral von Müller's diary

German attempts to let Russia put herself in the wrong

The mood is decidedly milder. It appears that the neutral tendency of England is having a very cooling effect on Russia and France.[186] On the other hand Austria will not have completed her mobilization till 12 August. Tendency of our policy: to keep quiet, letting Russia put herself in the wrong, but then not shying away from war.

John C.G. Röhl, 'Admiral von Müller and the Approach of War, 1911–1914, *Historical Journal*, 12, 1969, pp. 651–673, p. 669.

(268) 27 July: Berchtold to Ambassadors in St Petersburg and Rome

Austria-Hungary wants no territorial gains as long as war remains localized

I authorize Your Excellency, without however entering into any binding engagement, to declare vis-à-vis Sazonov and your Italian colleague that the Monarchy has no intentions for territorial annexations as long as the war between Austria-Hungary and Serbia remains localized.[187]

ÖUA, VIII, No. 10834.

186 See also (**266**).
187 Copies were also sent to the Ambassadors in Paris, London and Berlin.

9

'The machine is in motion'

28 July–30 July: Documents (269)–(332)

In the light of Serbia's unexpectedly conciliatory reply to Austria-Hungary's ultimatum, it should have been possible to avert the threatening war. However, Austria-Hungary's decision-makers were as determined as they had been right from the beginning of the crisis to use this opportunity for war (**321**). Austria-Hungary's leaders were dismayed by the Serbian reply, and to prevent any further attempts at a diplomatic solution being found, refused Britain's conference suggestion of 24 July, declared war on Serbia on 28 July and began hostilities by bombarding Belgrade from gunboats the next day (**291**). In London, Haldane dejectedly commented: 'The German General Staff is in the saddle.'[1] It seemed clear to him that Austria-Hungary would not have embarked on this course without the backing of her ally, and any chance of peace now seemed to have evaporated. Following a meeting with Grey and Asquith on 29 July, he wrote to his mother: 'The declaration of war by Austria against Serbia has made the situation very critical. [...] It is a time for calmness and decision.'[2]

And yet, even now a European war might still have been avoided. Cracks began to appear between Austria-Hungary and Germany. In Berlin, Wilhelm II concluded that following the Serbian reply there was no longer any reason for Austria-Hungary to go to war with Serbia. Instead, he advocated a 'halt in Belgrade' of Austro-Hungarian troops, and negotiations (**277**). However, this important attempt at conciliation was initially undermined by Bethmann Hollweg who delayed the Kaiser's instructions to Vienna and toned it down (**276**), (**277**). Instead, he focused his efforts on encouraging

1 Frederick Maurice, *Haldane 1856–1915*, Faber & Faber, London 1937, p. 353.
2 Ibid.

Wilhelm II to begin a series of telegraphic exchanges with his cousin, Tsar Nicholas II, drafted by Bethmann Hollweg and intended to pass the blame for a war to Russia.[3] The two Emperors exchanged numerous telegrams (the famous Willy-Nicky telegrams) in which they assured each other of their own government's peaceful intentions and tried to convince each other to stop military preparations and restrain their respective allies (**285**), (**288**), (**289**), (**313**), (**314**). While in the long run this had the desired effect of providing a useful smokescreen, it had no influence on the decisions being made in either Berlin or St Petersburg.

By 29 July Germany's Government was finally willing to discuss British mediation proposals, much to the dismay of Germany's military planners and of the Austro-Hungarian ally (**317**). In Vienna, it was momentarily feared that Germany might abandon her ally after all, as Berlin started to put pressure on Vienna not to rule out international mediation. Both Tschirschky and Berchtold initially misunderstood these confusing messages from Berlin, hardly surprising, given that until this point in the crisis they had been told that Berlin would pass on mediation proposals merely to save face, but did not support them.[4] But explicit warnings from Bethmann Hollweg on 30 July led to the realization in Vienna that it was still possible that the ally could abandon Austria-Hungary at the last minute.[5] Astonishingly, given Germany's strong support for Austria-Hungary, at this late point in the crisis, Bethmann Hollweg wondered which points of the ultimatum Serbia had actually rejected.[6]

However, despite the ally's cooling off, Austria's decision-makers were still determined to go to war. Berchtold rejected the 'halt in

3 As Bethmann Hollweg callously explained to the Kaiser, should war nonetheless result from the crisis, the existence of such telegrams would point clearly to Russia's guilt and would make it appear as if Germany had wanted to preserve peace in July 1914. Imanuel Geiss, *Julikrise*, Vol. II, No. 587. Letting Russia put herself in the wrong was a deliberate policy in Berlin. See for example (**267**). In his speech to the Reichstag on 4 August the Chancellor used these telegrams to make the case for Germany's desire for peace during the crisis (**416**).

4 As Kronenbitter argues, Tschirschky had been reprimanded early on in the crisis for trying to restrain the ally (**108**), and now did not approve of Bethmann Hollweg's attempts to diffuse the situation, not least because it undermined his own position in Vienna. Günther Kronenbitter, *'Krieg im Frieden'*, Oldenbourg, Munich 2003, p. 509, n. 380.

5 For details see Kronenbitter, *'Krieg im Frieden'*, pp. 506–507.

6 See marginal note on (**322**).

Belgrade' idea,[7] and Conrad spoke up against it during his meeting with Emperor Franz Joseph where he declared it 'impossible' to suspend the fighting with Serbia (**321**).

Bethmann Hollweg's change of heart was motivated by his continuing (and indeed renewed) hope for British neutrality, but those hopes rested on a combination of false news and wishful thinking shared by others in Berlin, not least Kaiser Wilhelm II (**281**), (**282**). However, Germany's political decision-makers became increasingly pessimistic about Britain's likely attitude (**297**), while her military leaders never shared the vain hope that Britain would remain neutral. Bethmann Hollweg made ill-advised direct appeals for British neutrality which were rejected by London, but in the process they revealed Germany's intention to violate Belgian neutrality and her determination to go to war (**301**).

In St Petersburg, Paris, Berlin and London, tensions began to show between the military planners (whose attitudes were uniformly impatient) and their civilian leaders, who attempted to delay mobilizations and preserve peace for as long as possible. In Russia, the military leaders were unable to get the Tsar's agreement on a declaration of general mobilization – it was nearly declared for 29 July, revoked on 30 July and finally implemented on 31 July (**271**), (**291**), (**328**). Vienna's military action against Serbia (following the declaration of war, Belgrade was bombarded from 29 July onwards) put pressure on St Petersburg to come to a decision. They estimated that Austria-Hungary would require 14 days from mobilization to complete their deployment against Russia, while Russia would require 25 days to be fully deployed.[8]

In Germany, the military leaders could not put into effect mobilization measures against the wishes of the Chancellor, who was convinced by Sazonov's explanation that Russian mobilization did not necessarily mean war and who shied away from issuing Germany's own mobilization order, a move that would make war unavoidable, for as long as possible (**292**). Instead, Bethmann Hollweg issued a request for Russia to stop her military preparations while insisting that the military leaders wait for Russia to make the first move (**290**).

---

7 See Kronenbitter, *'Krieg im Frieden'*, p. 507.

8 See Bruce Menning, 'Russian Military Intelligence' forthcoming. Russia's estimates for Germany's deployment were even more worrying, as they feared it could be as little as 10 days from mobilization.

In France, the Cabinet in Paris ruled firmly that only minimal military preparations could be made and that, crucially, French troops would be held back 10 kilometres from the border. This decision was based on their desire to ensure Britain would join the war on their side. In their effort to ensure that Germany would bear the responsibility for beginning any hostilities they overruled the objections of the military leaders[9] (**303**), (**332**).

At the same time, the French ambassador assured Sazonov of France's support (**272**), and in Paris, the willingness to fulfil the alliance obligation was also confirmed (**274**), (**315**), although there were differing opinions at the Quai d'Orsay. At this point in the crisis Poincaré seems to have accepted that war would be unavoidable and his aim was to enter the war under the most favourable conditions for France (**279**). Viviani, on the other hand, believed until almost the very last moment that Germany might change her mind and that war might still be averted, so much so that he was described by his colleagues as 'tortured' during a crucial ministerial council meeting on 31 July.[10] The French President set about trying to justify France's entry into the war as a defensive act, still mindful of the fact that Britain had not yet declared her support. It should be noted, however, that this policy was conducted against the background of the certainty that Germany was not restraining her ally. On 30 July, Poincaré recorded in his diary: 'If Germany seriously wanted to stop Austria and prevent a general conflict, she would speak a different language.'[11] Furthermore, French decision-making was motivated by not wanting to allow Austria even a limited military success. In this scenario, war was indeed unavoidable. Poincaré's views were shared by the Minister of War and the Chief of the General Staff, though they were also not accepted universally in the Council of Ministers or in the Foreign Office[12] (**299**). While Poincaré was motivated by Britain's likely attitude and did not want for France to appear non-conciliatory, Viviani's main concern was

9 For details of French anxiety over Britain's uncertain attitude and the French Cabinet's decision to implement the 10-kilometre restriction against Joffre's will, see for example Roy A. Prete, 'French Strategic Planning and the Deployment of the B.E.F. in France in 1914', *Canadian Journal of History*, XXIV, April 1989, pp. 42–62, pp. 49–50.

10 Stefan Schmidt, *Frankreichs Außenpolitik*, Oldenbourg, Munich 2007, p. 316.

11 Notes journalières, Poincaré papers, BNF, Nafr.16027, fol. 125, cited in ibid, pp. 312–14.

12 Ibid, pp. 314–15.

to act in the interest of general peace.[13]

In Britain, a 'critical cabinet meeting'[14] on 29 July set the tone for the remainder of the crisis. Sir Edward Grey tried to convince the Cabinet members that Britain should intervene in a likely European war (his hand had been strengthened by the news of Russia's partial mobilization, and indication that war was probably unavoidable), but the majority of members disagreed with his interpretation of the neutrality agreement of 1839.[15] The decision was taken to inform Germany and France that Britain would not commit herself one way or the other (**309**), leading to Grey having to tell the French 'Don't count on our coming in', and the Germans 'Don't count on our abstention' (**294**). The wait continued for Britain to declare her hand, although Grey was becoming increasingly convinced of the need for Britain to be involved (**273**). The Ulster question had receded into the background and public opinion was becoming aware of the seriousness of the international situation (**293**). In response to Russian and Austrian mobilization measures, the 'precautionary period' was ordered for the British army (**295**). The British Fleet had already been ordered on 28 July not to disperse after manoeuvres and had been sent to its war stations in the North Sea the next day.

By 30 July, Russia's suspended mobilization was becoming a problem and her military and diplomatic leaders agreed on the urgency of a general mobilization and attempted to persuade the Tsar to order it (**305**). One more time, however, the Tsar changed his mind and his order for a general mobilization was once again scaled down to a partial one (**327**). Eventually, the president of the Duma was asked to intervene and change the Tsar's mind, and mobilization was finally allowed to run its course (**328**), (**330**).

In Germany, the importance of ensuring that Russia would put herself in the wrong meant that Bethmann Hollweg insisted on mobilization being delayed for as long as possible (**319**). It was decided on 30 July that by midday on 31 July, Germany was to declare her mobilization, whether or not Russia had begun fully to mobilize

---

13 See ibid, p. 323; John F.V. Keiger, *France and the Origins of the First World War*, Macmillan, London, Basingstoke 1983, pp. 154–64.

14 As John Burns commented at the time. See Keith Wilson, 'Britain', in idem, *Decisions for War, 1914*, UCL Press, London 1995, p. 189. See also (**295**).

15 At the Treaty of London in 1839, Belgium's independence and neutrality had been guaranteed by the Great Powers.

(**323**). This move would make war inevitable, as Germany's military planners knew only too well. That same day, Moltke declared: 'This war will turn into a world war in which England will also intervene. Only few can have an idea of the extent, the duration and the end of this war. Nobody today can have a notion of how it is all going to end.'[16]

Italy had been largely ignored by Germany and Austria-Hungary throughout the crisis, and San Giuliano advised his Ambassadors in Berlin and Vienna that Italy would not take part in an 'unjustified war'.[17] The German Ambassador reported on 30 July that the *casus foederis* did not apply for Italy in this war of aggression (**326**). Germany was keen to change Italy's mind with concessions, but given that these would be made from Austro-Hungarian territory, Vienna was not willing to promise anything, much to Berlin's frustration. We can of course not ever know if concessions, judiciously offered at the right time, might have swayed Italy onto the Dual Alliance side. In the last days of July, Vienna's decision-makers were in any case so confident in their army's ability to wage their war against Serbia that concessions to Italy did not seem worth considering.

(269) 28 July: Sazonov to Benckendorff (1)

Germany appears to hold the key to defusing the crisis

Telegram No 1528
28/15 July 1914

From my discussions with the German Ambassador I have gained the impression that Germany rather encourages Austria's intransigence. The Cabinet in Berlin, which could halt the whole development of the crisis, seemingly exerts no influence on its ally. The Ambassador here [Pourtalès] considers Serbia's answer insufficient.

I consider such an attitude by Germany to be very alarming and think that England more than the other powers could undertake steps to put appropriate pressure on Berlin. The key to the situation lies

16 BA-MA, N35/1, Aufzeichnungen v. Haeften, p. 27.

17 Richard Bosworth, *Italy and the Origins of the First World War*, MacMillan, London 1983, p. 395.

undoubtedly in Berlin.[18]

Int. Bez., I, 5, No. 164.

(270) 28 July: Sazonov to Benckendorff (2)

Britain must speed up mediation if Austria's declaration of war on Serbia is not to escalate

In consequence of Austria's declaration of war on Serbia, direct discussions on my part with the Austrian Ambassador are obviously useless. It would be necessary for England to take action in view of mediation with all speed and for Austria to suspend military measures against Serbia at once. Otherwise mediation will only supply a pretext for delay in bringing the matter to a decision and make it possible for Austria in the meantime to annihilate Serbia completely.

Int. Bez., I, 5, No. 167.

(271) 28 July: Sazonov to Bronevski

Declaration of mobilization for 29 July

Telegram 1539
St Petersburg, 28 July 1914

Sent to Vienna, Paris, London and Rome

In consequence of Austria's declaration of war on Serbia, we shall declare mobilization in the military districts of Odessa, Kiev, Moscow and Kazan tomorrow. Kindly bring this to the attention of the German Government and emphasize the absence of any intentions of a Russian attack on Germany. Our Ambassador in Vienna is not being recalled from his post for the time being.

Int. Bez. I, 5, No. 168.

18 Benckendorff passed a French version of this telegram to Nicolson the same day. See BD, XI, No. 210, enclosure. The telegram was also sent to the Russian Ambassador in Paris.

(272) 28 July: Daily record of the Ministry of Foreign Affairs

France promises to support Russia

28/15 July 1914

The French Ambassador declares to Sazonov, on behalf of his Government, France's complete readiness to fulfil her alliance obligation if necessary.[19]

Int. Bez. I, 5, No. 172.

(273) 28 July: Benckendorff to Sazonov

Grey's language more determined; change in British public opinion

Telegram No. 213
London, 28/15 July 1914

Received telegram No. 1524.[20]

Personal

The feeling that you express[21] is exactly the same as that which has taken hold of Grey and which not only dictated his language vis-à-vis

19 The entry was made by Baron Schilling. See Alfred von Wegerer, 'Russian Mobilization of 1914', *Political Science Quarterly*, 43, 1928, pp. 201–228, p. 211. Unfortunately Paléologue appears to have omitted informing his Government of this conversation and exceeded his authority when giving this assurance. See Schmidt, *Frankreichs Außenpolitik*, p. 320. Paléologue's role in the crisis has been controversially discussed among his contemporaries and historians. On the basis of the available evidence Schmidt concludes that the French Ambassador adopted a 'policy of calculated half-truths' which began on 24/25 July. Over the next few days he knowingly omitted to inform his Government of the Russian decision for secret mobilization measures (**203**), (**300**), (**330**), for fear of Viviani's intervention. Schmidt, *Frankreichs Außenpolitik*, p. 338 (here also a discussion of the various interpretations and critiques of Paléologue's role). Crucially, he also did not immediately report Russia's decision for general mobilization on 30 July, although the reasons for the delay until 31 July remain unclear. Sazonov appears not to have informed him as early and as clearly as he might have, and Paléologue, who had in any case guessed the change in Russia's attitude, failed to communicate this to Paris (**349**).

20 See (**264**).

21 See (**264**).

Lichnowsky[22] and yesterday in the Chamber,[23] but which has also given him the necessary grounding for the determined position which he has adopted since Saturday. His language in the Chamber yesterday – which incidentally is based on the measures taken for the fleet – is being judged quite clearly by the English public. In the current moment it seems to me urgently necessary to feed this atmosphere and, if you can, to make easier for Grey the delicate situation which your answer in No. 1521 will perhaps cause.[24] Sudden change of public opinion quicker than I anticipated.

Int. Bez. I, 5, No. 174.

(274) 28 July: Ignatjev[25] to the Russian General Staff

France willing to fulfil alliance duty; some preparation of French army

Telegram No. 213
[Paris], 28/15 July 1914

Immediately following my arrival I was received by the Minister of War and the Chief of the General Staff, who expressed complete and lively willingness to fulfil the alliance duties faithfully. The mood is quiet, determined. The preparations of the French army consist of the following: 1. Today the movement of those parts of troops located in camps to their garrisons in the five border corps, the second, sixth, seventh, twentieth and twenty-first was finished around 6 o'clock in the

22 See (257).

23 See (258).

24 Benckendorff refers to Sazonov's telegram of 27 July (*Int. Bez.* No. 116) in which Sazonov informed the Russian Ambassadors in Paris and London (as well as Berlin, Vienna and Rome) that Grey had suggested a conference in London between Britain, France, Germany and Italy to find a solution to the crisis. Sazonov instructed his representatives in London and Paris: 'If this is about any kind of mediating pressure in St Petersburg then we reject this at the outset, because we have from the beginning adopted an attitude which we cannot change because we are already meeting all of Austria's acceptable demands.'

25 Russian military attaché in Paris. I am grateful to Robert Doughty for pointing out that there were, in fact, two Ignatjevs in Paris. One was a Russian colonel who was present during the July crisis, and the second was a Russian nobleman who was sent to replace him. Olivier Lahaie, in his dissertation on French intelligence during the First World War, notes that the first Ignatjev was a secret Russian agent in Germany between 1913 and 1915, where he used the pseudonyms 'CNE Istomine' as well as 'Boris Stomm'. Olivier Lahaie, 'Renseignement et Services de Renseignement en France pendant la Guerre de 1914–1918', PhD thesis, Sorbonne, Paris, 2006, p. 1026.

evening. In these corps the officers have been recalled from leave. 2. Granting of leave for the entire army has been suspended. 3. Measures have been taken for the increased protection of the railway lines and the most important military buildings, such as the Eiffel tower and the powder magazines. 4. The railway companies received a pre-prepared message that the mobilization period will be shortened by a few hours.

Int. Bez., I, 5, No. 180.

(275) 28 July: Bronevski to Sazonov

Serbian answer not widely made public in Germany

Telegram No. 136
Berlin, 28/15 July 1914

Wolff's [news] agency has not published the wording of the Serbian answer note which has been communicated to it, and until now it has not been published fully in any of the local papers which seemingly do not want to accord it any space in their columns because they are aware of the sobering impression that it would make in German reader circles.

Int. Bez., I, 5, No. 185.

(276) 28 July: Plessen's diary

Serbia's reply to the ultimatum, Wilhelm II no longer sees any reason for war

I am out riding with H.M. at 7.30 [a.m.]. He tells me that England views the Serbian reply to the Austrian ultimatum thus that with it basically all demands have been met, and thus any reason for war had actually been removed. I thought that Austria would at least get her hands on a hostage [*Faustpfand*] which could serve as a guarantee for sticking to the agreements.[26]

26 The Bavarian General Krafft von Dellmensingen commented in his diary after his return from Berlin to Munich on 30 July on the 'unfortunately noticeably peaceful news. The Kaiser absolutely wants peace and the Kaiserin is working towards it with all means. [...] He even wants to influence Austria and to stop her from continuing further. That would be the gravest disaster! We would lose all credit as allies.' BA-MA, W-10/50642, p. 2. Wilhelm instructed Plessen to inform the Chief of Staff

Cited in Holger Afflerbach, *Wilhelm II.*, Oldenburg, Munich 2005, p. 642.

(277) 28 July: Wilhelm II to Jagow

Following Serbia's reply, every cause for war has gone; suggests 'halt in Belgrade'

Hand-written letter
Neues Palais, 28 July 1914.
D. 10 a.m.
After reading over the Serbian reply, which I received this morning, I am convinced that by and large the wishes of the Danube Monarchy have been fulfilled. The few reservations that Serbia makes in regard with individual points could, in my opinion, be settled by negotiation. But it contains the announcement orbi et urbi of capitulation of the most humiliating kind, and as a result, *every cause for war has gone*. Nevertheless, the piece of paper, like its contents, can only be considered to be of limited value as long as it is not translated into *deeds*. The Serbs are Orientals, therefore full of lies, false, and masters of evasion. In order that these beautiful promises may turn into truth and facts, a gentle violence must be exercised. This should be so arranged that Austria would receive a *hostage* (Belgrade),[27] as a guarantee for the enforcement and carrying out of the promises, and should occupy it until the demands had actually been complied with. This is also necessary in order to give the army, now *unnecessarily* mobilized for the third time, the external satisfaction d'honneur of an ostensible success in the eyes of the world, and to make it possible for it to feel that it had at least stood on foreign soil. Without that the abandonment of a military campaign might be the cause of bad feeling against the dynasty, which would be cause great concern.

If Your Excellency shares my views, I propose: to say to Austria: Serbia's retreat has been forced through in a very humiliating manner, and we offer our congratulations. Naturally, as a result, *a cause for war no longer exists*. However, a *guarantee* is necessary that the promises would be *carried out*. That could be secured by means of the *temporary* military occupation of a portion of Serbia. Similar to the way we kept troops stationed in France in 1871 until the billions were paid. *On this basis*, I am ready to *mediate* for *peace* in Austria. [...]

of this decision. (**277**).

27 See (**276**).

Therefore Your Excellency will submit a proposal to me along the lines sketched out which shall be communicated to Vienna.[28] I have had Plessen write along the lines indicated to the Chief of the General Staff who is entirely in accord with my views.[29]

DD, No. 293.[30]

(278) 28 July: Lichnowsky to Jagow

Austrians reveal they want war; devastated by Serbia's reply

Tel. No. 171
London, 28 July 1914
D. 12.58 p.m.
R. 3.45 p.m.

The members of the Austrian Embassy here, including Count Mensdorff, have in their conversations with members of the [German] Embassy and with me never denied the fact that Austria is intent only on vanquishing Serbia, and that the Note [to Serbia] was deliberately composed so that it would have to be rejected. When the news was distributed here on Sunday evening by the 'Central News' that Serbia had given in[31] the said men were seemingly devastated; Count Mensdorff told me just yesterday confidentially that they absolutely wanted the war in Vienna, because Serbia was to be 'put down'. Said men also maintain that it is intended to give away parts of Serbia to Bulgaria (and probably also to Albania).[32]

DD, No. 301.

28 By delaying and altering the Kaiser's mediation proposal to Vienna, the Chancellor in the end ensured that the monarch was indeed no longer in a position to interfere. Bethmann even instructed Tschirschky 'to avoid very carefully giving rise to the impression that we wish to hold Austria back'. Imanuel Geiss (ed.), *July 1914*, Scribner, London 1967, No. 115. The substantial differences between the Kaiser's order and Bethmann's instruction to Vienna are analysed by Geiss in *Julikrise und Kriegsausbruch*, Vol. II, pp. 164f.

29 See (**276**).

30 English translation in Geiss, *July 1914*, No. 112, here with minor amendments.

31 See (**227**).

32 Bethmann Hollweg commented in the margin: 'The duplicitousness of Austria is unbearable. To us they deny explanation of their plans and tell us explicitly that Count Hoyos' explanations which culminated in a carving-up of Serbia had been purely private (**119**), in Petersburg they are the lambs who have no evil intentions, and in London their Embassy talks of giving away Serbian territory to Bulgaria and Albania.'

(279) 28 July: Joffre's Memoirs

France determined to let Germany take the blame for any hostilities; no military steps to be taken that had not also been taken by Germany

The main preoccupation of the French Government was to make no move which could be construed as anything except a reply to some step taken in Germany. This timid attitude was largely the result of the absence of the heads of the Government; nevertheless, under the pressure of circumstances, the necessary measures were taken little by little. For example, on the night July 27th/28th, orders were given for all troops absent from army corps stationed in the interior to return to their garrisons. [...]

Up to this moment [mobilization order in Austria; preliminary warning of mobilization in Germany] we had only taken what might be called passive measures of protection; it now became necessary to put our covering forces into position, and I urged upon the Minister [Messimy] that the safety of the country required that this step be taken without delay.[33] M. Messimy considered that we still had not sufficiently plain indications to justify such a measure; he thought it would be interpreted both in France and abroad as a bellicose manifestation which might embitter diplomatic conversations. Above all, this measure seemed to him of such gravity that he decided to delay its decision until the President of the Republic and the Premier had returned to France.

Joseph Joffre, *Memoirs*, 2 vols, Geoffrey Bles, London 1932, Vol. I, pp. 118–119.

33 On 28 July Joffre demanded the '*disposition de couverture*', i.e., the mobilization and deployment of five army corps on the Franco-German border. See Joseph Joffre, *Memoirs*, 2 vols, Vol. I, pp. 118–119; Ministère de la Guerre, *Les Armées françaises dans la Grande Guerre*, Vol. I, 1, pp. 59–64. Stefan Schmidt points out that at this point in time, Joffre had no news of any German measures which might have necessitated such a step on the French side. Even thought this was still the case on 29 July, Joffre nonetheless repeated his demand in conversation with Messimy. Schmidt, *Frankreichs Außenpolitik*, pp. 344–345.

(280) 28 July: Dobrorolski's memoirs

Austrian declaration of war on Serbia makes Russian mobilization inevitable

On 15/28 [July], the day of the Austro-Hungarian declaration of war against Serbia, Sazonov suddenly loses all optimism. It occurs to him that a general war is unavoidable, and he alerts Ianushkevitch to the fact that mobilization of our army should not be delayed any longer. According to Ianushkevitch, the language the Minister of Foreign Affairs used about the mobilization was now betraying some astonishment at the fact that it had not started earlier.

Sergei Dobrorolski, 'La mobilisation de l'Armée russe en 1914', *Revue d'Histoire* ..., 1, April–July 1923, p. 145.

(281) 28 July: Prince Henry to Wilhelm II

King George hoped that Germany would join the attempts to localize the conflict and assured Prince Henry that Britain would attempt to stay neutral

Kiel, 28 July 1914

My dear Wilhelm!

[...] Before my departure from London,[34] on Sunday morning, I had, upon my request, a short conversation with Georgie who was completely clear about the seriousness of the current situation and who assured me that he and his Government would not omit anything in order to localize the fight between Austria and Serbia, which is why his Government had made the suggestion, as you have long known, that Germany, England, France and Italy should intervene to try to hold back Russia[.] He hoped that Germany would be able, despite her alliance with Austria, to join this proposal in order to avoid the European war which we, as he said, were nearer to than ever before[.] His exact words were: 'we shall try all we can to keep out of this and shall remain neutral.' I am convinced

34 Prince Heinrich (Henry) visited England from 25–27 July and had an audience with King George V on 26 July. (**237**), Note 130. For details of the visit, see John Röhl, *Wilhelm II.*, Vol. 3: *Der Weg in den Abgrund, 1900–1941*, Beck, Munich 2008, 2009, pp. 1122ff., where he points out that Kaiser Wilhelm considered this conversation to have amounted to a 'clear and official declaration of neutrality'. See also (**296**). King's George's account was less definite (**250**).

that this statement was meant seriously, just as I am that England will remain neutral in the beginning, however if she will do so in the long run I cannot pass judgement on, though I have my doubts because of the relationship with France. –

Georgie was very serious, drew logical conclusions and had the most serious and most honest desire to avoid a possible world fire [*Weltbrand*], and he reckoned strongly with your support. [...] Lichnowsky, with whom I spent time on Sunday, has again assured me of the loyal and honest mood of Sir Edward Grey in regard to the current crisis.[35] [...]
Your faithful [and] obedient brother
Heinrich

DD, No. 374.

(282) 28 July: Müller's Diary

Auswärtiges Amt believes in possibility of British neutrality

28 July, out riding in the morning in the Tiergarten. Met the [Director of the political department Wilhelm von] Stumm from the *Auswärtiges Amt* and talked with him about England's attitude. Stumm, who is known as an England-expert, thinks that England would initially certainly remain neutral but would throw in her entire weight in favour of a quick peace agreement as soon as France is seriously in danger of being defeated.

Walter Görlitz, *The Kaiser and his Court, 1914–1918*, transl. M. Savill, MacDonald & Co., London 1961, p. 36.

35 See also (**296**) and Wilhelm II's marginal notes on this document. John Röhl has pointed to the 'fatal consequences' of Heinrich's interpretation of 'the King's word'. *Wilhelm II.*, Vol. 3, p. 1122. Much has been made by the Kaiser of Grey's alleged trap for him as he understood Heinrich to have ascertained that Britain would be neutral. In fact, in his diary Heinrich recorded the King's words as: 'We shall try & keep out of it, we shall probably remain neutral.' In his letter to the Kaiser, Heinrich omitted the crucial word 'probably'. In the diary, that sentence was a later addition, but we do not know when Heinrich made it. See ibid., p. 1123.

(283) 28 July: Moltke's memorandum about the political situation

Chief of Staff intervenes in political matters; puts pressure on civilian leaders to seek clarification of situation as military situation is deteriorating daily

[Received by Bethmann Hollweg on 29 July[36]]

It is without question that no state in Europe would show any other than human interest in the conflict between Austria and Serbia, were not inherent in it the danger of a general political entanglement which already threatens today to unleash a world war. For more than five years Serbia has been the cause of a European tension which has been pressing with simply intolerable weight on the political and economic life of the nations. With a patience approaching weakness, Austria has up to the present borne the continuous provocations and the political machinations aimed at the disruption of her own national stability by a people which has gone from regicide at home to the murder of princes in the neighbouring land. Only after the last gruesome crime did it reach for the ultimate means in order to lance with a red-hot iron the boil which continues to threaten to poison the body of Europe. All of Europe would have sighed a breath of relief if this mischief-maker could have been properly chastised and peace and order thereby been restored in the Balkans, but Russia placed herself at the side of this criminal nation. It was only then that the Austro-Serbian affair became the thunder cloud which may at any moment break over Europe.

Austria has declared to the European cabinets that she does not aim for territorial acquisitions at Serbia's cost nor to touch on the existence of that state, but that she only wanted to force the disquiet neighbour to accept the conditions which she considers necessary for a continuing existence side by side [...].

Austria has only mobilized a portion of her armed forces, eight army corps, against Serbia. Just enough to be able to carry out her punitive expedition. Against this, Russia has made all preparations to enable her to mobilize the army corps of the military districts of Kiev, Odessa and Moscow, twelve army corps in all, in the shortest period, and is ordering similar preparatory measures in the north also, along the German border and the Baltic Sea. She declares that she intends to mobilize when Austria marches into Serbia, as she cannot permit the destruction of Serbia by Austria, even though Austria has explained that she intends nothing of the sort.

What must and will be the further consequences? If Austria advances into Serbia she will have to face not only the Serbian army but also the

36 Moltke gave a copy of the memorandum to the Kaiser in the evening of 28 July.

vastly superior strength of Russia; thus she cannot enter upon a war with Serbia without securing herself against an attack by Russia. That means that she will be forced also to mobilize the other half of her army, for she cannot possibly surrender at discretion to a Russia all prepared for war. At the moment, however, in which Austria mobilizes her entire army, the collision between herself and Russia will become inevitable. But that is the *casus foederis* for Germany. If Germany does not want to be false to her word and permit her ally to suffer annihilation at the hands of Russian superiority, she too, must mobilize. This would result in the mobilization of the rest of Russia's military districts. But then Russia will be able to say: I am being attacked by Germany, and with that she will assure herself of the support of France, which is bound by treaty to take part in the war, should her ally, Russia, be attacked.[37] Thus the Franco-Russian agreement, so often praised as a purely defensive alliance, created only in order to meet the aggressive plans of Germany, will come into force, and the mutual butchery of the civilised states of Europe will begin.

It cannot be denied that the affair has been cunningly instigated by Russia. While giving continuous assurances that she was not yet 'mobilizing', but only making preparations 'for any eventuality', that 'up to now' she had not called up any reserves, she has been getting herself so prepared for war that, when she actually issues her mobilization orders, she will be ready to move her armies forward in a few days. [...]

Germany does not want to bring about this horrific war. However, the German Government knows that it would be fatefully violating the deep-rooted feelings of alliance loyalty [...] and would be setting itself in opposition to the sentiments of the [German] people if it did not come to the assistance of its ally at a moment which will necessarily decide on the latter's existence.

According to the information at hand, France also appears to be taking measures preparatory to an eventual mobilization.[38] It is apparent that Russia and France are moving hand in hand as far as regards their

37 Moltke omitted to mention that France would in any case become involved in the war, as German mobilization would lead to German troops being deployed on the Western Front for an immediate attack against France.

38 When the French President returned to Paris, he had a meeting with Messimy who, like his military counterparts in Russia, was convinced that war was inevitable. He briefed the President on the precautionary measures already implemented. He had been urging Russia to invade East Prussia, and on the 29th it was decided that French officers abroad should rejoin their corps, and frontier wireless stations were put on war footing. In Frederick Schumann's words, 'The French war preparations preliminary to mobilization had already progressed further than the German intelligence service had been able to discover and were further advanced than corresponding measures in Germany.' *War and Diplomacy*, Whittlesey House, London 1931, p. 228.

preparations.[39]

Thus, if the collision between Austria and Russia is inevitable, Germany will also mobilize and will be ready to take up the fight on two fronts.

With relation to the military measures we have in mind it is of the greatest importance to ascertain as soon as possible whether Russia and France intend to let it come to a war with Germany. The further the preparations of our neighbours are advancing, the quicker they will be able to complete their mobilization. Thus with every day the military situation is becoming increasingly unfavourable for us, and can, if our prospective opponents continue to prepare themselves undisturbed, lead to fateful consequences for us.[40]

DD, No. 349.[41]

(284) 28 July: Berchtold to Szögyény

Berchtold requests clear indication of likely German military actions to determine if Austrian troops can be deployed against Serbia only; suggests that Germany threaten Russia with military moves unless mobilization measures are revoked; suggests that Rumania joins the Triple Alliance as a way of intimidating Russia

Telegram No. 282
Vienna, 28 July 1914

39 This was in fact incorrect. Paris did not even learn of Russia's mobilization when it was first declared. See p. 405, n. 19 for details. See also (**349**).

40 The document's particular importance lies in the fact that a military leader took it upon himself to intervene in political decisions (the memorandum was even entitled 'An estimation of the political situation'), and put pressure on the civilian leaders just at the time when they were making at least a tentative step towards peace by encouraging Austria-Hungary to accept London's mediation proposals. For criticism of Moltke's document, see Luigi Albertini, *The Origins of the War of 1914*, 3 vols, Engl. transl., Oxford University Press, Oxford 1952–1957, Vol. 2, pp. 489–490, and particularly Geiss, *Julikrise*, Vol. 2, p. 236, who argues that with this memorandum Moltke 'decisively contributed to bringing out this "horrible war" with his robust intervention in German politics'. See also Annika Mombauer, *Helmuth von Moltke*, Cambridge University Press, Cambridge 2001, pp. 201ff.

41 English translation based on Geiss, *July 1914*, No. 125, here with additions and amendments.

D. 11.00 p.m.
Strictly confidential

Have received your Excellency's telegram No. 297 of 26th of the month.[42] I have received corresponding news from the Imp. and Roy. Military Attaché in St. Petersburg about Russian armaments. Your Excellency will report immediately to the Imperial Chancellor or the Secretary of State and report the following in my name: according to corresponding news from St Petersburg, Kiev, Warsaw, Moscow and Odessa, Russia is making extensive military preparations. Although Mr Sazonov and the Russian War Minister both gave their word of honour that a mobilization had not at present been ordered, the latter told the German military attaché that the military districts Kiev, Odessa, Moscow which border Austria-Hungary would be mobilized when our troops crossed the Serbian border.

Under these circumstances the Chief of the General Staff [Conrad] considers it absolutely necessary to obtain certainty whether we can march against Serbia with strong forces, or whether we must reserve our main strength to use against Russia.[43] On this question depends our entire campaign against Serbia. If Russia is really mobilizing the military districts in question, even just in view of the time she is gaining it is absolutely imperative that Austria-Hungary, and under present circumstances Germany also, should immediately take comprehensive counter-measures.

Baron Conrad's view seems to me to be most worthy of consideration and I would like to request the Berlin Cabinet to reflect urgently whether Russia should not, in a friendly manner, be reminded that the mobilization of the above-mentioned districts would amount to a threat vis-à-vis Austria-Hungary and thus, if it were really to occur, would have to be answered by military counter-measures by the Monarchy as well as by the allied German Empire.

To make a potential change of heart easier for Russia it seems to us advisable that such a step should initially be undertaken by Germany alone; but of course we would be prepared also to take this step together. I think that plain language would at this moment be the most effective means for alerting Russia to the consequences of a threatening demeanour.

It would also be worth considering if the favourable disposition which exists in Bucharest, according to news received by the Cabinet

42 ÖUA, VIII, No. 10717. Szögyény reported about news received in Berlin about Russian regiments having been recalled to their garrisons, and unsubstantiated reports that reserve troops had been called up. This, if true, was considered by the German General Staff to amount to a general mobilization in Russia. News that the military districts of Moscow, Warsaw, Kiev and Odessa had been mobilized was not yet substantiated.

43 See (**353**).

in Berlin (Your Excellency's telegram No. 389 from yesterday[44]) could also be used to exert pressure on Russia from Rumania. With this aim in mind it seems to me desirable that our and the German Minister in Bucharest should immediately be instructed to approach King Carol with the request, be it by solemn démarche in St. Petersburg (or perhaps also a secret telegram from King Carol to Tsar Nicholas) or by way of public announcement of the alliance, to declare openly that Rumania would fight against Russia on the side of the Triple Alliance in case of a European conflagration.[45] This clarification should, in order to be effective, be made at the latest on 1 August.

Your Excellency will conclude by saying that I trust those in authority in Germany will, in view of the threatening attitude of Russia against both Empires, agree with my propositions.[46]

ÖUA, VIII, No. 10863.[47]

(285) 28 July: Wilhelm II to Nicholas II

Appeals to common monarchic principle; regicide needs to be punished

Telegram (unnumbered)
Berlin, 28 July 1914
D. 29 July, 1.45 a.m.

[English original]
It is with the gravest concern that I hear of the impression which the action of Austria against Serbia is creating in your country. The unscrupulous agitation that has been going on in Serbia for years has resulted in the outrageous crime to which archduke Franz Ferdinand fell a victim. The spirit that led Serbians to murder their own king and his wife still dominates the country. You will doubtless agree with me that we both, you and me, have a common interest, as well as all Sovereigns, to insist that all the persons morally responsible for the dastardly murder should receive their deserved punishment. In this politics play no part at all.

On the other hand I fully understand how difficult it is for you and your Government to face the drift of your public opinion. Therefore, with regard to the hearty and tender friendship which binds us both

44 This should have said No. 289. See ÖUA, VIII, No. 10718.
45 See (**194**).
46 Germany took up Berchtold's suggestion the next day. See (**285**).
47 Engl. transl. based on Geiss, *July 1914*, No. 111, but here with amendments and additions.

from long ago with firm ties, I am exerting my utmost influence to induce the Austrians to deal straightly [*sic*] to arrive to a satisfactory understanding with you. I confidently hope you will help me in my efforts to smooth over difficulties that may arise.[48]

Your very sincere and devoted friend and cousin
Willy[49]

DD, No. 335.[50]

(286) 29 July: Nicholas II to Wilhelm II

Tsar appeals to Wilhelm II to intervene and stop the Austrians

Telegram (no number)
29 July 1914
D. 1:00 a.m.
R. 1.10 a.m.

[English original] [*Wilhelm II's emphases and marginal notes*]

Am glad you are back. In this most serious moment I appeal to you to help me. An ignoble war has been declared upon a weak country. The indignation in Russia shared fully by me is enormous. I foresee that very soon I shall be overwhelmed by the pressure upon me, and be forced to take extreme measures which will lead to war. To try and avoid such a calamity as a European war, I beg you in the name of our old friendship to do what you can to stop your allies from going too far.

[Margin, beside "ignoble": !]
[Margin, beside "allies": *ally!*]
[Margin, beside "going too far": *What would that be?*]

Nicky[51]

48 For the Tsar's reply see (**286**).
49 The infamous Willy-Nicky correspondence needs to be seen in context of both leaders' desire to pass the blame for a conflagration of the crisis to the other. This telegram crossed with (**286**). Chancellor Bethmann Hollweg repeatedly begged the Kaiser to send a telegram to the Tsar and on 28 July provided him with a draft. As he informed the Kaiser, 'such a telegram, should it come to war after all, would highlight Russia's guilt'. DD, No. 308.
50 Also in Geiss, *July 1914*, No. 117.
51 This telegram crossed with (**285**).

A confession of his own weakness, and an attempt to put the responsibility on my own shoulders.

The telegram contains a concealed threat! and an order-like summons to tie the hands of our ally. In case Your Excellency sent off my telegram yesterday evening, it must have crossed with this one.[52] *We shall see now what effect mine has. The expression 'ignoble war' does not indicate any sense of Monarchical unity in the Tsar, but rather a Pan Slavic conception; i.e. worry over a capitis diminutio in the Balkans in case of an Austrian success. This might well first be awaited for its overall result. There will always be time later for negotiation and perhaps for mobilization, for which now Russia has no reason at all. Instead of summoning us to check our allies, His Majesty should turn to the Emperor Franz Josef [sic] and deal with him in order to learn His Majesty's intentions. Should not copies of both telegrams be sent to His Majesty the King at London for his information? The Socialists [die Sozen] are making anti-military demonstrations in the streets; that must not be tolerated, in any event, not now; if they are repeated I shall proclaim a state of martial law and have the leaders one and all tutti quanti locked up.*

Instruct Loebell[53] *and Jagow*[54] *about this. We can tolerate no Socialist propaganda now!*
Wilhelm

DD, No. 332.[55]

(287) 29 July: Bethmann Hollweg to Pourtalès

Germany warns Russia not to continue mobilization measures, as per Austria's request[56]

Telegram No. 134
Berlin, 29 July 1914
D. 12.50 p.m.
R. 4.35 p.m.

Request you alert Mr Sazonov very seriously that further continuation of Russian mobilization measures would force us to mobilize, and that it would then scarcely be possible to avoid European war.[57]

52 The Kaiser was correct, the two documents did cross. See (**285**) and (**286**).
53 Prussian Minister of the Interior.
54 Berlin's Chief of Police, Traugott von Jagow.
55 Engl. transl. based on Geiss, *July 1914*, No. 116, here with minor amendments.
56 See (**284**).
57 According to Schilling's diary, the German Ambassador's rendering of this

DD, No. 342.

(288) 29 July: Wilhelm II to Nicholas II

Kaiser suggests that Russia can remain spectator

Telegram (no number)
Berlin, 29 July 1914
D. 29 July, evening

[English original]

I received your telegram[58] and share your wish that peace should be maintained. But as I told you in my first telegram,[59] I cannot consider Austria's action against Serbia an 'ignoble' war. Austria knows by experience that Serbian promises on paper are wholly unreliable. I understand its action must be judged as trending [*sic*] to get full guarantee that the Serbian promises shall become real facts. Thus my reasoning is borne out by the statement of the Austrian Cabinet that Austria does not want to make any territorial conquests at the expense of Serbia.[60] I therefore suggest that it would be quite possible for Russia to remain a spectator of the Austro-Serbian conflict without involving Europe in the most horrible war she ever witnessed. I think a direct understanding between your Government and Vienna possible and desirable and as I already telegraphed to you, my Government is continuing its exertions to promote it. Of course military measures on the part of Russia which would be looked on by Austria as threatening would precipitate a

---

instruction was even worse. 'If Russia continued her military preparations, even though she did not proceed to mobilize, Germany would find herself compelled to mobilize, *in which case she would immediately proceed to take the offensive*' [my italics]. Schillings diary cited in Menning, 'Russian military intelligence', forthcoming. See also DD, No. 378, (**283**) and (**312**). This instruction from Berlin confirmed Sazonov's view that Germany did not intend to intervene in Austria, and, following a short phone-call to the Tsar, mobilization was briefly declared, but revoked when Tsar Nicholas received a further telegram from Kaiser Wilhelm II which stressed the latter's peaceful intentions (**288**), (**290**), (**291**). According to Turner, Sazonov was so concerned by this request that he immediately sought permission from the Tsar to convene a meeting with the purpose of deciding on general mobilization. This meeting took place between 7 and 9 p.m. L.C.F. Turner, 'Russian Mobilisation', in P. Kennedy (ed.), *War Plans*, Allen & Unwin, London 1979, pp. 252–268, p. 265.

58 (**286**).

59 (**285**).

60 ÖUA, VIII, No. 10834, Berchtold to Ambassadors in St Petersburg, Rome, Paris, London, Berlin, 27 July 1914.

calamity we both wish to avoid and jeopardise my position as mediator which I readily accepted on your appeal to my friendship and my help.[61]

Willy

DD, No. 359.[62]

(289) 29 July: Nicholas II to Wilhelm II

Surprised at discrepancy between Kaiser's views and those of his Ambassador; suggests international conference could resolve the crisis

Telegram (no number)
29 July 1914
D. 8:20 p.m.
R. 8.42 p.m.
[English original]

[Wilhelm II's emphases and marginal notes]

Thanks for your telegram conciliatory and friendly.[63] Whereas official message presented today by your Ambassador to my Minister was conveyed in a very different tone.[64] Beg you to explain this divergency. *Oh! [Nanu!]* It would be right to give over the Austro-Serbian problem to the Hague conference. *!* Trust in your wisdom and friendship.

Thanks to you too. [Wilhelm]

DD, No. 366.[65]

61 For Tsar's reply see (**313**). As Bruce Menning argues, 'it was reading between the lines of the kaiser's seemingly conciliatory telegram that prompted the tsar at literally the eleventh hour in the evening of 16 (29) July to revert to the fall-back option for partial mobilization. The appropriate decree went out, and now was the time for nail biting'. 'Russian military intelligence', forthcoming.

62 Engl. transl. from Geiss, *July 1914*, No. 131.

63 See (**288**).

64 See (**291**).

65 For the reply see (**314**).

(290) 29 July: Sazonov to Isvolsky

Russia cannot comply with German request to stop military preparations; Russia grateful for declaration by Paléologue that French assistance will be forthcoming; British position still not clarified

Telegram 1551
St Petersburg, 29 July 1914
Urgent

The German Ambassador today informed me of the decision of his Government to mobilize, if Russia did not stop her military preparations.[66] Now, in point of fact, we only began these preparations in consequence of the mobilization already undertaken by Austria, and owing to her evident unwillingness to accept any means of arriving at a peaceful settlement of her dispute with Serbia.[67]

As we cannot comply with the wishes of Germany, we have no alternative but to hasten our own military preparations and to assume that war is probably inevitable. Please inform the French Government of this, and add that we are sincerely grateful to them for the declaration which the French Ambassador made to me on their behalf, to the effect that we could count fully upon the assistance of our ally, France.[68] In the existing circumstances, that declaration is especially valuable to us.

It would be extremely desirable if England were also without delay to align herself with France and Russia, since only in this manner could she succeed in preventing a dangerous disturbance of the balance of power in Europe.

Int. Bez. I, 5, No. 221.[69]

66 See (**287**) (**289**), (**291**).

67 This was not strictly true, as the Russian leadership had decided to implement partial mobilization measures as early as 24 July and had implemented these on 26 July (**206**), (**215**).

68 If this assurance was made then Paléologue transgressed his authority. See also p. 405, n. 19 on the debate about Paléologue's role in the July Crisis.

69 English translation based on Geiss, *July 1914*, No. 136, here with minor amendments.

(291) 29 July: Memorandum of the day of the Russian Ministry of Foreign Affairs

German Ambassador assures Russians that Berlin is trying to influence Vienna; Ministers doubt Germany's sincerity; Germany demands end to Russian partial mobilization measures under threat of German mobilization; contradictory telegram arrives from Kaiser Wilhelm II; partial mobilization decided upon, but later revoked by the Tsar

St Petersburg, 29 July 1914

At 9.30 this morning the German Ambassador called Baron Schilling on the telephone and said that he desired to see the Minister in order to make to him an 'agreeable communication'. Count Pourtalès, however, hastened to add, 'Toutefois pas trop d'optimisme'. Baron Schilling replied that latterly we had grown unaccustomed to 'pleasant' news from Berlin, and that therefore the Minister would certainly hear with pleasure what the Ambassador had to say.

S.D. Sazonov received Count Pourtalès at 11 a.m., who said that Germany was agreeable to continuing the attempts she had already made to induce the Vienna Cabinet to grant concessions. He requested, however, that strict secrecy should be maintained concerning this, as the announcement of such an intention on the part of the German Government might create the impression that the views of Austria and Germany were not fully in agreement in the present instance. In addition, the Ambassador insistently requested that the successful issue of the influence which Germany hoped to exercise in Vienna might not be hindered by a premature mobilization on our part.[70]

After the Ambassador's departure the above-mentioned communication made by him was discussed by the Minister with A.A. Neratov, Baron Schilling and Prince Troubetzkoi. The question was raised whether Germany really intended to exert serious pressure in Vienna or whether the communication which Count Pourtalès was instructed to make was only intended to lull us to sleep and so to postpone the Russian mobilization and thus gain time wherein to make corresponding preparations. The general impression was that even if the sincerity of the Germany Government could be admitted, under the circumstances the possibility of arriving at any practical results in this direction must be doubted, because if Austria had gone thus far without the cooperation, or at least the tacit approval, of Germany, then it must be supposed that the influence of the latter in Vienna had greatly declined, and that therefore the German

70 For Pourtalès' account see DD, No. 343.

Government would not succeed in effecting much there at present.

At 3 p.m.[71] the German Ambassador came again to the Minister and read to him a telegram from the Imperial Chancellor, in which it was stated that if Russia continued her military preparations, even though she did not proceed to mobilize, Germany would find herself compelled to mobilize, in which case she would immediately proceed to take the offensive.[72] To this communication S.D. Sazonov sharply replied, 'Maintenant je n'ai plus de doute sur les vraies causes de l'intransigeance autrichienne.'[73] Count Pourtalès jumped up from his seat, and also sharply exclaimed, 'Je proteste de toutes mes forces, M. le Ministre, contre cette assertion blessante.'[74]

The Minister drily replied that Germany still had an opportunity for proving the erroneousness of what he had said. The Minister and the Ambassador parted coolly.

Soon after the German Ambassador's departure, while A.A. Neratov and Baron Schilling were still in the Minister's cabinet, the telephone rang, and H.M. the Tsar personally informed S.D. Sazonov that he had just received a telegram from Kaiser Wilhelm, who urgently requested him not to allow events to develop into a war.[75] S.D. Sazonov utilized this opportunity to report to His Majesty concerning the announcement made to him a few minutes previously by Count Pourtalès, and pointed out how little the words of the Kaiser agreed with the instructions conveyed to his Ambassador. The Tsar said that he was instantly telegraphing to Berlin to ask for an explanation of this apparent contradiction.[76] His Majesty gave permission to S.D. Sazonov to discuss the question of our mobilization at once with the Minister for War and the Chief of the General Staff.

At this moment news was received of the commencement of the bombardment of Belgrade by the Austrians.[77]

The discussion between the three above-mentioned persons took place soon afterwards in the office of Lieutenant-General Ianushkevich. In the adjoining room were *Generalquartiermeister* Danilov, General Monkevitz, and the Assistant to the Chief of the Chancellery of the Foreign Minister, N.A. Basili, in readiness immediately to carry out the

71 According to Pourtalès this discussion took place between 5 and 7 p.m., and the telegram in question only reached the German Embassy at 4.35 p.m.

72 See (**287**).

73 'Now I have no further doubts as to the true cause of Austria's intransigence.'

74 'Minister, I protest with all my might against this insulting assertion.'

75 See (**288**).

76 See (**289**).

77 Austria-Hungary's declaration of war on 28 July was followed by the bombing of Belgrade from river monitors in the night of 28/29 July. See Strandtmann's telegram about the bombing of Belgrade in *Int. Bez.* I, 5, 257.

arrangements necessitated by the decisions about to be reached. Those decisions were awaited with some trepidation, since all concerned knew how important in respect of our military preparedness even a partial mobilization would be if it were ordered, and still more a general mobilization, as in the first case a partial mobilization would render difficult a general mobilization if such should prove subsequently necessary.

After examining the situation from all points, both the Ministers and the Chief of the General Staff decided that in view of the small probability of avoiding a war with Germany it was indispensable to prepare for it in every way in good time, and that therefore the risk could not be accepted of delaying a general mobilization later by effecting a partial mobilization now. The conclusion reached at at this conference was at once reported by telephone to the Tsar, who authorized the taking of steps accordingly. This information was received with enthusiasm by the small circle of those acquainted with what was in progress. Telegrams were at once dispatched to Paris and London to inform the respective Governments of the decision that had been arrived at.[78]

At the same time the Imperial Ambassador in Paris was instructed to thank the French Government for the declaration made by the French Ambassador yesterday.[79] The Imperial Ambassador in London was directed to address to the English Government a request 'to align itself with Russia and France without delay in order to prevent the European balance from being destroyed'.[80]

At about 11 p.m. the Minister for War informed the Foreign Minister by telephone that he had received orders from the Tsar to stop the general mobilization.

At about 1 a.m. the German Ambassador insistently requested the Minister to see him immediately, despite the lateness of the hour, on very pressing business.[81] S.D. Sazonov, who had already gone to bed, rose and received the Ambassador, who asked if we could not be satisfied with an assurance on the part of Austria not to violate the integrity of Serbia. The Minister replied that this would not suffice, and at the pressing request of the Ambassador drew up and handed to Count Pourtalès the text of a formula which set forth the conditions on which Russia would be willing to cease her armed preparations. [...]

Int. Bez. I, 5, No. 224.[82]

78 See (**290**).

79 See also Maurice Paléologue, *An Ambassador's Memoirs*, Doran, New York 1925, Vol. 1, pp. 38–41.

80 See (**290**).

81 But see DD, No. 401: Pourtalès to Jagow, 30 July: 'Just had one and a half hours' conference with Sazonov, who sent for me at midnight.'

82 Engl. transl. based on Geiss, *July 1914*, No. 137, with minor amendments.

(292) 29 July: Falkenhayn's Diary

Dispute over how to respond to Russia's partial mobilization measures

In the evening a discussion at the Imperial Chancellor's with Moltke and Jagow of the question whether Russia's announced mobilization for the military districts of Moscow, Kazan, Odessa [and] Kiev was for us a reason also to mobilize. It is answered negatively by the Imperial Chancellor, against quiet, very quiet objection from Moltke, because he [the Chancellor] is of the opinion that, according to Sazonov's declaration to Pourtalès, Russia's mobilization did not yet mean war, [and that] the *casus foederis* was not yet given. We must, however, wait for this to occur because otherwise we would not have public opinion for us, neither here nor in England. The latter was desirable because in the opinion of the Imperial Chancellor England would not be able to be on Russia's side if she unleashed the general fury of war by way of an attack on Austria, and thus took on board the responsibility for the big mess [*Kladderadatsch*].[83]

BA-MA, BArch RH 61/927.

(293) 29 July: Benckendorff to Sazonov

British public opinion becoming aware of seriousness of the situation

Telegram No. 218
London, 29/16 July 1914
(French Original)

War remains unpopular as public does not understand reasons [for it]; but seriousness of the situation is becoming apparent to the public. Ulster-affair has entirely receded to the background. Papers today are continuing their energetic campaign. In the liberal press a change is apparent, but this has consisted until now primarily of that they no longer know what to say. The vague expression: localization of the

83 Minister of War Falkenhayn had already advocated the declaration of '*Kriegsgefahrzustand*' on 28 July. Such a measure would have led to troop movements within 36 hours. BA-MA, W-10/50635. For details of these events see also Holger Afflerbach, *Falkenhayn*, Oldenbourg, Munich 1994, p. 157. See also (283), (323).

conflict is often repeated and haunts the minds. By the way, so far there is not a trace of any ill-intended hints at Russia, nor at her attitude. This attitude is highly esteemed in influential circles.

Int. Bez, I, 5, No. 228.

(294) 29 July: Pease's Diary

Cabinet discussion of British dilemma; how to abstain from European conflagration without disappointing the French and encouraging the Germans

Cabinet, [London] 29 July 1914

[...] European situation

Grey criticized Austria's conduct as 'brutal recklessness'. He read telegrams showing an indisposition of Austria to listen to Russia & [he] obviously regarded the situation as very grave. [...]

We were urged by France & Russia to come out with them to establish Peace. Germany & the triple alliance urged our neutrality & said this would alone preserve Peace. Evidently we could do nothing right, & that we should be held liable for anything that happened. The cabinet agreed we must do the best for our own interests, and that was the cause of Peace & was the course to be promoted. All the Powers were now building on were their hopes of our participation or abstention as suited them best.

Grey said if it had not been for his intervention they were hopelessly drifting into war, & none had any suggestion to make, he would continue to urge mediation by as many Powers as he could – and restrain Russia who was mobilizing from doing so opposite the German frontier. [...]

Grey said he must tell Cambon that our people thought the Austro-Serbian quarrel did not directly concern us, & that he would say to Cambon Don't count upon our coming in, & to Lichnowsky don't count on our abstention – & neither could then regard our inaction or action respectively as an Act of Treachery. This was assented to.[84] [...]

Keith M. Wilson, 'The Cabinet Diary of J.A. Pease', *Proceedings of the Leeds Philosophical Society*, XIX, III, 1983, pp. 41–51, pp. 43–45.

84 See (309).

(295) 29 July: Wilson's Diary[85]

Precautionary period ordered as result of Cabinet meeting

The Russians have ordered the mobilization of 16 Corps. The Austrians are mobilizing 12 Corps. The Germans and French remain quiet. At 3 p.m. a note came to Douglas from Asquith ordering the 'Precautionary Period'.[86] This we did. I don't know why we are doing it, because there is nothing moving in Germany. We shall see. Anyhow it is more like business than I expected of this Government.

Cited in Charles E. Callwell, *Field-Marshal Sir Henry Wilson*, 2 vols, Cassell, London 1927, Vol. 1, p. 152.

(296) 29 July: Lichnowsky to Jagow, with marginal notes by Wilhelm II

Russia unable to negotiate directly with Austria-Hungary following declaration of war on Serbia; Britain still keen on mediation; suggestion that Austria occupy Belgrade and then announce conditions for mediation; Grey warns that Britain will stay out of a conflict if it involves only Russia and Austria, but not if Germany and France become involved; British public opinion turning against Austria; a European war would be the greatest catastrophe

London, 29 July 1914[87]
[*Wilhelm II's marginal comments and emphases, 30 July*]

85 In the published version, this is dated 28 July, but this appears to be a mistake.

86 See (**309**), outlining decisions taken at the Cabinet meeting of 29 July – John Burns summarized the meeting: 'critical cabinet at 11.30 […] Situation seriously reviewed from all points of view. It was decided not to decide'. Burns Diary, 29 July 1914, John Burns diary, B.M. Add. MSS, 46336, cited in Zara Steiner and Keith Neilson, *Britain and the Origins of the First World War*, Macmillan, London 2003, p. 239. See also K.M. Wilson, 'The British Cabinet's Decision for War, 2 August 1914', in *British Journal for International Studies*, I, 1975, pp. 148–159, pp. 149–150.

87 The telegram was despatched at 6.39 p.m. and received at 9.12 p.m. Kaiser Wilhelm wrote his marginal comments and dated his copy as 30. VII. 14., 1 o'clock p.m.

The worst and most scandalous piece of English pharisaism that I ever saw! I will never enter into a naval convention with such scoundrels.	Sir E. Grey just sent for me again.[88] The Minister was entirely calm, but very grave, and received me with the words that the situation was continuing to grow more acute. Sazonov had stated that after the declaration of war he will no longer be in a position to negotiate with Austria
despite the Tsar's appeal to me!	directly, and had requested them here to take up the mediation efforts
that sets me out of the running	**again.**[89] The Russian Government regards the cessation of hostilities for the present as a necessary preliminary to mediation.
	Sir E. Grey repeated his suggestion already reported, that we take part in a mediation *à quatre*, such as we had already accepted in principle.[90]
good	It would seem to him to be a suitable basis for mediation, if Austria, after occupying Belgrade, for example, or other places, should announce her
we have been trying to accomplish this for days, in vain!	conditions. Should Your Excellency, however, undertake mediation, a prospect I was able early this morning to put before him, this would of course
Instead of mediation, a serious word to St Petersburg and Paris, to the effect that England would not help them would quieten the situation at once.	suit him equally well. But mediation seemed now to him to be urgently necessary, if a European catastrophe were not to result.
	Sir E. Grey then said to me that he had a friendly and private communication to make to me, namely, that he did not want our warm personal relations and the intimacy of our talks on all
aha! The common cheat!	political matters to lead me astray, and he would like to spare himself later *that remains!*

88 DD, No. 357, 29 July: Lichowsky to *Auswärtiges Amt.*

89 Underlined twice by Wilhelm II.

90 Note that the last part of this sentence was omitted from the version presented to the Kaiser which referred to an earlier telegram from Jagow authorizing Lichnowsky to assure Grey that Germany would join mediation efforts. Geiss, *July 1914*, No. 192.

the reproach [of] bad faith. The British Government desired now as before to cultivate our previous friendship, and it could stand aside as long as the conflict remained confined to Austria and Russia.

this means we are to leave Austria in the lurch. Mean and Mephistophelian! Thoroughly English, however

But if we and France should be involved, then the situation would immediately be altered, and the British Government would, under the circumstances, find itself forced to make up its mind quickly.

already made up

In that event it would not be practicable to stand aside and wait for any length of time.

this means they will attack us

'If war breaks out it will be the greatest catastrophe that the world has ever seen.' It was far from his desire to express any kind of a threat; he only wanted to protect me from disappointments and himself from the reproach of bad faith, and had therefore chosen the form of a private explanation.[91]

he has shown bad faith all these years just the same, down to his latest speech

an absolute failure

Sir E. Grey added also that the Government of course had to reckon with **public** opinion.

we too!

create it new!

Up to the present it had in general been in favour of Austria, as the justice of a certain satisfaction due her was recognised; but now it was beginning to turn completely to the other side, as a result of Austrian stubbornness.

if it wants to, it can turn and direct public opinion, as the press obeys it unconditionally

with the help of the jingo press

To my Italian colleague [Imperiali], who has just left me, Sir E. Grey said that he believed if mediation were accepted, that he would be able to secure for Austria every possible satisfaction; there was no longer any question of a humiliating retreat for Austria, as the Serbs would in any case be punished and compelled, with the consent of Russia, to subordinate themselves to Austria's wishes. Thus Austria could obtain guarantees for the future without a war that would jeopardize the peace of Europe.[92]

---

91 See Kaiser's marginal comments on (**312**).

92 See also (**316**). For Austria-Hungary's reaction see (**320**), (**357**).

[*Wilhelm II's notes:*]

England reveals herself in her true colours at a moment when she thinks that we are caught in the toils and, so to speak, finished with! That mean crew of shopkeepers has tried to trick us with dinners and speeches. The boldest deception, the words of the King to Heinrich [Prince Henry] for me: 'We shall remain neutral and try to keep out of this as long as possible.'[93] *Grey proves the King a liar, and his words to Lichnowsky are the outcome of a guilty conscience, because he feels that he has deceived us. At that, it is as a matter of fact a threat combined with a bluff, in order to separate us from Austria and to prevent us from mobilizing, and to shift the responsibility for the war. He knows perfectly well that, if he were to utter one single, serious, sharp and warning word in Paris and St Petersburg, and were to warn them to remain neutral, that both would immediately keep quiet. But he takes care not to speak the word, and threatens us instead! Common cur [Gemeiner Hundsfott]! England alone bears the responsibility for peace and war, not us any longer! That must also be made clear publicly, too.*

W[*ilhelm*]

DD, No. 368.[94]

(297) 29 July: Szögyény to Berchtold

Speculations about British position continue in Berlin

Telegram No. 324
Berlin, 29 July 1914
D. 11.40 a.m.
R. 11.30 p.m.

Secret. Under-Secretary of State told me that French Ambassador here declared today that England will without doubt place herself 'dès le premier coup de notre côté' (France, Russia). The Italian Ambassador has expressed the same conviction to Herr von Jagow. The Under-Secretary of State who had so far seemed convinced of England's neutrality, at least in the opening stages, this evening expressed himself pessimistically in this regard.

ÖUA, VIII, No. 10950.

93 See (**281**). This sentence is in English in the original.
94 Engl. transl. based on Geiss, *July 1914*, No. 130, here with minor amendments.

(298) 29 July: Mérey to Berchtold

Ambassador thinks Austria's harsh attitude towards Serbia will impress and intimidate Italy

Rome, 29 July 1914

Nothing impresses the Italians more than clear determination and ruthless energy which advances calmly and unstoppably towards its goal without flinching away from danger. Moreover, the Italians in particular – and perhaps also the Rumanians – must have had a slight horror when reading our note [to Serbia], because such a pointed attack against an irredentist movement practically demands the realization of a certain analogy – if on a totally different scale – and an interrogation of their own guilty conscience. If our determination is this time indeed serious and we hold our nerve, then this will be extremely useful for us in Italy in the future. Even a certain worsening of our relations will almost be compensated for by the respect which we will have created here.

ÖUA, VIII, No. 10989.

(299) 29 July: Poincaré's diary

Viviani still hopes for peaceful solution

Viviani, who, with worrying ease, lets himself be swayed by the most contradictory of impressions, is very serious at times and then at others, imagining a miracle can still solve everything, he becomes radiant.

'Notes journalières', Poincaré papers, BNF, Nafr. 16027, fol. 130, cited in Stefan Schmidt, *Frankreichs Außenpolitik in der Julikrise 1914*, Oldenbourg, Munich 2007, p. 315.

(300) 29 July: Paléologue's memoirs

Austro-Hungarian mobilization ordered; Russian military preparations ensued and general mobilization decided on later that day

Wednesday, 29 July 1914
I think we have reached the last scene of the prologue to the drama.

Yesterday evening the Austro-Hungarian Government ordered the general mobilization of the army. The Vienna cabinet is thus refusing the suggestion of direct conversations proposed by the Russian Government.

About three o'clock this afternoon, Pourtalès came to tell Sazonov that if Russia did not stop her military preparations at once Germany also would mobilize her army.[95] Sazonov replied that the preparations of the Russian General Staff were the result of the uncompromising obstinacy of the Vienna cabinet and the fact that eight Austro-Hungarian army corps were already on a war footing.

At eleven o'clock to-night, Nicholas-Alexandrovitch Basily, Deputy-Directory of the chancellery of the Foreign Office, appeared at my embassy. He came to tell me that the imperious language used by the German Ambassador this afternoon[96] has decided the Russian Government

(1) to order this very night the mobilization of the thirteen corps earmarked for operations against Austria-Hungary;

(2) secretly to commence general mobilization.

These last words made me jump: 'Isn't it possible for them to confine themselves – provisionally at any rate – to a partial mobilization?'

'No. The question has just been gone into thoroughly by a council of our highest military officers. They have come to the conclusion that in existing circumstances the Russian Government has no choice between partial and general mobilization as from the technical point of view a partial mobilization could be carried out only at the price of dislocating the entire machinery of general mobilization. So if to-day we stopped at mobilizing the thirteen corps destined for operations against Austria and to-morrow Germany decided to give her ally military support, we should be powerless to defend ourselves on the frontiers of Poland and East Prussia. Besides, isn't it as much to France's interest as our own that we should be able to intervene promptly against Germany?'

'Those are strong arguments but I still think that your General Staff should take no step without previous discussion with the French General Staff. Please tell M. Sazonov from me that I should like his most serious consideration of this matter and a reply in the course of the night.'

Maurice Paléologue, *An Ambassador's Memoirs*, Doran, New York 1925, Vol. 1, pp. 41–43.[97]

---

95 See (**291**).

96 See also the official account of this heated conversation in (**291**). Sazonov replied to Pourtalès: 'Now I have no more doubts as to the real cause of Austria's intransigence.'

97 Paléologue then composed a telegram to Paris to update the French Government about these developments. While it was being put into Russian cipher news was received of the Tsar's decision against general mobilization (**291**). The last paragraph of Paléologue's telegram was omitted and the French Govern-

(301) 29 July: Goschen to Grey

Bethmann Hollweg appeals for British neutrality; assures that Germany has no territorial ambitions in France, Belgium or the Netherlands

Berlin, 29 July 1914.
D. 20 July 1:20 a.m.
Tel. (No. 102.) Secret. Urgent.
R. 30 July, 9 a.m.

[?Austria and] Serbia. Chancellor having just returned from Potsdam sent for me again to-night and made the following strong bid for British neutrality in the event of war.[98] He said he was continuing his efforts to maintain peace,[99] but that [group omitted:? in the event of] a Russian attack on Austria, Germany's obligation as Austria's ally might, to his great regret, render a European conflagration inevitable, and in that case he hoped Great Britain would remain neutral. As far as he was able to judge key-note of British policy, it was evident that Great Britain would never allow France to be crushed. Such a result was not contemplated by Germany. The Imperial Government was ready to give every assurance to the British Government provided that Great Britain remained neutral that, in the event of a victorious war, Germany aimed at no territorial

---

ment was consequently only aware of the partial mobilization, not, however, of the fact that general mobilization had been so nearly decided on that day. Schuman, *War and Diplomacy*, pp. 227–228. See also Schmidt, *Frankreichs Außenpolitik*, p. 318.

98 Solicitor-general Buckmaster told Addison 'that, before the receipt of the German Chancellor's proposal [...] Simon, Harcourt, Pease, Burns and Morley as well as himself, had intended to resign if we became involved; but that, after its receipt, they decided to stick to the ship, with the exception of Morley and Burns'. Cited in Wilson, 'The British Cabinet's Decision', p. 157, who considers this account to be 'nonsense' and maintains that many of the members of the Cabinet simply sought an excuse not to resign, although he concedes that Germany's actions and the 'march of events' may have helped to confirm a decision already made (p. 159).

99 In a complete reversal of his previous position, Bethmann Hollweg finally tried to restrain Vienna, probably because he feared that Russia's partial mobilization meant there could be no more hope for a localization of the conflict. See also Mombauer, *Moltke*, p. 205. While Bethmann Hollweg was attempting to negotiate for peace, Moltke, behind his back, liaised with the Austrian General Staff, famously leading Berchtold to ask Conrad: 'Who rules in Berlin – Moltke or Bethmann?' See David Stevenson, *The First World War and International Politics*, Oxford University Press, Oxford 1988, p. 28; Holger Herwig, *The First World War*, Arnold, London et al. 1997, p. 28; F. Conrad, *Dienstzeit*, 5 vols, Rikola, Vienna et al. 1922–1925, Vol. IV, p. 152.

acquisitions at the expense of France.

In answer to a question from me, his Excellency said that it would not be possible for him to give such an assurance as regards colonies.

Continuing, his Excellency said he was, further, ready to assure the British Government that Germany would respect neutrality and integrity of Holland as long as they were respected by Germany's adversaries.

As regards Belgium, his Excellency could not tell to what operations Germany might be forced by the action of France, but he could state that, provided that Belgium did not take sides against Germany, her integrity would be respected after the conclusion of the war.[100]

Finally, his Excellency said that he trusted that these assurances might form basis of a further understanding with England which, as you well know, had been the object of his policy ever since he had been Chancellor.

An assurance of British neutrality in conflict which present crisis might possibly produce would enable him to look forward to a general neutrality agreement between the two countries, the details of which it would, of course, be premature to discuss at the present moment.

His Excellency asked me how I thought you would view his request. I replied that I thought that you would like to retain full liberty of action, and that personally I did not consider it likely that you would care to bind yourself to any course of action at this stage of events. [...][101]

MINUTE

The only comment that need be made on these astounding proposals is that they reflect discredit on the statesman who makes them.[102]

Incidentally it is of interest to note that Germany practically admits the intention to violate Belgian neutrality but to endeavour to respect that of Holland (in order to safeguard German imports via the Rhine and Rotterdam).

It is clear that Germany is practically determined to go to war, and that the one restraining influence so far has been the fear of England joining in the defence of France and Belgium. E.A.C[rowe]. 30 July.

BD, XI, No. 293.[103]

---

100 See (**302**), (**386**).

101 DD No. 373 contains the German Chancellor's record of this conversation. Asquith considered this 'a rather shameless attempt on the part of Germany to buy our neutrality', while Grey flew into a 'white heat of rage' upon learning of this conversation. See Wilson, 'Britain', p. 191.

102 Morley told Almeric Fitzroy on 2 August: 'the high-handed action of Germany was weakening the efforts of the peacemakers in the Cabinet'. Almeric Fitzroy, *Memoirs*, 2 vols, London 1925, Vol. II, pp. 559–560, cited in Wilson, 'The British Cabinet's Decision', p. 159.

103 For Grey's reply see (**331**).

(302) 29 July: Jagow to Below

German Government's ultimatum to Belgium drafted and sent to Below for presentation to the Belgian Government at suitable future point

Berlin, 29 July 1914

May I request that Your Excellency keep the enclosed document safely locked away, and only to open it when instructed to do so from here by telegram. Please will you confirm by telegram that you received this decree and enclosure.[104]

DD, No. 375.

(303) 30 July: Joffre's Memoirs

Cabinet decides that only minimal military preparations be allowed in France, despite signs of German preparations; French troops to remain 10 kilometres behind the border; Chief of Staff protests but without effect

[...] Faced by this menacing situation [of German war preparations], we had taken practically not a single measure for our defence, and I had not even received from the Government permission to establish our covering forces in one place. When I saw M. Messimy on the morning of the 30th, I once more urged the absolute necessity of the Government's taking this decision. He shortly afterwards went to a Cabinet meeting[105] and there informed his colleagues of my insistence. The séance was very long, but finally, after several hours of deliberation, the Minister of War sent to inform me that the Cabinet agreed that the covering troops should be put in place, but with the following reservations:

The only units to be moved up would be those which could reach their stations by march route, no movement by railway being authorized. No reservists were to be called up for the moment, and no requisitions made. Horses immediately needed to complete those on hand with the troops were to be bought in the open market. Lastly, no covering troops were to approach closer than 10 kilometres (6 miles) from the

104 The enclosed text was an ultimatum for Belgium, handed to the Belgian Government on 2 August (**386**). Below's telegram confirming receipt arrived in Berlin on 30 July in the afternoon.

105 See (**307**).

frontier, in order that contact between French and German patrols might be avoided.[106]

When the Minister communicated this decision to me, I strongly protested against the refusal to call up reservists and against the restriction imposed by limiting all movements to march route; I also represented to him that these half-way measures would in no fashion protect us from a sudden irruption across our frontier. In regard to the 10-kilometre limit, I made little objection, recognizing the strength of the motive dictating it and realizing, moreover, that this measure would in no way compromise our mobilization or our later operations.[107]

But my protest remained without effect. The decision had been taken at a Cabinet meeting and M. Messimy could not alter it on his own authority. All that I could obtain was that the troops destined for entraining should be moved up close to railway stations. I also pointed out that the necessity of our keeping back 10 kilometres from the frontier was too rigid, and I obtained authority for myself to indicate the line which was not to be crossed.

Joseph Joffre, *The Memoirs of Marshal Joffre*, 2 vols, Geoffrey Bles, London 1932, I, pp. 122–123.

(304) 30 July: Sazonov to Sverbejev

If Austria-Hungary drops unacceptable parts of conditions for Serbia, mobilization can still be suspended

Telegram 1554
St Petersburg, 30 July 1914
Very urgent

106 The main reason for this was to 'prove our pacifist intentions' to Britain, as Messimy explained in 1921 in conversation with the journalist Raymond Recouly, while Messimy's order of 1 August to the General commanders of the 2nd, 6th, 7th, 20th and 21st Army Corps was made 'in view of assuring ourselves of the collaboration of our English neighbour. Both cited in Schmidt, *Frankreichs Außenpolitik*, p. 346, n. 146. The decision to keep troops 10 kilometres behind the border was attributed to Viviani who was praised at this funeral for 'this gesture of sublime sincerity' which had become a symbol of French innocence in the events that led to war. Schumann, *War and Diplomacy*, p. 234, n. 4.

107 As Stefan Schmidt points out, militarily this did not give the opponents any advantage. *Frankreichs Außenpolitik*, p. 346. However, according to Berthelot's unpublished diary, Joffre objected that the move 'exposed valuable heights of land in the Vosges to the enemy and should be rescinded with the first German violation of the border'. See also Prete, 'French Strategic Planning', p. 50.

Communicated to Paris, London and Vienna
No. 1

Request urgent dispositions.

The German Ambassador, who has just seen me, enquired whether we could not be content with Austria's promise not to violate the integrity of the kingdom of Serbia. I replied that this declaration was insufficient.[108]

In response to the urgent request of the Ambassador to indicate on what conditions we would still agree to a suspension of our mobilization [*Rüstungen*] I dictated to him for urgent forwarding to Berlin the declaration contained under No. 2 in the telegram.[109]

Please telegraph urgently how the Germany Government will react to this new proof of our readiness to do the utmost for a peaceful settlement of the question, because we cannot allow such negotiations merely being used to buy time for Austria and Germany.

Int. Bez., I, 5, No. 277.

(305) 30 July: Daily record of Russian Foreign Ministry

Nicholas II resists military leaders' pressure to revoke his decision to stop general mobilization; finally gives in to pressure in the afternoon of 30 July

St Petersburg, 30 July 1914

Between 9 and 10 a.m. the Minister for Foreign Affairs spoke to the Minister for Agriculture [Krivoshein] by telephone. Both of them were greatly disturbed at the stoppage of the general mobilization,[110] as they fully realized that this threatened to place Russia in an extremely difficult position in the event of relations with Germany becoming acute. S.D. Sazonov advised A.V. Krivoshein to beg an audience of the Tsar in order to represent to His Majesty the dangers called forth by the change.

At 11 a.m. the Minister for Foreign Affairs again met the Minister for War and the Chief of the General Staff. Information received during the night still further strengthened the opinion which they all held that it was imperative to prepare for a serious war without loss of time. Accordingly the Ministers and the Chief of the Staff adhered to the view which they had expressed yesterday to the effect that it was indispensable to proceed to a general mobilization. Adjutant-General Sukhomlinov and General Ianushkevich again endeavoured by telephone to persuade the

108 See (**312**).
109 See (**312**).
110 See (**312**).

Tsar to revert to his decision of yesterday[111] to permit a general mobilization. His Majesty decidedly refused to do so, and finally shortly declared that the conversation was at an end. General Ianushkevich, who at this moment was holding the telephone receiver, only succeeded in reporting that the Minister for Foreign Affairs was there with him and asked to be allowed to say a few words to His Majesty. A somewhat lengthy silence ensued, after which the Tsar expressed his willingness to hear the Minister. S.D. Sazonov requested His Majesty to receive him today, to enable him to present a report concerning the political situation which admitted of no delay. After a silence, the Tsar asked: 'Is it all the same to you if I receive you at 3 o'clock, at the same time as Tatistchev, as otherwise I have not a free minute today?' The Minister thanked His Majesty and said that he would present himself at the hour named.

The Chief of the Staff heatedly pleaded with S.D. Sazonov to persuade the Tsar without fail to consent to a general mobilization in view of the extreme danger that would result for us if we were not ready for war with Germany should circumstances demand the taking of decisive measures by us after the success of a general mobilization had been compromised by recourse to a partial mobilization. General Ianushkevich requested the Minister that in the event of his succeeding in persuading the Tsar he would telephone to him to that effect from Peterhof, in order that he might immediately take the necessary steps, as it would be requisite first of all to stop as soon as possible the partial mobilization which had already commenced and substitute fresh orders for those which had been issued. 'After that,' said Ianushkevich, 'I shall go away, smash my telephone and generally adopt measures which will prevent anyone from finding me for the purpose of giving contrary orders which would again stop our general mobilization.'

On his return to the Foreign Office, S.D. Sazonov had an interview with the French Ambassador.[112]

Meanwhile A.V. Krivoshein informed S.D. Sazonov that in reply to his request that the Tsar would receive him he was told that His Majesty was so extremely occupied today that he could not see him. Krivoshein then expressed a desire to see S.D. Sazonov before the latter went to Peterhof. It was decided that they should breakfast together at Donon's, and at 12.30 they and Baron Schilling met in a private room there. The general state of mind was tense and the conversation was almost exclusively concerned with the necessity for insisting upon a general mobilization at the earliest possible moment, in view of the inevitability of war with Germany, which every moment became clearer. A.V. Krivoshein expressed the hope that S.D. Sazonov would succeed in persuading

111 See (**312**).

112 For Paléologue's account of this see DDF, 3e série, 11, No. 342.

the Tsar, as otherwise, to use his own words, we should be marching towards a certain catastrophe.

At 2 p.m. the Minister for Foreign Affairs left for Peterhof, together with Major-General Tatistchev, and both of them were received together there in the Alexander Palace by His Majesty. During the course of nearly an hour the Minister attempted to show that war was becoming inevitable, as it was clear to everybody that Germany had decided to bring about a collision, as otherwise she would not have rejected all the pacifying proposals that had been made and could easily have brought her ally to reason. Under these circumstances it only remained to do everything that was necessary to meet war fully armed and under the most favourable conditions for ourselves. Therefore it was better to put away any fears that our warlike preparations would bring about a war, and to continue these preparations carefully rather than by reason of such fears to be taken unawares by war.

The firm desire of the Tsar to avoid war at all costs, the horrors of which filled him with repulsion, led His Majesty in his full realization of the heavy responsibility which he took upon himself in this fateful hour to explore every possible means for averting the approaching danger. Consequently he refused for a long time to agree to the adoption of measures which, however indispensable from a military point of view, were calculated, as he clearly saw, to hasten a decision in an undesirable sense.

The tenseness of feeling experienced by the Tsar at this time found expression, amongst other signs, in the irritability most unusual with him, with which His Majesty interrupted General Tatistchev. The latter, who throughout had taken no part in the conversation, said in a moment of silence: 'Yes, it is hard to decide.' His Majesty replied in a rough and displeased tone: 'I will decide' – in order by this means to prevent the General from intervening any further in the conversation.

Finally the Tsar agreed that under the existing circumstances it would be very dangerous not to make timely preparations for what was apparently an inevitable war, and therefore gave his decision in favour of an immediate general mobilization.[113]

S.D. Sazonov requested the Imperial permission to inform the Chief of the General Staff of this immediately by telephone, and this being

113 See also (**328**), (**329**), (**330**) on the Tsar's change of mind. According to Sazonov, the Tsar stressed Austria-Hungary's mobilization as the main reason for his decision: 'If I agreed to Germany's demands [to end military preparations] now, we should find ourselves unarmed against the Austrian Army which is mobilized already.' Sergei Sazonov, *Fateful Years, 1909–1916*, New York 1928, p. 203. For details of the decision for mobilization, and for the difference between partial and full mobilization, see Menning, 'Russian Military Intelligence', forthcoming, who also points out that in fact, Austrian mobilization did not occur until 31 July, the day after Russia decided to mobilize.

granted, he hastened to the telephone on the ground floor of the palace. Having transmitted the Imperial order to General Ianushkevich, who was waiting impatiently for it, the Minister, with reference to their conversation that morning, added: 'Now you can smash your telephone.'

Meanwhile His Majesty still cherished the hope of finding some means of preventing the general mobilization from becoming an irrevocable *casus belli*. To this end the Tsar, in a telegram dispatched to Kaiser Wilhelm on this same day regarding the decision come to,[114] gave his solemn word that despite the mobilization referred to [...].[115]

Int. Bez., 1, 5, No. 284.[116]

(306) 30 July: Isvolsky to Sazonov

French request that Russian military measures be carried out with as little provocation as possible

Telegram No. 210
Paris, 30/17 July 1915
Copy to London
[...] Request urgent instructions.

Margerie, with whom I have just spoken, told me the French Government has no intention of interfering in our military preparations but thinks it extremely desirable, in view of the further pursuance of negotiations for the preservation of peace, that these preparations should be of as little overt and provocative a character as possible. Also, continuing the same theme, the Minister of War [Messimy] said to Count Ignatiev we could make a statement that in consideration of the overriding interests of peace we were prepared temporarily to slow down the measures for mobilization, which would, of course, not prevent us from continuing our military measures and even to conduct them more energetically, so long as we refrain, as far as possible, from mass transport of troops. At 9.30 a.m. there is to be a Cabinet meeting[117] presided over by Poincaré,

114 See (**313**).

115 The text ends abruptly. See also M.F. Schilling (ed.), *How the War Began in 1914. Being the Diary of the Russian Foreign Office from the 3rd to the 20th (Old Style) of July, 1914*, Allen & Unwin, London 1925, pp. 62ff. See also (**346**). For further background on the events of that day see also S.D. Sasonoff (Sazonov), *Sechs schwere Jahre*, Verlag für Kulturpolitik, Berlin 1927, pp. 246f. In English as in note 113.

116 Engl. transl. in Geiss, *July 1914*, No. 147.

117 See (**307**).

after which I shall immediately speak with Viviani.[118]

Int. Bez., I, 5, No. 291.

(307) 30 July: Abel Ferry's notes about the meeting of the French Council of Ministers

French want to wait for Germany to put herself in the wrong; in favour of Russian mobilization

Impressive cabinet. Solemn men.

1 For the sake of public opinion, let the Germans put themselves in the wrong

2 Do not stop Russian mobilization

Mobilize but do not concentrate

Cabinet calm, serious, orderly.

Archives privés de Abel Ferry, quoted in John F.V. Keiger, *Raymond Poincaré*, Cambridge University Press, Cambridge 1997, p. 175.[119]

118 As Albertini notes, this message summarizing Margerie's and Messimy's advice probably did not reach St Petersburg until after the Russian order for general mobilization had been issued. Yet, as Sidney B. Fay has noted, Paris sent St Petersburg no unequivocally clear message at this crucial moment about delaying general mobilization until all diplomatic efforts had failed. For a damning discussion of Paléologue's failings at this crucial point of the crisis, see Albertini, *Origins*, II, pp. 603ff. See also Schmidt, *Frankreichs Außenpolitik*, pp. 317ff.

119 Also in DDF, 3e série, XI, p. 262 n. 2. No formal minutes of the meeting exist, but Abel Ferry, the Under-Secretary of State for foreign affairs, recorded the main points. (He dated his notes: '30 July, Friday', but 30 July was a Thursday, so there is some uncertainty about when he wrote the note.) France did not offer Russia a blank cheque, but at this late point in the crisis she took only modest steps to defuse the Balkan crisis of July 1914 or restrain Russia. As John Keiger notes, the participants of the meeting were, however, 'quite unaware of how close to general mobilization Russia was' at that point in time. Previously, however, French policy had been focused on restraining Russia, so as to avoid any pretext which might allow Germany to go to war without appearing to be the aggressor. John F.V. Keiger, *Raymond Poincaré*, Cambridge University Press, Cambridge 1997, p. 175. See also Robert Doughty, 'France' in Hamilton and Herwig (eds), *War Planning 1914*, Cambridge University Press, Cambridge 2010, p. 167. On the other hand, Schmidt argues that France did not try to restrain her ally, and shows how the French were encouraging Russia to proceed 'secretly' with their measures prior to mobilization while outwardly declaring that she was slowing or even curtailing them. *Frankreichs Außenpolitik*, pp. 317f., p. 326.

(308) 30 July: Viviani to Paléologue and Paul Cambon

Viviani urges Russia not to take steps which will make her appear as the aggressor, but asserts France's commitment to fulfilling her alliance obligation

Telegram Nos 453, 373–374
Paris, 30 July 1914
D. 7 a.m. and 7.10 a.m.
Confidential

The Russian Ambassador has advised me tonight that the German Ambassador has notified M. Sazonov of his Government's decision to mobilize its armed forces if Russia does not stop her military preparations.[120] The Tsar's Foreign Minister points out that these preparations were only started after Austria's mobilization of eight army corps[121] and after this Power's refusal to settle peacefully her disagreement with Serbia. M. Sazonov states that, under these conditions: Russia has no choice but to hasten arming and to anticipate the imminence of war; that she is counting on France's allied help; and that she would like England to lose no time in joining Russia and France.

As I indicated to you in my telegram of the 27th of this month[122] the Government of the Republic is determined not to ignore any effort with a view to solving the conflict and to assist the Imperial Government's action in the interest of peace for all.

France is, moreover, committed to fulfilling all her obligations to the alliance.[123]

But, in the interest of peace for all and given the ongoing conversation between the less involved Powers, I think it advisable that, within the precautionary and defensive measures Russia thinks she should carry out, she should not, in the first instance, take any position that would give Germany a pretext for total or partial mobilization of her forces.[124]

DDF, 3e série, Vol. 11, No. 305.

120 See DDF, 3e série, 11, No. 301; (**287**), (**290**).

121 This was not true.

122 See DDF, 3e série, 11, No. 138.

123 See (**290**).

124 The reason for this warning was the telegram received by Isvolsky. See (**290**) in which the Russian Foreign Minister outlined that Russia's mobilization measures needed to be speeded up and in which he thanked the ally for Paléologue's promise of complete support. Viviani, Messimy and Poincaré (and, according to Poincaré, also the Navy Minister) met at 4 a.m. to discuss how to react to the telegram, and decided on the text of the message which was then despatched to Paléologue. See Schmidt, *Frankreichs Außenpolitik*, p. 322.

(309) 30 July: Asquith to King George V

Cabinet discussed treaty obligations vis-à-vis Belgium; Britain to inform Germany and France that she would not commit herself one way or the other; decision to despatch 'warning telegrams'

Mr Asquith, with his humble duty to Your Majesty, has the honour to report that the meeting of the Cabinet yesterday was mainly occupied with the diplomatic situation.[125]

At the moment the best hope of peace appeared to lie in the communications which the German Chancellor was making at Vienna.[126]

The Cabinet carefully reviewed the obligations of this country in regard to the neutrality, arising out of the two treaties of April 1839, and action which was taken by Mr Gladstone's Government in Aug[ust] 1870.

It is a doubtful point how far a single guaranteeing state is bound under the Treaty of 1839 to maintain Belgian neutrality if the remainder abstain or refuse.

The Cabinet advises that the matter if it arises will be rather one of policy than of legal obligation.

After much discussion it was agreed that Sir E. Grey should be authorised to inform the German and French Ambassadors that at this stage we were unable to pledge ourselves in advance, either under all conditions to stand aside, or in any condition to join in.

Mr Churchill described the hard steps which had already been taken, and it was resolved that the 'precautionary stage' had now arrived, and the 'warning telegram' should now be sent.

This was done immediately after the rising of the Cabinet, i.e. shortly before 2 p.m.[127]

TNA, CAB 41/35.

---

125 See (**294**). The Cabinet meeting on 1 August decided against despatching the BEF immediately and against immediate mobilization of the navy. Still 'no decision', Burns Diary, 1 August 1914, cited in Wilson, 'The British Cabinet's Decision', p. 150.

126 Unfortunately this hope was based on an illusion as the German Chancellor had until this point in the crisis not made any honest attempts to restrain Austria-Hungary. See also (**317**), for Kageneck's comment that Germany had 'rejected proudly' the English conference idea.

127 See (**295**).

(310) 30 July: King George V to Prince Henry of Prussia

British King supports 'halt in Belgrade' idea and is working to secure peace

Telegram
London, 30 July 1914
Thanks for telegram.[128] So pleased to hear of William's efforts to concert with Nicky to maintain peace.[129] Indeed I am earnestly desirous that such an irreparable disaster as a European war should be averted. My government is doing its utmost, suggesting to Russia and France to suspend further military preparations, if Austria will consent to be satisfied with occupation of Belgrade and the neighbouring Serbian territory as a hostage for satisfactory settlement of her demands[,] other countries meanwhile suspending their war preparations. Trust William will use his great influence to induce Austria to accept his proposal thus proving that Germany and England are working together to prevent what would be an international catastrophe. Pray assure William I am doing and shall continue to do all that lies in my power to preserve peace in Europe.

ÖUA, VIII, No. 11135.[130]

(311) 30 July: Henry Wilson's diary

War seems inevitable

The news is all bad today and war seems inevitable. Sazonov and the German Ambassador fell out last night, and the German went to Sazonov's house at 2 a.m. this morning in tears and said all was over. The Germans asked us to guarantee neutrality. Grey answers, 'Wait and see.' Nicolson, whom I saw several times, expects German mobilization tomorrow. I confess it looks like it. Panouse[131] to-night brought me a paper which

128 A copy of this telegram, dated 30 July, in which the Prince outlines that mobilization measures in Russia and France may force Germany's hand despite Wilhelm's best efforts is in the Royal Archives, PS/GV/Q 1549/5.

129 See **(288)**, **(313)**, **(314)**, **(289)**, **(330)**, **(347)**.

130 Copies were made of this telegram (one can be found in the Trotha papers, A257, in the Staatsarchiv Bückeburg, for example), and one must have been passed to Vienna. It was marked 'Ad acta. Alexander Hoyos' but was not dated. There is no copy of this telegram in BD, but it is contained in the files of the Royal Archives. For details of the meeting see also **(250)**.

131 General Vicomte Louis de la Panouse, French military attaché in London.

Cambon gave Grey this afternoon, showing German preparations.

Cited in Charles E. Callwell, *Field-Marshal Sir Henry Wilson: His Life and Diaries*, 2 vols, Cassell, London 1927, Vol.1, p. 152.

(312) 30 July: Pourtalès to Jagow

Peace still possible if Austria-Hungary willing to remove certain points from her list of demands for Serbia

Telegram 192
St Petersburg, 30 July 1914
D. 1.01 p.m.
R. 3.52 p.m.

Have just talked with Sazonov according to instructions in telegram 139.[132] Minister repeated his declaration of last night[133] that assurance of territorial disinterestedness on the part of Austria-Hungary did not satisfy Russia. Any other policy he could not at the present time advocate without endangering the life of the Tsar. I requested Sazonov – stating in advance, however, that I believed any prospect of the fulfilment of his wishes by Austria to be hopeless – to formulate them once more for me, and in writing, and to bear in mind that, if there were in any case to be the least prospect of a peaceful solution, he would absolutely have to agree to some sort of a compromise. Minister thereupon set down the following:

'If Austria declares that in recognition of the fact that her conflict with Serbia has assumed the character of a question of European interest, she declares herself ready to eliminate from her ultimatum those points which infringe on Serbia's sovereign rights, then Russia agrees to suspend all military preparations.'[134]

Even if these demands will scarcely prove acceptable, it is still remarkable that Sazonov's document should not contain a word requiring the immediate suspension of Austria's punitive expedition. The Minister would not, however, agree to my proposition that Russia might, perhaps, declare herself to be satisfied if Austria should give certain assurances

132 See DD, No. 380, Bethmann Hollweg to Pourtalés, 29 July 1914, in which the Chancellor outlined a proposal to Vienna to assure Russia that Austria-Hungary did not aim to claim any Serbian territory, and that such a declaration from Vienna would mean that 'Russia had achieved everything that she wants'.

133 See for example DD, No. 401 (Geiss, *July 1914*, No. 135) and DD, No. 412.

134 Sazonov also sent this text as a very urgent telegram to the Russian Ambassador in Berlin, copied to Paris, London and Vienna. See *Int. Bez.*, No. 278.

along these lines upon the *conclusion of peace*.[135]

DD, No. 421.[136]

(313) 30 July: Nicholas II to Wilhelm II

Military measures decided on in Russia on 25 July have now come into effect; Tsar hopes they won't interfere with Wilhelm II's attempts to mediate

Telegram (no number)
Peterhof Palace, 30 July 1914
D. 1.20 a.m.
R. 1.45 a.m.

[*Wilhelm II's marginal notes and emphases*]

* *Austria has only made a partial mobilization against Serbia in the south. On the strength of that the Tsar – as is openly admitted by him here – instituted 'milit. measures which have now come into force' against Austria and us and as a matter of fact 5 days ago. Thus it is almost a week ahead of us. And these measures are for defence against Austria, which is in no way attacking him!!! I cannot agree to any more mediation, since the Tsar who requested it has at the same time secretly mobilized behind my back. It is only a manoeuvre, in order to hold us back and to increase the start they have already got. My work is at an end!*

[English original]

Thank you heartily for your quick answer. Am sending Tatistchev this evening with instructions. The military measures* which have now come into force were decided five days ago for reasons of defence on account of Austria's preparations. I hope from all my heart that these measures won't in any way interfere with your part asmediator which I greatly value. We need your strong pressure on Austria to come to an understanding with us. *!* *No!*
Nicky

No! There is no thought of anything of that sort!!!

DD, No. 390.[137]

135 Bethmann Hollweg's marginal note: 'What point of the Austrian ultimatum has Serbia really rejected? To my knowledge only the cooperation of Austrian officials in the judicial proceedings. Austria could forgo this cooperation on the condition that she occupies parts of Serbia with her troops until the completion of negotiations.'

136 Engl. transl. based on Geiss, *July 1914*, No. 141a, here with minor amendments.

137 English translation in Geiss, *July 1914*, No. 132. See (**289**) and (**314**).

(314) 30 July: Wilhelm II to Nicholas II

Kaiser places responsibility for war or peace on Tsar

Telegram (no number)
30 July 1914, 3.30 pm

[English original]
Best thanks for telegram.[138] It is quite out of the question that my Ambassador's language could have been in contradiction with the tenor of my telegram. Count Pourtalès was instructed to draw the attention of your government to the danger & grave consequences involved by a mobilization; I said that same in my telegram to you. Austria has only mobilized against *Serbia* and only a *part* of her army. If, as it is now the case, according to the communication by you & your Government, Russia mobilizes against Austria, my rôle as mediator you kindly intrusted me with, & which I accepted at you[r] express prayer, will be endangered if not ruined. The whole weight of the decision lies solely on you[r] shoulders now, who have to bear the responsibility for Peace or War.[139]
Willy

DD, No. 420.

(315) 30 July: Ignatjev to the department of the General Quartermaster of the Russian General Staff

Messimy assures military attaché of French support, but urges to tone down mobilization and refrain from troop movements as way of trying to maintain peace

Telegram No. 227
Paris, 30/17 July

At three o'clock at night I gave the Minister of War the declaration by the German Ambassador to Sazonov[140] which I had received from the

138 See (**289**) and (**313**).

139 For Sazonov's reaction to this telegram see (**330**). Based on this telegram, Sazonov urged the Tsar to revoke the decision to delay the mobilization and at about 4 p.m. that day, the Tsar gave in to pressure from his military and political advisers and general mobilization was ordered.

140 See (**288**), and DD, Nos. 342, 378. Pourtalès' account also in Friedrich Pourtalès, *Meine Letzten Verhandlungen in St Petersburg Ende Juli 1914*, Deutsche Verlagsgesellschaft für Politik und Geschichte, Berlin 1927, pp. 43–44.

Ambassador [Isvolsky]. At six o'clock in the morning the Minister of War told me in general terms of the content of the answer telegram to Paléologue and declared that France would be ready to fulfil her alliance obligations exactly; it would however be desirable to use all means for maintaining peace, all the more as delaying a break would be useful for us. According to the thoughts of the Minister we could delay the course of our mobilization which would however not hinder us from continuing our preparations in reality and even to speed them up, as long as we made do without mass transports of troops where possible.

Int. Bez., I, 5, No. 293.

(316) 30 July: Bethmann Hollweg to Tschirschky

Berlin now urges Vienna to accept British mediation proposals

Telegram No. 192
Berlin, 30 July 1914
D. 2.55 a.m.
R. Midday
Urgent

[...] As a result [of Sir Edward Grey's forceful request for mediation[141]] we stand, in case Austria refuses all mediation, before a conflagration in which England will be against us; Italy and Romania to all appearances will not go with us, and we 2 shall be opposed by 4 Great Powers. Due to English opposition, the principal burden of the fight would fall on Germany. Austria's political prestige, the honour of her arms, as well as her just claims against Serbia, could all be sufficiently satisfied by an occupation of Belgrade or other places. Her position in the Balkans as well as vis-à-vis Russia would again be strengthened by the humiliation of Serbia. Under these circumstances we must urgently and impressively suggest to the consideration of the Vienna Cabinet the acceptance of mediation on the above-mentioned honourable conditions. The responsibility for the consequences that would otherwise follow would be an extremely heavy one both for Austria and for us.[142]

DD, No. 395.[143]

141 See (**278**).
142 See also (**317**).
143 Engl. transl. based on Geiss, *July 1914*, No. 133, here with minor changes.

(317) 30 July: Kageneck to Waldersee

Dismayed at news that Germany is backing British conference idea; worries about future of Alliance if Austria-Hungary is not supported and has to abandon her war against Serbia

Vienna, 30 July 1914
[Letter]
Your Highness will allow me to air my grievances. As I have just heard from the Ambassador [Tschirschky] we have once again sunk to our knees in front of Russia's and England's bluff. After I had not been in the Ministry of War this morning I now dare not go at all, where probably General von Conrad has already been informed of the fact that we are accepting the English conference proposal and thus are robbing the fine Austrian army again of its Serbian war. Just a few days ago our Government proudly proclaimed in Paris and Petersburg the point of view:[144] 1) the Austrian punitive expedition against Serbia is a just cause which we are backing, 2) we wish to keep the war localized, 3) should however a third power interfere then they will have to reckon with us. As soon as Russia rattles with the sabre and Grey with words then the mood tips straight away. [...]

Currently Berchtold's decisive audience with the Kaiser [Franz Joseph] is taking place in Schönbrunn where it will be decided whether Austria-Hungary will subject herself to the English conference idea (which *nota bene* we rejected proudly four days ago) and will order a stop to her troops. [...]

Unfortunately it will gradually transpire, indeed it cannot be kept a secret, that we have not drawn the final conclusion and in the Triple Alliance one will have learnt that we will never under any circumstances risk a war. What influence this latest phase will have on the alliance with Austria-Hungary cannot yet be fathomed today. Of course, the German army is unaffected by this, for until now only diplomacy has spoken, but only after an evaluation of the opposing powers. If one was uncertain in the diplomatic introduction of Italy and Rumania then one would have had to stop the sending of the ultimatum to Serbia at the 12th hour, then we would have saved ourselves the display vis-à-vis the world of our own weakness and fear of war. [...]

The disappointment of the *k.u.k.* army will be immense and I would not be surprised by cases of insubordination. Finally the declaration of war has occurred, and they have to stop at the border already. I entirely

144 See (**322**).

dread the first encounter with Conrad.[145]

Cited in Günther Kronenbitter, 'Die Macht der Illusionen', *Militärgeschichtliche Mitteilungen*, 57, 1998, pp. 539–541.

(318) 30 July: Moltke to Conrad

Suggests immediate mobilization and compensation for Italy

Berlin, 30 July 1914

Withstand Russian mobilization: Austria-Hungary must be preserved, immediately mobilize against Russia. Germany will mobilize. Force Italy to fulfil her alliance duty through compensations.

Cited in Winfried Baumgart, *Die Julikrise und der Ausbruch des Ersten Weltkrieges 1914*, Wissenschaftliche Buchgesellschaft, Darmstadt 1983, No. 132.

(319) 30 July: Nicolai's Diary

News about Russian mobilization received

[Berlin]

News about war measures in Russia and France leave no room for doubts. Intelligence officer in Allenstein (Volkmann) has posters about Russian total mobilization. Moltke still doubtful, wants to wait to receive those posters. [...] Mood in this circle [of General Staff officers] extremely tense, a longer wait is regarded as militarily unsustainable.

Special Archive Moscow, Nicolai Papers, Fond 1414: 1–10.[146]

---

145 As Günther Kronenbitter points out, 'even if the seriousness of the attempts of the imperial government to prevent a European war is disputed in the historiography, it is nonetheless clear to see how seriously one took in Vienna the danger of once again being left in the lurch by Berlin'. *'Krieg im Frieden'*, p. 507. Albertini also highlights the 'deep distrust of Berlin' that existed on 30 July. *Origins*, II, p. 671. Waldersee acknowledged receipt of the letter on 2 August: 'Thanks for your letter[.] Thank God all back on track[.] Charge[!] Waldersee'. AA-PA, BW/MA 247. I am very grateful to Günther Kronenbitter for making this citation available to me.

146 I am very grateful to Michael Epkenhans for making this unpublished source available to me in advance of a planned published edition of the Nicolai diaries.

(320) 30 July: Redlich's Diary[147]

Redlich recalls the events of July 1914 in conversation with Dietrich von Bethmann Hollweg, Secretary of Legation at the German Embassy in Vienna[148]

[...] First we spoke about his military experiences [...] Then we spoke about the staging [*Inszenesetzung*] of the war. I say that I consider him, next to Alek Hoyos, the main instigator of the war. He confirms this to me, and says that he had also had difficult hours on account of this, but that subsequent events which showed that it had been the last opportunity for us Germans had calmed him inwardly. It could not go on, that was the realization among all in the know. In the spring of 1913 his cousin [*sic*], the Imperial Chancellor [Theobald von Bethmann Hollweg] told him: 'I will not go to war over Scutari, the Germany people would not understand it.' Back then Dietrich von Bethmann Hollweg already said: 'Well, then another occasion will soon come.' Bethmann admits to me that the decisive dates are 7 and 30 July: He thinks, actually 6 July, for on that day the Kaiser and Bethmann agreed in Berlin that Germany would not 'let go' this time, and as far as I understand Bethmann's allusions it was clear and accepted in Berlin back then that we would do serious business with Serbia this time, no matter how much Russia threatened.[149] [...]

On 30 July the English mediation [proposal] arrived.[150] [Dietrich von] Bethmann Hollweg tells me that the long telegram, in cipher, arrived just at the time in the afternoon when Tschirschky was about to go to Berchtold for lunch.[151] Bethmann saw the beginning and the end of the telegram and realized what was up. He said to the Ambassador: 'A telegram has arrived from Berlin which is the most important telegram of the entire crisis, I will decipher it and bring it to you at Berchtold's.' And so it happened. Bethmann sat next to Berchtold when he read the telegram [...] and noticed that he turned deadly pale. The next day Alek Hoyos came to Bethmann's flat for lunch and asked him as 'friend' and 'German man of honour' if he thought it possible that Germany might now be capable of arranging with Russia a division of Austria-Hungary. Bethmann calmed him with the most energetic assurances of Germany's

147 Redlich recorded his conversation with Dietrich von Bethmann Hollweg on 13 June 1915.

148 Dietrich von Bethmann Hollweg was the nephew of Reich-Chancellor Theobald von Bethmann Hollweg.

149 See (**119**), (**120**).

150 See (**296**).

151 See (**316**).

complete loyalty. [...] The next day Germany's firm assurance arrived that she stood firmly behind Austria. Bethmann agrees with me that here Berchtold and Alek [Hoyos] actually made the war all by themselves, not the General Staff and Conrad. Berchtold was determined to have a war against Serbia, and perhaps also against Russia, from the moment of the murder of the Archduke. However Bethmann says that in his opinion Berchtold believed that the 'reckoning' with Serbia [*Züchtigung*] could have been carried out without Russia's declaration of war on us. Kaiser Franz Joseph was also of this opinion. And Bethmann thinks that this point of view was well justified, for in Petersburg they were not entirely determined to have war at that moment. That decision was only brought by England's intervention. In the beginning, Buchanan did not speak in Petersburg in a way that Sazonov could have been convinced of an English declaration of war. It appeared as if the mediation of England, reported here on 30 July, was not so impossible. [...] Bethmann now tells me how he was in Berlin in the last week of July, how his cousin,[152] the Imperial Chancellor, expressed to him his doubt whether the war would be 'popular', upon which Bethmann via a friend with the help of a few motor cars arranged a demonstration in front of the Imperial Chancellery in the *Wilhelmstrasse*. Bethmann told me that Under-Secretary of State Zimmermann also worked towards the war with all energy. [...]

Fritz Fellner and Doris Corradini (eds), *Schicksalsjahre Österreichs*, 3 vols, Vol. 1, Böhlau, Vienna et al. 2011, pp. 56ff.

(321) 30 July: Conrad's audience with Emperor Franz Joseph

Audience attended by Berchtold, Krobatin and Conrad; Chief of Staff advocates seizing Serbian territory

[...] At His Majesty's it was discussed what should be demanded of Serbia if she was now showing herself to be submissive.[153] She would have to accept the terms of our ultimatum word for word and reimburse

152 Redlich made a mistake. The German Chancellor was the uncle of Dietrich von Bethmann Hollweg.

153 At the audience Bethmann Hollweg's summary of news from London was discussed (DD, Vol. II, No. 357), in which Grey mentioned the possibility that Serbia would in fact accept all of Austria's demands. Based on this news, Bethmann Hollweg had instructed his Ambassador: 'We regard such compliance on the part of Serbia as suitable basis for negotiations on condition of an occupation of Serbian territory as a guarantee.' DD, Vol. II, No. 384: Bethmann Hollweg to Tschirschky.

all expenses resulting from the mobilization. I added that we should also demand cession of territory which would at least secure our military position: Belgrade and Šabać with adjacent territory for the construction of extensive fortifications, the costs of which would also be borne by Serbia.

His Majesty: 'That is something they will not agree to!'

Count Berchtold: 'Moreover Count Tisza desired that we should not demand cessions of territory.'[154]

I interjected that we could not suspend the hostilities against Serbia now that everything was under way – in view of the mood in the army this was not possible.[155] Germany would have to be told this.[156] If Russia mobilized, we would also have to mobilize.

Count Berchtold: 'That will cost millions.'

I: 'The Monarchy is at stake.'

Count Berchtold: 'If the army is in Galicia, it will mean war with Russia.'

I replied that if the Russians do us no harm, we need not harm them either. The position was not desperate if our own mobilization were ordered in good time; in that case there would at the beginning be about 27½ of our infantry divisions against about 33 Russian ones. [...]

The discussions at His Majesty's led to the following conclusion:

the war against Serbia shall be continued;

the English proposal will receive a very courteous reply, without accepting it on its merits;

general mobilization shall be ordered on 1 August, with 4 August as the first day of mobilization; however, tomorrow (31 July) there would be another discussion about this.

I remarked: 'Better tomorrow, but in the extreme case there would be time until 1 August.'

---

154 Tisza had insisted that no territory be seized (**134**). As Kronenbitter shows, Conrad chose not to record for posterity his remark: 'It's not about what Tisza said, but about what is being discussed here.' Kundmann's diary, cited in Kronenbitter, *'Krieg im Frieden'*, p. 507, n. 375. Kundmann also recorded: 'Chief said further in the office: It was not easy, I felt the whole weight of responsibility on me, if things go wrong the entire responsibility is mine.' I am very grateful to Günther Kronenbitter for making this additional unpublished citation available to me.

155 See (**317**) for a similar argument.

156 From 29 July onwards, Berlin had started to put pressure on Vienna not to rule out mediation as a way of dealing with Serbia, and on 30 July demands from Bethmann Hollweg to accept the idea of a 'halt in Belgrade' led to fears in Vienna that Germany had caved in to pressure (**317**). As Kronenbitter points out, while the seriousness of the German Government's attempts to restrain the ally this late in the crisis remains debated, there is clear evidence that a German change of heart was considered a distinct possibility in Vienna. *'Krieg im Frieden'*, p. 507.

Hereupon His Majesty approved my proposal that, in the event of general mobilization, [...] the Supreme Army Command should initially proceed to the Serbian theatre of war. In case of a subsequent outbreak of war against Russia it could still arrive early enough in Galicia.[157]

Franz Conrad von Hötzendorf, *Aus meiner Dienstzeit, 1906–1918*, 5 vols, Rikola Verlag, Vienna, Leipzig, Munich 1922–1925, Vol. IV, pp. 150–151.

(322) 30 July: Pourtalès to Jagow

Sazonov seeks German mediation in Austria-Hungary; Pourtalès has ruled this out

Telegram 189
St Petersburg, 30 July 1914
Urgent
D. 4.30 a.m.
R. 7.10 a.m.

[*Wilhelm II's marginal notes and emphases*]	
	Just had 1½ hours' conference with Sazonov, who sent for me at midnight. Minister's purpose was to persuade me to advocate participation by my Government in a conference of four, in order to
is Russian mobilization a friendly means?!	find a way to move Austria by friendly means to drop those demands which infringe on the sovereignty of Serbia. I confined myself to promising to report the conversation, and took the stand that any exchange of opinions appeared to me to be a very difficult if not an impossible matter now that
right	Russia had decided to take the fateful step of mobilization. Russia was demanding of us to do that to Austria which Austria was being reproached
very good	for doing to Serbia; to wit, infringing upon her

157 As Günther Kronenbitter argues, it appears that Conrad was playing for time in delaying the redeployment of the Second Army to Galicia, in the hope that Germany would perhaps still force Russia to back down. The results of this delaying tactic were damaging to Austria-Hungary military effectiveness and made 'an already difficult mission even more challenging'. Kronenbitter, 'Austria-Hungary', in Hamilton and Herwig (eds), *War Planning 1914*, p. 46. Undoubtedly Conrad also did not want to abandon 'his' war against Serbia.

rights of sovereignty. Since Austria had promised to consider Russian interests by her declaration of territorial disinterestedness, which, on the part of

good!

a nation at war meant a great deal, the Austro-Hungarian Monarchy ought to be let alone while settling her affairs with Serbia. It would be time enough to return the question of sparing Serbia's sovereign rights when *peace* was concluded. I added very earnestly that the whole Austro-Serbian matter took a back seat for the moment in

yes.

the face of the danger of a European conflagration. I took great pains to impress the magnitude of this danger upon the Minister. Sazonov was not to be

Nonsense! That kind of policy conceals within itself the greatest dangers for the Tsar!

diverted from the idea that Russia could not leave Serbia in the lurch. No Government could follow such a policy here without seriously endangering the Monarchy.

aha! As I already suspected!

During the course of the conversation Sazonov wanted to argue the inconsistency between the telegram of His Majesty the Kaiser to the Tsar[158] and Your Excellency's telegraphic instructions number 134.[159] I decidedly denied any, and pointed out

nothing done as yet.

that even if we had already mobilized, an appeal by my Most Gracious Master to the common interests of Monarchs would not be inconsistent

right.

with such a measure. I said that the communication I had made him this afternoon according to the instructions of Your Excellency had been no threat, but a friendly warning in the shape of a reference to the automatic effect that the mobilization here would have to have on us in consequence of the German-Austrian alliance. Sazonov stated that the order for mobilization could no longer

That was a partial mobilization of 6 corps for a limited purpose!

possibly be retracted, and that the Austrian mobilization was to blame for it.

From Sazonov's statements I received the impression that His Majesty's telegram did not fail to have an effect on the Tsar,[14] but that the Minister is busily striving to make sure that the Tsar stands firm.

158 See (**288**).
159 See (**286**).

[Wilhelm II's notes on the document]
If mobilization can no longer be retracted – which is not true – why, then, did the Tsar appeal for my mediation three days afterward without mention of the issuing of the mobilization order? That shows plainly that the mobilization appeared to him to have been precipitate, and that after it he made this move pro forma in our direction for the sake of quieting his uneasy conscience, although he knew that it would no longer be of any use, as he did not feel himself to be strong enough to stop the mobilization. Frivolity and weakness are to plunge the world into the most frightful war, which eventually aims at the destruction of Germany. For I have no doubt left about it: England, Russia and France have agreed among themselves – after laying the foundation of the casus foederis *for us through Austria – to take the Austro-Serbian conflict for an excuse for waging a war of extermination against us. Hence Grey's cynical observation to Lichnowsky 'as long as the war is confined to Russia and Austria, England would sit quiet, only when we and France are mixed up in it would he be compelled to make an active move against us'; i.e., either we are shamefully to betray our allies, sacrifice them to Russia – thereby breaking up the Triple Alliance, or we are to be attacked in common by the Triple Entente for our fidelity to our allies and punished, whereby they will satisfy their jealousy by joining in totally ruining us. That is the real naked situation in nuce, which, slowly and cleverly set going, certainly by Edward VII, has been carried on, and systematically built up by disowned conferences between England and Paris and St Petersburg; finally brought to a conclusion by George V and set to work. And thereby the stupidity and ineptitude of our ally is turned into a snare for us. So the famous 'encirclement' of Germany has finally become a complete fact, despite every effort of our politicians and diplomats to prevent it. The net has been suddenly thrown over our head, and England sneeringly reaps the most brilliant success of her persistently prosecuted purely anti-German world-policy, against which we have proved ourselves helpless, while she twists the noose of our political and economic destruction out of our fidelity to Austria, as we squirm isolated in the net. A great achievement, which arouses the admiration even of him who is to be destroyed as its result! Edward VII is stronger after his death than am I who am still alive! And there have been people who believed that England could be won over or pacified, by this or that puny measure!!! Unremittingly, relentlessly she has pursued her object, with notes, holiday proposals, scares, Haldane, etc., until this point was reached. And we walked into the net and even went into the one-ship-programme in construction with the ardent hope of thus pacifying England!!! All my warnings, all my pleas were voiced for nothing. Now comes England's so-called gratitude for it! From the dilemma raised by our fidelity to the venerable old Emperor*

of Austria we are brought into a situation which offers England the desired pretext for annihilating us under the hypocritical cloak of justice, namely, of helping France on account of the reputed 'balance of power' in Europe, i.e., playing the card of all the European nations in England's favour against us! This whole business must now be ruthlessly uncovered and the mask of Christian peacefulness publicly and brusquely torn from its face in public, and the pharisaical hypocrisy exposed on the pillory!! And our consuls in Turkey and India, agents, etc., must fire the whole Mohammedan world to fierce rebellion against this hated, lying, conscienceless nation of shop-keepers; for if we are to be bled to death, England shall at least lose India.

DD, No. 401.[160]

(323) 30 July: Falkenhayn's diary

Military measures decided upon regardless of whether Russian full mobilization is declared or not

---

Late in the evening[161] at the Imperial Chancellor's an argument between him and Moltke on the question of who will have to carry the responsibility for a possible war.[162] Moltke and I finally manage to assert that the decision over the declaration of 'impending danger of war' (*Kriegsgefahrzustand*)[163] must be made by tomorrow mid-day at the latest.[164] Moltke declares

160 Engl. transl. based on Geiss, *July 1914*, No. 135, here with minor amendments.
161 The meeting took place at 9 p.m.
162 See also (**292**). For a discussion of these events, see Mombauer, *Moltke*, p. 205.
163 The German military leadership had three different stages of mobilizing measures at its disposal, '*Verstärkung, drohende Kriegsgefahr und Mobilmachung*' (strengthening, imminent or impending danger of war, and mobilization). First troop movements were expected within 36 hours of the initial declaration of the state of impending war, so that this decision amounted to a declaration of mobilization. See for example BA-MA, PH3/720, General von Below to Falkenhayn, 6 June 1914.
164 This means that Germany's decision to mobilize was taken *before* Berlin had knowledge of Russia's decision to declare general mobilization, even though in the event Russia's mobilization preceded Germany's by a few hours. Just before the 12 o'clock deadline was approaching on 31 July, during an anxious wait, news was received confirming Russia's general mobilization. The Kaiser could no longer refuse the military demand that the state of impending danger of war be declared. The order for a German general mobilization was signed at 5 p.m. on 1 August in the *Sternensaal* of his Schloss in Berlin. The first mobilization day was to be 2 August. Geiss, *Julikrise*, Vol. II, Nos 999, 1000, Afflerbach, *Falkenhayn*, pp. 159f., Mombauer, *Moltke*, p. 207. See (**351**), (**367**).

himself decidedly in favour of war *sans phrase*. His changes of mood are hardly explicable, or not at all.

BA-MA, BArch RH 61/927.

(324) 30 July: Moltke in conversation with Haeften

Moltke torn between urgent need for mobilization and realization that this measure would mean war

[...] if we mobilize this means war. If Germany still continues to hesitate to implement this measure, for example in order to gain extra time for negotiations, then this means, in case that such negotiations fail – which is to be predicted – that Germany would enter the war under the worst conceivable circumstances. We would thus allow our opponents to carry the war into Germany. If we hesitate with mobilization, our situation will be worsening day by day and can lead to the most fateful results for us if our opponents can continue to prepare themselves undisturbed. [...]

This war will turn into a world war in which England will also intervene. Few can have any idea of the extent, the duration and the end of this war. Nobody today can have a notion of how it will all end.[165]

BA-MA, N35/1, pp. 26–7, Haeften: 'Generaloberst v. Moltke in der Nacht vom 30. zum 31. Juli 1914'.

(325) 30 July: Fleischmann[166] to Austro-Hungarian General Staff

Following an audience with Moltke, Fleischmann reports that Russian mobilization does not make war inevitable, but that German mobilization means war

Telegram
[Berlin, 30 July 1914]

165 This meeting occurred shortly after midnight on 30/31 July. Haeften thought the Chief of Staff was 'too pessimistic'; however, he was unaware of the additional pressure Moltke was under owing to the play to take Liège by *coup de main* before war had even been declared. See Mombauer, *Moltke*, p. 206.

166 Fleischmann had arrived in Berlin on 30 July as part of an effort to coordinate military matters between the German and Austrian General Staffs.

Russia's mobilization is not yet a reason for [German[167]] mobilization: only if war breaks out between the Monarchy [Austria-Hungary] and Russia. In contrast with the already habitual Russian mobilizations and de-mobilizations, Germany's mobilization would inevitable lead to war. Do not declare war on Russia, but await Russia's attack.[168]

Cited in Franz Conrad von Hötzendorf, *Aus meiner Dienstzeit, 1906–1918*, 5 vols, Rikola Verlag, Vienna, Leipzig, Munich 1922–1925, Vol. IV, p. 152.

(326) 30 July: Flotow to Jagow

San Giuliano declares that Italy is not obliged to participate in war of aggression; compensation might convince her otherwise, but Austrians oppose any consessions

Telegram 154
Rome, 30 July 1914
D. 11.45 a.m.
R. 3 p.m.

As Your Excellency knows Marquis di San Giuliano is not hiding the fact that he regards Austria's approach against Serbia as a war of aggression and that therefore Italy, according to the Triple Alliance Agreement, is not obligated to participate in a general world war resulting from this war. Also the violation of Article 7 of the Triple Alliance Treaty removes

167 Because this word had not been added for clarity, the effect in Vienna was one of confusion, as Conrad thought Moltke had advised Fleischmann that Russian mobilization did not necessitate one by Austria. See Albertini, *Origins*, Vol. II, p. 672.

168 The telegram is cited by Conrad, but is not among the official files. However, Fleischmann also summarized his conversation with Moltke in a letter of 30 July. See Albertini, Vol. 2, p. 672. For further details see also Afflerbach, *Falkenhayn*, p. 156; Mombauer, *Moltke*, p. 204. Moltke also urged Fleischmann that Austria should refrain from declaring war on Russia, 'to avoid producing any appearance of an aggressive move on our part in the eyes of Europe and because in the event of a Russian declaration of war, England would in no case cooperate within the framework of the Triple Entente', thus echoing Bethmann's views regarding possible British neutrality. Conrad felt somewhat belittled by this advice and replied indignantly: 'We will not declare war on Russia and will not start the war.' Conrad, *Dienstzeit*, IV, p. 152. For details of Russia's mobilization see for example Stephen J. Cimbala, 'Steering Through Rapids: Russian Mobilization and World War I', *Journal of Slavic Military History*, 9, 2, 1996, pp. 376–398.

Italy from the alliance duty.[169] In response to my refutation of this point of view he repeated stubbornly: 'I do not say that Italy will in the end not participate; I merely maintain that she is not obliged to do so.' It is becoming increasingly clear that Italy's intention is aimed at achieving something for Italy on this occasion, and therefore the question is worth investigating if it might appear politically advantageous in the current situation to offer the prospect of an advantage. In my opinion all Italian deductions about Article 7 of the Triple Alliance Treaty also have this aim. The decision will be Austria's. Unfortunately the Austrian Ambassador [Mérey] is decidedly against any kind of concession for Italy and yesterday had a very harsh discussion with Marquis di San Giuliano.[170]

DD, No. 419.

(327) 30 July: Dobrorolski's diary

Tsar revokes order for general mobilization at the last minute

[I]n my presence they began to type out the telegram on typewriters in order to send out the telegram over all the lines linking St. Petersburg with the main centre of the Empire. [...] Several dozen lines were waiting to receive the mobilization telegram. But at that moment – about 9.30 p.m. – General Ianushkevich called me to the telephone and ordered me to hold up the telegram until the arrival of Captain Tugan-Baranovski of the General Staff. [...] He arrived and announced that he had chased after me though the city to bring me the Imperial command not to dispatch the telegram about general mobilization. General mobilization, he said, was cancelled and His Majesty had issued the order to proceed instead to partial mobilization on the lines previously laid down.

Cited in Luigi Albertini, *The Origins of the War of 1914*, 3 vols, Oxford University Press, Oxford 1952–1957, Vol. 2, p. 557.

169 Article 7 required Austria to come to an agreement with Italy before making any territorial acquisitions on the Balkans, and to compensate Italy proportionally with territory.

170 Flotow reported along similar lines on 29 July and also commented: 'Things are bad between Baron von Mérey and Marquis di San Giuliano. They are both ill and stressed. The Austrian Ambassador is very violently against compensations for Italy and tries to influence Berchtold in this way.' DD, No. 363. See also (336).

(328) 30 July: Rodzianko's Memoirs

Sukhomlinov asks President of the Duma to change Tsar's mind about general mobilization

'I asked you to come and see me', said Sukhomlinov, 'because I am in an impossible situation. Imagine: the Tsar has suddenly started to waver and has given the order to stop the mobilization in those districts where we were to advance against Austria! I cannot find an explanation for this decision! If this intention is realized the situation can become absolutely catastrophic! All maps and mobilization orders have already been distributed to the responsible offices, they cannot be retracted and every delay must be disastrous! What shall I do? Advise me!'[171]

'Germany will in any case declare war on us', I answered the Minister, 'and if the slightest delay occurs the Germans will cross our border without the slightest resistance. When I drove through Wirballen I saw everywhere along the German border German cavalry in their war-kit, ready to pounce. You must report this to the Tsar immediately.' [...]

I advised immediately to go to Foreign Minister Sazonov. He was just about to go to Peterhof and seemingly knew nothing about the Tsar's change of heart. I asked Sazonov officially to tell the Tsar that I as head of the Duma declared most emphatically that the Russian people would never forgive the Government for such a waste of time which would become fateful for the Empire.

The report of the Foreign Minister, based on the weighty arguments of the Minister of War and the President of the Duma seems to have made the necessary impression. The Tsar gave up his intention.[172] The mobilization was not halted and ran its course. [...]

Michael Wladimirowitsch Rodzianko, *Erinnerungen*, Berlin 1926, pp. 96–97.

171 See (**305**), (**327**). Germany's military leaders faced a similar dilemma on 1 August when Kaiser Wilhelm II ordered a change of plan for the advance on the Western Front. See (**372**), (**373**), (**374**).

172 See (**330**).

(329) 30 July: Basily's Memoirs

Military arguments convince the Tsar that general mobilization must not be delayed any longer

In the early hours of that same afternoon, Sazonov was called to a meeting of the General Staff. [...] Sazonov took me with him. [...] Sukhomlinov, the minister of war, and General Ianushkevich, the chief of the General Staff, declared to Sazonov that, now that Germany seemed decided to make war, Russia was exposing herself to the greatest peril in failing to go beyond a partial mobilization that would render her powerless to assemble all her forces in time to resist the Central Powers. The war could be lost before it was even begun. The generals would implore Sazonov to use all his influence on the emperor to avert such danger.

[...] General Iurii Davilov, the quartermaster general [...] explained to me how the mechanism for partial mobilization would, from its second day – that is, the day after it went into effect – thwart the execution of a general mobilization, and how consequently the last moment was fast approaching, after which it would no longer be possible to correct the measures taken, especially those concerning transport. [...] As I walked back to the Ministry of Foreign Affairs with my chief, I related to him my conversation with the quartermaster general. Sazonov left immediately for Peterhof, where the Emperor awaited him. After listening to Sazonov, the Tsar capitulated to the arguments of the officers. The order for general mobilization was issued at dawn on 31 July. There was no other way.[173]

Nicolas de Basily, *Diplomat of Imperial Russia, 1903–1917: Memoirs*, Hoover Institution Press, Stanford University, Stanford, CA 1977, pp. 98–99.

(330) 30 July: Paléologue's Memoirs

Nicholas II orders Russian mobilization; France assures ally of support

[...] I had hardly got back to the Foreign Office before Sazonov rang up to ask me to send him my First Secretary, Chambrun,[174] 'to receive a very urgent communication'. At the same time my Military Attaché, General de Laguiche, was sent for by the General Staff. It was 11.45 p.m.

173 See (**348**).

174 First Secretary at the French Embassy.

The Tsar Nicholas had received a personal telegram from the Emperor William this evening and decided to suspend general mobilization as the Emperor William had told him 'that he is doing everything in his power to bring about a direct understanding between Austria and Russia'.[175] The Tsar has come to his decision on his own authority and in spite of the opposition of his generals who have once more insisted upon the difficulties, or rather the dangers of a partial mobilization. I have therefore informed Paris of the mobilization only of the thirteen Russian corps destined for eventual operations against Austria.[176]

We awoke this morning to find the papers announcing that yesterday evening the Austro-Hungarian army opened the attack on Serbia with the bombardment of Belgrade.[177]

The news has quickly spread among the public and produced intense excitement. I have been rung up from all quarters to ask if I have any detailed information on the matter, whether France has made up her mind to support Russia, and so forth. [...]

At two o'clock this afternoon Pourtalès went to the Foreign Office. Sazonov received him at once and from his first words I guessed that Germany would refuse to put in the restraining word at Vienna which could save peace.[178]

[...] 'For Heaven's sake,' he said to Sazonov, 'make me some proposal I can recommend to my government. It's my last hope!'

Sazonov at once put forward the following ingenious formula:

If Austria will recognize that the Austro-Serbian question has assumed the character of a European question and declare her readiness to delete from her ultimatum the points which encroach upon the sovereign rights of Serbia, Russia undertakes to stop her military preparations.

[...] An hour later Sazonov was ushered into Peterhof Palace to make his report to the Tsar. He found his sovereign sorely moved by a telegram the Emperor William had sent him during the night. Its tone was almost menacing.

If Russia mobilizes against Austria-Hungary the rôle of mediator which I have undertaken at your urgent request will be compromised, if not made impossible. The whole weight of the decision to be taken now rests on your shoulders and you will have to bear the responsibility for war or peace.[179]

Sazonov read and re-read this telegram and shrugged his shoulders in despair. 'We shall not escape war now! Germany is obviously evading the mediatorial intervention for which we asked her and all she is after

175 See (**288**).
176 See *Int. Bez.*, No. 284, p. 196.
177 The bombing of Belgrade had begun on 29 July. See (**291**).
178 See (**322**).
179 See also *Int. Bez.*, No. 299, p. 205; (**314**).

is to gain time to complete her military preparations in secret. In these circumstances I don't think Your Majesty can postpone the order for general mobilization any longer.'

The Tsar was deadly pale and replied in a choking voice. 'Just think of the responsibility you're advising me to assume! Remember it's a question of sending thousands and thousands of men to their death!'

Sazonov replied: 'Neither your Majesty's conscience nor mine will have anything to be reproached with if war breaks out. Your Majesty and the Government will have done everything to spare the world this terrible visitation. But now I feel certain that diplomacy has finished its work. We must henceforth think of the safety of the empire. If Your Majesty stops our preliminary mobilization all you will do is to dislocate our military organization and disconcert our allies. The war will break out just the same at Germany's appointed time – and will catch us in hopeless confusion.'

After a moment's reflection the Tsar said in a firm voice: 'Sergei Dimitrievitch, ring up the Chief of Staff and tell him I order general mobilization.'[180]

Sazonov went down to the hall of the palace where the telephone cabinet was and transmitted the imperial order to General Ianushkevitch.[181]

It was exactly four o'clock.

The battleship *France* with the President of the Republic and the President of the Council on board arrived yesterday at Dunkirk without calling at Copenhagen and Christiania as had been arranged.[182]

At six p.m. I received a telegram dispatched from Paris this morning and signed by Viviani. After once more emphasizing the pacific intentions of the French Government and imposing caution on the Russian Government, Viviani added: *France is determined to meet all the obligations of the alliance.*[183]

I went to tell Sazonov, who replied very simply: I was sure of France.'

Maurice Paléologue, *An Ambassador's Memoirs*, Doran, New York 1925, Vol. 1, pp. 43–46.

---

180 In Britain, news of Russian mobilization led both Government and opposition to postpone the second reading of the amendment bill on Irish Home Rule and, instead of being diverted by Irish matters as they had been previously, they now focused their attention on the European crisis, and put the maintaining of national unity before their dispute about Ireland. Frank McDonough, *The Conservative Party*, Macmillan, Basingstoke 2007, p. 129.

181 See also (**348**).

182 Poincaré and his party arrived in Dunkirk on 29 July, two days earlier than planned.

183 See DDF, 3e série, 11, No. 305.

(331) 30 July: Grey to Goschen

Britain cannot accept Germany's proposal for British neutrality; urges for both countries to work to preserve peace; suggests possibility of future arrangement if peace is maintained

Tel. (No. 231.)
D. 3:30 P.M.
Your telegram No. 102.[184]

You must inform German Chancellor that his proposal that we should bind ourselves to neutrality on such terms cannot for a moment be entertained.

He asks us in effect to engage to stand by while French colonies are taken and France is beaten so long as Germany does not take French territory as distinct from the colonies.

From the material point of view such a proposal is unacceptable, for France could be so crushed as to lose her position as a Great Power, and become subordinate to German policy without further territory in Europe being taken from her.

But apart from that, for us to make this bargain with Germany at the expense of France would be a disgrace from which the good name of this country would never recover.

The Chancellor also in effect asks us to bargain away whatever obligation or interest we have as regards the neutrality of Belgium. We could not entertain that bargain either.

Having said so much, it is unnecessary to examine whether prospect of a future general neutrality agreement between Germany and England would offer positive advantages sufficient to compensate us for tying our hands now. My answer must be that we must preserve our full freedom to act as circumstances may seem to us to require in any development of the present crisis, so unfavourable and regrettable, as the Chancellor contemplates.

You should add most earnestly that the one way of maintaining the good relations between England and Germany is to continue to work together to preserve the peace of Europe; if we succeed in this object, the mutual relations of Germany and England will, I believe, be ipso facto improved and strengthened. For that object His Majesty's Government will work in that way with all sincerity and goodwill.

And if the peace of Europe can be preserved, and this crisis be safely passed, my own endeavour would be to promote some arrangement to which Germany could be a party, by which she could be assured that no

184 See (**301**).

hostile or aggressive policy would be pursued against her or her allies by France, Russia, and ourselves, jointly or separately. I have desired this and worked for it, as far as I could, through the last Balkan crisis, and, Germany having a corresponding object, our relations sensibly improved. The idea has hitherto been too utopian to form the subject of definite proposals, but if this present crisis, so much more acute than any that Europe has had for generations, be safely passed, I am hopeful that the reaction and relief that will follow may make some more definite rapprochement between the Powers possible than was possible before.

BD, XI, No. 303.

(332) 30 July: Guillaume to Davignon

French General Staff in favour of war and considers the opportunity to be favourable; Government wants to attempt to preserve peace

Report
Copy
Paris, 30 July 1914
Major Collon saw Colonel Dupont today. The conversation revealed that the French Ambassador to Brussels this morning reported on the cautionary measures which Belgium has taken.[185] The General Staff shows itself to be satisfied by these measures. The mobilization of the French army has been postponed; the government wants to use all its trump cards with its diplomacy and put Germany in the wrong. This morning the order was confirmed that places in the East (Verdun, Toul, Epinal, Belfort) should be put on state of defensive. [...]

The French General Staff is for a war and has suggested in the Supreme Defence Council – the Ministerial Council under the leadership of the head of state – immediately to call up four years and to mobilize eight corps to secure the border opposite the German border. This suggestion was rejected. The Government wants to demonstrate its love of peace

185 On 29 July it was decided to place the Belgian army on a 'reinforced peace footing' which involved calling up three conscript classes, while the commander of Liège was authorized to defend the fortress. These were deliberately not called mobilization measures, but did essentially amount to it. For details of Belgium's military preparations see for example David Stevenson, 'Battlefield or Barrier? Rearmament and Military Planning in Belgium, 1902–1914', *International History Review*, XXIX, 3, September 2007, pp. 473–708, here p. 504.

and to undertake all efforts to secure peace; it only wants to mobilize if it is placed in front of the inevitable.[186]

The French General Staff wants the war because it considers the moment to be favourable and because one should finally make an end to it. They reckon with Italy's neutrality and with a possible alliance of Rumania against Austria.

The French General Staff does not intend in any way to violate Belgian territory or to include the violation of our territory in its strategic plans. [...]

In the Ministerial Council two directions have emerged: one, supported by the Chief of the General Staff, has spoken in favour of the mobilization measures outlined above. The second direction, which has asserted itself, wants to gain time and to preserve a peaceful attitude.

On the other hand the following attitude seems to be adopted by French diplomacy: treatment of the Austro-Serbian war as a Balkan conflict, similar to 1912, in order to localize it; fulfilment of Austria's wish for a punishment of Serbia, albeit under consideration of the integrity of that nation, but also of the Austrian need for economic expansion in the East (le 'Drang nach Oosten'); search for options which account for these requirements without encroaching upon the prestige of Russia and the powers of the Triple-Entente.

According to the personal opinion of Colonel Dupont, which reflects the opinion of the officers of the General Staff, war with Germany is unavoidable and is fortunate for the French army because the opportunity was favourable and because Germany herself wanted to end it all.

Imanuel Geiss (ed.), *Julikrise und Kriegsausbruch*, 2 vols, Hanover 1963/64, Vol. II, pp. 734–735.

186 See (**303**).

10
Mediation proposals and ultimatums

31 July–1 August: Documents (333)–(382)

The need for the potential enemy to be (or to appear as) the aggressors resulted in a waiting-game in France, Russia and Germany to see who could last out the longest before declaring a general mobilization. The French decision-makers were determined to let the Germans put themselves in the wrong; military plans were adapted accordingly, and their implementation delayed to ensure that France could not be accused of border violations and of starting hostilities. This was seen as particularly important, for in order to win Britain to France's side, she needed to be convinced that France was not acting aggressively (**303**). Little could contemporaries know just how important the timing of mobilization orders, of troop movements and of declarations of war would become in the passionately fought debate on the causes of the war, not only once war had broken out, but for decades to come.

A general mobilization, as demanded by the Chief of the General Staff Joffre on 31 July under threat of resignation (**338**), seemed too daring to the civilian leadership who were concerned about 'English susceptibilities', and the Council of Ministers did not decide on mobilization, but placated Joffre by ordering a partial mobilization (*disposition de couverture*) in the afternoon that day.[1] The timing of this decision, 5.15 pm, is important because it proves that this partial mobilization was not agreed in reaction to a similar German measure, as Poincaré and Messimy would later maintain. Rather, it was arrived at before the news of Germany's declaration of '*Kriegsgefahrzustand*' had been received in Paris, where the

1 Stefan Schmidt, *Frankreichs Außenpolitik in der Julikrise 1914*, Oldenbourg, Munich 2007, p. 347. See also Chapter 9, p. 410, n. 33, and (**303**).

French Ambassador's long telegram from Berlin had only arrived at 4.25 p.m. and would not have been deciphered and delivered to the Council meeting before the decision was made.[2] At this point, due to the never fully explained delay in the delivery of a telegram from Paléologue which informed the French of Russia's decision to mobilize,[3] the French did not yet know that their ally had ordered full mobilization.[4] Once Joffre learnt of the German decision, he immediately reiterated his demand for general mobilization which was agreed to (though with great reservations of a large part of the Council members, including Poincaré and Viviani) at a second Council of Ministers meeting at 9 p.m. The political leaders still hoped for a peaceful outcome and the final decision to begin general mobilization measures was not made until 4 p.m. on 1 August. This decision was made although at this point no clear indication had been received about Britain's military involvement in a European conflict. In order to ensure British support, French decision-makers stressed that their mobilization was not synonymous with war and that they continued to hope for a diplomatic solution.[5]

In Russia, as we have seen, the decision for general mobilization was first made and then revoked by Tsar Nicholas II who believed, based on a telegram by his German cousin Wilhelm II, that there was still a possibility that Germany might support negotiations in Vienna (**277**). Given that he could not have known that Wilhelm's telegrams were disingenuous, at this point in the crisis this was not an entirely unreasonable hope. At this late hour, Bethmann Hollweg finally tried to avert the now seemingly inevitable catastrophe by passing on Grey's mediation proposal to Vienna and encouraging the ally to accept it (**333**).[6]

As in Paris, Russian military decision-makers were exasperated, due to the change of heart of their monarch, and frustrated at seeing their military plans relegated behind diplomatic attempts at preserving peace. The documents in this volume show the surprising parallels that existed for the military planners in all European capi-

2 Schmidt, *Frankreichs Außenpolitik*, p. 349.

3 See Chapter 9, p. 433, n. 97 and p. 442, n. 118.

4 Conan Fischer makes the important point that when the French ordered their mobilization they did so in the mistaken belief that Germany had mobilized before Russia. *Europe between Democracy and Dictatorship*,Wiley-Blackwell, Oxford 2011, pp. 37–38.

5 Schmidt, *Frankreichs Außenpolitik*, pp. 351–353.

6 See Chapter 9, Introduction, p. 399.

tals during the crisis: the military leaders were keen to implement their plans, but to their frustration these were relegated, at least for a while, to diplomatic concerns. How long that relegation lasted depended to a large extent on the position the military occupied within the decision-making process of any one of the Great Powers: in Germany and Austria-Hungary, military reasoning outweighed political and diplomatic concerns first, while in Russia and France military leaders were held back longer, by their monarch in Russia's case, and by their civilian leadership in the case of France.[7] In London, where military leaders echoed their European colleagues' frustrations to some extent, they were not in a position to influence the decisions that were being made in the Cabinet in London (**354**).

While the Russian decision for mobilization was made, revoked, and then finally made in earnest, in Berlin the German decision-makers were eagerly hoping for news of a Russian mobilization. They had already decided on a deadline (at midnight on 31 July) when their own mobilization would have to be declared even if Russia had not yet implemented hers (**323**), and so as not to appear as the aggressor, they were hoping for conclusive evidence that Russia had beaten them to it and declared her own general mobilization first. That Russia's mobilization was indeed announced before Germany's was a fortuitous circumstance of which much would be made by apologists of Germany in the war-guilt debates that followed the outbreak of war, and to this day the argument that Russia started the war due to her general mobilization is one that can still be encountered.[8] It is true that Russia's mobilization was declared first (justified by an alleged secret mobilization order in Germany which had in fact

---

7 See for example (**400**), where resigned members of the *Auswärtiges Amt* explain to the Austrian Ambassador 'that now the Military had the word and that one could not interfere in this'.

8 Most recently, this argument has been advanced by Sean McMeekin who asserts that 'we must consider the possibility that they [the German General Staff] may have never put the hair-trigger Schlieffen Plan into action had their strict timetable not been threatened by Russia's secret early mobilization against Germany.' *The Russian Origins of the First World War*, Belknap Press, Cambridge, MA 2011, p. 72. For details of Russia's mobilization see for example Stephen Cimbala, 'Steering Through Rapids', *Journal of Slavic Military History*, 9, 2, 1996, pp. 376–398. For older accounts see Alfred von Wegerer, 'Russian Mobilization of 1914', *Political Science Quarterly*, 43, 1928, pp. 201–228; Sergei K. Dobrorolski, 'La mobilisation de l'Armée russe en 1914', *Revue d'Histoire de la Guerre Mondiale*, 1, April–July 1923, pp. 53–69.

not yet taken place![9]), but it is important to note that Germany had already decided on implementing her mobilization regardless, and that Germany's decision-makers just kept their fingers crossed that in the event the enemy would be the first to declare a general mobilization to ensure that Germany's moved appeared to be defensive. An early mobilization was necessitated by the demands of the German deployment plan (the so-called Schlieffen Plan), and not instigated in response to Russian moves. Russian mobilization was announced in the morning of 31 July (**348**), (**349**). The German Ambassador in St Petersburg was assured that Russian mobilization did not have to result in war and that while negotiations were continuing with Austria, Russia would not attack, but that they could not simply revoke the mobilization once it had been declared (**350**). Germany followed suit at 1 p.m. that day. Vienna was promptly informed of this measure, advised that this would 'probably' mean war within 48 hours, and told: 'We are expecting of Austria immediate active participation in the war against Russia.'[10]

On the same day as declaring her own mobilization, Germany made further appeals for neutrality to Britain, and issued ultimatums to Russia and France, demanding an end to their mobilization measures (**340**), (**342**). At the same time, Germany implored the alliance partner to ignore Serbia now in favour of fighting against the greater enemy, Russia. Austria-Hungary's war against Serbia was now relegated behind the looming war with Russia. Wilhelm II appealed to Franz Joseph: 'In this difficult struggle it is of utmost importance that Austria deploy her main troops against Russia and does not split them up by a simultaneous offensive against Serbia' (**353**).[11]

This was what Germany's military plan depended on, but in Vienna Conrad could not bring himself to abandon his long-desired war with Serbia (with whom Austria-Hungary had, after all, been at war since 28 July). At the Joint Ministerial Council meeting of 31

9 See for example Frederick Schuman, *War and Diplomacy in the French Republic*, Whittlesey House, London 1931, p. 233.

10 DD, No. 479, Bethmann Hollweg to Tschirschky, 31 July 1914, D. 1.45 p.m.

11 Fritz Fellner considers this telegram 'a shocking documentation of disregard for the interests of an ally who had been promised loyal friendship and protection'. Wilhelm II's telegram was 'monstrous in its wording, in its total disregard for the interests of the alliance partner, and it its complete misrepresentation of the situation'. Fellner, 'Austria-Hungary', in Keith Wilson (ed.), *Decisions for War, 1914*, UCL Press, London 1995, pp. 9–25, pp. 21–22.

July, Vienna's decision-makers discussed demands from Bethmann Hollweg to consider the British mediation proposal. It was decided that no negotiation could be entered upon if this required an end to the fighting in Serbia, and a diplomatic solution was considered 'odious' and undesirable (**333**). Even once Germany was at war with Russia, however, Austria-Hungary found it hard to relegate the war against Serbia behind the now more pressing conflict with Russia. As a result, she did not declare war on Russia until 6 August (**426**).

On 31 July, Wilhelm II appealed directly to Italy's King Victor Emanuel for support of the alliance partners (**335**), but in vain, as Italy still did not regard the *casus foederis* as given (**336**). It was thought that compensation might still get her on course (**364**), and at this late stage in the crisis, Austria-Hungary was finally willing to discuss this possibility (**333**), (**376**). However, it was too little, too late, and Italy's neutrality was officially declared on 1 August.

In Britain, there was still no decision for or against intervention, leading to frustration among the military leaders which echoed the impatience of their colleagues elsewhere in Europe (**354**). And of course, it led to frustration and worry in St Petersburg and Paris, where the nervous wait for a British declaration of support for her Entente partners continued. Nicholas II wrote anxiously to King George V: 'I trust that your country will not fail to support France and Russia in fighting to maintain the balance of power in Europe.'[12] But this trust was based on wishful thinking as Grey had not declared Britain's hand at this late stage in the crisis (**356**). The Cabinet continued to be divided, although Germany's intransigence was beginning to have an effect. Germany had refused to accept British mediation proposals (**334**), while Russia had twice accepted them. Now Britain raised the question of Belgian neutrality and asked both France and Germany to declare their intention to respect the neutral's borders. France immediately responded affirmatively, but Germany failed to declare her intentions (**355**), (**358**), (**359**).[13]

12 Nicholas II to George V, 1 August 1914, cited in Marina Soroka, *Britain, Russia and the Road to the First World War. The Fateful Embassy of Count Aleksandr Benckendorff (1903–1916)*, Ashgate, Farnham 2011, p. 254.

13 Prince Lichnowsky, who had worked tirelessly for peace in July 1914, summed up his frustration in January 1915: 'On our side nothing, absolutely nothing, was done to preserve peace, and when we at last decided to do what I had advocated from the first, it was too late. By then Russia, as a result of our harsh attitude and that of Count Berchtold, had lost all confidence and mobilized. The war party gained the upper hand. [...] Such a policy is comprehensible only

Britain would soon have to declare her hand, and the issue of Belgian neutrality would prove decisive in this.

Late in the crisis, it briefly appeared as if Berlin's desperate belief in British neutrality would fulfil itself, as a telegram from the German Ambassador in London seemed to offer the prospect that Britain would remain neutral if Germany respected French neutrality in turn (**370**). Astonishingly, in a second telegram that day, the news from London appeared even better. Britain would remain neutral even if Germany ended up at war with France and Russia, Lichnowsky reported (**371**). Bethmann Hollweg's desperate hope that Britain would stay out of the conflict seemed, for a moment, to have fulfilled itself, and Germany's military plans were briefly halted at the Kaiser's order. In the event, it turned out that this news had indeed been too good to be true and the misunderstanding of 1 August had resulted in nothing but brief confusion in Berlin, and a feeling of betrayal, particularly in the Kaiser (**371**). Later allegations of Grey's (and Britain's) alleged war guilt had their roots partly in this infamous misunderstanding.

(333) 31 July: Joint Ministerial Council meeting in Vienna

Ministers in Vienna reluctant to agree to English mediation proposal but pressurized to do so by Berlin Government; question of Italian compensation discussed but only reluctantly agreed to; mediation considered odious

---

Minutes of the Joint Council of Ministers held in Vienna on 31 July 1914 chaired by the Minister of the Imperial and Royal House and Minister for Foreign Affairs Count Berchtold.

Present: The Imperial and Royal President of the Council of Ministers Count Stürgkh, the Roy. Hungarian Premier Count Tisza, the Imp. and Roy. Joint Minister of Finances Ritter von Biliński, the Imp. and Roy. Minister of War *Feldzeugmeister* Ritter von Krobatin, the Royal Hungarian Minister at Court Baron Burián, the Deputy Chief of the Naval Staff, Rear-Admiral von Kailer

Minutes: Secretary of Legation Count Hoyos

---

if war was our aim, not otherwise.' Lichnowsky's memorandum cited in John C.G. Röhl (ed.), *1914: Delusion or Design? The Testimony of two German Diplomats*, Elek, London 1973, pp. 79ff.

Subject: Consultation about the English mediation proposal and about compensation to be granted to Italy

The Chair opens the session by reading a daily report of 30 inst.[14] of the following contents:

'Herr von Tschirschky has today in the name of the Imperial Chancellor transmitted a communication regarding a conversation between Sir E. Grey and Prince Lichnowsky in which the English Secretary of State informed the German Ambassador of the following facts:[15] Sazonov had informed the English Government that following Austria-Hungary's declaration of war on Serbia he was no longer in a position to negotiate directly with Austria-Hungary and therefore expressed the wish that England take up her mediation again; the Russian Government considered a temporary cessation of hostilities a condition. Regarding this Russian statement Sir E. Grey remarked to Prince Lichnowsky that England was thinking of a mediation à quatre and considered the same urgently necessary if a world war were not to ensue.

Privately Sir E. Grey had given the German Ambassador to understand that England might remain neutral if it were only a case of Russia's intervention, but that if Germany and France should also enter into action, she could not remain inactive but would be forced to take immediate decisions and actions. The English Cabinet must consider public opinion, which on account of the stubborn attitude on Austria's side was beginning to change.

To the Italian Ambassador, whom Sir E. Grey received shortly after Prince Lichnowsky, the English Secretary of State said he believed he could procure for Austria-Hungary every possible sort of satisfaction. A humiliating withdrawal of Austria-Hungary was out of the question as the Serbians had to be punished in any case and – with Russia's approval – be obliged to submit to the Austro-Hungarian wishes. Austria-Hungary could therefore obtain guarantees for the future without unleashing a world war.

Herr von Tschirschky was instructed to add to the above mentioned statements of Sir E. Grey the following considerations of the German Imperial Chancellor. If Austria-Hungary declined every sort of mediation, Austria-Hungary and Germany would find themselves opposed by a coalition of the whole of Europe, because neither Italy nor Rumania would go with them. Austria-Hungary's political prestige, the honour of her army and her justified claims on Serbia could be satisfied by the occupation of Belgrade and other points. Also her

14 ÖUA, VIII, No. 11025. Daily report about a conversation with the German Ambassador.

15 See (**316**), (**317**).

position on the Balkans – vis-à-vis Russia – would become a strong one due to the humiliation of Serbia. Under these circumstances the German Cabinet must urgently and earnestly request that the Imp. and Roy. Government accept the mediation of England under the said honourable conditions. It would be exceedingly difficult for Austria-Hungary and Germany to bear the responsibility for the consequences of a rejecting attitude.'[16]

Adding to this, Count Berchtold declares that he had, when the German Ambassador presented this English proposal to him, at once declared that a cessation of our hostilities against Serbia was impossible. He could not alone decide about the mediation proposal but must obtain His Majesty's orders on the subject and discuss the affair in the Ministerial Council.

He had then reported to His Imp. and Roy. Majesty on the contents of the démarche of the German Ambassador. His Majesty had instantly declared that the cessation of hostilities against Serbia was impossible. However, His Majesty had approved of the proposal carefully to avoid accepting the English offer on its merits, but agreed that we should in the form of our reply show that we desired to meet England's wishes and thus also meet the wishes of the German Imperial Chancellor by not offending the [German] Government.

The reply to the German Government had not yet been completed, but he could already say now that three fundamental principles would have to be observed in its wording, namely:

1. The warlike operations against Serbia must continue. 2. We cannot negotiate concerning the English offer as long as the Russian mobilization has not been stopped; and 3. Our conditions must be accepted integrally and we cannot agree to negotiate about them in any way.

Experience shows that in cases such as these the Powers always try to make reductions when passing on the demands made by one Power and it was probable that this would also now be tried, whereby in the present constellation France, England and also Italy would take Russia's side and we had a very doubtful support in the German representative in London. Anything might sooner be expected from Prince Lichnowsky than that he would warmly represent our interests. If this whole matter were to end now in nothing but a gaining of prestige, it would, in his opinion, have been undertaken altogether in vain. We would have no gain from a mere occupation of Belgrade, even if Russia were to give her approval. All this was moonshine [*Flitterwerk*], Russia would pose as the saviour of Serbia and especially of the Serbian army. The latter would remain intact and in two or thee years we could expect a renewed attack of Serbia under far more unfavourable conditions. He therefore

16 This daily report of 30 July can be found in ÖUA, VIII, No. 11025.

had the intention of replying most courteously to the English offer, but raising at the same time the aforementioned conditions and avoiding a discussion of any details [of the proposal].

The joint Minister for Finances [Biliński] points out that through our mobilization a completely new situation had been created. Proposals which might have been acceptable at an earlier date were now no longer acceptable.

The Royal Hungarian Prime Minister [Tisza] declares that he entirely shares the Chair's point of view and is also of the opinion that it would be dangerous to go into the details of the English proposal. Our military operations against Serbia must certainly continue. He asked himself, however, whether it was already necessary to inform the Powers of our new demands of Serbia and would propose to reply to the English suggestion by stating that we were ready to approach it in principle but only on the condition that our operations against Serbia be continued and the Russian mobilization stopped.

The Imp. and Roy. Prime Minister [Stürgkh] explains that the idea of a conference is so odious to him that he would want to avoid even seeming to accept it. He therefore finds Count Tisza's proposal the best. We must continue the war with Serbia and declare ourselves ready to continue negotiating with the Powers as soon as Russia stopped her mobilization.

Herr von Biliński finds Count Tisza's suggestion extremely clever and by posing the two conditions mentioned we would gain time. He too could not embrace the idea of a conference. The course of the London conference was so terrible a memory that public opinion would revolt against the repetition of such a performance. He too was of the opinion that the English offer must not be refused brusquely.

After Baron Burián had also expressed agreement, Count Tisza's proposal was unanimously accepted and it was established that the inclination was to accept the English proposal on the conditions formulated by Count Tisza.[17]

The Chair then highlights the importance of keeping Italy with the Triple Alliance. Now, however, Italy had taken the standpoint that we had provoked the conflict and that our proceedings against Serbia had an aggressive edge against Russia. From everything the Marquis di San Giuliano had said it was clear that the Italian attitude was inspired by a desire for compensation. Italy bases her wishes on the wording of

17 Later that day, Berchtold informed Kaiser Franz Joseph of the decision to accept the English proposal along these lines. ÖUA, VIII, No. 862. He also instructed his ambassadors in Berlin, London and St Petersburg that Austria-Hungary was willing 'for the safeguarding of world peace' to 'approach' Grey's proposal, under the two conditions that Austria's military action against Serbia continued and that Russia's mobilization be suspended.

Article VII of the Treaty of the Triple Alliance.[18] Our interpretation is that, according to this article, a right of compensation only exists if we occupied territories in the Balkans in perpetuity or temporarily, as according to the spirit of the Treaty there could only be talk of territories of the Ottoman Empire. Italy, however, maintains that as in one part of the text the words *dans les Balcans* are mentioned, the whole Balkan peninsula is meant. Although the Italian conception might be refuted by a series of reasons, he must point out that the German Government has also adopted the Italian point of view. In the course of the last week he had received daily démarches in order to induce the Imp. and Roy. Government to join the two other allied countries in their interpretation of the question of compensation.[19]

The Imp. and Roy. Minister for War [Krobatin] mentions that the Imp. and Roy. Military Attaché in Berlin had reported to him about conversations which he had had with Kaiser Wilhelm and the Chief of the General Staff Count Moltke, in which both had most urgently emphasized how important an active intervention of Italy was in the impending conflict, and that it would therefore be most desirable that the Imp. and Roy. Government meet the wishes of Italy in the compensation question.[20]

The Chair declares that word had been sent to him from Rome that the coming war was against Italian interests, as its successful ending would strengthen our position in the Balkans. Under these circumstances Italy could only then intervene actively if her claims were recognized. He had until now instructed the Imp. and Roy. Ambassador in Rome to reply to the demands concerning the compensation with vague phrases and to continue to emphasize the fact that any idea of territorial aggrandisement was quite beyond our intentions.[21] If, however, we should be forced against our will to undertake an occupation that was not just temporary, there would then still be time to approach the question of compensation. [...]

Herr von Biliński points out that the big fight which was before us would be a battle for life or death for the Monarchy. If in this fight effective help from Italy was really of such great value then one would have to make a sacrifice in order to buy such help. [...]

---

18 See (**196**), (**197**).

19 See for example DD No. 396; Imanuel Geiss, *July 1914*, Scribner, London 1967, No. 134. See also Geiss, *Julikrise*, 2 vols, Hanover 1963/64, Vol. 2, Nos 418, 500, 680, 696.

20 See for example Szögyény to Berchtold, ÖUA, VIII, Nos 11133, 11134; Geiss, *Julikrise*, Vol. 2, No. 868.

21 For documents which demonstrate Austria-Hungary's promise not to strive for territorial aggrandisement, see for example (**197**), (**223**), (**255**), (**283**), (**288**), (**322**), (**339**). But see (**119**) for a different point of view.

The Ministerial Council thereupon authorizes the Chair in principle to promise Italy compensation in the eventuality of a lasting occupation of Serbian territories on our part, and to speak of the relinquishing of Valona[22] to Italy if circumstances should demand it and if Italy actually fulfils her duties as an ally; in which case Austria-Hungary would assure herself the decisive influence in Northern Albania. [...]

ÖUA, VIII, No. 11203.[23]

(334) 31 July: Grey to Barclay[24]

Grey welcomes American mediation suggestions; informs British Ambassador that all mediation proposals have so far been rejected

Tel. No. 431
Foreign Office, 31 July 1914

The American Ambassador having written to me to say that his Government were willing to offer their services for mediation in the present European difficulties.[25] I saw him this afternoon and informed him how hitherto all suggestions of mediation in the dispute between Austria and Serbia, which was at the root of the European difficulties, had been refused. I should be only too delighted if any opportunity arose in which the good offices of the United States could be used. I had asked the German Government to suggest any means by which mediation could be applied, but had not yet received an answer. I asked Mr. Page whether the offer of the United States to mediate had been made in other capitals besides London. Of this he was not sure.

BD, XI, No. 370.

22 The Albanian city was called Valona in Italy, and Avlona in English.

23 Engl. transl. based on Geiss, *July 1914*, No. 154, but here with minor amendments and additions.

24 British Ambassador in Rumania.

25 Page to Grey, 29 July 1914, BD, XI, No. 259.

(335) 31 July: Wilhelm II to King of Italy

Appeals for ally support in expected European war

Telegram (no number)
[Berlin, 31 July 1914][26]

While I was trying with all my might to carry out the role of mediator between Austria-Hungary and Russia, and while I still exchanged telegrams about this with Tsar Nicholas, Russia mobilized her entire army and fleet and thus threatened Germany.[27] In order to safeguard the safety of the Empire I was forced to announce to Russia that I too would be forced to proclaim the mobilization unless Russia revoked all measures undertaken against me and Austria-Hungary. War with Russia seems to be imminent and inevitable for me. I will pose the question in Paris if France will remain neutral in a Russo-German war. The response, unfortunately, cannot be in any doubt.

In this decisive moment, and in view of the cordial relations of friendship and alliance which exist between us and our two countries, I turn to You in complete trust.

Your brother and ally
Wilhelm[28]

DD, No. 530.

(336) 31 July: Flotow to Jagow

Italy does not recognize *casus foederis* and declares her neutrality

Telegram 161
Rome, 31 July 1914

The Government here has already discussed Italy's attitude towards the war at the Ministerial Council held today. Marquis San Giuliano told me that the Italian Government had considered the question thoroughly,

26 Original text in French.

27 See (**323**).

28 Victor Emanuel's reply in DD 755: '[...] From the beginning [of the crisis] my Government let Your Government and that of Austria-Hungary know that, as the *casus foederis* allowed for in the Triple Alliance Treaty does not apply in the present situation, it would focus its entire diplomatic activities to represent the rightful interests of our allies and our own, and to work for peace.' Wilhelm II annotated the document with 'scoundrel', 'impertinence', and 'lies'.

and had again[29] come to the conclusion that Austria's procedure against Serbia must be regarded as an act of aggression, and that consequently a *casus foederis*, according to the terms of the Triple Alliance Treaty, did not exist. Therefore Italy would have to declare herself neutral. Upon my strong objections to this point of view, the Minister went on to state that Italy had not been informed in advance of Austria's procedure against Serbia, therefore she could even less be expected to take part in the war, as Italian interests were being directly injured by the Austrian proceeding. All that he could say to me now was that the Government here reserved the right to determine whether it might be possible for Italy to intervene later on behalf of the allies, if Italian interests were satisfactorily protected. The Minister, who was in a state of great agitation, added in explanation that the entire Ministerial Council, with the exception of himself, had shown a strong antipathy for Austria. It had been all the more difficult for him to contest this feeling because Austria, as I myself knew, was continuing persistently with a deliberate injury to Italian interests by violating Article 7 of the Triple Alliance Treaty,[30] and because she was declining to give a guarantee for the independence and integrity of Serbia. He regretted that the Imperial Government had not done more to intervene in this connection to persuade Austria to come to a timely agreement. I have the impression that it is not yet necessary to give up all hope for the future here, if the Italians should be met halfway with regard to the demands mentioned above, or rather if compensation should be offered them. Nevertheless, it cannot be denied that the attitude England has assumed has decidedly diminished prospects of Italian participation in our favour.

In the meanwhile, I pointed out to the Minister in the strongest manner possible the extremely regrettable impression which such a declaration would make on us, and then called to his attention the consequences which might develop for Italy in the future as a result.

DD, No. 534.

29 See (**326**).

30 This article required Austria to come to an agreement with Italy before making any territorial acquisitions on the Balkans, and to compensate Italy proportionally with territory.

(337) 31 July: Viviani to Paul Cambon

German army on French border and has even crossed into French territory; French army being held back 10 kilometres behind the frontier

Telegram No. 398
Paris, 31 July 1914
D. 12.30 p.m.

The German Army has its outposts right on our borders. Yesterday, Friday, German patrols crossed into our territory twice. Our outposts are 10 kilometres behind the frontier. The population thus abandoned to attack by the enemy army is protesting: but the Government is determined to show the public, and the English Government, that France will not, under any circumstances, be the aggressor.[31]

Metz's entire 16th Corps, reinforced by a section of the 8th that has come from Trèves [Trier] and Cologne, holds the front from Metz to Luxembourg. The 15th Corps from Strasburg has closed up at the frontier. People from the annexed countryside of Alsace-Lorraine cannot cross the border under threat of being shot. German reservists are being called up in their tens of thousands; this is the last stage before mobilization. And yet, we have not called up a single reservist. As you can see, Germany has done so. I might add that, in all, our information shows that German preparations began on Saturday, the same day as the delivery of the Austrian note.[32]

These points, added to those in my telegram of yesterday,[33] give you sufficient evidence to prove to the English Government the peaceful will of the one and the aggressive intentions of the other.[34]

DDF, 3e série, 11, No. 390.

31 See (**279**), (**303**).
32 This was not true.
33 See (**308**).
34 Cambon had already been informed of the various measures ordered by France in a telegram by Ferry the previous day. DDF, 3, 11, No. 316.

(338) 31 July: Joffre's memorandum for Messimy

Demands mobilization and threatens to resign[35]

31 July 1914
D. 3.30 p.m.
Approved. 5.15 p.m.
Minister of War

Measures taken until now are a long way behind similar measures that have been taken by the Germans, especially in the last forty-eight hours. These are ongoing.

Not satisfied with having put in place covering troops all along the frontier, most of the 8th, 16th, 21st, 15th and 14th Regiments have been assembled close to the frontier. Elsewhere, movements of troops by rail, coming from the 11th and 18th Regiments' territories, seem to indicate a strengthening of covering troops.

The call up for reservists has taken place and horses are being bought and requisitioned everywhere.

As matters stand, it is no longer possible to proceed with any new detailed measures other than those already ordered without causing serious disorder to the plans already made for covering troops, especially where the railway service is concerned.

If the state of tension continues and if the Germans, under the pretext of diplomatic conversations, continue to carry out their mobilization plan – the execution of which they have pursued while avoiding calling it such – it is absolutely essential that the Government knows that from this evening onwards any delay of twenty-four hours in calling up reservists and sending the *télégramme de couverture*[36] will mean a retreat from our concentration plan, in other words the first abandonment of part of our territory, around fifteen to twenty kilometres for every day we delay.

The Commander-in-Chief would not be able to accept this responsibility.[37]

---

35 According to Messimy, Joffre even demanded full mobilization in his meeting that day, a claim that Schmidt finds convincing: *Frankreichs Außenpolitik*, p. 347. The threat of Joffre's resignation led to the Council of Ministers' order of the *disposition de couverture* at 5.15 p.m., although this was not, as Poincaré and Messimy would later claim, the result of Germany's declaration of the 'state of threatening war' which only became known in Paris after this decision had been taken. See ibid, p. 349. For details of the decisions taken in Paris on this and the following days, see also Roy A. Prete, 'French Strategic Planning', *Canadian Journal of History*, XXIV, April 1989, pp. 42–62, pp. 49–50.

36 That is, ordering mobilization.

37 Text taken from a copy certified by Joffre which contains the following addi-

DDF, 3e série, 11, No. 401.[38]

(339) 31 July: Berthelot's note of a conversation with Szécsen

Austro-Hungarian Ambassador thinks it is not too late for negotiations; mobilization does not mean war

11.15 p.m. Count Szecsen calls and says that as Viviani has often asked what Austria wants, the Ambassador has told Count Berchtold this and has been instructed to say that the Austrian Government has declared at St. Petersburg it has no appetite for territorial possessions and will not infringe any sovereignty; that it has no intention of occupying the Sanjak, but that these declarations of disinterestedness are only good if the war remains localized, the eventualities of a European war being impossible to limit. Count Szecsen added, speaking for himself, that it was still possible to come to terms, as mobilization was not war and some days were left available for *pourparlers*, and that it behoved Serbia to ask Austria what conditions she would impose. Replied, quite privately, that it was rather late in the day. [...] It seems to me, then, that since the Russian Government accepts the British proposal (which implies the arrest of everybody's military preparations) peace might, even at this eleventh hour, be kept if at Berlin the desire for peace is really sincere.

Cited in Raymond Poincaré, *Memoirs*, William Heinemann, London 1926, pp. 259–260.

(340) 31 July: Bethmann Hollweg to Schoen

Germany has declared state of impending danger of war and delivered ultimatum to France with the demand to declare neutrality

Telegram 180
Urgent
Berlin, 31 July 1914
D. 3.30 p.m.

tional annotation: 'The Council of Ministers, convened the 31 July 1914 at 1700 hours, after having read the above note, has decided to send the telegram: "Order frontline troops to advance." The telegram was sent at 1800 hours.'

38 Also in Joseph Joffre, *Memoirs*, 2 vols, Geoffrey Bles, London 1932, Vol. I, p. 125. For details see also Raymond Poincaré, *Memoirs*, Heinemann, London 1926, p. 255; Prete, 'French Strategic Planning', pp. 49ff. See also (**378**).

In spite of our still pending mediation negotiations, and although we have ourselves taken no steps to mobilize, Russia has decided to mobilize her entire Fleet and Army, consequently also against us.[39] We have thereupon declared a state of 'threatening danger of war',[40] and mobilization will follow unless Russia suspends every military measure against us and Austria within the next twelve hours. Mobilization inevitably means war.[41] Please ask the French Government if it will remain neutral in case of a Russo-German war.[42] Answer must be given within eighteen hours. Immediately telegraph at what hour you put the question.[43] Utmost haste necessary.

Secret: If, as cannot be assumed, the French Government should declare neutrality, Your Excellency will inform the French Government that we must demand as a guarantee of neutrality the turning-over to us of the fortresses of Toul and Verdun, which we would occupy and return after the war with Russia is concluded. The answer to this question would have to be here by tomorrow afternoon at 4 o'clock.[44]

DD No. 491.[45]

---

39 However, Germany had decided on her own mobilization steps before knowing for certain of Russia's decision. See (**323**).

40 See (**351**).

41 Poincaré comments that Schoen did not reveal all of these instructions to Viviani as he found them so 'brutal in tone', and he did not tell him that 'mobilization inevitably means war'. The French managed to decipher the telegram later, although they initially struggled with the secret addition which had been put in a more complicated code. Poincaré, *Memoirs*, p. 251.

42 Poincaré comments in his memoirs: 'The question had not been unforeseen, and Viviani and I had agreed that if it were put, it would be wiser not to say offhand that France would do her duty as an Ally. Every moment which did not accentuate international differences might be a moment gained – for peace. Poincaré, *Memoirs*, p. 250.

43 See (**343**).

44 In his memoirs, Poincaré comments: 'Such would have been the reward for, and the price of, our neutrality if we had consented to break faith with our Allies! And without doubt, after such a beginning, we should have experienced many other humiliations. We should have allowed Germany to occupy our most important fortresses of the East, and when she had settled her account with Russia she would have had us easily at her mercy.' Poincaré, *Memoirs*, p. 251.

45 English translation based on Geiss, *July 1914*, No. 159, here with minor amendments.

(341) 31 July: Lyncker's diary

Information received shows that Russian mobilization cannot be halted; decision to send ultimatum to St Petersburg and Paris

Berlin, 31 July [19]14

[...] In the *Sternensaal* [of the Schloss in Berlin] the Kaiser stood with the Generals von Moltke, von Plessen, von Falkenhayn[46] and myself and again explained the situation to us based on new telegrams which culminated in the Tsar actually still protesting his love of peace, and in this regard gave his 'holy word of honour' in his latest telegram, but that on the other hand the Russian mobilization continued because, as the Tsar maintains apologetically, halting the military measures and in particular the mobilization was 'actually not possible'.[47] This shows most clearly that the Tsar has no will of his own and is being pushed by the Russian war party. During this conversation, which lasted about ¼ of an hour, the Imperial Chancellor who had been summoned, joined us and the calm conversation continued along the same lines. The Chancellor requested and received the authorization for two telegraphic requests in Petersburg and Paris whose wording, though not known here, has nonetheless been called a kind of ultimatum,[48] which had to be answered in twelve hours; it was around 4 o'clock in the afternoon when this happened and when the Chancellor telephoned State Secretary von Jagow with instructions to that effect.[49]

Imanuel Geiss, *Julikrise und Kriegsausbruch*, Hanover 1963/64, Vol. 2, No. 889.

46 See (**351**).

47 See (**346**), (**349**).

48 See (**340**), (**342**).

49 As the 12 o'clock deadline was approaching on 31 July, there was uncertainty over whether Russia had already declared mobilization, and while Moltke, Falkenhayn and the Kaiser waited for news, Moltke appeared to Falkenhayn 'unfortunately very nervous'. Just before the deadline, news was received confirming Russia's general mobilization and the state of impending mobilization was declared. For a detailed description of the events in Berlin, see Annika Mombauer, *Helmuth von Moltke*, Cambridge University Press, Cambridge 2001, pp. 206ff.

(342) 31 July: Lerchenfeld to Hertling (1)

Expectation that ultimatums to Paris and St Petersburg will be rejected; German General Staff confident of quick victory against France

Telegram from Berlin Embassy,
R. in Munich on 31 July 1914 at 8 p.m.

There are currently two ultimatums:

Petersburg 12 hours, Paris 18 hours. Petersburg query as to the reason for mobilization, Paris query if it will remain neutral.

Both will naturally be answered negatively. Mobilization on Saturday, 1 August at midnight at the latest.[50]

Prussian General Staff anticipates war with France with great confidence, reckons will be able to defeat France in 4 weeks;[51] in the French army no good spirit, few mortars and worse guns.[52]

Pius Dirr (ed.), *Bayerische Dokumente zum Kriegsausbruch*, 3rd edn, Oldenbourg, Munich and Berlin 1925, No. 67.

(343) 31 July: Schoen to Jagow

Demand for declaration of neutrality made, answer promised by the end of 18 hour deadline

Telegram 237
Paris, 31 July 1914

Question put at seven o'clock.[53]
The Premier [Viviani] said that he had no news of a general Russian mobilization, but only of precautionary measures.[54] He therefore did not

50 On Germany's decision to mobilize see (**323**), (**351**).

51 German military planning hinged on the planned enveloping movement in the West and foresaw a victory against France in 4–6 weeks. For details on German war planning, see for example Mombauer, 'German War Plans', in Richard Hamilton and Holger Herwig (eds), *War Planning 1914*, Cambridge University Press, Cambridge 2010, pp. 48–78.

52 This assessment would have been based on Senator Humbert's damaging revelations about the state of the French army. See Chapter 7, p. 252, n. 34.

53 See (**340**), Jagow to Schoen, 31 July.

54 Albertini argues that Paléologue deliberately kept Paris in the dark about this until 31 July. *Origins of the War of 1914*, 3 vols, Oxford University Press, Oxford

want to give up entirely the hope of avoiding the ultimate. He promised a reply to the question of neutrality by 1 o'clock tomorrow at the latest.[55]

DD, No. 528.

(344) 31 July: Viviani to Paléologue

Viviani briefs Paléologue about German request for French neutrality; requests information about alleged Russian mobilization at once; German 12-hour ultimatum to Russia

The German Government, pretending that the Russian Government has ordered total mobilization on land and water, has decided at noon to take all the military dispositions which compose what is called 'threat of war'. In communicating to me this decision at seven o'clock this evening Baron Schoen added that the Russian Government stipulated that Russia should demobilize, and that if the Russian Government had not given a satisfactory answer within twelve hours, Germany would mobilize herself. I told the German Ambassador that I knew nothing of the alleged general Russian mobilization which Germany invoked to justify the new military measures which she is taking today.[56] Baron Schoen wound up by asking me, in the name of his Government, what France would do in case of Russo-German war; I did not answer him, and he told me that he would come for my answer tomorrow at one o'clock. I have no intention of making any pronouncement on this subject, and I shall merely say that France will be guided by her own interests. The Government of the Republic surely need not tell anybody but her Ally what she intends to do. Pray communicate the above to Sazonov and let me know at once

1952–1957. Vol. 2, pp. 619–627. The cause of the delay of Paléologue's message to Paris about Russian's mobilization is discussed in Schuman, *War and Diplomacy*, p. 233. As Keiger argues, however, 'to proceed from this [delay] to saddle France with substantial blame for the outbreak of the First World War, as some historians have done, is quite unfounded', John Keiger, *France and the Origins of the First World War*, Macmillan, London, Basingstoke 1983, p. 160. (**344**), (**349**). See Stefan Schmidt, *Frankreichs Außenpolitik*, for a contradictory interpretation which places more emphasis on French responsibility for the outbreak of war.

55 The French apparently managed to decipher this telegram. Poincaré, *Memoirs*, p. 251. For the French reaction, see (**344**).

56 See (**340**), (**343**), (**349**). 30 hours after Russian mobilization had been declared, the Quai d'Orsay was still ignorant of what had been decided in St Petersburg. See also Schuman, *War and Diplomacy*, p. 237.

as to the alleged mobilization.[57] As I have already let you know, I am sure the Imperial Government, in the higher interests of peace, will do everything to avoid any inflammation of the crisis.

Raymond Poincaré, *Memoirs*, William Heinemann, London 1926, pp. 252–253.

(345) 31 July: Lerchenfeld to Hertling (2)

Russian mobilization has rendered mediation proposals redundant; uncertainty regarding Britain's attitude; speculation about Rumania's and Italy's attitudes, military circles in Germany optimistic; public mood calm; Social Democrats do not pose a problem

Berlin, 31 July 1914

[Private letter]

[...] The German-English mediation suggestion,[58] which had offered a certain amount of hope for keeping the peace, has been entirely finished with the mobilization in all of Russia. Sazonov demanded a few days ago that Austria-Hungary make do without the fulfilment of some points of her ultimatum.[59] This was impossible for Austria. The Anglo-German suggestions would have been acceptable in Vienna.

England's attitude is dark. A short while ago the King had assured the Prussian Prince Henry in London that England would initially remain neutral.[60] The article in the 'Westminster Gazette' that has been printed in our papers today also leads to this conclusion. As the editor of this paper is an intimate friend of Sir E. Grey the statements in the 'Westminster Gazette' are of some importance. Opposing this, however, is that Sir E. Grey has declared to Prince Lichnowsky that England could not look passively upon these events.[61] Whether the intention of this is to lead us to putting pressure on Austria, or if England has already decided in favour of supporting the other Entente powers remains to be seen.

While I am writing this it has already shown itself. England will go with the Entente.[62]

57 See (**349**).

58 See (**296**), (**316**).

59 See (**243**).

60 See (**250**), (**281**), (**296**).

61 See (**296**).

62 This decision had actually not yet been made.

Of Italy it is thought that she will remain with the Triple Alliance, however that she will want to acquire something during this opportunity. Not however Valona, this she rejects.[63]

Rumania should, according to the views of the *Auswärtiges Amt*, at least remain neutral. It is thought that we have enough means to put pressure on them to force them into it.

In military circles here one is of excellent spirit [*besten Mutes*]. The Chief of the General Staff Herr von Moltke already declared months ago that the current moment was militarily as favourable as it would not be again in the foreseeable future.[64] The reasons that he provides are:

1 Superiority of the German artillery. France and Russia do not own any howitzers and therefore cannot fight any troops in covered position with high-angle fire.
2 Superiority of the German infantry rifle.
3 Entirely inadequate training of the French army due to two-year service in the cavalry and the concurrent calling up of two years with all arms due to the reinstitution of the three-year service;[65] training must have suffered as a result.

Among the population the mood is also calm and optimistic. The Social Democrats have dutifully demonstrated in favour of peace, but are now keeping very quiet. A member of parliament, albeit of revisionist leaning, with whom the Chancellor has spoken, has assured him that nobody in the Social Democrat Party is thinking of disquiet or general strike.[66]

As regards the Kaiser I know that following some changes of mood at the beginning of the crisis he is now very serious and calm.[67] [...]

Pius Dirr (ed.), *Bayerische Dokumente zum Kriegsausbruch und zum Versailler Schuldspruch*, 3rd edn, Oldenbourg, Munich and Berlin 1925, No. 71.

---

63 For a different view, see (**336**).

64 For example during the War-Council meeting in December 1912 (**44**), (**46**), (**47**), or during his conversation with Jagow in May 1914 (**92**). For further evidence of Moltke's desire to have a war 'the sooner the better' and his fear of Russia's future strength, see Mombauer, *Moltke, passim*. See also Franz Conrad, *Aus meiner Dienstzeit*, 5 vols, Rikola Verlag, Vienna et al. 1922–1925, Vol. III, pp. 669ff. and (**84**).

65 For details see Gerd Krumeich, *Armaments and Politics in France on the Eve of the First World War. The Introduction of the Three-Year Conscription, 1913–1914*, Berg, London 1984.

66 Bethmann Hollweg had informed the meeting of the Prussian State Ministry on 30 July of his conversation to that effect with the Social Democrat Reichstag Member Albert Südekum. Geiss, *Julikrise*, Vol. 2, No. 784, p. 374.

67 On Wilhelm II during the July Crisis, see John Röhl, *Wilhelm II.*, Vol. 3: *Der Weg in den Abgrund, 1900–1941*, Beck, Munich 2008, 2009, pp. 1068–1172.

(346) 31 July: Nicholas II to Wilhelm II

Peace still possible if Germany mediates successfully in Vienna

Telegram (unnumbered)
St Petersburg, Palace, 31 July 1914
D. 2.55 p.m.
R. 2.52 p.m.
[original telegram composed in English]

I thank you heartily for your mediation which begins to give one hope that all may yet end peacefully. It is *technically* impossible to stop our military preparations which were obligatory owing to Austria's mobilisation. We are far from wishing war. So long as the negotiations with Austria on Serbia's account are taking place my troops shall not take any *provocative* action. I give you my solemn word for this. I put all my trust in God's mercy and hope in your successful mediation in Vienna for the welfare of our countries and for the peace of Europe.
Your affectionate Nicky[68]

Int. Bez. 1, 5, 338; DD. No. 487.[69]

(347) 31 July: Wilhelm II to Nicholas II

Peace still possible if Russia stops her military preparations

Telegram (unnumbered)
Berlin, 31 July 1914
D. 2.04 p.m.
[original telegram composed in English]

On your appeal to my friendship and your call for assistance I began to mediate between your and the Austro-Hungarian Governments. While this action was proceeding your troops were mobilised against Austria-Hungary, my ally. Thereby, as I have already pointed out to you, my mediation has been made almost illusory.

I have nevertheless continued my action. I now receive authentic news of serious preparations for war on my eastern frontier. Responsibility for the safety of my Empire forces preventive measures of defence upon me.[70] In my endeavours to maintain the peace of the world I have gone

68 This telegram crossed with (347).
69 Engl. transl. in Geiss, *July 1914*, No. 156.
70 But note how in fact the decision to declare 'impending state of mobilization'

to the utmost limit possible. The responsibility for the disaster which is now threatening the whole civilised world will not be laid at my door. In this moment it still lies in your power to avert it. Nobody is threatening the honour or power of Russia who can well afford to await the result of my mediation. My friendship for you and your Empire, transmitted to me by my grandfather on his deathbed, has always been sacred to me and I have honestly often backed up Russia when she was in serious trouble, especially in her last war.

The peace of Europe may still be maintained by you, if Russia will agree to stop the military measures which must threaten Germany and Austria-Hungary.

Willy

Int. Bez. 1, 5, 357.[71]

(348) 31 July: Daily record of the Russian Ministry for Foreign Affairs

Russian mobilization announced; Pourtalès assured that mobilization does not necessarily mean war and that mediation still possible

St Petersburg, 31/18 July 1914

In order to avoid rendering more acute our relations with Germany, the Minister for Foreign Affairs thought it desirable to proceed to the general mobilization as far as possible secretly and without making any public announcement.[72] However, it proved that this was technically

in Germany was done before Russia's mobilization had been declared (**292**), (**323**).

71 Also in DD, No. 480. Engl. transl. in Geiss, *July 1914*, No. 157.

72 Nicolas de Basily had been instructed to inform the French Ambassador of this decision on 29 July. His memoirs record his meeting with Paléologue: 'I explained to him the imperious reasons that militated against a partial mobilization. Since the order for the general mobilization would not appear until the next morning, it was important that this decision would not be made known in Berlin during the night, that is, before it became public in Russia.' Basily, *Diplomat of Imperial Russia*, Stanford University, Stanford , CA 1977, pp. 95–96. Basily points out that Paléologue's account of this conversation was not entirely accurate. Paléologue claimed that Basily had told him that the Russian Government had decided 'secretly to commence general mobilization' (Maurice Paléologue, *Memoirs*, Doran, New York 1925, Vol. 1, pp. 42–43). As Basily explains: 'A general mobilization obviously cannot be kept secret, even for a very short time; all we could hope for was that the news of our mobilization would not be known

impossible, and from the morning of 31/18 July announcements on red paper appeared in every street, summoning men to the colours.

This would of course cause excitement among the foreign representatives, and as one of the first the German Ambassador visited the Foreign Minister to demand an explanation. S.D. Sazonov explained to him that the decision taken by the Imperial Government merely constituted a precautionary measure necessitated by the intransigence manifested in Berlin and Vienna, but that on Russia's part nothing irrevocable would occur, and that, despite the mobilization, peace could be maintained if Germany would consent before it was too late to exercise a moderating influence upon her ally.

Count Pourtalès did not conceal his fears as to how the measure would be received in Berlin.

Int. Bez. 1, 5, 349.

(349) 31 July: Paléologue to Viviani

News of Russian mobilization received in Paris

Tel. No. 318
St Petersburg, 31 July 1914
Extremely urgent.
D. 10.43 a.m.
R. 8.30 p.m.

The general mobilization of the Russian army has been ordered.[73]

DDF, 3e série, 11, No. 432.[74]

by the German government before it had been made public in Russia the next day (July 30).' Basily, *Diplomat of Imperial Russia*, p. 96, note.

73 Due to an unfortunate and still not adequately explained delay, Paléologue's 'extremely urgent' telegram to Paris only arrived there at 8.30 in the evening, nearly 16 hours after the event (Mark Hayne, *The French Foreign Office*, Clarendon, Oxford 1993, p. 300; Schuman, *War and Diplomacy*, p. 233.) Schuman speculates that the delay was deliberately caused at the Quai d'Orsay, although he does not back up his claim with evidence. When confronted about Russia's moves by the German Ambassador Schoen in Paris and asked of France's reaction, Viviani could not reply (**337**), (**343**). Not only does this episode show how difficult communications could be at this time (trying to keep the telegram secret was apparently one of the reasons for its delay), but more importantly it also demonstrates that Paris had not encouraged or approved of Russian mobilization on that day. See John Keiger, *Raymond Poincaré*, Cambridge University Press, Cambridge 1997, pp. 176–177, and for details of Paléologue's deliberate deception see Albertini, *Origins*, Vol. 2, pp. 619–627. See also (**350**).

74 This telegram is as an example of the extent of the falsifications contained in

(350) 31 July: Paléologue's Diary

Russian mobilization; last minute negotiations between Tsar Nicholas and Kaiser Wilhelm; German ultimatum demanding Russian demobilization

Friday, July 31, 1914.

The mobilization decree was issued at dawn.[75] Enthusiasm is general in the city, in the working-class districts as much as in the rich and aristocratic quarters. I am told there is cheering in the Winter Palace Square and in front of Our Lady of Kazan.

The Tsar Nicholas and the Emperor William are continuing their telegraphic dialogue.[76] [...]

Sazonov, always on the look out to win over English opinion and anxious to do everything possible up to the last moment to avert war, has accepted without discussion certain changes Sir Edward Grey asked him to make in the proposal put forward to the Berlin Cabinet yesterday. The new draft runs:

---

the French *Yellow Book*. (See also Introduction, p. 3, n. 4). The version that was printed in the 1914 volume was fabricated so as to suggest that Russia's mobilization occurred in response to Austrian mobilization measures and German preparatory measures when in fact the actual telegram, which was not published in DDF until 1936, amounted to just the one line of information printed here. As Toscana asserts, 'mobilization was first ordered by the St Petersburg government, and not by Vienna, and [...] the French government knew of the exact sequence of events, thanks to the information sent to Paris by the French military attaché in Vienna'. Mario Toscano, *The History of Treaties*, Johns Hopkins Press, Baltimore 1966, p. 94; Sacha Zala, *Geschichte unter der Schere*, Oldenbourg, Munich 2001, p. 34.

75 As Stefan Schmidt shows, Paléologue claims to have sent the telegram to the telegraph office at 9 a.m., having first ascertained whether the mobilization order applied to the entire Russian Empire. He claimed that the transmission was delayed by the fact that he had to send the telegram via an alternative route through Scandinavia because he did not consider the one through Germany to be safe. Mark Hayne proves that the telegram was in fact not despatched until some time between 5 and 6 p.m. Hayne, *The French Foreign Office*, p. 301. A careful analysis leads Schmidt to conclude that the accusations of a deliberate delay on Paléologue's part are speculative and not supported by the available evidence. This, however, is not to detract from the fact that the Ambassador attempted to avoid any mediating intervention in St Petersburg by the French Government by keeping Paris in ignorance of the move towards general mobilization in Russia. Schmidt, *Frankreichs Außenpolitik*, pp. 341–343. For more details on this document see Introduction, p. 3, n. 4.

76 See (**346**), (**347**).

If Austria agrees to stop the march of her armies on Serbian territory and, recognizing that the Austro-Serbian conflict has assumed the character of a question interesting all Europe, allows the Great Powers to examine what satisfaction Serbia could give the Austro-Hungarian Government without prejudice to her rights as a sovereign state and her independence, Russia guarantees to maintain her waiting attitude.

[...] At eleven o'clock in the evening Pourtalès presented himself at the Foreign Office. He was received immediately and announced to Sazonov that if within twelve hours Russia did not suspend her mobilization, both on the German and Austro-Hungarian frontiers, the whole German army would be mobilized.[77]

Then with a glance at the clock which showed twenty-five minutes past eleven, he added: 'The time will expire at midday to-morrow.'

Without giving Sazonov time to make a single remark he continued in a trembling, hurried voice: 'Agree to demobilize!... Agree to demobilize!... Agree to demobilize!'

Sazonov, quite unruffled, replied: 'I could only confirm what His Majesty the Emperor has told you. As long as the conversations with Austria continue, as long as there's any chance of averting the war, we shall not attack. But it's technically impossible for us to demobilize without dislocating our entire military organization. It is a point the soundness of which your General Staff itself could not deny.'

Pourtalès went out, scared out of his wits.[78]

Maurice Paléologue, *Memoirs*, Doran, New York 1925, pp. 46–48.

77 See Sazonov to Isvolsky and Benckendorff, 1 August/19 July, in *Int. Bez.*, No. 385, p. 246: Telegram No 1601: 'At midnight the German Ambassador declared on behalf of his Government that if we did not, within the twelve hours – that is Sunday mid-day – proceed with a demobilization not just against Germany, but also against Austria, the German Government would be forced to give the order for mobilization. In response to my question if this equalled war the Ambassador answered this was not the case, but we were extremely close to war. Sazonov'. See also (**341**).

78 Mark Hayne comments: 'During the period 1–3 August, Paléologue appears to have been in the forefront of those who harangued the crowds around the French Embassy. It would, however, be a mistake to see him as a mere warmonger. He was deeply suspicious of Germany and convinced that war was unavoidable. His patriotism was undeniable. Unfortunately, it encouraged him to follow an extreme course which, whatever Germany's motives, did much to prevent a peaceful resolution of the July Crisis.' Hayne, *French Foreign Office*, p. 301.

(351) 31 July: Falkenhayn's Diary

Order of impending war signed

Between 2 and 3 o'clock to H.M. in the *Sternensaal*. He [gives] an exposé about the situation in which Russia is given the entire blame.[79] His composure and language is worthy of a Germany Kaiser! worthy of a Prussian King. The order about the impending danger of war is being signed in my hand, standing up. Then Moltke reads out the draft for a declaration to the people, written by Major v. Haeften,[80] delivered in such a way, sometimes with a voice that is almost suffocated by tears but yet energetic at the same time that it makes a superb impression.[81] [...] The declaration to the people is taken on by the Imperial Chancellor, who appeared in the meantime, and who expressed his displeasure in no uncertain terms that Moltke had infringed here upon his prerogative, which leads to a clash between the Imperial Chancellor and H.M. [...] I must remark that a telegram by the Tsar was received during these [negotiations] in which he implores H.M. to preserve the peace.[82] Russia's mobilization would have to be continued for technical reasons, but he gave his holiest word of honour that the Russian troops would not undertake any provocative actions against Germany.[83]

BA-MA, BArch RH 61/927.

79 Russia's general mobilization had been announced a few hours previously. See (**323**), (**348**).

80 Hans von Haeften, Moltke's personal adjutant, had been called to Moltke shortly after midnight in the night of 30/31 July and instructed to draft the Kaiser's soon-to-be-delivered declaration to the people, the army and the navy. BA-MA, N35/1, p. 26, 'Generaloberst v. Moltke in der Nacht vom 30. zum 31. Juli 1914', Aufzeichnung v. Haeften.

81 The Chief of Staff then declared to the officers of the General Staff: 'This means if the slight hope for the preservation of peace is not fulfilled, mobilization for tomorrow and thus the war.' Nicolai Diary, Sonderarchiv Moscow, Fond 1414: 1–10, 31.7.1914. (My thanks to Michael Epkenhans for making this unpublished diary available to me.)

82 See (**346**).

83 See also (**350**).

(352) 31 July: Davignon to Belgian Ministers at Berlin, Paris and London

France assures Belgian Government that French troops will not invade Belgium

Brussels, 31 July 1914.

The French Minister [Klobukowski] came to show me a telegram from the *Agence Havas* reporting a state of war in Germany, and said:

I seize this opportunity to declare that no incursion of French troops into Belgium will take place, even if considerable forces are massed upon the frontiers of your country. France does not wish to incur the responsibility, so far as Belgium is concerned, of taking the first hostile act. Instructions in this sense will be given to the French authorities.[84]

I thanked M. Klobukowski for his communication, and I felt bound to observe that we had always had the greatest confidence in the loyal observance by both our neighbouring States of their engagements towards us. We have also every reason to believe that the attitude of the German Government will be the same as that of the Government of the French Republic.

Belgian *Grey Book*, No. 9. Engl. transl. in *Collected Diplomatic Documents*, HMSO, London 1915, p. 304.

(353) 31 July: Wilhelm II to Franz Joseph

The Kaiser urges Austria not to get distracted by 'peripheral' Serbia

Telegram 208
Berlin, 31 July 1914
D. 4.40 pm
R 7 pm

The initial mobilization of my entire Army and my Navy, ordered by me today,[85] will be followed by the definite mobilization in the shortest time.[86] I anticipate that 2 August will be the first mobilization day and

84 See (**279**), (**303**).

85 See (**341**), (**351**). Admiral von Müller recorded with relief that war had 'at last' been decided on. John Röhl, 'Admiral von Müller and the Approach of War', *Historical Journal*, 12, 1969, pp. 651–673, p. 669.

86 Wilhelm II signed the order for general mobilization at 5 pm on 1 August.

am willing, in honouring my alliance duty,[87] immediately to begin the war against Russia and France. In this difficult struggle it is of utmost importance that Austria deploy her main troops against Russia and does not split them up by a simultaneous offensive against Serbia. This is all the more important because a large part of my Army will be tied up by France. Serbia's role in this gigantic fight, which we enter shoulder to shoulder, is completely peripheral and only requires the most basic defensive measures. I ask you further to do everything to entice Italy to take part by meeting her as much as possible, everything else has to take a backward role so that the Triple Alliance enters the war united.[88]

DD, No. 503.

(354) 31 July: Wilson's diary

Military leaders frustrated with Cabinet's indecision

No news when I called for my usual visit to Arthur Nicolson at 9 a.m. Later (11 a.m.) the Cabinet met. Later we began to suspect that the Cabinet was going to run away.

Later, 5 p.m., Eyre Crowe came to see me and told me that Germany had given Russia 12 hours to demobilize.[89] Russia's answer was an order for 'General Mobilization'. Germany was going to order mobilization tonight, followed by France; and we were doing nothing. Later Johnnie Baird[90] came in. I told him of the state of affairs and got him to write to Bonar Law who had gone to Wargrave, begging him to come up and see Asquith to-night.

Later I saw Panouse[91] and advised him to get Cambon to go to Grey

87 As Fritz Fellner points out, 'there were no alliance obligations demanding such an action'. Germany was merely required to come to the aid of her alliance partner, not to fight against Russia, and certainly not to fight against France. 'Austria-Hungary', p. 22.

88 For Franz Joseph's answer see (**376**). Fritz Fellner has argued that this request by the German ally to ignore Serbia in favour of Russia amounted to a German betrayal of Austria-Hungary. Fellner, 'Austria-Hungary' pp. 20–23. However, Kronenbitter points instead to 'deep-seated misunderstandings between the alliance partners', leading to doubts about the reliability of the ally both in Berlin and Vienna. Günther Kronenbitter, *'Krieg im Frieden'*, Oldenbourg, Munich 2003, p. 513. See (**360**).

89 See (**341**), (**342**).

90 Johnnie Baird, MP, was a leading Conservative/Unionist and was later Lord Stonehaven.

91 General Vicomte de la Panouse, French military attaché in London.

to-night and say that, if we did not join, he would break off relations and go to Paris. An awful day.

No C.I.D. has been held, no military opinion has been asked for by this Cabinet, who are deciding on a question of war.

Cited in Charles Callwell, *Field-Marshal Sir Henry Wilson*, 2 vols, Cassell, London 1927, Vol. 1, pp. 152–153.

(355) 31 July: Grey to Bertie (1)

Request to establish if France is willing to respect Belgian neutrality

Foreign Office, 31 July 1914
Telegram (No. 287.)
D. 5:30 P.M.

I still trust that situation is not irretrievable, but in view of prospect of mobilisation in Germany it becomes essential to His Majesty's Government, in view of existing treaties, to ask whether French Government is prepared to engage to respect neutrality of Belgium so long as no other Power violates it.[92]

A similar request is being addressed to German Government.[93] It is important to have an early answer.

BD, XI, No. 348.

(356) 31 July: Grey to Bertie (2)

Grey unwilling to pledge support to France at this point

Tel. (No. 290)
Foreign Office, 31 July 1914.
D. 7.30 p.m.

Your telegram No. 95 of 30th July:[94] European Crisis

I believe it to be quite untrue that our attitude has been decisive factor in situation. Germany does not expect our neutrality.[95]

92 For the answer see (**358**).
93 See BD, XI, No. 348 for the request, and (**359**) for the non-committal answer.
94 BD, XI, No. 318.
95 In fact, they did. See for example (**281**).

Nobody here feels that in this dispute, so far as it has gone yet, British treaties or obligations are involved. Feeling is quite different from what it was in Morocco question, which was a dispute directly involving France. In this case France is being drawn into a dispute which is not hers.

I have told French Ambassador that we cannot undertake a definite pledge to intervene in a war.[96]

He has urged that His Majesty's Government should reconsider this decision, and I have said they will certainly consider the situation again directly there is new development, but that we should not be justified in giving any pledge at this moment.

BD, XI, No. 352.

[357) 31 July: Communication from German Embassy to British Government

German Government blames Russian mobilization for failure of mediation attempts; issues ultimatums to Russia and France

Translation [German original]

Midnight, July 31, 1914

On the 29th July the Tsar asked His Majesty the Emperor by telegraph to mediate between Austria-Hungary and Russia.[97] The Emperor at once declared his readiness to do so; he so informed the Tsar by telegram,[98] and immediately took the necessary steps at Vienna. Without waiting for the result Russia then mobilized against Austria-Hungary, whereupon the Emperor at once informed the Tsar that such action rendered his mediation illusory; the Emperor further requested the Tsar to stop the military preparations against Austria.[99] This was, however, not done. The German Government nevertheless persevered with their mediation at Vienna. In putting forward the urgent proposals that she did, the German Government went to the utmost limit possible with a sovereign State which is her ally.[100] The suggestions made by the German Government at Vienna were entirely on the lines of those put forward by Great Britain, and the German Government recommended them for serious consideration at Vienna. They were considered this morning at

96 For Cambon's report on this conversation, see DDF, 3e série, 11, No. 363.
97 See (**286**).
98 See (**288**).
99 See (**314**).
100 See (**316**), (**317**).

Vienna. While the deliberations were taking place, and before they were even terminated, Count Pourtalès announced from St. Petersburg the mobilization of the whole Russian army and fleet.[101] This action on the part of Russia rendered any answer by Austria to the German proposal for mediation impossible. It also affected Germany, whose mediation had been solicited by the Tsar personally. We were compelled, unless we wished to abandon the safety of the Fatherland, to answer this action, which could only be regarded as hostile, with serious counter-measures. We could not idly watch Russia mobilizing on our frontier. We therefore told Russia that if she did not stop her warlike measures against Germany and Austria-Hungary within twelve hours we should mobilize, and that would mean war.[102] We asked France whether in a Russo-German war she would remain neutral.[103] [The German version, Bethmann Hollweg to Lichnowsky, included an additional sentence: 'Request that you work with all means so that these events also get noticed in the English press'.][104]

BD, XI, No. 372.

(358) 31 July: Bertie to Grey

France willing to respect Belgian neutrality

Paris, July 31, 1914.
D. August 1, 1:12 A.M.
Tel. (No. 104.)
R. August 1, 2:15 A.M.

Political Director has brought me the reply of the Minister for Foreign Affairs to your enquiry respecting the neutrality of Belgium.[105] It is as follows:

French Government are resolved to respect the neutrality of Belgium, and it would only be in the event of some other Power violating that neutrality that France might find herself under the necessity, in order to assure defence of her own security, to act otherwise. This assurance has been given several times. President of the Republic spoke of it to the King of the Belgians, and the French Minister at Brussels has spontaneously renewed the assurance to the Belgian Minister for Foreign Affairs to-day.

101 Pourtalès to AA, 31 July 1914, DD, No. 473.
102 Bethmann Hollweg to Pourtalès, 31 July 1914, DD, No. 490.
103 See (**340**). See also (**365**).
104 For German text see DD, No. 513. See also (**365**).
105 See (**355**).

MINUTES

France will respect Belgian neutrality, Germany will not. But Germany will delay a definite answer until it is too late for England to act effectively. E. A. C[rowe]. August 1.

We should take no reply or a postponed reply as a refusal. A. N[icolson].

BD, XI, No. 382.

(359) 31 July: Goschen to Grey

Germany refuses to commit to respecting Belgian neutrality

Berlin, 31 July 1914
D. 31 July, 2 a.m.
Tel. (No. 114.)
R. 1 August, 3:30 a.m.

Your telegram No. 287 of 31st July to Paris:[106] Belgian neutrality.

Secretary of State for Foreign Affairs said that he could not possibly give me an answer before consulting the Emperor and the Chancellor. I said that I hoped that the answer would not be too long delayed. He then gave me to understand he rather doubted whether they could answer at all, as any reply they might give could not fail, in the event of war, to have the undesirable effect of disclosing to a certain extent part of their plan of campaign. After taking note of your request, he told me in confidence that Belgium had already committed certain acts which he could only qualify as hostile. On my asking him for details, he gave me as an instance that the Belgian Government had already embargoed a consignment of grain destined for Germany.

In telling me that it was unlikely that the Imperial Government would be in a position to answer, he said that in any case it would be necessary for them to know what France replied to your enquiry.

I shall speak to him again on the subject to-morrow, but I am not very hopeful of obtaining a definite answer.

MINUTES

[…] telegraph to Sir Goschen: […] 'French Government state that they will respect neutrality of Belgium, unless it is violated by another Power which thereby may force France to take measures of self-defence. You should inform M[inister] F[oreign] A[ffairs].' G. R. C[lerk]. August 1, 1914.

106 BD, XI, No. 348. See also (355).

The Cabinet are discussing the question. Wait. E. A. C[rowe]. August 1.

I am not sure that we should inform German Government of French reply in any case without French consent. The two countries may very shortly be at war and we should not pass on anything from one to the other. If France asks us we can say we have had no reply from Germany. A. N[icolson].

The French Government have given the assurance to the Belgian Minister for Foreign Affairs so it is presumably no secret. I told the German Ambassador of it today.[107] *E. G[rey].*

BD, XI, No. 383.

(360) 31 July: Kageneck to Waldersee

Conrad not willing to change mobilization plans (and abandon the war against Serbia) to suit Germany's strategy

[...] Conrad is of the assumption that the war against S[erbia] has to be carried out with sufficiently strong forces in order to achieve a certain success down there. [...] Against Russia, however, he only wanted to make Galicia secure.[108] The justification behind the general mobilization stresses, after all, that no aggressive intention against Russia existed here, that it was a purely defensive measure vis-à-vis Russia's arming. Conrad said that otherwise it could happen that they did not achieve anything against S[erbia] and that they would stand opposite Russia in Galicia, guns at the ready, if Russia did not attack.[109]

107 BD, XI, No. 448. See (358) for French reply.

108 See (353).

109 This was indeed what happened. Austrian troops were initially deployed against Serbia, but then forces were redirected north where they arrived too late to prevent the collapse of the opening offensives. For details see for example Kronenbitter, *'Krieg im Frieden'*, pp. 514–516; Kronenbitter, 'Austria-Hungary', in Hamilton and Herwig (eds), *War Planning 1914*, 2010, pp. 24–47, p. 46; Norman Stone; 'Die Mobilmachung der österreichisch-ungarischen Armee 1914, *Militärgeschichtliche Mitteilungen*, 16, 1974, pp. 67–95; Graydon Tunstall, *Planning for War Against Russia and Serbia. Austro-Hungarian and German Military Strategies, 1871–1914*, New York 1993; Tunstall, 'The Habsburg Command Conspiracy: The Austrian Falsification of Historiography on the Outbreak of World War I, *Austrian History Yearbook*, 27, 1996, pp. 181–196. Austrians blamed the German ally for this muddle. On 10 January 1915, for example, Count Forgách wrote: In Serbia 'it was only the most insistent German pressure which, in full lack of political and military realisation of the importance of the Balkan theatre of war, forced us against our better judgement to throw everything towards

He received me with the words 'if only G[ermany] had declared herself 24 h[ours] earlier, then it would have been simple still to alter the measures against S[erbia].[110]

Cited in Günther Kronenbitter, 'Macht der Illusionen', *Militärgeschichtliche Mitteilungen*, 57, 1998, p. 541.

(361) 31 July: Crowe to Grey

Crowe in favour of British intervention on France's side

Private

[...] Memorandum by Sir E. Crowe, 31 July 1914

The theory that England cannot engage in a big war means her abdication as an independent State. She can be brought to her knees and made to obey the behests of any Power or group of Powers who can go to war, of whom there are several.

The theory further involves not only that there is no need for any British army or navy but also that there has been no such need for many years. It cannot have been right to impose on the country the upkeep at an enormous annual cost of an unnecessary because useless force.

If the theory were true, the general principle on which our whole foreign policy has hitherto been declared to rest would stand proclaimed as an empty futility. A balance of power cannot be maintained by a State that is incapable of fighting and consequently carries no weight.

---

the North and to undertake the first Serbian offensive with forces which were partly insufficient and partly too hesitantly deployed. If the offensive deployments against Lublin and Cholm in August, which had turned into Pyrrhic victories owing to retreats involving heavy losses, had not happened, then nothing much would have been different in the North, while more troops could have remained in the South and could have defeated Serbia decisively in 6–8 weeks. Bulgaria, in the first enthusiasm over the defeat of her mortal enemy, would have joined our side, as would Turkey; Rumania could hardly have hesitated then and today's entire dilemma would not have occurred. The embarrassing lack of success against Serbia is thus in part also due to Germany's advice.' Cited in Fritz Fellner, 'Zwischen Kriegsbegeisterung und Resignation – ein Memorandum des Sektionschefs Graf Forgách vom Jänner 1915', in Hermann Wiesflecker and Othmar Pickl (eds), *Beiträge zur Allgemeinen Geschichte. Alexander Novotny zur Vollendung seines 70. Lebensjahres*, Akademische Druck- und Verlagsanstalt, Graz 1975, pp. 153–162, p. 159.

110 Given his repeated demands for a war against Serbia in the preceding months, this was likely to have been a disingenuous statement.

The fact that British influence has on several momentous occasions turned the scale, is evidence that foreign States do not share the belief that England cannot go to war.

At the opening of any war in all countries there is a commercial panic.

The systematic disturbance of an enemy's financial organisation and the creation of panic is part of a well-laid preparation for war.

Commercial opinion is generally timid, and apt to follow pusillanimous counsels. The panic in the city has been largely influenced by the deliberate acts of German financial houses, who are in at least as close touch with the German as with the British Government, and who are notoriously in daily communication with the German Embassy.

It has been the unremitting effort of Germany to induce England to declare herself neutral in case Germany were at war with France and Russia. The object has been so transparent that His Majesty's Government have persistently declined to follow this policy, as incompatible with their duty to France and Russia and also to England herself. The proposal was again pressed upon us in a concrete form yesterday. It was rejected in words which gave the impression that in the eye of His Majesty's Government the German proposal amounted to asking England to do a dishonourable act.

If it be now held that we are entirely justified in remaining neutral and standing aside whilst Germany falls upon France, it was wrong yesterday to think that we were asked to enter into a dishonourable bargain, and it is a pity that we did not close with it. For at least terms were offered which were of some value for France and Belgium. We are apparently now willing to do what we scornfully declined to do yesterday, with the consequence that we lose the compensating advantages accompany in yesterday's offer.

The argument that there is no written bond binding us to France is strictly correct. There is no contractual obligation. But the Entente has been made, strengthened, put to the test and celebrated in a manner justifying the belief that a moral bond was being forged. The whole policy of the Entente can have no meaning if it does not signify that in a just quarrel England would stand by her friends. This honourable expectation has been raised. We cannot repudiate it without exposing our good name to grave criticism.

I venture to think that the contention that England cannot in any circumstances go to war is not true, and that any endorsement of it would be an act of political suicide.

The question at issue is not whether we are capable of taking part in a war, but whether we should go into the present war. That is a question firstly of right or wrong, and secondly of political expediency.

If the question were argued on this basis, I feel confident that our duty and our interest will be seen to lie in standing by France in her hour of need. France has not sought the quarrel. It has been forced upon her. E. A. C[rowe].

BD, XI, No. 369.

(362) 1 August: Isvolsky to Sazonov

Isvolsky reports that Messimy informed Russian military attaché of French cabinet's decision for war

Paris, 1 August 1914
D. 1 a.m.

He [Ignatjev] asked me to confirm the hope of the French General Staff that all our efforts would be directed against Germany and that Austria should be considered as a negligible quantity.[111]

Cited in Frederick Schuman, *War and Diplomacy in the French Republic*, Whittlesey House, London 1931, p. 240.

(363) 1 August 1914: Moltke's Memoirs

Moltke and *Auswärtiges Amt* did not expect French neutrality; a German declaration of war on France was inevitable even if only Russia declared war on Germany

In the early years the *Auswärtiges Amt* already told me that France could possibly remain neutral in a war between Germany and Russia. I had such little faith in this possibility that I explained even then that if Russia declared war on us we would have to declare war on [France] immediately if [her] attitude was in doubt.

Eliza von Moltke (ed.), *Helmuth von Moltke, Erinnerungen, Briefe, Dokumente*, Der Kommende Tag, Stuttgart 1922, p. 21.

111 At the same time, Germany was encouraging her ally to concentrate her efforts on the 'real enemy', Russia, and abandon her quarrel with Serbia (**353**).

(364) 1 August: Wenninger to Bavarian Minister of War

Waiting to hear what Russia and France will do; Britain's attitude still unclear; Italy makes compensation demands

No. 2697
Berlin, 1 August 1914
Confidential!
Report No. 6
Re: Political situation and military measures

The War Minister had yesterday requested that the Imperial Chancellor immediately give the order to mobilize in response to France's and Russia's answer, so that 1 August could still become the 1st mobilization day, and that also for Bavaria.

The night passed by, at 4 o'clock pm the afternoon the Russian deadline elapsed,[112] at 10 o'clock am the French deadline. Russia's answer was evasive and meaningless; from France there was a request for an extension of the deadline until 1 o'clock in the morning, 'because we first have to find out from St. Petersburg, whether it's true that Russia has mobilized; nobody knows anything about it.' (?!) That smacks worryingly of trying to gain time which actually should not be granted.[113] The Prussian War Ministry is very angry about the lost mobilization day.

In the meantime, however, England had declared that she must still 'keep her hands free'. This was a notable change that ought not to be ignored, even if it did only represent a trick. The declaration alone takes the wind out of France's sails, unless they possess an entirely different declaration from England.

Italy's position had recently caused upset in Austria and concerns here; she is not satisfied with the offer of Albania, and instead is said to demand the Trentino and Trieste.[114] Cambon explained that Italy is still not a certainty for the Triple Alliance.

Denmark, too, is said to have been sent a question with a deadline.[115]

In terms of news by mid-day:

1. From France: advance of stronger forces from Toul and Frouard towards the border, is said to be a move to protect the border.

112 Even before the deadline had passed, Moltke and Falkenhayn insisted that German mobilization needed to be implemented and were frustrated by the delay. Moltke wanted to 'proceed immediately'. See Mombauer, *Moltke*, p. 216.

113 In fact, Paris had really not been aware of Russia's mobilization. See (**343**), (**344**).

114 See for example Geiss, *Julikrise*, Vol. 2, Nos 981 and 991.

115 This was not true.

2. From Russia: The railway line Petersburg–Warsaw is said to be destroyed. Sabotage? Poland?

BHST-MA, MKr 1765, Berichte des K.B. Militärbevollmächtigten, Mobilmachung 1914.[116]

(365) 1 August: George V to Nicholas II

British attempts to keep mediation going

Telegram, 1 August/19 July

My Government has received the following statement from the German Government:

[Here follows the text of (**357**)]

I cannot help thinking that some misunderstanding has produced this deadlock. I am most anxious not to miss any possibility of avoiding the terrible calamity which at present threatens the whole world. I therefore make a personal appeal to you to remove the misapprehension which I feel must have occurred, and to leave still open ground for negotiation and possible peace. If you think I can in any way contribute to that all-important purpose, I will do everything in my power to assist in reopening the interrupted conversations between the Powers concerned. I feel confident that you are as anxious as I am that all that is possible should be done to secure the peace of the world.

Sent to Sir G. Buchanan by Sir Edward Grey (Tel. No. 423) on 1 August at 3.30 A.M.

Repeated to Paris No. 291 (3:45 A.M.): You should apply to the President at once for an audience, and communicate to him the following message sent by the King to the Emperor of Russia.

Int. Bez., No. 397; BD, XI, No. 384.

116 Also in Dirr (ed.), *Bayerische Dokumente*, p. 228.

(366) 1 August: Grey to Bertie

Last-minute attempts to stop escalation of crisis; Grey suggests possibility of French and German armies mobilized but not crossing border

Tel. (No. 297)
Foreign Office, 1 August 1914
D. 5.25 p.m.

The war. I have definitely refused all overtures to give Germany any promise of neutrality, and shall not entertain any such suggestion unless it were on conditions that seemed real advantages for France.[117]

German Ambassador here seemed to think it not impossible, when I suggested it, that after mobilisation on western frontier French and German armies should remain, neither crossing the frontier as long as the other did not do so.[118] I cannot say whether this would be consistent with French obligations under her alliance. If it were so consistent, I suppose French Government would not object to our engaging to be neutral as long as German army remained on frontier on the defensive.[119]

BD, XI, No. 419.

(367) 1 August: Müller's Diary

German Government manages to appear attacked

The mood is brilliant. The Government has succeeded very well in making us appear as the attacked.[120]

John Röhl, 'Admiral von Müller and the Approach of War, 1911–1914', *Historical Journal*, 12, 1969, pp. 651–673, p. 670.

117 See also (**356**).

118 The constraints within which Germany's deployment plan operated meant that this was not actually an option in 1914. For details see for example Mombauer, 'German War Plans', in Hamilton and Herwig (eds), *War Planning 1914*, pp. 48–78.

119 For Lichnowsky's account see (**375**). See also BD, XI, Nos 453, 460; DD Nos 630, 631.

120 See (**292**), (**323**), which show attempts to delay German mobilization until Russia had mobilized, so that Germany would not appear to be the aggressor.

(368) 1 August: Isvolsky to Sazonov

French President confirms French support for Russia

Telegram No. 225

Paris, 1 August/19 July 1914
Very secret.

3 o'clock at night. I have just returned from the President of the Republic who told me that the Ministerial Council had once again confirmed the decision to fulfil completely the duties which the alliance treaty demands of France. The Council recognized that the interests of both alliance partners demand that France, if possible, finalise her mobilization before military operations commence, which will require 10 days. Poincaré still fears that Germany will attack France immediately in order to make the finalizing of mobilization difficult for her. This information requires strictest secrecy.

Int. Bez., No. 412.

(369) 1 August: Krupenski to Sazonov

Italy declares neutrality

Telegram No. 52
Rome, 1 August/19 July 1914
Urgent

Following the Ministerial Council presided over by the King the Cabinet in Rome declared Italy's neutrality[121] and gave as reason for its decision that the war was neither a war of aggression nor a defensive war, and that the Cabinet in Rome had not been consulted by either Vienna or Berlin nor involved in their decisions.[122]

Int. Bez., No. 414.

121 The official publication of Italy's declaration of neutrality occurred on 3 August. See also BD, XI No. 406, No. 543. On 31 July it was already known officially in Berlin and Vienna that Italy did not regard the *casus belli* as given and therefore did not consider herself obliged to come to Austria-Hungary's aid, although such help was not yet ruled out categorically. See e.g. ÖUA, VIII, No. 11128.

122 See (**336**).

(370) 1 August: Lichnowsky to Jagow

Britain appears to offer possibility of British and French neutrality if Germany refrains from attacking France

Telegram 205
London, 1 August 1914
D. 11.14 am
R. 4.23 pm[123]

Sir E. Grey has just had me informed through Sir W. Tyrrell that he hopes, as the result of a Cabinet Meeting now in session, to be able to give me this afternoon some facts which may prove useful for the avoidance of the great catastrophe. Judging from Sir William's hints this would appear to mean that in case we did not attack France, England would remain neutral and would guarantee France's neutrality. I shall learn more this afternoon.

Sir E. Grey has just called me on the telephone and asked me if I thought I could assure him that in case France should remain neutral in a Russo-German war we would not attack France. I assured him that I could take the responsibility for such a guarantee, and he is to use this assurance at today's Cabinet session.

P.S. Sir W. Tyrrell requested from me urgently to ensure that our troops did not violate the French border. Everything depended on this. French troops had retreated when a [German] border-crossing occurred.

DD, No. 562.[124]

(371) 1 August: Lichnowsky to Jagow (2)

Britain may offer neutrality even if Germany is at war with Russia and France

Telegram No. 209
London, 1 August 1914

Further to Telegram 205.[125] Sir William Tyrrell was just here with me to tell me that Sir E. Grey would this afternoon want to make suggestions to me about England's neutrality, *even in case that we are at war with*

123 Wilhelm II had just signed the mobilization order at 5 p.m. when this telegram arrived at the Schloss.

124 Engl. transl. based on Geiss, *July 1914*, No. 170, here with minor amendments and additions.

125 See (**370**).

Russia and with France.[126] I will see Sir E. Grey at 3.30 and will report immediately.[127]

DD, No. 570.

(372) 1 August: Lyncker's Diary

Reaction in Berlin to British neutrality offer; Kaiser orders stop to deployment in the West

Moltke had just gone home when the Chancellor appeared with Jagow, with a telegram from Lichnowsky in London.[128] The contents was an incredible surprise. State Secretary Grey had explained to Lichnowsky that England would not only herself remain neutral, but would also ensure and guarantee that France would also remain neutral. This news impacted like a bomb. How could this be explained? and what did we have to do? Immediately the opinion was generally held that this request could under no circumstances be dismissed out of hand, even if the offer was only a bluff, which was after all possible. For firstly this might be the opportunity perhaps only to have to face 1 rather than 3 opponents, that is Russia, against whom war has already been declared today,[129] and

126 Kaiser's marginal note: 'Tell Rome immediately, as well as telegrams from this afternoon. As Italy will not go with the Triple Alliance as long as fear of England's opposition exists.'

127 At 5 p.m. on 1 August, the Kaiser signed the mobilization order in the presence of the Chancellor, Moltke, Falkenhayn, Tirpitz, Lyncker and Plessen. (Falkenhayn diary, 1 August 1914; see also (**373**) and Lerchenfeld to Hertling, 1 August 1914, in Ernst Deuerlein (ed.), *Briefwechsel Hertling-Lerchenfeld*, Harald Boldt Verlag, Boppard am Rhein 1973, doc. 114, p. 323). Moltke had already left the Schloss when Lichnowsky's fateful telegram arrived which threatened to overthrow all the careful military arrangements for the initial days of the war. The ambassador reported that Grey had informed him not only that England would remain neutral, but that it would guarantee French neutrality in a forthcoming war, too, if Germany refrained from hostilities against France. Bethmann Hollweg (DD, No. 578) and Jagow (DD, No. 579) sent separate telegrams to Lichnowsky thanking Britain for the suggestion, both at pains to point out that the suggestion had been received too late to stop German mobilization. 'We would however pledge not to cross the French border until Monday, 3 August, 7 pm, if until then affirmation from England has been received.' DD, No. 578. The Kaiser also wrote personally to King George: (**374**).

128 Britain's alleged suggestion that she would remain neutral if Germany did not attack France (**370**), (**371**). For details, see for example K.M. Wilson, 'Understanding the "Misunderstanding" of 1 August', *Historical Journal*, 37, 4, 1994, pp. 885–889.

129 See (**380**).

secondly the Kaiser must grasp the hand that is offered out of reasons of loyalty for the [German] people and the public and may not rebuff it. In the meantime, Moltke had returned and Falkenhayn had also been called. To everyone's astonishment Moltke declared that the westward deployment could no longer be halted and that despite everything France would have to be attacked. On this point there now developed an exceedingly lively and dramatic discussion [...].[130]

Cited in Imanuel Geiss, *Julikrise und Kriegsausbruch*, 2 vols, Hanover 1963/64, Vol. 2, No. 1000b.

(373) 1 August: Müller's Diary

Describes Moltke's frustration at being overruled by the Kaiser and forced to change deployment plan

[...] Any moment the announcement of a general mobilization is expected. Finally at 5 p.m. a telephone message from the Schloss that mobilization order had just been signed and that I was to come to the Schloss immediately. I drive there through a throng of people who raise repeated cheers to the Navy, and find in the Stern-Saal with the Kaiser already Tirpitz, Lyncker and Falkenhayn.

Soon the Imperial Chancellor and Jagow arrived with a despatch from London, according to which England also offered French neutrality under English guarantee.[131] Great, but delighted, astonishment.

The Chief of the General Staff who had already left is called back and the despatch is read to him. The Kaiser says: 'Of course we must go along with this and therefore stop the deployment in the West for the time being.' General v. Moltke: 'We cannot do that, if that were to happen, we would disrupt the whole army and would give up any chance of success.[132] Besides, our patrols have already entered Luxembourg and

130 There are several testaments to the events in the Kaiser's Schloss that day, collected in Geiss, *Julikrise*, Vol. 2, Nos 1000 a–e. See also (**373**). See also Alfred von Wegerer, *Der Ausbruch des Weltkrieges 1914*, 2 vols, Hamburg 1939, Vol. II, pp. 188ff. Haeften's accounts are particularly important, see BA-MA, N35/1, as well as his article in *Deutsche Allgemeine Zeitung*, 11 October 1921. For an analysis of these events, see also Albertini, *Origins*, Vol. 3, pp. 172ff; Marc Trachtenberg, 'The Coming of the First World War: a Reassessment', in idem, *History and Strategy*, Princeton University Press, Princeton, NJ, 1991, pp. 58ff., and Mombauer, *Moltke*, pp. 216ff.

131 See (**370**).

132 In 1919, Bethmann Hollweg commented on this situation in a letter to Jagow:

the Division from Trier is to follow immediately. The final straw would be if Russia now also fell away.'

But the Kaiser gives Plessen[133] the order immediately to set up the telephone line with Trier. Moltke is beside himself.[134] He says that, if the advance against France did not happen he could not take the responsibility for the war.[135] The Imperial Chancellor replied very excitedly: 'And I cannot take the responsibility for us not agreeing to the English offer.'

Now the Imperial Chancellor, Jagow and Moltke are ordered to compose an answer for England in the adjutants' room next door.[136] Before this Moltke had stopped the advance into Luxembourg as far as that was still possible. [...]

Then a new astonishing telegram arrived from England, in which Sir Edward Grey offered the possibility of English neutrality even in case of Germany ending up in a war with France.[137] (?) [*sic*]

What fabulous change! The Kaiser was very happy and asked for champagne to be brought. Tirpitz exclaimed – in my opinion very out of place – 'the risk-theory is working'.[138] Surely given the entire political

---

'Given that we did only have the one war plan, even in my estimation today our attitude back then was right. [...] I also consider the adherence of the military leaders to Schlieffen's war plan to have been right. An offensive in the East and defensive in the West would have amounted to the admission that we could at the absolute best expect a draw [*partie remise*]. With such a rallying call no army and no people could be lead into a battle for existence.' Cited in Wolfgang Schumann and Ludwig Nestler (eds), *Weltherrschaft im Visier. Dokumente zu den Europa- und Weltherrschaftsplänen des deutschen Imperialismus von der Jahrhundertwende bis Mai 1945*, VEB Deutscher Verlag der Wissenschaften, Berlin 1975, No. 19. See also Willibald Gutsche, *Sarajevo 1914. Vom Attentat zum Weltkrieg*, Dietz Verlag, Berlin 1984, p. 140. My thanks to John Röhl for alerting me to this document.

133 *Generaloberst* Hans von Plessen, Adjutant of the Kaiser and Commandant of the Headquarters.

134 For a different version of events, see Mutius, who remembers that the Kaiser did not undermine Moltke's authority and that Moltke ordered the suspension of the troop movements himself. He declared to Mutius: 'I always feared this would happen, we would have won the war on two fronts.' Memoirs of former Adjutant Mutius, cited in Holger Afflerbach, *Wilhelm II.*, Oldenbourg, Munich 2005, pp. 132–133, Anmerkung 36 (NL Mutius, BA-MA, N195, pp. 204–206).

135 In his own account of the events, Moltke recorded advising the Kaiser: 'If His Majesty insisted on leading the entire army to the East then he would not have an army that was ready to strike but a messy heap of disorderly, armed men without supplies.' Eliza von Moltke (ed.), *Helmuth von Moltke, Erinnerungen, Briefe, Dokumente*, Stuttgart 1922, p. 20.

136 At the same time, the Kaiser dictated a telegram to King George V. See (**374**).

137 See (**371**).

138 Tirpitz's plan for building the German navy had been publicly justified with the

situation there was no reason for England to shy away from the risk that her fleet would be deployed against us in a war. Rather the opposite![139]

Walter Görlitz, *Regierte der Kaiser?*, 2nd edn, Musterschmidt Verlag, Göttingen, Berlin, Frankfurt/Main 1959, pp. 38ff.[140]

(374) 1 August: Wilhelm II to George V

Germany willing to spare France if Britain is prepared to guarantee her neutrality

Telegram (no number)
Berlin, Schloss, 1 August 1914
Urgent!
[original telegram composed in English]

I just received the communication from your Government offering French neutrality under guarantee of Great Britain.[141] Added to this offer was the enquiry, whether under these conditions Germany would refrain from attacking France. On technical grounds my mobilisation which had already been proclaimed this afternoon must proceed against the two fronts east and west as prepared. This cannot be countermanded because I am sorry your telegram came so late. But if France offers me neutrality which must be guaranteed by the British fleet and army I shall of course refrain from attacking France and employ my troops elsewhere.

DD, No. 575.

'risk theory', the notion that Germany needed a navy large enough to deter a British attack.

139 Later that night, Moltke was summoned to the Schloss. The Kaiser had received a further telegram from Lichnowsky which outlined that no definitive promise of neutrality would be made. Moltke was finally given the go-ahead for the occupation of Luxembourg. According to Haeften, the Kaiser was already in bed when he told Moltke: '"As has now transpired, Lichnowsky's telegram was based on a misunderstanding." Turning over in the bed, he continued: "Now do as you please; I don't care either way".' Haeften, 'Meine Erlebnisse aus den Mobilmachungstagen 1914', BA-MA, N35/1, pp. 35f. Haeften's account makes the Kaiser's demeanour seem worse than it actually was. Moltke's own account relates that the Kaiser got out of bed and in fact gave Moltke the order to 'do as you please' in his dressing gown. See Röhl, *Wilhelm II.*, Vol. 3, p. 1164.

140 This translation differs from that in the English: Walter Görlitz (ed.), *The Kaiser and his Court*, Transl. Mervyn Savill, MacDonald, London 1961.

141 See (370).

(375) 1 August: Lichnowsky to Jagow (3)

British Cabinet concerned that Germany is not willing to guarantee Belgian neutrality; Lichnowsky still thinks Britain would like to stay out of the war if Germany can give guarantees to respect French and Belgian borders

Telegram 212
London, 1 August 1914
D 5.47 p.m.
R 10.02 p.m.

[Kaiser's marginal notes and emphases from 2 August]

Grey's drivel shows doesn't know what he is to do. We will now await England's decision. I just learn that England has already cut the cable to Emden.[143] *A war measure, then! While she is still negotiating*

Sir E. Grey has just read to me the following statement, which was unanimously drawn up by the Cabinet: [']The reply of the German Government with regard to the neutrality of Belgium[142] is a matter of very great regret, because the neutrality of Belgium does affect feeling in this country. If Germany could see her way to give the same positive reply as that which has been given by France,[144] it would materially contribute to relieve anxiety and tension here, while on the other hand, if there were a violation

142 See (**390**), (**396**), (**397**), (**404**).

143 Wilhelm II anticipated an event that in fact only occurred a few days later on 4 August, when the British General Post Office ship CS *Alert* sailed into the English Channel and physically lifted the five Atlantic submarine telegraph cables that linked Germany to the wider world. The crew severed these links with hammers, hatchets and hard labour. Germany was thereby cut off from all global telegraph communications except for those that could be arranged via neutral third parties (although she could still use Wireless Telegraphy, i.e. radio, which was, however, fraught with difficulty). I am very grateful to Matthew Seligmann for this information. Barbara Tuchman, who mistakenly names the *Telconia* as the ship which cut the cables, summed up the importance of this action: 'It was England's first offensive action of the war and was to have results more lethal than were dreamed of when the Committee of Imperial Defense planned the action back in 1912.' *The Zimmermann Telegram*, Papermac, London and Basingstoke, 1981 (1st edn 1958).

144 See (**359**).

of the neutrality of Belgium by one combatant while the other respected it, it would be extremely difficult to restrain public feeling in this country[']¹⁴⁵

To my question whether he could give me a definite declaration on the neutrality of Great Britain on the condition that we respected Belgian neutrality, the Minister replied that that would not be possible for him, though this question played an important role in connection with public opinion here. Should we violate Belgian neutrality in a war with France, a reversal of public feeling would certainly take place that would make it difficult for the Government here to adopt an attitude of friendly neutrality. For the present, there was not the slightest intention of proceeding to hostilities against us. But it would be difficult to draw a line beyond which we might not go without causing them on this side to step in. He kept returning to the question of Belgian neutrality and stated that in any case, this question would play an important role. He had also been wondering whether it would not be possible for us and France to remain facing each other under arms, without attacking each other, in the event of a Russian war. I asked him if he was in a position to say whether France would agree to a pact of that sort. Since we intended neither to ruin France nor to conquer any territory, I could imagine that we might enter upon that sort of an agreement, if it

[Left margin:] a false rascal, then!

[Right margin:] Unless an English equivalent is named!

[Left margin:] Humbug! it has not adopted it so far

[Right margin:] He lies! He told Lichnowsky so himself four days ago!

[Left margin:] Without naming an English countermeasure!

[Right margin:] !

[Left margin:] The guy is crazy or an idiot! Besides the French have begun the war and the violation of international law with their bomb-hurling places.[146]

[Right margin:] He already has my offer of yesterday afternoon, that is very plain! And there the King explains the misunderstanding!

145 BD, XI, No. 382.

146 Original English text.

assured us of Great Britain's neutrality. *Rubbish!*

The Minister said that he would inform himself, but he also did not underestimate the difficulty of retaining the soldiers of both sides in a state of inactivity.

My impression as a whole is that if it is possible in any way, they want here to keep out of the war, but that the reply of the Secretary of State to Sir Edward Goschen concerning Belgian neutrality has caused an unfavourable impression.[147]

My impression is that Mr Grey is a false dog who is afraid of his own meanness and false policy, but who will not come out into the open against us, but rather wants to be forced by us to do it. [148]

DD, No. 596.[149]

(376) 1 August: Franz Joseph I to Wilhelm II

Austria-Hungary willing to send troops to fight Russia; also to offer concessions to Italy

Telegram
Vienna (no date)

[...] As soon as my General Staff had learnt that You are determined to begin the war against Russia immediately and to conduct it with all strength, the decision was firm here, too, to amass the majority of troops against Russia.

With Italy negotiations are arranged on the part of the General Staff which aim at a continued [*sic*] participation of Italian troops in the Triple Alliance war; a supportive influencing in this regard on your part would be urgently desired.

You can be assured that on the part of My Army the utmost will be done to bring the great fight to a successful conclusion.

147 See (**366**), (**370**), (**371**).

148 The Kaiser only saw this document on 2 August in the afternoon, and his angry notes were influenced by what he had learned of British policy in the meantime.

149 English translation based on Geiss, *July 1914*, No. 174, with minor amendments.

My military attaché in Berlin reported today about his reception with You yesterday.[150] I am delighted and enthusiastic about Your extensive precautions to strengthen our military power with the inclusion of new allies.[151]

Due to the seriousness of the situation my Ambassador in Rome has been charged with explaining to the Italian Government that we are willing to accept their interpretation of Article VII of the [Triple Alliance] treaty if Italy now fully complies with her duty as an alliance partner.[152] I will personally telegraph to the King of Italy to tell him that after thirty years of peace work we count on the fact that the three allies will unite their armies for this decisive fight.

ÖUA, VIII, No. 11204.

(377) 1 August: Poincaré's Diary

France and Russia both want to be seen to be engaged in a defensive war

I do not despair; the English are slow to decide, methodical, reflective, but they know where they are going. […]

Germany clearly does not wish us to negotiate on an equal footing; she claims to agree to talk; but she does not want Russia and us to be able to defend ourselves in the talks.

[Following a conversation with Isvolsky he recorded] […] that we had an interest, Russia and us, that mobilization should be taken as far as possible before war was declared. I added that it would be better

150 At 5 p.m. on 31 July, Bienerth had been called to see the Kaiser who told the military attaché that 'Germany needed to turn the bulk of her [military] power initially against France and could only assume the offensive against Russia after [France's] defeat, therefore Austria-Hungary would have to withstand Russia's initial onslaught and reckon with at least fourteen corps against her as according to intelligence only six Russian corps are to be used against Germany.' He also told Bienerth that 'Germany would have to reckon with England's active involvement against the Triple Alliance'. Bienerth's account in Szögyény to Berchtold, ÖUA, VIII, 11133 and 11134 (also in Geiss, *Julikrise*, Vol. II, No. 868).

151 Wilhelm had told Bienerth that he had telegraphed the Kings of Rumania (DD 472) and Bulgaria (there is no record of this telegram) to try to convince them to support the Triple Alliance.

152 This meant that Italy would be compensated with territory in return for agreeing to Austria-Hungary making any territorial acquisitions on the Balkans.

that we should not be obliged to declare war ourselves and that it be declared on us. That was necessary for both military and domestic political reasons: a defensive war would raise the whole country; a declaration of war by us could leave some doubts about the alliance, amongst part of public opinion.

Raymond Poincaré, 'Notes journalières', cited in John Keiger, *Raymond Poincaré*, Cambridge University Press, Cambridge 1997, pp. 179, 182.

(378) 1 August: Messimy to French Military High Command

French troops still to stay 10 kilometres behind the border

Telegram
1 August 1914, 10.30 pm

The Ministry of War insists again, on behalf of the President of the Republic, and for serious diplomatic reasons, on the necessity of not crossing the demarcation line indicated by the telegram of 30 July and reiterated in a telegram of today.[153] This prohibition applies as much to the cavalry as to other units. No patrol, no reconnaissance, no post, no element whatsoever, must go east of said line. Whoever crosses it will be liable to court martial and it is only in the event of a full-scale attack that it will be possible to transgress this order, which will be communicated to all troops.[154]

153 On 30 July, Poincaré, Viviani, Messimy and Joffre had decided on a set of proposals designed to demonstrate France's defensive stance, including the condition not to deploy any troops closer than 10 kilometres from the Franco-German border. In Keiger's words, this was 'a remarkable gesture of restraint, the like of which there can be few cases in the history of warfare'. On 31 July Joffre advised the cabinet that each delay of twenty-four hours in mobilizing the eastern army corps meant losing 15–20 kilometres of French territory (**338**), and the next day he threatened to resign over this matter. However, Messimy later commented: 'Nothing made such an impression on British opinion (all accounts are agreed on that point), nothing was better proof of our pacific intentions than this decision to keep troops at a slight distance from the frontier.' Keiger, *Poincaré*, p. 180.

154 Following Joffre's request the cabinet agreed to lift the 10-kilometre withdrawal on 2 August at 2 p.m. Joffre's dispatch to the army commanders read: 'For national reasons of a moral nature and for imperious reasons of a diplomatic kind, it is indispensable that the Germans be left with full responsibility for hostilities. Consequently, and until further notice, covering troops will restrict themselves to expelling across the frontier any assault troops without giving chase any further and without encroaching on opposing territory.' Cited in Keiger, *Poincaré*, p. 183.

Cited in John Keiger, *Raymond Poincaré*, Cambridge University Press, Cambridge 1997, p. 181.

(379) 1 August: Joffre's note[155]

Joffre argues that Germany had an advantage of 2–3 days in her mobilization measures

1 August 1914, 9 a.m.

The serious risks indicated yesterday concerning the delayed departure of covering troops will become even greater if we delay the order of general mobilization.

German preparations continue, in effect, following a well-formulated plan, the basis of which we know from a report drawn up by the German High Command that came into our hands.

In particular the report says:

that they can proceed, with minimal notice, and without waiting for mobilization orders, to a discreet mobilization of personnel and extra equipment by calling up reservists and by purchasing or requisitioning horses, in order to start transporting army corps as soon as the mobilization order is received;

that the discreet preparation of mobilization, arrangements made for the call up, transportation, security measures (publication of the law on requisitions before mobilization begins) and the rapid execution of strategic transport ensure them advantages which will be difficult for the armies of the other nations to replicate;

that the objective which must be aimed for is to launch a superior offensive from the very first days; plans finalized this way allow the hope that the offensive can be launched as soon as the army has congregated in the Lower Rhine area. Before long, an ultimatum that must be followed up immediately with the invasion will sufficiently justify their actions from the point of view of international law.

Etc.

All this is clarified by information received:

Five classes of [German] reservist are called up for the 2nd August at the latest; requisitioning and purchasing of horses began from the 30th July, perhaps before.

We can thus say that on the 4th August, even without a mobilization order, the German army will be entirely mobilized[156] and will already

155 No recipient mentioned, but most likely written for Messimy.

156 In fact, on that day the German attack through Belgium began.

have a forty-eight hour, or even three day, advantage on ours.

DDF, 3e série, 11, No. 473.

(380) 1 August: Paléologue's memoirs

German declaration of war handed to Russia; emotional scenes in St Petersburg

During yesterday the Emperor William proclaimed Germany 'in danger of war.' The announcement of the *Kriegsgefahrzustand* means the immediate calling up of the reservists and the closing of the frontiers. If it is not the official mobilization it is at any rate the prelude and opening move.

On receiving this news the Tsar telegraphed to the Kaiser:

I understand that you are compelled to mobilize but I should like to have the same guarantee from you that I gave you myself – that these measures do not mean war and that we shall continue our negotiations to save the general peace so dear to our hearts. With God's help our long and tried friendship should be able to prevent bloodshed. I confidently await a reply from you.[157]

The time given by the ultimatum[158] expired at midday to-day, but it was not before seven this evening that Pourtalès appeared at the Foreign Office.

His eyes were swollen and he was very red in the face and choking with emotion as he solemnly handed Sazonov a declaration of war, which concluded with this theatrical and mendacious phrase: *His Majesty the Emperor, my august sovereign, in the name of the empire accepts the challenge and considers himself in a state of war with Russia.*[159]

Sazonov replied: 'This is a criminal act of yours. The curses of the nations will be upon you.' [...]

[Pourtalès:] 'We are defending our honour!'

157 See *Int. Bez.*, No. 384.

158 Germany had given Russia 18 hours to revoke her mobilization. See for example (**364**).

159 See also *Int. Bez.*, No. 396, Daily Record of the Russian Foreign Ministry: '[...] Count Pourtalès, who had lost all self-control, stood by the window [...], held his head, burst into tears and said: 'Je n'aurais jamais cru que je quitterais Pétersbourg dans ces conditions' (p. 252). Poincaré commented on the German declaration of war on 1 August: 'Thus Germany assumes full responsibility for a horrific war'. Poincaré, 'Notes journalières', cited in Keiger, *Poincaré*, p. 183.

'Your honour was not involved. You could have prevented the war by one word: you didn't want to. In all my efforts to save peace I haven't had the slightest help from you. But there's a divine justice!'

Pourtalès repeated in a dull voice, with a look of desperation: 'That's true ... there's a divine justice ... a divine justice!'

He went on muttering a few incomprehensible words and staggered towards the window which is on the right of the door, opposite the Winter Palace. There he leaned against the embrasure and burst into tears.

[...] Finally he rushed to the door, which he could hardly open with his trembling fingers, and went out murmuring: 'Goodbye! Goodbye!'

A few minutes later I went to Sazonov who described the scene. He also told me that Buchanan had just requested an audience of the Tsar to hand him a personal telegram from his sovereign. In this telegram,[160] King George makes a supreme appeal to the peace-loving nature of the Tsar and begs him to continue his efforts for conciliation. The step has no object now that Pourtalès has handed in the declaration of war. But the Tsar will receive Buchanan at eleven to-night in any case.

Maurice Paléologue, *Memoirs*, Doran, New York 1925, Paléologue, *Memoirs*, Vol. I, pp. 48–49.

(381) 1 August: Schoen to Jagow

France has still not declared if she will stay neutral; British mediation proposal received

Telegram 239
Paris, 1 August 1914
D. 1.05 p.m.
R. 6.10 p.m.
Urgent

[Wilhelm II's emphases and marginal notes]

Follow-up to Telegram[161]

To the definite and repeated question whether France would remain neutral in case of a Russo-German war, the Premier stated to me *hesitatingly*: France would do what her interests demanded. He based the uncertainty of this statement on the fact

160 *Int. Bez.*, No. 397.

161 See (**343**).

Do not know of any I have not received any

that he regarded the situation as changed since yesterday. It was officially reported here that *Sir E. Grey's proposal of a general suspension of military preparations* had in principle[162] been accepted by Russia, and that Austria-Hungary had declared that she would not infringe on Serbia's territory or sovereignty.

DD, No. 571.[163]

(382) 1 August: Davignon to Belgian Ministers at Berlin, Paris, and London

France pledges to respect Belgian neutrality in case of war

Brussels, 1 August 1914

I have the honour to inform you that the French Minister [Klobukowski] has made the following verbal communication to me:

'I am authorized to declare that, in the event of an international war, the French Government, in accordance with the declarations they have always made, will respect the neutrality of Belgium. In the even of this neutrality not being respected by another Power, the French Government, to secure their own defence, might find it necessary to modify their attitude.'

I thanked His Excellency and added that we on our side had taken without delay all the measures necessary to ensure that our independence and our frontiers should be respected.

Belgian *Grey Book*, No. 15.

162 The deciphering of this word is not certain (see DD, No. 571, note 6). Wilhelm II noted over the word 'principle': 'what does this mean?'

163 Engl. transl. based on Geiss, *July 1914*, No. 173, with minor amendments.

11
The European war becomes a reality

2 August–6 August: Documents (383)–(428)

On 2 August the long-awaited decision for war was finally taken in London when the Cabinet met twice that day and decided, in Walter Runciman's words, 'that war with Germany was inevitable' (**389**).[1] Initially, it did not look as if the Cabinet could agree. Prime Minister Asquith recorded: 'We had a long Cabinet from 11 to nearly 2, which very soon revealed that we are on the brink of a split. [...] There is a strong party including all the 'Beagles' and reinforced by Ll[oyd] George[,], Morley and Harcourt who are against any kind of intervention in any case.'[2] In the end, the Conservative Party leaders offered their support to the Government (**387**) and this was welcome news for Grey in his attempts to unite the Cabinet behind a decision for war. On 1 August, Balfour explained to Count Benckendorff's son-in-law 'that if it was purely a question of Serbia, [the Tories] were against war; it if was the [...] European issue, they were for it to a man.'[3] By now, Grey was even threatening to resign if Britain did not support France (**388**).

The next day, news was received of Germany's ultimatum to Belgium, delivered on 2 August (**386**). Asquith commented in a letter

1 Cited in Keith M. Wilson, 'The British Cabinet's Decision for War, 2 August 1914', in *British Journal for International Studies*, I, 1975, pp. 148–159, p. 150. See also Samuel R. Williamson, Jr., 'General Henry Wilson, Ireland, and the Great War', in William Roger Louis (ed.), *Resurgent Adventures with Britannia: Personalities, Politics and Culture in Britain*, London, I.B. Tauris, 2011, pp. 91–105, who argues that Wilson was instrumental and successful in getting the Tory leadership to put pressure on the Liberals, and that this pressure was almost as important as Belgium in leading to the decision to intervene.

2 Michael Brock and Eleanor Brock (eds), *H.H. Asquith. Letters to Venetia Stanley*, Oxford University Press, Oxford and New York 1985, p. 146.

3 Cited in Soroka, *Britain, Russia and the Road to the First World War*, p. 254.

to Venetia Stanley: 'The Germans, with almost Austrian crassness, have delivered an ultimatum to Belgium & forced themselves on to their territory, and the Belgian King has made an appeal to ours.'[4] Germany's action led to a change of heart among those who had still opposed Britain's entry into the war, most crucially, in Lloyd George, while others who had contemplated resigning (Simon and Beauchamp) were swayed to stay by Asquith.[5] In the end, two members of the Cabinet, Burns and Morley, resigned as a result of the decision to come to France's aid.[6] In a lengthy statement in the House of Commons, Grey outlined Britain's difficult position. He explained that France had declared herself willing to respect Belgium's neutrality (**382**), while Germany had refused to do so. Britain's prospects were bleak for, according to Grey, Britain was 'going to suffer, I am afraid, terribly in this war whether we are in it or whether we stand aside'(**401**). In the afternoon, when the House reconvened, he was able to tell its members about the German note, amounting to an ultimatum to Belgium (**302**), (**386**). At last, he was able to unite not only the Cabinet, but most of the country behind a war in defence of Belgium's honour. Without Germany's invasion of Belgium, Grey's task would have been far more difficult; fighting for Serbia would never have delivered the same unifying reason for war. The Russian Ambassador in London, Benckendorff, could report to St Petersburg a surprising reversal in public opinion in favour of war following the German declaration of war on Russia on 1 August, and invasion of Luxembourg the next day (**407**).

Belgium proved a great cause for going to war, but there is much evidence to suggest that it was not actually the reason why Grey wanted to convince the Cabinet to join France. Some contemporaries felt that 'Belgium did not determine Grey's attitude',[7] and this

---

4 Ibid., p. 148.

5 Ibid., p. 148: 'You will be relieved to hear that there is a slump in resignations. I wrote last night a strong appeal to the Impeccable, with the result that he & Beauchamp have returned to the fold, & attended the Cabinet this morning. J. M[orley] remains obstinate & I fear must go [...] Master C. Trevelyan also persists in his determination: happily, *il n'y a pas d'homme nécessaire*.'

6 For a moving account of these decisions, see K.M. Wilson, 'The Cabinet Diary of J.A. Pease', *Proceedings of the Leeds Philosophical Society*, XIX, III, 1983, pp. 41–51, p. 48. See also Asquith's letters to Venetia Stanley, 2, 3 and 4 August 1914, in Brock and Brock, *Asquith. Letters*, pp. 145–150.

7 Ramsay McDonald's memorandum, recalling a conversation with Lloyd George and Edwin Montagu on 7 October 1914, cited in Keith M. Wilson, 'Britain', in

impression seemed confirmed by the fact that Grey had

> threatened to resign if the Cabinet declared for neutrality on Wednesday 29 July [...] before Belgium was mentioned seriously (if at all) in the Cabinet discussions. [...] Belgium had nothing whatever to do with the Cabinet decisions. Without it there would have been more resignations but there still would have been war.[8]

In Germany, the news of Britain's decision came as a shock, particularly for Wilhelm II and Bethmann Hollweg. Admiral von Müller recorded after the war: 'For the Kaiser England's joining our enemies was indeed a serious blow. England-experts in the *Auswärtiges Amt* had reckoned that England would intervene during the course of the war if the French were doing badly, but only with the intention of reinstating peace soon without humiliating Germany.'[9]

Belgium's Crown Council meeting in the evening of 2 August unanimously decided to reject the German ultimatum presented to them that day (**399**). False news of French border violations and the dropping of French bombs in southern Germany did not help to sway the Belgian Government to accept Germany's conditions, nor did it lead to a change of heart in Rome (**392**), (**393**), (**396**). On 3 August Below forwarded the reply by the Belgian Government which rejected the claim that France had violated Belgium's borders and reaffirmed its desire to repel the infringement of Belgium's rights by any power (**406**).

France mobilized on 2 August, but troops were still not allowed to cross into enemy territory (**394**), (**395**). On 3 August Germany

---

Keith M. Wilson (ed.), *Decisions for War, 1914*, UCL Press, London 1995, pp. 175–208, p. 176.

8 Ramsay McDonald's memorandum, recalling a conversation with John Morley on 6 October 1914, cited in Wilson, 'Britain', p. 176. As Wilson points out, Belgium had in fact been mentioned in the meeting of 29 July, although it is also true that Grey threatened to resign, and that members of the Cabinet felt that 'Grey wishes to go to war without any violation of Belgium.' Harcourt to Lloyd George, 2 (?) August, cited in ibid., p. 177. See also (**387**). Asquith's letter of 4 August is revealing in this respect: 'We had an interesting Cabinet, as we got the news that the Germans had entered Belgium, & had announced to 'les braves Belges' that if necessary they wd. push their way through by force of arms. This simplifies matters, so we sent the Germans an ultimatum to expire at midnight [...]. Brock and Brock, *Asquith. Letters*, p. 150 (**386**).

9 Müller's marginal notes on a manuscript written by Vice-Admiral Freiherr von Keyserlingk after the war. Cited in Stephen Schröder, *Die englisch-russische Marinekonvention*, Vandenhoeck & Ruprecht, Göttingen 2004, p. 589.

declared war on France (her declaration of war on Russia had been made on 1 August[10]), again using the fabricated news of French bombs being dropped over German territory as pretext (**404**). Given that she was now at war with Russia, Germany's military deployment plan compelled her to launch an immediate attack in the West while in the East Russia was expected to be slow to mobilize. The French had been determined to leave the declaration of war to Germany so as not to appear as an aggressor (**377**). Their patience had paid off, leading Poincaré to comment in his diary on 3 August: 'never had a declaration of war been received with such satisfaction'.[11]

On 5 August, a 'historic' war council was held at No 10 Downing Street, during which the most important ministers, generals and admirals discussed how Britain would best come to France's military aid in the war in which they had finally decided to become involved (**425**).[12]

Britain's decision to support her Entente partner was a further factor in Italy's decision for neutrality in July 1914 (**410**). King Vittorio Emanuele III telegraphed to Wilhelm II on 3 August that the Italian Government did not accept that the *casus foederis* arose for Italy, which proved a shock for Germany's military leaders who had clung to the belief that Italy could be counted on, not necessarily for the military support they would bring, but because the Triple Alliance should be seen to stand united. (**398**) At the very least, Moltke insisted, Italy would have to be pressed to allow the import of food into Germany unhindered – this was a matter of 'life and death' for Germany (**412**).[13] It would have been difficult at the best of times to enthuse Italians for a war on Austria-Hungary's side, but in the circumstances of July 1914, when it appeared as if Austria

10 See (**380**).

11 Cited in Stefan Schmidt, *Frankreichs Außenpolitik*, Oldenbourg, Munich 2007, p. 354. See also (**403**), (**405**).

12 For details, see for example Roy Prete, 'French Strategic Planning', *Canadian Journal of History*, XXIV, April 1989, pp. 42–62, p. 54.

13 Moltke was concerned that the coming war would not be short, and had been at pains to ensure that it would be possible for Germany to continue the imports on which her population depended. This was one of the reasons why he was insistent on not violating the neutrality of the Netherlands. His fear of the fate of Germany's population in a long war was increased by the news of Britain's declaration of war. See (**420**). On Moltke's idea to use Holland as a windpipe, see also Annika Mombauer, *Helmuth von Moltke*, Cambridge University Press, Cambridge 2001, pp. 94–95.

was acting as the aggressor, the Italian Government could arguably not really have decided differently (**384**).[14] Italy's declaration of neutrality was drafted on 2 August and formally published on 3 August (**410**). That day, San Giuliano declared in conversation with the journalist Olindo Malagodi: 'Our decision depended necessarily on that of England.'[15] By 5 August, in Berlin hopes had changed from securing Italian involvement to ensuring that Italy would at least maintain neutrality and not actively become involved on the side of the Entente (**421**). By 6 August the Entente Powers were at war with the Dual Alliance. Now neither side wanted to settle for mediation (**428**). All governments were confident of victory and convinced that war, if still avoided now, would come in any case, but at a less convenient point in the future. Few, if any, Europeans anticipated either the length, the nature, or indeed the outcome and long-term consequences of this World War whose outbreak, as the documents clearly show, could easily have been avoided as it had on previous occasions. If they had been able to predict its ruinous nature and outcome, perhaps they would have chosen to avoid it once more.

(383) 2 August: Wenninger to Bavarian Minister of War Kress

War with Russia and France now certain; Britain's attitude still unclear; Italy will not participate

No. 2720, Berlin, 2 August 1914
Strictly confidential
Report No. 9

Re: Political situation and military measures

The fighting between the military and the diplomats continues;[16] the latter kept on postponing the decisive steps. Russia's infringements of

14 William A. Renzi, 'Italy and the Great War', *American Historical Review*, 73, 5 June 1968, pp. 1414–1432, p. 1420. Another important reason for Italy's policy in July 1914 was that the army was in poor shape and that 50,000 troops were still tied up in the war in Libya.

15 Olindo Malagodi, *Conversazioni della guerra, 1914–1919*, 2 vols, R. Ricciardi, Milan 1960, Vol. I, p. 17. San Giuliano declared as early as 30 July that he was certain England would fight on the side of France and Russia if war were to break out. See Flotow's Telegram, DD, 2, No. 414. See also (**423**).

16 See for example (**372**), (**373**) and Falkenhayn's diary entry of 21 July (**351**).

the border[17] at least clarified the situation on this side; this afternoon, following long discussions, the passports were sent to Russian Ambassador and the exequatur was withdrawn from the consuls, however it was declared that there was as yet no reason to undertake the same step vis-à-vis the French mission.

The Ministry of War was much put out about this, because all the general commandos sent queries about who was to be regarded as the enemy. Then the welcome news arrived from our Third Bavarian Army Corps about the bombing near Nuremberg by a French plane.[18] Now the Ministry of War and the General Staff declared France as an enemy without waiting for an act of diplomacy.

With regard to France and Russia politics now have to be silent. Only with regard to England do the arguments continue. England is alleged to have declared that she would remain neutral if the neutrality of Belgium and Holland would also be respected by Germany.[19] Moltke[20] remains determined only to be guided in this regard by military[21] considerations.

Italy's embarrassing change of heart occurred at the moment when England strengthened her Mediterranean fleet; Italy pretended concern about her unprotected coastline was the reason. At around the same time that Italy's uncertain attitude became known here a higher Italian naval officer arrived here and requested under order the German naval operations plan. He was not received.[22] This much is certain: whether Italy now joins in or not, the current war will be followed by an Austro-Italian war. [...]

---

17 On 2 August Bethmann Hollweg informed Kaiser Wilhelm II that the Russians had destroyed railway lines on the German border, and that two squadrons of Cossacks had been deployed into Johannisburg in East Prussia. See DD, No. 629. This does not seem to have been correct. There was an initial raid by the Russian 4th cavalry division into the south of East Prussia on 5 August, in which a rail station was wrecked. On 9 August elements of the same division (Dragoons and Cossacks) penetrated into Johannisburg before being turned back by local German formations. I am very grateful to Bruce Menning, who kindly consulted the archives in Moscow, as well as N.F. Evseev, *Avgustoskoe srazhenie 2–i russkoi armii v Vostochnoi Prussii* (Moscow 1936) to help clarify the initial moves of the Russian army.

18 This news was a fabrication. See (**390**), (**392**), (**393**), (**396**), (**397**).

19 Lichnowsky's telegram of 1 August: (**370**), (**371**).

20 In the unpublished version this reads: 'The General Staff'. Reports of the Royal Bavarian Military Plenipotentiary, BHST-MA, MKr 1765.

21 In the archive copy: military.

22 In the archive copy, but not in published version: 'Generally the death of Pollio is regretted, who would certainly have opposed the change of heart with all his might.' Ibid.

Pius Dirr (ed.), *Bayerische Dokumente zum Kriegsausbruch*, 3rd edn, Oldenbourg, Munich and Berlin 1925, No. 13, pp. 230–231.

(384) 2 August: San Giuliano to Avarna

Outlines Italy's difficult position

Rome, 2 August 1914

[...] It is superfluous to recount the sad consequences that a defeat of the Triple Alliance would produce; even if it gained a partial victory, it would not be able to give us adequate compensations; and if the Alliance won a decisive victory and reduced France and Russia to impotency for many years, there would be neither the interest not the desire to give us compensations in proportion to our sacrifices. [...][23]

DDI, 5th Series, I, No. 2.

(385) 2 August: Villiers to Grey

Belgium determined to defend herself without appealing to other Powers

Brussels, 2 August 1914
D. 12.15 p.m.
Tel. (No. 10.)
R. 1.25 p.m.

Minister for Foreign Affairs states that Belgian Government have no reason whatever to suspect Germany of an intention to violate neutrality. He says that Belgian Government have not considered idea of appeal to other guarantee Powers, nor of intervention should a violation occur; they would rely upon their own armed force as sufficient to resist aggression, from whatever quarter it might come.[24]

23 Similarly, Antonio Salandra wrote after the war: 'The kingdom of Italy, if [...] victorious with them [the Central Powers], would at best have been reduced to first among the vassal states of the [German] empire.' *La Neutralità italiana 1914. Ricordi e pensieri*, Mondadone, Milan 1928, p. 88, cited in Renzi, 'Italy and the Great War', p. 1420.

24 See (**382**).

MINUTE

It is impossible for the German troops to get out of Luxemburg without crossing Belgian territory except through a narrow bottle-neck into France.[25] *G. R.C. 2 August 1914.*

BD, XI, No. 476.

(386) 2 August: Note from the German to the Belgian Government

German Government alleges that French troops intend to march into Belgium; threatens Belgium with hostilities unless she maintains neutrality towards Germany

Imperial German Legation in Belgium-Brussels, 2 August 1914[26]

(Very Confidential.)

Reliable news has been received by the Imperial Government to the effect that French forces intend to march along the line of the Meuse by Givet and Namur. This information leaves no doubt as to the intention of France[27] to march through Belgian territory against Germany.[28]

25 In fact, even with the violation of Belgium the advance of German troops was made exceptionally difficult because they had to proceed through a narrow corridor in order to preserve Dutch neutrality. For details see Annika Mombauer, 'German War Plans', in Richard F. Hamilton and Holger H. Herwig (eds), *War Planning 1914*, Cambridge University Press, Cambridge et al., 2010, pp. 48–78, pp. 61–62.

26 This document was first drafted by Helmuth von Moltke and sent to the *Auswärtiges Amt* on 26 July. It was then amended slightly by Stumm, Zimmermann and Bethmann Hollweg, before being sent to Below on 29 July by special messenger with Jagow's instructions to keep it securely sealed and only to open it when thus instructed. See (**302**).

27 In Moltke's original draft, this read: 'France's intentions, having been joined by the British Expeditionary Corps'.

28 This was a mere fabrication, as pointed out in Imanuel Geiss, *July 1914*, Scribner, London 1967, p. 231, n. 4. This becomes even clearer if one considers that, when the text was drafted (26 July), there was no sign of French military moves against Germany (**392**), (**393**). Albertini comments 'on the hypocrisy and clumsy obtuseness displayed in this document by which the rulers of Germany thought to trick world opinion into believing that the German army had been unexpectedly compelled to enter Belgium because reliable news had been received that the French were invading that country. As if it were not self-evident that the German General Staff could embark on the venture of invading Belgium to take the French in the rear only as a result of having a plan

The Imperial Government cannot but fear the probability that Belgium, in spite of the best of intentions, will be unable, without assistance, to resist so considerable a French[29] invasion with sufficient prospect of success to afford an adequate guarantee against danger to Germany. It is essential for the self-defence of Germany that she should anticipate any such hostile attack. The German Government would, however, feel the deepest regret if Belgium regarded it as an act of hostility against herself if the measures of her opponents were to force Germany, for her own protection, to enter Belgian territory.

In order to avoid any misunderstanding, the German Government make the following declaration:

1 Germany contemplates no act of hostility against Belgium. In the event of Belgium being prepared in the coming war to maintain an attitude of benevolent neutrality towards Germany,[30] the German Government will bind itself to guarantee, at the conclusion of peace, [not only] the possessions and independence of the Kingdom in full, [but it will even be prepared to favour with the best of good will any possible claims of the Kingdom for territorial compensation at the expense of France.][31]
2 Germany undertakes, under the above-mentioned condition, to evacuate Belgian territory as soon as peace has been concluded.
3 If Belgium adopts a friendly attitude, Germany is prepared, in co-operation with the Belgian authorities, to purchase for cash all the necessities required by her troops against, and to make good any damage that may possibly have been caused by German troops.

Should Belgium oppose the German troops, and in particular throw obstacles in the way of their march by the resistance of the fortresses on the Meuse, or by destroying railways, roads, tunnels, or other similar works, Germany will, to her regret, be compelled to consider Belgium as an enemy. In this event, Germany can undertake no obligations towards Belgium, but the future regulation of the relations between the two States must be left to the decision of arms.

---

of concentration, a railway network, and an organization planned long years in advance'. Luigi Albertini, *The Origins of the War of 1914*, 3 vols, Oxford University Press, Oxford 1952–1957, Vol. III, p. 455. 'As an extra touch of knavery, the ultimatum was written in German so that the first thing the Belgian Government had to do was to have it translated. And this, be it noted, when the time allowed for the reply was only twelve hours – twelve night hours. Ibid.

29 In Moltke's original draft, this read 'Franco-(English)'.

30 In Moltke's draft, 'to be on Germany's side'.

31 The text in square brackets was not included in the version that was handed to the Belgian Government. See DD, No. 648. In November 1913, Moltke and Kaiser Wilhelm had already tried to persuade the Belgians to be on Germany's side (65), (67).

The Imperial Government, however, entertains the definite hope that this eventuality will not occur, and that the Belgian Government will know how to take the necessary measures to prevent any such occurrences as those mentioned. In this case the friendly ties which bind the two neighbouring States would grow stronger and more enduring.[32]

DD, No. 376.[33]

(387) 2 August: Bonar Law to Asquith

Conservative leaders offer support to the Government

Dear Mr. Asquith,
Lord Lansdowne and I feel it is our duty to inform you that in our opinion, as well as in that of all the colleagues with whom we have been able to consult, it would be fatal to the honour and security of the United Kingdom to hesitate in supporting France and Russia at the present moment; and we offer our unhesitating support to the Government in any measures they may consider necessary to that object.[34]

---

32 The instructions to Below contained the following additional paragraph: 'Your Highness are immediately to inform the Royal Belgian Government extremely confidentially and to ask them for an unambiguous answer within 24 hours.' The General Staff's version of this document had contained a harsher version: 'An unambiguous answer to this despatch much be given within 24 hours of receipt, otherwise hostilities will commence immediately.' In the event, this deadline was changed to 12 hours, and Below was instructed: 'Please assure Belgian Government urgently that, in spite of Paris's promises, all doubt as to the correctness of our news of French plans must be ruled out. For your personal information: Belgian reply must be here by tomorrow afternoon 2 p.m., German time. Will Your Excellency immediately wire reply to us here and also, immediately on receiving it, send it to General von Emmich, Union Hotel, Aix-la-Chapelle, by one of the Embassy staff, preferably the Military Attaché, by car. Belgian Government must receive impression that all instructions in this matter only reached you today. I further advise that you suggest to Belgian Government that it might retire with troops to Antwerp and that, if desired, we might take over protecting of Brussels against internal unrests.' (DD, No. 648). For Belgium's reaction see (**399**).

33 Also in Belgian *Grey Book*, No. 20. Engl. transl. based on Geiss, *July 1914*, No. 91, here with amendments.

34 This was one of two letters sent by conservative leaders to the Prime Minister following a meeting at Lansdowne House in the evening of 1 August. Interestingly, Belgium, the apparent reason for Britain's possible intervention, is not even mentioned. In his reply, Asquith pointed out that Britain was under 'no

Bonar Law Papers, 34/3/2, Law to Asquith, 2 August 1914, cited in Frank McDonough, *The Conservative Party and Anglo-German Relations*, Palgrave Macmillan, Basingstoke and New York 2007, p. 133.

(388) 2 August: Grey to Bertie

Summary of Cabinet meeting of 2 August: Britain still not decided

Foreign Office, 2 August 1914.
Tel. (No. 303.)
D. 4.45 p.m.

After the Cabinet this morning[35] I gave M. Cambon the following aide-mémoire:

'I am authorised to give an assurance that if the German fleet comes into the Channel or through the North Sea to undertake hostile operations against French coasts or shipping the British fleet will give all the protection in its power. This assurance is of course subject to the policy of His Majesty's Government receiving the support of Parliament and must not be taken as binding His Majesty's Government to take any action until the above contingency of action by the German fleet takes place.'

I pointed out that we had very large questions and most difficult issues to consider, and that the Government felt that they could not bind themselves to declare war upon Germany necessarily, if war broke out between France and Germany to-morrow, but it was essential to the French Government, whose fleet had long been concentrated in the

---

obligation' towards France or Russia. In a first emergency Cabinet meeting on 2 August (two were held that day), Asquith read out Bonar Law's letter and it was doubtless useful as a way of putting pressure on those members of the Cabinet who did not favour intervention. However, Asquith later denied that the letter had any influence on the Cabinet's decision. Brock and Brock, *Asquith. Letters*, p. 147, note 6.) During the same meeting, Grey threatened to resign if Britain did not come to the aid of France and Russia. Frank McDonough, *The Conservative Party and Anglo-German Relations*, Macmillan, Basingstoke and New York 2007, pp. 133–134. See also Wilson, who argues in 'The British Cabinet's Decision', pp. 150–151, that the support of the Conservatives provided Grey with much needed back-up for making his demands more forcefully.

35 There were two Cabinet meetings that day. This was 'the Fateful Sunday' (as Masterman recalled in a letter to Runciman on 14 February 1915) when the decision to intervene in a continental war was taken in the Cabinet. In a second Cabinet Meeting later that day it was decided that a violation of Belgian neutrality would 'compel us to take action'. See Wilson, 'The British Cabinet's Decision', p. 150, and Introduction, Note 88 (387), (389).

Mediterranean, to know how to make their dispositions with their north coast entirely undefended. We therefore thought it necessary to give them this assurance. It did not bind us to go to war with Germany unless the German fleet took the action indicated, but it did give a security to France that would enable her to settle the disposition of her own Mediterranean fleet.

M. Cambon asked me about the violation of Luxemburg. I told him the doctrine on that point laid down by Lord Derby and Lord Clarendon in 1867. He asked me what we should say about the violation of the neutrality of Belgium. I said that was a much more important matter; we were considering what statement we should make in Parliament to-morrow, in effect whether we should declare violation of Belgium neutrality to be a casus belli. I told him what had been said to the German Ambassador on this point. I also explained how at the beginning of a great catastrophe such as this European war, of which no one could foresee the consequences where we had such enormous responsibilities in our Empire, as in India, or as regards countries in our occupation such as Egypt, when even the conditions of naval warfare and the possibility of protecting our coast under these conditions were untried, it was impossible safely to send our military force out of the country.

M. Cambon asked whether this meant that we should never do it.

I replied that it dealt only with the present moment. He dwelt upon the moral effect of our sending only two divisions. But I said that to send so small a force as two or even four divisions abroad at the beginning of a war would entail the maximum of risk to them and produce the minimum of effect.[36]

BD, XI, No. 487.

(389) 2 August: Runciman's account of morning Cabinet Meeting

---

Decision made to regard German ships in Channel as hostile act; but still not committed to Belgium; Cabinet divided

---

Grey proposes definitely

(I) to announce to France and Germany that if the German ships enter the Channel we should regard that as a hostile act.

36 Later that day Grey sent the following additional message to Bertie: 'The war. My telegram No. 303 of 2nd August. Assurances as to action of British Fleet. You should impress on French Government that the assurance given to-day is very confidential till it has been announced in public to-morrow.' BD, XI, No. 495; Sir Edward Grey to Sir F. Bertie, 2 August 1914.

(II) on Belgian neutrality, we do not commit ourselves at present. We are consulting Parliament.

Crewe would not hesitate to go to war over the English Channel. Several others agreed.[37]

Runciman MS, cited in Keith M. Wilson, *The Policy of the Entente*, Cambridge University Press, Cambridge 1985, 2nd edn 2009, p. 139.

(390) 2 August: Goschen to Grey

German claims that French bombs have been dropped near Nuremberg

Berlin, 2 August 1914.
D. 2.15 p.m.
Tel. (No. 124.) Urgent. Secret.
R. 3.30 p.m.

Minister for Foreign Affairs tells me that judging from a report which has been received from General commanding the district, it seemed probable that French had already commenced hostilities by dropping bombs from an airship in the vicinity of Nuremberg.[38] His Excellency begged me not to mention this to any of my colleagues, but he himself had told Belgian Minister.

BD, XI, No. 477.

37 This meeting lasted from 11 a.m. to nearly 2 p.m. A second Cabinet meeting from 6.30 p.m. to 8 p.m. decided that 'a substantial violation of the neutrality of [Belgium] would place us in the situation [...] when interference with the Belgian independence [holds] us to take action'. Cited in Wilson, 'The British Cabinet's Decision', p. 150.

38 This was not true. In his diary, Poincaré called this 'an audacious invention'. Cited in John Keiger, *Raymond Poincaré*, Cambridge University Press, Cambridge 1997, p. 186. Although this news was a fabrication, it was nonetheless believed by contemporaries. Josef Redlich, for example, recorded in his diary on 3 August: 'The attempts to poison wells in Metz with cholera bacillus (committed by a French doctor) as well as the throwing of French bombs from planes onto Nuremberg cause horror and blind rage. From nationality to bestiality, said Grillparzer! The war with France was unleashed by itself because the French committed acts against international law.' Fritz Fellner and Doris Corradini (eds), *Schicksalsjahre Österreichs*, 3 vols, Böhlau, Vienna et al. 2011, Vol. 1, p. 621. See also **(390)**, **(396)**, **(397)**, **(408)**.

(391) 2 August: French Embassy to British Foreign Office

French claims that German troops have invaded France

Communication from French Embassy.
Foreign Office, 2 August 1914.
R. 4.40 p.m.

The French Embassy have just telephoned to say that they have received a telegram from the Havas Agency from Liège stating that 20,000 German troops have invaded France near Nancy.[39]

BD, XI, No. 486.

(392) 2 August: Jagow to Envoys in Brussels, The Hague and Ambassador in London

News of alleged French border violation

Telegram 43, 27, 211

Berlin, 2 August 1914

Please inform Government there that early this morning 80 French officers, dressed in Prussian officers' uniforms attempted with 12 cars to cross the German border near Walbeck west of Geldern.[40] This amounts most serious violation of neutrality on the part of France.

DD, No. 677.

39 This was not true. One border violation had, however, taken place, as the Chief of Staff informed the Chancellor: 'Of the French complaints about violations of the border on our part only one has to be admitted. Against explicit orders a patrol of the XIV's army corps, seemingly led by an officer, crossed the border on 2 August. It appears to be cut off, only one man has returned. But long before this single border infringement took place French aviators threw bombs onto our railway lines, all the way into Southern Germany [...].' The Chancellor quoted Moltke's statement in his Reichstag speech of 4 August to show that Germany was acting in self-defence and that France had started the war. *Stenographische Berichte über die Verhandlungen des Reichstags*, 13. Legislaturperiode, Vol. 306, 2nd session, 1914, p. 6.

40 This was not true.

(393) 2 August: Jagow to Below

More alleged French military actions against Germany; bombs and border crossings

Telegram 44

Berlin, 2 August 1914

The concerns which we have already expressed over France's procedure in our decree No. 87[41] are being further confirmed by the fact that today, under violation of international law, she has committed war-like actions (the throwing of bombs by aeroplanes, the crossing of borders by cavalry patrols) against us.[42]

Please inform the Government there immediately.

DD, No. 682.

(394) 2 August: Joffre's orders to the commanding generals of the 2nd, 6th, 20th, 21st, 7th Corps and the Cavalry Corps

Intelligence reports of German border violations; restrictions on movements of troops lifted, but still imperative that Germany appear as the aggressor, hence restriction to defensive actions

2 August 1914, 5:30 p.m.

General secret order for the front line

1. Intelligence reports indicate that the Germans have this morning violated the French frontier at three points: a. between Delle and Belfort's main square; b. in front of Cirey-sur-Vezouze; c. to the north and to the south of Longwy. Under these conditions, the ban on moving eastward

41 Refers to the note which Below handed to the Belgian Government on 2 August (**302**), (**386**).

42 This was not true. See (**397**). Albertini notes: 'The allegations were without foundation, as was later proved, but the trick was no more barefaced and puerile than its predecessors.' Albertini, *Origins*, Vol. III, p. 464. Bethmann Hollweg claimed in his Reichstag speech of 4 August that France had attacked Germany before war had been declared with 'bomb-throwing aeroplanes, cavalry patrols, French companies broken through to German territory'. These alleged crimes claims were greeting by outrage among the delegates. *Verhandlungen des Reichstags*, Vol. 306, 1914/16, p. 6.

beyond the 10 kilometre line indicated by telegram No. 129–3/11 of 30 July is lifted.

However, for national reasons of a moral nature and for urgent reasons of a diplomatic order, it is essential to leave all responsibility for the hostilities to the Germans.

Consequently, and until new orders are issued, forces will limit themselves to pushing all invading troops back over the border, without pursuing them further and without entering onto enemy territory. [...]

DDF, 3e série, 11, No. 594.

(395) 2 August: Paléologue's Memoirs

French mobilization ordered

Sunday, 2 August 1914

General mobilization of the French army. The order reached me by telegraph at two o'clock this morning.

So the die is cast! The part played by reason in the government of nations is so small that it has only taken a week to let loose world madness! I do not know – history will judge the diplomatic operation in which I have just been concerned with Sazonov and Buchanan; but all three of us have a right to claim that we have conscientiously done everything in our power to save the peace of the world without, however, sacrificing to it those two other and still more precious possessions, the independence and honour of our countries. [...]

Maurice Paléologue, *An Ambassador's Memoirs*, Doran, New York 1925, Vol. I, p. 50.

(396) 2 August: Jagow to Flotow

News of alleged French bombs around Nuremberg used to convince Italy to remain with the Alliance

Telegram 162
Berlin, 2 August 1914

According to news from the *Generalkommando* of the 3rd Bavarian Army Corps, French aviators are throwing bombs in the wider surroundings of Nuremberg. Moreover, French patrols have crossed the border.[43] These

43 This was not true. See (**397**).

hostile acts before a declaration of war amount to an attack by France on us. This means the *casus foederis*.[44]

Russia too has yesterday already opened hostilities,[45] before the declaration of war was issued.

DD, No. 664.

(397) 2 August: Treutler to Bethmann Hollweg

Bombs on Nuremberg just a myth

Munich, 2 August 1914
R. 3 August p.m.

The news, also spread here by the *Süddeutsche Korrespondenzbureau* [Southern German News Agency], that today French planes had dropped bombs near Nuremberg has so far not been confirmed.[46] There had merely been the sighting of unknown planes which were obviously not military ones. No dropping of bombs has been noted, even less of course whether the aviators were French.[47]

DD, No. 758.

44 Flotow replied from Rome on 2 August: 'Informed here of state of war. Marquis di San Giuliano replied that yesterday's Ministerial Council came to the conclusion that *casus foederis* did not apply as this was an aggressive war. Italy had not been asked beforehand and was therefore not obliged. [...] News of attack by Russian troops on German territory impressed him. However, when he chanced the remark that this was probably smaller border skirmishes which perhaps did not necessitate such a heavy response I clashed heavily with him. [...]' DD No. 675.

45 See for example DD, No. 628, Bethmann Hollweg to Flotow, 2 August: 'Yesterday at 5 p.m. H.M. the Kaiser declared general mobilization. Due to attack by Russian troops on German territory we are at war with Russia. [...] War with Russia will undoubtedly result in attack on us by France and war with her. We expect from Italy fulfilment of her alliance duties. [...]'. See also DD, No. 629, Bethmann Hollweg to Kaiser Wilhelm II, 2 August, alleging that the Russians had destroyed railway lines on the German border, and that two squadrons of Cossacks had been deployed into Johannisburg in East Prussia. This does not appear to have been correct. See Chapter 11, p. 530, n. 17.

46 These unsubstantiated allegations were published widely in the German press; for example, the *Hamburger Nachrichten* reported on 3 August under the heading 'Germany's just case' that 'dishonourable French officers in German uniforms [...] had attempted to cross the border. [...] French aviators [had] thrown bombs near Nuremberg'. Here also the myth that a French doctor had attempted to poison German wells with Cholera.

47 But see (**404**) on how these false allegations were used to justify the German declaration of war on France.

(398) 2 August: Moltke to Jagow

Moltke summarizes the current situation from a military point of view and makes demands of how German foreign policy should now be conducted

Berlin, 2 August 1914
R. 2 August, afternoon
Secret

I have the honour of presenting herewith to the *Auswärtiges Amt* some suggestions from a military-political nature, to which I attribute importance from a military point of view.

v. Moltke

Switzerland[48]
Switzerland has mobilized. Following reports which have arrived here she is already afraid of French violation of her neutrality, as evidenced by the accumulation of French troops on her western border. It will be of advantage to assure Switzerland that Germany is prepared to secure her neutrality with military help. For this eventuality a treaty of alliance with Switzerland has been prepared by me, one copy of which is in my hands and the other in the hands of the Chief of Swiss General Staff. This treaty, putting all Swiss armed forces under the control of the German High Command, needs only to be ratified and exchanged. This agreement has to be kept absolutely secret until a diplomatic discussion along these lines has taken place, lest premature publication should discredit the Chief of the Swiss General Staff in the eyes of his Government or expose him to the reproach of unilateral political action.[49]

Turkey
The alliance treaty with Turkey should be made public immediately. Turkey ought to <u>declare war on Russia as soon as possible</u>.

England
Attempts must be made to instigate an uprising in India if England takes a stand as our opponent.

48 This section on Switzerland was omitted from the DD collection. Geiss speculates that it was excised in 1919 so as not to bring ill-repute onto neutral Switzerland. See also Imanuel Geiss, *Julikrise*, 2 vols, Hanover 1963/64, Vol. 1, p. 32.

49 On the role of Switzerland in German military planning, see Hans Rudolf Fuhrer and Michael Olsansky, 'Die "Südumfassung": zur Rolle der Schweiz im Schlieffen und im Moltkeplan', in Hans Ehlert et al. (eds), *Der Schlieffenplan. Analysen und Dokumente*, Schöningh, Paderborn 2006, pp. 311–338.

The same should be attempted in Egypt; also in the Dominion of South Africa.

Should England make her neutrality in the German-Austro-Russo-French war dependent upon Germany's assurance 'that she would act with moderation in case of a victory over France' (*Ausw. Amt* No. 218 of 2 August 1914[50]) then this assurance can be given unconditionally and in the most binding form. It is not of consequence to us to smash France, only to defeat her. England's neutrality is of such importance to us that this concession can be made unconditionally.

Sweden

We should strive to get Sweden to mobilize her entire armed forces immediately and to proceed as soon as possible with her 6th Division against the Finnish border.[51] Sweden's undertakings should be so guided that her measures would inspire and maintain in Russia the fear of an attack by her on Finland, as well as the possible landing of Swedish troops on the Russian coast. We must promise unconditionally to fulfil all of Sweden's desires, whether they relate to regaining Finland or are in other directions, so far as they are compatible with German interests. If Sweden declares herself willing to enter upon a joint war with Germany, then notice of this should at once be given at Copenhagen, with the request to do the same as Sweden. Similar demands should be made of Norway, with allusion to Russia's aspiration – well recognized in Norway – to possess an ice-free harbour on the Norwegian coast, a wish that Russia would unquestionably turn at once into fact were she to emerge victorious from the current war. The Russian aspirations can be effectively blocked if the Scandinavian nations will join with Germany to oppose Russia's insatiable hunger for territory. Germany has absolutely no intention of infringing upon the political status of the Norwegian Kingdom, and would gladly oppose all Russia's schemes to this end, both at present and in the future.

Denmark

No further measures are necessary. Our already announced declaration agreeing to respect her neutrality remains, so long as our opponents' measures do not force us to counter-measures.

---

50 The quote is from Lichnowsky to Jagow, 2 August 1914, DD, No. 641: 'If we violate Belgium's neutrality and if a war against the Belgians results from this, then I do not think that the [English] Government will be in a position, faced with the storm which will erupt in public opinion here, to remain neutral for much longer. If we were to respect Belgian neutrality, however, it is at least possible that England will remain neutral if we act with moderation in case of a victory against France.'

51 See also General Staff, Section IIIb, to Jagow, 1 August, Geiss, *Julikrise*, Vol. 2, No. 1015a. For the navy, cooperation with Sweden was also desirable, as Pohl informed Jagow on the same day. Ibid., No. 1015b.

The Balkans

It is necessary as soon as possible to bring about a clarification of the situation in the Balkans. Austria must state frankly whether, under the present military situation, she will allow the agreements which she has made with Bulgaria to come into effect. The attitude of Greece, and that of Rumania, must also be entirely clarified.

All information that can be obtained by us concerning the Balkan States must be passed on to Austria and to Turkey immediately.

Should Italy join in the war she, too, should be kept permanently instructed as to the situation in the Balkans. The information which, to my knowledge, has been received here, that Rumania is forced to remain neutral in a Russo-Austrian conflict, but had faithfully promised that under no circumstances would she go over to Russia's side, is of the greatest importance to Austria and must be communicated to her at once.

Belgium

The reply to Germany's summary demand[52] has to be brought to my attention by tomorrow, Monday, 3 August, at 2 p.m. at the latest. I propose that time for the reply be limited to twelve hours. If in the opinion of the *Auswärtiges Amt* this should not be possible, the time set for presenting the demand should be altered accordingly. But I consider a twelve-hour time limit to be better.

Presentation of the note to Holland simultaneously with the copy of the note to Belgium.[53]

The same simultaneously to England, with the additional announcement that Germany, even in the event of a hostile clash with Belgium, will not threaten her status as a nation, but, on the other hand, will, after the conclusion of peace, guarantee that Belgium's integrity is preserved. England should be asked in this case to regard Germany's procedure merely as an act of self-defence against French threats to German territory.[54]

Italy

It is absolutely necessary that Italy be brought to declare immediately whether or not she is willing to take an active part in the approaching war, in accordance with the obligations of her alliance. To me it is of no importance that Italy should carry out to its full extent her agreement to despatch troops to Germany. If Italy, due to the general political

52 See (**393**), (**406**).

53 See (**302**) for the text of the note to Belgium which was sent to Below on 29 July in a sealed envelope. On 2 August he was instructed to hand over the note (DD, No. 648).

54 See DD 667, Jagow to Lichnowsky, despatched at 5.30 p.m. that day.

situation, can only send very few troops to Germany, and even if this were only one cavalry division, that would be sufficient for me. It is not important that Italy should support us actively with a strong force, but that the Triple Alliance as such should act united in the war. That would be shown by the smallest conceivable contribution of troops. [...]

Should Italy decide to take part in the war it is necessary for us to receive early information as to the military measures planned by Italy, as well as the announcement of the date of the first day of mobilization in Italy, which could be accomplished by direct communication between the two General Staffs.

Russia

A declaration of war against Russia or, respectively, of Russia against us, has become of no consequence owing to the Russian invasion across our eastern boundary.[55] If declaration of war from Russia has not yet reached us or was presented only after the Russian operations, then Russia has acted contrary to the Hague agreements.

France

Our possible declaration of war is entirely independent of the move made in Belgium. One does not necessarily lead to the other. I do not consider it necessary to deliver the declaration of war to France already;[56] rather, I am counting on the likelihood that, if it is held back for the present, France, on her part, will be forced by public opinion to organise warlike measures against Germany, even if a formal declaration of war has not been presented. Presumably France will move into Belgium in the role of the protector of Belgian neutrality, just as soon as the step taken by Germany against Belgium becomes known in Paris.[57]

On our side arrangements have been made so that the crossing of the French frontier will be avoided until activities on the part of France provoke this.

Japan

Japan is to be urged to use this favourable opportunity for satisfying her entire aspirations in the Far East now, preferably by means of a war against Russia tied up by a European war.

Any desires Japan believes she could perhaps accomplish with German

55 See Chapter 11, p. 530, n. 17 and p. 541, n. 45.

56 See also DD, No. 629, Bethmann Hollweg to Wilhelm II, 2 August: 'In accordance with understanding with Ministry of War and General Staff, presentation of declaration of war to France not necessary today for any military reasons. Consequently it will not be done, in the hope that the French will attack us.' Quoted in Geiss, *July 1914*, p. 353, n. 2. Germany finally declared war on France on 3 August.

57 See (**302**).

cooperation must be promised her. We can promise Japan anything that she wishes from us in this direction.

Persia
Persia should be urged to use the favourable opportunity for shaking off the Russian yoke, and, if possible, to go hand in hand with Turkey.

DD, No. 662.[58]

(399) 2 August: Broqueville's statement in the Belgian Crown Council meeting

Crown Council meeting at 10 p.m. decides unanimously to reject Germany's ultimatum[59]

[…] If die we must, better death with honour. We have no other choice. Our submission would serve no end. The stake for which Germany has begun this war is the freedom of Europe. Let us make no mistake about it, if Germany is victorious, Belgium, whatever her attitude, will be annexed to the Reich. […]

Cited in Luigi Albertini, *The Origins of the War of 1914*, 3 vols, Oxford University Press, Oxford 1952–1957, Vol. III, p. 458.

(400) 3 August: Szögyény to Berchtold

Concerned that Germany's invasion of Belgium will make Britain's enmity even more likely

Telegram No. 365
Berlin, 3 August 1914
D. 6.48 p.m.
R. 10 p.m.

Chiffre. Very secret

Belgium
The German army has adopted a plan – which is impossible to influence – to make the advance into France via Belgium. As a result German

58 Engl. transl. based on Geiss, *July 1914*, No. 179, here with substantial amendments.

59 See (**386**).

troops will march into Belgium soon, perhaps already today or tomorrow.[60]

In reply to my remark that in this case England would, agitated by the violation of neutrality, place herself even more on the side of our opponents, the *Auswärtiges Amt* explained 'that now the Military had the word and that one could not interfere in this'.

This morning, by the way, the German Government has already informed the Belgian Government officially of the intended march of German troops into Belgian territory, but declared at the same time that she would otherwise respect Belgium's full neutrality and *guarantee* that Belgium would receive her territory to the same extent during and after the war, also that any damage caused to Belgium by the German troop movements would be entirely compensated.[61]

Auswärtiges Amt hopes that Belgium will give an affirmative answer to the advance of German troops under these circumstances. But if [the answer] were to be unfavourable this would not change anything of the decision mentioned earlier.

For strategic reasons parts of the German VIIIth army corps advanced into Luxembourg yesterday to occupy the railway lines.

Die österreichisch-ungarischen Dokumente zum Kriegsausbruch. Diplomatische Aktenstücke, 3 vols, Bundesverlag, Vienna 1919, No. 114.

(401) 3 August: Grey's statement in the House of Commons (and response by Ramsay MacDonald)

Grey outlines the case for Britain joining the war to defend Belgium and France; Ramsay MacDonald remains unconvinced as Britain not in danger

Last week I stated that we were working for peace not only for this country, but to preserve the peace of Europe. To-day events move so rapidly that it is exceedingly difficult to state with technical accuracy the actual state of affairs, but it is clear that the peace of Europe cannot be preserved. Russia and Germany, at any rate, have declared war upon each other.

60 German troops entered Belgian territory on 4 August, in a hasty move necessitated by her deployment plan. For details of Germany's strategic plan see Mombauer, "German War Plans', in Hamilton and Herwig (eds), *War Planning 1914*, pp. 48–78.

61 That declaration had actually been made the previous day (**386**).

Before I proceed to state the position of His Majesty's Government, I would like to clear the ground so that [...] the House may know exactly under what obligations the Government is [...] in coming to a decision on the matter. First of all let me say, very shortly, that we have consistently worked with a single mind, with all the earnestness in our power, to preserve peace. The House may be satisfied on that point. We have always done it. During these last years, as far as His Majesty's Government are concerned, we would have no difficulty in proving that we have done so. [...]

In the present crisis, it has not been possible to secure the peace of Europe; because there has been little time, and there has been a disposition – at any rate in some quarters on which I will not dwell – to force things rapidly to an issue, at any rate, to the great risk of peace, and, as we now know, the result of that is that the policy of peace, as far as the Great Powers generally are concerned, is in danger. [...]

We shall publish Papers as soon as we can regarding what took place last week when we were working for peace; and when those Papers are published, I have no doubt that to every human being they will make it clear how strenuous and genuine and whole-hearted our efforts for peace were, and that they will enable people to form their own judgment as to what forces were at work which operated against peace.

I come first, now, to the question of British obligations. I have assured the House – and the Prime Minister has assured the House more than once – that if any crisis such as this arose, we should come before the House of Commons and be able to say to the House that it was free to decide what the British attitude should be, that we would have no secret engagement which we should spring upon the House, and tell the House that, because we had entered into that engagement, there was an obligation of honour upon the country. I will deal with that point to clear the ground first.

There has been in Europe two diplomatic groups, the Triple Alliance and what came to be called the 'Triple Entente', for some years past. The Triple Entente was not an Alliance – it was a Diplomatic group. The House will remember that in 1908 there was a crisis, also a Balkan crisis, originating in the annexation of Bosnia and Herzegovina. The Russian Minister, M. Isvolsky, came to London, or happened to come to London, because his visit was planned before the crisis broke out.[62] I told him definitely then, this being a Balkan crisis, a Balkan affair, I did not consider that public opinion in this country would justify us in promising to give anything more than diplomatic support. More was never asked from us, more was never given, and more was never promised.

62 Isvolsky visited London in October 1913.

In this present crisis, up till yesterday, we have also given no promise of anything more than diplomatic support [...]. Now I must make this question of obligation clear to the House. I must go back to the first Moroccan crisis of 1906. That was the time of the Algeciras Conference, and it came at a time of very great difficulty to His Majesty's Government when a General Election was in progress, and Ministers were scattered over the country, and I [...] was asked the question whether if that crisis developed into war between France and Germany we would give armed support. I said then that I could promise nothing to any foreign Power unless it was subsequently to receive the whole-hearted support of public opinion here if the occasion arose. I said, in my opinion, if war was forced upon France then on the question of Morocco – a question which had just been the subject of agreement between this country and France, an agreement exceedingly popular on both sides – that if out of that agreement war was forced on France at that time, in my view public opinion in this country would have rallied to the material support of France.

I gave no promise, but I expressed that opinion during the crisis [...] to the French Ambassador and the German Ambassador at the time. I made no promise, and I used no threats; but I expressed that opinion. That position was accepted by the French Government, but they said to me at the time – and I think very reasonably – 'If you think it possible that the public opinion of Great Britain might, should a sudden crisis arise, justify you in giving to France the armed support which you cannot promise in advance, you will not be able to give that support, even if you wish to give it, when the time comes, unless some conversations have already taken place between naval and military experts.' There was force in that. I agreed to it, and authorised those conversations to take place,[63] but on the distinct understanding that nothing which passed between military or naval experts should bind either Government or restrict in any way their freedom to make a decision as to whether or not they would give that support when the time arose. [...]

The Agadir crisis came – another Morocco crisis – and throughout that I took precisely the same line that had been taken in 1906. But subsequently, in 1912, after discussion and consideration in the Cabinet it was decided that we ought to have a definite understanding in writing, which was to be only in the form of an unofficial letter, that these conversations which took place were not binding upon the freedom of either Government; and on the 22nd of November, 1912, I wrote to the French Ambassador the letter which I will now read to the House, and I received from him a letter in similar terms in reply. [...]

---

63 Anglo-French military talks began during the First Moroccan Crisis. See also p. 34, (**10**).

'My dear Ambassador, – From time to time in recent years the French and British naval and military experts have consulted together. It has always been understood that such consultation does not restrict the freedom of either Government to decide at any future time whether or not to assist the other by armed force. We have agreed that consultation between experts is not and ought not to be regarded as an engagement that commits either Government to action in a contingency that has not yet arisen and may never arise. The disposition, for instance, of the French and British Fleets respectively at the present moment is not based upon an engagement to co-operate in war.

'You have, however, pointed out that, if either Government had grave reason to expect an unprovoked attack by a third Power, it might become essential to know whether it could in that event depend upon the armed assistance of the other.

'I agree that, if either Government had grave reason to expect an unprovoked attack by a third Power, or something that threatened the general peace, it should immediately discuss with the other whether both Governments should act together to prevent aggression and to preserve peace, and, if so, what measures they would be prepared to take in common'

[...] The situation in the present crisis is not precisely the same as it was in the Morocco question. [...] It has not originated as regards anything with which we had a special agreement with France; it has not originated with anything which primarily concerned France. It has originated in a dispute between Austria and Serbia. I can say this with the most absolute confidence – no Government and no country has less desire to be involved in war over a dispute with Austria and Serbia than the Government and the country of France. They are involved in it because of their obligation of honour under a definite alliance with Russia. Well, it is only fair to say to the House that that obligation of honour cannot apply in the same way to us. We are not parties to the Franco-Russian Alliance. We do not even know the terms of that Alliance. [...]

I now come to what we think the situation requires of us. For many years we have had a long-standing friendship with France. [An HON. MEMBER: 'And with Germany!'] [...].

The French fleet is now in the Mediterranean, and the Northern and Western coasts of France are absolutely undefended. [...] The French fleet is in the Mediterranean, and has for some years been concentrated there because of the feeling of confidence and friendship which has existed between the two countries. My own feeling is that if a foreign fleet engaged in a war which France had not sought, and in which she had not been the aggressor, came down the English Channel and bombarded and battered the undefended coasts of France, we could not stand aside and see this going on practically within sight of our eyes, with our arms folded, looking on dispassionately, doing nothing! I believe that would be the feeling of this country. [...]

But I also want to look at the matter without sentiment, and from the point of view of British interests [...]. If we say nothing at this moment, what is France to do with her Fleet in the Mediterranean? If she leaves it there, with no statement from us as to what we will do, she leaves her Northern and Western coasts absolutely undefended, at the mercy of a German fleet coming down the Channel, to do as it pleases in a war which is a war of life and death between them. If we say nothing, it may be that the French fleet is withdrawn from the Mediterranean. We are in the presence of a European conflagration; can anybody set limits to the consequences that may arise out of it? Let us assume that to-day we stand aside in an attitude of neutrality, saying, 'No, we cannot undertake and engage to help either party in this conflict.' Let us suppose the French fleet is withdrawn from the Mediterranean; and let us assume that the consequences – which are already tremendous in what has happened in Europe even to countries which are at peace – in fact, equally whether countries are at peace or at war – let us assume that out of that come consequences unforeseen, which make it necessary at a sudden moment that, in defence of vital British interests, we should go to war and let us assume – which is quite possible – that Italy, who is now neutral[64] – [HON. MEMBERS: 'Hear, hear!'] – because, as I understand, she considers that this war is an aggressive war, and the Triple Alliance being a defensive alliance her obligation did not arise – let us assume that consequences which are not yet foreseen – and which perfectly legitimately consulting her own interests – make Italy depart from her attitude of neutrality at a time when we are forced in defence of vital British interests ourselves to fight, what then will be the position in the Mediterranean? It might be that at some critical moment those consequences would be forced upon us because our trade routes in the Mediterranean might be vital to this country.

Nobody can say that in the course of the next few weeks there is any particular trade route the keeping open of which may not be vital to this country. What will be our position then? We have not kept a Fleet in the Mediterranean which is equal to dealing alone with a combination of other fleets in the Mediterranean. It would be the very moment when we could not detach more ships to the Mediterranean, and we might have exposed this country from our negative attitude at the present moment to the most appalling risk, I say that from the point of view of British interests. We feel strongly that France was entitled to know – and to know at once! – whether or not in the event of attack upon her unprotected

64 Italy's decision to remain neutral had been announced on 2 August (**410**).

Northern and Western Coasts she could depend upon British support. In that emergency, and in these compelling circumstances, yesterday afternoon I gave to the French Ambassador the following statement: -

'I am authorised to give an assurance that if the German Fleet comes into the Channel or through the North Sea to undertake hostile operations against the French coasts or shipping, the British Fleet will give all the protection in its power. This assurance is, of course, subject to the policy of His Majesty's Government receiving the support of Parliament, and must not be taken as binding His Majesty's Government to take any action until the above contingency of action by the German Fleet takes place.'

I read that to the House, not as a declaration of war on our part, not as entailing immediate aggressive action on our part, but as binding us to take aggressive action should that contingency arise. Things move very hurriedly from hour to hour. Fresh news comes in, and I cannot give this in any very formal way; but I understand that the German Government would be prepared, if we would pledge ourselves to neutrality, to agree that its fleet would not attack the Northern coast of France. I have only heard that shortly before I came to the House, but it is far too narrow an engagement for us. And, Sir, there is the more serious consideration – becoming more serious every hour – there is the question of the neutrality of Belgium.

I shall have to put before the House at some length what is our position in regard to Belgium. The governing factor is the Treaty of 1839, but this is a Treaty with a history – a history accumulated since. In 1870, [...] Prince Bismarck gave an assurance to Belgium that, confirming his verbal assurance, he gave in writing a declaration which he said was superfluous in reference to the Treaty in existence – that the German Confederation and its allies would respect the neutrality of Belgium, it being always understood that that neutrality would be respected by the other belligerent Powers. That is valuable as a recognition in 1870 on the part of Germany of the sacredness of these Treaty rights.

What was our own attitude? The people who laid down the attitude of the British Government were Lord Granville in the House of Lords, and Mr. Gladstone in the House of Commons. [...]

Mr. Gladstone spoke as follows: [...]

'There is, I admit, the obligation of the Treaty. [...] The circumstance that there is already an existing guarantee in force is of necessity an important fact, and a weighty element in the case to which we are bound to give full and ample consideration. There is also this further consideration, the force of which we must all feel most deeply, and that is, the common interests against the unmeasured aggrandisement of any Power whatever.'

The Treaty is an old Treaty – 1839 – and that was the view taken of it in 1870. It is one of those Treaties which are founded, not only on consideration for Belgium, which benefits under the Treaty, but in the interests of those who guarantee the neutrality of Belgium. The honour and interests are, at least, as strong to-day as in 1870, and we cannot take a more narrow view or a less serious view of our obligations, and of the importance of those obligations than was taken by Mr. Gladstone's Government in 1870.

I will read to the House what took place last week on this subject. When mobilisation was beginning, [...] I telegraphed at the same time in similar terms to both Paris and Berlin to say that it was essential for us to know whether the French and German Governments respectively were prepared to undertake an engagement to respect the neutrality of Belgium. [...] I got from the French Government this reply: -

'The French Government are resolved to respect the neutrality of Belgium, and it would only be in the event of some other Power violating that neutrality that France might find herself under the necessity, in order to assure the defence of her security, to act otherwise. This assurance has been given several times. The President of the Republic spoke of it to the King of the Belgians, and the French Minister at Brussels has spontaneously renewed the assurance to the Belgian Minister of Foreign Affairs to-day.'

From the German Government the reply was: -

'The Secretary of State for Foreign Affairs could not possibly give an answer before consulting the Emperor and the Imperial Chancellor.'

Sir Edward Goschen, to whom I had said it was important to have an answer soon, said he hoped the answer would not be too-long delayed. The German Minister for Foreign Affairs [Jagow] then gave Sir Edward Goschen to understand that he rather doubted whether they could answer at all, as any reply they might give could not fail, in the event of war, to have the undesirable effect of disclosing, to a certain extent, part of the then-plan of campaign.

I telegraphed at the same time to Brussels to the Belgian Government, and I got the following reply from Sir Francis Villiers: -

'The Minister for Foreign Affairs thanks me for the communication, and replies that Belgium will, to the utmost of her power, maintain neutrality, and expects and desires other Powers to observe and uphold it. He begged me to add that the relations between Belgium and the neighbouring Powers were excellent, and there was no reason to suspect their intentions, but that the Belgian Government believe, in the case of violation, they were in a position to defend the neutrality of their country.'

It now appears from the news I have received to-day [...] that an ultimatum has been given to Belgium by Germany, the object of which was to offer Belgium friendly relations with Germany on condition that she would facilitate the passage of German troops through Belgium. [...]

Shortly before I reached the House I was informed that the following telegram had been received from the King of the Belgians by our King – King George: -

'Remembering the numerous proofs of your Majesty's friendship and that of your predecessors, and the friendly attitude of England in 1870, and the proof of friendship she has just given us again, I make a supreme appeal to the Diplomatic intervention of your Majesty's Government to safeguard the integrity of Belgium.'

Diplomatic intervention took place last week on our part. What can diplomatic intervention do now? We have great and vital interests in the independence – and integrity is the least part – of Belgium. If Belgium is compelled to submit to allow her neutrality to be violated, of course the situation is clear. Even if by agreement she admitted the violation of her neutrality, it is clear she could only do so under duress. The smaller States in that region of Europe ask but one thing. Their one desire is that they should be left alone and independent. The one thing they fear is, I think, not so much that their integrity but that their independence should be interfered with. If in this war which is before Europe the neutrality of one of those countries is violated, if the troops of one of the combatants violate its neutrality and no action be taken to resent it, at the end of the war, whatever the integrity may be the independence will be gone.

I have one further quotation from Mr. Gladstone as to what he thought about the independence of Belgium. [...] Mr. Gladstone said:

'We have an interest in the independence of Belgium which is wider than that which we may have in the literal operation of the guarantee. It is found in the answer to the question whether under the circumstances of the case, this country, endowed as it is with influence and power, would quietly stand by and witness the perpetration of the direst crime that ever stained the pages of history, and thus become participators in the sin.'[65]

No, Sir, if it be the case that there has been anything in the nature of an ultimatum to Belgium, asking her to compromise or violate her neutrality, whatever may have been offered to her in return, her independence is gone if that holds. If her independence goes, the independence of Holland will follow. I ask the House from the point of view of British interests, to consider what may be at stake. If France is beaten in a struggle of life and death, beaten to her knees, loses her position as a great Power, becomes subordinate to the will and power of one greater than herself – consequences which I do not anticipate, because I am sure that France has the power to defend herself with all the energy and ability and patriotism which she has shown so often – still, if that were

65 Hansard, Volume 203, Page 1787.

to happen, and if Belgium fell under the same dominating influence, and then Holland, and then Denmark, then would not Mr. Gladstone's words come true, that just opposite to us there would be a common interest against the unmeasured aggrandisement of any Power? [...]

It may be said, I suppose, that we might stand aside, husband our strength, and that whatever happened in the course of this war at the end of it intervene with effect to put things right, and to adjust them to our own point of view. If, in a crisis like this, we run away from those obligations of honour and interest as regards the Belgian Treaty, I doubt whether, whatever material force we might have at the end, it would be of very much value in face of the respect that we should have lost. And do not believe, whether a great Power stands outside this war or not, it is going to be in a position at the end of it to exert its superior strength. For us, with a powerful Fleet, which we believe able to protect our commerce, to protect our shores, and to protect our interests, if we are engaged in war, we shall suffer but little more than we shall suffer even if we stand aside.

We are going to suffer, I am afraid, terribly in this war whether we are in it or whether we stand aside. Foreign trade is going to stop, not because the trade routes are closed, but because there is no trade at the other end. Continental nations engaged in war – all their populations, all their energies, all their wealth, engaged in a desperate struggle – they cannot carry on the trade with us that they are carrying on in times of peace, whether we are parties to the war or whether we are not. I do not believe for a moment, that at the end of this war, even if we stood aside and remained aside, we should be in a position, a material position, to use our force decisively to undo what had happened in the course of the war, to prevent the whole of the West of Europe opposite to us – if that had been the result of the war – falling under the domination of a single Power, and I am quite sure that our moral position would be such as to have lost us all respect. [...]

I have read to the House the only engagements that we have yet taken definitely with regard to the use of force. I think it is due to the House to say that we have taken no engagement yet with regard to sending an Expeditionary armed force out of the country. Mobilisation of the Fleet has taken place; mobilisation of the Army is taking place; but we have as yet taken no engagement, because I do feel that in the case of a European conflagration such as this, unprecedented, with our enormous responsibilities in India and other parts of the Empire, or in countries in British occupation, with all the unknown factors, we must take very carefully into consideration the use which we make of sending an Expeditionary Force out of the country until we know how we stand. [...]

The one bright spot in the whole of this terrible situation is Ireland. The general feeling throughout Ireland [...] does not make the Irish question a consideration which we feel we have now to take into account. [...]

What other policy is there before the House? There is but one way in which the Government could make certain at the present moment of keeping outside this war, and that would be that it should immediately issue a proclamation of unconditional neutrality. We cannot do that. We have made the commitment to France that I have read to the House which prevents us from doing that. We have got the consideration of Belgium which prevents us also from any unconditional neutrality, and, without those conditions absolutely satisfied and satisfactory, we are bound not to shrink from proceeding to the use of all the forces in our power. If we did take that line by saying, 'We will have nothing whatever to do with this matter' under no conditions – the Belgian Treaty obligations, the possible position in the Mediterranean, with damage to British interests, and what may happen to France from our failure to support France – if we were to say that all those things mattered nothing, were as nothing, and to say we would stand aside, we should, I believe, sacrifice our respect and good name and reputation before the world, and should not escape the most serious and grave economic consequences.

[...] I do not for a moment conceal, after what I have said, and after the information, incomplete as it is, that I have given to the House with regard to Belgium, that we must be prepared, and we are prepared, for the consequences of having to use all the strength we have at any moment – we know not how soon – to defend ourselves and to take our part. We know, if the facts all be as I have stated them, though I have announced no intending aggressive action on our part, no final decision to resort to force at a moment's notice, until we know the whole of the case, that the use of it may be forced upon us. As far as the forces of the Crown are concerned, we are ready. I believe the Prime Minister and my right hon. Friend the First Lord of the Admiralty have no doubt whatever that the readiness and the efficiency of those Forces were never at a higher mark than they are to-day, and never was there a time when confidence was more justified in the power of the Navy to protect our commerce and to protect our shores. The thought is with us always of the suffering and misery entailed from which no country in Europe will escape and from which no abdication or neutrality will save us. The amount of harm that can be done by an enemy ship to our trade is infinitesimal, compared with the amount of harm that must be done by the economic condition that is caused on the Continent.

The most awful responsibility is resting upon the Government in deciding what to advise the House of Commons to do. [...]. We have disclosed the issue, the information which we have, and made clear to the House, I trust, that we are prepared to face that situation, and that should it develop, as probably it may develop, we will face it. We worked for peace up to the last moment, and beyond the last moment. [...]

But that is over, as far as the peace of Europe is concerned. We are now face to face with a situation and all the consequences which it may yet have to unfold. We believe we shall have the support of the House at large in proceeding to whatever the consequences may be and whatever measures may be forced upon us by the development of facts or action taken by others. I believe the country, so quickly has the situation been forced upon it, has not had time to realise the issue. It perhaps is still thinking of the quarrel between Austria and Serbia, and not the complications of this matter which have grown out of the quarrel between Austria and Serbia. Russia and Germany we know are at war. We do not yet know officially that Austria, the ally whom Germany is to support, is yet at war with Russia. We know that a good deal has been happening on the French frontier. We do not know that the German Ambassador has left Paris.

The situation has developed so rapidly that technically, as regards the condition of the war, it is most difficult to describe what has actually happened. [...] I have put the vital facts before the House, and if, as seems not improbable, we are forced, and rapidly forced, to take our stand upon those issues, then I believe, when the country realises what is at stake, what the real issues are, the magnitude of the impending dangers in the West of Europe, which I have endeavoured to describe to the House, we shall be supported throughout, not only by the House of Commons, but by the determination, the resolution, the courage, and the endurance of the whole country.

[...][66]

Mr. RAMSAY MACDONALD

I should, had circumstances permitted, have preferred to remain silent this afternoon. But circumstances do not permit of that. I shall model what I have to say on the two speeches we have listened to, and I shall be brief. The right hon. Gentleman, to a House which in a great majority is with him, has delivered a speech the echoes of which will go down in history. The speech has been impressive, but however much we may resist the conclusion to which he has come, we have not been able to resist the moving character of his appeal. I think he is wrong. I think the Government which he represents and for which he speaks is wrong. I think the verdict of history will be that they are wrong. We shall see. The effect of the right hon. Gentleman's speech in this House is not to be its final effect. There may be opportunities, or there may not be opportunities for us to go into details, but I want to say to this House, and to say it without equivocation, if the right hon. Gentleman had come here to-day and told us that our country is in danger, I do not care what party

66 There were a number of comments at this point.

he appealed to, or to what class he appealed, we would be with him and behind him. If this is so, we will vote him what money he wants. Yes, and we will go further. We will offer him ourselves if the country is in danger. But he has not persuaded me that it is. He has not persuaded my hon. Friends who cooperate with me that it is, and I am perfectly certain, when his speech gets into cold print to-morrow, he will not persuade a large section of the country. If the nation's honour were in danger we would be with him. There has been no crime committed by statesmen of this character without those statesmen appealing to their nation's honour. We fought the Crimean War because of our honour. We rushed to South Africa because of our honour. The right hon. Gentleman is appealing to us to-day because of our honour. There is a third point. If the right hon. Gentleman could come to us and tell us that a small European nationality like Belgium is in danger, and could assure us he is going to confine the conflict to that question, then we would support him. What is the use of talking about coming to the aid of Belgium, when, as a matter of fact, you are engaging in a whole European War which is not going to leave the map of Europe in the position it is in now. The right hon. Gentleman said nothing about Russia. We want to know about that. We want to try to find out what is going to happen, when it is all over, to the power of Russia in Europe, and we are not going to go blindly into this conflict without having some sort of a rough idea as to what is going to happen. Finally, so far as France is concerned, we say solemnly and definitely that no such friendship as the right hon. Gentleman describes between one nation and another could ever justify one of those nations entering into war on behalf of the other. If France is really in danger, if, as the result of this, we are going to have the power, civilisation, and genius of France removed from European history, then let him so say. But it is an absolutely impossible conception, which we are talking about to endeavour to justify that which the right hon. Gentleman has foreshadowed. I not only know but I feel that the feeling of the House is against us. I have been through this before, and 1906 came as part recompense. It will come again. We are going to go through it all. We will go through it all. So far as we are concerned, whatever may happen, whatever may be said about us, whatever attacks may be made upon us, we will take the action that we will take of saying that this country ought to have remained neutral, because in the deepest parts of our hearts we believe that that was right and that that alone was consistent with the honour of the country and the traditions of the party that are now in office. [...]

Sitting suspended at twenty-five minutes before Five [...]. The House reassembled at Seven of the clock, Mr. SPEAKER in the Chair. [...]

Sir EDWARD GREY

I want to give the House some information which I have received, and which was not in my possession when I made my statement this afternoon. It is information I have received from the Belgian Legation in London, and is to the following effect: -

'Germany sent yesterday evening at seven o'clock a Note proposing to Belgium friendly neutrality, covering free passage on Belgian territory, and promising maintenance of independence of the kingdom and possession at the conclusion of peace, and threatening, in case of refusal, to treat Belgium as an enemy. A time limit of twelve hours was fixed for the reply. The Belgians have answered that an attack on their neutrality would be a flagrant violation of the rights of nations, and that to accept the German proposal would be to sacrifice the honour of a nation. Conscious of its duty, Belgium is firmly resolved to repel aggression by all possible means.'[67] [...]

Hansard, House of Commons Debates, 3 August 1914, Vol. 65, cc1809–32.

(402) 3 August: Klobukowski to Viviani

Suspects Germans are waiting for France to violate Belgian border first

Telegram No. 94.
Extremely urgent
Brussels, 3 August 1914
D. 5.23 p.m.
R. 6.25 p.m.

Extremely urgent

According to information that has reached me at the Legation, the Germans amassed near the Belgian border have not crossed over. It would be to our advantage to leave the initiative of the first breach up to them, just as they are perhaps trying to leave that responsibility to us. Commander Génie believes the Belgian Government is waiting for this breach in order to call on the help of the guaranteeing powers.[68]

DDF, 3e série, 11, No. 680.

67 See (**399**).

68 He sent another telegram an hour later: 'The impression is being confirmed that the ultimatum of Germany who, after threatening, has not acted, is a manoeuvre to induce us to be the first to intervene in Belgium, thus provoking an initial conflict between the Belgian army and our own.' DDF, 3, 11, No. 687.

(403) 3 August: Poincaré's Diary (1)

Looting and anti-German riots in Paris; German attack through Belgium expected; French troops continue to be prevented from crossing border

Yesterday Paris gave a sad spectacle which contrasts with the sang-froid of these last days and with the sang-froid of the whole of France. There were many incidents of pillaging of shops. The dairies of the Maggi company[69] were widely plundered; it is true that the cause of this violence is competition between this company and small milk suppliers. But, added to this, German and Austrian shops were looted; and the police stood passively by these scenes of disorder: officers even watched them with a certain complicity. I instructed [Minister of the Interior] Malvy to ask [Prefect of the Police] Hennion to be merciless and to maintain public order at all cost. The fomenters will appear before a war tribunal. [...]

We are expecting, of course, a German attack through Belgium, as our High Command has always predicted. We have constantly recommended to General Joffre not to permit any crossing of the Belgian frontier nor over-flying of Belgium until further notice. On that depends the support of England and the attitude of Belgium. When King Albert came to Paris, he promised that Belgium would defend herself against Germany.[70] Let us do nothing which could discourage that good will.

[...].[71]

Raymond Poincaré, 'Notes journalières', cited in John Keiger, *Raymond Poincaré*, Cambridge University Press, Cambridge 1997, pp. 184, 186.

69 Actually a Swiss-owned company mistaken for a German one.

70 Albert I and his wife Elisabeth went on an official state visit to Paris on 12 July 1910.

71 I am very grateful to Robert Doughty for supplying me with additional excerpts of this document. Poincaré expressed similar views about Belgium's neutrality in October 1911. See (**12**).

(404) 3 August: Schoen to Viviani

German declaration of war on France

3 August 3, 1914
[letter handed to the French President at 6.45 p.m.]

The German administrative and military authorities have noted a number of flagrantly hostile acts committed on German territory by French military aviators.[72] Several of these have seemingly violated the neutrality of Belgium by flying over the territory of that country. One has attempted to destroy railway installations near Wesel; others were seen over the district of the Eifel, another threw bombs on the railways near Karlsruhe and Nuremberg.

I am instructed, and I have the honour, to inform Your Excellency, that in consequence of these attacks the German Empire considers itself in a state of war with France due to France's actions.

At the same time I have the honour to inform Your Excellency that the German authorities will detain French mercantile vessels currently in German ports, but that they will release them if, within forty-eight hours, complete reciprocity is assured.

My diplomatic mission having thus come to an end it only remains for me to request Your Excellency to be good enough to hand me my passports, and to take the steps You consider suitable to assure my return to Germany, with the staff of the Embassy, as well as with the staff of the Bavarian Legation and of the German General Consulate in Paris.[73]

DD, No. 734.

(405) 3 August: Poincaré's Diary (2)

Relief at French Cabinet Meeting on evening of 3 August that German declaration of war reveals her as the aggressor

It was for all the members of the cabinet a real relief. Never before had a declaration of war been welcomed with such satisfaction.[74] France

72 This was not true. See (**397**).

73 Bethmann Hollweg's telegram to Schoen arrived incomplete in Paris, and Schoen put together this letter based on a certain amount of guesswork. See DD No. 734 for the original text, and No. 734a for the garbled message. The German government then published the original text via Wolff's press bureau, alleging that the text had possibly been deliberately garbled by the French telegraph office. See DD, No. 734 c.

74 See (**404**).

having done all that was incumbent upon her to maintain peace and war having never the less become inevitable, it was a hundred times better that we should not have been led, even by repeated violations of our frontiers, to declare it ourselves. It was indispensable that Germany, who was entirely responsible for the aggression, should be led into publicly confessing her intentions. If we had had to declare war ourselves, the Russian alliance would have been contested, national unanimity would have been smashed, it would probably have meant Italy would have been forced by the clauses of the Triple Alliance to side against us [...]'.[75]

Raymond Poincaré, 'Notes journalières', cited in John Keiger, *Raymond Poincaré*, Cambridge University Press, Cambridge 1997, p. 186.

(406) 3 August: Below to Jagow

Belgian Government rejects German request for neutrality

Telegram No. 29
Brussels, 3 August 1914
D. 12.35 p.m.
R. 7.58 p.m.
[Note from Belgian Government to Germany]

In their note of 2 August[76] the German Government advised that according to certain news the French army had the intention to advance via Givet and Namur against the Meuse and that Belgium, despite her best intentions, would not be in a position to halt the advance of the French troops without support.

The German Government felt compelled to pre-empt this attack and violate Belgian territory. [...][77]

This note has caused deep and painful astonishment in the King's Government. The intentions it ascribes to France are in contradiction with the explicit declaration made to us on 1 August by the Government of the Republic.[78]

---

75 As John Keiger points out, this excerpt was not included in the published version of Poincaré's diary: *Poincaré*, p. 186. On 8 January 1915, Poincaré reflected: 'I have always believed, of course, that the French did not want to declare war for Serbia. I even believed that France would not rise up united to keep the promises of the alliance with Russia and that, if we had been led into declaring war, the country would be cruelly divided. But I had never had doubts about France in the event of her being attacked, even if it was over Serbia.' Ibid., p. 189.

76 See (**386**).

77 The text of the Note was summarized here (**386**).

78 See (**382**).

If, moreover, contrary to our expectation, Belgian neutrality should be violated by France, then Belgium would fulfil all her international obligations and her army would offer vigorous resistance to the invader.

The Treaties of 1839, confirmed by the Treaties of 1871, solemnly acknowledge the independence and neutrality of Belgium under the guarantee of the Great Powers, and in particular of the Government of His Majesty, the King of Prussia.

Belgium has always been faithful to her international obligations, she has carried out her duties in a spirit of sincere impartiality, she has spared no effort to maintain her neutrality and enforce respect for it.

The attack on her independence with which the German Government threatens her would constitute a flagrant violation of international law. No strategic interest justifies such a breach of this law.

If the Belgian Government were to accept the proposals laid before it, it would sacrifice the nation's honour while at the same time violating its duties towards Europe.

Conscious of the part which has been played by Belgium in the civilization of the world for more than eighty years, the Government refuses to believe that Belgian independence can only be preserved at the price of the violation of her neutrality.

If this hope were disappointed, the Belgian Government is firmly resolved to repel every attack on its rights by all means in its power.[79]

DD, No. 779.

(407) 3 August: Benckendorff to Sazonov

Change of public opinion in Britain in favour of war

Telegram, 3 August/21 July 1914
Copy to Paris

Following news of declaration of war on Russia and occupation of Luxembourg by German army public opinion has suddenly changed completely. Pacifist demonstration in Trafalgar Square, which was due

79 Luigi Albertini considered the Belgian reply 'the noblest document produced by the whole crisis and redounds to the honor – both of those who were responsible for its substance and those who gave it its form which in brevity and self-restraint – even if the self-restraint were due to a lingering hope that Germany might yet refrain from violating Belgian neutrality – attains a solemnity worthy of the occasion. This was so clearly felt by the German Government that in the three editions of the German *White Book* it refrained from publishing the note, for which reason German public opinion felt amazed and indignant at the resistance put up by Liège.' Albertini, *Origins*, Vol. III, pp. 465–466.

to be impressive, was reduced to nothing. Excitement in London grows hourly, crowds of people have gone to the Royal Palace to bring ovations to the King. I consider the pacifist party to be exhausted. Great difficulties exist within the Cabinet. [...]

Int. Bez., I, 5, No. 486.

(408) 3 August: Goschen to Grey

Germany alleges French border violations occurred already, but that German troops have not crossed into French territory

Berlin, 3 August 1914.
D. 4.10 p.m.
Tel. (No. 131.)
R. 6.30 p.m.

Chancellor has made the following communication to me in writing, which he begs me to bring to your immediate notice: —

'The German troops have as yet received orders scrupulously to respect French frontier, and these orders have been everywhere strictly carried out. French news to the contrary is absolutely false. Up to this morning at 10 o'clock no German soldier has been on French territory. On the other hand, in spite of French agreement to 10 kilom[etre] zone, already yesterday French troops crossed German frontier at Altmunsterol, in Alsace, and by way of Schlucht Pass in Vosges, and are still at this moment on German territory. French aviator who must also have flown over Belgian territory was shot down yesterday during attempt to destroy railway at Wesel. It was established without doubt that several other French aviators flew over the Eifel yesterday; these aircraft also have flown over Belgian territory. French aviators yesterday threw bombs on railways in neighbourhood of Carlsruhe and Nuremberg.[80] We must accordingly state it as an undeniable fact that yesterday there have been breaches of peace on the part of French. Latter has likewise violated Belgian neutrality.'

The official who brought me this communication informed me verbally at the request of the Chancellor that in some cases as necessary measures of precaution German patrols had crossed German frontier. He added that news of French aviators having been shot down had not been confirmed.[81]

BD, XI, No. 553.

80 This news was fabricated. See (**397**), (**404**).
81 See (**397**).

(409) 3 August: Moltke to Jagow

Moltke asks that Belgian Government be informed that German troops are advancing into Belgium; still hopeful that Belgium might re-consider once she realizes the severity of the situation

Secret!
Berlin, 3 August 1914
R. 10 p.m.

On Tuesday, 4 August, at 6 o'clock a.m. the Belgian Government is to be informed that, to our regret, due to the negative attitude of the Royal Belgian Government towards our well-intentioned proposals[82] we shall be forced to put into operation the security measures against a French threat[83] which we have already shown to be unavoidably necessary, if need be by force of arms.

This announcement is necessary because our troops will already be entering Belgian territory tomorrow morning.[84] I consider this declaration sufficient as Belgium has advised us that she will oppose any invasion with force of arms. I do not consider a declaration of war desirable because I am still counting on coming to an understanding with Belgium when the Belgian Government has realized the gravity of the situation.[85]

DD, No. 788.[86]

82 See (**302**), (**386**), (**399**), (**406**).

83 This largely fabricated threat was outlined in the German note to Belgium of 2 August (**386**).

84 Due to the constraints of Germany's military plan which required that German troops took the fortifications of Liège by *coup de main* before war was even declared. For details see Mombauer, 'German War Plans', pp. 59ff, and Annika Mombauer, 'Der Moltke-Plan. Modifikation des Schlieffenplanes bei gleichen Zielen?', in Hans Ehlert et al. (eds), *Der Schlieffenplan. Analysen und Dokumente*, Schöningh, Paderborn 2006, pp. 79–99.

85 Jagow instructed Below accordingly in an urgent telegram which arrived 35 minutes later. See DD, No. 791; Geiss, *July 1914*, No. 182.

86 Slightly different English translation in Geiss, *July 1914*, No. 180.

(410) 3 August: San Giuliano to all Ambassadors, Envoys and Diplomatic Agents

Official declaration of Italian neutrality

Telegram 4474
Rome, 3 August 1914
D. 12.45 p.m.

Finding some of the powers of Europe in a state of war, and Italy being in a state of peace with all the belligerent powers, the Government of the King and the citizens and subjects of the Kingdom have the obligation to observe the duties of neutrality, according to existing legislation and the principles of international law.

Whoever shall violate these obligations will endure the consequences of their acts and will incur, whenever that may be, the relevant legal sanctions.

Please inform these Authorities and act on spreading this news.[87]

DDI, 5th Series, I, No. 30.

(411) 4 August: Maier, Russian Military Attaché in Belgium and the Netherlands, to the department of the Quartermaster-General of the Russian General Staff

Belgium will not join France in joint operations

Telegram No. 156

Vis-à-vis the town of Liège appear to be two German corps.[88] Belgium has today rejected joint operations with France and has declared it

87 On the same day, King Victor Emanuel III sent a telegram to Wilhelm II (DD, No. 755), stating that 'from the beginning my Government told your Government and that of Austria-Hungary that, because the *casus foederis* does currently not apply, it will use all its diplomatic action for the cause of our own rightful interests and those of our allies, and to work for the cause of peace'. Wilhelm II annotated the document with the word 'scoundrel'. Moltke was outraged at the betrayal by the ally. On 5 August, he wrote to Conrad: 'God grant you victory now so that later you will be able to settle accounts with these rascals.' Cited in John Gooch, 'Italy', in Richard Hamilton and Holger Herwig (eds), *War Planning 1914*, Cambridge University Press, Cambridge et al. 2010, pp. 198–225, p. 224.

88 The fortified town of Liège was the first target of the German deployment plan.

would regard anyone who crosses the border as an enemy and fight against him.

Int. Bez., I, 5, No. 545.

(412) 4 August: Moltke to Jagow

Importance of access to imports via Italy; need for explanation to London that Germany does not seek Belgian territory

Secret
Berlin, 4 August 1914
D. 6.00 a.m.

1. For the purpose of carrying out the war that has broken out it is of the very utmost importance and cannot be over-emphasized that the importation of foodstuffs into Germany through Italy remains unimpeded. Since Italy has not been willing to observe the obligations of her alliance, but has promised benevolent neutrality, the least she can do to prove this benevolence is to put no difficulties in our way in this regard.

I request that you act towards this end at Rome as soon as possible. It is a question of life or death for us.[89]

2. I request that the following be transmitted at once to London: Germany again emphasizes the fact that in her action in Belgium she was not guided by the intention of taking possession of Belgian territory on some frivolous pretext, even in the event of a hostile clash with Belgium. Germany's declaration to the Netherlands that she would not set foot on Dutch territory during this war, but, on the other hand, was determined to observe the strictest neutrality with regard to the Netherlands, is the best substantiation of the assurance just given.[90] The English Government is able to judge for itself that if Germany were harbouring any intention of acquiring Belgian territory, such an acquisition could only be of value if the same intention were being harboured towards Holland. It is here emphasised once again that German action in Belgium was compelled and had to be compelled, by the knowledge, acquired

89 A telegram was despatched to Flotow in Rome immediately. See DD, No. 806.

90 See DD, No. 426, n. 3. Under Moltke's leadership of the German General Staff, German war plans had been changed so that Dutch neutrality no longer needed to be violated by German troops on their way towards France. This was primarily motivated by wanting to use Holland as a 'windpipe' to allow Germany access to imports from the sea. See for example Mombauer, 'German War Plan', p. 59.

from reliable sources, of France's intended military operations. Germany could not afford to expose herself to the danger of attack by strong French forces in the direction of the Lower Rhine. Germany was forced to act on the principle that the offensive is the best defensive, which England, always ready to take the most energetic steps in time of war, should certainly understand better than anybody else. This war is for Germany not only a question of her whole national existence and of the continuation of the German Empire, created through such heavy bloody sacrifices, but also of the preservation and maintenance of German culture and civilization against uncivilized Slavdom.[91]

Germany is unable to believe that England will be willing to assist, by becoming an enemy of Germany, in destroying this civilization – a civilization in which English spiritual culture has always had such a prominent share. The decision about this lies in England's hands.

Note
I would ask that this despatch be sent to London uncoded, and that the Ambassador be advised to read it to Sir Edward Grey. It will not do us any harm if this note, by reason of its uncoded form, should also become known elsewhere.[92]

3. Note for the *Auswärtiges Amt*: Vis-à-vis the Belgian Government it is necessary continually to maintain, even after the German invasion has taken place, the stand that Germany is ready at any moment to hold out to Belgium the hand of a brother, and is ever willing to enter upon negotiations concerning an acceptable *modus vivendi*, subject to the prosecution of the war forced upon us by France's action.

The indispensable basis of these negotiations, however, would have to remain the opening of Liège to the passage of German troops,[93] and

91 Just two days earlier, on 2 August, German troops had committed atrocities against civilians, and near-enough destroyed the border city of Kalisz in Poland, appearing themselves to be the epitome of barbarism, rather than a harbinger of civilization. For details, see for example Joshua Sanborn, 'Military Occupation and Social Unrest: Daily Life in Russian Poland at the Start of World War I', in Golfo Alexopolous (eds), *Writing the Stalin Era: Sheila Fitzpatrick and Soviet Historiography*, Palgrave Macmillan, New York 2011, pp. 43–58, here pp. 52ff; Laura Engelstein, '"A Belgium of Our Own": The sack of Russian Kalisz, August 1914', *Kritika: Explorations in Russian and Eurasian History*, 10, 3, Summer 2009, pp. 441–473. More famous still are the atrocities committed by German troops in Belgium. For detail see John Horne and Alan Kramer, *German Atrocities, 1914: A History of Denial*, Yale University Press, New Haven, CT and London 2001.

92 Jagow instructed Lichnowsky on 4 August (see DD, No. 810, Geiss, *July 1914*, No. 185). He talked of 'absolutely unimpeachable information' regarding the French intention to attack Germany through Belgium. This news was a fabrication.

93 For the importance of Liège in Germany's war planning, see for example

Belgium's assurance that she would not undertake the destruction of any railroads, bridges or artificial structures. Other demands than these would not be required from a military point of view.

DD, No. 804.[94]

(413) 4 August: Haig to Haldane

Haig expects a long war and suggests increasing British Expeditionary Force

Personal

What an anxious time you must be having but what a satisfaction it must be to you [to] see that this Country is able to draw on her vast resources at the moment of crisis as a result of the thought & labour you spent on the problem when you were S[ecretary] of S[tate].

So I make so bold as to write & express a hope that you will, even at great personal inconvenience, return to the W[ar] O[ffice]. for as long as war lasts and preparations are necessary. No one knows the details of the problems of organization as you do! This war will last many months, possibly years, so I venture to hope that our only bolt (and that not a very big one) may not suddenly be shot on a project of which the success seems to me quite doubtful – I mean the checking of the German advance into France. Would it not be better to begin at once to enlarge our Exped[itionar]y Force by amalgamating less regular forces with it? In three months time we sh[oul]d have quite a considerable army so that when we do take the field we can act decisively and dictate terms which will ensure a lasting peace.

I presume of course that France can hold on (even though her forces have to fall back from the frontier) for the necessary time for us to create an army of say 300,000. [...]

National Library of Scotland, Haldane Papers, MS5910.[95]

Mombauer, 'German War Plans', p. 59.

94 Engl. transl. based on Geiss, *July 1914*, No. 184, here with some amendments.

95 I am grateful to the Trustees of the National Library of Scotland for granting permission to reproduce this extract, and to Keith Neilson for making this document available to me. See also Neilson, 'Great Britain', in Hamilton and Herwig (eds), *War Planning 1914*, p. 192.

(414) 4 August: Joffre's Memoirs

Possibility that false news of German violation of Belgium were spread to induce France into crossing the border

In Belgium things were moving rapidly. The news that the Germans had violated the frontier began to circulate on the evening of the 3rd in official circles in Brussels. It was stated, however, that the material fact of the frontier being crossed was questionable, that the partisans of an arrangement with the Germans were still numerous and powerful in Belgium and that, moreover, it was possible that Germany might be spreading false news in order to induce us to be the first to violate Belgian neutrality. The greatest circumspection was, therefore, still necessary. Another rumour persisted throughout the day, namely, that the Belgians were showing themselves just as hostile to our entrance upon their territory as they were to that of the Germans.[96]

Joseph Joffre, *Memoirs of Marshal Joffre*, 2 vols, Geoffrey Bles, London 1932, Vol. I, pp. 135–136.

(415) 4 August: Paléologue's Memoirs

Russian mobilization progressing well; war enthusiasm and anti-German demonstrations

Yesterday Germany declared war on France.[97]

General mobilization is in active progress throughout the [Russian] empire and without the least incident. As a matter of fact five or six hours has been gained on the time table of the covering troops. [...]

Every day processions, with flags and icons, have passed under the embassy windows, to a chorus of 'Vive la France! Vive la France!'

Very mixed crowds they are, too: workmen, priests, *moujiks*, students, male and female, servants, shop assistants, etc. Their enthusiasm seems genuine. But how far are the police responsible for these numerous demonstrations which take place at such regular intervals?[98]

I put this question to myself at ten o'clock this evening when I was

96 See (**406**).
97 See (**404**).
98 For a discussion of Russian war enthusiasm (and lack of) see Joshua Sanborn, 'The Mobilization of 1914 and the Question of the Russian Nation: a Reexamination', *Slavic Review*, 59, 2, Summer 2000, pp. 267–289.

told that a mob had attacked the German Embassy and sacked it from top to bottom.

The German Embassy is a *kolossal* edifice in the most important square of the city, between the Cathedral of St. Isaac and the Marie Palace. It has a heavy façade in Finland granite, massive architraves, cyclopean masonry. On the roof two enormous bronze horses, with giants holding their bridles, all but bring down the whole building. Hideous as a work of art it is none the less a powerful piece of symbolism. With its coarse and blatant eloquence it emphasizes Germany's claim to domination in Russia.

The mob has invaded the building, smashed the windows, torn down the tapestries, ripped up the pictures, thrown all the furniture (including the Renaissance marbles and bronzes which formed Pourtalès' admirable private collection) out of the windows. By way of conclusion the marauders hurled the equestrian group on the façade down into the street. The sack lasted more than an hour under the tolerant eye of the police.

Has this act of vandalism any symbolic meaning[?]

Can it be said to presage the ruin of German influence in Russia?

My Austro-Hungarian colleague, Count Szapary, is still in Petersburg and cannot understand why his government is apparently in so little of a hurry to break off relations with the Russian Government.[99]

Maurice Paléologue, *An Ambassador's Memoirs*, Doran, New York 1925, pp. 57–58.

(416) 4 August: Bethmann Hollweg's Reichstag's speech[100]

Germany is fighting a defensive war; admits that violation of Belgian neutrality contrary to international law

---

[...] Gentlemen, we are now acting in self-defence;
(Lively approval),
and needs must!
(Rapturous applause.)
Our troops have occupied Luxembourg
(Bravo!)
Perhaps they have already entered Belgian territory
(Bravo again.)

99 The Austro-Hungarian Government did not declare war on Russia until 6 August.

100 The Reichstag convened in the morning for a speech by the Kaiser, and reconvened for Bethmann Hollweg's speech at 3 p.m.

Gentlemen, this is contrary to international law. Although the French Government declared in Brussels that it would respect Belgium's neutrality as long as the opponent did so,[101] however, we knew that France was ready for the advance.
(Hear! Hear! On the right [side of the House])
France could wait, but we could not! A French attack on our flank on the lower Rhine could have been disastrous.
(Lively approval.)
Thus we were forced to ignore the justified protests of the Governments of Luxembourg and Belgium.
(Quite right!)
The wrong – I speak openly –, the wrong that we are thus committing we will try to make right again as soon as our military goal is reached.
(Bravo!)
[…]
Gentlemen, […] I repeat the words of the Kaiser: 'Germany enters the fight with a clear conscience!'
(Bravo!) […]
Our Army is in the field, our Navy is ready for battle – behind it is the entire German people!
(Continuous lively applause on all sides of the House […]. The Reichstag rises)
– The entire German people (towards the Socialists), unified to the last man!
(Repeated applause, lasting several minutes)

You, Gentlemen, know your duty in its full extent. The bills no longer require justification. I request their urgent approval.[102]
(Tumultuous applause)

Stenographische Berichte über die Verhandlungen des Reichstags, 13. Legislaturperiode, Vol. 306, 2nd session, 1914, pp. 5–7.

(417) 4 August: Grey to Goschen

British Government protests against German threats to Belgium's neutrality and demands clarification of Berlin's intentions

Telegram No. 266
Foreign Office, 4 August 1914
D. 9.30 a.m.

101 See (**352**).
102 The members of the Reichstag, including the Social Democrats, voted in support of the war and for war credits.

The King of the Belgians has made an appeal to His Majesty the King for diplomatic intervention on behalf of Belgium.

His Majesty's Government are also informed that the German Government has delivered to the Belgium Government [*sic*] a note proposing friendly neutrality entailing free passage through Belgian territory and promising to maintain the independence and integrity of the kingdom and its possessions at the conclusion of peace, threatening in case of refusal to treat Belgium as an enemy. An answer was requested within twelve hours.[103]

We also understand that Belgium has categorically refused this as a flagrant violation of the law of nations.[104]

His Majesty's Government are bound to protest against this violation of a treaty to which Germany is a party in common with themselves, and must request an assurance that the demand made upon Belgium will not be proceeded with, and that her neutrality will be respected by Germany. You should ask for an immediate reply.[105]

BD, XI, No. 573 (a).

(418) 4 August: Grey to Goschen

British ultimatum to Germany to uphold Belgian neutrality

Tel. No. 270
D. 2 p.m.

We hear that Germany has addressed note to Belgian Minister for Foreign Affairs stating that German Government will be compelled to carry out, if necessary by force of arms, the measures considered indispensable.

We are also informed that Belgian territory has been violated at Gemmenich.[106]

In these circumstances, and in view of the fact that Germany declined to give the same assurance respecting Belgium as France gave last week in reply to our request made simultaneously at Berlin and Paris,[107] we must repeat that request, and ask that a satisfactory reply to it and to my telegram No. 266 of this morning[108] be received here by 12 o'clock

103 See (**302**), (**393**), (**406**).
104 See (**399**), (**406**).
105 For an account of Goschen's discussions with Jagow and Bethmann Hollweg see (**419**).
106 German troops invaded the border town on 4 August.
107 (**331**).
108 (**417**).

to-night. If not, you are instructed to ask for your passports and to say that His Majesty's Government felt bound to take all steps in their power to uphold the neutrality of Belgium and the observance of a Treaty to which Germany is as much a party as ourselves.[109]

BD, XI, No. 594.[110]

(419) 4 August: Goschen's account of his final meeting with Bethmann Hollweg

The infamous 'scrap of paper' conversation[111]

[Goschen to Grey]
Berlin, 6 August 1914[112]
Received 19 August
No. 309

In accordance with the instructions contained in your telegram No. 266 of the 4th instant[113] I called upon the Under-Secretary of State[114]

109 This was communicated by Goschen as an aide-mémoire to Jagow in the afternoon that day, and acknowledged by the Kaiser at 7 p.m. See DD No. 823. Jagow added to the document: 'I answered Sir E. Goschen that we had to violate the Belgian neutrality for reasons of self-defence, I have explained all the reasons which forced our hand and have repeated again all the assurances already given in London.'

110 See also (**419**).

111 For a discussion of the controversy around this document, see Thomas G. Otte, 'A "German Paperchase": the "scrap of paper" controversy and the problem of myth and memory in international history', *Diplomacy & Statecraft*, 18, 1, 2007, pp. 53–87. Goschen had attended the Reichstag session that day (**416**), and in the meeting described here with the Chancellor before requesting his passport the infamous discussion about the neutrality of Belgium took place. When Goschen's report about these meetings was presented to Parliament on 27 August, it was immediately published as the *Blue Book Miscellaneous No. 6*. See Otte, 'A "German Paperchase"', pp. 57ff. See also above, Introduction, p. 12, n. 47.

112 As Otte shows this date is not correct and we do not know exactly when this account was drafted. The meeting described occurred on 4 August; this account was received in London on the 19th. The document printed in the British *Blue Book* is dated 8 August, the date in BD is 6 August. Goschen and the Embassy staff left Berlin on the morning of 6 August, and the date of 6 August on the original document appears to have been a later addition. Otte suspects the document may not have been drafted until 17 or 18 August. Otte, 'A "German Paperchase"', p. 73.

113 See (**417**).

114 This should have read Secretary of State (Jagow).

for Foreign Affairs that afternoon and enquired in the name of His Majesty's Government whether the Imperial Government would refrain from violating Belgian neutrality. Herr von Jagow at once replied that he was sorry to say that his answer must be 'No' as, in consequence of the German troops having crossed the frontier that morning, Belgian neutrality had been already violated.[115] Herr von Jagow again went into the reasons why the Imperial Government had been obliged to take this step – namely that they had to advance into France by the quickest and easiest way so as to be able to get well ahead with their operations and endeavour to strike some decisive blow as early as possible.[116] It was a matter of life and death for them, as if they had gone by the more southern route they could not have hoped, in view of the paucity of roads and the strength of the Fortresses, to have got through without formidable opposition entailing great loss of time. This loss of time would have meant time gained by the Russians for bringing up their troops to the German frontier. Rapidity of action was the great German asset while that of Russia was an inexhaustible supply of troops. I pointed out to Herr von Jagow that this fait accompli of the violation of the Belgian frontier rendered, as he would readily understand, the situation exceedingly grave and I asked him whether there was not still time to draw back and avoid possible consequences which both he and I would deplore. He replied that for the reasons he had given me it was now impossible for them to draw back.

During the afternoon I received your telegram No. 270[117] and, in compliance with the instructions therein contained, I again proceeded to the Imperial Foreign Office and informed the Secretary of State for Foreign Affairs that unless the Imperial Government could give the assurance by 12 o'clock that night that they would proceed no further with their violation of the Belgian frontier and stop their advance, I had been instructed to demand my passports and inform the Imperial Government that His Majesty's Government would have to take all steps in their power to uphold the neutrality of Belgium and the observance of a treaty to which Germany was as much a party as themselves.

Herr von Jagow replied that to his great regret he could give no

115 German troops entered Belgium on their way to take Liège by *coup de main*. Luxembourg's neutrality had already been violated on 2 August at the village and station of Trois-Vierges by a German detachment of infantry under Lieutenant Feldmann. See Poincaré, *Memoirs* p. 271.

116 This summarized the German deployment plan which envisaged a quick blow against France before turning on the more powerful, but initially slower to mobilize, enemy Russia. Jagow's argument shows to what extent military, rather than diplomatic, concerns determined German foreign policy at the end of the July Crisis.

117 (**418**).

other answer than that which he had given me earlier in the day, namely that the safety of the Empire rendered it absolutely necessary that the Imperial troops should advance through Belgium. I gave his Excellency a paraphrase of your telegram and, pointing out that you had mentioned 12 o'clock as the time when His Majesty's Government would expect an answer, asked him whether, in view of the terrible consequences which would necessarily ensue, it were not possible even at the last moment that their answer should be reconsidered. He replied that if the time given were even twenty four hours or more his answer must be the same. I said that in that case I should have to demand my passports. This interview would have taken place at about 7 o'clock. In a short conversation which ensued Herr von Jagow expressed his poignant regret at the crumbling of his entire policy and that of the Chancellor, which had been to make friends with Great Britain and then, through Great Britain to get closer to France. I said that this sudden end to my work in Berlin was to me also a matter of deep regret and disappointment, but that he must understand that under the circumstances and in view of our engagements His Majesty's Government could not possibly have acted otherwise than they had done.

I then said that I should like to go and see the Chancellor as it might be perhaps the last time I should have an opportunity of seeing him. He begged me to do so. I found the Chancellor very agitated. His Excellency at once began a harangue which lasted for about 20 minutes.[118] He said that the step taken by His Majesty's Government was terrible to a degree, just for a word 'neutrality' a word which in war time had so often been disregarded just for a scrap of paper, Great Britain was going to make war on a kindred nation who desired nothing better than to be friends with her. All his efforts in that direction had been rendered useless by this last terrible step, and the policy to which, as I knew, he had devoted himself since his accession to office, had tumbled down like a house of cards. What we had done was unthinkable; it was like striking a man from behind while he was fighting for his life against two assailants. He held Great Britain responsible for all the terrible events that might happen! I protested strongly against that statement and said that in the same way as he and Herr von Jagow wished me to understand that for strategical reasons it was a matter of life and death to Germany to advance through Belgium and violate her neutrality, so I would wish

118 The editors of BD added the following note: 'The question having been raised as to the language used in this conversation and in the statement by the Chancellor, an enquiry was addressed to Sir Horace Rumbold. He writes that according to private notes which he made at the time Sir Edward Goschen informed him on the same day that "the Chancellor made a set speech in English."' Quoted in Otte, 'A "German Paperchase"', p. 76.

him to understand that it was, so to speak, a matter of 'life and death' for the honour of Great Britain that she should keep her solemn engagement to do her utmost to defend Belgium's neutrality if attacked. That solemn compact simply had to be kept, or what confidence could anyone have in engagements given by Great Britain in the future? The Chancellor said 'But at what price will that compact have been kept. Has the British Government thought of that?' I hinted to his Excellency as plainly as I could that fear of consequences could hardly be regarded as an excuse for breaking solemn engagements, but his Excellency was so excited, so evidently overcome by the news of our action and so little disposed to hear reason, that I refrained from adding fuel to the flame by further argument. As I was leaving he said that the blow of Great Britain joining Germany's enemies was all the greater that almost up to the last moment he and his Government had been working with us and supporting our effort to maintain peace between Austria and Russia. I admitted that that had been the case and said that it was part of the tragedy which saw the two nations fall apart just at the moment when the relations between them had been more friendly and cordial than they had been for years. Unfortunately notwithstanding our efforts to maintain peace between Russia and Austria the war had spread and had brought us face to face with a situation which, if we held to our engagements, we could not possibly avoid, and which unfortunately entailed our separation from our late fellow-workers. He would readily understand that no one regretted this more than I.

After this somewhat painful interview[119] I returned to the embassy and drew up my telegram No. 137. This telegram was handed in at the Central Telegraph Office a little before 9 p.m. It was accepted by that office but apparently never despatched.

At about 9.0 p.m. Herr von Zimmermann, the Under-Secretary of State for Foreign Affairs came to see me. After expressing his deep regret that the very friendly official and personal relations between us were about to cease, he asked me casually whether a demand for passports was equivalent to a declaration of war. I said that such an authority on international law as he was known to be must know as well, or better than I what was usual in such cases. I added that there were many cases where diplomatic relations had been broken off and nevertheless

119 When the British Government, against diplomatic conventions, published details of this meeting in September 1914, Bethmann Hollweg was dismayed to find that Goschen had clearly neglected to point out that both men had been overcome by emotion and tearful during this fateful meeting. For details, see Egmont Zechlin, 'Deutschland zwischen Kabinetts- und Wirtschaftskrieg: Politik und Kriegsführung in den ersten Monaten des Weltkrieges 1914', *Historische Zeitschrift*, 199, 2, October 1964, pp. 347–458, p. 393.

war had not ensued, but that in this case he would have seen from my instructions of which I had given Herr von Jagow a paraphrase that His Majesty's Government expected an answer to a definite question by 12 o'clock that night, and that in default of a satisfactory answer they would be forced to take such steps as their engagements required. Herr Zimmermann said that that was in fact a declaration of war, as the Imperial Government could not possibly give the assurance required either that night or any other night.

The next morning I demanded my passports in writing. [...]

BD, XI, No. 671.

(420) 5 August: Lerchenfeld to Hertling

Moltke's briefing on current military situation; timing of war fortuitous as it would have come anyway when the opponents would have been stronger

I have just learnt that Chief of the General Staff *Generaloberst* von Moltke has expressed the following opinion about the current situation:

He knew most definitely that Russia, France and England had agreed among themselves on an offensive war against Germany for the year 1917.[120] Moltke considered Russia to be the instigator of these plans. It could be regarded as fortuitous that the murder of Sarajevo had exploded this mine planted by the three powers at a time when Russia was not ready and the French army was in a state of transition. Against the three states, when fully armed, Germany would have had a very hard stand. Germany was strong enough, if not a particular misfortune occurred, to withstand the war against Russia and France that we are now having to wage. England's joining with our opponents no doubt worsened our situation, because it might become difficult to ensure supplies for the civilian population should the war take longer. This point caused him some concern. Nonetheless he had emphatically counselled against buying English neutrality at the price of sparing Belgian territory even if this had been possible, which he doubted.[121] An attack from German territory would have cost the German army a full three months and

120 There is no evidence that suggests that such an agreement had been made. However, such arguments had frequently been advanced by Germany's military planners in an effort to achieve armament increases, and in order to push for war while time was still on Germany's side. For more details see for example Mombauer, *Moltke*, pp. 106ff.

121 See (370), (371), (372), (373), (375).

would have given Russia such a head start that one could no longer have hoped for success on both fronts. We had to advance towards Paris immediately, and with all might, via Belgium in order to deal with France quickly. This was the only way to victory.[122]

Generaloberst Moltke further explained that until now only unimportant fighting had occurred in Belgium. However, tomorrow Liège would be occupied, which was fortified, and would lead to losses.[123] A part of the German army had already marched into France. [...]

Ernst Deuerlein (ed.), *Briefwechsel Hertling-Lerchenfeld*, 2 vols, Boppard am Rhein 1973, No. 119.

(421) 5 August: Szögyény to Berchtold

Germany fears that Italy might join the Entente; advises Vienna to discuss compensation if necessary

Telegram No. 382
Berlin, 5 August 1914
D. 3.50 p.m.
R. 10 p.m.

Shared with State Secretary [Jagow] the contents of your Telegram No. 338,[124] [he] completely shares Your Excellency's view to put a brave face on vis-à-vis Italy [*gute Miene zum bösen Spiel*] and to explain to Marquis San Giuliano that, under the circumstances, we will be content with Italy's declaration of neutrality.

As regards the question of compensation, the Secretary of State and the Under-Secretary of State [Zimmermann] were of the opinion that it would not be right to answer evasively in case of this question being further raised by Italy.

---

122 This was a good summary of Germany's strategic dilemma and the rationale behind the 'Moltke-Plan'. For details, see for example Mombauer, 'Der Moltke-Plan', pp. 79–99; idem, *Moltke*, chapter 3.

123 However, the *coup de main* on Liège did not go according to plan, and German troops did not enter the city until 7 August. It took even longer to overcome the twelve reinforced forts; the last one was not taken until 16 August. For more details see for example Mombauer, 'German War Plans', p. 67; Mombauer, *Moltke*, pp. 230ff.

124 See *Die österreichisch-ungarischen Dokumente zum Kriegsausbruch. Diplomatische Aktenstücke*, ed. Republik Österreich, 3 vols, Bundesverlag, Vienna 1919, No. 117. Berchtold had suggested telling Italy that they would be content with a declaration of neutrality, and hoped that winning over Turkey and Rumania to accept the *casus foederis* as given might sway Italy into accepting the same.

Italy was close to not only staying [neutral[125]], but to go hand in hand with the enemies.[126]

Die österreichisch-ungarischen Dokumente zum Kriegsausbruch. Diplomatische Aktenstücke, 3 vols, Bundesverlag, Vienna 1919, No. 137.

(422) 5 August: Berchtold's memorandum for an audience with Kaiser Franz Joseph

Berchtold urges monarch to authorize declaration of war on France and Britain following German pressure

Vienna, 5 August 1914

Now that the war between the German Empire and France and England has already begun it no longer seems advisable for the Monarchy to maintain diplomatic relations with the French and British Governments and not also to declare war on them.

I therefore humbly ask Your Majesty most graciously to grant me permission in principle, following the usual agreement with Your Majesty's Army High Command, to address the enclosed declaration of war to the French Government and to pass a similarly worded declaration of war to the British Government as soon as this is regarded opportune by the Army High Command.

In view of the fact that hostilities between German and English ships have already begun in the Mediterranean – the cruiser *Goeben* is being blocked in Messina by 4 big English cruisers – a fight between our ships and English ones can ensue even without a declaration of war.

The German Imperial Chancellor, via Count Szögyény, has asked me today most urgently to dispatch the declaration of war to France and England as soon as possible.[127] With regard to maintaining the friendly mood towards the ally which exists in the German Empire I consider it very necessary that we proceed in every regard in parallel with the German Government and that we do not give rise for the suspicion among the German population that we might want to delay fulfilling our alliance obligation.

125 This chiffre was missing.

126 Italy finally entered the war on 26 April 1915 on the Entente's side.

127 On 5 August, Jagow also instructed Tschirschky 'urgently' to request that Austria-Hungary declare war on France, Russia and England immediately. DD, No. 874. Austria-Hungary's declaration of war on Russia was issued on 6 August (**427**). France declared war on Austria-Hungary on 11 August, and Britain on 12 August.

Die österreichisch-ungarischen Dokumente zum Kriegsausbruch. Diplomatische Aktenstücke, No. 147.

(423) 5 August: Giolitti to San Giuliano

Neutrality necessary as conflict with Britain had to be avoided

[Bardonecchia], 5 August 1914

Dearest Friend,

I have been in Vichy, Paris, and London, and I must confess that I did not think it possible that a European war could be provoked so lightheartedly. I was only convinced on July 31st and the day after I hurried back to Italy.

The manner in which Austria has precipitated the conflict is nothing less than brutal, and proves either a total lack of conscience on her part, or a direct intention to bringing on a European war. I may be mistaken, but my impression is that she will pay the penalty more than anyone else.

Happily matters were so ordered as fully to justify our neutrality. I make no concealment of the danger that we may also suffer thereby, but the Government now has no other alternative. A conflict between Italy and England is out of the question, and the way in which the war was brought about would have made it very difficult for our country to enter into it with enthusiasm. I may add that the ends Austria has in view are evidently not in keeping with our interests.

In my opinion, now more than ever, we should keep on good terms with England and should do our utmost to limit the duration and consequences of the conflict.

I also think we should keep ourselves in readiness from a military point of view. [...]

Giovanni Giolitti, *Memoirs of my Life*, Chapman and Dodd, London 1923, pp. 380–381.

(424) 5 August: Pease's Diary

Tearful good-bye to Lichnowsky; Britain still prepared to negotiate for peace

Cabinet Wednesday 5 August 1914

This is the 10th cabinet since 27th July. We were very businesslike. Agreed a lot of matters without discussion. [...]

Grey told some of us quietly that he had had a very harrowing goodbye scene the previous night with Lichnowsky, they had both wept – & he had told Lichnowsky he would find us at any moment prepared to enter into negotiations for Peace – & possibly economic forces might quickly work in that direction – if he saw his way at any moment to promote peace he should know we would respond, & would be always anxious to bring the war to an end consistent with honour.

Cited in Keith M. Wilson, 'The Cabinet Diary of J.A. Pease', *Proceedings of the Leeds Philosophical Society*, XIX, III, 1983, pp. 41–51, pp. 49–50.

(425) 5 August: Minutes of British War Council Meeting

Discussion of the terms of British intervention following the declaration of war

THE DESTINATION OF THE EXPEDITIONARY FORCE

THE PRIME MINISTER made a brief statement of the circumstances in which he had summoned this Council of the greatest soldiers in the country to assemble. The situation, he said, was not unlike one which had constantly been considered, but with regard to which no decision had ever been reached. The present situation, he said, was as follows: War had actually been declared between England and Germany, between Russia and Germany and between France and Germany but as yet Austria was not technically at war with any country except Serbia.[128] One unexpected factor in the situation was the neutrality of Italy. It must now be assumed that Italy would not stand in with Germany and Austria. A further unexpected factor in the situation was the action of Belgium and Holland. Belgium appeared to be offering a better [resistance?] than had been anticipated. Germany was reported to

128 See Chapter 11, p. 580, n. 127.

have violated Dutch [Limburg?][129] and was apparently determined to overwhelm all opposition.

SIR JOHN FRENCH said that the prearranged plan to meet this situation had been that the Expeditionary Force should mobilize simultaneously with the French and concentrate behind the French army at Maubeuge by the [fifteenth?] day of mobilization. The intention then had been for it to move eastwards towards the Meuse and act on the left of the French army against the right German flank. It had, however, always been felt that if we were late in commencing our mobilization, as had actually happened, we should have to change our plan. Maubeuge, in his opinion, was no longer a safe place to concentrate. He suggested that Amiens would now be a safer place at which to concentrate. The general tenor of his opinion was that the Expeditionary Force should be sent into France; a safe place for concentration should be selected, and events should be awaited. He added that, as an alternative, and owing to the existing conditions, he was inclined to consider a landing at Antwerp with a view to co-operation with the Belgians and Dutch. The three forces would form a considerable army, and would necessarily contain a large German force, and they might be able to advance southward. The feasibility of this plan, however, was largely a naval question. As an alternative to a landing at Antwerp he proposed a landing in France and a movement to Antwerp by the coast route.

MR CHURCHILL said that the convoy of the Expeditionary Force to Antwerp was a very different proposition from its transport to France, and depended very largely on the attitude of Holland, owing to the necessity of navigating the Scheldt, the mouth of which was wholly in Dutch territory. In any case, however, the voyage to Holland would be very exposed, one flank being entirely open, and the transports would incur great risks.

SIR CHARLES DOUGLAS pointed out that our arrangements were all made for the embarkation of the Expeditionary Force at Newhaven, Southampton and Bristol. The voyage from these ports to Antwerp would be much longer than the trip to the French coast, and consequently the railway time-table would be dislocated.

LORD ROBERTS suggested that the decision should depend upon what view the French might take of the situation.

SIR CHARLES DOUGLAS concurred with Lord Roberts.

SIR E GREY pointed out that the Belgians had now invited the French

129 This was an erroneous assumption. German troops had violated Belgian and Luxembourg neutrality, but the German military plan was based on not violating Dutch neutrality.

to enter Belgium. He had just seen the Dutch Minister, who thought that the violation of [Limburg?] was extremely unlikely, and been very firm as to Holland's intention to remain neutral. If the rumour that Dutch neutrality had been violated were true a very important new element would be introduced.

THE PRIME MINISTER suggested that Belgium appeared likely to become the terrain of the hostilities.

SIR JAMES GRIERSON said he had information which led him to believe that the French, when mobilized, would advance along the whole line.

GENERAL WILSON said that a month ago he had sent three officers to France. They had worked out an alternative scheme in co-operation with the French General Staff, according to which the British force might concentrate at Amiens, whence they could very easily be despatched in any direction, according as the situation might develop.[130]

SIR DOUGLAS HAIG said he had formulated a number of questions on which further information was required. They were as follows:

Is it possible to delay and take time to organize, or will the French be beaten if we don't go at once?

If the French are already falling back when we arrive, will our small Expeditionary Force be sufficient to turn the tables?

What is the state of the French army?

How do their numbers in the field compare with the German?

What is the state of Belgium: Can Liège hold out for days or weeks, or for how long?

Can we land at Antwerp and Ostend?

If we join the Belgians, what force could the Germans turn upon us?

Have we enough troops, with the Belgians, to wage an active campaign, or do we run excessive risk, at the moment, of defeat in detail?

Where can we act with most effect, and when?

Would it be of value to send a small force at once, say, two divisions and a cavalry brigade?

What do the French wish?

The trend of his remarks was that our best policy at the present time was to be ready to do as the French wished us.

---

130 According to Roy A. Prete, Wilson 'did not comprehend the intricacies of his own government's policy and decision-making. Right down until the famous war council of 5 August 1914 (**425**), which met to decide the terms of British intervention, he continued to believe as did the French that a British decision for war would mean automatic dispatch of the B.E.F.' 'French Strategic Planning and the Deployment of the B.E.F. in France in 1914', *Canadian Journal of History*, XXIV, April 1989, pp. 42–62, p. 47. On Wilson's role in the July Crisis, see also Williamson, 'General Henry Wilson', *passim*.

SIR IAN HAMILTON advised that we should concentrate on Amiens, leaving the decision on where we should go to the French.

MR CHURCHILL asked if the French had a reserve army. If so, he suggested that we might join up with the reserve army and release part of it to go to the front.

GENERAL WILSON said that the French General Staff had devised their plans on the anticipation that we should arrive on the fifteenth day of mobilization. They had therefore to dislocate their plans to some extent in order to obtain troops to fill the gap.

LORD KITCHENER thought that the co-operation between the French and English General Staff ought to be closer. He suggested that the French General Staff should be invited to send a senior Staff Officer with full information to confer with our General Staff.

MR CHURCHILL said that the Chief of the French Naval General Staff was due in London to-night to confer with the naval authorities.

THE PRIME MINISTER agreed with Lord Kitchener.

SIR CHARLES DOUGLAS undertook to take action accordingly.

SIR E GREY asked whether in the event of a complete collapse of the French army, it would be possible for us to extricate our Expeditionary Force.

SIR CHARLES DOUGLAS anticipated that this could be done.

SIR E GREY then raised the question of how many men could be spared from this country.

MR CHURCHILL referred to the Report of the recent Sub-Committee of the Committee of Imperial Defence on Invasion (C.I.D. Paper (62–A)). The situation, however, was far better than that promised in the Invasion Report, for the following reasons:-

1 Our Navy was in a state of complete readiness.
2 The Territorial Force was already embodied.
3 The Germans were a good deal more extended than we had anticipated owing to the Belgian resistance.
4 Our fortifications were now in a complete state of defence.

PRINCE LOUIS OF BATTENBERG said that, in these circumstances, he would not object if five divisions, or perhaps even six, were allowed to go. He asked, however, if a raid with the object of dislodging our arrangements for the despatch of the Expeditionary Force was not probable.

SIR CHARLES DOUGLAS thought that a raid by 10,000 men was possible, but at present the Germans could not spare a larger force for this purpose.

LORD ROBERTS said that Germany was in a worse situation than he had ever dared to hope. In the present circumstances he did not believe that an invasion was possible.

SIR CHARLES DOUGLAS said that the present arrangement was that five divisions should go at once. The sixth division should be concentrated near Harrow ready for any emergency in home defence, and could be sent to the Continent when the situation had cleared sufficiently.

EGYPT

MR CHURCHILL raised the question of bringing Indian troops to Egypt. The situation in the Mediterranean might shortly be expected to be so favourable that there would be no difficulty in transporting troops accumulated in Egypt to Marseilles to assist the French.

SIR CHARLES DOUGLAS said that there was only one white brigade to two native brigades in an Indian division.

LORD ROBERTS said his opinion had been asked by the Indian Office, and he had replied that it was most undesirable to employ native troops in a continental war.

LORD KITCHENER asked that one division from India might be sent at once to garrison Egypt. A second division and a cavalry brigade might be held in readiness to follow if they should be required.

SOUTH AFRICA

SIR CHARLES DOUGLAS said that the Union Government were most anxious to take over the responsibility of garrisoning Cape Colony and thereby set free the British troops.

LORD HALDANE said the Secretary of State for the Colonies was averse to the proposal of the Union Government owing to the native problem.

CONTINGENTS FROM THE DOMINIONS

LORD HALDANE said that offers of contingents had been received from Canada, Australia and New Zealand. The most advantageous use to which these contingents could be put would be as reliefs to oversea[s] garrisons. It would not, however, be popular in the Dominions.

THE PRIME MINISTER said that we should accept the offer and should leave it to each Dominion to decide the strength of the contingent which it is prepared to provide. The contingents should not be asked to relieve our oversea[s] garrison, but should be sent to England.

ULSTER

Discussion of the offer of the Ulster Volunteers for service either in Ireland or abroad was postponed.

Conclusions[131]

1. The War Office to make all arrangements for taking up the transports with a view to the embarkation of five divisions. The decision as to what our line of operations should be is postponed.
2. The Chief of the Imperial General Staff to communicate at once with the French War Office with a view to the despatch at the earliest possible [..?...] of a French Staff Officer of high standing to confer in London with the General Staff.
3. The War Office to apply to India for a division to reinforce the garrison of Egypt, and for a general division and a cavalry brigade to be held in readiness.
4. The proposal to withdraw the British troops from South Africa is not approved.
5. The Office to accept the offer of the Dominions to provide contingents, which should be concentrated in England.

TNA, Cab 42/1/4.

(426) 6 August: Minutes of British War Council Meeting

Decision to despatch the Expeditionary Corps to come to Belgium's aid

The Despatch of the Expeditionary Corps

THE PRIME MINISTER said that the Cabinet had decided to-day in principle to despatch the Expeditionary Force.[132] It remained to be decided of what force it should consist and where it should concentrate.

131 The BEF's mobilization already was three days behind that of the French when this war council met at 10 Downing Street to consider Britain's options. There was an immediate challenge to the plans that Henry Wilson and his staff had been designing since 1911. Sir John French, the commander-in-chief of the BEF, argued that the three-day gap between the British and French mobilizations rendered all pre-war plans obsolete, and suggested that the BEF be landed in Antwerp instead of at a French port, something that he had advocated as early as 1911. However, this was dismissed as impractical, as the Royal Navy could not promise to protect an expedition to Antwerp. For French's thinking, see William J. Philpott, 'The Strategic Ideas of Sir John French', *Journal of Strategic Studies* 12, 4 (1989), pp. 458–478. On French, see also Richard Holmes, *The Little Field-Marshal: Sir John French*, J. Cape, London 1981, and George H. Cassar, *The Tragedy of Sir John French*, University of Delaware Press, London 1985.

132 As Asquith informed the King on 6 August, the Cabinet had sanctioned the war council's decision in favour of the 'immediate dispatch of the Expeditionary Force' with little 'demur'. Cited in Prete, 'French Strategic Planning', p. 54.

LORD KITCHENER[133] said that under the prevailing uncertainty of conditions, it was [hardly politic to send more than] four divisions. These divisions should be sent as soon as possible and should be followed when circumstances permitted by a fifth division. The sixth division should be held as part of the force to follow.[134]

PRINCE LOUIS OF BATTENBERG said that the transport required for the troops first to embark would be ready on Friday evening the 7th August.

THE PRIME MINISTER asked if the Navy could guarantee a safe crossing.

MR CHURCHILL said that they could guarantee a passage across the Channel.

GENERAL WILSON said that owing to the interruption of the arrangements which had been worked out by the General Staff there would be a delay of two days before the railway programme could be set in motion. In consequence, the Expeditionary Force could not be concentrated and ready for action for another twenty days. It was necessary that concentration should take place not nearer than three days march from the enemy.

SIR J. FRENCH said that concentration ought not to be further forward than Amiens.

LORD KITCHENER agreed. He added that it was very important to deal with the attitude of Italy. If it were certain that the Italians would be neutral, the six French divisions which were guarding the Italian frontier could be moved up on the left of the French army and so secure our concentration.

SIR E. GREY said that he was certain that the French could uncover the Italian frontier, but he had no information whether they had done so.

SIR J. FRENCH said that he would like to press for five divisions. One

---

133 On 6 August, Kitchener became Secretary of State for War. The post had remained unfilled following Jack Seely's dismissal during the Curragh incident while the Prime Minister had acted as his own Secretary of State for War. See Neilson, 'Great Britain', p. 192–193, also for a discussion of Kitchener's position on 6 August. On the changes to Britain's military strategy which resulted from Kitchener's appointment, see Prete, 'French Strategic Planning', pp. 55 ff.

134 Berthelot recorded France's disappointment at the reduction of British troops for despatch to the Western Front in his diary on 7 August: 'After their hesitation to take up action on our side, and the time lost in deciding on the mobilization of their forces, the British Government reduces their co-operation to 4 infantry divisions and 5 cavalry brigades. [...] What are their second thoughts? And will we be able to count seriously on such allies?' Cited in Prete, 'French Strategic Planning', p. 57.

division was sufficient to secure the country against invasion, and all arrangements made by the General Staff was [*sic*] based on a force comprising five divisions.

GENERAL WILSON said that the programme was made out for five divisions, but the fifth division which was to start on the tenth day of mobilization could be left behind.

THE PRIME MINISTER said that everything was to be said for retaining two divisions. The domestic situation might be grave,[135] and Colonial Troops or Territorials could not be called on to aid the civil power.

LORD KITCHENER said that he attached great importance to the withdrawal of the British troops from South Africa. He understood that the Union Government would undertake to capture German South-West Africa with their own troops.

THE PRIME MINISTER said that the capture of German South-West Africa was not urgent. The War Office should telegraph to Sir James Wolfe Murray to ask how soon he could despatch the troops in South Africa.

LORD KITCHENER said that five or six ships would be required to convey the troops, which did not include the garrison of Cape Town. He would inform the Admiralty directly he heard when the troops would be able to embark. He would like to raise the question whether the garrisons in the Mediterranean could not be relieved by troops from India. There were two divisions under orders from India, and if they could relieve the garrisons in Egypt, Malta, and Gibraltar, there would be eleven divisions available for service on the Continent of Europe.

THE PRIME MINISTER said that the Cabinet was averse to sending native troops too far West, and he felt very strongly that it was undesirable. It had been suggested that the second Division from India should capture Dar-es-Salaam.

LORD KITCHENER said that the Secretary of State for India had informed him that there was an additional brigade available. He suggested that the capture of Dar-es-Salaam should be entrusted to this brigade, and that the Indian Government should make all the necessary arrangements.

SIR E. GREY said that it still remained to be decided what reply should be given to the Enquiry from the Belgian Government regarding the despatch of the Expeditionary Force.

THE PRIME MINISTER said that the Belgian Government should be informed that a force of over 100,000 men would be sent with the least possible delay, and that they would cooperate with the French for the

135 The Cabinet were still concerned about the Ulster question.

assistance of Belgium. He thought it inadvisable to commit ourselves to any more definite plan of operations.
Conclusions:
In accordance with the decisions reached by the Cabinet this morning –

1. The first instalment of the Expeditionary Force should consist of four divisions and the cavalry division.
2. Sir E. Grey to inform the Belgian Government that an Expeditionary Force of over 100,000 men will embark as soon as possible, and will act in concert with the French Army for the assistance of Belgium.
3. The imperial troops (6.000 – 7.000 men) to be brought home from South Africa. The War Office to inform the Admiralty as soon as possible as to the proposed arrangements and the sea-transport required.
4. The Indian Government to find the troops for the capture of Dar-es-Salaam, and they should preferable be distinct from the two divisions to be sent to Egypt.

TNA, Cab, 42/1/3.

(427) 6 August: Paléologue's Memoirs

Austro-Hungarian declaration of war to Russia; Germans advance into Poland

---

This morning my Austro-Hungarian colleague, Szapary, handed Sazonov a declaration of war. This declaration alleged two reasons: (1) the attitude adopted by the Russian Government in the Austro-Serbian dispute; (2) the fact that according to a communication from Berlin, Russia had taken it upon herself to commence hostilities against Germany.

The Germans are entering western Poland. Since the day before yesterday they have occupied Kalisz, Czenstschowa and Bendin.[136] This swift advance shows how wise the Russian General Staff were in 1910 in withdrawing their frontier garrisons and concentration zone a hundred kilometres further east – a step which met with vigorous criticism in France at the time.[137] […]

---

136 German troops had occupied Kalisz on 2 August. For details see Chapter 11, p. 568, n. 91.

137 For details of Russia's Mobilization Schedule 1910, and for Russian war planning, see for example Bruce W. Menning, 'War Planning and Initial Operations in the Russian Context', in Hamilton and Herwig (eds), *War Planning 1914*, pp. 80–142, pp. 115ff.

Maurice Paléologue, *An Ambassador's Memoirs*, Doran, New York 1925, p. 63.

(428) 6 August: Poincaré's Diary

The prospect of last-minute American mediation is discussed – and dismissed

I am warned, in Viviani's and Doumergue's presence, that the United States' ambassador wants to see me. 'That must be', I say, 'for an offer of mediation'. Viviani's face lights up. 'It would be', I add immediately, 'the greatest misfortune which could befall us, if mediation were to be accepted today by Germany. Doubtless the immediate war would not take place; but, as we are not victorious, the peace would not be in our favour, Germany would remain as powerful and we would be exposed, before long, to new threats'. Doumergue backs me up, and also Augagneur, and even Malvy. Messimy energetically supports me. In short, it is agreed that, it if is an offer of mediation which is brought to me, I shall reply:

1 that not being the aggressors, we cannot accept mediation;
2 that we cannot ever do anything other than with the agreement of Russia and England;
3 that there can be no question of mediation after the invasion of a neutral territory.

Herrick brings me this little piece of paper, which is not a firm proposal, but a platonic declaration, and he tells me himself that he thinks, for the present moment, all mediation impossible.[138]

Cited in John Keiger, *Raymond Poincaré*, Cambridge University Press, Cambridge 1997, p. 202.

138 This section is not included in the published diary. See Keiger, *Poincaré*, p. 202, note 23.

Appendix: Documents and their provenance

Document Number and Title	*Reference (full titles in bibliography)*
(1) 16 April 1911: Grey to Asquith	TNA, FO 800/100.
(2) 19 April 1911: Kiderlen-Wächter in conversation with Heinrich Class	Class, *Wider den Strom.* pp. 203–4.
(3) 20 July 1911: Crowe to Bertie	TNA, FO 800/160.
(4) 21 July 1911: Lloyd George's Mansion House Speech	*The Times*, 22 July 1911.
(5) 19 August 1911: Moltke to his wife	Moltke, *Erinnerungen*, p. 362.
(6) 23 August 1911: Minutes of the Committee of Imperial Defence meeting	TNA, Cab 2/2.
(7) 29 August: Wilson to Churchill	TNA, Adm. 116/3474.
(8) 30 August 1911: Churchill to Grey	Churchill, *World Crisis*, I, p. 47.
(9) 3 September 1911: Gebsattel to Kress	BayHSTA-KA, MKr41, Nr.1731.
(10) 8 September 1911: Grey to Asquith	TNA, Grey Papers, FO 800/100.
(11) 4 October 1911: Esher's diary	Esher Papers, ESHR 2/12, Churchill College Archives Centre, Cambridge.
(12) 11 October 1911: Minutes of the French Superior Council of Defence meeting	P.V., C.S.D.N., Séance du 11 octobre 1911, Fonds Messimy, AN 509 AP/5.
(13) October 1911: French assessment of future conflict	Doughty, 'France', p. 144.
(14) 16 November 1911: Asquith to the King	Bodleian Library, Oxford.
(15) 2 December 1911: Moltke to Bethmann Hollweg	BA-MA, BArch RH 61/406.
(16) 13 December 1911: Schlieffen to the editor of *Deutsche Revue*	PA Berlin, R 788.

(**17**) 9 January 1912: French Superior Council of National Defence meeting	C.S.D.N., Séance du 9 janvier 1912, pp. 4–5, AN 509AP/5.
(**18**) 12 January 1912: Goschen to Nicholson	TNA, FO371, 1373, f.116–9.
(**19**) 29 January 1912: Memorandum by Grey, Churchill, and Lloyd George	GP, 31, No. 98.
(**20**) 7 February 1912: Grey to Bertie	BD, VI, No. 499.
(**21**) 8 February 1912: Haldane's diary	BD, VI, No. 506.
(**22**) 8 February 1912: Minute by Crowe	TNA, FO 371/1572.
(**23**) 8 February 1912: Tirpitz to Müller	BA-MA Freiburg, *Nachlass* Tirpitz, N 253/26a.
(**24**) 9 February 1912: Haldane's diary	BD, VI, No. 506.
(**25**) 9 February 1912: Wilhelm II to Ballin	Cited in Röhl, *Wilhelm II.*, vol.3, p. 904.
(**26**) 10 February 1912: Haldane's diary	BD, VI, No. 506.
(**27**) 8–10 February 1912: Bethmann Hollweg's Memoirs	Bethmann Hollweg, *Betrachtungen zum Weltkrieg*, vol.1, pp. 48–53, 56f.
(**28**) 16 February 1912: Bertie's Memorandum	TNA, Bertie Papers, FO 800/188.
(**29**) 21 February 1912: Joffre's account of a secret meeting at the Quai d'Orsay	Joffre, *Memoirs*, I, pp. 49–51.
(**30**) 21 March 1912: Cambon to Paléologue	DDF, 3e série, 2, No. 240.
(**31**) 22 March 1912: Balfour to Churchill	Cited in Langhorne, 'The Naval Question', p. 361.
(**32**) 28 March 1912: Poincaré to Paul Cambon	DDF, 3e série, 2, No. 269.
(**33**) 9 April 1912: Grey to Bertie	BD, VI, No. 569.
(**34**) 10 April 1912: Bertie to Grey	BD, VI, No. 570.
(**35**) 15 April 1912: Nicolson to Grey	Nicolson, *Sir Arthur Nicolson*, pp. 268–269.
(**36**) 11 November 1912: Wilhelm II's Memorandum	GP, 33, No. 12349.
(**37**) 18 November 1912: Kageneck's report from Vienna	PA Berlin, R 8627, *Militär- und Marineangelegenheiten Österreichs*.
(**38**) 22 November 1912: Grey to Paul Cambon	BD, X, No. 416.

(**39**) 22 November 1912: Schemua's report about meeting Moltke and Wilhelm II	Cited in Helmreich, 'An Unpublished Report on Austro-German Military Conversations', pp. 205–207.
(**40**) 23 November 1912: Kokovtsov's account of a meeting between the Tsar and his military advisers	Kokovtsov, *Out of My Past*, pp. 345–6.
(**41**) 25 November 1912: Ludendorff's memorandum	BA-MA, BArch RH 61/996.
(**42**) 2 December 1912: Bethmann Hollweg's Reichstag speech	Stenographische Berichte des Reichstags, 13. Legislaturperiode, vol. 286, 2472.
(**43**) 3 December 1912: Lichnowsky's report from London	GP, 39, No. 15612.
(**44**) 8 December 1912: Admiral von Müller's diary	Cited in Röhl, 'Schwelle', doc. 4.
(**45**) 9 December 1912: Poincaré to George Louis	DDF, 3e série, vol.5, No. 22.
(**46**) 10 December 1912: Claparède's report about a conversation with Wilhelm II	Cited in Cole, 'The Records of the Swiss Embassy in Berlin', pp. 62–3.
(**47**) 15 December 1912: Wenninger to Bavarian Minister of War	Cited in Röhl, 'Schwelle', doc.22.
(**48**) 20 December 1912: Bethmann Hollweg to Eisendecher	Cited in Röhl, 'Schwelle', p. 124.
(**49**) 21 December 1912: Moltke to Bethmann Hollweg	*Kriegsrüstung, Anlagen*, No. 54, pp. 158ff.
(**50**) 31 December 1912: Wilson's Diary	Cited in Callwell, *Field-Marshal Sir Henry Wilson*, p. 121.
(**51**) January 1913: Moltke's memorandum	BA-MA, BArch RH 61/406.
(**52**) January or February 1913: Jagow in conversation with Moltke	PA Berlin, NL Gottlieb von Jagow, vol.8, part I, pp. 48ff.
(**53**) 29 January 1913: Falkenhayn to Hanneken	Cited in Afflerbach, *Falkenhayn*, p. 102.
(**54**) 31 January 1913: Cartwright to Nicolson	BD, IX, II, No. 582.
(**55**) 22 February 1913: San Giuliano's speech to the Chamber of Deputies	Cited in Bosworth, *Italy*, p. 359.
(**56**) 23 February 1913: Otto von Ritter to Hertling	BayHStA, MA 2567.

(**57**) 24 February 1913: Nicolson to Grey	BD, IX, No. 656.
(**58**) 28 April 1913: Jagow to Tschirschky	PA/AA, Botschaft Wien, vol. 6/I.
(**59**) 6 May 1913: Sazonov to Russian Minister in Belgrade Hartwig	Cited in Stieve, *Isvolsky and the World War*, p. 180.
(**60**) 23 May 1913: Cartwright to Nicolson	BD, IX, No. 994.
(**61**) 25 May 1913: Lord Stamfordham's notes of his conversation with Wilhelm II	RA GV/M 450/18.
(**62**) 25 May 1913: Lord Stamfordham's notes of a conversation with Jagow	RA, PS/GV/M 450/18.
(**63**) 12 June 1913: Guillaume to Belgian Government	Cited in Stieve, *Isvolsky and the World War*, p. 169.
(**64**) 15 November 1913: Schoen to Bethmann Hollweg	GP, 39, No. 15657.
(**65**) 22 November 1913: Jules Cambon to Pichon	DDF, 3e série, 8, No. 517.
(**66**) 23 November 1913: Jagow to Wilhelm II; Wilhelm II's marginal note	GP, 38, No. 15452.
(**67**) 24 November 1913: Jules Cambon to Pichon	DDF, 3e série, 8, No. 522.
(**68**) 25 November 1913: O'Beirne to Grey	BD, X, I, No. 379.
(**69**) 27 December 1913: Goschen to Grey	BD, X, I, No. 450.
(**70**) 12 January 1914: Poincaré's conversation with the French journalist Judet	Georges Louis' diary, cited in Hölzle, *Quellen*, p. 178.
(**71**) 21 January 1914: Buchanan to Nicolson	BD, X, II, No. 469.
(**72**) February 1914: P. N. Durnovo, 'Memorandum to Tsar Nicholas II'	Cited in Golder (ed.) *Documents of Russian History*, pp. 12–19.
(**73**) 26 February 1914: Jagow to Lichnowsky	GP, 37/I, No. 14697.
(**74**) 18 March 1914: Buchanan to Grey	BD, X, II, No. 528.
(**75**) 18 March 1914: Buchanan to Nicolson	BD, X, II, No. 529.

(76) 23 March 1914: Carl von Weizsäcker's notes	HStA Stuttgart, NL Weizsäcker, Q 1/18, Bü. 41.
(77) 24 March 1914: Colonel Knox's Memorandum for Henry Wilson	TNA, WO 105/1039.
(78) 30 March 1914: Nicolson to de Bunsen	TNA FO 800/373.
(79) 3 April 1914: Buchanan to Grey	BD, X, II, No. 537.
(80) 4 April 1914: Paléologue to Doumergue	DDF, 3e série, 10, No. 69.
(81) 16 April 1914: Buchanan to Nicolson	BD X, II, No. 538.
(82) 24 April: Goschen to Nicolson	TNA, FO 800/374, cited in Steiner and Nielson, *Britain*, p. 135.
(83) 1 May 1914: Grey to Bertie	BD, X, II, No. 541.
(84) 12 May 1914: Conrad and Moltke meet in Karlsbad	Conrad, *Dienstzeit*, vol.3, pp. 669–673.
(85) 18 May 1914: Waldersee's memorandum 'on Germany's military position'	BA-MA, BArch RH 61/577.
(86) 18 May 1914: Nicolson to Goschen	BD, X, II, No. 510.
(87) 28 May 1914: Sazonov to Benckendorff	Cited in Stieve, *Isvolsky and the World War*, p. 201.
(88) 29 May 1914: Edward House reports from Berlin	House, *Intimate Papers*, vol.I, pp. 254ff.
(89) 31 May 1914: Waldersee to Kageneck	Cited in Kronenbitter, 'Macht der Illusionen', pp. 525–6.
(90) May 1914: Moltke to Bethmann Hollweg	BA-MA, BArch RH 61/577.
(91) May 1914: Pollio in conversation with Zitzewitz	Cited in Wolfgang Foerster, 'Der deutsche und der italienische Generalstab vor dem Weltkriege', pp. 877–8.
(92) May or June 1914: Jagow recalls conversation with Moltke	Cited in Röhl, *From Bismarck to Hitler*, p. 70.
(93) 1 June 1914: Eckardstein's Memoirs	Eckardstein, *Lebenserinnerungen*, vol.III, p. 186.
(94) 4 June 1914: Lerchenfeld to Hertling	Deuerlein, *Briefwechsel*, doc.97.
(95) 11 June 1914: Nicolson to Hardinge	TNA, Nicolson papers, FO 800/374.

(**96**) 16 June 1914: Wenninger to Kress	Bay. HStA Munich, Abt. IV, Mkr. 41.
(**97**) 16 June 1914: Bethmann Hollweg to Lichnowsky	DD, No. 3.
(**98**) 24 June 1914: Pollio to Italian Ministry of War	Cited in Mazzetti, *L'esercito italiano nella triplice alleanza*, pp. 409–12.
(**99**) 24 June 1914: Grey to Goschen	BD, XI, No. 4.
(**100**) 25 June 1914: Grey to Buchanan	BD, XI, No. 5.
(**101**) 26 June 1914: Hoyos to Pallavicini	ÖUA, VIII, No. 9926.
(**102**) 27 June 1914: Bertie Memorandum	TNA, FO 800/171.
(**103**) 28 June: Nicolai's Diary	*Sonderarchiv* Moscow, NL Nicolai, Fond 1414: 1–10.
(**104**) 28 June: Salandra's conversation with San Guiliano	Salandra, *Italy*, p. 18.
(**105**) 29 June 1914: Conrad's conversation with Berchtold	Conrad, *Dienstzeit*, IV, pp. 33–4.
(**106**) 29 June: Bunsen to Grey	BD, XI, No. 21.
(**107**) 30 June 1914: Jovanović to Pašić	*Serbian Blue Book*, No. 2.
(**108**) 30 June: Tschirschky to Bethmann Hollweg	DD, No. 7.
(**109**) 30 June: Bollati to San Giuliano	DDI, 4th series, XII, No. 25.
(**110**) 1 July: Ferry's note about conversation with Serbian Ambassador Vesnić	DDF, 3e série, 10, No. 466.
(**111**) 1 July: Tisza to Franz Joseph	ÖUA, VIII, No. 9978.
(**112**) 2 July: Lichtenau to Vitzthum	Bach, *Gesandtschaftsberichte*, No. 2.
(**113**) 2 July: Dumaine to Viviani	DDF, 3e série, 10, No. 470.
(**114**) 3 July: Leuckart to Carlowitz	Bach, *Gesandtschaftsberichte*, No. 3.
(**115**) 3 July: Rumbold to Grey	BD, XI, No. 26.
(**116**) 3 July 1914: Henderson to Rumbold	Seligmann (ed.), *Naval Intelligence*, doc. 219.
(**117**) 5 July: Matscheko-Memorandum	ÖUA, VIII, No. 9984.
(**118**) 5 July: Conrad's audience with Emperor Franz Joseph in Schönbrunn	Conrad, *Dienstzeit*, IV, 36–38.

(**119**) 5 July: Hoyos' personal account of his 'mission' to London	Cited in Fellner, 'Die "Mission Hoyos"', pp. 311–313.
(**120**) 5 July: Szögyény to Berchtold	ÖUA, VIII, No. 10058.
(**121**) 5 July: Bollati to San Giuliano	DDI, 4th series, XII, No. 78.
(**122**) 5 July: Plessen Diary	Bach, *Gesandtschaftsberichte*, p. 14.
(**123**) 5 July: Falkenhayn to Moltke	DD, 2nd edn, 1927, p.XII.
(**124**) 5 July: Haldane to Grey	Cited in Maurice, *Haldane 1856–1915*, p. 348.
(**125**) 6 July: Hopman to Tirpitz	Berghahn and Deist, 'Kaiserliche Marine', No. 1.
(**126**) 6 July: Berthold Molden's memorandum	Cited in Solomon Wank, 'Desperate Council in Vienna in July 1914', pp. 281–310.
(**127**) 6 July: Wilhelm II in conversation with Krupp von Bohlen und Halbach	Cited in Fischer, *Griff*, p. 51.
(**128**) 6 July: Grey to Rumbold	BD, XI, No. 32.
(**129**) 6 July: Conrad's conversation with Berchtold and Forgách	Conrad, *Dienstzeit*, IV, pp. 39–40.
(**130**) 6 July: Szögyény to Berchtold	ÖUA, VIII, No. 10076.
(**131**) 6 July: Forgách to Tisza	ÖUA, VIII, No. 10091.
(**132**) 7 July: Kageneck to Moltke	Cited in Kronenbitter, 'Macht der Illusionen', pp. 530–531.
(**133**) 7 July: Vesnić to Pašić	*Serbian Blue Book*, No. 13.
(**134**) 7 July: Minutes of the Council of Ministers for Common Affairs	ÖUA, VIII, No. 10118.
(**135**) 7 July: Riezler Diary	Erdmann (ed.), *Kurt Riezler, Tagebücher*, pp. 181–3.
(**136**) 7 July: Nicolson to Grey	Nicolson, *Sir Arthur Nicolson*, pp. 407–8.
(**137**) 7 July: Jovanović to Pašić	*Serbian Blue Book*, No. 17.
(**138**) 8 July: Riezler Diary	Erdmann (ed.), *Kurt Riezler, Tagebücher*, p. 184.
(**139**) 8 July: Berchtold to Tisza	ÖUA, VIII, No. 10145.
(**140**) 8 July: Forgách to Mérey	HHStA, NL Mérey, K.10.
(**141**) 9 July: Hopman to Tirpitz	Berghahn and Deist, 'Kaiserliche Marine', No. 4.
(**142**) 9 July: Soden to Hertling	Deuerlein, *Briefwechsel*, No. 103.
(**143**) 9 July: Lichnowsky to Bethmann Hollweg	DD, No. 30.

(**144**) 10 July: Tschirschky to *Auswärtiges Amt*	DD, No. 29.
(**145**) 10 July: Dumaine to Viviani	DDF, 3e série, 10, No. 493.
(**146**) 11 July: Tschirschky to *Auswärtiges Amt*	DD, 2nd edn, No. 34a.
(**147**) 11 July: Riezler Diary	Erdmann (ed.), *Kurt Riezler, Tagebücher*, pp. 184–5.
(**148**) 12 July: Szögyény to Berchtold	ÖUA, VIII, No. 10215.
(**149**) 13 July: Wiesner to Berchtold	ÖUA, VIII, No. 10252/53.
(**150**) 13 July: Hopman to Tirpitz	Berghahn/Deist, 'Kaiserliche Marine', p. 50.
(**151**) 13 July: Bunsen to Grey	BD, XI, No. 55.
(**152**) 13 July: Crackanthorpe to Grey	BD, XI, No. 62.
(**153**) 14 July: Berchtold to Franz Joseph	ÖUA, VIII, No. 10272.
(**154**) 14 July: Tschirschky to Bethmann Hollweg	DD, No. 50.
(**155**) 14 July: Letter by Pourtalès	PA/AA, R 2062.
(**156**) 15 July: Berchtold to Szögyény	ÖUA, VIII, No. 10276.
(**157**) 15 July: Redlich's Diary	Fellner (ed.), *Das politische Tagebuch Joseph Redlichs*, vol. 1, pp. 237–8.
(**158**) 15 July: Kageneck to Waldersee	BA-MA W-10/50891.
(**159**) 15 July: Dumaine to Viviani	DDF, 3e série, 10, No. 516.
(**160**) 16 July: Memorandum by F. Bertie	TNA, FO 800, 161.
(**161**) 16 July: Bunsen to Grey (1)	BD, XI, No. 50.
(**162**) 16 July: Bunsen to Grey (2)	BD, XI, No. 65.
(**163**) 16 July: Granville to Grey	BD, XI, No. 52.
(**164**) 16 July: San Giuliano to Averna, Bollati, Carlotti and Squitti	DDI, 4th series, XII, No. 272.
(**165**) 17 July: Crackanthorpe to Grey	BD, XI, No. 53.
(**166**) 17 July: Biedermann to Vitzthum	Bach, *Gesandtschaftsberichte*, No. 4.
(**167**) 17 July: Jagow to Tschirschky	DD, No. 61.
(**168**) 17 July: Bunsen to Nicolson	BD, XI, No. 56.
(**169**) 17 July: French military intelligence report	DDF 3e série, X, No. 558.
(**170**) 18 July: Buchanan to Grey	BD, XI, No. 60.
(**171**) 18 July: Schoen to Hertling	DD, 2nd edn, App. IV, No. 2.
(**172**) 18 July: Memorandum of the Russian Ministry for Foreign Affairs	*Int. Bez.* I, 4, 272.

(**173**) 18 July: Stolberg to Jagow	DD, No. 87.
(**174**) 18 July: Granville to Grey	BD, XI, No. 66.
(**175**) 18 July: Rumbold to Grey	BD, XI, No. 63.
(**176**) 18 July: Pašić to Serbian Ministers	Dedijer & Anić (eds), *Dokumenti o spolnoj politici Kraljevine Srbije*, No. 462.
(**177**) 19 July: Minutes of the Austro-Hungarian Joint Council of Ministers meeting	ÖUA, VIII, No. 10393.
(**178**) 19 July: Crackanthorpe to Grey	BD, XI, No. 61.
(**179**) 19 July: French military intelligence report	DDF, 3e série, 11, No. 32.
(**180**) 20 July: Berchtold to Giesl	ÖUA, VIII, No. 10395.
(**181**) 20 July: Riezler Diary	Erdmann (ed.), *Kurt Riezler. Tagebücher*, p. 187.
(**182**) 21 July: Jules Cambon to Bienvenu-Martin (1)	DDF, 3e série, 10, No. 548.
(**183**) 21 July: Lyncker to his wife	Afflerbach, *Wilhelm II*, pp. 125/127.
(**184**) 21 July: Jules Cambon to Bienvenu-Martin (2)	DDF, 3e série, 10, No. 539.
(**185**) 21 July: Poincaré's Diary	Poincaré papers, BNF, Nafr.106026, f.104.
(**186**) 22 July: Cambon to Bienvenu-Martin	DDF, 3e série, X, No. 551.
(**187**) 22 July: Dumaine to Bienvenu-Martin	DDF, 3e série, X, No. 554.
(**188**) 22 July: Bienvenu-Martin to the French Ambassadors at London, St. Petersburg, Vienna, Rome	DDF, 3e série, 10, No. 555.
(**189**) 22 July: Lyncker to his wife	Afflerbach, *Wilhelm II.*, p. 127.
(**190**) 23 July: Paléologue's Memoirs	Paléologue, *Memoirs*, pp. 27–28.
(**191**) 23 July: Giesl to Berchtold	ÖUA, VIII, No. 10526.
(**192**) 23 July: Lyncker to his wife	Afflerbach, *Wilhelm II*, p. 128
(**193**) 23 July: Hoyos to Haldane	Maurice, *Haldane 1856–1915*, pp. 349–52.
(**194**) 23 July: Fascotti to San Giuliano	DDI, 4th series, XII, No. 443.
(**195**) 24 July: Otto von Ritter to Hertling	BayHStA, GPS 918 and MA2568.
(**196**) 24 July: San Giuliano to Bollati and Varna	DDI, 4th series, XII, No. 488.

(**197**) 24 July: Flotow to Jagow	DD, Nos 156 and 168.
(**198**) 24 July: Churchill remembers the arrival of the ultimatum	Churchill, *World Crisis*, I, pp. 154–5.
(**199**) 24 July: Viviani to Bienvenu-Martin	DDF, 3e série, 11, No. 1.
(**200**) 24 July: Sazonov to Strandtmann	*Int. Bez*, I, 5, 22.
(**201**) 24 July: Memorandum of the day of the Russian Ministry for Foreign Affairs	*Int. Bez.*, I, 5, 25.
(**202**) 24 July: Buchanan to Grey	BD, XI, No. 101.
(**203**) 24 July: Paléologue to Bienvenu-Martin	DDF, 3e serié, 11, No. 21.
(**204**) 24 July: Paul Cambon to Bienvenu-Martin	DDF, 3e série, 11, No. 23.
(**205**) 24 July: Joseph Redlich's diary	Fellner, *Schicksalsjahre*, pp. 238–9.
(**206**) 24 July: Russian Council of Ministers meeting	*Int. Bez.*, I, 5, No. 19.
(**207**) 24 July: A.V. Krivoshein's summary of Russian Council of Ministers meeting of 24 July 1914	Cited in Lieven, *Russia*, pp. 142–3.
(**208**) 24 July: Peter Bark's account of his meeting with Tsar Nicholas II	Cited in Lieven, *Nicholas II*, pp. 199–200.
(**209**) 25 July: Cambon to Bienvenu-Martin	DDF, 3e série, 11, No. 33.
(**210**) 25 July: Cambon to Bienvenu-Martin	DDF, 3e série, 11, No. 60.
(**211**) 25 July: Theodor Wolff's Diary	Sösemann (ed.), *Theodor Wolff*, No. 3.
(**212**) 25 July: Bienvenu-Martin to Dumaine	DDF, 3e série, 11, No. 36.
(**213**) 25 July: Cambon to Bienvenu-Martin	DDF, 3e série, 11, No. 45.
(**214**) 25 July: de Fleuriau to Bienvenu-Martin	DDF, 3e série, 11, No. 46.
(**215**) 25 July: Special Journal of the Russian Council of Ministers	*Int. Bez.*, I, 5, No. 42.
(**216**) 25 July: Pourtalès to Sasonov	*Int. Bez.*, I, 5, No. 46.
(**217**) 25 July: Draft report of the Russian Foreign Minister for Nicholas II	*Int. Bez.*, No. 47.
(**218**) 25 July: Sazonov to Benckendorff	*Int. Bez.*, I, 5, No. 48.

(**219**) 25 July: Sazonov to Strandtmann and Benckendorff	*Int. Bez.*, I, 5, No. 49.
(**220**) 25 July: Grey to Buchanan	BD, XI, No. 132.
(**221**) 25 July: Benckendorff to Sazonov (1)	*Int. Bez.*, I, 5, No 55.
(**222**) 25 July: Benckendorff to Sazonov (2)	*Int. Bez.* I, 5, No. 56.
(**223**) 25 July: Bronevski to Sazonov	*Int. Bez.* I, 5, No. 63.
(**224**) 25 July: Grey to Rumbold	BD, XI, No. 116.
(**225**) 25 July: Szögyény to Berchtold	ÖUA, VIII, No. 10656.
(**226**) 25 July: Tisza's report to Kaiser Franz Joseph	ÖUA, VIII, No. 10708.
(**227**) 25 July: Serbian Government to Giesl	ÖUA, VIII, No. 10648.
(**228**) 25 July: Czernin to Berchtold	ÖUA, VIII, No. 10662.
(**229**) 25 July: Journal of the Russian General Staff Committee	*Int. Bez.* I, 5, No. 79.
(**230**) 25 July: Szögyény to Berchtold (2)	ÖUA, VIII, No. 10655.
(**231**) 25 July: Lyncker to his wife	Afflerbach, *Wilhelm II.*, pp. 128–9.
(**232**) 26 July: Lothar Freiherr von Ritter to Herling	Dirr (ed.), *Bayerische Dokumente*, No. 31.
(**233**) 26 July: Otto Freiherr von Ritter to Hertling	BayHStA, MA 2568.
(**234**) 26 July: Benckendorff to Sazonov	*Int. Bez.*, I, 5, No. 91.
(**235**) 26 July: Captain Berens to Chief of Russian General Staff Russin	*Int. Bez,* I, 5, No. 99.
(**236**) 26 July: Grey to Missions in Paris, Vienna, St Petersburg, Niš, Berlin and Rome	BD, XI, No. 140.
(**237**) 26 July: Nicolson to Grey	BD, XI, No. 144.
(**238**) 26 July: Henry Wilson's Diary	Cited in Callwell, *Field-Marshal Sir Henry Wilson*, vol.1, pp. 151–2.
(**239**) 26 July: Bronevski to Sazonov	*Int. Bez.*, I, 5, No. 96.
(**240**) 26 July: San Giuliano to Salandra	DDI, 4th series, XII, No. 560.
(**241**) 26 July: Berchtold to Kral	ÖUA, VIII, No. 10728.
(**242**) 26 July: Szécsen to Berchtold	ÖUA, VIII, No. 10740.
(**243**) 26 July: Szápáry to Berchtold	ÖUA, VIII, No. 10835.
(**244**) 26 July: Messimy's Diary	Messimy, *Mes Souvenirs*, pp. 131–5.

(**245**) 26 July: Berthelot's note for Bienvenu-Martin	DDF, 3e série, 11, No. 109.
(**246**) 26 July: Paléologue to Bienvenu-Martin	DDF, 3e série, 11, No. 89.
(**247**) 26 July: Carlotti to San Giuliano	DDI, 4th series, XII, No. 537.
(**248**) 26 July: Bunsen to Grey (1)	BD, XI, No. 150.
(**249**) 26 July: Bunsen to Grey (2)	BD, XI, No. 166.
(**250**) 26 July: King George's record of his conversation with Prince Henry	Cited in Nicolson, *King George V*, p. 327.
(**251**) 27 July: Lichnowsky to Jagow	DD, No. 258.
(**252**) 27 July: Pourtalés to Jagow	DD, No. 242.
(**253**) 27 July: Bertie to Grey	BD, XI, No. 183
(**254**) 27 July: Goschen to Grey	BD, XI, No. 185.
(**255**) 27 July: Rodd to Grey	BD, XI, No. 202.
(**256**) 27 July: Bunsen to Grey	BD, XI, No. 175
(**257**) 27 July: Grey to Goschen	BD, XI, No. 176.
(**258**) 27 July: Grey addresses the House of Commons	BD, XI, No. 190.
(**259**) 27 July: British Cabinet Meeting, Viscount Morley's account	Morley, *Memorandum on Resignation*, pp. 11–4; 6.
(**260**) 27 July: Szögyény to Berchtold	ÖUA, VIII, No. 10793.
(**261**) 27 July: Viviani to Bienvenu-Martin	DDF, 3e série, 11, No. 127.
(**262**) 27 July: Joffre's Memoirs	Joffre, *Memoirs*, I, pp. 117–8.
(**263**) 27 July: Messimy's Diary	Messimy, *Mes Souvenirs*, pp. 135.
(**264**) 27 July: Sazonov to Russian Embassies	*Int. Bez.*, I, 5, No. 119.
(**265**) 27 July: Paŝić's Minute	*DSP*, No. 588, cited in Cornwall, 'Serbia', p. 83.
(**266**) 27 July: Plessen's Diary	Bach, *Gesandtschaftsberichte*, p. 22.
(**267**) 27 July: Admiral von Müller's diary	Cited in Röhl, 'Admiral von Müller', p. 669.
(**268**) 27 July: Berchtold to Ambassadors in St. Petersburg and Rome	ÖUA, VIII, No. 10834.
(**269**) 28 July: Sazonov to Benckendorff (1)	*Int. Bez.*, I, 5, No. 164.
(**270**) 28 July: Sazonov to Benckendorff (2)	*Int. Bez.*, I, 5, No. 167.

(**271**) 28 July: Sazonov to Bronevski	*Int. Bez.* I, 5, 168.
(**272**) 28 July: Daily record of the Ministry of Foreign Affairs	*Int. Bez.* I, 5, No. 172.
(**273**) 28 July: Benckendorff to Sazonov	*Int. Bez.* I, 5, No. 174.
(**274**) 28 July: Ignatjev to the Russian General Staff	*Int. Bez.*, I, 5, No. 180.
(**275**) 28 July: Bronevski to Sazonov	*Int. Bez.*, I, 5, No. 185.
(**276**) 28 July: Plessen's diary	Afflerbach, *Wilhelm II.*, p. 642.
(**277**) 28 July: Wilhelm II to Jagow	DD, No. 293.
(**278**) 28 July: Lichowsky to Jagow	DD, No. 301.
(**279**) 28 July: Joffre's Memoirs	Joffre, *Memoirs*, I, pp. 118–9.
(**280**) 28 July: Dobrorolski's memoirs	Dobrorolski, 'La mobilisation de l'Armée russe en 1914', p. 145.
(**281**) 28 July: Prince Henry to Wilhelm II	DD, No. 374.
(**282**) 28 July: Müller's Diary	Görlitz, *The Kaiser and his Court, 1914–1918*, p. 36.
(**283**) 28 July: Moltke's memorandum about the political situation	DD, No. 349.
(**284**) 28 July: Berchtold to Szögyény	ÖUA, VIII, No. 10863.
(**285**) 28 July: Wilhelm II to Nicholas II	DD, No. 335.
(**286**) 29 July: Nicholas II to Wilhelm II	DD, No. 332.
(**287**) 29 July: Bethmann Hollweg to Pourtalés	DD, No. 342.
(**288**) 29 July: Wilhelm II to Nicholas II	DD, No. 359.
(**289**) 29 July: Nicholas II to Wilhelm II	DD, No. 366.
(**290**) 29 July: Sazonov to Isvolsky	*Int. Bez.* I, 5, No. 221.
(**291**) 29 July: Memorandum of the day of the Russian Ministry for Foreign Affairs	*Int. Bez.* I, 5, No. 224.
(**292**) 29 July: Falkenhayn's Diary	BA-MA, BArch RH 61/927.
(**293**) 29 July: Benckendorff to Sazonov	*Int. Bez*, I, 5, No. 228.
(**294**) 29 July: Pease's Diary	Wilson, 'The Cabinet Diary of J.A.Pease, pp. 43–45.
(**295**) 29 July: Wilson's Diary	Cited in Callwell, *Field-Marshal Sir Henry Wilson*, vol.1, p. 152.
(**296**) 29 July: Lichnowsky to Jagow, with marginal notes by Wilhelm II	DD, No. 368.
(**297**) 29 July: Szögyény to Berchtold	ÖUA, VIII, No. 10950.
(**298**) 29 July: Mérey to Berchtold	ÖUA, VIII, No. 10989.

(**299**) 29 July: Poincaré's diary	Poincaré papers, BNF, Nafr. 16027, fol.130, cited in Schmidt, *Frankreichs Außenpolitik*, p. 315.
(**300**) 29 July: Paléologue's memoirs	Paléologue, *Memoirs*, pp. 41–43.
(**301**) 29 July: Goschen to Grey	BD, XI, No. 293.
(**302**) 29 July: Jagow to Below	DD, No. 375.
(**303**) 30 July: Joffre's Memoirs	Joffre, *Memoirs*, I, pp. 122–3.
(**304**) 30 July: Sazonov to Sverbejev	*Int. Bez.* I, 5, No. 277.
(**305**) 30 July: Daily record of Russian Foreign Ministry	*Int. Bez.* 1, 5, 284.
(**306**) 30 July: Isvolsky to Sazonov	*Int. Bez*, I, 5, No. 291.
(**307**) 30 July: Abel Ferry's notes about the meeting of the French Council of Ministers	Cited in Keiger, *Poincaré*, p. 175.
(**308**) 30 July: Viviani to Paléologue and Paul Cambon	DDF, 3e serie, vol.11, No. 305.
(**309**) 30 July: Asquith to King George V	TNA, CAB 41/35.
(**310**) 30 July: King George V to Prince Henry of Prussia	ÖUA, VIII, No. 11135.
(**311**) 30 July: Henry Wilson's diary	Cited in Callwell, *Field-Marshal Sir Henry Wilson*, vol.1, p. 152.
(**312**) 30 July: Pourtalès to Jagow	DD, No. 421.
(**313**) 30 July: Nicholas II to Wilhelm II	DD, No. 390; Geiss, *July 1914*, No. 132.
(**314**) 30 July: Wilhelm II to Nicholas II	DD, No. 420.
(**315**) 30 July: Ignatjev to the department of the General Quartermaster of the Russian General Staff	*Int. Bez*, I, 5, No. 293.
(**316**) 30 July: Bethmann Hollweg to Tschirschky	DD, No. 395.
(**317**) 30 July: Kageneck to Waldersee	Cited in Kronenbitter, 'Macht der Illusionen', pp. 539–541.
(**318**) 30 July: Moltke to Conrad	Cited in Baumgart, *Julikrise*, No. 132.
(**319**) 30 July: Nicolai's Diary	Special Archive Moscow, Nicolai Papers, Fond 1414: 1–10.
(**320**) 30 July: Redlich's Diary	Fellner (ed.), *Das politische Tagebuch Josef Redlichs*, vol. 2, pp. 43–44.

(**321**) 30 July: Conrad's audience with Emperor Franz Joseph	Conrad, *Dienstzeit*, IV, pp. 150–1.
(**322**) 30 July: Pourtalés to Jagow	DD, No. 401.
(**323**) 30 July: Falkenhayn's diary	BA-MA, BArch RH 61/927.
(**324**) 30 July: Moltke in conversation with Haeften	BA-MA, N35/1, pp. 26–7.
(**325**) 30 July: Fleischmann to Austro-Hungarian General Staff	Cited in Conrad, *Dienstzeit*, IV, p. 152.
(**326**) 30 July: Flotow to Jagow	DD, No. 419.
(**327**) 30 July: Dobrorolsky's diary	Cited in Albertini, *Origins*, vol.2, p. 557.
(**328**) 30 July: Rodzianko's Memoirs	Rodzianko, *Erinnerungen*, pp. 96–97.
(**329**) 30 July: Basily's Memoirs	Basily, *Diplomat of Imperial Russia*, pp. 98–99.
(**330**) 30 July: Paléologue's Memoirs	Paléologue, *Memoirs*, pp. 43–46.
(**331**) 30 July: Grey to Goschen	BD, XI, No. 303.
(**332**) 30 July: Guillaume to Davignon	Geiss, *Julikrise*, II, pp. 734–5.
(**333**) 31 July: Joint Ministerial Council meeting in Vienna	ÖUA, VIII, No. 11203.
(**334**) 31 July: Grey to Barclay	BD, XI, No. 370.
(**335**) 31 July: Wilhelm II to King of Italy	DD, No. 530.
(**336**) 31 July: Flotow to Jagow	DD, No. 534.
(**337**) 31 July: Viviani to Paul Cambon	DDF, 3e série, 11, No. 390.
(**338**) 31 July: Joffre's Memorandum for Messimy	DDF, 3e série, 11, No. 401.
(**339**) 31 July: Berthelot's note of a conversation with Szecsen	Cited in Poincaré, *Memoirs*, pp. 259–60.
(**340**) 31 July: Bethmann Hollweg to Schoen	DD No. 491.
(**341**) 31 July: Lyncker's diary	Geiss, *Julikrise*, vol.2, No. 889.
(**342**) 31 July: Lerchenfeld to Hertling (1)	*Bay. Dok*, No. 67.
(**343**) 31 July: Schoen to Jagow	DD, No. 528.
(**344**) 31 July: Viviani to Paléologue	Poincaré, *Memoirs*, pp. 252–3.
(**345**) 31 July: Lerchenfeld to Hertling (2)	*Bay. Dok*. No. 71.
(**346**) 31 July: Nicholas II to Wilhelm II	*Int. Bez.* 1, 5, 338.
(**347**) 31 July: Wilhelm II to Nicholas II	*Int. Bez.* 1, 5, 357.
(**348**) 31 July: Daily record of the Russian Ministry for Foreign Affairs	*Int. Bez.* 1, 5, 349.

(**349**) 31 July: Paléologue to Viviani	DDF, 3e série, 11, No. 432.
(**350**) 31 July: Paléologue's Diary	Paléologue, *Memoirs*, pp. 46–48.
(**351**) 31 July: Falkenhayn's Diary	BA-MA, BArch RH 61/927.
(**352**) 31 July: Davignon to Belgian Ministers at Berlin, Paris and London	*Collected Diplomatic Documents*, p. 304.
(**353**) 31 July: Wilhelm II to Franz Joseph	DD, No. 503.
(**354**) 31 July: Wilson's diary	Cited in Callwell, *Field-Marshal Sir Henry Wilson*, vol.1, pp. 152–3.
(**355**) 31 July: Grey to Bertie (1)	BD, XI, No. 348.
(**356**) 31 July: Grey to Bertie (2)	BD, XI, No. 352.
(**357**) 31 July: Communication from German Embassy to British Government	BD, XI, No. 372.
(**358**) 31 July: Bertie to Grey	BD, XI, No. 382.
(**359**) 31 July: Goschen to Grey	BD, XI, No. 383.
(**360**) 31 July: Kageneck to Waldersee	Kronenbitter, 'Macht der Illusionen', p. 541.
(**361**) 31 July: Crowe to Grey	BD, XI, No. 369.
(**362**) 1 August: Isvolsky to Sazonov	Cited in Schumann, *War and Diplomacy*, p. 240.
(**363**) 1 August 1914: Moltke's Memoirs	Moltke (ed.), *Erinnerungen*, p. 21.
(**364**) 1 August: Wenninger to Bavarian Minister of War	BHST-MA, MKr 1765.
(**365**) 1 August: George V to Nicholas II	*Int. Bez*, No 397; BD, XI, No. 384.
(**366**) 1 August: Grey to Bertie	BD, XI, No. 419.
(**367**) 1 August: Müller's Diary	Röhl, 'Admiral von Müller', p. 670.
(**368**) 1 August: Isvolsky to Sazonov	*Int. Bez.*, No. 412.
(**369**) 1 August: Krupenski to Sazonov	*Int. Bez.*, No. 414.
(**370**) 1 August: Lichnowsky to Jagow	DD, No. 562.
(**371**) 1 August: Lichnowsky to Jagow (2)	DD, No. 570.
(**372**) 1 August: Lyncker's Diary	Cited in Geiss, *Julikrise*, vol. 2, doc.1000b.
(**373**) 1 August: Müller's Diary	Müller, *Regierte der Kaiser?*, pp. 38ff.
(**374**) 1 August: Wilhelm II to King George V	DD, No. 575.

(375) 1 August: Lichnowsky to Jagow (3)	DD, No. 596.
(376) 1 August: Franz Joseph I to Wilhelm II	ÖUA, VIII, No. 11204.
(377) 1 August: Poincaré's Diary	Cited in Keiger, *Poincaré*, pp. 179, 182.
(378) 1 August: Messimy to French Military High Command	Cited in Keiger, *Poincaré*, p. 181.
(379) 1 August: Joffre's note	DDF, 3e série, 11, No. 473.
(380) 1 August: Paléologue's memoirs	Paléologue, *Memoirs*, vol. I, pp. 48–49.
(381) 1 August: Schoen to Jagow	DD, No. 571.
(382) 1 August: Davignon to Belgian Ministers at Berlin, Paris, and London	*Belgian Grey Book*, No. 15.
(383) 2 August: Wenninger to Bavarian Minister of War Kress	*Bay. Dok.*, Ergänzungen und Nachträge, No. 13.
(384) 2 August: San Giuliano to Avarna	DDI, 5th Series, I, No. 2.
(385) 2 August: Villiers to Grey	BD, XI, No. 476.
(386) 2 August: Note from the German to the Belgian Government	DD, No. 376.
(387) 2 August: Bonar Law to Asquith	Cited in McDonough, *The Conservative Party*, p. 133.
(388) 2 August: Grey to Bertie	BD, XI, No. 487.
(389) 2 August: Runciman's account of morning Cabinet Meeting	Cited in Wilson, 'The British Cabinet's Decision for War, 2 August 1914', p. 152.
(390) 2 August: Goschen to Grey	BD, XI, No. 477.
(391) 2 August: French Embassy to British Foreign Office	BD, XI, No. 486.
(392) 2 August: Jagow to Envoys in Brussels, The Hague and Ambassador in London	DD, No. 677.
(393) 2 August: Jagow to Below	DD, No. 682.
(394) 2 August: Joffre's Orders to the Commanding Generals of the 2nd, 6th, 20th, 21st, 7th Corps and the Cavalry Corps	DDF, 3e série, 11, No. 594.
(395) 2 August: Paléologue's Memoirs	Paléologue, *Memoirs*, vol. I, p. 50.
(396) 2 August: Jagow to Flotow	DD, No. 664.
(397) 2 August: Treutler to Bethmann Hollweg	DD, No. 758.

(398) 2 August: Moltke to Jagow	DD, No. 662.
(399) 2 August: Broqueville's statement in the Belgian Crown Council meeting	Cited in Albertini, *Origins*, III, p. 458.
(400) 3 August: Szögyény to Berchtold	*Die österreichisch-ungarischen Dokumente zum Kriegsausbruch*, No. 114.
(401) 3 August: Grey's statement in the House of Commons (and response by Ramsay MacDonald)	Hansard, House of Commons Debates, 3 August 1914, vol. 65, cc1809–42.
(402) 3 August: Klobukowski to Viviani	DDF, 3e série, 11, No. 680.
(403) 3 August: Poincaré's Diary (1)	Cited in Keiger, *Poincaré*, pp. 184, 186.
(404) 3 August: Schoen to Viviani	DD, No. 734.
(405) 3 August: Poincaré's Diary (2)	Cited in Keiger, *Poincaré*, p. 186.
(406) 3 August: Below to Jagow (Belgian Government to German Government)	DD, No. 779.
(407) 3 August: Benckendorff to Sazonov	*Int. Bez.*, I, 5, No. 486.
(408) 3 August: Goschen to Grey	BD, XI, No. 553.
(409) 3 August: Moltke to Jagow	DD, No. 788.
(410) 3 August: San Giuliano to all Ambassadors, Envoys and Diplomatic Agents	DDI, 5th Series, I, No. 30.
(411) 4 August: Maier, Russian Military Attaché in Belgium and the Netherlands, to the department of the Quartermaster-General of the Russian General Staff	*Int. Bez.*, I, 5, No. 545.
(412) 4 August: Moltke to Jagow	DD, No. 804.
(413) 4 August: Haig to Haldane	National Library of Scotland, Haldane Papers, MS5910.
(414) 4 August: Joffre's Memoirs	Joffre, *Memoirs*, I, pp. 135–6.
(415) 4 August: Paléologue's Memoirs	Paléologue, *Memoirs*, pp. 57–58.
(416) 4 August: Bethmann Hollweg's Reichstag's speech	*Verhandlungen des Reichstags*, vol.306, 1914/16, pp. 55–7.
(417) 4 August: Grey to Goschen	BD, XI, No. 573 (a).
(418) 4 August: Grey to Goschen	BD, XI, No. 594.
(419) 4 August: Goschen's account of his final meeting with Bethmann Hollweg	BD, XI, No. 671.

(**420**) 5 August: Lerchenfeld to Hertling	Deuerlein, *Briefwechsel*, No. 119.
(**421**) 5 August: Szögyény to Berchtold	*Die österreichisch-ungarischen Dokumente zum Kriegsausbruch*, No. 137.
(**422**) 5 August: Berchtold's memorandum for an audience with Kaiser Franz Joseph	*Die österreichisch-ungarischen Dokumente zum Kriegsausbruch*, No. 147.
(**423**) 5 August: Giolitti to San Giuliano	Giolitti, *Memoirs*, pp. 380–381.
(**424**) 5 August: Pease's Diary	Wilson, 'The Cabinet Diary of J.A. Pease, 24 July – 5 August 1914', pp. 41–51, pp. 49–50.
(**425**) 5 August: Minutes of British War Council Meeting	TNA, Cab 42/1/4.
(**426**) 6 August: Minutes of British War Council Meeting	TNA, CAB, 42/1/3.
(**427**) 6 August: Paléologue's Memoirs	Paléologue, *Memoirs*, p. 63.
(**428**) 6 August: Poincaré's Diary	Cited in Keiger, *Poincaré*, p. 202.

Bibliography

Afflerbach, Holger, *Falkenhayn. Politisches Denken und Handeln im Kaiserreich*, Oldenbourg, Munich 1994

Afflerbach, Holger, *Der Dreibund: Europäische Großmacht- und Allianzpolitik vor dem Ersten Weltkrieg*, Böhlau, Munich 2003

Afflerbach, Holger, *Kaiser Wilhelm II. als oberster Kriegsherr im Ersten Weltkrieg: Quellen aus der militärischen Umgebung des Kaisers 1914–1918*, Oldenbourg, Munich 2005

Afflerbach, Holger and Stevenson, David (eds), *An Improbable War? The Outbreak of World War I and European Political Culture before 1914*, Berghahn Books, New York 2007

Aksakal, Mustafa, *The Ottoman Road to War in 1914. The Ottoman Empire and the First World War*, Cambridge University Press, Cambridge 2008

Albertini, Luigi, *The Origins of the War of 1914*, 3 vols, Engl. transl., Oxford University Press, Oxford 1952–57 (reprint: Enigma, New York 2005)

Alff, Wilhelm (ed.), *Deutschlands Sonderung von Europa, 1862–1945*, Peter Lang, Frankfurt am Main, Bern, New York 1984

Allain, J.-C., *Agadir 1911: Une crise impérialiste en Europe pour la conquête du Maroc*, Université de Paris I Panthéon-Sorbonne, coll. 'Publications de la Sorbonne', 'série internationale' No. 7, Paris 1976

Angelow, Jürgen, 'Vom 'Bündnis' zum 'Block'. Struktur, Forschungsstand und Problemlage einer Geschichte des Zweibundes 1879–1914', *Militärgeschichtliche Mitteilungen*, 54, 1995, pp. 129–170

Angelow, Jürgen, *Kalkül und Prestige. Der Zweibund am Vorabend des Ersten Weltkrieges*, Böhlau, Cologne, Weimar, Vienna 2000

Angelow, Jürgen, *Der Weg in die Urkastrophe. Der Zerfall des alten Europa 1900–1914*, Be.bra Verlag, Berlin 2010

Asquith, Herbert H., *The Genesis of the War*, Cassell and Co., London, New York et al. 1923

Bach, August (ed.), *Deutsche Gesandtschaftsberichte zum Kriegsausbruch*, Quaderverlag, Berlin 1937

Baraclough, Geoffrey, *From Agadir to Armageddon. Anatomy of a Crisis*, London 1982

Barlow, Ima Christina, *The Agadir Crisis*, University of North Carolina Press, Chapel Hill 1940, reprint 1971

Barros, Andrew and Frédéric Guelton, 'Les imprévus de l'histoire instrumentalisée: le livre jaune de 1914 et les Documents Français sur les Origines de la Grande Guerre, 1914–1918', *Revue d'histoire diplomatique*, 1, 2006, pp. 3–22.

Basily, Nicolas de, *Diplomat of Imperial Russia, 1903–1917: Memoirs*, Hoover Institution Press, Stanford University, Stanford, CA 1977

Bauer, Max, *Der große Krieg in Feld und Heimat, Erinnerungen und Betrachtungen*, Tübingen 1921

Baumgart, Winfried, *Quellenkunde zur deutschen Geschichte der Neuzeit von 1500 bis zur Gegenwart*, Vol. 5: *Das Zeitalter des Imperialismus und des ersten Weltkrieges (1871–1918)*, Part 1: *Akten und Urkunden*; Part 2: *Persönliche Quellen*, Wissenschaftliche Buchgesellschaft, Darmstadt 1977, 2nd edn 1991

Baumgart, Winfried, *Die Julikrise und der Ausbruch des Ersten Weltkrieges 1914. Auf der Grundlage der von Erwin Hölzle hrsg. 'Quellen zur Entstehung des Ersten Weltkrieges. Internationale Dokumente 1901–1914' für den Studiengebrauch bearbeitet von Winfried Baumgart.* Wissenschaftliche Buchgesellschaft, Darmstadt 1983

Bayern, Kronprinz Rupprecht von, *In Treue fest. Mein Kriegstagebuch*, ed. Eugen von Frauenholz, 3 vols, Deutscher Nationalverlag, Munich 1929

Behnen, Michael, *Quellen zur deutschen Außenpolitik im Zeitalter des Imperialismus, 1890–1911*, Wissenschaftliche Buchgesellschaft, Darmstadt 1977

Bergh, Max van den, *Das deutsche Heer vor dem Weltkriege*, Sanssouci Verlag, Berlin 1934

Berghahn, Volker R., 'Zu den Zielen des deutschen Flottenbaus unter Wilhelm II.', *Historische Zeitschrift*, 210, 1970, pp. 34–100

Berghahn, Volker R., *Der Tirpitzplan. Genesis und Verfall einer innenpolitischen Krisenstrategie unter Wilhelm II.*, Düsseldorf 1971

Berghahn, Volker R., *Germany and the Approach of War in 1914*, Macmillan, London 1973

Berghahn, Volker R., *Imperial Germany 1871–1914. Economy, Society, Culture and Politics*, Berghahn, Oxford 1994, 2nd edn 2005

Berghahn, Volker R. and Wilhelm Deist, 'Kaiserliche Marine und Kriegsausbruch 1914. Neue Dokumente zur Juli-Krise', *Militärgeschichtliche Mitteilungen*, 4, 1970, pp. 37–58

Berghahn, Volker R. and Wilhelm Deist (eds), *Rüstung im Zeichen wilhelminischer Weltpolitik. Grundlegende Dokumente 1890–1914*, Droste, Düsseldorf 1988

Bergsträsser, Ludwig, 'Die diplomatischen Kämpfe vor Kriegsausbruch. Eine kritische Studie auf Grund der offiziellen Veröffentlichungen aller beteiligten Staaten', *Historische Zeitschrift*, 114, 1915, pp. 489–592

Bestuzhev, I.V., 'Russian Foreign Policy, February to June 1914', *Journal of Contemporary History*, 1, 3, July 1966, pp. 93–112

Bethmann Hollweg, Theobald von, *Betrachtungen zum Weltkrieg*, 2 vols, Vol.1, *Vor dem Kriege*, Hobbin, Berlin 1919

Bihl, Wolfdieter (ed.), *Deutsche Quellen zur Geschichte des Ersten Weltkrieges*, Wissenschaftliche Buchgesellschaft, Darmstadt 1991

Bittner, Ludwig, Alfred T. Pribram et al. (eds), *Österreich-Ungarns Aussenpolitik von der bosnischen Krise bis zum Kriegsausbruch 1914*, 9 vols, Österreichische Bundesanstalt für Unterricht, Wissenschaft und Kultur, Vienna and Leipzig 1930

Blänsdorf, Agnes, 'Der Weg der Riezler-Tagebücher. Zur Kontroverse über die Echtheit der Tagebücher Kurt Riezlers', *Geschichte in Wissenschaft und Unterricht*, 35, 1984, pp. 651–684

Blinkley, Robert C., 'New Light on Russia's War Guilt', *Current History*, 23, 4, January 1926, pp. 531–533

Boghitschewitsch, Milos (ed.), *Die auswärtige Politik Serbiens 1903–1914*, 3 vols, Brückenverlag, Berlin 1928–1931

Bosworth, Richard J.B., *Italy, the Least of the Great Powers: Italian Foreign Policy before the First World War*, Cambridge University Press, Cambridge, New York et al. 1979

Bosworth, Richard J.B., *Italy and the Origins of the First World War*, Macmillan, London 1983

Brock, Michael and Eleanor Brock (eds), *H.H. Asquith: Letters to Venetia Stanley*, Oxford University Press, Oxford, New York 1985

Bülow, Bernhard Fürst von, *Denkwürdigkeiten*, 4 vols, Ullstein, Berlin 1930f

Burkardt, Johannes et al. (eds), *Lange und kurze Wege in den Ersten Weltkrieg. Vier Beiträge zur Kriegsursachenforschungen*, Ernst Vögel, Munich 1996

Burz, Ulfried, 'Austria and the Great War. Official Publications in the 1920s and 1930s' in Keith M. Wilson (ed.), *Forging the Collective Memory. Governments and International Historians through two World Wars*, Berghahn, Providence, RI and Oxford 1996, pp. 178–191.

Caillaux, Joseph, *Mes Mémoires*, Plon, Paris 1947

Callwell, Charles E., *Field-Marshal Sir Henry Wilson: His Life and Diaries*, 2 vols, Cassell, London 1927

Cassar, George H., *The Tragedy of Sir John French*, University of Delaware Press, London 1985

Churchill, Winston S., *The World Crisis, 1911–1918*, 2 vols, Odhams Press, London 1938

Cimbala, Stephen J., 'Steering Through Rapids: Russian Mobilization and World War I', *The Journal of Slavic Military History*, 9, 2, 1996, pp. 376–398

Clark, Christopher, *The Sleepwalkers. How Europe went to War in 1914*, Allen Lane, London 2012

Class, Heinrich, *Wider den Strom. Vom Werden und Wachsen der nationalen Opposition im alten Reich*, Koehler, Leipzig 1932

Cole, Terence F., 'German Decision-Making on the Eve of the First World War. The Records of the Swiss Embassy in Berlin', in John Röhl (ed.), *Der Ort Kaiser Wilhelm II. in der deutschen Geschichte*, Munich 1991, pp. 53–76

Collected Diplomatic Documents Relating to the Outbreak of the European War, HMSO, London 1915

Conrad von Hötzendorf, Franz, *Aus meiner Dienstzeit, 1906–1918*, 5 vols, Rikola Verlag, Vienna, Leipzig, Munich 1922–1925

Conrad von Hötzendorf, Franz, *Private Aufzeichnungen. Erste Veröffentlichungen aus den Papieren des k.u.k. Generalstabschefs*, edited by Kurt Peball, Amalthea, Vienna, Munich 1977

Coogan, John W. and Peter F. Coogan, 'The British Cabinet and Anglo-French Staff Talks, 1905–1914: Who Knew What and When did he Know it?' *Journal of British Studies*, 24, 1, 1985, pp. 110–131

Cornwall, Mark, 'Serbia', in Keith M. Wilson (ed.), *Decisions for War, 1914*, UCL Press, London 1995, pp. 55–96

Cramon, August von, *Unser Österreichisch-Ungarischer Bundesgenosse im Weltkriege. Erinnerungen aus meiner vierjährigen Tätigkeit als bevollmächtigter deutscher General beim k.u.k. Armeeoberkommando*, Mittler, Berlin 1920

Dedijer, Vladimir and Života Anić (eds), *Dokumenti o spolnoj politici Kraljevine Srbije*, VII/2, Srpska akademija nauka i umetnosti, Odeljenje istorijskih nauka, Belgrade 1980

Delbrück, Hans, 'Die deutsche Kriegserklärung und der Einmarsch in Belgien', *Preußische Jahrbücher*, CLXXV, 175, January–March 1919

Deuerlein, Ernst (ed.), *Briefwechsel Hertling-Lerchenfeld, 1912–1917. Dienstliche Privatkorrespondenz zwischen dem bayerischen Ministerpräsidenten Georg Graf von Hertling und dem bayerischen Gesandten in Berlin Hugo Graf von und zu Lerchenfeld*, 2 vols, Harald Boldt Verlag, Boppard am Rhein 1973

Die deutschen Dokumente zum Kriegsausbruch. Vollständige Sammlung der von Karl Kautsky zusammengestellten amtlichen Aktenstücke mit einigen Ergänzungen, ed. Graf Max Montgelas and Walter Schücking, 5 vols, Deutsche Verlagsgesellschaft für Politik und Geschichte, Berlin-Charlottenburg 1919

Die Grosse Politik der Europäischen Kabinette, 1871–1914. Sammlung der Diplomatischen Aktenstücke des Auswärtigen Amtes, ed. (on behalf of the *Auswärtiges Amt*) by Johannes Lepsius, Albrecht Mendelssohn Bartholdy and Friedrich Thimme, 40 vols, Deutsche Verlagsgesellschaft für Politik und Geschichte, Berlin 1922–27

Die österreichisch-ungarischen Dokumente zum Kriegsausbruch. Diplomatische Aktenstücke zur Vorgeschichte des Krieges 1914. Ergänzungen und Nachträge zum österreichisch-ungarischen Rotbuch, ed. Republik

Österreich, Staatsamt für Äusseres, 3 vols, Bundesverlag, Vienna 1919
Dirr, Pius (ed.), *Bayerische Dokumente zum Kriegsausbruch und zum Versailler Schuldspruch*, 3rd edn, Oldenbourg, Munich and Berlin 1925
Dobrorolski, S.K., *Die Mobilmachung der russischen Armee, 1914*, Deutsche Verlagsgesellschaft für Politik und Geschichte, Berlin 1922
Dobrorolski, S.K., 'La mobilisation de l'Armée russe en 1914', *Revue d'Histoire de la Guerre Mondiale*, 1, April–July 1923, pp. 153–169
Dockrill, Michael L., 'British Policy During the Agadir Crisis of 1911', in F.H. Hinsley (ed.), *British Foreign Policy Under Sir Edward Grey*, Cambridge University Press, Cambridge 1977, pp. 271–287
d'Ombrain, Nicholas, 'The Imperial General Staff and the Military Policy of a "Continental Strategy" during the 1911 International Crisis', *Military Affairs*, 34, 3, October 1970, pp. 88–93
Doughty, Robert A., 'France', in Richard F. Hamilton and Holger H. Herwig (eds), *War Planning 1914*, Cambridge University Press, Cambridge et al. 2010, pp. 143–174
Dülffer, Jost, *Regeln gegen den Krieg? Die Haager Friedenskonferenzen von 1899 und 1907 in der internationalen Politik*, Ullstein, Berlin 1981
Dülffer, Jost, Martin Kröger and Rolf-Harald Wippich (eds), *Vermiedene Kriege. Deeskalation und Konflikte der Großmächte zwischen Krimkrieg und Erstem Weltkrieg (1856–1914)*, Oldenbourg, Munich 1997
Duroselle, Jean-Baptiste, *La Grande Guerre des Français: l'incompréhensible*, Perrin, Paris 1994
Eckardstein, Hermann Frhr. von, *Lebenserinnerungen und Politische Denkwürdigkeiten*, 3 vols, Paul List, Leipzig 1921
Ehlert, Hans, Michael Epkenhans and Gerhard P. Groß (eds), *Der Schlieffenplan. Analysen und Dokumente*, Schöningh, Paderborn 2006
Emperor William II, *My Memoirs, 1878–1818*, Engl. transl., Cassell, London 1922
Engelstein, Laura, '"A Belgium of Our Own": The sack of Russian Kalisz, August 1914', *Kritika: Explorations in Russian and Eurasian History*, 10, 3, Summer 2009, pp. 441–473
Epkenhans, Michael (ed), *Albert Hopman. Das ereignisreiche Leben eines 'Wilhelminers'. Tagebücher, Briefe, Aufzeichnungen 1901 bis 1920*, Oldenbourg, Munich 2004
Erdmann, Karl Dietrich (ed.), *Kurt Riezler. Tagebücher, Aufsätze, Dokumente*, Vandenhoeck & Ruprecht, Göttingen 1972 (reprinted 2008)
Erdmann, Karl Dietrich, 'Die Tagebücher sind echt. Streit um ein historisches Dokument, das ins Zwielicht geraten ist. Eine Antwort', *Die Zeit*, No. 28, 8 July 1983
Evseev, N.F., *Avgustoskoe srazhenie 2–i russkoi armii v Vostochnoi Prussii*, Moscow 1936
Fay, Sidney Bradshaw, *The Origins of the World War*, 2 vols, Macmillan 1928, 3rd edn, Ishi Press, New York and Tokyo 2010

Fellner, Fritz (ed.), *Schicksalsjahre Österreichs 1908–1919. Das politische Tagebuch Josef Redlichs*. 2 vols, Böhlau, Graz, Cologne 1953

Fellner, Fritz, 'Zwischen Kriegsbegeisterung und Resignation – ein Memorandum des Sektionschefs Graf Forgách vom Jänner 1915', in Hermann Wiesflecker and Othmar Pickl (eds), *Beiträge zur Allgemeinen Geschichte. Alexander Novotny zur Vollendung seines 70. Lebensjahres*, Akademische Druck- und Verlagsanstalt, Graz 1975, pp. 153–162

Fellner, Fritz, 'Die Mission Hoyos', in Wilhelm Alff (ed.), *Deutschlands Sonderung von Europa, 1862–1945*, Peter Lang, Frankfurt am Main, Bern, New York 1984, pp. 283–316

Fellner, Fritz, 'Austria-Hungary', in Keith M. Wilson (ed.), *Decisions for War, 1914*, UCL Press, London 1995, pp. 9–25

Fellner, Fritz and Doris A. Corradini (eds), *Schicksalsjahre Österreichs. Die Erinnerungen und Tagebücher Josef Redlichs, 1869–1936*, 3 vols, Vol. 1: *Erinnerungen und Tagebücher 1869–1914*, Böhlau, Vienna, Cologne, Weimar 2011

Ferguson, Niall, 'Germany and the Origins of the First World War: New Perspectives', *Historical Journal*, 35, 3, 1992, pp. 725–752

Ferguson, Niall, *The Pity of War*, Allen Lane, London 1998

Fischer, Conan, *Europe between Democracy and Dictatorship, 1900–1945*, Wiley-Blackwell, Oxford 2011

Fischer, Eugen, *Die kritischen 39 Tage von Sarajevo bis zum Weltbrand*, Ullstein, Berlin 1928

Fischer, Fritz, *Griff nach der Weltmacht. Die Kriegszielpolitik des kaiserlichen Deutschlands, 1914/18*, first published 1961. Nachdruck der Sonderausgabe 1967, Droste, Düsseldorf 1984 (Engl. transl.: *Germany's Aims in the First World War*, London 1967)

Fischer, Fritz, *Juli 1914: Wir sind nicht hineingeschlittert. Das Staatsgeheimnis um die Riezler Tagebücher*, Rowohlt, Reinbek 1983

Fischer, Fritz, *Krieg der Illusionen. Die deutsche Politik von 1911–1914*, paperpack reprint of 2nd edn 1970 (1st edn 1969), Droste, Düsseldorf 1987 (Engl. transl.: *War of Illusions. German Policies from 1911–1914*, Norton, London 1975)

Fischer, Jörg-Uwe, *Admiral des Kaisers. Georg Alexander von Müller als Chef des Marinekabinetts Wilhelms II.*, Peter Lang, Frankfurt 1992

Fitzroy, Almeric, *Memoirs*, George H. Doran Co., London, 2 vols, 1925

Foerster, Wolfgang, 'Der deutsche und der italienische Generalstab vor dem Weltkriege', *Deutscher Offizier-Bund*, No. 20, 1926, pp. 874–878

Forsbach, Ralf, *Alfred von Kiderlen-Wächter (1852–1912). Ein Diplomatenleben im Kaiserreich*, 2 vols, Vandenhoeck & Ruprecht, Göttingen 1997

Frantz, Gunther, *Rußlands Eintritt in den Weltkrieg. Der Ausbau der russischen Wehrmacht und ihr Einsatz bei Kriegsausbruch*, Deutsche Verlagsgesellschaft für Politik und Geschichte, Berlin 1924

Frantz, Gunther, 'Wie Rußland mobil machte', *Berliner Monatshefte*, 14, 1,

April 1936, pp. 277–319

Frauenholz, Eugen von (ed.), *Kronprinz Rupprecht von Bayern. In Treue fest. Mein Kriegstagebuch*, 3 vols, Deutscher Nationalverlag, Munich 1929

French Yellow Book, No. 17, Engl. transl. in *Collected Diplomatic Documents on the Outbreak of the European War.*

French, David and Brian Holden Reid (eds), *The British General Staff. Reform and Innovation, 1890–1939*, Frank Cass, London and Portland, OR 2002

Fuhrer, Hans Rudolf and Michael Olsansky, 'Die "Südumfassung": zur Rolle der Schweiz im Schlieffen und im Moltkeplan', in Hans Ehlert et al. (eds), *Der Schlieffenplan. Analysen und Dokumente*, Schöningh, Paderborn 2006, pp. 311–338

Geiss, Imanuel (ed.), *Julikrise und Kriegsausbruch. Eine Dokumentensammlung*, 2 vols, Verlag für Literatur und Zeitgeschehen, Hanover 1963/64

Geiss, Imanuel (ed.), *Hermann Kantorowitz: Gutachten zur Kriegsschuldfrage*, Europäische Verlagsanstalt, Frankfurt/M. 1967

Geiss, Imanuel (ed.), *July 1914. The Outbreak of the First World War. Selected Documents*, B.T. Batsford, London 1967

Geiss, Imanuel, *German Foreign Policy 1871–1914*, Routledge and Keegan Paul, London, Boston 1976

Geiss, Imanuel, *Der Lange Weg in die Katastrophe. Die Vorgeschichte des Ersten Weltkrieges, 1815–1914*, Piper, Munich 1990

Geppert, Dominik and Andreas Rose, 'Machtpolitik und Flottenbau vor 1914. Zur Neuinterpretation britischer Außenpolitik im Zeitalter des Hochimperialismus', *Historische Zeitschrift*, 293 (2011), pp. 401–437

Giesl, Wladimir von, 'Konnte die Annahme der serbischen Antwortnote den Ausbruch des Weltkrieges verhindern?' *Berliner Monatshefte*, May 1933, pp. 454–469

Gilbert, Bentley B., 'Pacifist to Interventionist: David Lloyd George in 1911 and 1914. Was Belgium an Issue?', *Historical Journal*, 28, 4, 1985, pp. 863–885

Giolitti, Giovanni, *Memoirs of my Life*, Chapman and Dodd, London 1923

Golder, Frank (ed.), *Documents of Russian History, 1914–1917*, The Century Co., New York and London 1927

Gooch, G.P., *Recent Revelations of European Diplomacy*, Longman, London 1940

Gooch, John, *The Plans of War: The General Staff and British Military Strategy, c.1900–1916*, Wiley, London 1974

Gooch, John, 'Italy', in Richard F. Hamilton and Holger H. Herwig (eds), *War Planning 1914*, Cambridge University Press, Cambridge et al. 2010, pp. 198–225

Görlitz, Walter, *Regierte der Kaiser? Kriegstagebücher, Aufzeichnungen und Briefe des Chefs des Marinekabinetts, Admiral Georg Alexander von Müller 1914–1918*, 2nd edn, Musterschmidt Verlag, Göttingen, Berlin, Frankfurt/Main 1959

Görlitz, Walter, *The Kaiser and his Court. The diaries, note books and letters of Admiral Georg Alexander von Müller, chief of the naval cabinet, 1914–1918*, transl. Mervyn Savill, MacDonald & Co, London 1961

Görlitz, Walter, *Der Kaiser ... Aufzeichnungen des Chefs des Marinekabinetts Admiral Georg Alexander von Müller über die Ära Wilhelms II.*, Musterschmidt Verlag, Göttingen 1965

Grau, Bernhard, *Kurt Eisner 1867–1919. Eine Biographie*, Beck, Munich 2001

Great Britain and the European Crisis, London 1914 (*British Blue Book*)

Grey, Edward; *Twenty-Five Years, 1892–1916*, 2 vols, Stokes, New York 1925

Gutsche, Willibald, *Sarajevo 1914. Vom Attentat zum Weltkrieg*, Dietz Verlag, Berlin 1984

Hall, Richard C., 'Serbia', in Richard F. Hamilton and Holger H. Herwig (eds), *The Origins of World War I*, Cambridge University Press, Cambridge 2003, pp. 92–111

Hamilton, Keith, *Bertie of Thane: Edwardian Ambassador*, RHS/Boydell Press, Woodbridge 1990

Hamilton, Keith, 'The Historical Diplomacy of the Third Republic', in Keith M. Wilson (ed.), *Forging the Collective Memory*, Berghahn, Oxford 1996, pp. 29–62

Hamilton, Keith, 'The Pursuit of "Enlightened Patriotism". The British Foreign Office and Historical Researchers During the Great War and its Aftermath', in Keith M. Wilson (ed.), *Forging the Collective Memory*, Berghahn, Oxford 1996, pp. 192–229

Hamilton, Keith, 'Falsifying the Record: Entente Diplomacy and the Preparation of the Blue and Yellow Books on the War Crisis of 1914', *Diplomacy & Statecraft*, 18, 2007, pp. 89–108

Hamilton, Richard F. and Holger H. Herwig (eds), *The Origins of World War I*, Cambridge University Press, Cambridge 2003

Hamilton, Richard F. and Holger H. Herwig (eds), *War Planning 1914*, Cambridge University Press, Cambridge 2010

Hayne, Mark B., *The French Foreign Office and the Origins of the First World War, 1898–1914*, Clarendon Press, Oxford 1993

Headlam-Morley, J.W., *England, Germany and Europe*, Macmillan, London 1914

Headlam-Morley, J.W., *The History of Twelve Days, July 24–August 4 1914. Being an account of the Negotiations preceding the Outbreak of War based on the official publications*, T. Fisher Unwin, London 1915

Helmreich, E.C., 'An Unpublished Report on Austro-German Military Conversations of November, 1912', *Journal of Modern History*, V, 2, June 1933, pp. 197–207

Hermann, Carl Hans, *Deutsche Militärgeschichte*, Bernard und Graefe, Frankfurt/Main, 2nd edn 1968

Herrmann, David G., *The Arming of Europe and the Making of the First World War*, paperback edn, Princeton University Press, Princeton, NJ 1997

Herwig, Holger H., 'Disjointed Allies: Coalition Warfare in Berlin and Vienna, 1914', *Journal of Military History*, 54, July 1990

Herwig, Holger H., 'Clio Deceived. Patriotic Self-Censorship in Germany after the Great War', in Keith M. Wilson (ed.), *Forging the Collective Memory*, 1996, pp. 87–127

Herwig, Holger H., *The First World War. Germany and Austria-Hungary 1914–1918*, Arnold, London, New York, Sydney, Auckland 1997

Herwig, Holger H. and Richard Hamilton (eds), *The Outbreak of World War I. Causes and Responsibilities*, 5th edn, Cambridge University Press, Lexington, MA 1991

Herzfeld, Hans, 'Die Limankrise und die Politik der Grossmächte in der Jahreswende 1913–1914', *Berliner Monatshefte*, September 1933, pp. 837–858; October 1933, pp. 973–993

Hildebrand, Klaus, 'Julikrise 1914: Das europäische Sicherheitsdilemma. Betrachtungen über den Ausbruch des Ersten Weltkrieges', *Geschichte in Wissenschaft und Unterricht*, 1985/7

Hildebrand, Klaus, *Deutsche Aussenpolitik 1871–1914*, Oldenbourg, Munich 1989

Hildebrand, Klaus, *Das Vergangene Reich. Deutsche Außenpolitik von Bismarck bis Hitler, 1871–1945*, Deutsche Verlagsanstalt, Stuttgart 1995

Hillgruber, Andreas, 'Kurt Riezlers Theorie des "kalkulierten Risikos" und Bethmann Hollwegs politische Konzeption in der Julikrise 1914', *Historische Zeitschrift*, 202, 1966

Hinsley, F.H. (ed.), *British Foreign Policy under Sir Edward Grey*, Cambridge University Press, Cambridge 1977

Höbelt, Lothar, 'Schlieffen, Beck, Potiorek und das Ende der gemeinsamen deutsch-österreich-ungarischen Aufmarschpläne im Osten', *Militärgeschichtliche Mitteilungen*, 2/1984

Hobson, Rolf, *Imperialism at Sea: Naval Strategic Thought, the Ideology of Sea Power, and the Tirpitz Plan, 1875–1914*, Brill, Boston 2002.

Hoetsch, Otto (ed.), *Die Internationalen Beziehungen im Zeitalter des Imperialismus. Dokumente aus den Archiven der Zarischen und der Provisorischen Regierung*, Reihe 1: *Das Jahr 1914 bis zum Kriegsausbruch*, 5 vols, Reimar Hobbing, Berlin 1931–1934 (German edition of M.N. Pokrovskii/Kommissiya po izdaniyu dokumentov epokha imperialisma (eds), *Mezhdunarodnyye otnosheniya v epokhu imperialisma. Dokumenty iz arkhivov tsarskogo i vremennogo pravitel'stv*, Series III, vol. 1, Moscow 1931–1934)

Hoffmann, Dieter, *Der Sprung ins Dunkle. Oder wie der 1. Weltkrieg entfesselt wurde*, Militzke Verlag, Leipzig 2010

Holmes, Richard, *The Little Field-Marshal: Sir John French*, J. Cape, London, 1981

Hölzle, Erwin (ed.), *Quellen zur Entstehung des Ersten Weltkrieges. Internationale Dokumente, 1901–1914*, Wissenschaftliche Buchgesellschaft, Darmstadt 1978

Horne, John and Alan Kramer, *German Atrocities, 1914: A History of Denial*, Yale University Press, New Haven, CT and London 2001

House, Edward, *The Intimate Papers of Colonel House*, 2 vols, Houghton Mifflin, London 1926, Vol. I, *Behind the Political Curtain*, 1912–1915

Janssen, Karl-Heinz, 'August' 14: Wahrheit auf Raten. Zwei Historiker streiten um Tagebücher: Wurde die deutsche Kriegsschuld am Ersten Weltkrieg im nationalen Interesse verschleiert?', *Die Zeit*, No. 24, 10 June 1983

Jarausch, Konrad, 'The Illusion of Limited War: Bethmann Hollweg's calculated risk, July 1914', *Central European History*, 2, 1, 1969, pp. 48–76

Jarausch, Konrad, *The Enigmatic Chancellor. Bethmann Hollweg and the Hubris of Imperial Germany*, Yale University Press, New Haven, London 1973

Jean Stengers, 'Guillaume II et le Roi Albert à Potsdam en novembre 1913', *Bulletin de la Classe des Lettres et des Sciences Morales et Politiques*, 7–12, 1993, pp. 227–253

Jerábek, Rudolf, 'Die österreichische Weltkriegsforschung', in Wolfgang Michalka (ed.), *Der Erste Weltkrieg. Wirkung, Wahrnehmung, Analyse*, Piper, Munich 1994, pp. 953–971

Joffre, Joseph J.C., *The Memoirs of Marshal Joffre*, transl. Colonel T. Bentley Mott, 2 vols, Geoffrey Bles, London 1932

Joll, James and Gordon Martel, *The Origins of the First World War*, Longman, London, 3rd edn, 2007

Kantorowitz, Hermann, *Gutachten zur Kriegsschuldfrage* (1927), ed. Imanuel Geiss, Deutsche Verlagsanstalt, Frankfurt/M. 1967

Keiger, John F.V., *France and the Origins of the First World War*, Macmillan, London, Basingstoke 1983

Keiger, John F.V., 'Jules Cambon and Franco-German Détente, 1907–1914', *Historical Journal*, 26, 3, 1983

Keiger, John F.V., *Raymond Poincaré*, Cambridge University Press, Cambridge 1997

Kennedy, Paul M. (ed.), *The War Plans of the Great Powers, 1880–1914*, George Allen & Unwin, London 1979

Kiesling, Eugenia, 'France', in Holger Herwig and Richard Hamilton (eds), *The Outbreak of World War I. Causes and Responsibilies*, 5th rev. edn, Cambridge University Press, Lexington, MA, Toronto 1991, pp. 227–265

Kießling, Friedrich, *Gegen den 'großen Krieg?' Entspannung in den interna-*

tionalen Beziehungen, 1911–1914, Oldenbourg, Munich 2002.

Klein, Fritz, 'Über die Verfälschung der Historischen Wahrheit in der Aktenpublikation "Die Grosse Politik der Europäischen Kabinette 1871–1914"', in *Zeitschrift für Geschichtswissenschaft*, 7, 1959, pp. 318–330

Kokovtsov, Vladimir N., *Out of My Past. The Memoirs of Count Kokovtsov*, transl. Laura Matveev, Stanford University Press, Stanford, London, Oxford 1935

Koss, Stephen E., *Lord Haldane. Scapegoat for Liberalism*, Columbia University Press, New York, London 1969

Kröger, Martin, 'Letzter Konflikt vor der Katastrophe: Die Liman-von-Sanders-Krise 1913/14', in Jost Dülffer, Martin Kröger and Ralf-Harald Wippich (eds), *Vermiedene Kriege: Deeskalation von Konflikten der Grossmächte zwischen Krimkrieg und Erstem Weltkrieg, 1856–1914*, Oldenbourg, Munich 1997, pp. 657–71

Kronenbitter, Günther, '"Nur los lassen!" Österreich-Ungarn und der Wille zum Krieg', in Johannes Burkhardt et al. (eds), *Lange und kurze Wege in den Ersten Weltkrieg*, Ernst Vögel, Munich 1996

Kronenbitter, Günther, 'Bundesgenossen? Zur militärpolitischen Kooperation zwischen Berlin und Wien 1912–1914', in W. Bernecker/V. Dotterweich (eds), *Deutschland in den internationalen Beziehungen des 19. und 20. Jahrhunderts. Festschrift für Josef Becker*, E. Vögel, Munich 1996

Kronenbitter, Günther, 'Austria-Hungary and World War I', in Günther Bischof and Anton Pelinka (eds), *Austrian Historical Memory and National Identity*, Contemporary Austrian Studies, Vol. 5, Transaction Publishers, New Brunswick and London 1997

Kronenbitter, Günther, 'Die Macht der Illusionen. Julikrise und Kriegsausbruch 1914 aus der Sicht des deutschen Militärattachés in Wien, *Militärgeschichtliche Mitteilungen*, 57, 1998

Kronenbitter, Günther, *'Krieg im Frieden'. Die Führung der k.u.k. Armee und die Großmachtpolitik Österreich-Ungarns 1906–1914*, Oldenbourg, Munich 2003

Kronenbitter, Günther, 'Austria-Hungary', in Richard F. Hamilton and Holger H. Herwig (eds), *War Planning 1914*, Cambridge University Press, Cambridge et al. 2010, pp. 24–47

Krumeich, Gerd, *Armaments and Politics in France on the Eve of the First World War. The Introduction of the Three-Year Conscription, 1913–1914*, Berg, Leamington Spa 1984

Lahaie, Olivier, 'Renseignement et Services de Renseignement en France pendant la Guerre de 1914–1918', PhD thesis, Sorbonne, Paris 2006

Langdon, John W., *July 1914. The Long Debate 1918–1990*, Berg, New York, Oxford 1991

Langer, William L., Review of *Österreich-Ungarns Aussenpolitik von der bosnischen Krise bis zum Kriegsausbruch 1914*, *Foreign Affairs*, April 1930

Langhorne, R.T.B., 'The Naval Question in Anglo-German Relations, 1912–1914', *Historical Journal*, XIV, 2, 1970, pp. 359–370

Lepsius, Johannes, Albrecht Mendelsohn-Bertholdy and Friedrich Thimme (eds), *Die Große Politik der Europäischen Kabinette 1871–1914*. Sammlung der Diplomatischen Akten des Auswärtigen Amtes, 40 vols, Deutsche Verlagsgesellschaft für Politik und Geschichte, Berlin 1922–1927

Leslie, John D., 'Österreich-Ungarn vor dem Kriegsausbruch. Der Ballhausplatz in Wien im Juli 1914 aus der Sicht eines österreichisch-ungarischen Diplomaten', in Ralph Melville et al. (eds), *Deutschland und Europa in der Neuzeit. Festschrift für Karl Otmar Frh. von Aretin zum 65. Geburtstag*, 2. Halbband, F. Steiner Verlag, Stuttgart 1988, pp. 661–684

Leslie, John D., 'The Antecedents of Austria-Hungary's War Aims. Policies and Policy-making in Vienna and Budapest before and during 1914', *Wiener Beiträge zur Geschichte der Neuzeit*, 20, 1993, pp. 307–94

Lichnowsky, Karl Max Prince von, *My Mission to London, 1912–14*, Cassell & Co., London 1918

Lieven, Dominic, *Russia and the Origins of the First World War*, St Martin's Press, New York 1983

Lieven, Dominic, *Nicholas II. Twilight of the Empire*, St Martins Griffin, New York 1993

Lloyd George, David, *War Memoirs*, Vol. I, Odhams Press, London 1938

Mackey, Richard W., *The Zabern Affair, 1913–1914*, University Press of America, Lanham 1991

Mackintosh, John P., 'The Role of the Committee of Imperial Defence before 1914', *English Historical Review*, 77, July 1962, pp. 490–503

Malagodi, Olindo, *Conversazioni della guerra, 1914–1919*, 2 vols, R. Ricciardi, Milan 1960

Mann, Josef, 'FML Blasius Schemua. Chef des Generalstabes am Vorabend des Weltkrieges 1911–1912', PhD Dissertation, University of Vienna 1978

Maurice, Frederick, *Haldane 1856–1915. The Life of Viscount Haldane of Cloan*, Faber & Faber, London 1937

May, Ernest R. (ed.), *Knowing One's Enemies: Intelligence Assessment before the two World Wars*, Princeton University Press, Princeton 1984

Mayer, Martin, *Geheime Diplomatie und öffentliche Meinung. Die Parlamente in Frankreich, Deutschland, und Großbritannien und die erste Marokkokrise 1904–1905*, Droste, Düsseldorf 2002

Mazzetti, Massimo, *L'esercito italiano nella triplice alleanza*, Edizioni Scientifiche Italiane, Naples 1974

McDonald, David M., 'The Durnovo Memorandum in Context: Official Conservatism and the Crisis of Autocracy', *Jahrbücher für die Geschichte Osteuropas*, 44, 4, 1996, pp. 481–502

McDonough, Frank, *The Conservative Party and Anglo-German Relations, 1905–1914*, Palgrave, Macmillan, Basingstoke, New York 2007

McMeekin, Sean, *The Berlin-Baghdad Express: The Ottoman Empire and Germany's Bid for World Power, 1898–1918*, Allen Lane, London 2010

McMeekin, Sean, *The Russian Origins of the First World War*, Belknap Press of Harvard University Press, Cambridge, MA 2011

Menning, Bruce W., 'War Planning and Initial Operations in the Russian Context', in Richard F. Hamilton and Holger H. Herwig (eds), *War Planning 1914*, Cambridge University Press, Cambridge et al. 2010, pp. 80–142

Menning, Bruce W., 'Russian Military Intelligence, July 1914: What St Petersburg Perceived and Why It Mattered', unpublished article MS, forthcoming

Messimy, Adolphe, *Mes Souvenirs*, Librairie Plon, Paris 1937

Meyer, Thomas, *'Endlich eine Tat, eine befreiende Tat ...'. Alfred von Kiderlen-Wächters 'Panthersprung nach Agadir' unter dem Druck der öffentlichen Meinung*, Mathiesen, Husum 1996

Meyer-Arndt, Lüder, *Die Julikrise 1914. Wie Deutschland in den ersten Weltkrieg stolperte*, Böhlau, Cologne, Weimar, Vienna 2006

Mezhdunarodnye Otnosheniya v Epokhu Imperializma. Dokumenty iz arkhivov tsarskogo i vremennogo pravitel'stv, published also under the German title *Die Internationalen Beziehungen im Zeitalter des Imperialismus*

Michalka, Wolfgang, *Der Erste Weltkrieg. Wirkung, Wahrnehmung, Analyse*, Piper, Munich 1994

Ministère de la Guerre. État-major de l'armée, Service Historique (eds), *Les armées françaises dans la Grande Guerre*, 103 vols. Imprimerie nationale, Paris 1922–1938

Ministère des Affaires Etrangères, *Documents diplomatiques 1914: la Guerre européenne, I, Pièces relatives aux négociations qui ont precédés les déclarations de guerre de l'Allemagne à la Russie (1er Août 1914) et à la France (3 Août 1914). Declaration du 4 Septembre 1914*, Imprimerie Nationale, Paris 1914 (*French Yellow Book*)

Moltke, Eliza von (ed.), *Helmuth von Moltke, Erinnerungen, Briefe, Dokumente 1877–1916. Ein Bild vom Kriegsausbruch, erster Kriegsführung und Persönlichkeit des ersten militärischen Führer des Krieges*, Der Kommende Tag, Stuttgart 1922

Mombauer, Annika, 'A Reluctant Military Leader? Helmuth von Moltke and the July Crisis of 1914', *War in History*, 6, 4, 1999, pp. 417–446

Mombauer, Annika, *Helmuth von Moltke and the Origins of the First World War*, Cambridge University Press, Cambridge 2001

Mombauer, Annika, *The Origins of the First World War. Controversies and Consensus*, Longman, Harlow 2002

Mombauer, Annika, 'Of War Plans and War Guilt: the Debate Surrounding the Schlieffen Plan, *Journal of Strategic Studies*, 28, 5, October 2005, pp. 857–885

Mombauer, Annika, 'Der Moltke-Plan. Modifikation des Schlieffenplanes by gleichen Zielen?', in Hans Ehlert et al. (eds), *Der Schlieffenplan. Analysen und Dokumente*, Schöningh, Paderborn 2006, pp. 79–99

Mombauer, Annika, 'German War Plans', in Richard F. Hamilton and Holger H. Herwig (eds), *War Planning 1914*, Cambridge University Press, Cambridge et al., 2010, pp. 48–78

Mombauer, Annika, 'The Fischer Controversy, Documents and the "Truth" about the Origins of the First World War', *Journal of Contemporary History*, forthcoming 2013.

Mommsen, Wolfgang J., *Der autoritäre Nationalstaat. Verfassung, Gesellschaft und Kultur im deutschen Kaiserreich*, Fischer, Frankfurt/Main 1990

Mommsen, Wolfgang J., 'Der Topos vom unvermeidlichen Krieg: Außenpolitik und öffentliche Meinung im Deutschen Reich im letzten Jahrzehnt vor 1914', in idem, *Der autoritäre Nationalstaat*, Frankfurt/Main 1990, pp. 380–406

Mommsen, Wolfgang J., *Großmachtstellung und Weltpolitik 1870–1914. Die Außenpolitik des Deutschen Reiches*, Ullstein, Frankfurt/Main, Berlin 1993

Morley, John Viscount, *Memorandum on Resignation, August 1914*, Macmillan, London 1928

Mulligan, William, 'We Can't Be More Russian Than the Russians: British Policy During the Liman Von Sanders Crisis, 1913–1914', *Diplomacy & Statecraft* 17, 2, 2006, pp. 261–282

Mulligan, William, *The Origins of the First World War*, Cambridge University Press, Cambridge 2010

Neiberg, Michael S., *Dance of the Furies. Europe and the Outbreak of World War I*, Belknap/Harvard University Press, Cambridge MA, London 2011

Neilson, Keith, 'Great Britain', in Richard F. Hamilton and Holger H. Herwig (eds), *War Planning 1914*, Cambridge University Press, Cambridge et al., 2010, pp. 175–197

Nicolson, Harold, *Sir Arthur Nicolson, First Lord Carnock. A Study in the Old Diplomacy*, Constable & Co., London 1930

Nicolson, Harold, *King George V*, Constable & Co., London 1952, 2nd edn 1967

Oncken, Emily, *Panthersprung nach Agadir. Die deutsche Politik während der Zweiten Marokkokrise*, Droste, Düsseldorf 1981

Otte, Thomas G., 'The Elusive Balance. British Foreign Policy and the French Entente before the First World War', in Alan Sharp and Glyn Stone (eds), *Anglo-French Relations in the Twentieth Century: Rivalry and Cooperation*, Routledge, London and New York, 2000, pp. 23–26

Otte, Thomas G., 'A "German Paperchase": the "Scrap of Paper" Controversy and the Problem of Myth and Memory in International History', *Diplomacy & Statecraft*, 18, 1, 2007, pp. 53–87

Paléologue, Maurice, *An Ambassador's Memoirs*, transl. F.A. Holt, George H. Doran Co., New York 1925

Parsons, Frederick V., *The Origins of the Morocco Question 1880–1900*, Duckworth, London 1976

Pédroncini, Guy, 'Stratégie et relations internationales: La séance du 9 janvier 1912 au conseil supérieur de la défense nationale', *Revue d'histoire diplomatique*, 91, 1977, pp. 143–158

Peter, Matthias and Hans-Jürgen Schröder, *Einführung in das Studium der Zeitgeschichte*, Schöningh, Paderborn 1994

Petersson, H. Bertil A, 'Das österreichisch-ungarische Memorandum an Deutschland vom 5. Juli 1914', *Scandia*, 29, 1963, pp. 138–190

Philpott, William J., 'The Strategic Ideas of Sir John French', *Journal of Strategic Studies* 12, 4, 1989, pp. 458–478

Poincaré, Raymond, *Au Service de la France: neuf années de souvenirs*, 10 vols, Librairie Plon, Paris 1926–1933

Poincaré, Raymond, *The Memoirs of Raymond Poincaré (1913–1914)*, Transl. and adapted by Sir George Arthur, William Heinemann, London 1926

Pommerin, Reiner and Michael Fröhlich (eds), *Quellen zu den deutsch-britischen Beziehungen, 1815–1914*, Wissenschaftliche Buchgesellschaft, Darmstadt 1997

Pourtalès, Friedrich, *Meine Letzten Verhandlungen in St Petersburg Ende Juli 1914. Tagesaufzeichnungen und Dokumente*, Deutsche Verlagsgesellschaft für Politik und Geschichte, Berlin 1927

Prete, Roy A., 'French Strategic Planning and the Deployment of the B.E.F. in France in 1914', *Canadian Journal of History*, XXIV, April 1989, pp. 42–62

Prete, Roy A., *Strategy and Command. The Anglo-French Coalition on the Western Front, 1914*, McGill-Queen's University Press, Montreal et al. 2009

Rauchensteiner, Manfried, *Der Tod des Doppeladlers. Österreich-Ungarn und der Erste Weltkrieg*, Styria Verlag, Graz, Vienna, Cologne 1993

Rauh, Manfred, 'Die britisch-russische Militärkonvention von 1914 und der Ausbruch des Ersten Weltkrieges', *Militärgeschichtliche Mitteilungen*, 41, 1987

Renzi, William A. 'Italy and the Great War', *American Historical Review*, 73, 5, June 1968, pp. 1414–1432

Rodzianko, Michael W., *Erinnerungen*, Berlin 1926

Rodzianko, M.W., *The Reign of Rasputin: An Empire's Collapse: Memoirs of M. V. Rodzianko*, Philpot, London 1927

Röhl, John C.G., 'Admiral von Müller and the Approach of War, 1911–1914, *Historical Journal*, 12, 1969, pp. 651–673

Röhl, John C.G. (ed.), *From Bismarck to Hitler. The Problem of Continuity in German History*, Barnes & Noble, London 1970

Röhl, John C.G. (ed.), *1914: Delusion or Design? The Testimony of two German Diplomats*, Elek, London 1973

Röhl, John C.G. (ed.), *Philipp Eulenburgs Politische Korrespondenz*, 3 vols, Boldt Verlag, Boppard/Rhein 1976–1983

Röhl, John C.G., 'An der Schwelle zum Weltkrieg: Eine Dokumentation über den 'Kriegsrat' vom 8. Dezember 1912', *Militärgeschichtliche Mitteilungen,* 21, 1, 1977

Röhl, John C.G., 'Die Generalprobe. Zur Geschichte und Bedeutung des 'Kriegsrates' vom 8. Dezember 1912', in D. Stegmann, B.J. Wendt and P.-C. Witt (eds), *Industrielle Gesellschaft und politisches System. Beiträge zur politischen Sozialgeschichte. Festschrift für Fritz Fischer zum 70. Geburtstag*, Verlag Neue Gesellschaft, Bonn 1978

Röhl, John C.G., *Wilhelm II.* Vol. I: *Die Jugend des Kaisers 1859–1888*, Beck, Munich 1993; Vol. II: *Der Aufbau der persönlichen Monarchie, 1888–1900*, Beck, Munich, 2001, 2nd edn 2012; Vol. III: *Der Weg in den Abgrund, 1900–1941*, Beck, Munich 2008, 2nd edn 2009. Engl. transl.: *Young Wilhelm. The Kaiser's Early Years*, Cambridge University Press, Cambridge 1998; *Wilhelm II. The Kaiser's Personal Monarchy, 1888–1900*, Cambridge University Press, Cambridge 2004; *Wilhelm II. Into the Abyss of War and Exile, 1900–1941*, Cambridge University Press, Cambridge 2013

Röhl, John C.G., *Kaiser, Hof und Staat. Wilhelm II. und die deutsche Politik*, Beck, Munich 1988 (English translation: *The Kaiser and his Court*, Cambridge University Press, Cambridge 1995)

Röhl, John C.G. (ed.), *Der Ort Kaiser Wilhelm II. in der deutschen Geschichte*, Beck, Munich 1991

Röhl, John C.G., *The Kaiser and his Court*, Cambridge University Press, Cambridge 1994

Röhl, John C.G., 'Germany', in Keith Wilson (ed.), *Decisions for War 1914*, UCL Press, London 1995, pp. 27–54

Romberg, Gisbert Freiherr von (ed.), *Die Fälschungen des russischen Orangebuches: der wahre Telegrammwechsel Paris–Petersburg bei Kriegsausbruch*, Vereinigung Wissenschaftlicher Verleger, Berlin, Leipzig 1922 (Engl. transl. *The Falsification of the Russian Orange-Book*, Allen & Unwin, London, New York 1923)

Rose, Andreas, *Zwischen Empire und Kontinent – Zur Transformation britischer Außen- und Sicherheitspolitik im Vorfeld des Ersten Weltkrieges*, Veröffentlichungen des Deutschen Historischen Instituts London, Vol. 70, Munich 2011

Salandra, Antonio, *La Neutralità italiana 1914. Ricordi e pensieri*, Mondadone, Milan 1928

Salandra, Antonio, *Italy and the Great War*, Edward Arnold, London 1932

Sanborn, Joshua, 'The Mobilization of 1914 and the Question of the Russian Nation: a Reexamination', *Slavic Review*, 59, 2, Summer 2000, pp. 267–289

Sanborn, Joshua, 'Military Occupation and Social Unrest: Daily Life in Russian Poland at the Start of World War I', in Golfo Alexopolous, Julie Hessler and Kiril Tomoff (eds), *Writing the Stalin Era: Sheila Fitzpatrick and Soviet Historiography*, Palgrave Macmillan, New York 2011, pp. 43–58

Sazonov, Sergei D., *Sechs schwere Jahre*, Verlag für Kulturpolitik, Berlin, 2nd edn, 1927

Sazonov, Sergei, *Fateful Years, 1909–1916*, New York 1928

Schäfer, Theobald von, 'Generaloberst von Moltke in den Tagen vor der Mobilmachung und seine Einwirkung auf Österreich-Ungarn', *Die Kriegsschuldfrage. Berliner Monatshefte für Internationale Aufklärung*, August 1926

Schilling, M.F. (ed.), *How the War Began in 1914, Being the Diary of the Russian Foreign Office from the 3rd to the 20th (Old Style) of July, 1914*, Allen & Unwin, London 1925

Schmidt, Stefan, *Frankreichs Außenpolitik in der Julikrise 1914. Ein Beitrag zur Geschichte des Ausbruchs des Ersten Weltkrieges*, Oldenbourg, Munich 2007

Schmitt, Bernadotte E., 'France and the Outbreak of the World War', in *Foreign Affairs*, 15, 1937, pp. 516–536

Schoenbaum, David, *Zabern 1913. Consensus Politics in Imperial Germany*, Allen & Unwin, London 1982

Schöllgen, Gregor, 'Kriegsgefahr und Krisenmanagement vor 1914. Zur Außenpolitik des kaiserlichen Deutschland', *Historische Zeitschrift*, 267, 2, 1998

Schröder, Stephen, *Die englisch-russische Marinekonvention. Das Deutsche Reich und die Flottenverhandlungen der Triple-Entente am Vorabend des Ersten Weltkriegs*, Vandenhoeck & Ruprecht, Göttingen 2004

Schroeder, Paul, 'Romania and the Great Powers before 1914', *Revue Roumaine d'Histoire*, XIV, 1, 1975, pp. 39–53

Schulte, Bernd-Felix, 'Neue Dokumente zum Kriegsausbruch und Kriegsverlauf 1914', *Militärgeschichtliche Mitteilungen*, 25, 1, 1979

Schulte, Bernd-Felix, 'Zu der Krisenkonferenz vom 8. Dezember 1912 in Berlin', *Historisches Jahrbuch*, 102, 1982

Schulte, Bernd-Felix, *Europäische Krise und Erster Weltkrieg. Beiträge zur Militärpolitik des Kaiserreichs 1871–1914*, Peter Lang, Frankfurt/Main 1983

Schulte, Bernd-Felix, *Die Verfälschung der Riezler Tagebücher. Ein Beitrag zur Wissenschaftsgeschichte der 50er und 60er Jahre*, Peter Lang, Frankfurt/M., Bern and New York 1985

Schuman, Frederick L., *War and Diplomacy in the French Republic*, Whittlesey House, London 1931

Schumann, Wolfgang and Ludwig Nestler (eds), *Weltherrschaft im Visier.*

Dokumente zu den Europa- und Weltherrschaftsplänen des deutschen Imperialismus von der Jahrhundertwende bis Mai 1945, VEB Deutscher Verlag der Wissenschaften, Berlin 1975

Schwertfeger, Berhard (ed.), *Amtliche Aktenstücke zur Geschichte der Europäischen Politik 1885–1914. Die Belgischen Dokumente zur Vorgeschichte des Weltkrieges 1885–1914. Vollständige Ausgabe der vom Deutschen Auswärtigen Amt herausgegebenen Diplomatischen Urkunden aus den Belgischen Staatsarchiven*, 5 vols, Deutsche Verlagsgesellschaft für Politik und Geschichte, Berlin 1919

Schwertfeger, Bernhard, *Der Weltkrieg der Dokumente. Zehn Jahre Kriegsschuldforschung und ihr Ergebnis*, Deutsche Verlagsgesellschaft für Politik und Geschichte, Berlin 1929

Seligmann, Matthew (ed.), *Naval Intelligence from Germany. The Reports of the British Naval Attachés in Berlin, 1906–1914*, Ashgate, Naval Records Society, Aldershot 2007

Seligmann, Matthew, *The Royal Navy and the German Threat, 1901–1914: Admiralty Plans to protect Britain's Trade in a War against Germany*, Oxford University Press, Oxford 2012

Seyfert, Gerhard, 'Die militärischen Beziehungen und Vereinbarungen zwischen dem deutschen und dem österreichischen Generalstab vor und bei Beginn des Weltkrieges', PhD Diss. Leipzig 1934

Sharp, Alan and Glyn Stone (eds), *Anglo-French Relations in the Twentieth Century: Rivalry and Cooperation*, Routledge, London and New York 2000

Siebert, Benno von, *Diplomatische Aktenstücke zur Geschichte der Ententepolitik der Vorkriegsjahre*, de Gruyter, Berlin/Leipzig 1921 (Engl. edn, transl. G.A. Schreiner, *Entente Diplomacy and the War*, G.P. Putnam's & Sons, New York 1922)

Silberstein, Gerard E., 'The Serbian Campaign of 1915: Its Diplomatic Background', *American Historical Review*, 73, 1, October 1967, pp. 51–69

Smith, David James, *One Morning in Sarajevo, 28 June 1914*, Phoenix, London 2008

Sondhaus, Lawrence, *Franz Conrad von Hötzendorf: Architect of the Apocalypse*, Humanities Press, Boston, Leiden, Cologne 2000

Sondhaus, Lawrence, *World War One. The Global Revolution*, Cambridge University Press, Cambridge 2011

Soroka, Marina, *Britain, Russia and the Road to the First World War. The Fateful Embassy of Count Aleksandr Benckendorff (1903–1916)*, Ashgate, Farnham 2011

Sösemann, Bernd (ed.), *Theodor Wolff. Tagebücher 1914–1918*, 2 vols, H. Boldt, Boppard/Rhein 1984

Sösemann, Bernd (ed.), *Theodor Wolff. Der Chronist. Krieg, Revolution und Frieden im Tagebuch 1914–1919*, Econ, Düsseldorf, Munich 1997

Spring, Derek, 'Russian Documents on the Origins of the First World War', in Keith M. Wilson (ed.), *Forging the Collective Memory. Governments and International Historians through two World Wars*, Berghahn, Providence, RI and Oxford, 1996, pp. 63–86

Staatsamt für Äusseres, Wien (ed.), *Die österreichisch-ungarischen Dokumente zum Kriegsausbruch. Diplomatische Aktenstücke zur Vorgeschichte des Krieges 1914*, Nationalverlag Vienna 1919, reprint Berlin 1922

Steinberg, John W. et al. (eds), *The Russo-Japanese War in Global Perspective. World War Zero*, Brill, Leiden, Boston 2005

Steinberg, Jonathan, 'Diplomatie als Wille und Vorstellung: Die Berliner Mission Lord Haldanes im Februar 1912', in H. Schottelius and W. Deist (eds), *Marine und Marinepolitik im Kaiserlichen Deutschland 1871–1914*, Droste, Düsseldorf 1972

Steiner, Zara and Keith Neilson, *Britain and the Origins of the First World War*, Palgrave Macmillan, London 2003

Stengers, Jean, 'Guillaume II et le Roi Albert à Potsdam en novembre 1913', *Bulletin de la Classe des Lettres et des Sciences Morales et Politiques*, 7–12, 1993, pp. 227–253

Stevenson, David, *The First World War and International Politics*, Oxford University Press, Oxford 1988

Stevenson, David, *Armaments and the Coming of War. Europe 1904–1914*, Clarendon, Oxford 1996

Stevenson, David, *The Outbreak of the First World War. 1914 in Perspective*, Macmillan, London 1997

Stevenson, David, 'Battlefield or Barrier? Rearmament and Military Planning in Belgium, 1902–1914', *International History Review*, XXIX, 3, September 2007, pp. 473–708

Stieve, Friedrich, *Isvolsky and the World War. Based on the Documents recently published by the German Foreign Office*, transl. E.W. Dickes, Allen & Unwin, London 1926

Stone, Norman, 'Die Mobilmachung der österreichisch-ungarischen Armee 1914', *Militärgeschichtliche Mitteilungen*, 16, 2, 1974, pp. 67–95

Stone, Norman, 'Moltke-Conrad: Relations between the Austro-Hungarian and German General Staffs, 1909–1914', *Historical Journal*, 9, 1966, pp. 201–228 (also in P.M. Kennedy (ed.), *The War Plans of the Great Powers, 1880–1914*, Allen & Unwin, London 1979)

Strachan, Hew, *European Armies and the Conduct of War*, Routledge, London 1983

Strachan, Hew, *The First World War*, Vol. 1: *To Arms*, Oxford University Press, Oxford 2001

Strachan, Hew, 'The British Army, its General Staff and the Continental Commitment 1904–14', in David French and Brian Holden Reid (eds), *The British General Staff. Reform and Innovation, 1890–1939*, Frank Cass, London and Portland, OR 2002, pp. 75–94

Temperley, H.W.V. and L.M. Penson, *A Century of Blue Books 1814–1914*, Cambridge University Press, Cambridge 1938

Tirpitz, Alfred von, *Erinnerungen*, Hase & Kohlen, Leipzig 1919

Tirpitz, Alfred von, *Der Aufbau der deutschen Wehrmacht*, Cotta'sche Buchhandlung, Stuttgart, Berlin 1924

Torre, A., Ministero degli affari esteri. Commissione per la pubblicazione dei documenti diplomatici (eds), *I documenti diplomatici Italiani,* Series 1–9 (1861–1943), Istituto Poligrafico e Zecca dello Stato, Rome 1954ff

Torrey, Glenn E., 'The Rumanian-Italian Agreement of 23 September 1914', *Slavonic and East European Review*, 44, 103, 1966, pp. 403–420

Toscano, Mario, *The History of Treaties and International Politics: The Documentary and Memoir Sources*, Johns Hopkins Press, Baltimore 1966

Trachtenberg, Marc, 'The Meaning of Mobilization in 1914', *International Security* 15, 3, Winter 1990/91

Trachtenberg, Marc, 'The Coming of the First World War: a Reassessment', in idem, *History and Strategy*, Princeton University Press, Princeton, NJ, 1991

Trumpener, Ulrich, 'War premeditated? German Intelligence Operations in July 1914', *Central European History*, 9, 1, 1976, pp. 58–85

Tuchman, Barbara, *The Zimmermann Telegram*, Papermac, London and Basingstoke 1981 (1st edn 1958)

Tunstall, Graydon A. Jr, 'The Schlieffen Plan: the Diplomacy and Military Strategy of the Central Powers in the East, 1905–1914', PhD Diss. Rutgers University, New Brunswick, N.J. 1974

Tunstall, Graydon A. Jr, *Planning for War Against Russia and Serbia: Austro-Hungarian and German Military Strategies, 1871–1914*, Columbia University Press, New York 1993

Tunstall, Graydon A Jr, 'The Habsburg Command Conspiracy: The Austrian Falsification of Historiography on the Outbreak of World War I', *Austrian History Yearbook*, 27, 1996, pp. 181–196

Turner, L.C.F., *The Origins of the First World War,* Edward Arnold, London 1970

Turner, L.C.F., 'The Russian Mobilization in 1914', in Paul M. Kennedy (ed.), *The War Plans of the Great Powers, 1880–1914*, Allen & Unwin, London 1979, pp. 252–268

Turner, L.C.F., 'The Significance of the Schlieffen Plan', in Paul M. Kennedy (ed.), *The War Plans of the Great Powers, 1880–1914*, Allen & Unwin, London 1979, pp. 199–221

Ullrich, Volker, 'Das deutsche Kalkül in der Julikrise 1914 und die Frage der englischen Neutralität', *Geschichte in Wissenschaft und Unterricht*, 34, 1983

Ullrich, Volker, 'Der Sprung ins Dunkle – Die Julikrise 1914 und ihre aktuellen Lehren, *Geschichtsdidaktik*, 2, 1984

Ullrich, Volker, *Die nervöse Großmacht 1871–1918. Aufstieg und Unter-*

gang des deutschen Kaiserreiches, S. Fischer, Frankfurt 1997

Valiani, Leo, 'Verhandlungen zwischen Italien und Österreich-Ungarn, 1914 – 1915', in Wolfgang Schieder (ed.), *Erster Weltkrieg. Ursachen, Entstehung und Kriegsziele*, Kiepenheuer & Wietsch, Cologne, Berlin 1969

Vierhaus, Rudolf (ed.), *Das Tagebuch der Baronin Spitzemberg. Aufzeichnungen aus der Hofgesellschaft des Hohenzollernreiches*, Vandenhoeck & Ruprecht, Göttingen 1960

Wank, Solomon, 'Desperate Council in Vienna in July 1914: Berthold Molden's Unpublished Memorandum', *Central European History*, 26, 3, 1993, pp. 281–310

Watts, D.C., 'The British Reactions to the Assassination at Sarajevo', *European Studies Review*, 1, 3, 1971, pp. 233–247

Wegerer, Alfred von, 'Russian Mobilization of 1914', *Political Science Quarterly*, 43, 1928, pp. 201–228

Wegerer, Alfred von, *Der Ausbruch des Weltkrieges 1914*, 2 vols, Hanseatische Verlagsanstalt, Hamburg 1939

William II, *My Memoirs, 1878–1818*, Engl. transl., Cassell, London 1922

Williamson, Samuel R. Jr, *The Politics of Grand Strategy. Britain and France Prepare for War, 1904–1914*, Harvard University Press, Cambridge, MA 1969 (paperback edn, Ashfield Press, London and Atlantic Highlands, NJ 1990)

Williamson, Samuel R. Jr, 'Joffre Reshapes French Strategy', in Paul M. Kennedy (ed.), *The War Plans of the Great Powers, 1880–1914*, Allen & Unwin, London 1979, pp. 133–154

Williamson, Samuel R. Jr, *Austria-Hungary and the Origins of the First World War*, Macmillan, London 1991

Williamson, Samuel R. Jr, 'General Henry Wilson, Ireland, and the Great War', in William Roger Louis (ed.), *Resurgent Adventures with Britannia: Personalities, Politics and Culture in Britain*, I.B. Tauris, London 2011, pp. 91–105

Williamson, Samuel R. Jr and Russel van Wyk, *July 1914. Soldiers, Statesmen and the Coming of the Great War. A Brief Documentary History*, Bedford/St Martin's, New York 2003

Wilsberg, Klaus, *'Terrible ami – aimable ennemi'. Kooperation und Konflikt in den deutsch-französischen Beziehungen 1911–1914*, Bouvier Verlag, Bonn 1998

Wilson, Keith M., 'The Agadir Crisis, the Mansion House Speech, and the Double-Edgedness of Agreements', *Historical Journal*, XV, 3, 1972, pp. 513–532

Wilson, Keith M., 'The British Cabinet's Decision for War, 2 August 1914', in *British Journal for International Studies*, I, 1975, pp. 148–159, reprinted in Keith M. Wilson, *The Policy of the Entente*, 2nd edn, Cambridge University Press, Cambridge 2009

Wilson, Keith M., 'The War Office, Churchill and the Belgian Option: August to December 1911', in *Bulletin of the Institute of Historical Research*, 50, 122, 1977, pp. 218–228

Wilson, Keith M., 'The Cabinet Diary of J.A. Pease, 24 July–5 August 1914', *Proceedings of the Leeds Philosophical Society*, XIX, III, 1983, pp. 41–51

Wilson, Keith M., *The Policy of the Entente. Essays on the Determinants of British Foreign Policy, 1904–1914*, 1985, 2nd edn, Cambridge University Press, Cambridge 2009

Wilson, Keith M., 'Hankey's Appendix: Some Admiralty Manoeuvres During and After the Agadir Crisis', *War in History*, 1, 1, 1994, pp. 81–97

Wilson, Keith M., 'Understanding the 'Misunderstanding' of 1 August', *Historical Journal*, 37, 4, 1994, pp. 885–889

Wilson, Keith M. (ed.), *Decisions for War, 1914*, UCL Press, London 1995

Wilson, Keith M., 'Britain', in K.M. Wilson (ed.), *Decisions for War, 1914*, UCL Press, London 1995, pp. 175–208

Wilson, Keith M. (ed.), *Forging the Collective Memory. Governments and International Historians through two World Wars*, Berghahn, Providence, RI and Oxford 1996

Zala, Sacha, *Geschichte unter der Schere politischer Zensur. Amtliche Aktensammlungen im internationalen Vergleich*, Oldenbourg, Munich 2001

Zechlin, Egmont, 'Die Adriakrise und der "Kriegsrat" vom 8. Dezember 1912', in idem, *Krieg und Kriegsrisiko. Zur Deutschen Politik im Ersten Weltkrieg*, Droste, Düsseldorf 1979

Zechlin, Egmont, *Krieg und Kriegsrisiko. Zur Deutschen Politik im Ersten Weltkrieg*, Droste, Düsseldorf 1979

Zedler, Jörg, 'Das Rittertelegramm. Bayern und der Heilige Stuhl in der Julikrise 1914', in Jörg Zedler (ed.), *Der Heilige Stuhl in den internationalen Beziehungen 1870–1939*, Herbert Utz Verlag, Munich 2010, pp. 175–202

Index